D1088270

Saddle Aces of the Cinema

Also by BUCK RAINEY

The Saga of Buck Jones
The Fabulous Holts
The Cowboy: Sixshooters, Songs and Sex
Shoot-Em-Ups

Saddle Aces of the Cinema

Buck Rainey

SAN DIEGO • NEW YORK
A. S. BARNES & COMPANY, INC.
IN LONDON:
THE TANTIVY PRESS

First Edition
Manufactured in the United States of America

For information write to:
A.S. Barnes & Company, Inc.
P.O. Box 3051
La Jolla, California 92038

The Tantivy Press
Magdalen House
136-148 Tooley Street
London, SE1 2TT, England

Library of Congress Cataloging in Publication Data

Rainey, Buck.
    Saddle aces of the cinema.

    Includes filmographies and index.
    CONTENTS: Roy Stewart.—Wally Wales/Hall
Taliaferro.—Tom Mix. [etc.]
    1.   Western films—History and criticism.   2.   Western
films—Catalogs.   3.   Moving-picture actors and actresses—
United States.   I.   Title.
PN1995.9.W4R34   1980   791.43′028′0922   78-75328
ISBN 0-498-02341-9

1 2 3 4 5 6 7 8 9   84 83 82 81 80

In Memory of
Reb Russell

. . . A pardner fittin' to ride the range with. . . in fair weather or foul, a true-blue cowboy always ready to hit the leather for a friend.

Reb Russell and "Rebel," the epitome of cowboy heroism and equine courage in yesteryear's world of heroes.

Contents

Preface

It is sad, the passing of an era—a genre, a group of entertainers the likes of which the world will never see again. I speak of the programmer Westerns, lovingly referred to as "hoss operas," "sagebrushers," "giddyups," "cactus capers," "shoot-em-ups," and "Bs," and of a group of thrillmakers who primarily made movies for what was referred to as the "grinds" and the "splits" (or "double harness" or "dualers") market, where audiences wanted plenty of action and only a modicum of romance and talk.

The low-budget Western as a distinct type of film survived and prospered for fifty years before being gunned down by television, urbanization, and escalating production costs. In that half century scores of sarsaparilla-drinking cowboy heroes rode the celluloid range on their sometimes equally famous mounts, dispensed justice right and left, and weekly saved heroines from a "fate worse than death"—or at least from mortgage foreclosure at the hands of Hairbreath Harry and his scallywags.

Tom Mix and "Tony," Buck Jones and "Silver," Reb Russell and "Rebel," Jack Perrin and "Starlight," Gene Autry and "Champion," Ken Maynard and "Tarzan," Fred Thomson and "Silver King"—these and a hundred other saddle aces and their trusty steeds left us memories that have admirably withstood the weathering of time, even though the old-fashioned shoot-'em-ups which provided yesteryear's vicarious thrills and goosepimples (and generated a mythical conception of the American cowboy) are evidently gone forever.

America has had its heroes—athletes, military leaders, explorers, politicians, scientists, astronauts—but no group has ever come close to matching the sustained idolization heaped on the heroes of the Saturday matinee. Their popularity and influence on the youth of the 1920s, 1930s, and 1940s was nothing short of phenomenal.

This book is about fifteen of those movie cowboys of yesteryear who had earned their spurs and a respected place in the hearts of Western film lovers way back when . . . . Some of these stalwarts of the cacti have been selected for inclusion here because their stories or records of their film credits have not been adequately documented before. Most of the cowboys written about here have made both silent and sound films; some only silents, others only talkies. Emphasis is on those whose careers overlapped both eras.

The selection of cowboys was mine alone, and I must confess to choosing those who had a special fascination for me. But what is more important, I chose those whose career stories and film credits I felt should be made a part of the history of the Western cinema, and at the same time include a few favorites for each generation of Western fans, from the era prior to World War I to the end of the genre in 1954.

The knowledgeable film buff will readily agree, I think, that no other book has presented comparable filmographies for the fifteen cowboy aces whose stories are told in this volume. This book, then, fills a gap in the history of the achievements of specific cowboy personalities. It should aid Western film devotees to more objectively evaluate these personalities in a truer perspective, offsetting to some extent, as this book does, the erroneous conclusion many have gathered from reading current nostalgia publications which play up as all-important the Western stars of the late 1940s and early 1950s. In no sense would I take away from the achievements and popularity of those stars, for I love them. But students of Western film history should realize that in granddad's, or great-granddad's day, many other cowboys were just as famous and popular as the later generation gun packers and guitar pluckers.

To my knowledge, this is the only book that has attempted a complete presentation of the films of a given cowboy star from his earliest walk-ons to his last fade-out, both Western and non-Western, silent and sound. The filmographies are believed to be the most complete ever put together for these fifteen stars, and it is this painstakingly assembled data that makes this book unique and, I believe, a valuable contribution to movie history.

Regretfully a single book can be only so long, and I had to leave out of this one many favorites whose film careers need to be recorded and preserved for future generations interested in the history of the Western motion picture and its personalities. My hope is to write another book that would include these other saddle aces who romped through Western after Western to the whoops, whistles, shrills, hand-clapping, and foot-stomping of thousands of blood-shot-eyed front-row youngsters, and their slightly less vocal parents in the mid-rows, who trudged to the cinema on a weekly basis in the halcyon years of the Western genre. Certainly the film careers of all those who have the hearts of the public are no less important in Western movie history than those contained herein, and a complete record of the work of these great saddle aces should be documented.

It is my sincere hope that you will enjoy this book, and through it come to appreciate even more the achievements of the great group of cowboy aces discussed herein. For many it will be a nostalgic journey that they will want to take time after time. As a reference book for researchers and writers, it should prove valuable for many years.

BUCK RAINEY
Tishomingo, Oklahoma

Acknowledgments

A special tip of the Rainey sombrero is extended to these good friends and fellow film historians who labored beyond the obligations of mere friendship in providing continuous assistance in this project:

LES ADAMS   JOSE SIMOES
                   FILHO
JANUS BARFOED   BILL McDOWELL
WAYNE J.   W. C. WILSON
   CAMPBELL

Their enthusiasm and dedication to the accurate recording and preservation of western film data is deeply appreciated, as are the many hours they worked on behalf of this book.

I am also indebted to the following persons for their cooperation and assistance in bringing this book to the point of publication:

Gene Autry	Al Hoxie
Rex Bell, Jr.	Don Miller
Johnny Bond	Cyril Nicholls
Elizabeth Burbridge	George O'Brien
Harry Carey, Jr.	Mrs. Jack Perrin
Olive Carey	Dorothy Revier
Maxine Jones Firfires	Carl (Dusty) Rhodes
Bob Harmon	Reb Russell
Berdee Holt	William Russell
Jennifer Holt	Wally Wales
Tim Holt	Ray Whitley
Mrs. Buck Jones	Nick Williams

In addition, I want to acknowledge and express my indebtedness to the authors and publishers of the following books and magazines consulted in the preparation of this book:

AFI Catalog of Feature Films, 1921–1930 (R. R. Bowker Co., 1971).

AFI Catalog of Feature Films, 1961–1970 (R. R. Bowker Co., 1976).

American Film Index, 1903–1915, by Einar Lauritzen and Gunnar Lundquist (Film-Index, Stockholm, Sweden, 1976).

Catalog of Copyright Entries, Motion Pictures, 1912–1939 (Copyright Office, Library of Congress, 1951).

Continued Next Week, by Kalton C. Lahue (University of Oklahoma Press, 1964).

The Cowboy: Six-Shooters, Songs, and Sex, Edited by Charles Harris and Buck Rainey (University of Oklahoma Press, 1976).

The Fabulous Holts, by Buck Rainey (Western Film Collectors Press 1976).

The Filming of the West, by Jon Tuska (Doubleday Publishers, 1976).

Hollywood Corral, by Don Miller (Popular Library, 1976).

The "It" Girl, by Joe Morella and Edward Z. Epstein (Delacorte Press, 1976).

The Saga of Buck Jones, by Buck Rainey (Western Film Collectors Press, 1975).

Shoot-'Em-Ups, by Les Adams and Buck Rainey (Arlington House Publishers, 1978).

The Life and Legend of Tom Mix, by Paul E. Mix (A. S. Barnes and Co., 1972).

Winners of the West, by Kalton C. Lahue (A. S. Barnes and Co., 1970).

Cinema Trails (Publisher, Bill McDowell).

Classic Film Collector, (Publisher, Samuel Rubin).

Film Collectors Registry (Publisher, Earl Blair).

Filmograph (Publisher, Murray Summers).

Films in Review (Editor, Charles Reilly).

Nostalgia Monthly (Publisher, Snuff Garrett).

Nostalgia News (Publisher, Larry Herndon).

Remember When (Publisher, Larry Herndon).

Screen Thrills (Publisher, Jerry Burke).

Under Western Skies (Publisher, Ron Downey).

Views and Reviews (Publisher, Jon Tuska).

Western Film Collector (Publisher, Packy Smith).

Western Revue (Publisher, William Russell).

Wild West Stars (Publisher, Jim Ward).

Wrangler's Roost (Publisher, Colin Momber).

Yesterday's Saturdays (Publisher, Les Adams).

Motion picture reviews published over a period of fifty years in *The Film Daily, Hollywood Reporter, Moving Picture World, Photoplay, Variety,* and *Wid* were also consulted in the preparation of this book. Finally, deserving special mention, is my wife, Rosalva Rainey, whose unselfish devotion and patience made this book possible.

Key to Filmography Abbreviations

Director	D
Story	S
Screenplay	SP
Scenario	Scen
Producer	P
Adaptation	Adapt
Camera	C
Continuity	Cont
Supervision	Supv
Writer	W
Associate Producer	AP
Assistant Director	AD

Photographic Illustrations

All photographs used in this book are from the collection of the author, Buck Rainey.

Saddle Aces of the Cinema

1 • ROY STEWART

Dynamo of Ruggedness

Roy Stewart, a salubrious progenitor of rustic Westerns, is a good example of a first-rate performer from the movies' infancy whose films, for the most part, are in the "lost" group and whose personal life is largely impenetrable. The average semiknowledgeable movie buff is insensible to the name, and many self-styled experts on the Western are likewise nescient regarding this Western favorite of granddad's day. But when pictures flickered, the guns silently belched smoke, the piano beneath the screen groaned, the girls squealed, the popcorn sizzled, and the coming attraction and intermission slides served as a singular thrill in themselves, Roy Stewart thundered across the prairie in the horse opera's adolescence.

Fame is indeed ephemeral, its transience a respecter of no individual; and so the masses forget as they are caught up in the adoration of new screen personalities. But for the favored few who delve into the history of Western filmdom, Roy Stewart will be remembered as one of the pioneers of the genre—a man who molded and nourished the "B" programmer in its infancy years, and helped to give it the strength which later allowed it to withstand a decade of bastardization before biting the dust in the early 1950s as a unique art form and an industry within an industry.

San Diego was the site of Roy's birth in 1884, and, like several other thespians of the time, following his grammar school days he attended the University of California at Berkeley and he graduated with honors. Desire, mentality, and physique aided him in deciding on a stage career and Roy joined a traveling stock company playing West Coast cities. For one season he was with the road company producing *Florodora*, a popular hit of the day. But constant traveling did not especially appeal to homeloving Roy. Seeking the opportunity to settle down in his native state, he found it in motion pictures.

His first movie experience came in 1913 with the American Company at National City. Later he was with the Majestic Company at Los Angeles and played in all productions of the Masterpiece Film Company. His principal part was that of "Bud Means" in *The Hoosier School Master*, supporting Max Figman. Roy also played leads for the Robin Company, releasing through Universal, in the early pre-World War I days.

Good-looking, with a fine bearing and abounding with youth, Stewart easily found work in the studios when pictures were first "looking up." For several seasons he held the single-scull championship of the West Coast, was an amateur boxer of ability, rode and swam well, and was adept in other athletic acts which he performed before the cameras.

Hal Roach, just getting his start as "King of the Laughmakers," used Roy in several films in 1914, casting him opposite Jane Novak and Harold Lloyd in such two-reelers as *Just Nuts, The Hungry Actors,*

Roy Stewart

and *Into the Light*. At this time Stewart commanded ten dollars a day in salary, as contrasted with five dollars by Lloyd.

In 1915 Universal engaged Roy to play the part of "Blake" in the serial *The Diamond from the Sky*, and he appeared in all sixty reels of the cliffhanger. One of the long-talked-about big punches of this serial was the fight scene staged by Stewart and star William Russell. According to reports of the day, it was a real whing-ding. The following year, Roy appeared in the first Western serial, *Liberty*, along with Marie Walcamp, Jack Holt, and Neal Hart.

Roy did not come into real prominence, however, until he moved to Triangle. It was then that he was signed to a Western series as a replacement for the departing William S. Hart. It was a lucky move for both Hart and Stewart; Bill received more money and freedom under the Paramount banner, and Roy became a major Western star at Triangle in films such as *The Law's Outlaw, Keith of the Border, The Learnin' of Jim Benton, One-Shot Ross, Wolves of the Border, The Devil Dodger,* and *Boss of the Lazy Y.*

Cliff Smith, who would eventually work with most of the major Western stars of the 1920s and become the top action director of the decade, directed most of the Stewart films. One of Roy's better non-Western performances was in *The House Built on Sand,* playing opposite Lillian Gish and proving that there was more to his talents than riding a horse and pounding the daylights out of ruffians engaged in egregious violence.

In 1919–1920 Roy made several good Westerns—released through Hodkinson Pictures—that were based on the stories of Zane Grey and other western writers. His versatility as an actor was displayed opposite Katherine MacDonald in *Beauty Market* (First National, 1919), with Betty Compson in *Prisoners of Love* (Goldwyn, 1920), and with Kathlyn Williams in *Just a Wife* (National, 1920).

Roy free-lanced during 1920–1921, and appeared as star in a variety of films, both Western and non-Western. *The Radio King* (1922) found Roy as the star of Universal's first ten-chapter cliffhanger—a story of the early days of radio and the attempts of an international gang to steal certain inventions. Roy was not only able to thwart nefarious thugs but also found romance with the beauteous and petite Louise Lorraine.

Stewart was solidly built, six feet two inches tall, and weighed 195 pounds. And for the record, he had brown hair and eyes. He was an impressive figure, whether slapping leather as a Western gunfighter or having a tête-à-tête with a bounteously beautiful nymph in her boudoir. Somewhat like John Wayne in physique, his sinewy frame did not lend itself to dancing the *Zapateado*, and his mere presence in a room seemed to fill it.

During the years 1921–1927 Roy periodically wandered off the range to take assorted roles in dramatic films. But it was the Western for which Stewart is now remembered, and rightly he should be. His unfeigned portrayals, coupled with solid stories and lots of action, made possible his continuation as a cowboy star when the screen was overrun with the likes of Mix, Jones, Hart, Carey, Acord, Farnum, and a score of other competent range galahads. Although Roy never made it into the ranks of the elite, he remained on the periphery as a cowboy favorite of the independent market.

For no especial reason, unless it is the unusual title, *Back to Yellow Jacket* (Arrow, 1922) is one of

17

THE MEDICINE MAN
TRIANGLE PLAY

Roy Stewart and Aaron Edwards mix it up in *The Medicine Man* (Triangle, 1917).

Roy's films most often mentioned by those who know enough even to comment on his career. Equally good 1922 Westerns were *The Sagebrush Trail* (with no less than Wallace Beery as the villain), *One Eighth Apache*, and *The Snowshoe Trail*, all produced by small independent companies.

It was in 1922–1923 that Roy thundered through his two turbulent, titillating series of two-reelers for Universal. The first, known as the *Lumberjack* or *Timber Tales* series, presented Roy as a valorous hero undaunted by the forces of evil pitted against him as he fought for life, love, and justice in the great northwest woods country. Trepidity reigned supreme as lethargy and serenity were shuttled to

the sidelines in a demonstration of the supremacy of Universal's know-how in making short films. But generally the *Tales of the Old West* series of 1923 was a more rollicking and rigorous one. In films such as *God's Law, A Fight for A Mine, Showdown, Forced to Fight*, and *The Secret Code*, Roy agitatedly and sometimes ferociously set about to quell the bestial qualities of his fellowman. Although sometimes he tried pacification, Roy's sedative moments were usually short-lived and his rampageous tendencies detonated before very many minutes of the two-reelers had slipped by. Audiences could count on blusterous action in a Stewart oater, often realistic and unsubdued in its intensity.

Roy's Universal features, such as *Burning Words, Pure Grit,* and *The Love Brand,* were more reticent in raw action; but his tenacity of purpose was undaunted and he always remained uncompromising —a "standpatter for righteousness" in a day when morality and noble heroes were respected by movie audiences. On the screen, Stewart's magnanimous personality sometimes caused him to be taken in by the machinations of incorrigible individuals; but once he learned of the impropriety of those whom he trusted, his revenge was usually swift and, if justified, tempered with mercy—especially if a comely lady was involved.

In 1924 Roy and sensuous Bessie Love found romance along the trail to Mexico in First National's *Sundown,* a nine-reeler about a last-desperate cattle drive to Mexico by ranchers driven from the open range by homesteaders. It was one of the major Westerns of the year.

With Kit Carson Over the Great Divide (1925) was the first of Roy's historicals for Sunset Productions, followed in 1926 by *With Buffalo Bill on the U.P. Trail, With Daniel Boone Thru the Wilderness,* and *With General Custer at Little Big Horn.* These features have held up well and are worthy of viewing today. They remain Stewart's most remembered work and perhaps his best. Although not enjoying the luxury of lavish budgets or big studio release, the production values are consistently above average, and the casts comprise talented performers. More so than in later and more expensively mounted productions, basically the Stewart historicals were truthful depictions of the frontier stories they espoused to portray.

After 1927, as the transition to talking pictures began and Westerns slipped into disrepute, Roy made the change to featured roles. *Stormy Waters* (1928), a sea melodrama, was one of his better films of the post-1927 years.

Roy was adept at playing different roles with considerable aplomb, a talent that kept him working as a featured player when other cowboys were swelling the ranks of "B" Western extras in low-budget quickies. In 1929 he was a Viking king in *The Viking* for MGM, and a commandant in *In Old Arizona,* the "Cisco Kid" yarn that won Warner Baxter an academy award at Fox. He appeared in several George O'Brien vehicles, and also was featured in Westerns with Ken Maynard, Tom Keene, and Tom Mix. His last film was *Zoo in Budapest,* a 1933 Fox film starring Loretta Young and Gene Raymond.

At his death Roy Stewart was only forty-nine years of age. Given a normal lifespan, he could have continued working throughout the "B" era. Undoubtedly his talents would have greatly contributed to the enjoyment of many sagebrushers and non-Westerns alike.

ROY STEWART *Filmography*

THE WASP (Selig, October 10, 1914).
Roy Stewart, Vivian Rich, Walter Spencer, Hugh Bennett
D: Edward J. Le Saint
S: J. A. Lacy

THE HUNGRY ACTORS (Universal-Rex, 1914).
Harold Lloyd, Jane Novak, *Roy Stewart,* Martha Maddox, Bobby Vernon, Neely Edwards

THE DIAMOND FROM THE SKY (American, May 3, 1915) 30 Chapters.
Lottie Pickford, Irving Cummings, William Russell, Charlotte Burton, Eugenie Ford, George Periolat, Orral Humphrey, W. J. Tedmarsh, *Roy Stewart,* Lillian Buckingham
D: William Desmond Taylor, Jacques Jaccard
S: Roy L. McCardell
Chapter Titles: (1) The Heritage of Hate, (2) An Eye for an Eye, (3) The Silent Witness, (4) The Prodigal's Progress, (5) For the Sake of a False Friend, (6) Shadows at Sunrise, (7) The Fox and the Pig, (8) A Mind in the Past, (9) A Runaway Match, (10) Old Foes with New Faces, (11) The Web of Destiny, or Plaything of the Papoose, (12) To the Highest Bidder, (13) The Man in the Mask, (14) For Love and Money, (15) Desperate Chances, (16) The Path of Peril, (17) King of Diamonds and the Queen of Hearts, (18) Charm Against Harm, (19) Fire, Fury, and Confusion, (20) The Soul Stranglers, (21) The Lion's Bride, (22) The Rose in the Dust, (23) The Double-Cross, (24) The Mad Millionaire, (25) A House of Cards, (26) The Garden of the Gods, (27) Mine Own People, (28) The Falling Aeroplane, (29) A Deal with Destiny, (30) The American Earl

FROM ITALY'S SHORE (Universal, May 13, 1915) 2 Reels.
Harold Lloyd, Jane Novak, *Roy Stewart*
D: Otis Turner
S: James Dayton

A BROKEN CLOUD (American, 1915).
Roy Stewart, Lizette Thorne, Alfred Vosburgh, Perry Banks

THE SILVER LINING (American, 1915).
Roy Stewart

INTO THE LIGHT (Universal-Rex, June 10, 1915) 2 Reels.
Harold Lloyd, *Roy Stewart*, Jane Novak, Violet MacMillan

JUST NUTS (Hal Roach, 1915).
Harold Lloyd, Jane Novak, *Roy Stewart*

THE EXILE OF BAR-K RANCH (American, August, 1915)
2 Reels.
Vivian Rich, *Roy Stewart*

THE MIGHTY HOLD (American, August 14, 1915).
Roy Stewart, Helen Rosson, Perry Banks, Beatrice Van
D: William Bertram
S: Joseph F. Poland

THE TERROR OF TWIN MOUNTAINS (American, September 25, 1915) 2 Reels.
E. Forrest Taylor, Helene Rosson, *Roy Stewart*
D: William Bertram

THE GREATER COURAGE (Universal, October 14, 1915)
2 Reels.
Roy Stewart, Jane Novak

THE SOLUTION OF THE MYSTERY (American, December 11, 1915) 2 Reels.
Vivian Rich, Alfred Vosburgh, Charles Newton, *Roy Stewart*
D: Reaves Eason

THE OTHER SIDE OF THE DOOR (American, January 6, 1916) 5 Reels.
Harold Lockwood, Mae Allison, Harry von Meter, Dick La Reno, *Roy Stewart*, Josephine Humphreys
D: Thomas Ricketts
S: Clifford Howard

LIBERTY (Universal, August 14, 1916) 20 Chapters.
Marie Walcamp, Jack Holt, Neal Hart, G. Raymond Nye, L. M. Wells, Eddie Polo, Hazel Buckham, *Roy Stewart*, Maude Emory, Bertram Grassby
D: Jacques Jaccard, Henry McRae
P/S/Adapt: Jacques Jaccard
Chapter Titles: (1) The Fangs of the Wolf, (2) Riding with Death, (3) American Blood, (4) Dead or Alive, (5) Love and War, (6) The Desert of Lost Souls, (7) Liberty's Sacrifice, (8) Clipped Wings, (9) Trapped, (10) The Human Target, (11) A Daughter of Mars, (12) For the Flag, (13) Strife and Sorrow, (14) A Modern Joan of Arc, (15) The Flag of Truce, (16) Court-Martialled, (17) A Trail of Blood, (18) The Wolf's Nemesis, (19) An Avenging Angel, (20) A Daughter of the U.S.A.

THE INNER STRUGGLE (American-Mutual, June 1916)
5 Reels.
Roy Stewart, Winifred Greenwood, Franklyn Ritchie
D: Edward Sloman
S: Julian La Mothe

THE BRUISER (American, 1916).
Roy Stewart

LYING LIPS (American, May 1916) 5 Reels.
Roy Stewart, Winifred Greenwood, Franklin Ritchie, Eugenia Forde, Clarence Burton, George Webb
S: Karl Coolidge

THE BLINDNESS (American, 1916).
Roy Stewart, William Stowell, Dodo Newton, Warren Ellsworth, Rhea Mitchell

LITTLE HERO (Universal, 1916).
Roy Stewart, Vivian Rich

THE CRAVING (American, 1916).
Roy Stewart

THE WINNING PAIR (Universal, 1916).
Roy Stewart

MIXED BLOOD (Universal-Red Feather, December 1916)
5 Reels.
Roy Stewart, Claire McDowell, George Beranger, Wilbur Higby, Jessie Arnold, Harry Archer, Mrs. Emmons
P: Charles Swickard
S: William Mack
Adapt: J. Grubb Alexander

JUNGLE GENTLEMAN (Universal, 1916).
Roy Stewart, Hobart Henley
D: Hobart Henley

JUNE MADNESS (Universal-Gold Seal, January 15, 1917)
3 Reels.
Roy Stewart, Wadsworth Harris, Frank Brownlee, Gypsy Hart, Lloyd Whitlock
D: Hobart Henley
Scen: Willis Woods

THE BOSS OF THE LAZY Y (Fine Arts/Triangle, April 7, 1917).
Roy Stewart, Josie Sedgwick, Graham Pette, Frank McQuarrie, Aaron Edwards, Walt Whitman, Frankie Lee, William Ellingford, Bill Patton
D: Cliff Smith
S: Charles Alden Seltzer
Scen: Cinema Exchange
C: Steve Rounds

A YOUNG PATRIOT (Universal-Gold Seal, June 1917)
3 Reels.
Roy Stewart
D: Louis William Chaudet
S: M. and W. Pigott
Scen: E. J. Clawson

COME THROUGH (Universal, July 11, 1917) 7 Reels.
Herbert Rawlinson, Alice Lake, *Roy Stewart*, Jean Hathaway,
George Webb, Charles Mailes, Bill Dyer
D: Jack Conway
S: George Bronson Howard
Scen: Fred Myton

THE DOUBLE STANDARD (Universal-Butterfly, July 13,
1917) 5 Reels.
Roy Stewart
D: Phillips Smalley
S: Brand Whitlock
Scen: E. J. Clawson

FOLLOW THE GIRL (Universal-Butterfly, July 26, 1917)
5 Reels.
Roy Stewart, Ruth Stonehouse, Jack Dill, Claire Dubley, Alfred
Allen
D: Louis William Chaudet
S: Fred Myton

THE WINNING PAIR (Universal-Gold Seal, August 1917)
3 Reels.
Roy Stewart
D: Louis W. Chaudet
S: Eugene B. Lewis

A DAUGHTER OF THE POOR (Fine Arts/Triangle, 1917).
Roy Stewart, Bessie Love, Carl Stockdale, Max Davidson,
George Belanger
D: D. W. Griffith

THE DOLL SHOP (Fine Arts/Triangle, 1917).
Roy Stewart

THE FUGITIVE (Fine Arts/Triangle, January 1917).
Roy Stewart, Harry Carter, Louise Lovely, F. D. Crittenden,
Vester Pegg
S: E. Magnus Ingleton
P: Fred A. Kelsey

THE HOUSE BUILT ON SAND (Fine Arts/Triangle, 1917)
5 Reels.
Lillian Gish, *Roy Stewart*, William H. Brown, Bessie Buskirk,
Jack Brammel, Josephine Crowell, Kate Bruce
D: Edward Morrisey
S: Mary H. O'Connor

Lillian Gish, Roy Stewart, and Kate Bruce in *House Built Upon Sand* (Triangle, 1917).

ONE SHOT ROSS (Fine Arts/Triangle, October 1917).
Roy Stewart, Josie Sedgwick, Jack Richardson, Louis Durham,
William Ellingford, Leo Willis, Belle Bennett
D: Cliff Smith

THE LEARNIN' OF JIM BENTON (Fine Arts/Triangle,
1917).
Roy Stewart, Fritzie Ridgeway, Walter Perry, Edward J.
Brady, William Ellingford, Thornton Edwards, Harry Ratten-
berry
D: Cliff Smith
S: Al Nietz

BOND OF FEAR (Fine Arts, Triangle, September 1917)
5 Reels.
Roy Stewart, Belle Bennett, Melbourne McDowell, George
Webb, John Lince
D: Jack Conway

THE DEVIL DODGER (Fine Arts/Triangle, September 23,
1917) 5 Reels.
Roy Stewart, Jack (John) Gilbert, Carolyn Wagner, John Lince,
Anna Dodge, George Willis
D: Cliff Smith

THE MEDICINE MAN (Fine Arts/Triangle, November
1917) 5 Reels.
Roy Stewart, Aaron Edwards, Ann Kronan, Percy Challenger,
Carl Ulman, Wilbur Higby
D: Cliff Smith
SP: Alvin H. Neitz
S: Jack Cunningham

Roy Stewart and Kathlyn Williams in *The U.P. Trail* (Hodkinson/Pathe, 1919).

THE SILENT RIDER (Fine Arts/Triangle, December 1, 1917) 5 Reels.
Roy Stewart, Ethel Fleming, Leo Willis
D: Cliff Smith
S: C. M. Clark
C: Steve Rounds

THE LAW'S OUTLAW (Triangle, January 13, 1918).
Roy Stewart, Fritzie Ridgeway, Harry Rattenberry, Herbert Giles
D: Cliff Smith
S: Ethel and James Dorrance

FAITH ENDURIN' (Triangle, March 17, 1918).
Roy Stewart, Fritzie Ridgeway, W. A. Jeffries, Joe Bennett, Edward Brady, Walter Perkins, Graham Pette, Walter Perry
D: Cliff Smith

KEITH OF THE BORDER (Triangle, February 17, 1918).
Roy Stewart, Josie Sedgwick, Herbert Giles, Alberta Lee, Wilbur Higby, Pete Morrison, William Ellingford
D: Cliff Smith
S: Randall Parrish

BY PROXY (Triangle, 1918).
Roy Stewart, Maude Wayne
D: Cliff Smith

CACTUS CRANDALL (Triangle, August 11, 1918).
Roy Stewart, Marion Marvin, William Ellingford, Pete Morrison, Joe Rickson
D: Cliff Smith
S: *Roy Stewart*

THE FLY GOD (Triangle, 1918).
Roy Stewart, Edward Peil, Claire Anderson, Aaron Edwards,
Percy Challenger, Walter Perry
D: Cliff Smith
S: Red Saunders

IRISH EYES (Triangle, 1918).
Roy Stewart, Pauline Stazke

PAYING HIS DEBT (Triangle, April 28, 1918).
Roy Stewart, Josie Sedgwick, Dixie Doll, Harry Yamamoto,
Walter Perkins, William Ellington, William Dyer, Arthur
Millett
D: Cliff Smith
S: Alvin J. Neitz
C: Steve Rounds

RED-HAIRED CUPID (Triangle, 1918) 5 Reels.
Roy Stewart, Peggy Peace, Charles Dorian, Ray Griffith, Aaron
Edwards, Walter Perry
D: Cliff Smith
S: Henry Wallace Phillips

WOLVES OF THE BORDER (Triangle, 1918).
Roy Stewart, Josie Sedgwick, Jack Curtis, Frank McQuarrie,
Willis Jeffries, Lewis Durham, Curly Baldwin
D: Cliff Smith
S: Alvin J. Neitz

THE GUN WOMAN (Triangle, 1918).
Texas Guinan, *Roy Stewart*, Kingsley Benedict
D: Frank Borzage

UNTAMED (Triangle, September 1, 1919) 5 Reels.
Roy Stewart, H. N. Dudgeon, May Giraci, Graham Pette,
H. C. Simmons, Ethel Flemming, John Lynce, Jimmy Weil,
Eagle Eye
D: Cliff Smith
S: Kenneth B. Clark

THE U.P. TRAIL (Zane Grey Pictures/Hodkinson, 1919).
Roy Stewart, Kathlyn Williams, Robert McKim, Joseph J.
Dowling, Margerite De La Motte, Frederick Starr, Charles
Murphy, Virginia Caldwell, Walter Perry
D: Jack Conway
S: Zane Grey
P: B. B. Hampton

THE WESTERNERS (Great Authors Pictures/Hodkinson,
1919).
Roy Stewart, Mildred Manning, Robert McKim, Mary Jane
Irving, Graham Pettie, Wilfrid Lucas, Frankie Lee, Dorothy
Hagan
D: Edward Sloman
S: Stewart Edward White
P: B. B. Hampton

Roy Stewart and Marguerite de LaMotte in *The Sage-brusher* (Hodkinson, 1920).

BEAUTY MARKET (Katherine MacDonald Pictures/First
National, December 22, 1919) 6 Reels.
Katherine MacDonald, *Roy Stewart*, Winter Hall, Bob Brewster,
Wedgewood Nowell, Kathleen Kirkham
D: Colin Campbell
S: Margery Land May - "The Bleeders"

PRISONERS OF LOVE (Goldwyn, January 8, 1920).
Betty Compson, *Roy Stewart*, Ralph Lewis, Clara Horton,
Claire McDowell, Kate Toncry, Emory Johnson, Betty Marie
Schade
D: Arthur Rossen
S: Catherine Henry
P: Betty Compson

THE SAGEBRUSHER (Great Authors Pictures/Hodkinson,
February 11, 1920).
Roy Stewart, Marguerite De La Motte, Noah Beery, Betty
Bruce
D: Edward Sloman
Scen: William H. Clifford
P: Benjamin B. Hampton

JUST A WIFE (National, February 23, 1920) 5 Reels.
Roy Stewart, Kathlyn Williams, Leatrice Joy, Albert Van,
William West
D: Howard Hickman
Scen: Katherine Reed
S: Eugene Walters

RIDERS OF THE DAWN (Zane Grey Pictures/Hodkinson, May 31, 1920) 7 Reels.
Roy Stewart, Claire Adams, Norman Kerry, Robert McKim, Frederick Star, Violet Scham, Frank Brownlee, Marie Messenger
D: Hugh Ryan Conway
Scen: William H. Clifford, L. V. Jefferson
S: Zane Grey - "The Desert of Wheat"
P: Benjamin B. Hampton

THE LONE HAND (Alexander Productions, 1920) 5 Reels.
Roy Stewart, Josie Sedgwick, Harry Von Meter, Wilbur Higby
D: Cliff Smith
S: Alvin J. Neitz

THE MONEY CHANGERS (Benjamin B. Hampton Productions/Pathe, October 5, 1920).
Roy Stewart, Robert McKim, Claire Adams
D: Jack Conway
Scen: Upton Sinclair
Adapt: Benjamin B. Hampton

THE DEVIL TO PAY (Robert Brunton Productions/Pathe, November 10, 1920).
Roy Stewart, Fritzie Brunette, Robert McKim, Joseph Dowling, George Fisher, Evelyn Selbie, Richard Lepan, Mark Fenton, William Marion
D: Ernest C. Warde
Scen: Jack Cunningham
S: Frances Nimmo Green

THE MISTRESS OF SHENSTONE (R-C Pictures, February 27, 1921) 6 Reels.
Roy Stewart, Pauline Frederick, Emmett C. King, Arthur Clayton, John Willink, Helen Wright, Rosa Gore, Helen Muir, Lydia Yeamans Titus
D: Henry King
Scen: Florence L. Barclay
S: Florence L. Barclay - "The Mistress of Shenstone"

THE HEART OF THE NORTH (Quality Film Productions/C.B.C. Film Sales, September 10, 1921) 6 Reels.
Roy Stewart, Louise Lovely, Harry von Meter, Roy Justi, William Leon West, Betty Marvyn
D: Harry Revier
S: Edward Dowling

HER SOCIAL VALUE (Katherine MacDonald Pictures/Associated First National, October 24, 1921) 6 Reels.
Katherine MacDonald, *Roy Stewart*, Bertram Grassby, Betty Ross Clark, Winter Hall, Joseph Girard, Lillian Rich, Vincent Hamilton, Helen Raymond, Violet Phillips, Arthur Gibson
D: Jerome Storm
Scen: Gerald Duffy, Jerome Storm
S: B. P. Fineman, J. A. Barry

A MOTION TO ADJOURN (Ben Wilson Productions/Arrow Film Corp., November 2, 1921) 6 Reels.
Roy Stewart, Harry Rattenberry, Sidney D'Albrook, Evelyn Nelson, Norval MacGregor, Marjorie Daw, Peggy Blackwood, William Carroll, Charles L. King, Bill White, Jim Welsh
D/Scen: Roy Clements
S: Peter B. Kyne - "A Motion to Adjourn"

LIFE'S GREATEST QUESTION (Quality Film Productions: C.B.C. Film Sales, December 10, 1921) 5 Reels.
Roy Stewart, Louise Lovely, Harry von Meter, Dorothy Valegra, Eugene Burr
D/S/Scen: Harry Revier

THE INNOCENT CHEAT (Ben Wilson Production/Arrow Film Corp., December 26, 1921) 6 Reels.
Roy Stewart, Sidney De Gray, George Hernandez, Rhea Mitchell, Kathleen Kirkham
D/P: Ben Wilson
Adapt: J. Grubb Alexander
S: Peter B. Kyne

RECKLESS CHANCES (Playgoers Pictures, December 31, 1921).
Roy Stewart

BACK TO YELLOW JACKET (Ben Wilson Productions/Arrow Film Corp., March 14, 1922) 6 Reels.
Roy Stewart, Kathleen Kirkham, Earl Metcalfe, Jack Pratt
P/D: Ben Wilson
Adapt: J. Grubb Alexander
S: Peter B. Kyne

THE SAGEBRUSH TRAIL (Western Pictures Exploitation Co., May, 1922) 5 Reels.
Roy Stewart, Marjorie Daw, Johnny Walker, Wallace Beery
D: Robert R. Thornby
S/Scen: H. H. Van Loan
P: Hugh B. Evans

ONE-EIGHTH APACHE (Berwilla Film Corp./Arrow Film Corp., July 15, 1922) 6 Reels.
Roy Stewart, Kathleen Kirkham, Wilbur McGaugh, George M. Daniel, Dick La Reno
D: Ben Wilson
Scen: J. Grubb Alexander
S: Peter B. Kyne

THE SNOWSHOE TRAIL (Chester Bennett Productions/FBO, September 17, 1922) 6 Reels.
Roy Stewart, Jane Novak, Lloyd Whitlock, Herbert Prior, Kate Toncray, Spottiswoode Aiken, Chai Hung
D: Chester Bennett
Scen: Marion Fairfax
S: Edison Marshall - "The Snowshoe Trail"

GIANTS OF THE OPEN (Universal, September 26, 1922)
2 Reels.
("Timber Tales" Series)
Roy Stewart
D: Duke Worne

BLUE BLOOD AND RED (Universal, October 11, 1922)
2 Reels.
("Timber Tales" Series)
Roy Stewart
D: Duke Worne

RUSTLERS OF THE REDWOODS (Universal, October 28,
1922) 2 Reels.
("Timber Tales" Series)
Roy Stewart
D: Duke Worne

THE RADIO KING (Universal, October 30, 1922) 10 Chapters.
Roy Stewart, Louise Lorraine, Al Smith, Sidney Bracey, Clark
Comstock, Ernest Butterworth, Jr.
D: Robert F. Hill
S/Scen: Robert Dillon
Chapter Titles: (1) A Cry for Help, (2) The Secret of the Air,
(3) A Battle of Wits, (4) Warned by Radio, (5) Ship of Doom,
(6) S.O.S., (7) Saved by Wireless, (8) The Master Wave, (9)
The Trail of Vengeance, (10) Saved by Science

TIMBERLAND TREACHERY (Universal, November 13,
1922) 2 Reels.
("Timber Tales" Series)
Roy Stewart, Esther Ralston
D: Duke Worne

KINGS OF THE FOREST (Universal, December 1, 1922)
2 Reels.
("Timber Tales" Series)
Roy Stewart
D: Duke Worne

THE DOOMED SENTINEL (Universal, December 23, 1922)
2 Reels.
("Timber Tales" Series)
Roy Stewart
D: Duke Worne

HEARTS OF OAK (Universal, January 18, 1923) 2 Reels.
("Timber Tales" Series)
Roy Stewart
D: Duke Worne

KNIGHTS OF THE TIMBER (Universal, February 10,
1923) 2 Reels.
("Timber Tales" Series)
Roy Stewart
D: Duke Worne

ONE OF THREE (Universal, February 19, 1923) 2 Reels.
("The Further Adventures of Yorke Norroy" Series)
Roy Stewart, Hayden Stevenson, Jack Perrin, Lucille Ricksen,
Fontaine La Rue
D: Duke Worne
S: George Bronson Howard

GOD'S LAW (Universal, February 28, 1923) 2 Reels.
("Tales of the Old West" Series)
Roy Stewart
D: Duke Worne

UNDER SECRET ORDERS (Universal, March 6, 1923)
2 Reels.
("The Further Exploits of Yorke Norroy" Series)
Roy Stewart, Esther Ralston, Jack Perrin, William Welsh
D: Duke Worne
S: George Bronson Howard

GUILTY HAND (Universal, March 16, 1923) 2 Reels.
("Tales of the Old West" Series)
Roy Stewart
D: Duke Worne

THE SECRET CODE (Universal, March 24, 1923) 2 Reels.
("The Further Adventures of Yorke Norroy" Series)
Roy Stewart
D: Duke Worne
S: George Bronson Howard

THE RADIO-ACTIVE BOMB (Universal, April 1923)
2 Reels.
Roy Stewart
D: Duke Worne
S: George Bronson Howard

TRIMMED IN SCARLET (Universal, April 9, 1923)
5 Reels.
Kathlyn Williams, *Roy Stewart*, Lucille Rickson, Robert Agnew,
David Torrence, Phillips Smalley, Eve Southern, Bert Sprotte,
Grace Carlyle, Gerrald Grassby, Raymond Hatton, Philo
McCullough
D: Jack Conway
Scen: Edward T. Lowe, Jr.
S: William Hurlbut

HARD TO BEAT (Universal, May 5, 1923) 2 Reels.
("Tales of the Old West" Series)
Roy Stewart, Leonard Clapham (Tom London)
D: Duke Worne

A FIGHT FOR A MINE (Universal, May 5, 1923) 2 Reels.
("Tales of the Old West" Series)
Roy Stewart
D: Duke Worne

Roy Stewart looked every bit the rugged individualist in *A Fight For a Mine* (Universal, 1923).

BETTER THAN GOLD (Universal, May 16, 1923) 2 Reels.
("Tales of the Old West" Series)
Roy Stewart
D: Duke Worne

BURNING WORDS (Universal, May 27, 1923) 5 Reels.
Roy Stewart, Laura La Plante, Harold Goodwin, Edith Yorke, Alfred Fisher, William Welsh, Noble Johnson, Eve Southern, Harry Carter, George McDaniels
D: Stuart Paton
S/Scen: Harrison Jacobs

THE SHOWDOWN (Universal, 1923) 2 Reels.
("Tales of the Old West" Series)
Roy Stewart
D: Duke Worne

FORCED TO FIGHT (Universal, 1923) 2 Reels.
("Tales of the Old West" Series)
Roy Stewart
D: Duke Worne

THE LOVE BRAND (Universal, August 13, 1923) 5 Reels.
Roy Stewart, Wilfrid North, Margaret Landis, Arthur Hull, Sidney De Grey, Marie Wells, Boris Karloff
D: Stuart Paton
S/Scen: Adrian Johnson

PURE GRIT (Universal, December 31, 1923) 5 Reels.
Roy Stewart, Esther Ralston, Jere Austin, Jack Mower, Verne Winter
D: Nat Ross
Scen: Isadore Bernstein
S: William MacLeod Raine - "A Texas Ranger"

TALL TIMBER (Universal, 1923) 2 Reels.
Roy Stewart, Esther Ralston

THE WOMAN ON THE JURY (Associated First National, April 20, 1924) 7 Reels.
Sylvia Breamer, Frank Mayo, Lew Cody, Bessie Love, Mary Carr, Hobart Bosworth, Myrtle Stedman, Henry B. Walthall, *Roy Stewart*
D: Harry O. Hoyt
Adapt: Mary O'Hara
S: Bernard K. Burns - "Woman on the Jury"
Supv: Earl Hudson

SUNDOWN (First National, November 23, 1924) 9 Reels.
Bessie Love, *Roy Stewart*, Hobart Bosworth, Arthur Hoyt, Charles Murray, Jere Austin, Charles Crockett, E. J. Radcliffe, Margaret McWade, Bernard Randall, Charles Sellon
D: Laurence Trimble, Harry O. Hoyt
S: Earl Hudson
Scen: Frances Marion, Kenneth B. Clarke
Supv: Earl Hudson

KIT CARSON OVER THE GREAT DIVIDE (Sunset Productions/Aywon, September 3, 1925) 6 Reels.
Roy Stewart, Henry B. Walthall, Marguerite Snow, Sheldon Lewis, Earl Metcalfe, Charlotte Stevens, Jack Mower, Arthur Hotaling, Lew Meehan, Billy Franey, Nelson McDowell
D/Scen: Frank S. Mattison
P: Anthony J. Xydias

TIME, THE COMEDIAN (Metro-Goldyn-Mayer, November 8, 1925) 5 Reels.
Mae Busch, Lew Cody, Gertrude Olmsted, Rae Ethelyn, *Roy Stewart*, Paulette Duval, Creighton Hale, Nellie Parker, Robert Ober, David Mir, Templar Saxe, Mildred Vincent
D: Robert Z. Leonard
Adapt: Frederick Hatton, Fanny Hatton
S: Kate Jordan - "Time, the Comedian"

WHERE THE WORST BEGINS (Co-Artists Productions/Truart Film Co., November, 1925) 6 Reels.
Ruth Roland, Alec B. Francis, Matt Moore, Grace Darmond, *Roy Stewart*, Derelys Perdue, Theodore Lorch, Ernie Adams, J. P. Lockney, Robert Burns, Floyd Shackelford
D: John McDermott
Adapt: Joseph Anthony Roach
S: George Frank Worts - "Out Where the Worst Begins"

THE LADY FROM HELL (Stuart Paton Productions/Associated Exhibitors, January 7, 1926) 6 Reels.
Roy Stewart, Blanche Sweet, Ralph Lewis, Frank Elliott, Edgar Norton, Margaret Campbell, Ruth King, Mickey Moore
D: Stuart Paton
Adapt/Cont: J. Grubb Alexander
S: Norton S. Parker - "My Lord of the Double B"

BUFFALO BILL ON THE U.P. TRAIL (Sunset Productions, March 1, 1926) 6 Reels.
Roy Stewart, Kathryn McGuire, Cullen Landis, Sheldon Lewis, Earl Metcalfe, Milburn Morante, Hazel Howell, Fred De Silva, Felix Whitefeather, Jay Morley, Eddie Harris, Dick La Reno, Harry Fenwick
D: Frank S. Mattison
P: Anthony J. Xydias

DANIEL BOONE THRU THE WILDERNESS (Sunset Productions, May 1, 1926) 6 Reels.
Roy Stewart, Kathleen Collins
D: Robert N. Bradbury
P: Anthony J. Xydias

GENERAL CUSTER AT LITTLE BIG HORN (Sunset Productions, September 15, 1926) 6 Reels.
Roy Stewart, Helen Lynch, John Beck, Edmund Cobb
D: Harry L. Fraser
S: Carrie E. Rawles
P: Anthony J. Xydias

SPARROWS (Pickford Corp./United Artists, September 19, 1926) 9 Reels.
Mary Pickford, Gustav von Seyffertitz, *Roy Stewart*, Mary Louise Miller, Charlotte Mineau, Spec O'Donnell, Lloyd Whitlock, A. L. Schaeffer, Mark Hamilton, Monty O'Grady, Muriel McCormac, Billy Jones, Cammilla Johnson, Mary McLane, Billy Butts, Jack Lavine, Florence Rogan, Seesel Ann Johnson, Sylvia Bernard
D: William Beaudine
Adapt: C. Gardner Sullivan
S: Winifred Dunn

YOU NEVER KNOW WOMEN (Paramount/Famous Players Lasky Corp., September 20, 1926) 6 Reels.
Florence Vidor, Lowell Sherman, Clive Brook, El Brendel, *Roy Stewart*, Joe Bonomo, Irma Kornelia, Sidney Bracy
D: William Wellman
SP: Benjamin Glazer
S: Ernest Vajda

THE MIDNIGHT WATCH (Trem Carr Productions/Rayart, February 1927) 6 Reels.
Roy Stewart, Mary McAllister, David Torrence, Ernest Hilliard, Marcella Daly
D: Charles Hunt
S: Trem Carr

ROARING FIRES (Elbee Pictures, July 29, 1927) 6 Reels.
Roy Stewart, Alice Lake, Lionel Belmore, Bert Berkeley, Raymond Turner, Spottiswoode Aitken, Culvert Curtis
D: W. T. Lackey
S/Scen: A. B. Barringer

ONE WOMAN TO ANOTHER (Paramount/Famous Players-Lasky Corp., September 17, 1927) 5 Reels.
Florence Vidor, Theodore von Eltz, Marie Shotwell, Hedda Hopper, *Roy Stewart*, Joyce Coad, Jimmy Boudwin
D: Frank Tuttle
S: Frances Nordstrom—"The Ruined Lady"
SP: J. L. Campbell

ACROSS THE BORDER (Vitaphone, September 1928) 2 Reels. (Sound)
Roy Stewart, Sara Padden, Frank Campeau

STORMY WATERS (Tiffany/Stahl Productions, June 1, 1928) 6 Reels.
Eve Southern, Malcolm McGregor, *Roy Stewart*, Shirley Palmer, Olin Francis, Norbert Myles, Bert Apling
D: Edgar Lewis
Adapt/Cont: Harry Dittmar
S: Jack London—"Yellow Handkerchief"
Supv: Roy Fitzroy

THE CANDY KID (Dailey Productions, 1928) 7 Reels.
Rex Lease, Pauline Garon, Frank Campeau, Harry Woods, *Roy Stewart*, Charlotte Merriam, Paul Panzer
D: David Kirkland
Scen: Rex Lease

IN OLD ARIZONA (Fox, January 20, 1929) 7 Reels.
Edmund Lowe, Dorothy Burgess, Warner Baxter, Farrell MacDonald, Fred Warren, Henry Armetta, Frank Campeau, Tom Santschi, Pat Hartigan, *Roy Stewart*, James Bradbury, Jr., John Dillon, Frank Nelson, Duke Martin, James Marcus, Joe Brown, Alphonse Ethier, Soledad Jiminez, Helen Lynch, Ivan Linow
D: Raoul Walsh, Irving Cummings
S/SP: Tom Barry

PROTECTION (Fox, May 5, 1929) 7 Reels.
Robert Elliott, Paul Page, Dorothy Burgess, Ben Hewlett, Dorothy Ward, Joe Brown, *Roy Stewart*, William H. Tooker, Arthur Hoyt
D: Benjamin Stoloff
Scen: Frederick Hazlitt Brennan
S: J. Clarkson Miller

THE GREAT DIVIDE (First National, September 15, 1929) 8 Reels.
(Sound)
Dorothy Mackaill, Ian Keith, Myrna Loy, Lucien Littlefield, Creighton Hale, George Fawcett, Claude Gillingwater, *Roy Stewart*, Ben Hendricks, Jr., Jean Laverty
D: Reginald Barker
Scen: Fred Myton, Paul Perez
S: William Vaughn Moody—"The Great Divide"
P: Robert North

Sara Padden, Roy Stewart, and Frank Campeau in
Across the Border (Vitaphone, 1928).

THE VIKING (Metro-Goldwyn-Mayer, November 2, 1929)
9 Reels.
(Music Score and Sound Effects) (Technicolor)
Donald Crisp, Pauline Starke, LeRoy Mason, Anders
Randolph, Richard Alexander, Harry Woods, *Roy Stewart,*
Torben Meyer, Claire McDowell, Julia Swayne Gordon
D: R. William Neill
Scen: Jack Cunningham
S: Ottilia Adelina Liljencrantz—"The Thrall of Leif the
Lucky: A Story of Viking Days"

THE LONE STAR RANGER (Fox, January 5, 1930) 7 Reels.
George O'Brien, Sue Carol, Walter McGrail, Warren Hymer,
Russell Simpson, *Roy Stewart,* Lee Shumway, Richard
Alexander, Elizabeth Patterson, William Steele, Bob Flem-
ing, Caroline Rankin, Joel Franz, Colin Chase, Oliver
Eckhardt, Billy Butts, Ralph Le Fevre, Joe Rickson, Delmar
Watson
D: A. F. Erickson
SP: Seton Miller
S: Zane Grey

MEN WITHOUT WOMEN (Fox, January 31, 1930) 9 Reels.
Kenneth MacKenna, Frank Albertson, Paul Page, Walter
McGrail, Warren Hymer, J. Farrell MacDonald, Stuart
Erwin, George Le Guere, Ben Hendricks, Jr., Harry Tenbrook,
Warner Richmond, *Roy Stewart,* Charles Gerard, Pat Somerset,
Robert Parrish, John Wayne
D: John Ford
SP: Dudley Nichols
S: John Ford, James Kevin McGuinness
AP: James Kevin McGuinness

THE ARIZONA KID (Fox, April 27, 1930) 9 Reels.
Warner Baxter, Mona Maris, Carol Lombard, Theodore von
Eltz, Arthur Stone, Solidad Jiminez, Walter P. Lewis, Jack
Herrick, Wilfred Lucas, Hank Mann, James Gibson, De Sacia
Mooers, Larry McGrath, *Roy Stewart,* Charles Gerard
D: Alfred Santell
S/Scen: Ralph Block

28

BORN RECKLESS (Fox, May 11, 1930) 9 Reels.
Edmund Lowe, Catherine Dale Owen, Warren Hymer, Marguerite Churchill, Lee Tracy, William Harrigan, Frank Albertson, Paul Page, Ferike Boros, Paul Porcasi, Joe Brown, Eddie Gribbon, Mike Donlin, Ben Bard, Pat Somerset, J. Farrell MacDonald, *Roy Stewart,* Jack Pennick, Ward Bond, Yola D'Avril
D: John Yord
SP: Dudley Nichols
S: Donald Henderson Clarke—"Louis Beretti"
AP: James K. McGuinness

ROUGH ROMANCE (Fox, June 15, 1930) 6 Reels.
George O'Brien, Helen Chandler, Antonio Moreno, Harry Cording, David Hartford, Noel Francis, Eddie Borden, *Roy Stewart,* Frank Lanning, John Wayne
D: A. F. Erickson
Scen: Elliott Lester
S: Kenneth B. Clarke—"The Girl Who Wasn't Wanted"

FIGHTING CARAVANS (Paramount, February 14, 1931) 91 Mins.
Gary Cooper, Lita Damita, Ernest Torrence, Fred Kohler, Tully Marshall, Eugene Pallette, Syd Saylor, *Roy Stewart,* May Boley, James Farley, James Marcus, Eve Southern, Donald MacKenzie, Charles Winninger, Frank Hagney, Frank Campeau, E. Allyn Warren, Merrill McCormick, Tiny Sanford, Jane Darwell, Irving Bacon, Harry Semels, Iron Eyes Cody, Chief Big Tree
D: Otto Brower, David Burton
SP: Edward E. Paramore, Keene Thompson, Agnes Brand Leahy
S: Zane Grey

MYSTERY RANCH (Fox, July 1, 1932) 65 Mins.
George O'Brien, Cecilia Parker, Charles Middleton, *Roy Stewart,* Charles Stevens, Forrest Harvey, Virginia Herdman, Noble Johnson, Russell Powell
D: David Howard
S: Edward White—"The Killer"
SP: Al Cohn

COME ON, TARZAN (World Wide, September 11, 1932) 61 Mins.
Ken Maynard, Kate Campbell, *Roy Stewart,* Niles Welch, Ben Corbett, Bob Kortman, Jack Rockwell, Nelson McDowell, Jack Mower, Merna Kennedy, Edmund Cobb, Robert Walker, Hank Bell, Jim Corey, Slim Whitaker, Al Taylor, Jack Ward, Bud McClure, "Tarzan"
D/SP: Alan James
P: Burt Kelley, Sam Bischoff, William Saal

COME ON DANGER (RKO-Radio, September 23, 1932) 60 Mins.
Tom Keene, Julie Hayson, Rosco Ates, Robert Ellis, Wade Boteler, William Scott, Roy Stewart, Harry Tenbrook, Bud Osborne, Frank Lacteen, Neil Craig, Monte Montague, "Flash"
D: Robert Hill
S/SP: Bennett Cohen

EXPOSED (Eagle, 1932) 63 Mins.
William Collier, Jr., Barbara Kent, Raymond Hatton, Bobby Hutchins, Walter McGrail, Jack Quinn, *Roy Stewart,* Billy Engles
D: Albert Herman
SP: Mauri Grashin

RUSTLER'S ROUNDUP (Universal, March 16, 1933) 56 Mins.
Tom Mix, Diane Sinclair, Noah Beery, Jr., Douglass Dumbrille, *Roy Stewart,* William Desmond, Gilbert Holmes, Bud Osborne, Frank Lackteen, William Wanger, Nelson McDowell, Walter Brennan, "Tony, Jr."
D: Henry MacRae
S: Ella O'Neill
SP: Frank Clark, Jack Cunningham

ZOO IN BUDAPEST (Fox, April 28, 1933) 85 Mins.
Loretta Young, Gene Raymond, O. P. Heggie, Wally Albright, Paul Fix, Ruth Warren, Russ Powell, *Roy Stewart,* Murray Kinnell, Frances Rich, Lucille Ward
D: Rowland V. Lee
S: Melville Baker, John Kirkland
SP: Dan Totheroh, Louise Long, Rowland V. Lee

FARGO EXPRESS (World Wide/Fox, November 20, 1933) 61 Mins.
Ken Maynard, Helen Mack, *Roy Stewart,* William Desmond, Paul Fix, Jack Rockwell, Bud McClure, Hank Bell, Ben Corbett, Blackjack Ward, Charles King, "Tarzan"
D: Alan James
SP: Alan James, Earle Snell
P: Burt Kelly, Sam Bischoff, William Saal

Wally Wales/Hal Taliaferro

2 • WALLY WALES / HAL TALIAFERRO

Rider of Many Trails

Floyd Taliaferro Alderson, in a thirty-eight-year film career, has certainly earned himself a niche in any patrician listing of "B" Western personalities. He was never a major star; nevertheless, as a minor star and character actor on the periphery of Western film immortality he outlasted most, if not all, of the first-magnitude stars. Perhaps the name is not one that you recognize or associate with Westerns. For although he came to the screen as Floyd Alderson and Floyd Taliaferro, and later was billed in a few pictures as Walt Williams, from 1925 to 1936 Floyd was generally known as Wally Wales and then as Hal Taliaferro for the remainder of his career.

Floyd worked with them all—the great, the competent, and those whose careers quickly tumbled into the abyss of oblivion. And when his own star had descended, during the last fifteen years of its life he quietly became one of the "B" genre's most beloved character actors.

Wally, if we may call him that, was born on November 13, 1895, and grew up on Hanging Woman Creek in Montana. He went on his first roundup in 1908 as a cook's helper with the outfit belonging to Senator John V. Kendrick of Wyoming. Despite his tender age, he quickly became a herd wrangler and cowpuncher and worked roundups for the next five years. In time he went back to develop the old Alderson ranch and to lay the foundations for the dude ranch which subsequently

was developed by his younger brothers. While Wally was still ramrodding the Bones Brothers Ranch ("Bones" was a name given by cowboys to the three Taliaferro brothers as children; Wally was called "Bigger Bones," his brother Allen "Big Bones," and the younger brother Ervin, "Little Bones"), the world first heard of him through the popular pen of Mary Roberts Rinehart who told her readers about Wally and his brothers and their picturesque ranch in a story called "Riding Circle on Hanging Woman Creek" in her book *Nomad's Land*, serialized in *The Saturday Evening Post*.

In the spring of 1914 Wally left the Montana country with a pack outfit headed for Yellowstone Park, where he obtained a job as a stage driver for Shore and Hopkins out of Cody, Wyoming. In the fall of 1915 he bummed his way to San Francisco to see the World's Fair, then drifted down to Hollywood where it was easy enough for a good rider to get work at the Universal studio ranch helping with the horses in the "cavalry." Later he began to pick up jobs as an extra, then played bits in Harry Carey and Tom Mix Westerns. But the titles in which Wally appeared are not known and so cannot be included in the Wales filmography.

In 1917 Wally entered the army, serving in the 91st Division and in the Spruce Division until 1919, spending his service time in stateside duty. After the war he picked up his Hollywood career, such as it was, eeking out an exiguous living mostly in bit parts. But a few featured roles did come his way. As Floyd Taliaferro, he had a meaty role in Associated Photoplay's *Western Hearts* of 1921. That same year he supported Pete Morrison in *Crossing Trails* at the same studio, and in 1922 was billed in Pinnacle's *The Kingfisher's Roost* and Paramount's *Travelin' On* as Floyd Alderson.

But until 1925 Wally's film work was mostly minor roles. To supplement his income he worked in the oil fields, as a night watchman, as a railroad deputy, and at assorted other jobs. It was while working in the oil fields that his friend, Shorty Hendricks, got him an interview with Lester F. Scott, Jr., founder of Action Pictures, who was already producing series with Buddy Roosevelt and Buffalo Bill, Jr., (Jay Wilsey). On July 7, 1925, Scott signed Floyd Alderson to a contract and changed his name to Wally Wales—a stage sobriquet compounded of his remarkable resemblance to Wallace Reid and the Prince of Wales—surmising that the name would attract attention. Sure enough, it did—and favorably.

Tearin' Loose, released in September 1925, was Wally's first starring venture. Story was by Betty Burbridge and direction by Richard Thorpe, both of whom would often serve him throughout his three years with Scott. The Wales pictures were brought in for $10,000 to $20,000 and were initially released by Weiss Artclass on the states' rights market, later by Pathe. Wally received $500 a picture as star.

By the time Wally attained stardom, William S. Hart had retired, and the realism he had injected into Westerns was in disfavor. Audiences had tired of seeing grubby-looking actors and seedy characters in bleak and near-desperate stories with tragic endings; the 1920s were beginning to roar, and audiences wanted lighthearted entertainment. And so, in the movies of Wales, Tom Mix, Buck Jones, and confreres, the Western began to give audiences what the producers sensed they wanted—a mythical conception of the West and its occupants.

Wally had the ability to play a whimsical kind of comedy and sufficient talent and facets to his screen character to make viewing his films an enjoyable adventure. Certainly his was not a linear screen personality with little opportunity to explore and develop offshoots from that straight line; thus

Burbridge and Thorpe were able to work considerable magic with the Wales films, in spite of cramped budgets. Wally was handsome, a good athlete, and a better-than-average actor who on a lesser scale demonstrated some of the qualities with which Buck Jones and John Wayne were endowed. Viewed today, the Wales films stand up well in comparison to other "indies" of the time.

Wally became a lovable, virile daredevil of countless giddyups, his histrionic talents embellished in the sound era by the charm of his low-pitched burr-twanging bass voice, with all cactus-land unfolding in the pronunciation of a sentence! It was a voice with the accent and color of a cowpuncher's lingo, although deep and with good tonal qualities. Good-looking he was, but as a sure-'nuff cowboy and bronco-bustin' ranch-ranger he was as good for the first five reels of his quick-on-the-trigger Westerns as he was in the final fadeout with the heroine neatly clasped in his swashbuckling embrace.

With the advent of sound, Wales kept right on grinding out entertaining sagebrushers for the cheaper cinema houses. Beginning with a featured role in *Overland Bound* (1929), one of the first sound Westerns employing sound-on-disc, Wally remained employed through the early depression years as a star of Big 4 and Imperial horse operas. He had the distinction of starring in the first all-sound serial, *Voice from the Sky*, a film that has long been lost to the film world and which received only limited bookings. Apparently no copies of this "cinematic first" exist today.

Like Yakima Canutt, Jack Perrin, Buddy Roosevelt, and other lesser cowboys of the 1930s, Wally altered among starring, featured, and minor roles. But he remained active and in demand, and that was the name of the game when millions of people were standing in breadlines.

Wales' Imperial and Big 4 Westerns are available for inspection today and, after viewing them, one is impressed with this fine cowboy who obviously had much more talent than most of the cowpunchers of his own or later eras. It was just bad breaks that kept him confined to the independents instead of finding a stall with the major studios that could have promoted him into another Maynard or Jones, for there was a charisma about Wally Wales that is evident even now when viewing his films of fifty years ago. *Film Daily*, the trade publication that more often than not was unkind in its reviews of "B" Westerns, said in its August 16, 1931 review of *Riders of the Cactus* that pictorially it was one of the finest Westerns ever produced and that it was Wally Wales at his best. Few independent Westerns ever received such a good review.

In the mid-1930s Wally became a character actor and second lead, and played with just about every cowboy star and star-aspirant in the business. His last starring effort was *The Way of the West* (Superior, 1934); thereafter he switched to character parts and, in 1936, made the name change to Hal Taliaferro. For several years he continued to receive third, fourth, and fifth billing in the Westerns of just about every studio and cowboy star who was then working. He quickly became one of the best heavies on the screen, and his face and voice were as welcome to two generations of matinee audiences as a valley of lush green grass to a hungry buffalo herd.

In his off-hours away from the camera Wally loved to paint—about the West, naturally—and his canvases have adorned many an art exhibit. He was quite good at painting and was one of Hollywood's most noted celebrity painters. His research into ancient religions and philosophies give an insight, perhaps, into his mental fiber. For pure relaxation he resorted to the sea in his boat.

His last great fling as a hero was as "Bob Stuart" in *The Lone Ranger*, Republic's classic serial of 1938. He had a lot of people convinced that he was the masked hero for much of the film. Throughout the 1940s Taliaferro continued to excel in his brand of villainy, menacing all the Republic and Columbia cowboys, and sometimes straying onto the ranges and backlots of other studios to lend a helping hand in frightening heroines into the arms of white-stetsoned heroes.

When the Western series bit the dust in the early 1950s, Wally left the glamour capital to work for a construction firm in Alaska. After a year or two he returned to Montana, where he practiced cowboyin' for twenty years on the ranch of a nephew. After he turned seventy-five, Wally would work in Arizona during the winter months to escape the extreme cold of Montana. But spring always found him back in southeastern Montana where no screen cowboy, other than himself, has trod. Working outdoors kept him lean and healthy until he was eighty, and he took a lot of pride in being able to pay his own way and take care of himself.

Wally Wales is a throwback, retaining the cowboy's pride and preferring to hoist his aching bones into the saddle and riding the trails of the Southwest rather than sitting at the hitchin' rail spittin' tobacco juice and remembering the "good old days." His trails have not always been downhill and shady; but he never expected that they would be. Philosophically, he meets life head on and merely shrugs his shoulders at temporary setbacks. For tomorrow is a brand-new day, possibly destined to be as unique as the one when his trail crossed that of Lester F. Scott, Jr., or the day William Witney directed his death scene in *The Lone Ranger*, or the days back in 1903 when he would sit by the creek and watch the Sioux ride by his dad's ranch.

Wally suffered a crippling stroke in 1976 and, as of this writing (June, 1979), is confined to a nursing home in Sheridan—a sad ending for a spirit still undaunted.

WALLY WALES/HAL TALIAFERRO *Filmography*

THE NEW ADVENTURES OF TERRENCE O'ROURKE (Universal Special, November 1915).
(Series of three 2-reel films which included "Palace of Dust," "When a Queen Loved O'Rourke," and "The Road to Paradise")
J. Warren Kerrigan, Floyd Alderson (*Wally Wales*)
(Wales' part was only a bit)

THE UNDERCURRENT (Universal, 1915).
Jane Bernoudy, Floyd Alderson (*Wally Wales*)
(No other information available. Wales' part would have been only a bit)

THE ADVENTURES OF PEG O' THE RING (Universal, May 1, 1916) 15 Chapters.
Francis Ford, Grace Cunard, Ruth Stonehouse, Peter Gerald, Charles Mann, G. Raymond Nye, Eddie Polo, Mark Fenton, Jean Hathaway, Floyd Alderson (*Wally Wales*)
D: Francis Ford, Jacques Jaccard
Chapter Titles: (1) The Leopard's Mark, (2) A Strange Inheritance, (3) In the Lion's Den, (4) The Circus Mongrels, (5) The House of Mystery, (6) The Cry for Help, or Cry of the Ring, (7) The Wreck, (8) Outwitted, (9) The Leap, (10) In the Hands of the Enemy, (11) The Stampede, (12) On the High Seas, (13) The Clown Act, (14) The Will, (15) Retribution

WESTERN HEARTS (Cliff Smith Productions/Associated Photoplays, September 1921) 5 Reels.
Art Straton, Josie Sedgwick, Floyd Taliaferro (*Wally Wales*), Hazel Hart, Edward Moncrief, Bert Wilson, Clark Comstock
D: Cliff Smith
S/SP: Cliff Smith, Alvin J. Neitz

CROSSING TRAILS (Cliff Smith Productions/Associated Photoplays, November 23, 1921) 5 Reels.
Pete Morrison, Esther Ralston, John Hatton, Lew Meehan, Floyd Taliaferro (*Wally Wales*), James B. Warner, Billie Bennett
D: Cliff Smith
S: L. V. Jefferson
SP: L. V. Jefferson, Alvin J. Neitz

THE KINGFISHER'S ROOST (Pinnacle, February 20, 1922) 5 Reels.
Neal Hart, Yvette Mitchell, William Quinn, Ben Corbett, Chet Ryan, James Fosher, Floyd Alderson (*Wally Wales*), W. S. Weatherwax, John Judd, Earl Simpson, Earl Dwyer
D/S/SP: Louis Chaudet, Paul Hurst

TRAVELIN' ON (William S. Hart Company/Paramount, March 5, 1922) 7 Reels.
William S. Hart, James Farley, Ethel Grey Terry, Brinsley Shaw, Mary Jane Irving, Robert Kortman, Willis Marks, Floyd Alderson (*Wally Wales*)
D/Adapt: Lambert Hillyer
S: William S. Hart

TEARIN' LOOSE (Action Pictures/Weiss Artclass, September 4, 1925) 5 Reels.
Wally Wales, Jean Arthur, Charles Whitaker, Alfred Newston, Polly Vann, Harry Belmour, Bill Ryno, Vester Pegg, Frank Ellis, Shorty Hendricks
D: Richard Thorpe
SP: Frank L. Inghram

HURRICANE HORSEMAN (Action Pictures/Weiss Artclass, October 14, 1925) 5 Reels.
Wally Wales, Jean Arthur, Vester Pegg, Charles Whitaker, Bob Chandler, Bob Fleming, Kewpie King
D: Richard Thorpe
SP: A. E. Serrao, Katherine Fanning

GALLOPING ON (Action Pictures/Weiss Artclass, November 23, 1925) 5 Reels.
Wally Wales, Jessie Cruzon, Louise Lester, Charles Whitaker, Richard Belfield, Gretchen Waterman, Art Phillips
D: Richard Thorpe
SP: Frank L. Inghram

Wally Wales and Jean Arthur in *The Fighting Cheat* (Action/Artclass, 1926).

ROARING RIDER (Action Pictures/Weiss Artclass, January 2, 1926) 5 Reels.
Wally Wales, Jean Arthur, Bert Lindley, Frank Ellis, Hazel Rodgers, Charles Whitaker
D: Richard Thorpe
SP: Reginald C. Barker

THE FIGHTING CHEAT (Action Pictures/Weiss Artclass, February 11, 1926) 5 Reels.
Wally Wales, Jean Arthur, Ted Rackerby, Fanny Midgley, Charles Whitaker, V. L. Barnes, Al Taylor
D: Richard Thorpe
S: Betty Burbridge
SP: Frank L. Inghram

VANISHING HOOFS (Action Pictures/Weiss Artclass, March 28, 1926) 5 Reels.
Wally Wales, Alma Rayford, William Ryno, Hazel Keener, Frank Ellis, William Dunn, Jane Sherman, Charles Whitaker, W. J. Willett, Robert Kortman, Dutch Malloy
D: J. P. McCarthy
S: L. V. Jefferson
SP: Betty Burbridge

RIDING RIVALS (Action Pictures/Weiss Artclass, May 2, 1926) 5 Reels.
Wally Wales, Jean Arthur, Charles Colby, Frank Ellis, Fanny Midgely, Charles Whitaker, William H. Turner, Lafe McKee
D: Richard Thorpe
SP: Betty Burbridge

DOUBLE DARING (Action Pictures/Weiss Artclass, June 11, 1926) 5 Reels.
Wally Wales, Jean Arthur, J. P. Lockney, Hank Bell, Charles Whitaker, Toby Wing, Vester Pegg, Shorty Hendricks
D: Richard Thorpe
S: Betty Burbridge
SP: Frank L. Inghram

TWISTED TRIGGERS (Action Pictures/Associated Exhibitors, July 11, 1926) 5 Reels.
Wally Wales, Jean Arthur, Al Richmond, Art Winkler, J. P. Lockney, William Bertram, Harry Belmour, Lawrence Underwood
D: Richard Thorpe
S: Tommy Gray
SP: Betty Burbridge

ACE OF ACTION (Action Pictures/Associated Exhibitors, November 28, 1926) 5 Reels.
Wally Wales, Alma Rayford, Charles Colby, Hank Bell, Fanny Midgley, Charles Whitaker, William Hayes, Frank Ellis
D: William Bertram
S/SP: Betty Burbridge

THE CYCLONE COWBOY (Action Pictures/Pathe, January 2, 1927) 5 Reels.
Wally Wales, Violet Bird, Raye Hampton, Richard Lee, Ann Warrington, George Magrill, Andrew Huyregis
D: Richard Thorpe
S: Tommy Gray
SP: Betty Burbridge

George F. Marion, Harry Todd, and Wally Wales in *Skedaddle Gold* (Action/Pathe, 1927).

TEARIN' INTO TROUBLE (Action Pictures/Pathe, March 20, 1927) 5 Reels.
Wally Wales, Olive Hasbrouck, Walter Brennan, Tommy Bay, Nita Cavalier, Violet Bird
D: Richard Thorpe
S: John Harold Hamlin
SP: Betty Burbridge

THE MEDDLIN' STRANGER (Action Pictures/Pathe, June 12, 1927) 5 Reels.
Wally Wales, Nola Luxford, Charles K. French, Mabel Van Buren, James Marcus, Boris Karloff
D: Richard Thorpe
S/SP: Christopher B. Booth

SKEDADDLE GOLD (Action Pictures/Pathe, July 31, 1927) 5 Reels
Wally Wales, Betty Baker, Robert Burns, George F. Marion, Harry Todd, Gordon Standing
D: Richard Thorpe
S: James French Dorrance
SP: Frank L. Inghram

WHITE PEBBLES (Action Pictures/Pathe, August 7, 1927) 5 Reels.
Wally Wales, Olive Hasbrouck, Walter Maly, Tom Bay, Harry Todd, K. Nambu, Kelly Gafford, Andrew Huyregis
D: Richard Thorpe
S: Reginald C. Barker—"Boss of the Bar None"
SP: Betty Burbridge

Wally Wales looks worried in this scene with an unidentified player from *Vanishing Hoofs* (Action/Artclass, 1926).

Wally Wales in *The Meddlin' Stranger* (Action/Pathe, 1927).

SODA WATER COWBOY (Action Pictures/Pathe, September 25, 1927) 5 Reels.
Wally Wales, Beryl Roberts, J. P. Lockney, Charles Whitaker, Al Taylor, Lafe McKee, Harry Belmour, Frank Ellis, Wallace Roberts, Kelly Gafford, Andrew Huyregis
D: Richard Thorpe
S: Tommy Gray
SP: Betty Burbridge

THE DESERT OF THE LOST (Action Pictures/Pathe, December 18, 1927) 5 Reels.
Wally Wales, Peggy Montgomery, William J. Dyer, Edward Cecil, Richard Neill, Kelly Gafford, Ray Murro, George Magrill, Charles Whitaker, Lafe McKee, Tom Bay
D: Richard Thorpe
S: Walter J. Coburn—"The Survival of Slim"
SP: Frank L. Inghram

DESPERATE COURAGE (Action Pictures/Pathe, January 15, 1928) 5 Reels.
Wally Wales, Olive Hasbrouck, Tom Bay, Lafe McKee, Fanchon Frankel, Bill Dyer, Charles Whitaker, Al Taylor, S. S. Simon
D: Richard Thorpe
S: Grant Taylor
SP: Frank L. Inghram

SADDLE MATES (Action Pictures/Pathe, August 5, 1928) 5 Reels.
Wally Wales, Peggy Montgomery, Hank Bell, J. Gordon Russell, Charles Whitaker, Lafe McKee, Edward Cecil, Lillian Allen
D: Richard Thorpe
SP: Frank L. Inghram
S: Harrington Strong—"Saddle Mates"

THE FLYING BUCKAROO (Action Pictures/Pathe, November 25, 1928) 5 Reels.
Wally Wales, Duane Thompson, Jack D'Oise, J. P. Lockney, Fanny Midgely, Mabel Van Buren, Charles K. French, Charles Whitaker, Helen Marlowe, Bud McClure
D: Richard Thorpe
S: Frank L. Inghram
SP: Betty Burbridge

THE VOICE FROM THE SKY (Ben Wilson Productions/ G.Y.B. Films, 1929) 10 Chapters.
Wally Wales, Jean Dolores (Neva Gerber), Robert Walker, J. P. Lockney, Al Haskell, Cliff Lyons, John C. McCallum, Merle Farris
D: Ben Wilson
S/Dial: Robert Dillon
C: William Nobles
Chapter Titles: (1) Doomed, (2) The Cave of Horror, (3) The Man from Nowhere, (4) Danger Ahead, (5) Desperate Deeds, (6) Trail of Vengeance, (7) The Scarlet Scourge, (8) Trapped by Fate, (9) The Pit of Peril, (10) Hearts of Steel
(Note: This was the first 100% sound and talking serial)

OVERLAND BOUND (Rayton Talking Pictures/Presido, November 23, 1929) 5,200 ft.
Jack Perrin, *Wally Wales,* Leo Maloney, Allene Ray, Lydia Knott, Charles K. French, R. J. Smith, Joe Maloney, William Dyer, "Bullet," "Starlight"
D: Leo Maloney
SP: Ford Beebe, Joseph Kane
P: Leo Maloney

BAR L RANCH (Big 4, July 1, 1930) 60 Mins.
Buffalo Bill, Jr., *Wally Wales,* Yakima Canutt, Betty Baker, Ben Corbett, Fern Emmett, Robert Walker
D: Harry S. Webb
S: Bennett Cohen
SP: Bennett Cohen, Carl Krusada
P: F. E. Douglas

CANYON HAWKS (National Players/Big 4, August 26, 1930) 5,400 ft.
Wally Wales, Buzz Barton, Rene Borden, Yakima Canutt, Cliff Lyons, Bobby Dunn, Bob Reeves, Robert Walker
D: J. P. McGowan, Alvin J. Neitz (Alan James)
S/SP: Henry Taylor, Alvin J. Neitz
P: F. E. Douglas

TRAILS OF PERIL (National Players/Big 4, September 30, 1930) 63 Mins.
(Title changed from "Trails of Danger")
Wally Wales, Virginia Brown Faire, Frank Ellis, Lew Meehan, Jack Perrin, Joe Rickson, Buck Connors, Bobby Dunn, Pete Morrison, Hank Bell
D: Alvin J. Neitz
SP: Henry Taylor and Alvin J. Neitz
P: F. E. Douglas
S: Alvin J. Neitz

Wally Wales seems to have the advantage over Cliff Lyons in this scene from *Red Fork Range* (Big 4, 1931)

BREED OF THE WEST (Big 4, November 12, 1930) 5,400 ft.
Wally Wales, Buzz Barton, Virginia Brown Faire, Robert Walker, Lafe McKee, Bobby Dunn, George Gerwin, Hank Cole (Hank Bell)
D: Alvin J. Neitz (Alan James)
SP: Henry Taylor, Alvin J. Neitz
P: F. E. Douglas

RED FORD RANGE (Big 4, January 12, 1931) 59 Mins.
Wally Wales, Ruth Mix, Al Ferguson, Cliff Lyons, Bud Osborned, Lafe McKee, Will Armstrong, George Gerwin, Jim Corey, Chief Big Tree
D: Alvin J. Neitz (Alan James)
S: Jenry Taylor
SP: Alvin J. Neitz

WESTWARD BOUND (Syndicate, January 25, 1931) 60 Mins.
Buffalo Bill, Jr., Buddy Roosevelt, Allene Ray, Yakima Canutt, Ben Corbett, Fern Emmett, Tom London, Robert Walker, Pete Morrison, Henry Rocquemore, *Wally Wales*
D: Harry Webb
S: Carl Krusada
P: Harry Webb and F. E. Douglas

HELL'S VALLEY (National Players/Big 4, March 7, 1931) 60 Mins.
Wally Wales, Virginia Brown Faire, Walter Miller, Franklyn Farnum, Vivian Rich, Lafe McKee, Jack Phipps, Frank Lackteen, Bobby Dunn
D: Alvin J. Neitz
S/SP: Alvin J. Neitz

Wally Wales connects on the chin of Sam Garrett in *Flying Lariats* (Big 4, 1931).

SO THIS IS ARIZONA (Big 4, April 24, 1931) 5 Reels.
Wally Wales, Lavaine Levoe, Fred Church, Buzz Barton, Kate Brady, Don Wilson, Gus Anderson, Jack Russell, Joe Lawliss
D: David Kirkland
S: Joe Lawliss

RIDERS OF THE CACTUS (Big 4, July 7, 1931) 60 Mins.
Wally Wales, Buzz Barton, Lorraine LaVal, Fred Church, Ed Cartwright, Don Wilson, Joe Lawliss, Tete Brady, Etta Delmas, Gus Anderson
D: David Kirkland
S: Charles Connell
SP: David Kirkland

FLYING LARIATS (Big 4, August 25, 1931) 60 Mins.
Wally Wales, Buzz Barton, Bonnie Gray, Sam Garrett, Etta Dalmas, Joe Lawliss, Fred Church, Tete Brady
D: David Kirkland
S: Henry Taylor
SP: Alvin J. Neitz

LAW AND LAWLESS (Majestic, November 30, 1932) 59 Mins.
Jack Hoxie, Hilda Moore, *Wally Wales*, Yakima Canutt, Julian Rivero, Jack Mower, J. Frank Glendon, Edith Fellows, Helen Gibson, Robert Burns, Alma Rayford, Joe De LaCruz, Fred Burns, Elvero Sonchez, William Quinn, Al Taylor, Dixie Starr
D: Armand Schaefer
S/SP: Oliver Drake
P: Larry Darmour

DEADWOOD PASS (Freuler/Monarch, May 5, 1933) 62 Mins.
Tom Tyler, Alice Dahl, *Wally Wales*, Buffalo Bill, Jr., Lafe McKee, Bud Osborne, Edmund Cobb, Slim Whitaker, Merrill McCormack, Charlote (Carlotta) Monti, Duke Lee, Blackie Whiteford, Bill Nestell
D: J. P. McGowan
S: John Wesley Patterson
SP: Oliver Drake
P: Burton King

THE FIGHTING TEXANS (Monogram, July 26, 1933)
55 Mins.
Rex Bell, Luana Walters, Betty Mack, George Hayes, *Wally Wales*, Yakima Canutt, Lafe McKee, Anne Howard, Al Bridge, Frank LaRue, George Nash
D: Armand Schaefer
SP: Wellyn Totman, Charles Roberts
P: Trem Carr

SECRETS OF HOLLYWOOD (Lester F. Scott Productions, August 1933) 58 Mins.
Mae Busch, *Wally Wales*, June Walters, George Cowl, Norbert Myles, David Callis, Tom Francis, Ernest Adams and film clips from old silent movies featuring Colleen Moore, Charles Ray, John Gilbert, Wallace Beery, Douglas McLean, Doris May and Leo White, Edmund Lowe, Florence Vidor, Madge Bellamy, Noah Beery, Cullen Landis, Enid Bennett, Matt Moore
D: George M. Merrick, Holbrook Todd
SP: Betty Burbridge

THE TRAIL DRIVE (Universal, September 4, 1933)
60 Mins.
Ken Maynard, Cecilia Parker, William Gould, *Wally Wales*, Ben Corbett, Lafe McKee, Alan Bridge, Bob Kortman, Frank Rice, Fern Emmett, Jack Rockwell, Slim Whitaker, Frank Ellis, Hank Bell, Edward Coxen, Bob Reeves, Art Mix, Jack Kirk, Buck Bucko, Roy Bucko, Bud McClure, "Tarzan"
D: Alan James
S: Ken Maynard, Nate Gatzert
SP: Nate Gatzert
P: Ken Maynard

SAGEBRUSH TRAIL (Lone Star/Monogram, December 15, 1933) 58 Mins.
John Wayne, Lane Chandler, Nancy Shubert, *Wally Wales*, Yakima Canutt, Henry Hall, William Dyer, Earl Dwire, Art Mix, Hank Bell, Slim Whitaker, Robert Burns, Hal Price
D: Armand Schaefer
SP: Lindsley Parsons
P: Paul Malvern

MYSTERY SQUADRON (Mascot, December 22, 1933)
12 Chapters.
Bob Steele, Guinn (Big Boy) Williams, Jack Mulhall, Lucile Browne, Robert Frazer, Purnell Pratt, J. Carrol Naish, Robert Kortman, Lafe McKee, Edward Hearn, Edward Piel, Kernan Cripps, Jack Mower, Jack Perrin, Lew Meehan, Frank Ellis, *Wally Wales*
D: Colbert Clark and David Howard
S: Sherman Lowe, Al Martin
SP: Barney Sarecky, Colbert Clark, David Howard, Wyndham Gittens
Chapter Titles: (1) The Black Ace, (2) The Fatal Warning, (3) The Black Ace Strikes, (4) Men of Steel, (5) The Death Swoop, (6) Doomed, (7) Enemy Signals, (8) The Canyon of Calamity, (9) The Secret of the Mine, (10) Clipped Wings, (11) The Beast at Bay, (12) The Ace of Aces

Wally Wales, Mae Bush, and June Walters in *Secrets of Hollywood* (Lester Scott Productions, 1933).

POTLUCK PARDS (B 'n' B Pictures/Reliable, January 15, 1934).
Walt Williams, (*Wally Wales*), Ben Corbett, Josephine Hill, Harry Myers, James Aubrey, Robert Walker, George Chesebro, Murdock McQuarrie
D/P: Bernard B. Ray
SP: Bennett Cohen

WHEELS OF DESTINY (Universal, February 19, 1934)
63 Mins.
Ken Maynard, Dorothy Dix, Philo McCullough, Fred McKay, Jay Wilsey (Buffalo Bill, Jr.), Fred Sale, Jr., Jack Rockwell, Frank Rice, Nelson McDowell, William Gould, Ed Coxen, Merrill McCormack, Slim Whitaker, Hank Bell, Robert Burns, Artie Ortego, *Wally Wales*, Jack Evans, Helen Gibson, Bud McClure, Fred Burns, Chief Big Tree, Roy Bucko, Chuck Baldro, Arkansas Johnny, Bobby Gun, Blackjack Ward, "Tarzan"
D: Alan James
S/SP: Nate Gatzert
P: Ken Maynard

NEVADA CYCLONE (B 'n' B Pictures/Reliable, March 15, 1934) 33 Mins.
Fred Humes, Ben Corbett, Frances Morris, Lafe McKee, Walt Williams, (*Wally Wales*), George Chesebro, Lew Meehan
D/P: Bernard B. Ray
SP: Bennett Cohen

THE LOST JUNGLE (Mascot, March 22, 1934) 12 Chapters.
Clyde Beatty, Cecilia Parker, Syd Saylor, Wheeler Oakman, Edward LeSaint, Warner Richmond, Lew Meehan, Mickey Rooney, George "Gabby" Hayes, *Wally Wales*, Ernie Adams, Maston Williams, Jim Corey, Charles Whitaker, Lloyd Whitlock, Lloyd Ingraham, Henry Hall, J. Crauford Kent, Max Wagner, Wes Warner, Jack Carlyle, Lionel Backus,

Josephine Hill finds Wally Wales fascinating company in *Potluck Pards* (Reliable, 1934), one of the few pictures in which Wally was billed as Walt Williams.

Harry Holman, Wilfrid Lucas
D: Armand Schaefer and David Howard
S: Sherman Lowe, Al Martin
SP: Barney Sarecky, David Howard, Armand Schaefer, Wyndham Gittens
Chapter Titles: (1) Noah's Ark Island, (2) Nature in the Raw, (3) The Hypnotic Eye, (4) The Pit of Crocodiles, (5) Guerrilla Warfare, (6) The Battle of Beasts, (7) The Tiger's Prey, (8) The Lion's Brood, (9) Eyes of the Jungle, (10) Human Hyenas, (11) The Gorilla, (12) Take Them Back Alive

HONOR OF THE RANGE (Universal, April 16, 1934) 61 Mins.
Ken Maynard, Cecilia Parker, Fred Kohler, Jack Rockwell, Frank Hagney, James Marcus, Franklyn Farnum, Al Bridge, Jack Kirk, Art Mix, Eddie Barnes, Albert J. Smith, Charles Whitaker, Fred McKaye, *Wally Wales,* Hank Bell, Lafe McKee, William Patton, Bud McClure, Nelson McDowell, Ben Corbett, Pascale Perry, Jack Ward, Roy Bucko, Buck Bucko, Fred Burns, "Tarzan"
D: Alan James
S/SP: Nate Gatzert
P: Ken Maynard

SMOKING GUNS (Universal, June 11, 1934) 62 Mins.
Ken Maynard, Gloria Shea, Walter Miller, Harold Goodwin, William Gould, Bob Kortman, Jack Rockwell, Etta Mc-Daniels, Martin Turner, Ed Coxen, Slim Whitaker, Hank Bell, Horace B. Carpenter, Blue Washington, *Wally Wales,* Edmund Cobb, Bob Reeves, Fred McKaye, Jim Corey, Roy Bucko, Buck Bucko, Ben Corbett, Jack Ward, Bud McClure, "Tarzan"
D: Alan James
S/SP: Nate Gatzert
P: Ken Maynard

THE FIGHTING ROOKIE (Mayfair, June 1934) 67 Mins.
Jack LaRue, Ada Ince, DeWitt Jennings, Matthew Betz, Arthur Belasco, Thomas Brewer, *Wally Wales*
D: Spencer Gordon Bennet
S: Homer King Gordon
SP: George Morgan
P: Lester F. Scott, Jr.

FIGHTING THROUGH (Kent, August 29, 1934) 55 Mins.
Reb Russell, Lucille Lund, Yakima Canutt, Edward Hearn, Chester Gans, Steve Clemente, Bill Patton, Frank McCarroll, Ben Corbett, Hank Bell, Slim Whitaker, Nelson McDowell, Lew Meehan, Jack Jones, Jack Kirk, Chuck Baldra, *Wally Wales,* "Rebel"
D: Harry Fraser
S/SP: Harry Fraser
P: Willis Kent

THE LAW OF THE WILD (Mascot, August 1934) 12 Chapters
"Rex" (King of Wild Horses), "Rin-Tin-Tin, Jr.," Bob Custer, Ben Turpin, Lucile Browne, Richard Crammer, Ernie Adams, Edmund Cobb, Slim Whitaker, Dick Alexander, Jack Rockwell, *Wally Wales,* Charles King, Lafe McKee, Hank Bell, Art Mix, Bud Osborne, Glenn Strange, Silver Harr, Al Taylor
D: B. Reeves Eason, Armand Schaefer
S: Ford Beebe, John Rathmell, Al Martin
SP: Sherman Lowe, B. Reeves Eason
P: Nat Levine
Chapter Titles: (1) The Mankiller, (2) The Battle of the Strong, (3) The Cross-Eyed Goony, (4) Avenging Fangs, (5) A Dead Man's Hand, (6) Horse Thief Justice, (7) The Death Stampede, (8) The Canyon of Calamity, (9) Robber's Roost, (10) King of the Range, (11) Winner Takes All, (12) The Grand Sweepstakes

THE OIL RAIDER (Mayfair, August 1934) 7 Reels.
Buster Crabbe, Gloria Shea, George Irving, Max Wagner, Emmett Vogan, Harold Minjir, *Wally Wales,* Tom London
D: Spencer Gordon Bennet
S: Rex Taylor
P: Lester F. Scott, Jr.

MYSTERY MOUNTAIN (Mascot, December 1, 1934)
12 Chapters
Ken Maynard, Verna Hillie, Edward Earle, Edmund Cobb, Lynton Brent, Syd Saylor, Carmencita Johnson, Lafe McKee, Al Bridge, Edward Hearn, Bob Kortman, Gene Autry, Lester "Smiley" Burnette, *Wally Wales,* Tom London, George Chesebro, Philo McCullough, Frank Ellis, Steve Clark, James Mason, Lew Meehan, Jack Rockwell, Art Mix, William Gould, "Tarzan"
D: B. Reeves Eason, Otto Brower
S: Sherman Lowe, Barney Sarecky, B. Reeves Eason
SP: Bennett Cohen, Armand Schaefer
P: Nat Levine
Chapter Titles: (1) The Rattler, (2) The Man Nobody Knows, (3) The Eye That Never Sleeps, (4) The Human Target, (5) Phantom Outlaws, (6) The Perfect Crime, (7) Tarzan the Cunning, (8) The Enemy's Stronghold, (9) The Fatal Warning, (10) The Secret of the Mountain, (11) Behind the Mask, (12) The Judgment of Tarzan

ARIZONA CYCLONE (Imperial, 1934).
Wally Wales, Franklyn Farnum, Sally Darling, Fred Parker, Barney Beasley, "Silver King"
D: Robert Emmett (Tansey)
SP: Robert Emmett (Tansey)
P: William Pizor

CARRYING THE MAIL (Imperial, 1934).
Wally Wales, Peggy Djarling, Yakima Canutt, Al Hoxie, Sherry Tansey, Franklyn Farnum, "Silver King"
D: Robert Emmett
SP: Al Lane
P: William Pizor

DESERT MAN (Imperial, 1934).
Wally Wales, Peggy Djarling, Yakima Canutt, Franklyn Farnum, Sherry Tansey, Al Hoxie, "Silver King"
D: Robert Emmett
SP: Robert Emmett
P: William Pizor

THE LONE BANDIT (Empire, 1934).
Lane Chandler, Doris Brook, *Wally Wales,* Slim Whitaker, Ray Gallagher, Ben Corbett, Philo McCullough, Jack Prince
D: J. P. McGowan
S: Buck Parsons
SP: Ralph Consumana
P: Nathan Hirish

THE LONE RIDER (Imperial, 1934).
Wally Wales, Marla Bratton, Franklyn Farnum, James Sheridan (Sherry Tansey), Fred Parker, "Silver King"
D: Robert Emmett
SP: Al Lane
P: William Pizor

PALS OF THE WEST (Imperial, 1934).
Wally Wales, Dorothy Gritten, Yakima Canutt, Franklyn Farnum, Al Hoxie, James Sheridan (Sherry Tansey), Fred Parker, "Silver King"
D: Robert Emmett
SP: Robert Emmett
P: William Pizor

THE SUNDOWN TRAIL (Imperial, 1934).
Wally Wales, Fay McKenzie, James Sheridan (Sherry Tansey), Barney Beasley, Jack Kirk, "Silver King"
D: Robert Emmett
SP: Al Lane
P: William Pizor

THE WAY OF THE WEST (Empire/Superior, 1934).
Wally Wales, Marla Bratton, Bobby Nelson, William Desmond, Fred Parker, Sherry Tansey, Art Mix, Bill Patton, Tex Jones, Harry Beery, Helen Gibson, Tiny Skelton, Gene Laymond, Jimmy Aubrey
S/P: Robert Emmett (Tansey)
S: Barry Barringer
SP: Al Lane

WEST OF THE LAW (Imperial, 1934).
Wally Wales, Marla Bratton, Franklyn Farnum, James Sheridan (Sherry Tansey), Fred Parker, "Silver King"
D: Robert Emmett (Tansey)
SP: Al Lane
P: William Pizor

RUSTLERS OF RED DOG (Universal, January 1935)
12 Chapters.
Johnny Mack Brown, Raymond Hatton, Joyce Compton, Walter Miller, Harry Woods, Charles K. French, Fred McKaye, William Desmond, *Wally Wales,* Chief Thunder Cloud, Slim Whitaker, Art Mix, Jim Corey, Bill Patton, Cliff Lyons, Tex Cooper, Ben Corbett, Hank Bell, Bud Osborne, Edmund Cobb, J. P. McGowan, Monte Montague, Lafe McKee, Artie Ortego, Jim Thorpe, Chief Thunderbird, Ann D'Arcy, Fritzi Brunette, Grace Cunard, Virginia Ainsworth
S: Louis Friedlander (Lew Landers)
S: Nathaniel Eddy
SP: George Plympton, Basil Dickey, Ella O'Neill, Nate Gatzert, Vin Moore
Chapter Titles: (1) Hostile Redskins, (2) Flaming Arrows, (3) Thundering Hoofs, (4) Attack at Dawn, (5) Buried Alive, (6) Flames of Vengeance, (7) Into the Depths, (8) Paths of Peril, (9) The Snake Strikes, (10) Riding Wild, (11) The Rustlers Clash, (12) Law and Order

WILLIAM M. PIZOR presents

WALLY WALES

IN "CARRYING THE MAIL"

Shown at upper left of lobby card is the famed horse "Silver King," formerly owned by Fred Thomson. Wally Wales is shown in circle at lower right, while the center photo shows Franklyn Farnum, Al Hoxie, Wally Wales, Yakima Canutt, Peggy Djarling, Sherry Tansey, and unidentified player (Imperial, 1934).

UNCONQUERED BANDIT (Reliable/William Steiner, January 8, 1935) 57 Mins.
Tom Tyler, Lillian Gilmore, Slim Whitaker, William Gould, John Elliott, Earl Dwire, Joe De LaCruz, George Chesebro, Lew Meehan, Dick Alexander, George Hazle, Ben Corbett, *Wally Wales,* Colin Chase
D: Harry S. Webb
Story: Carl Krusada
Screenplay: Rose Gordon, Lou C. Borden
P: Bernard B. Ray
Assoc. P: Harry S. Webb

SIX GUN JUSTICE (Spectrum, February 1, 1935) 57 Mins.
Bill Cody, *Wally Wales,* Ethel Jackson, Budd Buster, Donald Reed, Ace Cain, Frank Morgan, Bert Young, Buck Morgan, Roger Williams, Jimmy Aubrey, Blackie Whiteford
D: Robert Hill
SP: Oliver Drake
P: Ray Kirkwood

THE PHANTOM EMPIRE (Mascot, February 23, 1935) 12 Chapters. Gene Autry, Frankie Darro, Betsy King Ross, Dorothy Christie, Wheeler Oakman, Charles K. French,

Wally Wales, Bobby Nelson, and Marla Bratton in *The Way of the West* (Superior, 1934).

Warner Richmond, J. Frank Glendon, Smiley Burnette, William Moore, Edward Peil, Jack Carlyle, *Wally Wales,* Jay Wilsey (Buffalo Bill, Jr.), Stanley Blystone, Richard Talmadge, Frank Ellis, Peter Potter, Bob Burns, Bob Card, Bruce Mitchell, "Champion"
D: Otto Brower, B. Reeves Eason
S: Wallace MacDonald, Gerald Geraghty, Hy Freedman, Maurice Geraghty
SP: John Rathmell, Armand Schaefer
P: Nat Levine
Chapter Titles: (1) The Singing Cowboy, (2) The Thunder Riders, (3) The Lightning Chamber, (4) Phantom Broadcast, (5)Beneath the Earth, (6) Disaster from the Skies, (7) From Death to Life, (8) Jaws of Jeopardy, (9) Prisoners of the Ray, (10) The Rebellion, (11) A Queen in Chains (12) The End of Murania (Two feature versions edited from this serial: MEN WITH STEEL FACES and RADIO RANCH)

RANGE WARFARE (Kent, March 1935).
Reb Russell, Lucille Lund, *Wally Wales,* Lafe McKee, Roger Williams, Slim Whitaker, Ed Boland, Dick Botiller, Chief Blackhawk, Ed Porter, Gene Alsace (Rocky Camron)
D: S. Roy Luby
P: Willis Kent

THE COWBOY AND THE BANDIT (International/ Superior, April 3, 1935) 57 Mins.
Rex Lease, Bobby Nelson, Janet Morgan (Blanche Mehaffey), Dick Alexander, Ada Belle Driver, Bill Patton, *Wally Wales,* William Desmond, Franklyn Farnum, Art Mix, Lafe McKee, Ben Corbett, Vic Potel, George Chesebro, Alphonse Martel, Jack Kirk, Fred Parker
D: Al Herman
SP: Jack Jevne
P: Louis Weiss

THE SILVER BULLET (Reliable/William Steiner, May 11, 1935) 58 Mins.
Tom Tyler, Jayne Regan, Lafe McKee, Charles King, Slim Whitaker, Franklyn Farnum, George Chesebro, Lew Meehan, Walt Williams (*Wally Wales*), Nelson McDowell, Robert Brower, Blackie Whiteford, Hank Bell, Allen Greer
D: Bernard B. Ray
S: William L. Nolte
SP: Rose Gordon, Carl Krusada
P: B. B. Ray

CALL OF THE SAVAGE (Universal, June 1935) 12 Chapters.
Noah Beery, Jr., Dorothy Short, Harry Woods, Walter Miller, Bryant Washburn, Frederic MacKaye, John Davidson, Eddie Kane, Stanley Andrews, Russ Powell, William Desmond, Frank Glendon, Viva Tattersall, Grace Cunard, Gwendolyn Logan, Don Brodie, H. Burroughs, Dick Jones, *Wally Wales*, Al Ferguson, Buddy Roosevelt, J. P. McGowan
D: Louis Friedlander
S: Otis Adelbert Kline—"Jan of the Jungle"
SP: Nate Gazert, George Plympton, Basil Dickey
Chapter Titles: (1) Shipwrecked, (2) Captured by Cannibals, (3) Stampeding Death, (4) Terrors of the Jungle, (5) The Plunge of Peril, (6) Thundering Waters, (7) The Hidden Monster, (8) Jungle Treachery, (9) The Avenging Fire God, (10) Descending Doom, (11) The Dragon Strikes, (12) The Pit of Flame

THE LARAMIE KID (Reliable/William Steiner, June 1935) 57 Mins.
Tom Tyler, Alberta Vaughn, Al Ferguson, Murdock McQuarrie, George Chesebro, Snub Pollard, Steve Clark, Artie Ortego, *Wally Wales*, Nelson McDowell, Budd Buster, Jimmy Aubrey
D: Harry S. Webb
S: C. C. Church
SP: Carl Krusada, Rose Gordon
P: Bernard B. Ray
Assoc. P: Harry S. Webb

THE VANISHING RIDERS (Spectrum, July 3, 1935).
Bill Cody, Ethel Jackson, *Wally Wales*, Bill Cody, Jr., Budd Buster, Milburn Morante, Donald Reed, Francis Walker, Roger Williams, Bert Young, Buck Morgan, Ace Cain, Colin Chase, Bud Osborne
D: Bob Hill
S/SP: Oliver Drake
P: Ray Kirkwood

POWDERSMOKE RANGE (RKO, September 27, 1935) 6 Reels.
(First of the "3 Mesquiteers" films)
Harry Carey, Hoot Gibson, Bob Steele, Tom Tyler, Guinn "Big Boy" Williams, Boots Mallory, *Wally Wales*, Sam Hardy, Adrian Morris, Buzz Barton, Art Mix, Frank Rice, Buddy Roosevelt, Buffalo Bill, Jr., Franklyn Farnum, William Desmond, William Farnum, Ethan Laidlaw, Eddie Dunn, Ray Meyer, Barney Furey, Bob McKenzie, James Mason, Irving Bacon, Henry Rocquemore, Phil Dunham, Silver Tip Baker, Nelson McDowell, Frank Ellis
D: Wallace Fox
S: William Colt MacDonald
SP: Adele Buffington
P: Cliff Reid

LAWLESS RIDERS (Columbia, December 6, 1935) 57 Mins.
Ken Maynard, Geneva Mitchell, Harry Woods, Frank Yaconelli, Hal Taliaferro (*Wally Wales*), Slim Whitaker, Frank Ellis, Jack Rockwell, Bob McKenzie, Hank Bell, Bud Jamison, Horace B. Carpenter, Jack King, Bud McClure, Pascale Perry, Oscar Gahan, "Tarzan"
D: Spencer G. Bennet
S/SP: Nate Gatzert
P: Larry Darmour

SWIFTY (Diversion, December 12, 1935) 58 Mins.
Hoot Gibson, June Gale, George Hayes, Ralph Lewis, *Wally Wales*, Art Mix, Bob Kortman, Lafe McKee, "Starlight"
D: Alan James
S: Stephen Payne
SP: Bennett Cohen
P: Walter Futter

HEIR TO TROUBLE (Columbia, December 17, 1935) 59 Mins.
Ken Maynard, Joan Perry, Harry Woods, *Wally Wales*, Martin Faust, Harry Brown, Dorothy Wolbert, Fern Emmett, Pat O'Malley, Art Mix, Frank Yaconelli, Frank LaRue, Hal Price, Jim Corey, Lafe McKee, Jack Rockwell, Slim Whitaker, Roy Bucko, Buck Bucko, Jack Ward, Bud McClure, Artie Ortega, "Tarzan"
D: Spencer G. Bennet
S: Ken Maynard
SP: Nate Gatzert
P: Larry Darmour

DANGER TRAILS (Beacon/First Division, 1935) 55 Mins.
Big Boy Williams, Marjorie Gordon, *Wally Wales*, John Elliott, Ace Cain, Edmund Cobb, Steve Clark, George Chesebro
D: Bob Hill
S: Guinn "Big Boy" Williams
SP: Rock Hawley (Bob Hill)
P: Max and Arthur Alexander

FIGHTING CABALLERO (Merrick/Superior, 1935).
Rex Lease, Dorothy Gulliver, Earl Douglas, George Chesebro, Robert Walker, *Wally Wales*, Milburn Morante, George Morrell, Pinky Barnes, Carl Mathews, Barney Furey, Franklyn Farnum, Marty Joyve, Paul Ellis
D: Elmer Clifton
SP: Elmer Clifton, George M. Merrick
P: Louis Weiss

FIVE BAD MEN (Sunset, 1935).
Noah Beery, Jr., Buffalo Bill, Jr., Sally Darling, *Wally Wales*, William Desmond, Art Mix, Pete Morrison, Bill Patton, Edward Coxen, Billy Franey
D: Cliff Smith

GUN PLAY (Beacon/First Division, 1935) 59 Min.
(Also known as "Lucky Boots")
Big Boy Williams, Marion Shilling, *Wally Wales*, Frank Yaconelli, Tom London, Charles K. French, Roger Williams, Julian Rivero, Barney Beasley, Dick Botiller, Gordon Griffith, Si Jenks
D: Al Herman
S/SP: William L. Nolte
P: Arthur Alexander

THE MIRACLE RIDER (Mascot, 1935) 15 Chapters.
Tom Mix, Joan Gale, Charles Middleton, Jason Robards, Edward Hearn, Pat O'Malley, Robert Frazer, Ernie Adams, *Wally Wales*, Bob Kortman, Chief Standing Bear, Charles King, Tom London, Niles Welch, Edmund Cobb, George Chesebro, Jack Rockwell, Max Wagner, Stanley Price, George Burton, Lafe McKee, "Tony, Jr."
D: B. Reeves Eason, Armand Schaefer
S: Barney Scarecky, Wellyn Totman, Gerald Geraght
SP: John Rathmell
P: Nat Levine
Chapter Titles: (1) The Vanishing Indian, (2) The Firebird Strikes, (3) The Flying Knife, (4) A Race with Death, (5) Double-Barreled Doom, (6) Thundering Hoofs, (7) The Dragnet, (8) Guerrilla Warfare, (9) The Silver Band, (10) Signal Fires, (11) A Traitor Dies, (12) Danger Rides with Death, (13) The Secret of X-94, (14) Between Two Fires, (15) Justice Rides the Plains

THE PECOS KID (Commodore, 1935).
Fred Kohler, Jr., Ruth Findlay, Roger Williams, Edward Cassidy, *Wally Wales*, Earl Dwire, Francis Walker, Budd Buster, Rose Plummer, Clyde McClary, Robert Walker, Jack Evans
D/P: William Berke
S: Ted Tuttle
SP: Henry Hess

SILENT VALLEY (Reliable/William Steiner, 1935).
Tom Tyler, Nancy DeShon, *Wally Wales*, Charles King, Alan Bridge, Murdock McQuarrie, Art Miles, George Chesebro, Charles Whitaker, Jimmy Aubrey
D/P: Bernard B. Ray
SP: Carl Krusada, Rose Gordon

TRIGGER TOM (Reliable/William Steiner, 1935).
Tom Tyler, Al St. John, Bernadine Hayes, William Gould, John Elliott, Bud Osborne, Lloyd Ingraham, *Wally Wales*
D: Henri Samuels (Harry S. Webb)
S: George Cory Franklin—"The Swimming Herd"
SP: Tom Gibson
P: Bernard B. Ray

WESTERN RACKETEERS (Aywon, 1935).
Bill Cody, Edna Aslin, *Wally Wales*, Ben Corbett, Budd Buster, George Chesebro, Bud Osborne, Frank Clark, Gilbert (Pee-Wee) Holmes, Robert Sands, Tom Dwaine, Dick Cramer, Billy Franey
D: Robert J. Horner
P: Nathan Hirsch

LUCKY TERROR (Diversion/Grand National, February 20, 1936) 61 Mins.
Hoot Gibson, Lona Andre, Charles Hill, George Chesebro, Bob McKenzie, *Wally Wales*, Art Mix, Horace Murphy, Hank Bell
D: Alan James
S: Roger Allman
SP: Rose Gordon, Carl Krusada
P: Bernard B. Ray

THE PHANTOM RIDER (Universal, July 6, 1936) 15 Chapters.
Buck Jones, Marla Shelton, Diana Gibson, Joe Ray, Harry Woods, Frank LaRue, George Cooper, Eddie Gribbon, Helen Shipman, James Mason, Jim Corey, Lee Sumway, Charles LeMoyne, Clem Bevins, Cecil Weston, Matt McHugh, Jim Thorpe, Charles King, Curtis McPeters (Cactus Mack), Charles K. French, Tom London, *Wally Wales*, Slim Whitaker, Frank Ellis, Bob Fite, "Hi Pockets" Busse, Bill Scott, Jimmy Carroll, Hank Bell, Lafe McKee, Priscilla Lawson, Drew Stanfield, Art Mix, George Plues, Tom Carter, Scoop Martin, Fred Warren, Olin Francis, Iron Eyes Cody, Paul Regas, Eva McKenzie, Orrin Burke, George Ovey, Cliff Lyons, "Silver"
D: Ray Taylor
Original SP: George Plympton, Basil Dickey, Ella O'Neill
P: Henry MacRae
Chapter Titles: (1) Dynamite, (2) The Maddened Herd, (3) The Brink of Disaster, (4) The Phantom Rides, (5) Trapped by Outlaws, (6) Shot Down, (7) Stark Terror, (8) The Night Attack, (9) The Indian Raid, (10) Human Targets, (11) The Shaft of Doom, (12) Flaming Gold, (13) Crashing Timbers, (14) The Last Chance, (15) The Outlaw's Vengence

AVENGING WATERS (Columbia, July 8, 1936) 57 Mins.
Ken Maynard, Beth Marion, Ward Bond, John Elliott, Zella Russell, *Wally Wales*, Tom London, Edmund Cobb, Edward Hearn, Buck Moulton, Glenn Strange, Cactus Mack, Buffalo Bill, Jr., Sterling Holloway, Jack King, Buck Bucko, Bud McClure, "Tarzan"
D: Spencer G. Bennet
S/SP: Nate Gatzert
P: Larry Darmour

HEROES OF THE RANGE (Columbia, August 18, 1936) 58 Mins.
Ken Maynard, June Gale, Harry Woods, Harry Ernest, Bob Kortman, Bud McClure, Tom London, Bud Osborne, Frank Hagney, Jack Rockwell, Lafe McKee, *Wally Wales,* Jay Wilsey (Buffalo Bill, Jr.), Jerome Ward, Bud McClure, Bud Jamison, Bob Reeves, Jack King, "Tarzan"
D: Spencer G. Bennet
S/SP: Nate Gatzert
P: Larry Darmour

THE TRAITOR (Puritan, August 29, 1936) 56 Mins.
Tim McCoy, Frances Grant, *Wally Wales,* Karl Hackett, Jack Rockwell, Pedro Regas, Frank Melton, Dick Curtis, Dick Botiller, Edmund Cobb, Wally West, Tina Menard, Soledad Jiminez, J. Frank Glendon, Frank McCarroll
D: Sam Newfield
S: John Thomas Neville
SP: Joseph O'Donnell
P: Sigmund Neufeld, Leslie Simmonds

AMBUSH VALLEY (Reliable/William Steiner, November 1, 1936) 57 Mins.
Bob Custer, Victoria Vinton, Vane Calvert, Eddie Phillips, *Wally Wales,* Oscar Gahan, Ed Cassidy, Denver Dixon, Wally West, Roger Williams, John Elliott
D: Raymond Samuels (B. B. Ray)
S/SP: Bennett Cohen
P: Bernard B. Ray

LAW AND LEAD (Colony, November 15, 1936) 60 Mins.
Rex Bell, Harley Wood, *Wally Wales,* Lane Chandler, Earl Dwire, Soledad Jiminez, Lloyd Ingraham, Roger Williams, Karl Hackett, Edward Cassidy, Donald Reed, Lew Meehan
D: Bob Hill
S: Rock Hawley (Bob Hill)
SP: Basil Dickey
P: Arthur and Max Alexander

THE UNKNOWN RANGER (Columbia, December 1, 1936) 57 Mins.
Bob Allen, Martha Tibbets, Hal Taliaferro (*Wally Wales*), Harry Woods, Robert (Buzz) Henry, Edward Hearn
D: Spencer G. Bennet
SP: Nate Gatzert
P: Larry Darmour

RIO GRANDE RANGER (Columbia, December 11, 1936) 54 Mins.
Bob Allen, Iris Meredith, Hal Taliaferro (*Wally Wales*), Paul Sutton, Robert (Buzz) Henry, John Elliott, Tom London, Slim Whitaker, Jack Rockwell, Dick Botiller, Art Mix, Frank Ellis, Jack Ingram, Al Taylor, Jim Corey, Henry Hall, Jack C. Smith, Edward Cassidy, Ray Jones
D: Spencer G. Bennet
S: Jacques Jaccard, Ceila Jaccard
SP: Nate Gatzert
P: Larry Darmour

HAIR-TRIGGER CASEY (Atlantic, 1936) 59 Mins.
Jack Perrin, Betty Mack, *Wally Wales,* Fred Toones, Phil Dunham, Edward Cassidy, Robert Walker, Dennis Meadows (Moore), Vi Wong, "Starlight"
D: Harry Fraser
S/SP: Monroe Talbot
P: William Berke

THE GUN RANGER (Republic, February 9, 1937) 56 Mins.
Bob Steele, Eleanor Stewart, John Merton, Ernie Adams, Earl Dwire, Budd Buster, Frank Ball, Horace Murphy, Lew Meehan, Hal Taliaferro (*Wally Wales*), Horace B. Carpenter, Jack Kirk, George Morrell, Tex Palmer
D: R. N. Bradbury
S: Homer Gordon
SP: George Plympton
P: A. W. Hackel

LAW OF THE RANGER (Columbia, May 11, 1937) 57 Mins.
Bob Allen, Elaine Shepard, *Hal Taliaferro,* Lafe McKee, John Merton, Tom London, Lane Chandler, Slim Whitaker, Ernie Adams, Bud Osborne, Jimmy Aubrey
D: Spencer G. Bennet
S: Jesse Duffy, Joseph Levering
SP: Nate Gatzert
P: Larry Darmour

ROOTIN' TOOTIN' RHYTHM (Republic, May 12, 1937) 60 Mins.
Gene Autry, Smiley Burnette, Armida, Monte Blue, Ann Pendleton, *Hal Taliaferro,* Charles King, Max Hoffman, Jr., Frankie Marvin, Nina Campana, Charles Mayer, Karl Hackett, Al Clauser and his Oklahoma Outlaws, Jack Rutherford, "Champion"
D: Mack Wright
S: Johnston McCulley
SP: Jack Natteford
P: Armand Schaefer

THE PAINTED STALLION (Republic, June 5, 1937) 12 Chapters
Ray Corrigan, Hoot Gibson, LeRoy Mason, Duncan Renaldo, Sammy McKim, *Hal Taliaferro,* Jack Perrin, Ed Platt, Lou Fulton, Julia Thayer, Yakima Canutt, Maston Williams, Duke Taylor, Loren Riebe, George DeNormand, Gordon DeMain, Charles King, Vinegar Roan, Lafe McKee, Frank Leyva, Frankie Marvin, John Big Tree, Pascale Perry, Don Orlando, Henry Hale, Edward Piel, Sr., Horace Carpenter, Lee White, Joe Yrigoyen, Paul Lopez, Monte Montague, Gregg Star Whitespear, Ralph Bucko, Roy Bucko, Leo Dupee, Babe DeFreest, Jose Dominguez, Jack Padjan, Al Haskell, Augie Gomez
D: William Witney, Alan James, Ray Taylor
SP: Barry Shipman, Winston Miller
SP: J. Laurence Wickland
Chapter Titles: (1) Trail to Empire, (2) The Rider of the Stallion, (3) The Death Trap, (4) Avalanche, (5) Valley of Death, (6) Thundering Wheels, (7) Trail Treachery, (8) The Whispering Arrow, (9) The Fatal Message, (10) Ambush, (11) Tunnel of Terror, (12) Human Targets

ONE MAN JUSTICE (Columbia, July 1, 1937) 59 Mins.
Charles Starrett, Barbara Weeks, *Hal Taliaferro* (Wally Wales), Jack Clifford, Al Bridge, Walter Downing, Mary Gordon, Jack Lipson, Edmund Cobb, Dick Curtis, Maston Williams, Harry Fleischman, Art Mix, Hank Bell, Steve Clark, Frank Ellis, Ethan Laidlaw, Eddie Laughton, Ted Mapes, Lew Meehan, Merrill McCormack
D: Leon Barsha
S: William Colt MacDonald (credited to Peter B. Kyne)
SP: Paul Perez

THE RANGERS STEP IN (Columbia, August 8, 1937) 58 Mins.
Bob Allen, Eleanor Stewart, Jay Wilsey (Buffalo Bill, Jr.), John Merton, Hal Taliaferro (*Wally Wales*), Jack Ingram, Jack Rockwell, Lafe McKee, Bob Kortman, Billy Townsend, Ray Jones, Lew Meehan, Tommy Thompson
D: Spencer G. Bennet
S: Jesse Duffy, Joseph Levering
P: Larry Darmour

HEART OF THE ROCKIES (Republic, September 6, 1937) 56 Mins.
("3 Mesquiteers" Series)
Bob Livingston, Ray Corrigan, Max Terhune, Lynn Roberts, Sammy McKim, J. P. McGowan, Yakima Canutt, Hal Taliaferro (*Wally Wales*), Maston Williams, Guy Wilkerson, Ranny Weeks, George Simmons, George Pierce, Nelson McDowell, Herman's Mountaineers
D: Joseph Kane
S: Bernard McConville
SP: Jack Netteford, Oliver Drake
P: Sol C. Siegel

THE TRIGGER TRIO (Republic, October 18, 1937) 60 Mins.
("3 Mesquiteers" Series)
Ray Corrigan, Max Terhune, Ralph Byrd, Sandra Corday, Hal Taliaferro (*Wally Wales*) Robert Warwick, Cornelius Keefe, Sammy McKim, Jack Ingram, Willie Fung, "Buck"
D: William Witney
S: Houston Branch, Joseph Poland
SP: Oliver Drake, Joseph Poland
P: Sol C. Siegel

THE LONE RANGER (Republic, March, 1938) 15 Chapters.
Lee Powell, Chief Thunder Cloud, Lynne Roberts, *Hal Taliaferro* (Wally Wales), Herman Brix (Bruce Bennett), Lane Chandler, George Letz (George Montgomery), Stanley Andrews, Billy Bletcher (voice of Lone Ranger only), William Farnum, George Cleveland, John Merton, Sammy McKim, Tom London, Raphael Bennett, Maston Williams, Charles Thomas, Allan Cavan, Reed Howes, Walter James, Francis Sayles, Murdock McQuarrie, Jame Keckley, Phillip Armenta, Ted Adams, Jimmy Hollywood, Jack Kirk, Art Dillard, Millard McGowan, Frank Ellis, Carl Stockdale, Bud Osborne, Fred Burns, Inez Cody, Duke Green, Forbes Murray, Edna Lawrence, Charles King, Jack Perrin, Frank Leyva, George Mari, Charles Whitaker, Edmund Cobb, Jack Rockwell, J. W. Cody, Oscar Hancock, Buck Hires, Roy Kennedy, Al

Lorenzen, Karry Mack, Frankie Marvin, Lafe McKee, Henry Olivas, Perry Pratt, Charles Williams, Wally Wilson, Ben Wright, Gunner Johnson, Bill Jones, Robert Kortman, Ralph LeFever, Ike Lewin, Elmer Napier, Post Parks, George Plues, Loren Riebe, Al Rimpau, Vinegar Roan, John Slater, George St. Leon, Burl Tatum, Al Taylor, Duke Taylor, Bobby Thompson, Blackie Whiteford, Shorty Woods, Bill Yrigoyen, Joe Yrigoyen, "Silver Chief"
D: William Witney, John English
S: Fran Striker
SP: Barry Shipman, George Worthing Yates, Franklyn Adreon, Ronald Davidson, Lois Eby
AP: Sol C. Siegel
Supervisor: Robert Beche
Chapter Titles: (1) Heigh-yo Silver (2) Thundering Earth (3) The Pitfall, (4) Agent of Treachery, (5) The Steaming Cauldron, (6) Red Man's Courage, (7) Wheels of Disaster, (8) Fatal Treasure, (9) The Missing Spur. (10) Flaming Fury, (11) The Silver Bullet, (12) Escape, (13) The Fatal Plunge, (14) Messenger of Doom, (15) Last of the Rangers

STAGECOACH DAYS (Columbia, June 20, 1958) 58 Mins.
Jack Luden, Eleanor Stewart, Harry Woods, Hal Taliaferro, Slim Whitaker, Jack Ingram, Lafe McKee, Bob Kortman, Dick Botiller, Blackjack Ward, "Tuffy" (a dog)
D: Joseph Levering
SP: Nate Gatzert
P: Larry Damour

THE GREAT ADVENTURES OF WILD BILL HICKOK (Columbia, June 30, 1938) 15 Chapters. Gordon Elliott (Bill Elliott), Monte Blue, Carole Wayne, Frankie Darro, Dickie Jones, Sammy McKim, Kermit Maynard, Roscoe Ates, Monte Collins, Reed Hadley, Chief Thunder Cloud, George Chesebro, Mala (Ray Mala), Walter Wills, J. P. McGowan, Eddy Waller, Alan Bridge, Slim Whitaker, Walter Miller, Lee Phelps, Robert Fiske, Earle Hodgins, Earl Dwire, Ed Brady, Ray Jones, Edmund Cobb, Art Mix, *Hal Taliaferro*, Blackie Whiteford
D: Mack V. Wright, Sam Nelson
SO: George Rosener, Charles Arthur Powell, George Arthur Durlam
P: Harry Webb
Chapter Titles: (1) The Law of the Gun, (2) Stampede, (3) Blazing Terror, (4) Mystery Canyon, (5) Flaming Brands, (6) The Apache Killer, (7) Prowling Wolves, (8) The Pit, (9) Ambush, (10) Savage Vengeance, (11) Burning Waters, (12) Desperation, (13) Phantom Bullets, (14) The Lure, (15) Trail's End

PIONEER TRAIL (Columbia, July 15, 1938) 59 Mins.
Jack Luden, Joan Barclay, Slim Whitaker, Leon Beaumon, *Hal Taliaferro*, Marin Sais, Eve McKenzie, Hal Price, Dick Botiller, Tom London, Tex Palmer, Art Davis, Fred Burns, Bob McKenzie, "Tuffy" (a dog)
D: Joseph Levering
S/SP: Nate Gatzert
P: Larry Darmour

47

Bob Baker and Hal Taliaferro (Wally Wales) in *Prairie Justice* (Universal, 1938).

SOUTH OF ARIZONA (Columbia, July 28, 1938) 56 Mins.
Charles Starrett, Iris Meredith, Bob Nolan, Dick Curtis, Robert Fiske, Edmund Cobb, Art Mix, Dick Botiller, Lafe McKee, Ed Coxen, Hank Bell, *Hal Taliaferro*, George Morrell, Steve Clark, John Tyrell, Sons of the Pioneers (Pat Brady, Hugh and Carl Farr, Lloyd Perryman)
D: Sam Nelson
SP: Bennett Cohen

PHANTOM GOLD (Columbia, August 31, 1938) 56 Mins.
Jack Luden, Beth Marion, Barry Downing, Charles Whitaker, *Hal Taliaferro*, Art Davis, Jimmy Robinson, Jack Ingram, Buzz Barton, Marin Sais, "Tuffy" (a dog)
D: Joseph Levering
S/SP: Nate Gatzert
P: Larry Darmour

BLACK BANDIT (Universal, September 16, 1938) 57 Mins.
Bob Baker, Marjorie Reynolds, *Hal Taliaferro*, Jack Rockwell, Forrest Taylor, Glenn Strange, Arthur Van Slyke, Carleton Young, Dick Dickinson, Schyler Standish, Rex Downing, Jack Montgomery, Tom London, Slim Whitaker, Jack Ingram, Tex Palmer
D: George Waggner
SP: Joseph West
AP: Paul Malvern

WEST OF THE SANTA FE (Columbia, October 3, 1938) 58 Mins.
Charles Starrett, Iris Meredith, Dick Curtis, Robert Fiske, LeRoy Mason, Bob Nolan and the Sons of the Pioneers, Hank Bell, Edmund Cobb, Clem Horton, Dick Botiller, Edward Hearn, Edward J. LeSaint, Buck Connors, Bud Osborne, Blackie Whiteford, *Hal Taliaferro*
D: Sam Nelson
SP: Bennett Cohen

GUILTY TRAIL (Universal, October 21, 1938) 57 Mins.
Bob Baker, Marjorie Reynolds, *Hal Taliaferro*, Jack Rockwell, Carleton Young, Forrest Taylor, Georgia O'Dell, Glenn Strange, Murdock McQuarrie, Tom London, Tex Palmer, Jack Kirk
D: George Waggner
SP: Joseph West
AP: Paul Malvern

PRAIRIE JUSTICE (Universal, November 4, 1938) 57 Mins.
Bob Baker, Dorothy Fay, *Hal Taliaferro*, Jack Rockwell, Carleton Young, Jack Kirk, Forrest Taylor, Glenn Strange, Tex Palmer, Slim Whitaker, Jimmy Phillips, Murdock McQuarrie
D: George Waggner
S/SP: Joseph West
AP: Paul Malvern

RIO GRANDE (Columbia, December 8, 1938) 58 Mins.
Charles Starrett, Ann Doran, Bob Nolan and the Sons of the Pioneers, Dick Curtis, Hank Bell, Art Mix, George Chesebro, Lee Prather, *Hal Taliaferro*, Edward J. LeSaint, Ed Piel, Sr., Ted Mapes, Harry Strang, Fred Burns, Forrest Taylor, Stanley Brown, George Morrell, John Tyrell, Fred Evans
D: Sam Nelson
SP: Charles Francis Royal

THE THUNDERING WEST (Columbia, January 12, 1939) 57 Mins.
Charles Starrett, Iris Meredith, Bob Nolan and the Sons of the Pioneers, *Hal Taliaferro*, Dick Curtis, Hank Bell, Edward J. LeSaint, Blackie Whiteford, Art Mix, Robert Fiske, Edmund Cobb, Ed Piel, Sr., Slim Whitaker, Steve Clark, Fred Burns
D: Sam Nelson
SP: Bennett Cohen

FRONTIERS OF '49 (Columbia, January 19, 1939) 54 Mins.
Bill Elliott, Juana DeAlcaniz, *Hal Taliaferro*, Charles King, Slim Whitaker, Al Ferguson, Jack Walters, Octavio Giraud, Carlos Villarias, Joe de LaCruz, Kit Guard, Bud Osborne, Jack Ingram, Lee Shumway, Ed Cassidy, Tex Palmer
D: Joseph Levering
SP: Nate Gatzert
P: Larry Darmour

TRAPPED IN THE SKY (Columbia, February 16, 1939) 6 Reels.
Jack Holt, Katherine DeMille, Sidney Blackmer, C. Henry Gordon, Ralph Morgan, Iron Lebedeff, Paul Evarton, Regis Toomey, Holmes Herbert, *Hal Taliaferro*, Harry Woods
D: Lewis D. Collins
SP: Eric Taylor, Gordon Rigby
P: Larry Darmour

NORTH OF THE YUKON (Columbia, March 30, 1939) 64 Mins.
Charles Starrett, Linda Winters (Dorothy Comingore), Bob Nolan and the Sons of the Pioneers, Lane Chandler, Paul Sutton, Robert Fiske, Vernon Steele, Edmund Cobb, Tom London, Dick Botiller, Kenne Duncan, Harry Cording, *Hal Taliaferro*, Ed Brady
D: Sam Nelson
SP: Bennett Cohen

MAN OF CONQUEST (Republic, May 15, 1939) 97 Mins.
Richard Dix, Gail Patrick, Joan Fontaine, Edward Ellis, George Hayes, Victor Jory, Robert Barrat, Ralph Morgan, C. Henry Gordon, Robert Armstrong, Max Terhune, Janet Beecher, George Letz (Mongomery), Guy Wilkerson, Charles Stevens, *Hal Taliaferro*, Lane Chandler, Ethan Laidlaw, Edmund Cobb, Billy Benedict, Tex Cooper, Leon Ames, Ferris Taylor, Kathleen Lockhart
D: George Nichols, Jr.
S: Harold Shumate, Wells Root
SP: Wells Root, E. E. Paramore, Jr.
P: Sol C. Siegel

WESTERN CARAVANS (Columbia, June 15, 1939) 58 Mins.
Charles Starrett, Iris Meredith, Bob Nolan and the Sons of the Pioneers, Russell Simpson, *Hal Taliaferro*, Dick Curtis, Hank Bell, Sammy McKim, Edmund Cobb, Ethan Laidlaw, Steve Clark, Herman Hack, Charles Brinley
D: Sam Nelson
SP: Bennett Cohen

RIDERS OF THE FRONTIER (Monogram, August 16, 1939) 58 Mins.
Tex Ritter, Jack Rutherford, *Hal Taliaferro*, Jean Joyce, Marin Sais, Mantan Moreland, Olin Francis, Roy Barcroft, Merrill McCormack, Maxine Leslie, Nolan Willis, Nelson McDowell, Charles King, Forrest Taylor, Robert Frazer, "White Flash"
D: Spencer Bennet
S/SP: Jesse Duffy, Joseph Levering
P: Edward Finney

OVERLAND WITH KIT CARSON (Columbia, August, 1939) 15 Chapters.
Bill Elliott, Iris Meredith, Richard Diske, Bobby Clack, James Craig, *Hal Taliaferro*, Trevor Bardette, LeRoy Mason, Olin Francis, Frances Sayles, Kenneth MacDonald, Dick Curtis, Dick Botiller, Ernie Adams, Flo Campnell, Joe Garcia, Stanley Brown, Hank Bell, Art Mix, John Tyrell, Lee Prather, Irene Herndon, Jack Rockwell, Edward J. LeSaint, Martin Garralaga, Iron Eyes Cody, Carl Stockdale, Eddie Foster, Francisco Moran, Arnold Clack, Del Lawrence, J. W. Cody, Robert Fiske
D: Sam Nelson, Norman Deming
SP: Morgan Cox, Joseph Poland, Ned Dandy
P: Jack Fier

Hal Taliaferro (Wally Wales) in his favorite role as Charles Goodyear in *Mr. Goodyear* (second film in "Fools Who Made History" series) (Columbia, 1939).

Chapter Titles: (1) Doomed Men, (2) Condemned to Die, (3) Fight for Life, (4) The Ride of Terror, (5) The Path of Doom, (6) Rendezvous with Death, (7) The Killer Stallion, (8) The Devil's Nest, (9) Blazing Peril, (10) The Black Raiders, (11) Foiled, (12) The Warning, (13) Terror in the Night, (14) Crumbling Walls, (15) Unmasked

OUTPOST OF THE MOUNTIES (Columbia, September 14, 1939) 63 Mins.
Charles Starrett, Iris Meredith, Stanley Brown, Kenneth MacDonald, Edmund Cobb, Bob Nolan, Lane Chandler, Dick Curtis, Albert Morin, *Hal Taliaferro*, Pat O'Hara, Sons of the Pioneers
D: C. C. Coleman, Jr.
SP: Paul Franklin

FOOLS WHO MADE HISTORY NO. 2 (Columbia, October 2, 1939) 1 Reel.
Hal Taliaferro
D: Jan Leman

SAGA OF DEATH VALLEY (Republic, November 17, 1939) 58 Mins.
Roy Rogers, George Hayes, Donald Barry, Doris Day, Frank M. Thomas, Jack Ingram, *Hal Taliaferro*, Lew Kelly, Fern Emmett, Tommy Baker, Buzz Buckley, Horace Murphy, Lane Chandler, Fred Burns, Jimmy Wakely, Johnny Bond, Dick Rinehart, Peter Frago, Ed Brady, Bob Thomas, Matty Roubert, Pasquel Perry, Cactus Mack, Art Dillard, Horace B. Carpenter, Hooper Atchley, Frankie Marvin, "Trigger"
D/AP: Joseph Kane
S/SP: Karen DeWolf, Stuart Anthony

THE STRANGER FROM TEXAS (Columbia, December 18, 1939) 54 Mins.

Charles Starrett, Lorna Gray (Adrian Booth), Richard Fiske, Dick Curtis, Edmund Cobb, Bob Nolan, Al Bridge, Jack Rockwell, *Hal Taliaferro*, Edward J. LeSaint, Buel Bryant, Art Mix, George Chesebro

D: Sam Nelson

S: Ford Beebe—"The Mysterious Avenger"

SP: Paul Franklin

BULLETS FOR RUSTLERS (Columbia, March 5, 1940) 58 Mins.

Charles Starrett, Lorna Gray (Adrian Booth), Bob Nolan, Dick Curtis, Jack Rockwell, Kenneth MacDonald, Edward J. LeSaint, Francis Walker, Eddie Laughton, Lee Frather, *Hal Taliaferro*, Sons of the Pioneers

D: Sam Nelson

SP: John Rathmell

PIONEERS OF THE WEST (Republic, March 12, 1940) 56 Mins.

("3 Mesquiteers" Series)

Robert Livingston, Raymond Hatton, Duncan Renaldo, Noah Beery, Beatrice Roberts, Lane Chandler, George Cleveland, *Hal Taliaferro*, Yakima Canutt, John Dilson, Joe McGuinn, Earl Askam, George Chesebro, Jack Kirk, Bob Burns, Tex Terry, Chuck Baldra, Hansel Warner, Art Dillard, Ray Jones, Artie Ortego, Herman Hack

D: Les Orlebeck

SP: Jack Natteford, Karen DeWolf, Gerald Geraghty

Based on William Colt MacDonald's characters

AP: Harry Grey

DARK COMMAND (Republic, April 5, 1940) 94 Mins.

Claire Trevor, John Wayne, Walter Pidgeon, Roy Rogers, George Hayes, Porter Hall, Marjorie Main, Raymond Walburn, Joseph Sawyer, Helen MacKellar, J. Farrell MacDonald, Trevor Bardette, Tom London, Dick Alexander, Yakima Canutt, *Hal Taliaferro*, Edmund Cobb, Edward Hearn, Ernie Adams, Jack Rockwell, Al Bridge, Glenn Strange, Harry Woods, Harry Cording, Frank Hagney, Dick Rich, John Dilson, Clinton Rosemond, Budd Buster, Howard Hickman, John Merton, Al Taylor, Mildred Gover, Jack Low, Ferris Taylor, Edward Earle, Dick Alexander, Joe McGuinn, Harry Strang, Tex Cooper, Jack Mongomery

D: Raoul Walsh

S: W. R. Burnett

SP: F. Hugh Herbert, Grover Jones, Lionel Houser

AP: Sol C. Siegel

HI-YO SILVER (Republic, April 10, 1940) 69 Mins.

(Feature edited from 1938 serial "The Lone Ranger")

Lee Powell, Herman Brix (Bruce Bennett), Chief Thunder Cloud, Lynne Roberts, Stanley Andrews, Hal Taliaferro (*Wally Wales*), Lane Chandler, George Cleveland, George Letz (Montgomery), John Merton, Sammy McKim, Tom London, Raphael Bennett, Maston Williams, Raymond Hatton, Dickie Jones

(This feature version had new footage with Raymond Hatton telling the story to young Dickie Jones. Neither were in the original serial. For additional credits see the cast listing under "The Lone Ranger")

D: William Witney, John English

SP: Barry Shipman, George Washington Yates

Based on the Lone Ranger radio serial

AP: Sol C. Siegel

THE DARK COMMAND (Republic, April 15, 1940) 94 Mins.

John Wayne, Claire Trevor, Walter Pidgeon, Roy Rogers, George Hayes, Porter Hall, Marjorie Main, Raymond Walburn, Joseph Sawyer, Helen MacKellar, J. Farrell MacDonald, Trevor Bardette, Harry Woods, Al Bridge, Glenn Strange, Jack Rockwell, Ernie Adams, Edward Hearn, Edmund Cobb, *Hal Taliaferro*, Yakima Canutt, Dick Alexander, Tom London, John Merton, Dick Rich, Harry Cording, Al Taylor, Harry Strang, Tex Cooper, Joe McGuinn, Jack Montgomery

D: Raoul Walsh

2nd Unit D: Yakima Canutt, Cliff Lyons

SP: Grover Jones, Lionel Houser, F. Hugh Herbert

S: W. R. Burnett

Adapt: Jan Fortune

AP: Sol C. Siegel

COLORADO (Republic, September 15, 1940) 57 Mins.

Roy Rogers, George Hayes, Pauline Moore, Milburn Stone, Maude Eburne, *Hal Taliaferro*, Vester Pegg, Fred Burns, Lloyd Ingraham, Jay Novello, Chuck Baldra, Tex Palmer, Joseph Crehan, Edward Cassidy, George Rosenor, Robert Fiske, "Trigger"

D/AP: Joseph Kane

SP: Louis Stevens, Harrison Jacobs

YOUNG BILL HICKOK (Republic, October 21, 1940) 59 Mins.

Roy Rogers, George Hayes, Jacqueline Wells, John Miljan, Sally Payne, Archie Twitchell, Monte Blue, *Hal Taliaferro*, Ethel Wales, Jack Ingram, Monte Montague, Iron Eyes Cody, Fred Burns, Frank Ellis, Slim Whitaker, Jack Kirk, Hank Bell, Henry Wills, Dick Elliott, William Desmond, John Elliott, Jack Rockwell, Bill Wolfe, Tom Smith

D/AP: Joseph Kane

SP: Olive Cooper, Norton S. Parker

TEXAS TERRORS (Republic, November 22, 1940) 57 Mins.

Donald Barry, Julie Duncan, Al St. John, Arthur Loft, Ann Pennington, Eddy Waller, William Ruhl, Sammy McKim, Reed Howes, Robert Fiske, Fred Toones, *Hal Taliaferro*, Edmund Cobb, Al Haskell, Jack Kirk, Jimmy Wakely and his Rough Riders, Ruth Robinson, Blackjack Ward

D/AP: George Sherman

SP: Doris Schroeder, Anthony Coldeway

THE BORDER LEGION (Republic, December 5, 1940)
58 Mins.
Roy Rogers, George Hayes, Carol Hughes, Joseph Sawyer, Maude Eburne, Jay Novello, *Hal Taliaferro*, Dick Wessell, Paul Porcasi, Robert Emmett Keane, Ted Mapes, Fred Burns, Post Parks, Art Dillard, Chick Hannon, Charles Baldra
D/AP: Joseph Kane
S: Zane Grey
SP: Olive Cooper, Louis Stevens

THE GREAT TRAIN ROBBERY (Republic, February 28, 1941) 61 Mins.
Bob Steele, Claire Carleton, Milburn Stone, Helen MacKeller, Si Jenks, Monte Blue, *Hal Taliaferro*, George Guhl, Jay Novello, Dick Wessel, Yakima Canutt, Lew Kelly, Guy Usher
D: Joseph Kane

BORDER VIGILANTES (Paramount, April 18, 1941)
62 Mins.
William Boyd, Russell Hayden, Andy Clyde, Victor Jory, Morris Ankrum, Frances Gifford, Ethel Wales, Tom Tyler, *Hal Taliaferro*, Jack Rockwell, Britt Wood, Hank Worden, Hank Bell, Edward Earle, Al Haskell, Curley Dresden, Chuck Morrison, Ted Wells
D: Derwin Abrahams
SP: J. Benton Cheney
Based on characters created by Clarence E. Mulford in the "Hopalong Cassidy" stories
P: Harry Sherman

SHERIFF OF TOMBSTONE (Republic, May 7, 1941)
56 Mins.
Roy Rogers, George Hayes, Elyse Knox, Harry Woods, *Hal Taliaferro*, Jay Novello, Roy Barcroft, Jack Rockwell, Addison Richards, Sally Payne, Zeffie Tilbury, Jack Ingram, George Rosenor, Jack Kirk, Frank Ellis, Art Dillard, Herman Hack, Vester Pegg, Al Haskell, Ray Jones, Jess Cavan, "Trigger"
D/AP: Joseph Kane
S: James Webb
SP: Olive Cooper

LAW OF THE RANGE (Universal, June 20, 1941) 59 Mins.
Johnny Mack Brown, Fuzzy Knight, Nell O'Day, Roy Harris (Riley Hill), Pat O'Malley, Elaine Morley, Ethan Laidlaw, Al Bridge, *Hal Taliaferro*, Jack Rockwell, Charles King, Lucile Walker, Terry Frost, Jim Corey, Bud Osborne, Slim Whitaker, Bob Kortman, the Texas Rangers
D: Ray Taylor
AP: Will Cowan

UNDER FIESTA STARS (Republic, August 25, 1941)
64 Mins.
Gene Autry, Smiley Burnette, Carol Hughes, Frank Darien, Joe Straugh, Jr. , Pauline Drake, Ivan Miller, Sam Flint, Elias Gamboa, John Merton, Jack Kirk, Inez Palange, Curley Dresden, *Hal Taliaferro*, "Champion"
D: Frank McDonald
S: Karl Brown
SP: Karl Brown, Eliot Gibbons
AP: Harry Grey

BAD MAN OF DEADWOOD (Republic, September 5, 1941)
61 Mins.
Roy Rogers, George Hayes, Carol Adams, Sally Payne, Henry Brandon, Herbert Rawlinson, *Hal Taliaferro*, Jay Novello, Horace Murphy, Monte Blue, Ralf Harolde, Jack Kirk, Yakima Canutt, Curley Dresden, Fred Burns, Lynton Brent, Lloyd Ingraham, George Lloyd, Robert Frazer, Archie Twitchell, Karl Hackett, Harry Harvey, Eddie Acuff, Tom London, Jack Rockwell, Ernie Adams, Jack O'Shea, George Morrell, Wally West, Bob Woodward, "Trigger"
D/AP: Joseph Kane
SP: James R. Webb

RIDERS OF THE TIMBERLINE (Paramount, September 17, 1941) 59 Mins.
("Hopalong Cassidy" Series)
William Boyd, Brad King, Andy Clyde, J. Farrell MacDonald, Eleanor Stewart, Anna Q. Nilsson, Edward Keane, *Hal Taliaferro*, Victor Jory, Tom Tyler, Mickey Essia, Hank Bell, The Guardsman Quartet
D: Lesley Selander
SP: J. Benton Cheney
Based on characters created by Clarence E. Mulford
P: Harry Sherman

ROARING FRONTIERS (Columbia, October 16, 1941)
60 Mins.
Bill Elliott, Tex Ritter, Ruth Ford, Frank Mitchell, *Hal Taliaferro*, Bradley Page, Tris Coffin, Francis Walker, Joe McGuinn, George Chesebro, Charles Stevens, Charles King, Lew Meehan, Hank Bell, George Eldredge, Fred Burns, Ernie Adams
D: Lambert Hillyer
SP: Robert Lee Johnson
AP: Leon Barsha

JESSE JAMES AT BAY (Republic, October 17, 1941)
56 Mins.
Roy Rogers, George Hayes, Gale Storm, Sally Payne, Pierre Watkins, *Hal Taliaferro*, Roy Barcroft, Jack Kirk, Billy Benedict, Jack O'Shea, Rex Lease, Edward Piel, Sr., Jack Rockwell, Kit Guard, Curley Dresden, Hank Bell, Bill Wolfe, Ivan Miller, Lloyd Ingraham, Karl Hackett, Budd Buster, Fred Burns, Ray Jones, Fern Emmett, Bob Woodward, Chick Morrison, "Trigger"
D/AP: Joseph Kane
S: Harrison Jacobs
SP: James R. Webb

RED RIVER VALLEY (Republic, December 12, 1941)
62 Mins.
Roy Rogers, George Hayes, Salley Payne, Trevor Bardette,
Bob Nolan, Gale Storm, Robert Homans, *Hal Taliaferro*,
Lynton Brent, Pat Brady, Edward Piel, Sr., Dick Wessell,
Jack Rockwell, Ted Mapes, Sons of the Pioneers
D/AP: Joseph Kane
SP: Malcolm Stuart Boylin

BULLETS FOR BANDITS (Columbia, February 12, 1942)
55 Mins.
Bill Elliott, Tex Ritter, Frank Mitchell, Dorothy Short, Forrest
Taylor, Ralph Theodore, Edythe Elliott, Eddie Laughton,
Joe McQuinn, Tom Moray, Art Mix, Harry Harvey, *Hal
Taliaferro*, Ed Laughton, John Tyrrell, Bud Osborne
D: Wallace Fox
SP: Robert Lee Johnson
P: Leon Barsha
AD: Milton Carter

ROMANCE ON THE RANGE (Republic, May 18, 1942)
63 Mins.
Roy Rogers, George Hayes, Sally Payne, Linda Hayes, Bob
Noland and the Sons of the Pioneers, Edward Pawley, *Hal
Taliaferro*, Harry Woods, Glenn Strange, Roy Barcroft, Jack
Kirk, Pat Brady, Jack O'Shea, Dick Wessell, Dick Alexander,
"Trigger"
D/AP: Joseph Kane
SP: J. Benton Cheney

TOMBSTONE—THE TOWN TOO TOUGH TO DIE
(Paramount, June 13, 1942) 79 Mins.
Richard Dix, Kent Taylor, Edgar Buchanan, Frances Gifford,
Don Castle, Clem Bevins, Victor Jory, Rex Bell, Chris-Pin
Martin, Jack Rockwell, Charles Stevens, *Hal Taliaferro*, Wallis
Clark, James Ferrara, Paul Sutton, Dick Curtis, Harvey
Stevens, Charles Middleton, Don Curtis, Beryl Wallace
D: William McGann
S: Dean Franklin, Charles Beisner
SP: Albert Shelby LeVino, Edward E. Paramore
P: Harry Sherman

SONS OF THE PIONEERS (Republic, July 2, 1942) 61 Mins.
Roy Rogers, George Hayes, Maris Wrixon, Sons of the Pioneers,
Forrest Taylor, *Hal Taliaferro*, Minerva Urecal, Bradley Page,
Jack O'Shea, Frank Ellis, Tom London, Bob Woodward,
Fern Emmett, Chester Conklin, Ken Cooper, Karl Hackett,
Fred Burns, "Trigger"
D/AP: Joseph Kane
S: Mauri Grashin, Robert T. Shannon
SP: M. Coates Webster, Mauri Grashin, Robert T. Shannon

KING OF THE MOUNTIES (Republic, October 10, 1942)
15 Chapters.
Allan Lane, Gilbert Emery, Russell Hicks, Peggy Drake,
George Irving, Abner Biberman, William Vaughn, Nestor
Paiva, Bradley Page, Douglass Dumbrille, William Bakewell,
Duncan Renaldo, Francis Ford, Jay Novello, Anthony Warde,
Norman Nesbitt, John Hiestand, Allen Jung, Paul Fung,

Arvon Dale, Ken Terrell, John Roy, Bud Weiser, Duke Taylor,
Frank Wayne, Peter Katchenaro, Harry Cording, Carleton
Young, Tom Steele, Kam Tong, Earl Bunn, *Hal Taliaferro*,
Duke Green, Stanley Price, Tommy Coats, Duke Taylor, Duke
Green, Bob Jamison, Jack Kenney, Sam Serrano, King Kong,
Joe Chambers, Forrest Taylor, David Sharpe
D: William Witney
SP: Taylor Caven, Ronald Davidson, William Lively, Joseph
O'Donnell, Joseph Poland
AP: W. J. O'Sullivan
S: Zane Grey
Chapter Titles: (1) Phantom Invaders, (2) Road to Death, (3)
Human Target, (4) Railroad Saboteurs, (5) Suicide Dive,
(6) Blazing Barrier, (7) Perilous Plunge, (8) Electrocuted,
(9) Reign of Terror, (10) The Flying Coffin, (11) Deliberate
Murder, (12) On to Victory

LITTLE JOE THE WRANGLER (Universal, November 13,
1942) 64 Mins.
Johnny Mack Brown, Tex Ritter, Fuzzy Knight, Jennifer
Holt, *Hal Taliaferro*, Glenn Strange, Florine McKinney, James
Craven, Ethan Laidlaw, Jimmy Wakely Trio (Jimmy Wakely,
Johnny Bond, Scotty Harrell)
D: Lewis Collins
S: Sherman Lowe
SP: Sherman Lowe, Elizabeth Beecher
AP: Oliver Drake

AMERICAN EMPIRE (United Artists, December 11, 1942).
Richard Dix, Leo Carrillo, Preston Foster, Frances Gifford,
Guinn (Big Boy) Williams, Robert Barrat, Jack LaRue, Cliff
Edwards, Guy Rodin, Chris-Pin Martin, Richard Webb, Wil-
liam Farnum, Etta McDaniel, *Hal Taliaferro*, Tom London
D: William McGann
SP: J. Robert Bren, Glady Atwater, Ben Crauman Kohn
P: Harry Sherman

RIDIN' DOWN THE CANYON (Republic, December 30,
1942) 55 Mins.
Roy Rogers, George Hayes, Bob Nolan and the Sons of the
Pioneers (Pat Brady, Hugh and Earl Farr, Tim Spencer and
Lloyd Perryman), Dee "Buzzy" Henry, Linda Hayes, Addison
Richards, Lorna Gray (Adrian Booth), Olin Howlin, James
Seay, *Hal Taliaferro*, Forrest Taylor, Roy Barcroft, Art Mix,
Art Dillard, "Trigger"
D: Joseph Kane
S: Robert Williams, Norman Houston
SP: Albert DeMond
AP: Harry Grey

IDAHO (Republic, March 10, 1943) 70 Mins.
Roy Rogers, Smiley Burnette, Bob Nolan and the Sons of
the Pioneers, Virginia Grey, Harry J. Shannon, Ona Munson,
Dick Purcell, The Robert Mitchell Boychoir, Onslow Stevens,
Arthur Hohl, *Hal Taliaferro*, Rex Lease, Tom London, Jack
Ingram, James Bush, "Trigger"
D: Joseph Kane
Assoc. P: Joseph Kane
SP: Roy Chanslor, Olive Cooper

HOPPY SERVES A WRIT (United Artists, March 12, 1943) 67 Mins.
("Hopalong Cassidy" Series)
William Boyd, Andy Clyde, Jay Kirby, Victor Jory, George Reeves, Jan Christy, Forbes Murray, Robert Mitchum, Earle Hodgins, *Hal Taliaferro*, Roy Barcroft, Byron Foulger, Ben Corbett, Art Mix
D: George Archainbaud
SP: Gerald Geraghty
P: Harry Sherman
Based on characters created by Clarence E. Mulford

LEATHER BURNERS (THE) (United Artists, May 28, 1943) 58 Mins.
("Hopalong Cassidy" Series)
William Boyd, Andy Clyde, Jay Kirby, Victor Jory, George Reeves, S. Spencer, George Givot, Bobby Larson, *Hal Taliaferro*, Forbes Murray, Bob Mitchum, Bob Kortman, Herman Hack
D: Joseph E. Henabery
S: Bliss Lomax
SP: Joe Pagano
P: Harry Sherman
Based on characters created by Clarence E. Mulford

ITS A GREAT LIFE (Columbia, July 2, 1943) 66 Mins.
Penny Singleton, Arthur Lake, Hugh Herbert, Larry Simms, Jonathan Hale, Donald Mummert, Alan Dinehart, Douglas Leavitt, Irving Bacon, Douglas Wood, Andrew Tombes, Stanley Andrews, Gilbert Emery, Ray Walker, Emory Parnell, Frank Sully, Alec Craig, Hal Price, *Hal Taliaferro*
P/D: Frank Strayer
SP: Connie Lee and Karen DeWolf

SILVER SPURS (Republic, August 12, 1943) 65 Mins.
Roy Rogers, Smiley Burnette, John Carradine, Phyllis Brooks, Jerome Cowan, Joyce Compton, Bob Nolan and the Sons of the Pioneers, *Hal Taliaferro,* Jack Kirk, Kermit Maynard, Dick Wessell, Forrest Taylor, Byron Foulger, Charles Wilson, Jack O'Shea, Slim Whitaker, Arthur Loft, Eddy Waller, Tom London, Bud Osborne, Fred Burns, Henry Wills, "Trigger"
D: Joseph Kane
SP: John K. Butler, J. Benton Cheney
AP: Harry Grey

COWBOY IN THE CLOUDS (Columbia, December 23, 1943).
Charles Starrett, Dub Taylor, Julie Duncan, Jimmy Wakely, *Hal Taliaferro*, Charles King, Lane Chandler, Davidson Clark, Dick Curtis, Ed Cassidy, Ted Mapes, John Tyrell, Paul Zarema
D: Benjamin Kline
SP: Elizabeth Beecher
P: Jack Fier

THE WOMAN OF THE TOWN (United Artists, December 31, 1943) 90 Mins.
Claire Trevor, Albert Dekker, Barry Sullivan, Henry Hull, Marion Martin, Porter Hall, Percy Kilbride, Beryl Wallace, Arthur Hohl, Clem Bevins, Teddi Sherman, George Cleveland,

Russell Hicks, Herbert Rawlinson, Marlene Mains, Dorothy Granger, Dewey Robinson, Wade Crosby, *Hal Taliaferro*, Glenn Strange, Charley Foy, Claire Whiteney, Russell Simpson, Eula Gay, Frances Morris
D: George Archainbaud
SP: Aeneas MacKenzie
P: Harry Sherman

THE FIGHTING SEABEES (Republic, March 10, 1944) 100 Mins.
John Wayne, Dennis O'Keefe, Susan Hayward, William Frawley, Leonid Kinskey, J. M. Kerrigan, Grant Withers, Paul Fix, Ben Welden, William Forrest, Addison Richards, Jay Norris, Duncan Renaldo, Tom London, *Hal Taliaferro*, Crane Whitley
D: Edward Ludwig
SP: Borden Chase, Aeneas MacKenzie
S: Borden Chase

LUMBERJACK (United Artists, April 28, 1944) 65 Mins.
("Hopalong Cassidy" Series)
William Boyd, Andy Clyde, Jimmy Rogers, Douglass Dumbrille, Ellen Hall, Francis McDonald, Herbert Rawlinson, Ethel Wales, John Whitney, *Hal Taliaferro,* Henry Wills, Charles Morton, Frances Morris, Jack Rockwell, Bob Burns, Hank Worden, Earle Hodgins, Pierce Lyden
D: Lesley Selander
SP: Norman Houston, Barry Shipman
Based on characters created by Clarence E. Mulford
P: Harry Sherman

THE COWBOY AND THE SENORITA (Republic, May 12, 1944) 78 Mins.
Roy Rogers, Mary Lee, Dale Evans, John Hubbard, Guinn "Big Boy" Williams, Fuzzy Knight, Dorothy Christy, Lucien Littlefield, *Hal Taliaferro*, Jack Kirk, Jack O'Shea, Jane Beebe, Ben Rochelle, Bob Nolan and the Sons of the Pioneers, Rex Lease, Lynton Brent, Julian Rivero, Hob Wilke. Wally West, Tito and Corinne Valdes, "Trigger"
D: Joseph Kane
S: Bradford Ropes
SP: Gordon Kahn
AP: Harry Grey

FORTY THIEVES (United Artists, June 23, 1944) 60 Mins.
("Hopalong Cassidy" Series)
William Boyd, Andy Clyde, Jimmy Rogers, Louise Currie, Douglass Dumbrille, Kirk Alyn, Herbert Rawlinson, Robert Frazer, Glenn Strange, Jack Rockwell, Bob Kortman, *Hal Taliaferro*
D: Lesley Selander
SP: Michael Wilson, Bernie Kamins
Based on characters created by Clarence E. Mulford
P: Harry Sherman

YELLOW ROSE OF TEXAS (Republic, June 24, 1944) 69 Mins.

Roy Rogers, Dale Evans, George Cleveland, Harry Shannon, Grant Withers, Bob Nolan and the Sons of the Pioneers, William Haade, Weldon Heyburn, *Hal Taliaferro*, Lom London, Dick Botiller, Janet Martin, Don Kay Reynolds, Bob Wilke, Jack O'Shea, Rex Lease, Emmett Vogan, John Dilson, "Trigger"

D: Joseph Kane
SP: Jack Townley
AP: Harry Grey

VIGILANTES OF DODGE CITY (Republic, November 14, 1944) 54 Mins.

("Red Ryder" Series)

Bill Elliott, Bobby Blake, Alice Fleming, Linda Stirling, LeRoy Mason, *Hal Taliaferro*, Tom London, Stephen Barclay, Bud Geary, Kenne Duncan, Bob Wilke, Horace B. Carpenter, Stanley Andrews

DL: Wallace Grissell
S: Norman S. Hall
SP: Norman S. Hall, Anthony Coldeway
AP: Stephen Auer

ZORRO'S BLACK WHIP (Republic, December 16, 1944) 12 Chapters.

George J. Lewis, Linda Stirling, Lucien Littlefield, Francis McDonald, *Hal Taliaferro*, John Merton, John Hamilton, Tom Chatterton, Tom London, Jack Kirk, Jay Kirby, Si Jenks, Stanley Price, Tom Steele, Duke Green, Dale Van Sickel, Cliff Lyons, Roy Brent, Bill Yrigoyen, Forrest Taylor, Fred Graham, Marshall Reed, Augie Gomez, Carl Sepulveda, Horace Carpenter, Herman Hack, Carey Loftin, Cliff Parkinson, Ken Terrell, Duke Taylor, Cliff Parkinson, Vinegar Roan, Roy Brent, Babe DeFreest

D: Spencer G. Bennet, Wallace Grissell
SP: Basil Dickey, Jesse Duffey, Grant Nelson, Joseph Poland
AP: Ronald Davidson

Chapter Titles: (1) The Masked Avenger, (2) Tomb of Terror, (3) Mob Murder, (4) Detour to Death, (5) Take Off That Mask!, (6) Fatal Gold, (7) Wolf Pack, (8) The Invisible Victim, (9) Avalanche, (10) Fangs of Doom, (11) Flaming Juggernaut, (12) Trail of Tyranny

HAUNTED HARBOR (Republic, 1944) 15 Chapters.

Kane Richmond, Kay Aldridge, Roy Barcroft, Clancy Cooper, Marshall Reed, Forrest Taylor, *Hal Taliaferro*, Oscar O'Shea, George J. Lewis, Edward Keane, Kenne Duncan, Bud Geary, Robert Homans, Duke Green, Dale Van Sickel, Rico de Montez, Robert Wilke, Tom Steele, Fred Graham, Bud Wolfe, Carey Loftin, Charles Hayes, Kit Guard, Jack O'Shea, Ken Terrell, Nick Thompson, Eddie Parker, Pietro Sosso, Fred Cordova, Dick Botiller, Harry Wilson

D: Spencer Bennet and Wallace Grissell
SP: Royal Cole, Basil Dickey, Jesse Duffy, Grant Nelson, Joseph Poland
S: Dayle Douglas
AP: Ronald Davidson

Chapter Titles: (1) Wanted for Murder, (2) Flight to Danger, (3) Ladder of Death, (4) The Unknown Assassin, (5) Harbor of Horror, (6) Return of the Fugitive, (7) Journey Into Peril, (8) Wings of Doom, (9) Death's Door, (10) Crimson Sacrifice, (11) Jungle Jeopardy, (12) Fire Trap, (13) Monsters of the Deep, (14) High Voltage, (15) Crucible of Justice

FEDERAL OPERATOR 99 (Republic, March 1945) 12 Chapters

Marten Lamont, Helen Talbot, George J. Lewis, Lorna Gray, *Hal Taliaferro*, LeRoy Mason, Bill Stevens, Maurice Cass, Kernan Cripps, Elaine Lange, Frank Jaquet, Forrest Taylor, Jay Novello, Tom London, Jack Ingram, Frederick Howard, Craig Lawrence, Rex Lease, Jack George, Jack O'Shea, Harry Strang, Michael Gaddis, Duke Green, Nolan Leary, Tom Steele, Edmund Cobb, Fred Graham, Dale Van Sickel, Jimmy Zaner, Stanley Price, Ernie Adams, George Chesebro, Walter Shumway, Curt Barrett, Frank Marlowe

D: Spencer Bennet, Wallace A. Grissell, Yakima Canutt
SP: Albert DeMond, Basil Dickey, Jesse Duffy, Joseph Poland
AP: Ronald Davidson

Chapter Titles: (1) The Case of the Crown Jewels, (2) The Case of the Stolen Ransom, (3) The Case of the Lawful Counterfeit, (4) The Case of the Telephone Code, (5) The Case of the Missing Expert, (6) The Case of the Double Trap, (7) The Case of the Golden Cat, (8) The Case of the Invulnerable Criminal, (9) The Case of the Torn Blueprint, (10) The Case of the Hidden Witness, (11) The Case of the Stradivarius, (12) The Case of the Musical Clue

WHERE DO WE GO FROM HERE? (20th Century Fox, June 1945) 77 Mins.

Fred MacMurray, Joan Leslie, June Haver, Gene Sheldon, Anthony Quinn, Carlos Ramirez, Alan Mobray, Fortunio Bonanova, Herman Bing, Otto Preminger, John Davidson, Rosina Galli, Fred Essler, Cyril Ring, Hope Landid, Joe Bernard, Walter Bonn, Max Wagner, Arno Frey, Larry Thompson, Norman Field, *Hal Taliaferro*

D: Gregory Ratoff
S: Morrie Ryskind, Syd Herzig
SP: Morrie Ryskind
P: William Perlberg

SPRINGTIME IN TEXAS (Monogram, June 2, 1945) 55 Mins.

Jimmy Wakely, Dennis Moore, Lee "Lasses" White, Marie Harmon, Rex Lease, Pearl Early, Horace Murphy, I. Stanford Jolley, *Hal Taliaferro*, Budd Buster, Roy Butler, Johnny Bond, Lloyd Ingraham, The Callahan Brothers and their Blue Ridge Mountain Folks

D/P: Oliver Drake
SP: Frances Kavanaugh

George J. Lewis and Hal Taliaferro (Wally Wales) in *Federal Operator 99* (Republic, 1945).

THE CHEATERS (Republic, July 15, 1945) 87 Mins.
Joseph Schildkraut, Billie Burke, Eugene Pallette, Ona Munson, Raymond Walburn, Ann Gillis, Ruth Terry, Robert Livingston, David Holt, Robert Greig, St. Luke's Choristers, *Hal Taliaferro*
D/AP: Joseph Kane
SP: Frances Hyland, Albert Ray

THE PHANTOM RIDER (Republic, January 26, 1946) 12 Chapters.
Robert Kent, Peggy Stewart, LeRoy Mason, George J. Lewis, Kenne Duncan, *Hal Taliaferro*, Chief Thunder Cloud, Tom London, Roy Barcroft, Monte Hale, John Hamilton, Hugh Prosser, Jack Kirk, Rex Lease, Tommy Coats, Joe Yrigoyen, Bill Yrigoyen, Jack O'Shea, Walt LaRue, Cliff Parkinson, Carl Sepulveda, Art Dillard, Bud Bailey, George Carleton, Dale Van Sickel, Tom Steele, George Chesebro, Wayne Burson, Cliff Lyons, Post Parks, Fred Graham, Bob Duncan, Augie Gomez, Robert Wilke, John Roy, Cactus Mack, Eddie Parker,

Ted Mapes, Duke Taylor, Hal Price, James Linn, Tex Cooper, Henry Wills
D: Spencer G. Bennet, Fred Brannon
SP: Albert DeMond, Basil Dickey, Jesse Duffy, Lynn Perkins, Barney Sarecky
AP: Ronald Davidson
Chapter Titles: (1) The Avenging Spirit, (2) Flaming Ambush, (3) Hoofs of Doom, (4) Murder Masquerade, (5) Flying Fury, (6) Blazing Peril, (7) Gauntlet of Guns, (8) Behind the Mask, (9) The Captive Chief, (10) Beasts at Bay, (11) The Death House, (12) The Last Stand

DUEL IN THE SUN (Selznick/Metro-Goldwyn-Mayer, March 1946) 134 Mins.
(Technicolor)
Jennifer Jones, Joseph Cotten, Gregory Peck, Lionel Barrymore, Herbert Marshall, Lillian Gish, Walter Huston, Charles Bickford, Harry Carey, Tilley Losch, Joan Tetzel, Sidney Blackmer, Francis McDonald, Victor Kilian, Griff Barnett, Butterfly McQueen, Frank Cordell, Scott McKay, Dan White, Otto Kruger, Steve Dunhill, Lane Chandler, Lloyd Shaw, Thomas Dillon, Robert McKenzie, Charles Dingle, Si Jenks, Kermit Maynard, *Hal Taliaferro*, Hank Worden, Guy Wilkerson, Rose Plummer
D: King Vidor
S: Niven Busch
SP: Oliver H. P. Garrett
P: David O. Selznick

IN OLD SACRAMENTO (Republic, May 31, 1946) 89 Mins.
William (Bill) Elliott, Constance Moore, Hank Daniels, Ruth Donnelly, Eugene Pallette, Lionel Stander, Jack LaRue, Grant Withers, Bobby Blake, Charles Judels, Paul Hurst, Victoria Horne, Dick Wessel, *Hal Taliaferro*, Jack O'Shea, H. T. Tsiang, Marshall Reed, Wade Crosby, Eddy Waller, William Haade, Boyd Irwin, Lucien Littlefield, Ethel Wales, Elaine Lange, William B. Davidson, Ellen Corby, Fred Burns.
D/AP: Joseph Kane
S: Jerome Odlum
SP: Frances Lyland, Frank Gruber

HEADING WEST (Columbia, August 15, 1946) 54 Mins.
("Durango" Kid Series)
Charles Starrett, Smiley Burnette, Doris Houch, Norman Willis, Nolan Leary, Bud Geary, Frank McCarroll, John Merton, Tom Chatterton, *Hal Taliaferro*, Stanley Price, Tommy Coates, Hank Penny and his Plantation Boys
D: Ray Nazarro
SP: Ed Earl Repp
P: Colbert Clark

RAMROD (Enterprise/United Artists, May 2, 1947) 94 Mins.
Joel McCrea, Veronica Lake, Ian MacDonald, Charlie Ruggles, Preston Foster, Arleen Whelan, Lloyd Bridges, Donald Crisp, Rose Higgens, Chic York, Sarah Padden, Don DeFore, Nestor Pavia, Cliff Parkinson, Trevor Bardette, John Powers, Ward Wood, *Hal Taliaferro*, Wally Cassell, Ray Teal, Jeff Corey
D: Andre De Toth
S: Luke Short
SP: Jack Moffitt, Graham Baker, Cecile Kramer
P: Harry Sherman

WEST OF SONORA (Columbia, March 25, 1948) 52 Mins.
("Durango Kid" Series)
Charles Starrett, Smiley Burnette, Steve Darrell, George Chesebro, Anita Castle, *Hal Taliaferro*, Bob Wilke, Emmett Lynn, Lynn Farr, Lloyd Ingraham, The Sunshine Boys
D: Ray Nazarro
SP: Barry Shipman
P: Colbert Clark

THE GALLANT LEGION (Republic, May 24, 1948) 88 Mins.
William (Bill) Elliott, Adrian Booth, Joseph Schildkraut, Bruce Cabot, Andy Devine, Jack Holt, Grant Withers, Adele Mara, James Brown, Hal Landon, Max Terry, Lester Sharpe, *Hal Taliaferro*, Russell Hicks, Herbert Rawlinson, Marshall Reed, Steve Drake, Harry Woods, Roy Barcroft, Bud Osborne, Hank Bell, Jack Ingram, George Chesebro, Rex Lease, Noble Johnson, Emmett Vogan, John Hamilton, Trevor Bardette, Gene Stutenroth, Ferris Taylor, Iron Eyes Cody, Kermit Maynard, Jack Kirk, Merrill McCormack, Augie Gomez, Cactus Mack, Fred Kohler, Glenn Strange, Tex Terry, Joseph Crehan, Peter Perkins
D/AP: Joseph Kane
S: John K. Butler, Gerald Geraghty
SP: Gerald Adams

RED RIVER (Monterey/United Artists, September 17, 1948) 125 Mins.
John Wayne, Montgomery Clift, Joanne Dru, Walter Brennan, Coleen Gray, John Ireland, Noah Beery, Jr., Chief Yowlachie, Harry Carey, Sr., Harry Carey, Jr., Mickey Kuhn, Paul Fix, Hank Worden, Ivan Parry, *Hal Taliaferro*, Paul Fiero, Billy Self, Ray Hyke, Glenn Strange, Tom Tyler, Dan White, Lane Chandler, Lee Phelps, George Lloyd, Shelley Winters
D/P: Howard Hawks
S: Borden Chase—"The Chisholm Trail" (Also titled "Red River")
SP: Borden Chase, Charles Schnee

BRIMSTONE (Republic, August 15, 1949) 90 Mins.
Rod Cameron, Adrian Booth, Walter Brennan, Forrest Tucker, Jack Holt, Jim Davis, James Brown, Guinn "Big Boy" Williams, Charlita, *Hal Taliaferro*
D/AP: Joseph Kane
S: Norman S. Hall
SP: Thames Williams

THE SAVAGE HORDE (Republic, May 22, 1950) 90 Mins.
William (Bill) Elliott, Adrian Booth, Grant Withers, Barbara Fuller, Noah Beery, Jr., Jim Davis, Douglass Dumbrille, Bob Steele, Will Wright, Roy Barcroft, Earle Hodgins, Stuart Hamblen, *Hal Taliaferro*, Lloyd Ingraham, Marshall Reed, Crane Whitley, Charles Stevens, James Flavin, Edward Cassidy, Kermit Maynard, George Chesebro, Jack O'Shea, Monte Montague, Bud Osborne, Reed Howes
D/AP: Joseph Kane
S: Thames Williams and Gerald Geraghty
SP: Kenneth Gamet

COLT 45 (Warner Brothers, May 27, 1950) 70 Mins.
(Technicolor)
Randolph Scott, Zachary Scott, Ruth Roman, Lloyd Bridges,
Alan Hale, Ian MacDonald, Chief Thundercloud, Walter Coy,
Luther Crockett, Charles Evans, Buddy Roosevelt, *Hal
Taliaferro*, Art Miles, Barry Reagan, Howard Negley, Aurora
Navarro, Paul Newland, Franklin Farnum, Ed Peil, Sr.,
Jack Watt, Carl Andre, Royden Clark, Clyde Hudkins, Jr.,
Leroy Johnson, Ben Corbett, Kansas Moehring, Warren Fisk,
Forrest R. Colee, Artie Ortego, Richard Brehm, Dick Hudkins,
Leo McMahon, Bob Burrows, William Steele
D: Edward L. Marin
S/SP: Thomas Blackburn
P: Saul Elkins

CALIFORNIA PASSAGE (Republic, December 15, 1950)
90 Mins.
Forrest Tucker, Adele Mara, Estelita Rodriguez, Jim Davis,
Peter Miles, Charles Kemper, Bill Williams, Rhys Williams,
Paul Fix, Francis McDonald, Eddy Waller, Charles Stevens,
Iron Eyes Cody, Alan Bridge, Ruth Brennan, *Hal Taliaferro*
D/AP: Joseph Kane
SP: James Edward Grant

JUNCTION CITY (Columbia, July 12, 1952) 54 Mins.
("Durango Kid" Series)
Charles Starrett, Smiley Burnette, Jack (Jock) Mahoney,
Kathleen Case, John Dehner, Steve Darrell, George Chesebro,
Anita Castle, Mary Newton, Robert Brice, Hal Price, *Hal
Taliaferro*, Chris Alcaide, Bob Woodward, Frank Ellis
D: Ray Nazarro
SP: Barry Shipman
P: Colbert Clark

Tom Mix

3 • TOM MIX

Showman Nonpareil

After funeral services in the Little Church of the Flowers, and as Rudy Vallee sang "Empty Saddles," Tom Mix—perhaps the greatest cowboy actor produced by the movies—was lowered to his final resting place in a tree-shaded grave on a hillside in Forest Lawn Memorial Park in Los Angeles, in a section known as "Whispering Pines." Tom had been killed in a freak one-car accident a few miles north of Florence, Arizona, on October 12, 1940, as he zipped across the Arizona landscape in his custom-built Cord roadster with the same frenzy he used to ride "Old Blue" and "Tony" in those scores of Westerns that made his name a household word around the world. "Tony" was grazing in a pasture many miles away on this clear beautiful day, plagued with the infirmities of old age, and could not know that Tom was riding the last long trail without him. It was just as well.

The legend of Tom Mix's premovie heroics would live on for decades. And although not true, millions would go on believing that Tom had been a war hero in the Spanish-American War, a soldier of fortune in the Boer War, a hero of the Phillipine Insurrection, a Texas Ranger who slew bad men a la Bill Hickok, a United States marshal, a sheriff, and the Lord only knows what else. The stories of Tom's early life were mostly myth, the product of studio publicity departments and of Tom himself— who was caught up in the ecstasy of it all. But his fabulous career and heroics after 1910 remain

unequaled, and it is as the silent screen's greatest cowboy ace that he deserves to be remembered.

Tom Mix was 60 years old at his death. "Tony," who rode with him to fame in countless movies, outlived Tom by four years and was finally put to sleep at the advanced horse age of thirty-four years. Ivon D. Parker, a close friend, had been willed "Tony" and all Tom's personal effects, and had taken care of the horse until the infirmities of old age and approaching blindness suggested a merciful death.

Tom's last movie, Mascot's serial *The Miracle Rider*, was made in 1935, at which time he had come out of a three-year retirement to star in the 15-episode thriller about Texas Rangers, a secret explosive, and "hanky-panky" on an Indian reservation. The first chapter alone ran nearly 45 minutes. It was the longest serial ever turned out by Nat Levine's serial factory, and Tom was paid $10,000 a week for putting his tired fifty-five-year-old body through the paces once more. The Mix name was still magic even if the body was showing evidence of being held together with bailing wire, and the $40,000 paid Tom was a wise investment by Levine. The serial was a money-maker even though the movie critics panned it.

In spite of making only ten Westerns in the last decade of his life, Tom was still the best-known movie cowboy in the world. He was taken to his final resting place with all the showmanship that marked his long career, his body resting in a silver casket with his initials "T.M." engraved on the side. Over 5,000 mourners paid their respects, men and women from all walks of life and the children who worshiped him. Old movie cronies, such as Buck Jones, Harry Carey, and George O'Brien, were there, even saddle-crooners Gene Autry and Tex Ritter. But they all stayed in the background of this last crowd-drawing performance of the world's greatest movie cowboy who had paved the way for them all.

Tom Mix had been the embodiment of the world's yearning for a bigger-than-life hero—a strange, unbelievable fate for an army deserter shoving drinks across the mahogany in an Oklahoma City bar when Colonel Joe Miller blew into town for a cowman's convention in 1905. After a little sipping, chewing and jawing, the irascible colonel hired the twenty-two-year-old intractable kid who envisioned himself a cowboy. For cash wages of fifteen dollars a month and room and board, Tom went to work as a wrangler of tenderfeet on the 101 dude ranch and quickly worked his way up to livestock foreman of the vast enterprise. Before long he had won the respect of the professional cowboys, such as Bill Pickett, and was entering rodeos and holding his own with the best of them.

Much has been written about Tom's early life—some of it true, much of it myth. His birthplace was Mix Run, Pennsylvania, and the date was January 6, 1880. His father was a lumberman and teamster, and Tom grew up in the scenic hill country of Pennsylvania around DuBois. When war was declared against Spain in 1898, Tom immediately joined the army and served out the war in Delaware and Pennsylvania. He was never wounded charging up San Juan Hill, as has been reported; neither was he a hero of the Philippine Insurrection of 1892–1901. He was stationed in Virginia at that time. When he was discharged in 1901 as a sergeant, he immediately reinlisted, hoping to see action in the Boer War. He didn't. What he did do was to find romance for the first time. In 1902 he married a girl named Grace Allin, deserted the army that same year, and took his bride to the wilds of Oklahoma. The marriage was soon annulled. A marriage to Kitty Perrine in 1905 lasted but a year, and in 1907 he married Olive Stokes.

During the years 1905 to 1912 Tom performed with the 101 Ranch Show, Wilderman Wild West Show, Will A. Dickey's Circle D. Wild West Show, Kit Carson Buffalo Ranch Show, Vernon Seaver's Buffalo Ranch Show, and briefly had his own show at the Seattle Expositon of 1909. He returned to the 101 Ranch Show late in 1910 and remained for the 1911 season. In 1912 he traveled to Canada to headline the Weadick Wild West Show.

Stories about Mix indicate that he had been a Texas Ranger, sheriff in Oklahoma and Kansas, and deputy U.S. Marshal from 1905 through 1910. Most of these stories seem to be highly exaggerated. Documentary evidence does exist that he was a deputy sheriff and night marshal in Dewey, Oklahoma.

Tom and Olive had a small spread in the Cherokee Territory, and it was this fact that led to his entrance into the movies. The Selig Company was looking for a ranch on which to shoot a picture and for someone who knew the surrounding country. Tom Mix volunteered his ranch and himself. The result was *Ranch Life in the Great Southwest*, released in 1910. Tom was hired to handle stock and act as safety man, but he asked director Francis Boggs for a chance to be featured in the film. Boggs consented, and Tom was cast in a "bronco busting" sequence. His bombastic career as a motion picture actor was launched.

In the summers of 1910 and 1911 he made motion pictures in Canon City, Colorado, and often appeared in the films of William Duncan, famed serial king of the Twenties.

Tom rose to stardom in the years 1913–1914 in one- and two-reeler action flicks which appealed to the multitudes. Selig hastened to appease the public's seemingly insatiable thirst for blood-and-guts film entertainment by keeping Tom and his horse "Old Blue" (Tom acquired "Tony" after he retired "Old Blue" in 1915) as constantly in front of the camera as possible. Tom Mix's strong, handsome figure and virile qualities made him an appealing star. The dialogue subtitles were sometimes overdone, in the manner of Western pulp fiction; but the stories were surprisingly strong, and the films themselves were nicely directed, sometimes by Tom himself. Photography and editing were usually good, and the action content was always vigorous. Sometimes things happened that were not in the scripts, such as the time, in 1910, while filming a jungle thriller titled *Back to the Primitive*, that Tom bare-handedly wrestled a leopard that had attacked the heroine, Kathlyn Williams. Often he performed feats which not even later-day stuntmen of the calibre of Yak Canutt, Dave Sharpe, Tom Steele, or Cliff Lyons would perform without considerable thought and planning—if they performed them at all. It was all in the day's work for Tom, and over the years he proceeded to break many bones in carrying out the "day's work."

By 1916 Mix had become Selig's top Western star, and his brand of oater was catching on, although he was still several years away from overtaking the ultrarealist, William S. Hart, in popularity. Tom was still making only one- and two-reelers. He established a formula for the sexless Western that lasted into the 1950s, when the new realism returned it a little in films like *High Noon* and *Shane*. Cowboys, from Hoot Gibson and Ken Maynard to Roy Rogers and Gene Autry, were all heir to the Mix "flirt-and-run" legacy and these Mixian heroes, to the glee of youngsters who bought comic books and cap guns embossed with their names, were more infatuated with horses and pearl-handled revolvers than with their leading ladies.

In 1917 Tom was induced by William Fox to come to work for him, and it was at Fox that Tom made his greatest Westerns. By 1920 he had overtaken Hart in popularity and remained the most popular screen cowboy until the advent of sound. Tom was not a Western "purist," as was Hart. He tended to go overboard on stunting and trick riding and comedy. His movies were streamlined and showy, specialized in action for its own sake, and presented a superficial and glamorized picture of the West. His clothing definitely had a dude-like appearance. He wore a frilly cowboy suit and flamboyant ten-gallon hat which made the simple cowboy togs of other cowboys seem ragged in comparison. But Tom himself was no phony. He was tough, and most of his stunts, if not all, were performed without a double. He prided himself on this fact. When it came to hell-for-leather and thrill-a-second action, Tom was no slouch and needed no assistance. Gradually his Westerns took on the characteristics of a three-ring circus, with Tom performing simultaneously in all three rings. The Mix vehicles moved!

Tom was not a hero to be circumscribed by ordinary rules and conventions. He did the ordinary thing as well as any hero could but did not hesitate to add a little bit more, as in *The Cyclone* (1920) where, in the closing stunt, he rides Tony up three flights of stairs in a Chinatown gambling house and proceeds to carry off the heroine a la Lochinvar. Regardless of whether or not such scenes could stand an analytical test, they did give the spectators a new and pleasing thrill.

Tom could be counted on for his usual ripsnortin' boisterously harmless broncho-bustin' stunts in every picture, stirring up the Western dust literally and figuratively and injecting a modicum of pep into what would otherwise be vigor-lacking situations. His movie love affairs were always with the ranch-owner's daughter or the schoolteacher, and nothing happened that could not be explained by a small boy's mother at the table the night the minister had supper there.

The Tom Mix charm and personality endeared him to millions of people of all ages and classes. His white-stockinged chestnut horse "Tony" was an intelligent animal whose own personality complemented that of Tom. Together they shaped the traditions of the action Western in its formative years and gave the genre showmanship. Most important of all, they gave the Western to the kids and the young at heart.

Thirty-day shooting schedules were common for the Mix Westerns, which were usually filmed on location in picturesque settings and with adequate money spent on them. Tom's films were a veritable heaven for those millions who loved the escapist adventures of this sagebrush cavalier who inexorably galloped through film after film filled with exploding six-shooters, bone-crunching fist fights, and unbelievable stuntwork. There was nothing that he and "Tony" couldn't do, and their near-miraculous tricks kept the old Fox film studio solvent in its infancy years and enabled it to grow into the giant it became.

Ruth Mix was born to Tom and wife, Olive Stokes, on July 13, 1912 (Ruth died on September 21, 1977). But the marriage to Olive ended in divorce in 1917, and in 1918 Tom married actress Victoria Forde. To this union was born Thomasina, on February 12, 1922. The marriage lasted until the end of 1930 when Victoria obtained a divorce on

Tom Mix and "Tony"

grounds of mental cruelty. In early 1932 Tom married Mabel Ward, an aerialist with the Sells-Floto Circus.

Tom's $17,500-a-week salary, Beverly Hills mansion, lavish parties, expensive wardrobes, flashy cars, high-stepping personal life, and other symbols of his phenomenal success have been much publicized over the years; consequently no further comment on these manifestations of his wealth and personality will be made here.

As the 1920s came to a close, the movies gained a voice. Fox discontinued Westerns, after building the studio primarily on the earnings of the Mix films. Tom made a silent series for FBO in 1929, a series which did only average business at the box office. That same year he toured with the Sells-Floto Circus as its stellar attraction and remained with Sells-Floto for three seasons (1929–1931) before trying a movie comeback at Universal. His nine talkies proved popular enough, but he was seriously injured during the filming of *Rustler's Roundup* (1932) when "Tony, Jr." fell with him, and once again Tom retired from movie-making. For the next

eight years he traveled the sawdust trail, first with the Sam B. Dill Circus and then with his own.

As already mentioned, Tom took time to make his last movie in 1935 to raise money to keep his circus on the road. At fifty-five, however, Tom showed his age and had to be doubled by Cliff Lyons in some of the action scenes. The money Tom earned paid pressing circus bills, and the current release of the serial helped to keep alive the Mix name.

For several seasons his circus was successful, but 1938 was a disaster for all circuses—Tom Mix notwithstanding. The Mix Circus foundered in Pecos, Texas, on September 10. What might have been has no place in this chronicle. The show fell apart at the end; but for over four seasons it was a lusty, thriving thing and brought great circus to millions of people. Few shows survived the debacle of 1938, and this one outlived most of them. To people to whom Mix was a childhood hero, the Ralston straight-shooter of films and radio, the wish might occur that the show had had a neater and less ignominious end—but that is the stuff of fiction, not history. Tom Mix scored personal successes in the final two years of his life by making personal appearances with "Tony, Jr." in Europe.

It's sweet to remember . . . those yesteryears when today's grandfathers played at being Tom Mix astride "Tony" as they slapped their thighs and galloped off across the neighborhood range of streets, mud puddles, and empty lots in pursuit of fantasy adventures that only boys can find.

TOM MIX *Filmography*

RANCH LIFE IN THE GREAT SOUTHWEST (Selig, August 9, 1909) 1 Reel.
Pat Long, Charles Fuqua, Johnny Mullins, *Tom Mix*, Henry Grammar
D: Frank Boggs

BRITON AND BOER (Selig, October 30, 1909) 1 Reel.
Tom Mix

ON THE LITTLE BIG HORN OR CUSTER'S LAST STAND (Selig, November 27, 1909) 1 Reel.
Hobart Bosworth, Betty Harte, *Tom Mix*, Frank Waish
D: Frank Boggs
SP: Lannier Bartlett

THE RANGE RIDER (Selig, 1910) 1 Reel.
Tom Mix
D: Lynn Reynolds

AN INDIAN WIFE'S DEVOTION (Selig, 1910) 1 Reel.
Tom Mix

THE LONG TRAIL (Selig, 1910) 1 Reel.
Tom Mix, Frank Waish
D: Frank Boggs

THE MILLIONAIRE COWBOY (Selig, 1910).
Tom Mix

TAMING WILD ANIMALS (Selig, 1910).
Tom Mix
D: Frank Boggs

THE TRIMMING OF PARADISE GULCH (Selig, 1910).
Tom Mix
D: Frank Boggs
SP: Lannier Bartlett

UP SAN JUAN HILL (Selig, 1910).
Tom Mix

PRIDE OF THE RANGE (Selig, circa 1910) 1 Reel.
Tom Mix, Tom Santschi, Betty Harte, Hoot Gibson, Milt Brown, Al Green
D: Francis Boggs

CAPTAIN KATE (Selig, 1911).
Kathlyn Williams, Tom Santschi, Charles Clary, *Tom Mix*
D: Frank Boggs
SP: Edward McWade

LOST IN THE JUNGLE (Selig, 1911).
("Captain Kate" Series)
Kathlyn Williams, Tom Santschi, Charles Clary, *Tom Mix*
D: Frank Boggs
SP: Edward McWade

THE TOTEM MARK (Selig, 1911).
("Captain Kate" Series)
Kathlyn Williams, Tom Santschi, Charles Clary, *Tom Mix*
D: Frank Boggs
SP: Edward McWade

THE WHEELS OF JUSTICE (Selig, 1911).
("Captain Kate" Series)
Kathlyn Williams, Tom Santschi, Charles Clary, *Tom Mix*
D: Frank Boggs
SP: Edward McWade

BACK TO THE PRIMITIVE (Selig, May 11, 1911).
("Captain Kate" Series)
Kathlyn Williams, Tom Santschi, Charles Clary, *Tom Mix*, Joseph Girard
D: Frank Boggs
SP: Edward McWade

LOST IN THE ARCTIC (Selig, 1911).
("Captain Kate" Series)
Kathlyn Williams, Tom Santschi, Charles Clary, *Tom Mix*
D: Frank Boggs
SP: Edward McWade

RESCUED BY HER LIONS (Selig, 1911).
("Captain Kate" Series)
Kathlyn Williams, Tom Santschi, Charles Clary, *Tom Mix*
D: Frank Boggs
SP: Edward McWade

KIT CARSON'S WOOING (Selig, 1911).
Hobart Bosworth, Betty Harte, *Tom Mix*, Tom Santschi
D: Frank Boggs
SP: Lannier Bartlett

IN THE DAYS OF GOLD (Selig, 1911).
Hobart Bosworth, Betty Harte, Roy Watson, Frank Richardson, Tom Santschi, *Tom Mix*
D: Frank Boggs
SP/P: Hobart Bosworth and F. E. Montgomery

IN OLD CALIFORNIA WHEN THE GRINGOS CAME (Selig, 1911).
Kathlyn Williams, Tom Santschi, *Tom Mix*
D: Frank Boggs
SP: Lannier Bartlett

A ROMANCE OF THE RIO GRANDE (Selig, 1911) 1 Reel.
Tom Mix, Betty Harte
D: Colin Campbell
SP: Lannier Bartlett

THE SCHOOLMASTER OF MARIPOSA (Selig, 1911) 1 Reel.
Hobart Bosworth, Betty Harte, *Tom Mix*
D: Frank Boggs
SP: Lannier Bartlett

WESTERN HEARTS (Selig, 1911) 1 Reel
Tom Mix, "Old Blue"

THE TELLTALE KNIFE (Selig, November 25, 1911) 1 Reel.
William Duncan, *Tom Mix*, "Old Blue"
D: William Duncan

OUTLAW REWARD (Selig, 1912) 1 Reel.
Tom Mix, "Old Blue"

A RECONSTRUCTED REBEL (Selig, May 1912) 1 Reel.
Tom Mix, Hobart Bosworth, Betty Harte
D: Colin Campbell
SP: Lannier Bartlett

HOW IT HAPPENED (Selig, February 1, 1913) 1 Reel.
William Duncan, *Tom Mix*, Myrtle Stedman, Lester Cuneo, "Old Blue"
D: William Duncan
S: William Duncan

THE RANGE LAW (Selig, February 19, 1913) 1 Reel.
William Duncan, Myrtle Stedman, *Tom Mix*, Lester Cuneo,
"Old Blue"
D/S: William Duncan

JUGGLING WITH FATE (Selig, March 10, 1913).
Tom Mix, Myrtle Stedman, Rex de Roselli
S: Edward McWade

THE SHERIFF OF YAWAPAI COUNTY (Selig, March
15, 1913) 1 Reel.
William Duncan, Myrtle Stedman, *Tom Mix*, Lester Cuneo,
Rex De Rosselli, "Old Blue"
D/Scen: William Duncan

THE LIFE TIMER (Selig, March 22, 1913).
William Duncan, Myrtle Stedman, *Tom Mix*, Florence Dye,
Lester Cuneo, "Old Blue"
P/D/S: William Duncan

PAULINE CUSHMAN, THE FEDERAL SPY (March 27,
1913) 2 Reels.
Winifred Greenwood, Charles Clary, T. J. Commerford,
Lafayette McKee, Harry Lonsdale, Grant Foreman, Walter
Roberts, *Tom Mix*

A PRISONER OF CABANAS (Selig, April 3, 1913) 1 Reel.
Tom Mix, Tom Santschi, Bessie Eyton, "Old Blue"
D: Colin Campbell
SP: R. L. Terwillige

THE SHOTGUN MAN AND THE STAGE DRIVER
(Selig, April 5, 1913) 1 Reel.
William Duncan, *Tom Mix*, "Old Blue"
D/Scen: William Duncan

HIS FATHER'S DEPUTY (Selig, May 17, 1913) 1 Reel.
William Duncan, *Tom Mix*, Lester Cuneo, Rex De Rosselli,
"Old Blue"
P/D/S: William Duncan

THE NOISY SIX (Selig, May 21, 1913) 1 Reel.
Tom Mix, Betty Harte, "Old Blue"
D: Colin Campbell
SP: O. A. Nelson

RELIGION AND GUN PRACTICE (Selig, May 24, 1913)
1 Reel.
William Duncan, Myrtle Stedman, *Tom Mix*, "Old Blue"
D: William Duncan
Adapt: A. W. Corey

THE WORDLESS MESSAGE (Selig, May 29, 1913) 1 Reel.
Tom Mix, Tom Santschi, "Old Blue"
D: Colin Campbell
SP: Hettie Gray Baker

THE LAW AND THE OUTLAW (Selig, June 7, 1913)
1 Reel.
William Duncan, *Tom Mix*, Myrtle Stedman, Lester Cuneo,
"Old Blue"
D: William Duncan
S: *Tom Mix* and U. E. Hungerford

THE MARSHAL'S CAPTURE (Selig, June 28, 1913) 1 Reel.
William Duncan, *Tom Mix*, "Old Blue"
D: William Duncan
S: Elizabeth Frazer

SONGS OF TRUCE (Selig, June 28, 1913) 1 Reel.
Tom Mix, Tom Santschi, Kathlyn Williams
D: Colin Campbell
SP: Hettie Gray Baker

SALLIE'S SURE SHOT (Selig, June 28, 1913) 1 Reel.
William Duncan, *Tom Mix*, "Old Blue"
D: William Duncan
Adapt: Cornelius Shea

BUDD DOBLE COMES BACK (Selig, July 11, 1913) 1 Reel.
Tom Mix, Tom Santschi, "Old Blue"
D: Colin Campbell
SP: Frank Howard Clark

MADE A COWARD (Selig, July 11, 1913).
William Duncan, *Tom Mix*, "Old Blue"
S: A. W. Collins

THE TAMING OF TEXAS PETE (Selig, July 24, 1913)
1 Reel.
William Duncan, *Tom Mix*, "Old Blue"
P/D: William Duncan
S: Joseph F. Poland

AN APACHE'S GRATITUDE (Selig, August 1, 1913) 1 Reel.
William Duncan, Myrtle Stedman, *Tom Mix*, Jim Robson,
Rex DeRosselli, "Old Blue"
D/Scen: William Duncan

THE STOLEN MOCCASINS (Selig, August 9, 1913) 1 Reel.
William Duncan, Myrtle Stedman, *Tom Mix*, Lester Cuneo
"Old Blue"
P/D: William Duncan
S: Cornelius Shea

THE GOOD INDIAN (Selig, August 13, 1913) 1 Reel.
William Duncan, *Tom Mix*, "Old Blue"
D: William Duncan
Adapt: Ethel C. Unland

TOBIAS WANTS OUT (Selig, September 11, 1913) 1 Reel.
Tom Mix, "Old Blue"
P: Oscar Eagle
S: Arthur Preston Hankins

SAVED BY THE PONY EXPRESS (Selig, 1913) 1 Reel.
Tom Mix, "Old Blue"

THE SHERIFF AND THE RUSTLER (Selig, 1913) 2 Reels.
Tom Mix, Lester Cuneo, George Panky, Res de Roselli, Neal Broaded, Vic Firth, B. L. Jones, "Old Blue"
D: William Duncan
S: *Tom Mix*

A MUDDLE IN HORSE THIEVES (Selig, October 25, 1913) 1 Reel.
Tom Mix, "Old Blue"
S: Elizabeth Frazer

THE CHILD OF THE PRAIRIE (Selig, November 8, 1913) 1 Reel.
Tom Mix, "Old Blue"
S: *Tom Mix*

THE ESCAPE OF JIM DOLAN (Selig, November 13, 1913) 1 Reel.
Tom Mix, Betty Harte, Tom Santschi, "Old Blue"
D: Colin Campbell
S: *Tom Mix*
SP: Gilson Willets

LOCAL COLOR (Selig, November 21, 1913) 1 Reel.
Tom Mix, "Old Blue"
D/S: *Tom Mix*

THE LITTLE SISTER (Selig, February 2, 1914) 1 Reel.
Tom Mix, "Old Blue"
S: Merla Marion Metcalfe

SHOTGUN JONES (Selig, April 14, 1914) 2 Reels.
Tom Mix, "Old Blue"
D: Colin Campbell
SP: Bertha M. Bower

ME AN' BILL (Selig, June 6, 1914) 2 Reels.
Tom Mix, Tom Santschi, "Old Blue"
D/SP: Colin Campbell

THE LEOPARD'S FOUNDLING (Selig, June 11, 1914) 2 Reels.
Kathlyn Williams, *Tom Mix*
D: F. J. Grandon
SP: Mabel Heckes Justice

IN DEFIANCE OF THE LAW (Selig, June 13, 1914) 3 Reels.
Tom Mix, "Old Blue"
P: Colin Campbell
S: James Oliver Curwood—"Isabel"

HIS FIGHT (Selig, June 20, 1914) 1 Reel.
Tom Mix, Tom Santschi, Kathlyn Williams, "Old Blue"
D/SP: Colin Campbell

WIGGS TAKES THE REST CURE (Selig, June 26, 1914) 1 Reel.
Tom Mix, "Old Blue"
D: F. J. Grandon
SP: Walter E. Wing

THE WILDERNESS MAIL (Selig, June 26, 1914) 2 Reels.
Tom Mix, Kathlyn Williams, "Old Blue"
D/SP: Colin Campbell
S: James Oliver Curwood

WHEN THE COOK FELL ILL (Selig, July 9, 1914) 1 Reel.
Tom Mix, Wheeler Oakman, Frank Clark, "Old Blue"
D: Colin Campbell
S: B. M. Bower

ETIENNE OF THE GLAD HEART (Selig, July 15, 1914) 2 Reels.
Tom Mix, "Old Blue"
P: Colin Campbell
S: Maibelle Heikes Justice

THE REVELER (Selig, July 31, 1914) 1 Reel.
Tom Mix, "Old Blue"
D: Colin Campbell
SP: Bertha M. Bower (pseud. of Bertha Muzzy Sinclair)

THE WHITE MOUSE (Selig, August 4, 1914) 2 Reels.
Tom Mix, "Old Blue"
P: Colin Campbell
S: James Oliver Curwood

CHIP OF THE FLYING U (Selig, August 12, 1914) 3 Reels.
Tom Mix, Kathlyn Williams, Frank Clark, Wheeler Oakman, Bessie Eyton, Fred Huntley, "Old Blue"
D: Colin Campbell
SP: B. M. Bower (pseud. of Bertha Muzzy Sinclair)

TO BE CALLED FOR (Selig, August 19, 1914) 1 Reel.
Tom Mix, "Old Blue"
D: F. J. Grandon
SP: Wallace Clifton

THE FIFTH MAN (Selig, August 31, 1914) 3 Reels.
Tom Mix, Tom Santschi, Frank Walsh, Charles Clary, Bessie Eyton, Lafe McKee, Roy Watson, "Old Blue"
D: F. J. Grandon
S: James Oliver Curwood

JIM (Selig, September 2, 1914) 1 Reel.
Tom Mix, "Old Blue"
D: F. J. Grandon
SP: Wallace C. Clifton

THE LONESOME TRAIL (Selig, September 2, 1914) 1 Reel.
Tom Mix, Kathlyn Williams, "Old Blue"
D; Colin Campbell
SP: B. M. Bower

THE LIVID FLAME (Selig, September 3, 1914) 2 Reels.
Tom Mix, "Old Blue"
D: F. J. Grandon
SP: Walter E. Wing

FOUR MINUTES LATE (Selig, September 10, 1914) 1 Reel.
Tom Mix, "Old Blue"
D/SP: F. J. Grandon
S: James Oliver Curwood

THE REAL THING IN COWBOYS (Selig, September 10, 1914) 1 Reel.
Tom Mix, "Old Blue"
D: *Tom Mix*
S: Hettie Gray Baker

HEARTS AND MASKS (Selig, September 16, 1914) 3 Reels.
Tom Mix, Kathlyn Williams, "Old Blue"
D/SP: Colin Campbell
S: Harold MacGrath

THE MOVING PICTURE COWBOY (Selig, September 16, 1914) 2 Reels.
Tom Mix, Elinor (Peggy) Blevins, Lester Cuneo, Sid Jordan, "Old Blue"
D: *Tom Mix*
S: *Tom Mix*

THE WAY OF THE REDMAN (Selig, September 16, 1914) 1 Reel.
Tom Mix, "Old Blue"
D/SP: *Tom Mix*

THE MEXICAN (Selig, September 24, 1914) 1 Reel.
Tom Mix, Lillian Wade, "Old Blue"
D/SP: *Tom Mix*
S: Lynn Reynolds

THE GOING OF THE WHITE SWAN (Selig, September 28, 1914) 2 Reels.
Tom Mix, Frank Clark, Bessie Eyton, Wheeler Oakman, "Old Blue"
P: Colin Campbell
S: Gilbert Parker

JIMMY HAYES AND MURIEL (Selig, September 30, 1914) 1 Reel.
Tom Mix, "Old Blue"
D: *Tom Mix*
S: Sidney Porter

GARRISON'S FINISH (Selig, October 1, 1914) 3 Reels.
Tom Mix, "Old Blue"
D: F. J. Grandon
SP: W. B. M. Ferguson

WHY THE SHERIFF IS A BACHELOR (Selig, October 10, 1914) 1 Reel.
Tom Mix, "Old Blue"
D/SP: *Tom Mix*

THE LOSING FIGHT (Selig, October 15, 1914) 1 Reel.
Tom Mix, "Old Blue"
D/SP: Colin Campbell

THE RANGER'S ROMANCE (Selig, October 15, 1914) 1 Reel.
Tom Mix, Goldie Colwell, Roy Watson, Inez Walker, "Old Blue"
D/SP: *Tom Mix*

THE TELLTALE KNIFE (Selig October 15, 1914) 1 Reel.
Tom Mix, Goldie Colwell, Harry Loverin, Leo Maloney, "Old Blue"
D/SP: *Tom Mix*

IF I WERE YOUNG AGAIN (Selig, October 24, 1914) 2 Reels.
Tom Mix, "Old Blue"
D: F. J. Grandon
SP: Gelson Willets

OUT OF PETTICOAT LANE (Selig, October 24, 1914) 2 Reels.
Tom Mix, "Old Blue"
D/SP: F. J. Grandon

THE SHERIFF'S REWARD (Selig, October 24, 1914) 1 Reel.
Tom Mix, Goldie Colwell, Leo Maloney, Roy Watson, "Old Blue"
D/S/SP: *Tom Mix*

THE SCAPEGOAT (Selig, October 24, 1914) 1 Reel.
Tom Mix, Goldie Colwell, Leo Maloney, "Old Blue"
D/S/SP: *Tom Mix*

YOUR GIRL AND MINE (Selig, October 31, 1914) 7 Reels.
Kathlyn Williams, *Tom Mix*, "Old Blue"
D: F. J. Grandon
SP: Gilson Willets

IN THE DAYS OF THE THUNDERING HERD (Selig, November 12, 1914) 5 Reels.
Tom Mix, Bessie Eyton, Red Wing, Wheeler Oakman, John Bowers, Major Gordon (Pawnee Bill) Lillie, "Old Blue"
D: Colin Campbell
SP: Gilson Willets

THE RIVAL STAGE LINES (Selig, November 12, 1914) 1 Reel.
Tom Mix, Goldie Colwell, Leo Maloney, Sid Jordan, "Old Blue"
D: *Tom Mix*
S: Allen A. Martin

SAVED BY A WATCH (Selig, November 19, 1914) 1 Reel.
Tom Mix, Goldie Colwell, Leo Maloney, Inez Walker, "Old Blue"
D/S/SP: *Tom Mix*

THE SOUL MATE (Selig, November 19, 1914) 1 Reel.
Tom Mix, Kathlyn Williams
D: F. J. Grandon
SP: Mark Reardon

THE MAN FROM THE EAST (Selig, November 28, 1914) 1 Reel.
Tom Mix, Goldie Colwell, Leo Maloney, Pat Chrisman, Inez Walker, Hoot Gibson, "Old Blue"
D/SP: *Tom Mix*

WADE BRENT PAYS (Selig, December 8, 1914) 1 Reel.
Tom Mix, Tom Santschi, "Old Blue"
D: F. J. Grandon
SP: Marie Wing, F. J. Grandon

CACTUS JAKE, HEARTBREAKER (Selig, December 10, 1914) 1 Reel.
Tom Mix, Goldie Colwell, Leo Maloney, Josephine Miller, "Old Blue"
D: *Tom Mix*

BUFFALO HUNTING (Selig, 1914).
Tom Mix and "Old Blue"
D: F. J. Grandon
SP: Gilson Willets

THE LURE OF THE WINDIGO (Selig, 1914).
Tom Mix and "Old Blue"
D: F. J. Grandon
SP: Mabel Heikes Justice

THE TELLTALE KNIFE (Selig, November 7, 1914) 1 Reel.
Tom Mix
D/Scen: *Tom Mix*

THE FLOWER OF FAITH (Selig, December 10, 1914) 2 Reels.
Kathlyn Williams, *Tom Mix*
D: F. J. Grandon
SP: Will M. Hough

A MILITANT SCHOOL MA'AM (Selig, December 28, 1914) 1 Reel.
Tom Mix, Goldie Colwell, Leo Maloney, Sid Jordan, "Tony"
D: *Tom Mix*
S: Edwin Ray Coffin

HAROLD'S BAD MAN (Selig, January 2, 1915) 1 Reel.
Tom Mix, Goldie Colwell, Leo Maloney, Pat Chrisman, "Tony"
D: *Tom Mix*
S: Edwin Ray Coffin

CACTUS JIM'S SHOPGIRL (Selig, January 9, 1915) 1 Reel.
Tom Mix, Goldie Colwell, Lynn Reynolds, "Tony"
D: *Tom Mix*
S: Edwin Ray Coffin

THE GRIZZLY GULCH CHARIOT RACE (Selig, January 13, 1915) 1 Reel.
Tom Mix, Inez Walker, Sid Jordan, Dick Crawford, Roy Watson, "Tony"
D: *Tom Mix*
S: O. A. Nelson

HEART'S DESIRE (Selig, January 13, 1915) 1 Reel.
Tom Mix and "Tony"
D: F. J. Grandon
SP: Wallace Clifton

FORKED TRAILS (Selig, January 16, 1915) 1 Reel.
Tom Mix, Goldie Colwell, Sid Jordan, Pat Chrisman, "Tony"
D: *Tom Mix*
S: William MacLeod Raine

ROPING A BRIDE (Selig, January 26, 1915) 1 Reel.
Tom Mix, Goldie Colwell, Sid Jordan, C. W. Beakman, Roy Watson, Inez Walker, "Tony"
D: *Tom Mix*
S: E. Lynn Summers

BILL HAYWOOD, PRODUCER (Selig, February 1, 1915) 1 Reel.
Tom Mix, Mabel Van Buren, Sid Jordan, Goldie Colwell, Roy Watson, George Fawcett, Pat Chrisman, "Tony"
D/SP: *Tom Mix*

HEARTS OF THE JUNGLE (Selig, February 11, 1915) 1 Reel.
Tom Mix
D: F. J. Grandon
SP: Wallace Clifton

SLIM HIGGINS (Selig, February 11, 1915) 1 Reel.
Tom Mix, Goldie Colwell, Roy Watson, Pat Chrisman, "Tony"
D/SP: *Tom Mix*

THE MAN FROM TEXAS (Selig, February 24, 1915) 1 Reel.
Tom Mix, Leo Maloney, Hoot Gibson, "Tony"
D/SP: *Tom Mix*

A CHILD OF THE PRAIRIE (Selig, February 24, 1915) 2 Reels.
Tom Mix, Louella Mexam (later Lola Maxam), Baby Norma, Ed J. Brady, Fay Robinson, Rose Robinson, "Tony"
D/S: *Tom Mix*

THE STAGECOACH DRIVER AND THE GIRL (Selig, February 26, 1915) 1 Reel.
Tom Mix, Goldie Colwell, Louella (later Lola) Maxam, Sid Jordan, Ed Brady, Ed "King Fisher" Jones, "Tony"
D/SP: *Tom Mix*

THE PUNY SOUL OF PETER RAND (Selig, March 6, 1915) 1 Reel.
Tom Mix, Tom Santschi, "Tony"
D: F. J. Grandon
SP: Walter E. Wing

SAGEBRUSH TOM (Selig, March 8, 1915) 1 Reel.
Tom Mix, Myrtle Stedman, Goldie Colwell, Ed J. Brady, "Tony"
D/S: *Tom Mix*

THE OUTLAW'S BRIDE (Selig, March 13, 1915) 1 Reel.
Tom Mix, Eugenia Ford, Ed J. Brady, Pat Chrisman, "Tony"
D: *Tom Mix*
S: Cornelius Shea

JACK'S PALS (Selig, March 16, 1915) 1 Reel.
Tom Mix and "Tony"
D: F. J. Grandon
SP: C. B. Murphy

THE LEGAL LIGHT (Selig, March 20, 1915) 1 Reel.
Tom Mix, Eugenie Ford, Ed J. Brady, "Tony"
D: *Tom Mix*
S: Edwin Ray Coffin

MA'S GIRLS (Selig, March 20, 1915) 2 Reels.
Tom Mix, Eugenie Ford, Goldie Colwell, Ed J. Brady, Louella (later Lola) Maxam, "Tony"
D/S: *Tom Mix*

GETTING A START IN LIFE (Selig, March 29, 1915) 1 Reel.
Tom Mix and "Tony"
D: *Tom Mix*
SP: James Oliver Curwood

MRS. MURPHY'S COOKS (Selig, April 3, 1915) 1 Reel.
Tom Mix, Louella Maxam, "Tony"
D/SP: *Tom Mix*

THE CONVERSION OF SMILING TOM (Selig, April 10, 1915) 1 Reel.
Tom Mix, Sid Jordan, "Tony"
D: *Tom Mix*
S: Emma Bell

THE FACE AT THE WINDOW (Selig, April 10, 1915) 1 Reel.
Tom Mix, "Tony"
D: F. J. Grandon
SP: Wallace Clifton

AN ARIZONA WOOING (Selig, April 26, 1915) 1 Reel.
Tom Mix, Bessie Eyton, Sid Jordan, "Tony"
D: *Tom Mix*
S: William MacLeod Raine

A MATRIMONIAL BOOMERANG (Selig, April 30, 1915) 1 Reel.
Tom Mix, Louella Maxam, "Tony"
D: *Tom Mix*
S: Edith Blumer

PALS IN BLUE (Selig, May 26, 1915) 3 Reels.
Tom Mix, Ada Gleason, Sid Jordan, Howard Farrell, Pat Chrisman, Edward Brady, Bob Anderson, Al Merrill, Eugenia Ford, "Tony"
D/S: *Tom Mix*

SAVED BY HER HORSE (Selig, May 26, 1915) 1 Reel.
Tom Mix, Louella Maxam, "Tony"
D: *Tom Mix*
S: Cornelius Shea

THE HEART OF THE SHERIFF (Selig, June 8, 1915), 1 Reel.
Tom Mix, "Tony"
P/D/S: *Tom Mix*

WITH THE AID OF THE LAW (Selig, June 11, 1915) 1 Reel.
Tom Mix, "Tony"
P/D: *Tom Mix*
S: Marshall E. Gamon

THE PARSON WHO FLED WEST (Selig, July 3, 1915) 1 Reel.
Tom Mix, "Tony"
D: Burton L. King
SP: Malcolm Douglas

THE FOREMAN OF BAR Z RANCH (Selig, July 10, 1915) 1 Reel.
Tom Mix, "Tony"
D: *Tom Mix*
SP: Wallace C. Clifton

THE CHILD, THE DOG, AND THE VILLAIN (Selig, July 17, 1915) 1 Reel.
Tom Mix, "Tony"
D: *Tom Mix*
SP: Campbell MacCulloch

THE TAKING OF MUSTANG PETE (Selig, July 24, 1915) 1 Reel.
Tom Mix, "Tony"
D: *Tom Mix*
SP: Emma Bell

THE GOLD DUST AND THE SQUAW (Selig, July 31, 1915) 1 Reel.
Tom Mix, "Tony"
D: *Tom Mix*
SP: Cornelius Shea

A LUCKY DEAL (Selig, August 7, 1915) 1 Reel.
Tom Mix, "Tony"
D/P/S: *Tom Mix*

NEVER AGAIN (Selig, August 28, 1915) 1 Reel.
Tom Mix, "Tony"
P/D/S: *Tom Mix*

HOW WEARY WENT WOOING (Selig, September 4, 1915) 1 Reel.
Tom Mix, Victoria Forde, Sid Jordan, Leo Maloney, "Tony"
P/D: *Tom Mix*
S: B. M. Bower

THE AUCTION SALE OF RUN-DOWN RANCH (Selig, September 11, 1915) 1 Reel.
Tom Mix, "Tony"
D: *Tom Mix*
SP: Cornelius Shea

THE RANGE GIRL AND THE COWBOY (Selig, September 11, 1915) 1 Reel.
Tom Mix, Victoria Forde, Leo Maloney, Sid Jordan, "Tony"
D/SP: *Tom Mix*

NEVER AGAIN (Selig, September 11, 1915) 1 Reel.
Tom Mix, Victoria Forde, Sid Jordan, Leo Maloney, "Tony"
D/Scen: *Tom Mix*

HER SLIGHT MISTAKE (Selig, September 18, 1915) 1 Reel.
Tom Mix, Howard Farrell, Leo Maloney, Mrs. Chrisman, "Tony"
D: *Tom Mix*
S: Epes Winthrop Sargent

THE GIRL AND THE MAIL BAG (Selig, September 25, 1915) 1 Reel.
Tom Mix, Victoria Forde, "Tony"
D: *Tom Mix*
S: Cornelius Shea

THE BRAVE DESERVE THE FAIR (Selig, October 9, 1915) 2 Reels.
Tom Mix, "Tony"
D/SP: *Tom Mix*

THE STAGECOACH GUARD (Selig, October 9, 1915) 1 Reel.
Tom Mix, "Tony"
D/S/SP: *Tom Mix*

THE RACE FOR A GOLD MINE (Selig, October 16, 1915) 1 Reel.
Tom Mix, Victoria Forde, Sid Jordan, Pat Chrisman, "Tony"
D: *Tom Mix*
S: Cornelius Shea

THE FOREMAN'S CHOICE (Selig, October 20, 1915) 1 Reel.
Tom Mix, "Tony"
P/D: *Tom Mix*
S/SP: Cornelius Shea

ATHLETIC AMBITIONS (Selig, October 23, 1915) 1 Reel.
Tom Mix, "Tony"
D/SP: *Tom Mix*

THE TENDERFOOT'S TRIUMPH (Selig, October 29, 1915) 1 Reel.
Tom Mix, Hazel Daly, Joe Simkins, Sid Jordan, Pat Chrisman, "Tony"
D: *Tom Mix*
S/SP: Cornelius Shea

THE CHEF AT CIRCLE G (Selig, October 30, 1915) 1 Reel.
Tom Mix, "Tony"
P/D: *Tom Mix*
S: Edwin Ray Coffin

THE IMPERSONATION OF TOM (Selig, November 6, 1915) 1 Reel.
Tom Mix, "Tony"
P/D: *Tom Mix*
S: Cornelius Shea

BAD MAN BOBBS (Selig, November 13, 1915) 1 Reel.
Tom Mix, "Tony"
P/D: *Tom Mix*
S: Edwin Ray Coffin

ON THE EAGLE TRAIL (Selig, November 27, 1915) 1 Reel.
Tom Mix, Victoria Forde, Joe Simkins, Sid Jordan, "Tony"
P/D: *Tom Mix*
S: Cornelius Shea

THE DESERT CALLS ITS OWN (Selig, January 15, 1916) 1 Reel.
Tom Mix, "Tony"
P/D: *Tom Mix*
S: W. E. Wing

A MIX-UP IN MOVIES (Selig, January 22, 1916) 1 Reel.
Tom Mix, "Tony"
P/D/S: *Tom Mix*

MAKING GOOD (Selig, January 29, 1916) 1 Reel.
Tom Mix, "Tony"
P/D/S: *Tom Mix*

THE PASSING OF PETE (Selig, February 19, 1916) 1 Reel.
Tom Mix, "Tony"
P/D/S: *Tom Mix*

TRILBY'S LOVE DISASTER (Selig, March 4, 1916) 1 Reel.
Tom Mix, Victoria Forde, "Tony"
P/D/S: *Tom Mix*

A FIVE-THOUSAND-DOLLAR ELOPEMENT (Selig, March 16, 1916) 1 Reel.
Tom Mix, Victoria Forde, Sid Jordan, Joe Ryan, "Tony"
P/D: *Tom Mix*
S: Cornelius Shea

ALONG THE BORDER (Selig, March 18, 1916) 1 Reel.
Tom Mix, Victoria Forde, Sid Jordan, Joe Ryan, Joe Simkins, "Tony"
P/D/S: *Tom Mix*

TOO MANY CHEFS (Selig, April 1, 1916) 1 Reel.
Tom Mix, Victoria Forde, Joe Ryan, "Tony"
P/D/S: *Tom Mix*

THE MAN WITHIN (Selig, April 15, 1916) 3 Reels.
Tom Mix, Victoria Forde, Sid Jordan, Pat Chrisman, Joe Ryan, "Tony"
D: *Tom Mix*
S: E. Lynn Summers

THE SHERIFF'S DUTY (Selig, April 22, 1916) 1 Reel.
Tom Mix, "Tony"
P/D/S: *Tom Mix*

COOKED TRAILS (Selig, May 13, 1916) 1 Reel.
Tom Mix, Victoria Forde, Pat Chrisman, Joe Ryan, Sid Jordan, "Tony"
P/D/S: *Tom Mix*

GOING WEST TO MAKE GOOD (Selig, May 20, 1916) 1 Reel.
Tom Mix, Victoria Forde, "Tony"
P/D/S: *Tom Mix*

THE COWPUNCHER'S PERIL (Selig, May 27, 1916) 1 Reel.
Tom Mix, Victoria Forde, Pat Chrisman, Joe Ryan, "Tony"
P/D/S: *Tom Mix*

TAKING A CHANCE (Selig, June 3, 1916) 1 Reel.
Tom Mix, Victoria Forde, Pat Chrisman, Joe Ryan, "Tony"
P/D/S: *Tom Mix*

THE GIRL OF GOLD GULCH (Selig, June 10, 1916) 1 Reel.
Tom Mix, Victoria Forde, Joe Ryan, Ed Jones, "Tony"
P/D: *Tom Mix*
S: Cornelius Shea

SOME DUEL (Selig, June 17, 1916) 1 Reel.
Tom Mix, Victoria Forde, Joe Ryan, Sid Jordan, "Tony"
D/S/P: *Tom Mix*

LEGAL ADVICE (Selig, June 24, 1916) 1 Reel.
Tom Mix, Sid Jordan, "Tony"
P/D/S: *Tom Mix*

SHOOTING UP THE MOVIES (Selig, July 1, 1916) 2 Reels.
Tom Mix, Victoria Forde, Sid Jordan, Howard Farrell, Hazel Daly, Joe Ryan, "Tony"
D/S: *Tom Mix*

LOCAL COLOR (Selig, July 8, 1916) 1 Reel.
Tom Mix, Victoria Forde, Sid Jordan, "Tony"
D/S/P: *Tom Mix*

AN ANGELIC ATTITUDE (Selig, July 15, 1916) 1 Reel.
Tom Mix, Victoria Forde, Joe Ryan, "Tony"
D/P: *Tom Mix*
S: Edwin Ray Coffin

A WESTERN MASQUERADE (Selig, July 22, 1916) 1 Reel.
Tom Mix, Victoria Forde, Sid Jordan, "Tony"
P/D/S: *Tom Mix*

A BEAR OF A STORY (Selig, July 29, 1916) 1 Reel.
Tom Mix, Victoria Forde, "Tony"
D/P/S: *Tom Mix*

ROPING A SWEETHEART (Selig, August 5, 1916) 1 Reel.
Tom Mix, Victoria Forde, Sid Jordan, "Tony"
P/D/S: *Tom Mix*

TOM'S STRATEGY (Selig, August 12, 1916) 1 Reel.
Tom Mix, Victoria Forde, "Tony"
P/D/S: *Tom Mix*

THE TAMING OF GROUCHY BILL (Selig, August 19, 1916) 1 Reel.
Tom Mix, "Tony"
P/D/S: *Tom Mix*

THE PONY EXPRESS RIDER (Selig, August 26, 1916) 2 Reels.
Tom Mix, Pat Chrisman, Sid Jordan, Victoria Forde, "Tony"
P/D/S: *Tom Mix*

A CORNER IN WATER (Selig, September 2, 1916) 1 Reel.
Tom Mix, "Tony"
P/D/S: *Tom Mix*

THE RAIDERS (Selig, September 9, 1916) 1 Reel.
Tom Mix, "Tony"
P/D/S: *Tom Mix*

THE CANBY HILL OUTLAWS (Selig, September 16, 1916) 1 Reel.
Tom Mix, Pat Chrisman, "Tony"
P/D/S: *Tom Mix*

A MISTAKE IN RUSTLERS (Selig, September 23, 1916) 1 Reel.
Tom Mix, "Tony"
P/D/S: *Tom Mix*

AN EVENTFUL EVENING (Selig, September 30, 1916) 1 Reel.
Tom Mix, Victoria Forde, Betty Keller, Pat Chrisman, "Tony"
P/D: *Tom Mix*
S: Victoria Forde

THE WAY OF THE REDMAN (Selig, October 3, 1916) 1 Reel.
Tom Mix, "Tony"
D/Scen: *Tom Mix*

A CLOSE CALL (Selig, October 7, 1916) 1 Reel.
Tom Mix, Victoria Forde, "Tony"
P/D/S: *Tom Mix*

TOM'S SACRIFICE (Selig, October 14, 1916) 1 Reel.
Tom Mix, "Tony"
P/D/S: *Tom Mix*

WHEN CUPID SLIPPED (Selig, October 21, 1916) 1 Reel.
Tom Mix, Pat Chrisman, Victoria Forde, "Tony"
P/S: Victoria Forde

THE SHERIFF'S BLUNDER (Selig, November 4, 1916) 3 Reels.
Tom Mix, Sid Jordan, Victoria Forde, "Tony"
P/D/S: *Tom Mix*

MISTAKES WILL HAPPEN (Selig, November 11, 1916) 1 Reel.
Tom Mix, Victoria Forde, Pat Chrisman, Sid Jordan, "Tony"
P/D/S: *Tom Mix*

TWISTED TRAILS (Selig, November 25, 1916) 3 Reels.
Tom Mix, Bessie Eyton, George Clark, Eugenie Besserer, Sid Jordan, Frank LeRoy, Olcott Byrnes, "Tony"
P/D: *Tom Mix*
S: Edwin Ray Coffin

THE GOLDEN THOUGHT (Selig, December 9, 1916) 2 Reels.
Tom Mix, Victoria Forde, Sid Jordan, Earl Deming, Alice Burke, "Tony"
P/D: *Tom Mix*
S: J. A. Lacy

STARRING IN WESTERN STUFF (Selig, December 23, 1916) 2 Reels.
Tom Mix, "Tony"
P/D/S: *Tom Mix*

IN THE DAYS OF DARING (Selig, 1916).
Tom Mix, Goldie Colwell, "Tony"
P/D: *Tom Mix*

THE SADDLE GIRTH (Selig, January 23, 1917) 1 Reel.
Tom Mix, Louella Maxam, Sid Jordan, "Tony"
P/D/S: *Tom Mix*

THE LUCK THAT JEALOUSY BROUGHT (Selig, January 24, 1917) 1 Reel.
Tom Mix, Louella Maxam, Sid Jordan, Pat Chrisman, "Tony"
P/D: *Tom Mix*
S: Cornelius Shea

THE HEART OF TEXAS RYAN (Selig, February 10, 1917) 5 Reels.
Tom Mix, Bessie Eyton, George Fawcett, Goldie Colwell, Frank Campeau, William Rhyno, Leo Maloney, Charles Gerard, Sid Jordan, "Tony"
D: E. A. Martin
SP: Gilsen Willets

HEARTS AND SADDLES (Fox, March 11, 1917) 2 Reels.
Tom Mix, Victoria Forde, Sid Jordan, Pat Chrisman, Victor Potel, "Tony"
D: *Tom Mix*, Bob Eddy
S: *Tom Mix*

A ROMAN COWBOY (Fox, May 6, 1917) 2 Reels.
Tom Mix, Sid Jordan, "Tony"
D/S/SP: *Tom Mix*

SIX CYLINDER LOVE (Fox, June 10, 1917) 2 Reels.
Tom Mix, "Tony"
D/S/SP: *Tom Mix*

A SOFT TENDERFOOT (Fox, July 5, 1917) 2 Reels.
Tom Mix, Victoria Forde, "Tony"
D/S/SP: *Tom Mix*

DURAND OF THE BAD LANDS (Fox, August 12, 1917) 5 Reels.
Dustin Farnum, *Tom Mix*, Winifred Kingston, Frankie Lee
D: Richard Stanton
S: Maibelle Heikes Justice

TOM AND JERRY MIX (Fox, September 2, 1917) 2 Reels.
Tom Mix, Victoria Forde, "Tony"
S/SP/D: *Tom Mix*

CUPID'S ROUNDUP (Fox, January 13, 1918) 5 Reels.
Tom Mix, Wanda Petit (Wanda Hawley), Roy Watson, E. B. Tilton, Edwin Booth, Verne Mersereau, Al Padgett, Fred H. Clark, Eugenia Ford, Barney Furey, "Tony"
D: Edward Le Saint
S: George Scarborough
SP: Charles Kenyon

SIX SHOOTER ANDY (Fox, February 24, 1918) 5 Reels.
Tom Mix, Enid Markey, Sam de Grasse, Pat Chrisman, Bert Woodruff, Bob Fleming, Jack Planck, Ben Hammer, George Stone, Lewis Sargent, Buddy Messinger, Raymond Lee, Virginia Lee Corbin, Violet Radcleffe, Vivian Planck, Beulah Burns, Charles Stevens, Thelma Burns, "Tony"
D: Chester M. Franklin, Sidney A. Franklin
S/SP: Bernard McConville

WESTERN BLOOD (Fox, April 14, 1918) 5 Reels.
Tom Mix, Victoria Forde, Barney Furey, Frank H. Clark, Pat Chrisman, Buck Jones, "Tony"
D/SP: Lynn F. Reynolds
S: *Tom Mix*

ACE HIGH (Fox, June 9, 1918) 5 Reels.
Tom Mix, Kathleen O'Connor, Virginia Lee Corbin, Pat Chrisman, Lawrence Payton, Lloyd Pearl, Lewis Sargent, Colin Chase, Jay Morley, Georgie Johnson, "Tony"
D/S/SP: Lynn Reynolds

WHO'S YOUR FATHER? (Fox, July 7, 1918) 2 Reels.
Tom Mix, "Tony"
P: Henry Lehrman
D: *Tom Mix*

MR. LOGAN, U.S.A. (Fox, September 8, 1918) 5 Reels.
Tom Mix, Kathleen O'Connor, Smoke Turner, Dick La Reno, Val Paul, Maude Emory, "Tony"
D/SP: Lynn F. Reynolds

FAME AND FORTUNE (Fox, November 8, 1918) 5 Reels.
Tom Mix, Kathleen O'Connor, Virginia Lee Corbin, Jay Morley, Pat Chrisman, Laurence Peyton, Colin Chase, Virginia Brown Faire, Lewis Sargent, Lloyd Pearl, George Nichols, Jack Dill, Annette deFoe, "Tony"
D: Lynn F. Reynolds
SP: Bennett R. Cole
S: Charles Alden Seltzer

TREAT 'EM ROUGH (Fox, January 5, 1919) 5 Reels.
Tom Mix, Jane Novak, Smoke Turner, Charles LeMoyne, Jack Curtis, Val Paul, "Tony"
D/SP: Lynn F. Reynolds
S: Charles Alden Seltzer

HELL-ROARIN' REFORM (Fox, February 16, 1919) 5 Reels.
Tom Mix, Kathleen O'Connor, Smoke Turner, George Berrell, Jack Curtis, Cupid Morgan, "Tony"
D: Edward J. Le Saint
S: Anthony J. Roach
SP: Charles Kenyon

FIGHTING FOR GOLD (Fox, March 30, 1919) 5 Reels.
Tom Mix, Lucille Young, Teddy Sampson, Sid Jordan, George Nichols, Jack Nelson, Harry Lonsdale, Robert Dunbar, Hattie Buskirk, Frank H. Clark, "Tony"
D: Edward J. Le Saint
S: William MacLeod Raine—"The Highgrader"
SP: Charles Kenyon

THE COMING OF THE LAW (Fox, May 11, 1919) 5 Reels.
Tom Mix, Jane Novak, Brownie Vernon, George Nichols, Jack Curtis, Sid Jordan, Smoke Turner, Charles Le Moyne, Pat Chrisman, Lewis Sargent, Harry Dunkinson, Jack Nelson, Jack Dill. Gordon Marr, "Tony"
D: Authur Rosson
SP: Denison Clift
S: Charles Alden Seltzer

THE WILDERNESS TRAIL (Fox, July 6, 1919) 5 Reels.
Tom Mix, Colleen Moore, Sid Jordan, Frank H. Clark, Pat Chrisman, Jack Nelson, Lulu Warrenton, Buck Jones, "Tony"
D: Edward J. Le Saint
S: Frank Williams
SP: Charles Kenyon

ROUGH-RIDING ROMANCE (Fox, August 24, 1919) 5 Reels.
Tom Mix, Juanita Hansen, Jack Nelson, Pat Chrisman, Sid Jordan, Spottiswoode Aitken, "Tony"
D: Arthur Rosson
S/SP: Charles Kenyon

THE SPEED MANIAC (Fox, October 19, 1919) 5 Reels.
Tom Mix, Eva Novak, Charles K. French, Ernest Shields, Jack Curtis, Charles H. Mailes, Hayward Mack, Helen Wright, Pat Harmon, Lee C. Shumway, George E. Stone, George Hackathorne, Buck Jones, "Tony"
D: Edward J. Le Saint
SP: Denison Clift
S: H. H. Van Loan

THE FEUD (Fox, December 7, 1919) 5 Reels.
Tom Mix, Eva Novak, Claire McDowell, J. Arthur Mackey, John Cossar, Mollie McConnell, Lloyd Bacon, Joseph Bennett, Jean Calhoun, Frank Thorne, Sid Jordan, Nelson McDowell, Lucretia Harris, Guy Eakins, "Tony"
D: Edward J. Le Saint
S/SP: Charles Kenyon

THE CYCLONE (Fox, January 25, 1920) 5 Reels.
Tom Mix, Colleen Moore, William Ellingford, Buck Jones, Henry Herbert, "Tony"
D: Cliff Smith
SP: J. Anthony Roach

THE DAREDEVIL (Fox, March 7, 1920) 5 Reels.
Tom Mix, Eva Novak, Lucille Young, Pat Chrisman, Charles K. French, Lee C. Shumway, Sid Jordan, Harry Dunkinson, Lafe McKee, George Hernandez, "Tony"
D/S/SP: *Tom Mix*
C: J. D. Jennings

DESERT LOVE (Fox, April 11, 1920) 5 Reels.
Tom Mix, Eva Novak, Francelia Billington, Lester Cuneo, Charles K. French, Jack Curtis, "Tony"
D/SP: Jacques Jaccard
S: *Tom Mix*

THE TERROR (Fox, May 16, 1920) 5 Reels.
Tom Mix, Francelia Billington, Lester Cuneo, Lucille Young, Joseph G. Bennett, Charles K. French, Wilbur Higby, "Tony"
D/SP: Jacques Jaccard
S: *Tom Mix*

Tom Mix and Charles La Moyne in *Coming of the Law* (Fox, 1919).

THREE GOLD COINS (Fox, July 4, 1920) 5 Reels.
Tom Mix, Margaret Loomis, Bert Hadley, Frank Whitson, Bonnie Hill, Walt Robbins, Sylvia Jocelyn, Dick Rush, Sid Jordan, Margaret Cullington, Pat Chrisman, "Tony"
D: Clifford Smith
SP: Alvin J. Neitz
S: H. H. Van Loan

THE UNTAMED (Fox, September 5, 1920) 6 Reels.
Tom Mix, Pauline Starke, George Siegman, Philo McCullough, James Barrows, Charles K. French, Sid Jordan, Pat Chrisman, Gloria Hope, Robert Walker, Frank H. Clark, Joe Connelly, Major J. A. McGuire, "Tony"
D: Emmett J. Flynn
S: Max Brand
C: Frank Good, Irving Rosenberg

THE TEXAN (Fox, October 31, 1920) 5 Reels.
Tom Mix, Gloria Hope, Robert Walker, Charles K. French, Sid Jordan, Ben Corbett, Pat Chrisman, "Tony"
D: Lynn Reynolds
S: James B. Hendryx
SP: Lynn F. Reynolds and Jules Furthman

PRAIRIE TRAILS (Fox, December 26, 1920) 5 Reels.
Tom Mix, Kathleen O'Connor, Robert Walker, Charles K. French, Sid Jordan, Gloria Hope, William Elmer, Harry Dunkinson, "Tony"
D: George Marshall
S: James B. Hendryx
SP: Frank Howard Clark

THE ROAD DEMON (Fox, February 20, 1921) 5 Reels.
Tom Mix, Claire Anderson, Charles K. French, George Hernandez, Lloyd Bacon, Sid Jordan, Charles Arpling, Harold Goodwin, Billy Elmer, Frank Tokawaja, Lee Phelps, "Tony"
D/S/SP: Lynn Reynolds

HANDS OFF (Fox, April 3, 1921) 5 Reels.
Tom Mix, Pauline Curley, Charles K. French, Lloyd Bacon, Frank H. Clark, Sid Jordan, William McCormick, Virginia Warwick, J. Webster Dill, Marvin Loback, "Tony"
D: George E. Marshall
SP: Frank H. Clark
S: William MacLeod Raine

A RIDIN' ROMEO (Fox, May 22, 1921) 5 Reels.
Tom Mix, Rhea Mitchell, Pat Chrisman, Sid Jordan, Harry Dunkinson, Eugenie Ford, "Tony"
D/SP: George E. Marshall
S: Tom Mix

BIG TOWN ROUND-UP (Fox, June 26, 1921) 5 Reels.
Tom Mix, Ora Carew, Gilbert Holmes, Harry Dunkinson, Laura La Plante, William Buckley, William Elmer, William Crinley, "Tony"
D/SP: Lynn Reynolds
S: William MacLeod Raine—"Big Town Round-Up"

AFTER YOUR OWN HEART (Fox, August 7, 1921) 5 Reels.
Tom Mix, Ora Carew, George Hernandez, William Buckley, Sid Jordan, Betty Jewell, Charles K. French, Duke Lee, James Mason, J. Gordon Russell, E. C. Robinson, Bill Ward, "Tony"
D: George Marshall
Scen: John Montague, *Tom Mix*
S: William Wallace Cook

THE NIGHT HORSEMEN (Fox, September 4, 1921) 5 Reels.
Tom Mix, May Hopkins, Harry Lonsdale, Joseph Bennett, Sid Jordan, Bert Sprotte, Cap Anderson, Lon Poff, Charles K. French, "Tony"
D/Scen: Lynn F. Reynolds
S: Max Brand—"The Night Horseman"

THE ROUGH DIAMOND (Fox, October 30, 1921) 5 Reels.
Tom Mix, Eva Novak, Hector Sarno, Edwin J. Brady, Sid Jordan, "Tony"
D/SP: Edward Sedgwick
S: *Tom Mix*, Edward Sedgwick

TRAILIN' (Fox, December 11, 1921) 5 Reels.
Tom Mix, Eva Novak, Bert Sprotte, James Gordon, Sid Jordan, William Duvall, Duke Lee, Harry Dunkinson, Al Fremont, Bert Hadley, Carol Holloway, Jay Morley, Cecil Van Auker, J. Farrell MacDonald, "Tony"
D/Adapt: Lynn F. Reynolds
S: Max Brand—"Trailin' "

SKY HIGH (Fox, January 22, 1922) 5 Reels.
Tom Mix, Eva Novak, J. Farrell MacDonald, Sid Jordan, William Buckley, Adele Warner, Wynn Mace, Pat Chrisman, "Tony"
D/SP/S: Lynn Reynolds

CHASING THE MOON (Fox, February 26, 1922) 5 Reels.
Tom Mix, Eva Novak, William Buckley, Sid Jordan, Elsie Danbric, Wynn Mace, "Tony"
D: Edward Sedgwick
S: *Tom Mix*, Edward Sedgwick

UP AND GOING (Fox, April 2, 1922) 5 Reels.
Tom Mix, Eva Novak, William Conklin, Sid Jordan, Tom O'Brian, Pat Chrisman, Paul Weigel, Cecil Van Auker, Carol Holloway, "Tony"
D/SP: Lynn Reynolds
S: *Tom Mix*, Lynn Reynolds

THE FIGHTING STREAK (Fox, May 14, 1922) 5 Reels.
Tom Mix, Patsy Ruth Miller, Gerald Pring, Al Fremont, Sid Jordan, Bert Sprotte, Robert Fleming, "Tony"
D/SP: Arthur Rosson
S: George Owen Baxter—"Free Range Lanning"

FOR BIG STAKES (Fox, June 18, 1922) 5 Reels.
Tom Mix, Patsy Ruth Miller, Sid Jordan, Bert Sprotte, Joe Harris, Al Fremont, Earl Simpson, "Tony"
D/SP: Lynn Reynolds

JUST TONY (Fox, August 20, 1922) 5 Reels.
Tom Mix, Claire Adams, J. P. Lockney, Duke Lee, Frank Campeau, Walt Robbins, "Tony"
D/SP: Lynn F. Reynolds
S: Max Brand—"Alcatraz"

DO AND DARE (Fox, October 1, 1922) 5 Reels.
Tom Mix, Claire Adams, Dulcie Cooper, Claude Peyton, Jack Rollins, Hector Sarno, Wilbur Higby, Bob Klein, Gretchen Hartman, "Tony"
D/SP: Edward Sedgwick
S: Marion Brooks

TOM MIX IN ARABIA (Fox, November 5, 1922) 5 Reels.
Tom Mix, Claire Adams, George Hernandez, Norman Selby, Edward Peil, Ralph Yearsley, Hector Sarno, Eugene Corey
D/SP: Lynn Reynolds
S: *Tom Mix*, Lynn Reynolds

CATCH MY SMOKE (Fox, December 3, 1922) 5 Reels.
Tom Mix, Lillian Rich, Claude Peyton, Gordon Griffith, Harry Griffith, Robert Milash, Pat Chrisman, Cap Anderson, Ruby Lafayette, "Tony"
D: William Beaudine
SP: Jack Strumwasser
S: Joseph Bushnell Ames—"Shoe Bar Stratton"

ROMANCE LAND (Fox, February 11, 1923) 5 Reels.
Tom Mix, Barbara Bedford, Frank Brownlee, George Webb,
Pat Chrisman, Wynn Mace, "Tony"
D: Edward Sedgwick
SP: Joseph Franklin Poland
S: Kenneth Perkins—"The Gun Fanner"

THREE JUMPS AHEAD (Fox, March 25, 1923) 5 Reels.
Tom Mix, Alma Bennett, Edward Peil, Joe Girard, Virginia
True Boardman, Margaret Joslin, Frank Forde, Harry Todd,
"Tony"
D/S: Jack (John) Ford

STEPPING FAST (Fox, May 13, 1923) 5 Reels.
Tom Mix, Claire Adams, Donald MacDonald, Hector Sarno,
Edward Peil, George Siegmann, Tom S. Guire, Edward
Jobson, Ethel Wales, Minna Redman, "Tony"
D: Joseph J. Franz
S/SP: Bernard McConville

SOFT-BOILED (Fox, August 26, 1923) 8 Reels.
Tom Mix, Billie Dove, Joseph Girard, Lee C. Shumway, Tom
Wilson, Frank Beal, Jack Curtis, Charles Hill Mailes, Harry
Dunkinson, Wilson Hummell, "Tony"
D/SP: J. G. Blystone
S: J. G. Blystone, Edward Moran

THE LONE STAR RANGER (Fox, September 9, 1923)
6 Reels.
Tom Mix, Billie Dove, Lee C. Shumway, Stanton Heck,
Edward Peil, Frank H. Clark, Minna Redman, Francis
Carpenter, William Conklin, Tom Lingham, "Tony"
D/SP: Lambert Hillyer
S: Zane Grey—"The Lone Star Ranger"

MILE-A-MINUTE ROMEO (Fox, October 28, 1923)
6 Reels.
Tom Mix, Betty Jewel, J. Gordon Russell, James Mason, Duke
Lee, James Quinn, "Tony"
D: Lambert Hillyer
SP: Robert N. Lee
S: Max Brand—"Gun Gentleman: A Western Story"

NORTH OF HUDSON BAY (Fox, November 18, 1923)
5 Reels.
Tom Mix, Kathleen Key, Jennie Lee, Frank Campeau, Eugene
Pallette, Will Walling, Frank Leigh, Fred Kohler
D: Jack (John) Ford
S/SP: Jules Furthman

EYES OF THE FOREST (Fox, December 30, 1923) 5 Reels.
Tom Mix, Pauline Starke, Sid Jordan, Buster Gardner, J. P.
Lockney, Tom Lingham, Edwin Wallock, "Tony"
D: Lambert Hillyer
SP: LeRoy Stone
S: Shannon Fife

Tom Mix and Pauline Stark in *Eyes of the Forest* (Fox,
1923).

LADIES TO BOARD (Fox, February 3, 1924) 6 Reels.
Tom Mix, Gertrude Olmstead, Philo McCullough, Pee Wee
Holmes, Gertrude Claire, Dolores Rousse, "Tony"
D: J. G. Blystone
SP: Donald W. Lee
S: William Dudley Pelley

THE TROUBLE SHOOTER (Fox, May 4, 1924) 6 Reels.
Tom Mix, Kathleen Key, Frank Currier, J. Gunnis Davis,
Mike Donlin, Dolores Rousse, Charles McHugh, Al Fremont,
Earle Fox, Howard Truesdel, "Tony"
D: Jack Conway
S/SP: Frederic Hatton, Fanny Hatton

THE HEART BUSTER (Fox, July 6, 1924) 5 Reels.
Tom Mix, Esther Ralston, Cyril Chadwick, William Court-
wright, Frank Currier, Tom Wilson, "Tony"
D: Jack Conway
SP: John Stone
S: George Scarborough

THE LAST OF THE DUANES (Fox, August 24, 1924)
7 Reels.
Tom Mix, Marion Nixon, Brinsley Shaw, Frank Nelson, Lucy
Beaumont, Harry Lonsdale, "Tony"
D: Lynn Reynolds
SP: Edward J. Montayne
S: Zane Grey—"The Last of the Duanes"

OH, YOU TONY! (Fox, September 21, 1924) 7 Reels.
Tom Mix, Claire Adams, Dick La Reno, Earle Foxe, Dolores
Rousse, Charles K. French, Pat Chrisman, Miles McCarthy,
Mathilda Brundage, May Wallace, "Tony"
D: J. G. Blystone
S/SP: Donald W. Lee

TEETH (Fox, November 2, 1924) 7 Reels.
Tom Mix, Lucy Fox, George Bancroft, Edward Peil, Lucien Littlefield, "Tony," "Duke" (a dog)
D: John Blystone
SP: Donald W. Lee
S: Clinton H. Stagge—"Teeth" and Virginia Hudson Brightman—"Sonny"

THE DEADWOOD COACH (Fox, December 7, 1924) 7 Reels.
Tom Mix, Doris May, George Bancroft, De Witt Jennings, Buster Gardner, Lucien Littlefield, Norma Wills, Sid Jordan, Nora Cecil, Frank Coffyn, Jane Keckley, Clyde Kinney, Ernest Butterworth, "Tony"
D/SP: Lynn Reynolds
S: Clarence E. Mulford—"The Orphan"

DICK TURPIN (Fox, February 1, 1925) 7 Reels.
Tom Mix, Kathleen Myers, Philo McCullough, James Marcus, Lucille Hutton, Alan Hale, Bull Montana, Fay Holderness, Jack Herrick, Fred Kohler, Buck Jones (unbilled cameo)
D: John G. Blystone
SP: Charles Kenyon
S: Charles Darnton, Charles Kenyon

RIDERS OF THE PURPLE SAGE (Fox, March 15, 1925) 6 Reels.
Tom Mix, Beatrice Burnham, Arthur Morrison, Seesel Ann Johnson, Warner Oland, Fred Kohler, Charles Newton, Joe Rickson, Mabel Ballin, Charles Le Moyne, Harold Goodwin, Marion Nixon, Dawn O'Day, Wilfred Lucas, "Tony"
D: Lynn Reynolds
SP: Edfrid Bingham
S: Zane Grey—"Riders of the Purple Sage"

THE RAINBOW TRAIL (Fox, May 24, 1925) 6 Reels.
Tom Mix, Anne Cornwall, George Bancroft, Lucien Littlefield, Mark Hamilton, Vivian Oakland, Thomas Delmar, Fred De Silva, Steve Clemento, Doc Roberts, Carol Holloway, Diana Miller, Fred Dillon, "Tony"
D/SP: Lynn Reynolds
S: Zane Grey—"The Rainbow Trail"

LAW AND THE OUTLAW (Exclusive Features, May 26, 1925) 5 Reels.
Tom Mix
(An expansion of the 1913 Selig 2-reeler of the same title; some different Mix footage involved)

THE LUCKY HORSESHOE (Fox, August 30, 1925) 5 Reels.
Tom Mix, Billie Dove, Malcolm Waite, J. Farrell MacDonald, Clarissa Selwynne, Ann Pennington, J. Gunnis Davis, "Tony"
D: J. G. Blystone
SP: John Stone
S: Robert Lord

THE EVERLASTING WHISPER (Fox, October 11, 1925) 6 Reels.
Tom Mix, Alice Calhoun, Robert Cain, George Berrell, Walter James, Virginia Madison, Karl Dane, "Tony"
D: J. G. Blystone
SP: Wyndham Gittens
S: Jackson Gregory—"The Everlasting Whisper"

THE BEST BAD MAN (Fox, November 29, 1925) 5 Reels.
Tom Mix, Clara Bow, Buster Gardner, Cyril Chadwick, Tom Kennedy, Frank Beal, Judy King, Tom Wilson, Paul Panzer, "Tony"
D: J. G. Blystone
SP: Lillie Hayward
S: Max Brand—"Senor Jingle Bells"

A CHILD OF THE PRAIRIE (Exclusive Features, December 22, 1925) 5 Reels.
Tom Mix, Rose Bronson, Ed Brady, Mort Thompson, John Maloney, Fay Robinson, "Tony"
D/SP: Tom Mix
(Expansion of a Selig 2-reeler of the same title released in 1915 and with additional footage added from an unidentified Mix western)

THE YANKEE SENOR (Fox, January 10, 1926) 5 Reels.
Tom Mix, Olive Borden, Tom Kennedy, Francis McDonald, Margaret Livingston, Alec B. Francis, Kathryn Hill, Martha Mattox, Raymond Wells, Eugene Pallette, Harry Seymour, Joseph Franz, "Tony"
D: Emmett Flynn
SP: Eve Unsell
S: Katherine Fullerton Gerould—"Conquistador"

MY OWN PAL (Fox, February 28, 1926) 5 Reels.
Tom Mix, Olive Borden, Tom Santschi, Virginia Marshall, Bardson Bard, William Colvin, Virginia Warwick, Jay Hunt, Hedda Nova, Tom McGuire, Helen Lynch, Jacques Rollens, "Tony"
D: J. G. Blystone
SP: Lillie Hayward
S: Gerald Beaumont—"My Own Pal"

TONY RUNS WILD (Fox, April 18, 1926) 6 Reels.
Tom Mix, Jacqueline Logan, Lawford Davidson, Duke Lee, Vivian Oakland, Edward Martindel, Marion Harlan, Raymond Wells, Richard Carter, Arthur Morrison, Lucien Littlefield, Jack Padjan, "Tony"
D: Thomas Buckingham
SP: Edfrid Bingham, Robert Lord
S: Henry Herbert Knibbs

HARD-BOILED (Fox, June 6, 1926) 6 Reels.
Tom Mix, Helene Chadwick, William Lawrence, Charles Conklin, Emily Fitzroy, Phyllis Haver, Dan Mason, Walter "Spec" O'Donnell, Ethel Grey Terry, Edward Sturgis, Eddie Boland, Emmett Wagner, "Tony"
D: J. G. Blystone
SP: Charles Darnton, John Stone
S: Shannon Fife

NO MAN'S GOLD (Fox, August 29, 1926) 6 Reels.
Tom Mix, Eva Novak, Frank Campeau, Forrest Taylor, Harry Grippe, Malcolm Waite, Mickey Moore, Tom Santschi, "Tony"
D: Lewis Seiler
Adapt/SP: John Stone
S: J. Allen Dunn—"Dead Man's Gold"

THE GREAT K & A TRAIN ROBBERY (Fox, October 17, 1926) 5 Reels.
Tom Mix, Dorothy Dwan, William Walling, Harry Grippe, Carl Miller, Edward Piel, Curtis McHenry, "Tony"
D: Lewis Seiler
SP: John Stone
S: Paul Leicester Ford—"The Great K & A Train Robbery"

THE CANYON OF LIGHT (Fox, December 5, 1926) 6 Reels.
Tom Mix, Dorothy Dwan, Carl Miller, Ralph Sipperly, Barry Norton, Carmelita Geraghty, William Walling, Duke Lee, "Tony"
D: Benjamin Stoloff
SP: John Stone
S: Kenneth Perkins—"The Canyon of Light"

THE LAST TRAIL (Fox, January 23, 1927) 6 Reels.
Tom Mix, Carmelita Geraghty, William Davidson, Frank Hagney, Lee Shumway, Robert Brower, Jerry the Giant, Oliver Eckhardt, "Tony"
D: Lewis Seiler
SP: John Stone
S: Zane Grey—"The Last Trail"

THE BRONCHO TWISTER (Fox, March 13, 1927) 6 Reels.
Tom Mix, Helene Costello, George Irving, Dorothy Kitchen, Paul Nicholson, Doris Lloyd, Malcolm Waite, Jack Pennick, Otto Fries, "Tony"
D: Orville O. Dull
SP: John Stone
S: Adela Rogers St. Johns

OUTLAWS OF RED RIVER (Fox, May 8, 1927) 6 Reels.
Tom Mix, Marjorie Daw, Arthur Clayton, William Conklin, Duke Lee, Francis McDonald, Johnny Downs, Virginia Marshall, "Tony"
D: Lewis Seiler
SP: Harold Shumate
S: Gerald Beaumont

Tom Mix and Helene Chadwick in *Hard Boiled* (Fox, 1926).

THE CIRCUS ACE (Fox, June 26, 1927) 5 Reels.
Tom Mix, Natalie Joyce, Jack Baston, Duke Lee, James Bradbury, Stanley Blystone, Dudley Smith, Buster Gardner, "Tony," "Clarence" (a kangaroo)
D: Ben Stoloff
SP: Jack Jungmeyer
S: Harold Shumate

TUMBLING RIVER (Fox, August 21, 1927) 5 Reels.
Tom Mix, Dorothy Dwan, William Conklin, Stella Essex, Elmo Billings, Edward Peil, Wallace MacDonald, Buster Gardner, Harry Gripp, "Tony," "Buster" (a horse)
D: Lewis Seiler
SP: Jack Jungmeyer
S: Jesse Edward Grinstead—"The Scourge of the Little C"

SILVER VALLEY (Fox, October 2, 1927) 5 Reels.
Tom Mix, Dorothy Dwan, Philo McCullough, Jocky Hoefli, Tom Kennedy, Lon Poff, Harry Dunkinson, Clark Comstock, "Tony"
D: Ben Stoloff
SP: Harold B. Lipsitz
S: Harry Sinclair Drago

THE ARIZONA WILDCAT (Fox, November 20, 1927) 5 Reels.
Tom Mix, Dorothy Sebastian, Ben Bard, Gordon Elliott, Monte Collins, Jr., Cissy Fitzgerald, Doris Dawson, Marcella Daly, "Tony"
D: R. William Neill
SP: John Stone
S: Adela Rogers St. Johns

Tom Mix and "Tony," Sells-Floto Circus, 1929 (Courtesy Circus World Museum, Baraboo, Wisconsin).

LIFE IN HOLLYWOOD #4
(1927) 10 Mins.
John Barrymore, Ernst Bubitsch, Harry Myers, Mae Marsh, William Seiter, Monte Blue, Baby Priscilla Moran, Marie Prevost, Alice Calhoun, *Tom Mix*, Shirley Mason, Buck Jones, Francis MacDonald, Bessie Love, Hal Goodwin, L. C. Wellman, Alan Hale, Corrinne Griffith, "Tony"

DAREDEVIL'S REWARD (Fox, January 15, 1928) 5 Reels.
Tom Mix, Natalie Joyce, Lawford Davidson, Billy Bletcher, Harry Cording, William Welch, "Tony"
D: Eugene Forde
S/SP: John Stone

A HORSEMAN OF THE PLAINS (Fox, March 11, 1928) 5 Reels.
Tom Mix, Sally Blane, Heinie Conklin, Charles Byer, Lew Harvey, Grace Marvin, William Ryno, "Tony"
D: Benjamin Stoloff
SP: Fred Myton
S: Harry Sinclair Drago

HELLO CHEYENNE (Fox, May 13, 1928) 5 Reels.
Tom Mix, Caryl Lincoln, Jack Baston, Martin Faust, Joseph Girard, Al St. John, William Caress, "Tony"
D: Eugene Forde
SP: Fred Kennedy Myton
S: Harry Sinclair Drago

PAINTED POST (Fox, July 1, 1928) 5 Reels.
Tom Mix, Natalie Kingston, Philo McCullough, Al St. John, Fred Gamble, "Tony"
D: Eugene Forde
SP: Buckleigh F. Oxford
S: Harry Sinclair Drago

HOLLYWOOD TODAY #4
(Circa late 1920s) 1 Reel.
Tom Mix, Bessie Love, Buck Jones, "Tony"

SON OF THE GOLDEN WEST (FBO, October 1, 1928) 6 Reels.
Tom Mix, Sharon Lynn, Tom Lingham, Duke R. Lee, Lee Shumway, Fritzi Ridgeway, Joie Ray, Mark Hamilton, Wynn Mace, "Tony"
D: Eugene Forde
S/Cont: George W. Pyper

KING COWBOY (FBO, November 26, 1928) 7 Reels.
Tom Mix, Sally Blane, Lew Meehan, Barney Furey, Frank Leigh, Wynn Mace, Robert Fleming, "Tony"
D: Robert DeLacey
SP: Frank Howard Clark
S: S. E. V. Taylor

OUTLAWED (FBO, January 1929) 7 Reels,
Tom Mix, Sally Blane, Frank M. Clark, Al Smith, Ethan Laidlaw, Barney Furey, Al Ferguson, "Tony"
D: Eugene Forde
S/Cont: George W. Pyper

THE DRIFTER (FBO, March 18, 1929) 6 Reels.
Tom Mix, Dorothy Dawn, Barney Furey, Al Smith, Ernest Wilson, Frank Austin, Joe Rickson, Wynn Mace, "Tony"
D: Robert De Lacy
S: Oliver Drake, Robert De Lacy
SP: George W. Pyper

THE BIG DIAMOND ROBBERY (FBO, May 13, 1929) 7 Reels.
Tom Mix, Kathryn McGuire, Frank Beal, Martha Mattox, Ernest Hilliard, Barney Furey, Ethan Laidlaw, "Tony"
D: Eugene Forde
SP: John Stuart Twist
S: Frank Howard Clark

VOICE OF HOLLYWOOD #1 (Tiffany, January 8, 1930) 1 Reel.
(Sound)
Don Alvarado, Betty Compton, *Tom Mix*, Ruth Roland, John Boles, Louise Fazenda, Mickey Danisho, Mary Kornman, Lupe Velez, Weber and Fields

Newspaper advertisement for Sells-Foto Circus, 1930 season (Courtesy Circus World Museum, Baraboo, Wisconsin).

Tom Mix in *The Rider of Death Valley* (Universal, 1932).

VOICE OF HOLLYWOOD #2 (Tiffany, January 8, 1930)
1 Reel.
(Sound)
Andy Clyde, Buddy Rogers, Ernest Torrence, Sessue
Hayakawa, *Tom Mix,* Slim Summerville, Richard Arlen,
Jackie Coogan, Edwina Booth, Dickie Moore, Rex Bell,
George Marshall, Douglas Fairbanks, "Tony"

THE RIDER OF DEATH VALLEY (Universal, May 26,
1932) 78 Mins.
Tom Mix, Lois Wilson, Fred Kohler, Forrest Stanley, Willard
Robertson, Edith Fellows, Mae Busch, Edmund Cobb, Max
Asher, Pete Morrison, Otis Harlan, Iron Eyes Cody, "Tony,
Jr."
D: Albert Rogell
S: Stanley Bergerman and Jack Cunningham
SP: Jack Cunningham

TEXAS BAD MAN (Universal, June 30, 1932) 60 Mins.
Tom Mix, Lucille Powers, Fred Kohler, Edward J. Le Saint,
Willard Robertson, Dick Alexander, C. E. Anderson, Lynton
Brent, Franklyn Farnum, Joseph Girard, Bob Milash, Buck
Moulton, James Burtis, Slim Cole, Booth Howard, Frances
Sayles, Richard Sumner, "Tony, Jr."
D: Edward Laemmle
S/SP: Jack Cunningham

DESTRY RIDES AGAIN (Universal, July 24, 1932)
61 Mins.
Tom Mix, Claudia Dell, Zasu Pitts, Stanley Fields, Earle Fox,
Edward Peil, Sr., Francis Ford, Frederick Howard, George
Ernest, John Ince, Andy Devine, Edward J. LeSaint, Charles
K. French, "Tony, Jr."
D: Ben Stoloff
S: Max Brand
SP: Richard Schayer, Isadore Bernstein

MY PAL, THE KING (Universal, August, 1932) 74 Mins. *Tom Mix,* Noel Francis, Mickey Rooney, Paul Hurst, Finis Barton, Stuart Holmes, James Kirkwood, Jim Thorpe, Christian Frank, Wallis Clark, Clarissa Selwynne, Ferdinand Schumann-Heink, "Tony, Jr."
D: Kurt Neumann
S: Richard Schayer
SP: Jack Natteford, Tom J. Crizer

THE FOURTH HORSEMAN (Universal, September 25, 1932) 63 Mins. *Tom Mix,* Margaret Lindsay, Fred Kohler, Raymond Hatton, Rosita Marstini, Buddy Roosevelt, Edmund Cobb, Richard Cramer, Herman Nolan, Paul Shawhan, Donald Kirke, Harry Allen, Duke Lee, C. E. Anderson, Helene Millard, Martha Mattox, Frederick Howard, Grace Cunard, Walter Brennan, Pat Harmon, Hank Mann, Jim Corey, Delmar Watson, Fred Burns, Bud Osborne, Harry Tenbrook, Charles Sullivan, Sandy Sallee, Nip Reynolds, Henry Morris, Clyde Kinney, Jim Kinney, Ed Hendershot, Joe Balch, Art Bowden, Augie Gomez, Frank Guskie, Roy Bucko, Buck Bucko, "Tony, Jr."
D: Hamilton MacFadden
S: Nina Wilcox Putnam
SP: Jack Cunningham

HIDDEN GOLD (Universal, November 3, 1932) 60 Mins. *Tom Mix,* Judith Barrie, Raymond Hatton, Eddie Gribbon, Donald Kirke, Willis Clark, Roy Moore, Jay Wilsey (Buffalo Bill, Jr.), "Tony, Jr."
D: Arthur Rosson
S: Jack Natteford
SP: Jack Natteford, James Mulhauser

Tom Mix, Mickey Rooney, and player in *My Pal the King* (Universal, 1932).

FLAMING GUNS (Universal, December 22, 1932) 57 Mins. *Tom Mix,* Ruth Hall, William Farnum, George Hackathorne, Clarence Wilson, Bud Osborne, Duke Lee, Pee Wee Holmes, Jimmy Shannon, William Steele, Walter Patterson, Fred Burns, Slim Whitaker, Clyde Kinney, Jim Corey, Tex Phelps, "Tony, Jr."
D: Arthur Rosson
S: Peter B. Kyne—"Oh, Promise Me"
SP: Jack Cunningham

HOLLYWOOD ON PARADE #3
(Paramount, October 25, 1932) 1 Reel.
Eddie Kane, Wheeler and Woolsey, Anna May Wong, Jackie Cooper, Roscoe and Dorothy Ates, *Tom Mix,* Douglas Fairbanks, Jr., Billie Dove, Bebe Daniels, Jimmy Durante, Helen Kane, Ben Lyon
P: Louis Lewyn

HOLLYWOOD ON PARADE #4
(Paramount, November 25, 1932) 1 Reel.
Eddie Borden, Richard Arlen, Mary Pickford, *Tom Mix,* Bing Crosby, "Tony Jr."
P: Louis Lewyn

TERROR TRAIL (Universal, February 2, 1933) 57 Mins. *Tom Mix,* Naomi Judge, Raymond Hatton, Francis McDonald, Arthur Rankin, Bob Kortman, Lafe McKee, John St. Polis, Frank Brownlee, Hank Bell, Jay Wilsey (Buffalo Bill, Jr.), Harry Tenbrook, W. J. Holmes, Leonard Trainer, Jim Corey, "Tony, Jr."
D: Armand Schaefer
S: Grant Taylor—"The Rider of the Terror Trail"
SP: Jack Cunningham

Tom Mix, Fred Kohler, and players in *The Fourth Horseman* (Universal, 1932).

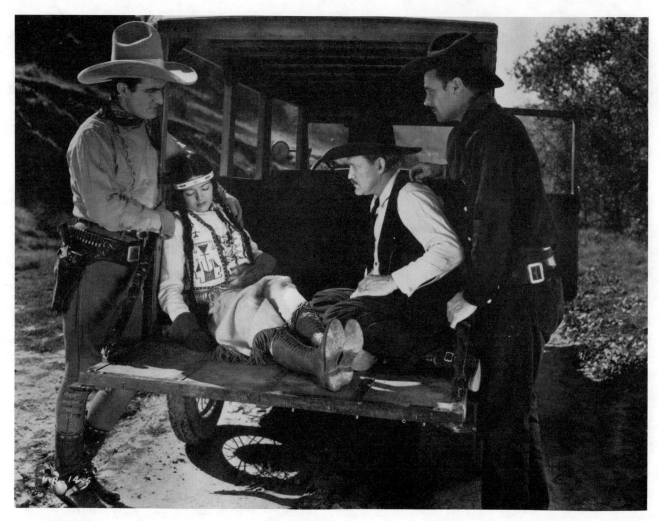

Tom Mix, Joan Gale, Jack Rockwell, and Wally Wales
in *The Miracle Rider* (Mascot, 1935).

RUSTLER'S ROUNDUP (Universal, March 16, 1933) 56
Mins.
Tom Mix, Diane Sinclair, Noah Beery, Jr., Douglass Dumbrille, Roy Stewart, William Desmond, Gilbert Holmes, Bud Osborne, Frank Lackteen, William Wagner, Nelson McDowell, Walter Brennan, "Tony, Jr."
D: Henry MacRae
S: Ella O'Neill
SP: Frank Clark, Jack Cunningham

THE MIRACLE RIDER (Mascot, 1935) 15 Chapters.
Tom Mix, Joan Gale, Charles Middleton, Jason Roberts, Edward Hearn, Pat O'Malley, Robert Frazer, Ernie Adams, Wally Wales, Bob Kortman, Chief Standing Bear, Charles King, Tom London, Niles Welch, Edmund Cobb, George Chesebro, Jack Rockwell, Max Wagner, Stanley Price, Hank Bell, George Burton, Lafe McKee, Edward Earle, Black Hawk, Tex Cooper, Buffalo Bill Jr. (Jay Wilsey), Charles Whitaker, Dick Curtis, Frank Ellis, George Magrill, Dick Alexander, "Tony, Jr."
D: B. Reeves Eason, Armand Schaefer
S: Barney Sarecky, Wellyn Totman, Gerald Geraghty
SP: John Rathmell
P: Nat Levine
Chapter Titles: (1) The Vanishing Indian, (2) The Firebird Strikes, (3) The Flying Knife, (4) A Race with Death, (5) Double-Barreled Doom, (6) Thundering Hoofs, (7) The Dragnet, (8) Guerrilla Warfare, (9) The Silver Band, (10) Signal Fires, (11) A Traitor Dies, (12) Danger Rides with Death, (13) The Secret of X-94, (14) Between Two Fires, (15) Justice Rides the Plains

4 • JACK PERRIN

Fastidious Hero on a White Charger

Jack Perrin is not a name to conjure up nostalgic heartwarming visions in most people, even the average Western movie buff. In fact he is little remembered, having been just another figure in the passing parade of cowboy actors that stretched from Bronco Billy Anderson and William S. Hart at one end of the spectrum to John Wayne and Clint Eastwood at the other. Yet, like each cowboy hero, he achieved a following of loyal fans and made his own unique contribution to the fascinating field of cactus and cliffhanger capers.

Western devotees whose memories go back only to the early 1940s might well ask, "Who was Jack Perrin?" And it is sad to think that such questioners did not have the opportunity to "grow up with" Jack, who won his spurs as an audaciously daring portrayer of Western heroes in the silent picture days.

Perrin was a prolific cowboy ace in the 1920s and 1930s, turning out oaters at a fast pace and consistently remaining in the second echelon of popular Western and serial stars and at the same time achieving some stature as a dramatic actor. Perrin was undoubtedly one of the most underrated of all action stars, and his up-and-down career is one of the most interesting of all Hollywood cowboys.

Born in Three Rivers, Michigan, on July 25, 1896, Jack—whose real name was Lyman Wakefield Perrin—moved with his parents to Hollywood when he was three years old. His father was in real

estate and investments. Jack went to grammar school in the Sunset and Alvarado district and received his high-school education at Manual Arts High. After graduation he went to work in the property department at one of the studios, and it was there that he was noticed by the right people; thus his mode of entry into pictures was exactly like that of John Wayne twelve years later.

Perrin is credited with first appearing before the cameras as a Keystone Kop for Mack Sennett back in 1915–1916, but his first important role was in Triangle's *Toton the Apache* in 1917. World War I temporarily put a stop to his film activities, and Jack served in the submarine service throughout the war.

Returning to Hollywood, Jack was given a contract by Universal and cast as a juvenile heavy in the Eddie Polo "Cyclone Smith" two-reelers before he got his first meaty role in Eric Von Stroheim's *Blind Husbands* (1919). Then came his big break. He was picked to co-star with Kathleen O'Connor in Universal's 18-chapter serial, *The Lion Man* (1919), a tasty morsel for the serial-hungry public, with the lion's share of homage going to Jack for his all-around daredevil performance. The initial episode served to create an interest that was well maintained through all 18 chapters. The film gave Jack the needed experience but did little to promote his career other than to win him favor with serial audiences. It remained for *Pink Tights* (1920)

Jack Perrin

But it was in the series of two-reelers produced by Edward Laemmle that Jack Perrin made a name for himself, and it was not long before his fame as an action ace was bruited abroad. These snappy little Westerns, constructed with careful technical skill, had a common-sense air of production about them and made up in speed what they lacked in footage. Perrin was emphatically the right man in the right place, and directors were quick to realize that in him they had found a film treasure in the person of one who, besides possessing an unusual degree of dramatic talent, was also a trained athlete capable of performing bewilderingly dangerous stunts of agility and had the ability to ride anything in the shape of horseflesh that confronted him. And Jack was no slouch when it came to displaying dazzling virtuosity with a six-gun, either. Hoot Gibson appeared with him in several of these thrill-a-minute prairie dramas; and Louise Lorraine and Josephine Hill, whom he married, were often the prairie flowers among the cacti.

Jack left Universal in 1923 to make two serials for Arrow Pictures. The first was *The Fighting Skipper,* a rousing sea yarn directed by serial star Francis Ford (brother of John) and featuring pretty Peggy O'Day. The second was *The Santa Fe Trail,* featuring serial queen Neva Gerber as the lovely Sunbonnet Sue Jack was forever saving from the clutches of menacing cutthroats. Both were wild-and-woolly affairs, putting to shame some of the powder-puff cliffhangers of the sound era in which stuntmen handled all the tough assignments. Jack projected well, and certainly had the physical attributes necessary for serial stardom.

During the years 1923–1926 Jack starred in independent feature Westerns for Harry Webb, releasing through Aywon and Arrow, and also did a series for Morris R. Schlank, releasing through Rayart. Featured with Jack was his beautiful white horse "Starlight," an exceptionally intelligent animal that could easily hold his own against other actors—man or beast. "Starlight" was every bit as good as the more famous mounts—"Silver," "Tarzan," "Silver King," "Tony," "Champion," and "Trigger"—and even commanded title recognition in films such as *Starlight the Untamed,* and *Starlight's Revenge.* Cracking into fiery action almost from the start, Perrin shoots, rides, and fights to

to give him a needed push. Good-looking, fastidious in appearance and soft-spoken (which seemed to project on the screen even though films were still silent), Jack was at ease in "drawing-room" dramas and made a number of such films. He was soon starring in *Lahoma* (1920), a Pathe Western, followed by Metro's *The Match-Breaker* (1921), a romantic comedy, and Irving W. Willat's *Partners of the Tide* (1921), a roaring sea adventure.

At Universal Jack co-starred with Eva Novak in *The Torrent,* a story dealing with high adventure and love in the south seas. Jack was "Mr. Good Guy" who gets the girl in the end after her brute of a husband kills himself in remorse for the way he had treated her. And in *The Rage of Paris* (1921) we find the same basic theme—Jack again the All-American gentleman who falls heir to the girl after her tyrannical husband is killed during an Arabian sandstorm. A change of pace was provided by *The Guttersnipe* (1922), a romantic satire, and *The Dangerous Little Demon* and *The Trouper,* both comedy dramas.

the expected delectation of Western patrons in these minor independent plains operas, built along conventional lines with sufficient rough-and-ready action to bet by on double-feature programs in low-admission houses.

Riders of the Plains (Arrow, 1924) was Jack's fourth serial, and it followed the general formula of successful serial construction with heroism, melodrama, action, villainy, climactic endings in each chapter, and a mild, mild love angle, with Marilyn Mills playing the garden-fresh sweetheart part.

In 1927 Jack was signed once more by Universal, and appeared in both a Northwest Mounted Police series of two-reelers and feature Westerns. The mountie two-reelers were especially good, and through them Jack acquired a considerable coterie of fans. Silhouetted against picturesque backgrounds, and clothed in a mountie uniform, Jack presented a beautiful portrait of heroic masculinity. The five-reel features were equally good and did average business. Jack was not a personality with a unique charisma and as a consequence was never able to break into the front ranks of Western stardom. It was his lot to ride the periphery of Western immortality, never quite able to leap into the real winner's circle of big names and big budgets.

One interesting aspect of Jack's Universal features, however, was the inclusion of "Rex, King of Wild Horses" in the cast, along with "Starlight." Both horses got a lot of good footage and provided some novel twists to the stories. And Henry Mac-Rae's direction spotlighted the characterizations and the factual incidents, never resorting to over-dramatics. His staging was masterful, and he gripped his audience at the tee/off and held them through what could have been mawkish endings.

Nat Levine cast Jack in the lead of Mascot's *The Vanishing West* (1928) a zingy Western serial with Leo Maloney, Jack Dougherty, and Yak Canutt in the cast. It was a silent. But in his next, *Overland Bound* (1929), Jack easily made the transition to sound. He played second lead in Leo Maloney's last Western with an ease and naturalness in his role that set him far ahead of the average slick-haired younger fellar.

Universal followed up by starring Jack in his sixth serial, *The Jade Box*, released in both silent and sound versions. Unlike many actors, Jack made

Jack Perrin and "Starlight"

the transition to talkies successfully but found work only at the small independents. But work he did, as he and "Starlight" streaked across the plains to the delight of audiences in the hinterlands of America during the early depression years in cheapie Westerns for such undistinguished studios as Big 4, Cosmos, Robert J. Horner, and National. The stories were the Western stereotype, stripped right down to the mare's back, made for a few thousand dollars, and released on the independent market—truly cow-dung products, but Jack and "Starlight" managed to stand out in these mediocre sagebrushers. Jack's films were sometimes criticized for being too predictable, and it was said that he personally was a fashion-plate cowboy who never got dirty or lost his hat. Yet he was able to keep working when greater names, like Tom Mix, Jack Hoxie, Art Acord, and Hoot Gibson were unable to get series.

It was relaxing to spend a Saturday afternoon watching Jack and "Starlight" win out over the forces of evil in the cinematic Wild West; and, if one were lucky, he might also get to see Jack giving a different gang of hoodlums a hard time in the serial following his feature. Certainly it was enough to set pulses throbbing, young hearts to beating madly, and indelibly etch scenes in one's memory of this fastidious hero on a white charger that would last a lifetime.

In 1934 Jack teamed up with Ben Corbett in the popular series of "Bud 'n' Ben" three-reelers produced by B. B. Ray for Astor release. Then came a series of feature Westerns in 1935–1936 for Reliable and Atlantic. But after 1936 it was all downhill. He had a featured role in Republic's serial *The Painted Stallion* (1937), but his parts became smaller and smaller as the years went by. Jack adjusted, worked hard and did his best right on up to the early 1960s at whatever jobs he got.

On a personal level Jack was a devoted family man, orderly in his business dealings, and successful in various real estate transactions. During the 1920s and 1930s he turned down offers to tour as headliner of circuses because he wanted to be with his family. In later years he mildly regretted not having had the circus experience and not investing in a ranch, which he always felt he would have enjoyed. He loved fine clothes, good music, new automobiles, and dining in fine restaurants. His marriage to Josephine Hill ended in divorce around 1937. A daughter, Patricia, was born of this union. In 1943 he married the chief telephone operator at Universal, and remained happily married until his death from a heart attack on December 17, 1967. He had retired from acting in 1962 and lived on a modest income during his final years.

Jack had a charming personality and was a credit to his profession. He had a deep and lasting respect for the milieu in which he worked, and those who knew him and worked with him loved him for it. He loved the good old Hollywood and was always loyal to it. Jack Perrin and "Starlight" ceased riding the range of neighborhood theatres before most of the readers of this book were born. But his star can still be found on the Walk of Stars on Vine Street, north of Hollywood Boulevard—a fine tribute to one of yesterday's more interesting saddle aces.

JACK PERRIN *Filmography*

TOTON THE APACHE (Triangle, 1917).
Jack Perrin, Olive Thomas, Norman Keery, Francis MacDonald
D: Frank Borzage
SP: Catherine Carr

TWO MEN OF TINTED BUTTE (Universal, May 14, 1919) 2 Reels.
Jack Perrin, Patricia Fox, Walt Whitman
D: Norman Dawn

CYCLONE SMITH'S COMEBACK (Universal Special, May 21, 1919) 2 Reels
Eddie Polo, *Jack Perrin*
D: Jacques Jaccard
S: Jacques Jaccard

CYCLONE SMITH PLAYS TRUMPS (Universal Special, June 7, 1919) 2 Reels
Eddie Polo, *Jack Perrin*
D: Jacques Jaccard
S: Jacques Jaccard, George Hively

CYCLONE SMITH'S PARTNER (Universal Special, June 25, 1919) 2 Reels
Eddie Polo, *Jack Perrin*
D: Jacques Jaccard
Scen: George Hively
S: Jacques Jaccard, George Hively

THE FIGHTING HEART (Universal, August 5, 1919) 2 Reels.
Jack Perrin, Hoot Gibson, Josephine Hill, William Pathe
D: Reeves Eason
S: William Piggott
SP: Anthony Coldeway

THE FOUR BIT MAN (Universal, August 21, 1919) 2 Reels.
Jack Perrin, Hoot Gibson, Josephine Hill, Andrew Waldron, William Dyer
D: Reeves Eason
S: Judith and Eric Howard
SP: Anthony Coldeway

THE JACK OF HEARTS (Universal, September 2, 1919) 2 Reels.
Jack Perrin, Hoot Gibson, Josephine Hill
D: Reeves Eason
S: Dorothy Rockfort
SP: Anthony Coldeway

BLIND HUSBANDS (Universal, October 21, 1919) 8 Reels.
Erich Von Strohein, Sam DeGrasse, Fiancilla Bellington, Gibson Gowland, *Jack Perrin*, Valerie Germonprez
D/Adapt/Scen: Erich Von Strohein
S: ErichVon Strohein—"The Pinnacle"

THE LION MAN (Universal, December 29, 1919) 18 Chapters.
Kathleen O'Connor, *Jack Perrin*, Mack V. Wright, J. Barney Sherry, Gertrude Astor, Henry Barrows, Leonard Clapham (Tom London), Robert Walker, Slim Padgett, William Carroll
D: Albert Russell, Jack Wells
SP: Karl Coolidge
S: Randall Parrish—"The Strange Case of Cavendish"
Chapter Titles: (1) Flames of Hate, (2) Rope of Death, (3) Kidnappers, (4) A Devilish Device, (5) In the Lions Den, (6) House of Horrors, (7) Doomed, (8) Dungeon of Despair, (9)

Sold into Slavery, (10) Perilous Plunge, (11) At the Mercy of Monsters, (12) Jaws of Destruction, (13) When Hell Broke Loose, (14) Desperate Deeds, (15) Furnace of Fury, (16) Relentless Renegades, (17) In Cruel Clutches, (18) In the Nick of Time

ONE HE MAN (Universal, April 1920) 2 Reels.
Jack Perrin
D: Henry Murray
Scen: Henry Murray
S: George Hively

THE ADORABLE SAVAGE (Universal, August 6, 1920) 7 Reels.
Jack Perrin, Edith Roberts, Dick Cummings, Noble Johnson, Lucille Moulton
D: Norman Dawn
Scen: Doris Schroeder
S: Ralph Stock

LAHOMA (Pathe, August 6, 1920).
Jack Perrin, Louise Burnham, Wade Boteler, Russell Simpson, Peaches Jackson, Lurline Lyons, S. B. Phillips, Will Jeffries, Yvette Mitchell, Jack Carlyle, H. M. Lindley
S: John Breckenridge Ellis
D/P: Edgar Lewis

PINK TIGHTS (Universal, September 25, 1920) 5 Reels.
Jack Perrin, Gladys Walton, Dave Dyas, Reeves Eason, Jr., Stanton Heck
P/D: Reeves Eason
S: J. U. Geisty
Scen: Philip Hurn

THE TORRENT (Universal, December 23, 1920) 5 Reels.
Eva Novak, Oleta Ottis, *Jack Perrin*, L. C. Shumway, Jack Curtis, Harry Carter, Bert Alpino
D: Stuart Paton
Adapt: Philip Hurn
S: George Rix—"Out of the Sunset"

THE GRIP OF THE LAW (Universal, January 27, 1921) 2 Reels.
Jack Perrin
D: Edward Laemmle
S: Carl R. Coolidge
SP: Ford Beebe

THE TRIGGER TRAIL (Universal, February 7, 1921) 2 Reels.
Jack Perrin, Louise Lorraine, Jim Corey
P/D: Edward Laemmle
S: James Edward Hungerford
Scen: George W. Plympton

BIG BOB (Universal, February 25, 1921) 2 Reels.
Jack Perrin, Ruby Lafayette, Jim Corey
D/S: Edward Laemmle
Scen: George Morgan

THE MIDNIGHT RAIDERS (Universal, March 16, 1921) 2 Reels.
Jack Perrin, Louise Lorraine
D: Edward Laemmle
S: James Ed Hungerford
SP: Robert Dillon

PARTNERS OF THE TIDE (Irvin V. Willat Productions/W. W. Hodkinson Corp., March 20, 1921) 7 Reels.
Jack Perrin, Marion Faducha, Gordon Mullen, Daisy Robinson, Gertrude Norman, J. P. Lockney, Joe Miller, Bert Hadley, Fred Kohler, Florence Midgley, Ashley Cooper
D: L. V. Jefferson
P/Writer: Irvin V. Willat

THE KNOCKOUT MAN (Universal, March 25, 1921) 2 Reels.
Jack Perrin, Louise Lorraine, Jim Corey
P/D: Edward Laemmle
S: Fred V. Williams
Scen: George H. Plympton

THE GUILTY TRAIL (Universal, April 7, 1921) 2 Reels.
Jack Perrin
P/D: Edward Laemmle
S: Malcolm Stuart Boylan
Scen: George Morgan

THE OUTLAW (Universal, April 27, 1921) 2 Reels.
Jack Perrin, Louise Lorraine
D: Edward Laemmle
S/Scen: George Morgan

DOUBLE-CROSSED (Universal, 1921) 2 Reels.
Jack Perrin
(No further credits available.)

FIGHTING BLOOD (Universal, May 16, 1921) 2 Reels.
Jack Perrin
D: Lee Kohlmar
S: Fred W. Williams
SP: George H. Plympton

STAND UP AND FIGHT (Universal, May 28, 1921) 2 Reels.
Jack Perrin
P/D: Edward Laemmle
S: Burl Armstrong
Scen: George Morgan

THE VALLEY OF THE ROGUES (Universal, July 21, 1921).
Jack Perrin, Louise Lorraine
P/D: Edward Laemmle
S/SP: George Morgan

THE DANGER MAN (Universal, July 29, 1921) 2 Reels.
Jack Perrin, Jim Corey
D: Edward Laemmle
S/SP: George Morgan

BOTH BARRELS (Universal, August 12, 1921) 2 Reels.
Jack Perrin, Magda Lane, Jim Corey
P/D: Edward Laemmle
S/Scen: Robert Dillon

RIM OF THE DESERT (Universal, August 19, 1921)
2 Reels
Jack Perrin
P/D: Edward Laemmle
S: Fred V. Williams
Scen: George Morgan

THE MATCH-BREAKER (Metro Pictures, September 19, 1921) 5 Reels.
Viola Dana, *Jack Perrin*, Edward Jobson, Julia Calhoun, Wedgewood Nowell, Kate Tonery, Lenore Lynard, Fred Kelsey, Arthur Millett
D: Dallas M. Fitzgerald
Scen: Arthur J. Zellner
S: Meta White—"The Match-Breaker"

IN THE NICK OF TIME (Universal, September 28, 1921) 2 Reels.
Jack Perrin, Jim Corey
P/D: Edward Laemmle
S/Scen: Robert Dillon

THE RAGE OF PARIS (Universal, October 3, 1921) 5 Reels.
Miss Du Pont, Elinor Hancock, *Jack Perrin*, Leo White, Ramsey Wallace, Freeman Wood, Eve Southern, Mathilda Brundage, J. J. Lance
D: Jack Conway
Scen: Lucien Hubbard, Douglas Doty
S: Du Vernet Rabell—"The White Peacock Feathers"

A BATTLE OF WITS (Universal, December 16, 1921) 2 Reels.
Jack Perrin
D: Edward Kull
S/SP: George Morgan and George H. Plympton

THE PHANTOM TERROR (Universal, January 13, 1922) 2 Reels.
Jack Perrin, Gertrude Olmsted
P/D: William J. Craft
S/Scen: Robert Dillon, Thomas Berrien

THE GUTTERSNIPE (Universal Special, January 30, 1922) 5 Reels.
Gladys Walton, Walter Peery, Kate Price, *Jack Perrin*, Sidney Franklin, Carmen Phillips, Edward Cecil, High Saxon, Seymour Zeliff, Eugene Corey, Lorraine Weiler, Christian J. Frank
D: Dallas M. Fitzgerald
Scen: Wallace Clifton
S: Percival Wilde

A BLUE-JACKET'S HONOR (Universal, February 8, 1922) 2 Reels.
Jack Perrin, Gertrude Olmsted
P/D: William J. Craft
S/Scen: Robert Dillon, Thomas Berrien

THE DANGEROUS LITTLE DEMON (Universal Special, March 27, 1922) 5 Reels.
Marie Prevost, *Jack Perrin*, Robert Ellis, Anderson Smith, Fontaine La Rue, Edward Martindel, Lydia Knott, Herbert Prior
D: Clarence G. Badger
Scen: Doris Schroeder
S: Mildred Considine

THE TROUPER (Universal, July 23, 1922) 5 Reels.
Jack Perrin, Gladys Walton, Thomas Holding, Kathleen O'Connor, Roscoe Karns, Mary Philbin, Mary True, Tom S. Guise, Florence D. Lee
D: Harry B. Harris
S/Scen: A. P. Younger

THE LONE HORSEMAN (A. B. Maescher Productions/ Arrow Film Corp., January 1, 1923) 5 Reels
Jack Perrin, Josephine Hill
D/SP: Fred Caldwell

ONE OF THREE (Universal, February 19, 1923) 2 Reels.
("The Further Adventures of Yorke Norroy" Series)
Roy Stewart, Hayden Stevenson, *Jack Perrin*, Lucille Ricksen, Fontaine LaRue
D: Duke Worne
S: George Bronson Howard

UNDER SECRET ORDERS (Universal, March 6, 1923) 2 Reels.
("The Further Adventures of Yorke Norroy" Series)
Roy Stewart, Esther Ralston, *Jack Perrin*, William Welsh
D: Duke Worne
S: George Bronson Howard

GOLDEN SILENCE (Sylvanite Productions/Kipling Enterprises, March 19, 1923) 5 Reels.
Jack Perrin, Hedda Nova
D: Paul Hurst

THE FIGHTING SKIPPER (Arrow, April 1923) 15 Chapters.
Jack Perrin, Peggy O'Day, Bill White, Francis Ford, Steve Murphy
D: Francis Ford
Chapter Titles: (1) Pirates of Pedro, (2) Harbor of Hate, (3) Pirates' Playground, (4) In the Fog, (5) Isle of Intrigue, (6) Trapped, (7) Silent Valley, (8) House of Mystery, (9) Snowbound, (10) The Mystery Car, (11) Across the Border, (12) Secret of Buoy #3, (13) Human Plunder, (14) Lost Island, (15) Love and Law

Neva Gerber and Jack Perrin in *The Santa Fe Trail* (Arrow, 1924).

MARY OF THE MOVIES (Columbia Productions/R-C Pictures Corp./FBO, May 27, 1923) 7 Reels.
Marion Mack, Florence Lee, Mary Kane, Harry Cornelli, John Geough, Raymond Cannon, Rosemary Cooper, Creighton Hale, Francis McDonald, Henry Burrows, John McDermott, *Jack Perrin*, Ray Harford
D: John McDermott
Scen: Louis Lewyn
Supv: Louis Lewyn, Jack Cohn

THE SANTA FE TRAIL (Arrow, July 15, 1923) 15 Chapters.
Jack Perrin, Neva Gerber, James Welch, Elias Bullock, Wilbur McGaugh, Clark B. Coffey, Jose De La Cruz, Maria Laredo, Ned Jarvis
D: Ashton Dearholt, Robert Dillon

Chapter Titles: (1) Mystery of the Trail, (2) Kit Carson's Daring Ruse, (3) Wagon of Doom, (4) The Half-Breed's Treachery, (5) The Gauntlet of Death, (6) Ride for Life, (7) Chasm of Fate, (8) Pueblo of Death, (9) The Red Menace, (10) A Duel of Wits, (11) Buried Alive, (12) Cavern of Doom, (13) Scorching Sands, (14) Mission Bells, (15) End of the Trail

WESTERN JUSTICE (A. B. Maescher/Arrow Film Corp., November 15, 1923) 5 Reels.
Jack Perrin, Josephine Hill
D/S/SP: Fred Caldwell

VIRGINIAN OUTCAST (Robert J. Horner Productions/ Aywon Film Corp., February 1924) 5 Reels.
Jack Perrin, Marjorie Daw, "Starlight" (The Wonder Horse)
D: Robert J. Horner

Jack Perrin in a frame enlargement from *Riders of the Plains* (Arrow, 1924).

THOSE WHO DANCE (Thomas H. Ince Productions/First National, April 27, 1924) 8 Reels.
Blanche Sweet, Bessie Love, Warner Baxter, Robert Agnew, John Sainpolis, Lucille Ricksen, Matthew Betz, Lydia Knott, Charles Delaney, W. S. McDonough, *Jack Perrin*, Frank Campeau.
D: Lambert Hillyer
Adapt: Lambert Hillyer, Arthur Statter
S: George Kibbe
Supv: Thomas H. Ince

COYOTE FANGS (Harry Webb Productions/Aywon Film Corp., August 21, 1924) 5 Reels.
Jack Perrin, Josephine Hill, "Starlight"
D: Harry Webb

CRASHIN' THROUGH (Robert J. Horner Productions/ Anchor Film Distributors, September 10, 1924) 5 Reels.
Jack Perrin, Jean Riley, Jack Richardson, Steve Clemento, Dick La Reno, Taylor Graves, Peggy O'Day, "Starlight"
D/SP: Alvin J. Neitz

RIDERS OF THE PLAINS (Arrow, October 1, 1924) 15 Chapters.
Jack Perrin, Marilyn Mills, Ruth Royce, Charles Brinley, Kingsley Benedict, Running Elke, Robert Miles, Rhody Hathaway, Clark Comstock, "Starlight"
D: Jacques Jaccard
S: Karl Coolidge, Jacques Jaccard
Chapter Titles: (1) Red Shadows [3 Reels], (2) Dangerous Hazards, (3) A Living Death, (4) Flames of Fury, (5) Morgan's Raid, (6) Out of the Past, (7) A Fighting Gamble, (8) A Prisoner of War, (9) Pawns of Destiny, (10) Riding for Life, (11) In Death's Shadow, (12) Flaming Vengeance, (13) Thundering Hoofs, (14) Red Talons, (15) The Reckoning

SHOOTIN' SQUARE (Anchor Film Distributors, November 15, 1924) 5 Reels.
Jack Perrin, Peggy O'Day, Alfred Hewston, S. J. Bingham, Horace Carpenter, Milburn Moranti, David Dunbar, "Starlight"
P: Robert J. Horner

RIDIN' WEST (Harry Webb Productions/Aywon Film Corp., November 17, 1924) 5 Reels.
Jack Perrin, "Starlight"
D: Harry Webb

LIGHTNIN' JACK (Anchor Film Distributors, December 22, 1924) 5 Reels.
Jack Perrin, Josephine Hill, Lew Meehan, Jack Richardson, Jack Phipps, Horace B. Carpenter, Jack Foster, "Starlight"

TRAVELIN' FAST (Anchor Film Distributors, December 30, 1924) 5 Reels. *Jack Perrin*, Jean Arthur, Peggy O'Day, Lew Meehan, John Pringle, Horace B. Carpenter, "Starlight"

DESERT MADNESS (Harry Webb Productions/Aywon Film Corp., January 13, 1925) 5 Reels.
Jack Perrin, "Starlight"
D: Harry Webb

CANYON RUSTLERS (Harry Webb Productions/Aywon Film Corp., March 18, 1925) 5 Reels.
Jack Perrin, "Starlight"
D: Harry Webb

WINNING A WOMAN (Harry Webb Productions/Rayart Pictures, April 1925) 5 Reels.
Jack Perrin, Josephine Hill, "Starlight"
D: Harry Webb

DOUBLE-FISTED (Harry Webb Productions/Rayart Pictures, July 9, 1925) 5 Reels.
Jack Perrin, Molly Malone, "Starlight"
D: Harry Webb

BORDER VENGEANCE (Harry Webb Productions/Aywon Film Corp., August 12, 1925) 5 Reels.
Jack Perrin, Josephine Hill, Minna Redman, Vondell Darr, Jack Richardson, Leonard Clapham (Tom London), "Starlight"
D: Harry Webb
S/Scen: Forrest Sheldon

THE KNOCKOUT KID (Harry Webb Productions/Rayart Pictures, September 1, 1925) 5 Reels.
Jack Perrin, Molly Malone, Eva Thatcher, Bud Osborne, Martin Turner, Ed Burns, Jack Richardson, "Starlight"
D: Albert Rogell
Scen: Forrest Sheldon

STARLIGHT, THE UNTAMED (Harry Webb Productions/Rayart Pictures, September 2, 1925) 5 Reels.
Jack Perrin, "Starlight"
D: Harry Webb

SILENT SHELDON (Harry Webb Productions/Rayart Pictures, October 7, 1925) 5 Reels.
Jack Perrin, Josephine Hill, Lew Meehan, Robert MacFarland, Martin Turner, Whitehorse, Lew Meehan, Leonard Clapham (Tom London), "Rex" (a dog), "Starlight"
D: Harry Webb
S/Scen: Pierre Couderc

DANGEROUS FISTS (Harry Webb Productions/Aywon Film Corp., November 27, 1925) 5 Reels.
Jack Perrin, "Starlight"
D: Harry Webb

CACTUS TRAILS (Harry Webb Productions/Aywon Film Corp., December 28, 1925) 5 Reels.
Jack Perrin, "Starlight"
D: Harry Webb

THE THUNDERBOLT STRIKES (Harry Webb Productions/Rayart Pictures, January 29, 1926) 5 Reels.
Jack Perrin, "Starlight"
D: Harry Webb

MIDNIGHT FACES (Otto K. Schreier Productions/Goodwill Pictures, March 25, 1926) 5 Reels.
Francis X. Bushman, Jr., *Jack Perrin*, Kathryn McGuire, Edward Piel, Sr., Charles Belcher, Nora Cecil, Martin Turner, Eddie Dennis, Al Hallett, Andy Waldron, Larry Fisher
D/Writer: Bennett Cohen

MISTAKEN ORDERS (Larry Wheeler Productions/Rayart Pictures, May 5, 1926) 5 Reels.
Helen Holmes, *Jack Perrin*, Henry Ballows, Cecil Kellogg, Hal Walters, Harry Tenbrook, Mack V. Wright, Arthur Millett, Alice Belcher
D: J. P. McGowan

STARLIGHT'S REVENGE (Harry Webb Productions/Rayart Pictures, May 21, 1926) 5 Reels.
Jack Perrin, "Starlight"
D: Harry Webb

DANGEROUS TRAFFIC (Otto K. Schreier Productions/Goodwill Pictures, June 7, 1926) 5 Reels.
Jack Perrin, Francis X. Bushman, Jr., Mildred Harris, Leonard Clapham (Tom London), Ethan Laidlaw, Hal Walters
D/Writer: Bennett Cohen

THE MAN FROM OKLAHOMA (Harry Webb Productions/Rayart Pictures, August 4, 1926) 5 Reels.
Jack Perrin, Josephine Hill, Martin Turner, "Starlight"
D: Forrest Sheldon

WEST OF THE RAINBOW'S END (George Blaisdell Productions/Rayart Pictures, August 13, 1926) 5 Reels.
Jack Perrin, Pauline Curley, Billy Lamar (Buzz Barton), James Welch, Tom London, Milburn Moranti, Chief Whitehorse, "Starlight," "Rex" (a dog)
D: Bennett Cohen
Scen: Daisy Kent
S: Victor Rousseau

THE GREY DEVIL (George Blaisdell Productions/Rayart Pictures, August 14, 1926) 5 Reels.
Jack Perrin, Lorraine Eason, Tom London, Andy Waldron, Jerome La Grasse, Milburn Morante, "Starlight"
D: Bennett Cohen
S/Scen: Henry Ziegler

Jack Perrin and players in an unidentified two-reeler from the Northwest Mounted Police series (Universal, 1927–1928).

HI-JACKING RUSTLERS (Ben Wilson Productions/Rayart Pictures, November 1926) 5 Reels.
Jack Perrin, Josephine Hill, Billy Lamar (Buzz Barton), Leonard Trainor, Bud Osborne, Al Ferguson, Walter Shumway, "Starlight," "Rex" (a dog)
D: Bennett Cohen

A RIDIN' GENT (Ben Wilson Productions/Rayart Pictures, December 1926) 5 Reels.
Jack Perrin, "Starlight"
D: Bennett Cohen

THE OPEN SWITCH (Morris R. Schlank Productions/California Studios/Rayart Pictures, 1926).
Helen Holmes, *Jack Perrin*, Charles (Slim) Whitaker, Max Ascher, Mack V. Wright, Arthur Millett, Henry Roquemore
D: J. P. McGowan

WHERE THE NORTH HOLDS SWAY (Morris R. Schlank Productions/Rayart Pictures, January 1927) 5 Reels.
Jack Perrin, "Starlight"
D: Bennett Cohen

THE LAFFIN' FOOL (Morris Schlank Productions/Rayart Pictures, February 1927) 5 Reels.
Jack Perrin, Billy Lamar (Buzz Barton), "Starlight"
D: Bennett Cohen

THUNDERBOLT'S TRACKS (Morris R. Schlank Productions/Rayart Pictures, April 1927) 5 Reels.
Jack Perrin, Pauline Curley, Billy Lamar (Buzz Barton), Jack Henderson, Lew Meehan, Harry Tenbrook, Ethan Laidlaw, Ruth Royce, "Starlight"
D: Bennett Cohen
Scen: Bennett Cohen

CODE OF THE RANGE (Morris R. Schlank Productions/Rayart Pictures, May 6, 1927) 5 Reels.
Jack Perrin, Nelson McDowell, Pauline Curley, Lew Meehan, Chic Olsen, "Starlight," "Rex" (a dog)
D: Bennett Cohen, Morris R. Schlank
S: Cleve Meyer

FIRE AND STEEL (Elbee Pictures, July 1, 1927) 6 Reels.
Jack Perrin, Philo McCullough, Mary McAllister, Burr McIntosh, Cissy Fitzgerald, Frank Newburg
D: Bertram Bracken
S: A. B. Barringer

DANGER AHEAD (Universal, September 3, 1927) 2 Reels.
Jack Perrin, "Starlight"
D: Bruce Mitchell
S/Cont: Basil Dickey

SOUTH OF NORTHERN LIGHTS (Universal, September 30, 1927) 2 Reels.
("Northwest Mounted Police" Series)
Jack Perrin, "Starlight"
D: Josef Levigard
S/Cont: Arthur Henry Gooden

BLIND MAN'S BLUFF (Universal, October 27, 1927) 2 Reels.
("Northwest Mounted Police" Series)
Jack Perrin, "Starlight"
D: Bruce Mitchell
S/Cont: Arthur Henry Gooden

KING OF HEARTS (Universal, November 23, 1927) 2 Reels.
("Northwest Mounted Police" Series)
Jack Perrin, "Starlight"
D: Josef Levigard
S/Cont: Basil Dickey

BARE FISTS (Universal, December 20, 1927) 2 Reels.
("Northwest Mounted Police" Series)
Jack Perrin, "Starlight"
D: Josef Levigard
S/Cont: George Morgan

SEALED ORDERS (Universal, January 18, 1928) 2 Reels.
("Northwest Mounted Police" Series)
Jack Perrin, "Starlight"
D: Josef Levigard
S/Cont: Arthur Henry Gooden

MADDEN OF THE MOUNTED (Universal, February 16, 1928) 2 Reels.
("Northwest Mounted Police" Series)
Jack Perrin, "Starlight"
D: Josef Levigard
S: Thomas Malloy
Cont: William Lester

PLUNGING HOOFS (Universal, April 10, 1928) 5 Reels.
Jack Perrin, Barbara Worth, J. P. McGowan, David Dunbar, "Starlight," "Rex" (King of Wild Horses)
D: Henry MacRae
Scen: George Morgan
S: Basil Dickey, William Lord Wright

THE CODE OF THE MOUNTED (Universal, April 13, 1928) 2 Reels.
("Northwest Mounted Police" Series)
Jack Perrin, "Starlight"
D: Josef Levigard
S/Cont: William Lester

THE RING LEADER (Universal, May 14, 1928) 2 Reels.
("Northwest Mounted Police" Series)
Jack Perrin, "Starlight"
D: Josef Levigard
S/Cont: George W. Pyper

HOOFBEATS OF VENGEANCE (Universal, June 4, 1928) 5 Reels.
Jack Perrin, Helen Foster, Al Ferguson, "Starlight," "Rex" (King of Wild Horses)
D: Henry MacRae
Scen: George H. Plympton
S: George H. Plympton, William Lord Wright

THE IRON CODE (Universal, June 6, 1928) 2 Reels.
("Northwest Mounted Police" Series)
Jack Perrin, "Starlight"
D: Josef Levigard
S/Cont: Arthur Henry Gooden

YUKON GOLD (Universal, July 3, 1928) 2 Reels.
("Northwest Mounted Police" Series)
Jack Perrin, "Starlight"
D: Josef Levigard
S/Cont: Arthur Henry Gooden

THE RUSE (Universal, August 3, 1928) 2 Reels.
("Northwest Mounted Police" Series)
Jack Perrin, "Starlight"
D: Josef Levigard
S/Cont: Lola D. Moore

THE WATER HOLE (Famous Players-Lasky/Paramount, September 9, 1928) 7 Reels.
(Some scenes in Technicolor)
Jack Holt, Nancy Carroll, John Boles, Montague, Shaw, Ann Christy, Lydia Yeamans Titus, *Jack Perrin*, Jack Mower, Paul Ralli, Tex Young, Bob Miles, Greg Whitespear
D: R. Richard Jones
S: Zane Grey—"The Water Hole"

GUARDIANS OF THE WILD (Universal, September 16, 1928) 5 Reels.
Jack Perrin, Ethlyne Clair, Al Ferguson, Bernard Siegel, Robert Homans, "Starlight," "Rex" (King of Wild Horses)
D: Henry MacRae
Cont: Basil Dickey
S/Scen: George Morgan

THE VANISHING WEST (Mascot, Octobr 15, 1928) 10 Chapters.
Jack Perrin, Jack Daugherty, Leo Maloney, Yakima Canutt, William Fairbanks, Eileen Sedgwick, Fred Church, Mickey Bennett, Helen Gibson, Harry Lorraine, Aaron Edwards, Bob Burns, Tom Bay, Ed Waldron
D: Richard Thorpe
SP: Wyndham Gittens
P: Nat Levine

A DANGEROUS TRAIL (Universal, 1928) 2 Reels.
Jack Perrin, "Starlight"
D: Josef Levigard
S/Cont: Wallace Clifton

THE TWO OUTLAWS (Universal, November 18, 1928) 5 Reels.
Jack Perrin, Kathleen Collins, J. P. McGowan, Cuyler Supplee, "Starlight," "Rex" (King of Wild Horses)
D/S: Henry MacRae
Adapt/Cont: George Morgan

WILD BLOOD (Universal, February 10, 1929) 5 Reels.
Jack Perrin, Ethlyne Clair, Theodore Lorch, Nelson McDowell, "Starlight," "Rex" (King of Wild Horses)
D: Henry MacRae
S/Cont: George Morgan

THE HARVEST OF HATE (Universal, August 4, 1929) 5 Reels.
Jack Perrin, Helen Foster, Tom London, Jim Corey, "Starlight," "Rex" (King of Wild Horses)
D: Henry MacRae
Cont: George H. Plympton
S: William Lord Wright, George H. Plympton

OVERLAND BOUND (Rayton Talking Pictures/Presido, November 23, 1929) 5 Reels.
Leo Maloney, Allene Ray, *Jack Perrin*, Wally Wales, Lydia Knott, Charles K. French, R. J. Smith, Joe Maloney, William Dyer, "Bullet" (a dog), "Starlight"
D/P: Leo Maloney
S/SP: Ford Beebe, Joseph Kane

THE JADE BOX (Universal, March 24, 1930) 10 Chapters.
(released in both silent and sound versions)
Jack Perrin, Eileen Sedgwick, Monroe Salisbury, Francis Ford
D: Ray Taylor
S: Fred Jackson

Jack Perrin restrains Al Ferguson as Ethlyn Clair and an unidentified lady look on in *Guardians of the Wild* (Universal, 1928).

Chapter Titles: (1) The Jade of Jeopardy! (2) Buried Alive! (3) The Shadow Man, (4) The Fatal Prophecy, (5) The Unseen Death, (6) The Haunting Shadow, (7) The Guilty Man, (8) The Grip of Death, (9) Out of the Shadows, (10) The Atonement

OVERLAND BOUND (Rayton Talking Pictures/Presido, November 23, 1929) 5,200 ft.
Jack Perrin, Wally Wales, Leo Maloney, Allene Ray, Lydia Knott, Charles K. French, R. J. Smith, Joe Maloney, William Dyer, "Bullet," "Starlight"
D: Leo Maloney
SP: Ford Beebe, Joseph Kane
P: Leo Maloney

BEYOND THE RIO GRANDE (Biltmore Productions/Big 4, April 12, 1930) 5,400 ft.
Jack Perrin, Buffalo Bill, Jr., Charlene Burt, Pete Morrison, Franklyn Farum, Edmund Cobb, Henry Rocquemore, Emma Tansey, Henry Taylor, "Starlight"
D: Harry Webb
SP: Carl Krusada
P: F. E. Douglas

RIDIN' LAW (Big 4, May 24, 1930) 5,600 ft.
Jack Perrin, Yakima Canutt, Rene Borden, Jack Mowers, Ben Corbett, Pete Morrison, Fern Emmett, Olive Young, Robert Walker, "Starlight"
D: Harry S. Webb
SP: Carl Krusada
P: Harry S. Webb, F. E. Douglas

TRAILS OF PERIL (National Players/Big 4, September 30, 1930) 5,400 ft.
(Title changed from "Trails of Danger")
Wally Wales, Viriginia Brown Faire, Frank Ellis, Lew Meehan, *Jack Perrin*, Joe Rickson, Buck Connors, Bobby Dunn, Pete Morrison, Hank Bell, "Starlight"
D: Alvin J. Neitz
S: Henry Taylor
P: F. E. Douglas

PHANTOM OF THE DESERT (Syndicate, November 1, 1930) 5,220 ft.
Jack Perrin, Eve Novak, Josef Swickard, Lila Eccles, Ben Corbett, Edward Earle, Robert Walker, Pete Morrison, "Starlight"
D: Harry S. Webb
SP: Carl Krusada
P: Harry Webb/F. E. Douglas

THE APACHE KID'S ESCAPE (Robert J. Horner Productions, November 22, 1930) 4,600 ft.
Jack Perrin, Josephine Hill, Fred Church, Virginia Ashcroft, Henry Rocquemore, Bud Osborne, "Starlight"
D: Robert J. Horner

WILD WEST WHOOPEE (Cosmos/Associated Film Exchange, March 8, 1931) 57 Mins.
Jack Perrin, Josephine Hill, Buzz Barton, Fred Church, Horace B. Carpenter, John Ince, George Chesebro, Henry Rocquemore, Ben Corbett, Charles Austin, Walt Patterson
P: Robert J. Horner
D: Robert J. Horner
SP: Robert J. Horner

RIDER OF THE PLAINS (Syndicate, May 3, 1931) 57 Mins.
Tom Tyler, Andy Shuford, Lillian Bond, Alan Bridge, Gordon DeMain, *Jack Perrin*, Ted Adams, Fern Emmett, Slim Whitaker
D: J. P. McCarthy
S/SP: Wellyn Totman

THE KID FROM ARIZONA (Cosmos, May 10, 1931) 55 Mins.
Jack Perrin, Josephine Hill, Robert Walker, Henry Rocquemore, George Chesebro, Ben Corbett, "Starlight"
D/S: Robert L. Horner
SP: Robert Walker

THE SHERIFF'S SECRET (Cosmos, June 14, 1931) 58 Mins.
Jack Perrin, Dorothy Bauer, George Chesebro, Jimmy Aubrey, Fred Hargraves, Joe Marba, Billy Franey, Monte Jones, "Starlight"
D: James Hogan
S/SP: James Hogan

LARIATS AND SIXSHOOTERS (Cosmos, October 25, 1931) 65 Mins.
Jack Perrin, Ann Lee, George Chesebro, Art Mix, Virginia Bell, Lafe McKee, Dick Cramer, Olin Francis, Jimmy Aubrey, Gloris Joy, "Starlight"
D: Alvin J. Neitz
S/SP: Carl Krusada

THE SIGN OF THE WOLF (Metropolitan, 1931) 10 Chapters. (Reissued in 1932 as feature called "The Lone Trail")
Rex Lease, Virginia Brown Faire, Joe Bonomo, Jack Mower, Al Ferguson, Josephine Hill, Robert Walker, Edmund Cobb, Harry Todd, Billy O'Brien, *Jack Perrin*, "King" (a dog)
D: Forrest Sheldon, Harry S. Webb
S/SP: Betty Burbridge, Bennett Cohen (credited for the feature version, whereas Karl Krusada is credited for the serial version)
P: Harry S. Webb
Chapter Titles: (1) Drums of Doom, (2) The Dog of Destiny, (3) The Wolf's Fangs, (4) The Fatal Shot, (5) The Well of Terror, (6) The Wolf Dogs, (7) Trapped, (8) The Secret Mark, (9) Tongues of Flame, (10) The Lost Secret

HELL-FIRE AUSTIN (Tiffany, March 3, 1932) 70 Mins.
Ken Maynard, Ivy Merton, *Jack Perrin*, Charles LeMayne, Lafe McKee, Nat Pendleton, Allan Roscoe, William Robyns, Fargo Bussey, Jack Rockwell, Jack Ward, Bud McClure, Lew Meehan, Ben Corbett, *Jack Perrin*
D: Forrest Sheldon
S: Forrest Sheldon
SP: Betty Burbridge

SON OF OKLAHOMA (Sono Art/World Wide, July 17, 1932) 55 Mins.
Bob Steele, Carmen LaRoux, Earl Dwire, Julian Rivero, Josie Sedgwick, Robert Homans, Henry Rocquemore, *Jack Perrin*
D: Robert N. Bradbury
S: Wellyn Totman
SP: Burl Tuttle, George Hull
P: Trem Carr

DYNAMITE RANCH (KBS/World Wide, July 31, 1932) 59 Mins.
Ken Maynard, Ruth Hall, *Jack Perrin*, Arthur Hoyt, Allan Roscoe, Al Smith, John Beck, George Pierce, Lafe McKee, Martha Mattox, Edmund Cobb, Charles Le Moyne, Cliff Lyons, Kermit Maynard (stuntman and double), "Tarzan"
D: Forrest Sheldon
S/SP: Barry Barrington, Forrest Sheldon
P: Burt Kelly, Sam Bischoff, William Saal

MOVIE CRAZY (Harold Lloyd Corp./Paramount, September 14, 1932) 84 Mins.
Harold Lloyd, Constance Cummings, Kenneth Thompson, Sydney Jarvis, Eddie Fetherstone, Robert McWade, Louise Closser Hale, Harold Goodwin, DeWitt Jennings, Lucy Beaumont, Arthur Housman, Mary Doran, Noah Young, Constantine Romanoff, Spencer Charters, Fred Kohler, Jr.,

Jack Perrin, Edward Peil, Blackie Whiteford, Bill O'Brien, Wallace Howe, Grady Sutton, Elinor Vanderveer, Gus Leonard, Dick Rush
D: Clyde Bruckman
S: Agnes Christine Johnston, John Grey, Felix Adler
Cont: Clyde Bruckman, Frank Terry, Lex Neal
SP: Vincent Lawrence

BETWEEN FIGHTING MEN (KBS/World Wide, October 16, 1932) 62 Mins.
Ken Maynard, Ruth Hall, Josephine Dunn, Wallace MacDonald, Albert J. Smith, Walter Law, James Bradbury, Jr., John Pratt, Charles King, Edmund Cobb, Jack Rockwell, Jack Kirk, Bud McClure, Roy Bucko, Jack Ward, *Jack Perrin*, "Tarzan"
D: Forrest Sheldon
S/SP: Betty Burbridge, Forrest Sheldon
P: Burt Kelly, Sam Bischoff, William Saal

TEX TAKES A HOLIDAY (Argosy/First Division, December 2, 1932) 60 Mins.
(Natural Color)
Wallace MacDonald, Virginia Brown Faire, Ben Corbett, Olin Francis, George Chesebro, James Dillon, Claude Peyton, George Gerwing, *Jack Perrin*
D: Alvin J. Neitz
S: Robert Walker

FORTY-FIVE CALIBRE ECHO (Horner Productions, 1932) 60 Mins.
Jack Perrin, Ben Corbett, Eleanor Fair, Olin Francis, Dick Cramer, George Chesebro, Jimmy Aubrey, C. H. Bussey, Ruth Rennick, "Starlight"
D: Bruce Mitchell
S: Carl Krusada
P: Robert J. Horner

THE LOST TRAIL (Syndicate, 1932).
(Feature version of 1931 serial "The Sign of the Wolf")
Rex Lease, Virginia Brown Faire, Joe Bonomo, Jack Mower, Josephine Hill, Al Ferguson, Robert Walker, Edmund Cobb, Harry Todd, Billy O'Brien, *Jack Perrin*, "King" (a dog)
D: Forrest Sheldon, Harry S. Webb
SP: Betty Burbridge, Bennett Cohen
P: Harry S. Webb

THE BIG RACE (Showmens Pictures/Screencraft, February 1933) 68 Mins.
Boots Mallory, John Darrow, Paul Hurst, Frankie Darro, Phillips Smalley, Kathlyn Williams, Georgie O'Dell, James Flavin, Skipper Zellan, Richard Terry (*Jack Perrin*), Ted Adams, Horace B. Carpenter
D: Fred Newmeyer
SP: Hugh Cummings
S: Hugh Cummings
Supv: Al Alt

JAWS OF JUSTICE (Principal, December 4, 1933) 58 Mins.
Richard Terry (*Jack Perrin*), Ruth Sullivan, Gene Tolar, Lafe McKee, Robert Walker, "Kazan" (a dog)
D: Spencer G. Bennet
S: Joseph Anthony Roach
P: Sol Lesser

GIRL TROUBLE (B 'n' B Pictures/Reliable, December 15, 1933).
Jack Perrin, Ben Corbett, Lola Tate, Mary Draper, Wally Turner
D: Bernard B. Ray
SP: Bennett Cohen
P: Bernard B. Ray

MYSTERY SQUADRON (Mascot, December 22, 1933) 12 Chapters.
Bob Steele, Guinn Williams, Jack Mulhall, Lucile Browne, Robert Frazer, Purnell Pratt, J. Carrol Naish, Robert Kortman, Lafe McKee, Edward Hearn, Edward Piel, Kernan Cripps, Jack Mower, *Jack Perrin*, Lew Meehan, Frank Ellis, Wally Wales
D: Colbert Clark, David Howard
S: Sherman Lowe, Al Martin
SP: Barney Sarecky, Colbert Clark, David Howard, Wyndham Gittens
Chapter Titles: (1) The Black Ace, (2) The Fatal Warning, (3) The Black Ace Strikes, (4) Men of Steel, (5) The Death Swoop, (6) Doomed, (7) Enemy Signals, (8) The Canyon of Calamity, (9) The Secret of the Mine, (10) Clipped Wings, (11) The Beast at Bay, (12) The Ace of Aces

THE WHISPERING SHADOW (Mascot, 1933) 12 Chapters.
Bela Lugosi, Henry B. Walthall, Karl Dane, Viva Tattersall, Malcolm MacGregor, Robert Warwick, Roy D'Arcy, George Lewis, Ethel Clayton, Lloyd Whitlock, Bob Kortman, Tom London, Lafe McKee, *Jack Perrin*
D: Albert Herman, Colbert Clark
P: Nat Levine
Chapter Titles: (1) The Master Magician, (2) The Collapsing Room, (3) The All-Seeing Eye, (4) The Shadow Strikes, (5) Wanted for Murder, (6) The Man Who was Czar, (7) The Double Doom, (8) The Red Circle, (9) The Fatal Secret, (10) The Death Warrant, (11) The Trap, (12) King of the World

MYSTERY RANCH (Reliable/William Steiner, April 12, 1934) 56 Mins.
Tom Tyler, Roberta Gale, Jack Gable, (*Jack Perrin*), Frank Hall Crane, Louise Gabo, Charles King, Tom London, George Chesebro, Lafe McKee, "Starlight"
D: Ray Bernard (Bernard B. Ray)
S: J. K. Henry
SP: Rose Gordon, Carl Krusada
P: Bernard B. Ray

Jack Perrin (billed as Richard Terry), Ruth Sullivan, and "Kazan" in *Jaws of Justice* (Principal, 1933).

ARIZONA NIGHTS (B 'n' B Pictures/Reliable, April 15, 1934).
Jack Perrin, Ben Corbett, Al Ferguson, Charles K. French, "Starlight"
D: Bernard B. Ray
SP: Bennett Cohen
P: Bernard B. Ray

RAWHIDE MAIL (Reliable/William Steiner, June 8, 1934) 59 Mins.
Jack Perrin, Lillian Gilmore, Lafe McKee, Dick Cramer, Chris-Pin Martin, Nelson McDowell, George Chesebro, Jimmy Aubrey, Robert Walker, Lew Meehan, "Starlight"
D/P: Bernard B. Ray
S: Bennett Cohen
SP: Rose Gordon, Betty Burbridge

RAINBOW RIDERS (Astor, June 15, 1934) 31 Mins.
Jack Perrin, Ben Corbett, Virginia Brown Faire, Ethan Laidlaw, Jim Corey, Jack Ward, Mack Wright, Grace Woods, "Starlight"
D: Bennett Cohen
SP: Bennett Cohen
P: Bernard B. Ray

RIDIN' GENTS (Astor, August 15, 1934) 32 Mins.
Jack Perrin, Ben Corbett, Doris Hill, George Chesebro, Alex Franks, Harry Myers, Lafe McKee, Charles K. French, Slim Whitaker, "Starlight"
D: Bennett Cohen
SP: Bennett Cohen
P: Bernard B. Ray

Lafe McKee, George Chesebro, Jack Perrin, Charles Whitaker, and Ben Corbett in *Ridin' Gents* (Astor, 1934). Player in background is unidentified.

THE CACTUS KID (Reliable/William Steiner, 1934).
Jack Perrin, Jayne Regan, Tom London, Slim Whitaker, Fred Humes, Philo McCullough, Joe De LaCruz, Kit Guard, Tina Menard, Lew Meehan, "Starlight"
D: Harry S. Webb
S/SP: Carl Krusada
P: Bernard B. Ray

LOSER'S END (Reliable/William Steiner, 1934).
Jack Perrin, Tina Menard, Frank Rice, William Gould, Fern Emmett, Elias Lazaroff, Robert Walker, Jimmy Aubrey, Rosemary Joye, Slim Whitaker, "Starlight"
D: Bernard B. Ray
S: Harry Semeles (Harry S. Webb)
SP: Rose Gordon, Carl Krudada
P: Bernard B. Ray

NORTH OF ARIZONA (Reliable/William Steiner, 1935) 60 Mins.
Jack Perrin, Blanche Mehaffey, Lane Chandler, Al Bridge, Murdock McQuarrie, George Chesebro, Artie Ortego, Budd Buster, Frank Ellis, Blackie Whiteford, "Starlight"
D: Harry S. Webb
SP: Carl Krusada
P: Bernard B. Ray

TEXAS JACK (Reliable/William Steiner, 1935) 52 Mins.
Jack Perrin, Jayne Regan, Nelson McDowell, Robert Walker, Budd Buster, Cope Borden, Lew Meehan, Blackie Whiteford, Oscar Gahan, Jim Oates, Steve Clark, "Starlight"
D/P: Bernard B. Ray
SP: Carl Krusada

WOLF RIDERS (Reliable/William Steiner, 1935).
Jack Perrin, Lillian Gilmore, Lafe McKee, Nancy DeShon, William Gould, George Chesebro, Earl Dwire, Budd Buster, Slim Whitaker, Frank Ellis, Robert Walker, George Morrell, Blackie Whiteford, "Starlight"
D: Harry S. Webb
SP: Carl Krusada
P: Bernard B. Ray

GUN GRIT (Atlantic, 1936).
Jack Perrin, Ethel Beck, David Sharpe, Roger Williams, Ralph Peters, Frank Hagney, Jimmy Aubrey, Edward Cassidy, Phil Dunham, Oscar Gahan, Earl Dwire, Horace Murphy, Baby Lester, Budd Buster, "Starlight," "Braveheart" (a dog)
D: Lester Williams (William Berke)
S: Allen Hall, Gordon Phillips
P: William Berke

HAIR-TRIGGER CASEY (Atlantic, 1936) 59 Mins.
Jack Perrin, Betty Mack, Wally Wales, Fred Toones, Phil Dunham, Edward Cassidy, Robert Walker, Dennis Meadows (Moore), Vi Wong, "Starlight"
D: Harry Fraser
S/SP: Monroe Talbot
P: William Berke

DESERT JUSTICE (Atlantic, 1936) 58 Mins.
Jack Perrin, David Sharpe, Warren Hymer, Budd Buster, Dennis Meadows (Moore), Maryan Downing, Roger Williams, William Gould, Fred Toones, Earl Dwire, "Starlight," "Braveheart" (a dog)
D: Lester Williams (William Berke)
S: Allan Hall
SP: Gordon Phillips, Lewis Kingdom
P: William Berke

Jack Perrin acting a little peeved at Lew Meehan in *Texas Jack* (Reliable, 1935).

Jack Perrin and Charles Whitaker in *The Cactus Kid* (Reliable, 1934). Player in background unidentified.

WILDCAT SAUNDERS (Atlantic, 1936) 60 Mins.
Jack Perrin, Blanche Mehaffey, William Gould, Fred Toones, Roger Williams, Tom London, Edward Cassidy, Bud Osborne, Jim Corey, Earl Dwire, Dennis Moore, J. P. McGowan, Tex Palmer, Francis Walker, "Starlight"
D: Harry Fraser
S: Miller Easton
SP: Monroe Talbot
P: William Berke

RECKLESS RANGER (Columbia, May 30, 1937) 56 Mins.
Bob Allen, Louise Small, *Jack Perrin,* Harry Woods, Mary MacLaren, Buddy Cox, Jack Rockwell, Jay Wilsey, Slim Whitaker, Roger Williams, Bud Osborne, Jim Corey, Tom London, Hal Price, Al Taylor, Tex Cooper, Bob McKenzie, Lane Chandler, Frank Ball, George Plues, Lafe McKee, Tex Palmer, Victor Cox, Chick Hannon, "Starlight"
D: Spencer G. Bennet
S: Joseph Levering, Jesse Duffy
SP: Nate Gatzert
P: Larry Darmour

Jack Perrin and player in *Wolf Riders* (Reliable, 1935).

THE PAINTED STALLION (Republic, June 5, 1937)
12 Chapters.
Ray Corrigan, Hoot Gibson, LeRoy Mason, Duncan Renaldo,
Sammy McKim, Hal Taliaferro, *Jack Perrin*, Ed Platt, Lou
Fulton, Julia Thayer, (Jean Carmen), Yakima Canutt,
Maston Williams, Duke Taylor, Loren Riebe, George De-
Normand, Gordon DeMain, Charles King, Vinegar Roan,
Lafe McKee, Frank Leyva, Frankie Marvin, John Big Tree,
Pascale Perry, Don Orlando, Henry Hale, Edward Piel, Sr.,
Horace Carpenter, Lee White, Joe Yrigoyen, Paul Lopez,
Monte Montague, Gregg Star Whitespear, Ralph Bucko, Roy
Bucko, Leo Dupee, Babe Defreest, Jose Dominguez, Jack
Padjan, Al Haskell, Augie Gomez
D: William Witney, Alan James, Ray Taylor
SP: Barry Shipman, Winston Miller
AP: J. Laurence Wickland
Chapter Titles: (1) Trail to Empire, (2) The Rider of the
Stallion, (3) The Death Trap, (4) Avalanche, (5) Valley of
Death, (6) Thundering Wheels, (7) Trail Treachery, (8) The
Whispering Arrow, (9) The Fatal Message, (10) Ambush,
(11) Tunnel of Terror, (12) Human Targets

THE LAST TRAIN FROM MADRID (Paramount, June 11,
1937) 77 Mins.
Lew Ayres, Dorothy Lamour, Gilbert Roland, Lionel Atwill,
Karen Morley, Helen Mack, Robert Cummings, Lee Bow-
man, Olympe Bradna, Anthony Quinn, Evelyn Brent,
Jack Perrin
D: James Hogan
S: Paul Hervey Fox, Elsie Fox
SP: Louis Stevens, Robert Wyler
P: George Arthur

THE ROAD BACK (Universal, June 1937) 12 Reels,
103 Mins.
Richard Cromwell, John King, Slim Summerville, Andy
Devine, Barbara Read, Louise Fazenda, Noah Beery, Jr.,
Jack Perrin
D: James Whale
SP: R. C. Sherriff, Charles Kenyon
S: Erich Maria Remarque

THE WRONG ROAD (Republic, October 11, 1937) 62 Mins.
Richard Cromwell, Helen Mack, Lionel Atwill, Horace
MacMahon, Russ Powell, Billy Bevan, Marjorie Main, Rex
Evans, Joseph Crehan, Arthur Hoyt, Syd Saylor, Selmer
Jackson, Chester Clute, *Jack Perrin*
D: James Cruze
SP/S: Gordon Rigby
AP: Colbert Clark

THE MYSTERIOUS PILOT (Columbia, 1937) 15 Chapters.
Frank Hawks, Dorothy Sebastian, Rex Lease, Guy Bates
Post, Kenneth Harlan, Yakima Canutt, Frank Lackteen,
Robert Terry, George Rosener, Clara Kimball Young, Harry
Harvey, Tom London, Ted Adams, Earl Douglas, Robert
Walker, Roger Williams, Esther Ralston, *Jack Perrin*
D: Spencer Gordon Bennet
Cont: George Rosener, George M. Merrick
S: William Byron Mowery—"The Silver Hawk"
Chapter Titles: (1) The Howl of the Wolf, (2) The Web
Tangles, (3) Enemies of the Air, (4) In the Hands of the Law,
(5) The Crackup, (6) The Dark Hour, (7) Wings of Destiny,
(8) Battle in the Sky, (9) The Great Flight, (10) Whirlpool of
Death, (11) The Haunted Mill, (12) The Lost Trail, (13) The
Net Tightens, (14) Vengeance Rides the Airways, (15)
Retribution

THE PURPLE VIGILANTES (Republic, January 24, 1938)
58 Mins.
("3 Mesquiteers " Series)
Bob Livingston, Ray Corrigan, Max Terhune, Joan Barclay,
Jack Perrin, Earle Hodgins, Earl Dwire, Frances Sayles,
George Chesebro, Robert Fiske, Ernie Adams, William Gould,
Harry Strang, Ed Cassidy, Frank O'Connor
D: George Sherman
SP: Betty Burbridge, Oliver Drake
AP: Sol C. Siegel
Based on characters created by Wm. Colt MacDonald

THE SECRET OF TREASURE ISLAND (Columbia,
March, 1938) 15 Chapters.
Don Terry, Gwen Gaze, Grant Withers, Hobart Bosworth,
William Farnum, Walter Miller, George Rosener, Dave
O'Brien, Yakima Canutt, Warner Richmond, Bill Boyle,
Sandra Karina, Joe Caits, Colin Campbell, Patrick J. Kelly,
Jack Perrin
D: Elmer Clifton
S: L. Ron Hubbard

Cont: George Rosener, Elmer Clifton, George Merrick
Chapter Titles: (1) The Isle of Fear, (2) The Ghost Talks, (3) The Phantom Duel, (4) Buried Alive, (5) The Girl Who Vanished, (6) Trapped by the Flood, (7) The Cannon Roars, (8) The Circle of Death, (9) The Pirate's Revenge, (10) The Crash, (11) Dynamite, (12) The Bridge of Doom, (13) The Mad Flight, (14) The Jaws of Destruction, (15) Justice

THE LONE RANGER (Republic, March, 1938) 15 Chapters.
Lee Powell, Chief Thunder Cloud, Lynn Roberts, Hal Taliaferro (Wally Wales), Herman Brix (Bruce Bennett), Lane Chandler, George Letz (George Montgomery), Stanley Andrews, Billy Bletcher (voice of Lone Ranger only), William Farnum, George Cleveland, John Merton, Sammy McKim, Tom London, Raphael Bennett, Maston Williams, Charles Thomas, Allan Cavan, Reed Howes, Walter James, Francis Sayles, Murdock McQuarrie, Jane Keckley, Phillip Armenta, Ted Adams, Jimmy Hollywood, Jack Kirk, Art Dillard, Millard McGowan, Frank Ellis, Carl Stockdale, Bud Osborne, Fred Burns, Inez Cody, Duke Green, Forbes Murray, Edna Lawrence, Charles King, *Jack Perrin*, Frank Leyva, George Mari, Charles Whitaker, Edmund Cobb, Jack Rockwell, J. W. Cody, Oscar Hancock, Buck Hires, Ray Kennedy, Al Lorenzen, Karry Mack, Frankie Marvin, Lafe McKee, Henry Olivas, Perry Pratt, Charles Williams, Wally Wilson, Ben Wright, Gunner Johnson, Bill Jones, Robert Kortman, Ralph LeFever, Ike Lewin, Elmer Napier, Post Parks, George Plues, Loren Riebe, Al Rimpau, Vinegar Roan, John Slater, George St. Leon, Burl Tatum, Al Taylor, Duke Taylor, Bobby Thompson, Blackie Whiteford, Shorty Woods, Bill Yrigoyen, Joe Yrigoyen—"Silver Chief"
D: William Witney, John English
S: Fran Striker
SP: Barry Shipman, George Worthing Yates, Franklyn Adreon, Ronald Davidson, Lois Eby
AP: Sol C. Siegel
Supervisor: Robert Beche
Chapter Titles: (1) Heigh-yo-Silver, (2) Thundering Earth, (3) The Pitfall, (4) Agent of Treachery, (5) The Steaming Cauldron, (6) Red Man's Courage, (7) Wheels of Disaster, (8) Fatal Treasure, (9) The Missing Spur, (10) Flaming Fury, (11) The Silver Bullet, (12) Escape, (13) The Fatal Plunge, (14) Messenger of Doom, (15) Last of the Rangers

THE GREAT ADVENTURES OF WILD BILL HICKOK (Columbia, June 30, 1938) 15 Chapters.
Gordon Elliott (Bill Elliott), Monte Blue, Carole Wayne, Frankie Darro, Dickie Jones, Sammy McKim, Kermit Maynard, Roscoe Ates, Monte Collins, Reed Hadley, Chief Thunder Cloud, George Chesebro, Mala (Ray Mala), Walter Wills, J. P. McGowan, Eddy Waller, Alan Bridge, Slim Whitaker, Walter Miller, Lee Phelps, Robert Fiske, Earle Hodgins, Earl Dwire, Ed Grady, Ray Jones, Edmund Cobb, Art Mix, Hal Taliaferro, Blackie Whiteford, *Jack Perrin*
SP: George Rosener, Charles Arthur Powell, George Arthur Durlam

D: Mack V. Wright, Sam Nelson
P: Harry Webb
Chapter Titles: (1) The Law of the Gun, (2) Stampede, (3) Blazing Terror, (4) Mystery Canyon, (5) Flaming Brands, (6) The Apache Killer, (7) Prowling Wolves, (8) The Pit, (9) Ambush, (10) Savage Vengeance, (11) Burning Waters, (12) Desperation, (13) Phantom Bullets, (14) The Lure, (15) Trail's End

THE TEXANS (Paramount, August 12, 1938) 92 Mins.
Randolph Scott, Joan Bennett, May Robson, Walter Brennan, Robert Cummings, Robert Barrat, Harvey Stephens, Francis Ford, Raymond Hatton, Clarence Wilson, Jack Moore, Chris-Pin-Martin, Anna Demetrio, Richard Tucker, Ed Gargan, Otis Harlan, Spencer Charters, Archie Twitchell, William Haade, Irving Bacon, Bill Roberts, Francis MacDonald, William B. Davidson, *Jack Perrin*, Richard Denning, John Qualen, Ester Howard, Philip Morris, Harry Woods, Wheeler Oakman, Dutch Hendrian, Vers Steadman, Kay Whitehead, Ralph Remley, Frank Cordell, Ernie Adams, Edward LeSaint, Ed Brady, Scoop Martin, Oscar Smith, James Quinn, Everett Brown, Margaret McWade, Virginia Jennings, Jim Burris, Lon Poff, Laurie Lane
D: James Hogan
S: Emerson Hough—"North of '36"
SP: Bertrand Millhouser, Paul Sloane, William Wister Haines
P: Lucien Hubbard

ANGELS WITH DIRTY FACES (Warner Brothers/First National, September 14, 1938) 97 Mins.
James Cagney, Pat O'Brien, Humphrey Bogart, Ann Sheridan, George Bancroft, Billy Halop, Bobby Jordan, Leo Gorcey, Gabriel Dell, Huntz Hall, Bernard Punsley, Joe Dowing, Edward Pawley, Adrian Morris, Frankie Burke, William Tracy, Marilyn Knowlden, William Worthington, Earl Dwire, Mary Gordon, Harry Hayden, Dick Rich, Joe Devlin, Dick Wessel, Frank Hagney, Lee Phelps, Emory Parnell, Ralph Sanford, Robert E. Homans, Jack C. Smith, Frank Coghland, *Jack Perrin*, The St. Brendan's Church Choir
D: Michael Curtis
SP: John Wexley, Warren Duff
S: Rowland Brown
P: Sam Bischoff

WESTERN JAMBOREE (Republic, December 2, 1938) 56 Mins.
Gene Autry, Smiley Burnette, Jean Rouveral, Esther Muir, Frank Darien, Joe Frisco, Kermit Maynard, *Jack Perrin*, Jack Ingram, Margaret Armstrong, Harry Holman, Edward Raquello, Bentley Hewitt, George Walcott, Ray Teal, Frank Ellis, Eddie Dean, Davidson Clark, "Champion"
D: Ralph Staub
S: Patricia Harper
SP: Gerald Geraghty
AP: Harry Grey

BULLDOG DRUMMOND'S BRIDE (Paramount, June 30, 1939) 55 Mins.
John Howard, Heather Angel, H. B. Warner, Reginald Denny, E. E. Clive, Elizabeth Patterson, Eduardo Cianelli, Gerald Hamer, John Sutton, Neil Fitzgerald, Louis Mercier, Adrienne D'Ambricourt, Adia Kuznetzoff, *Jack Perrin*
D: James Hogan
AP: Stuart Walker
SP: Stuart Palmer, Garnett Weston
S: H. C. "Sapper" McNeile—"Bulldog Drummond and the Oriental Mind"

$1,000 A TOUCHDOWN (Paramount, September 22, 1939) 71 Mins.
Joe E. Brown, Martha Raye, Eric Blore, Susan Hayward, John Hartley, Syd Saylor, Joyce Mathews, George McKay, Tom Dugan, Matt McHugh, *Jack Perrin*, Don Wilson, Edward Gargan, Frank M. Thomas, William Haade, Charles Middleton, Adrian Morris
D: James Hogan
AP: William C. Thomas
SP: Delmer Davies

ETERNALLY YOURS (Walter Wanger Productions/United Artists, October 3, 1939) 95 Mins.
Loretta Young, David Niven, Hugh Herbert, C. Aubrey Smith, Billie Burke, Broderick Crawford, Raymond Walburn, ZaSu Pitts, Virginia Field, Ralph Graves, Eve Arden, Lionel Pope, Dennie Moore (the actress, not to be confused with Dennis Moore), May Beatty, Douglas Wood, Leyland Hodgson, Frank Jacquet, Billy Wayne, Ralph Norwood, Paul Le Paul, Tay Garnett, George Cathrey, Mary Field, *Jack Perrin*, Fred Keating, Hillary Brooke, Walter Sande
D: Tay Garnett
S/SP: Gene Towne, Graham Baker
P: Walter Wanger

THE PAL FROM TEXAS (Metropolitan, November 1, 1939) 56 Mins.
Bob Steele, Claire Rochelle, *Jack Perrin*, Josef Swickard, Betty Mack, Ted Adams, Charleton Young, Jack Ingram, Robert Walker
D/P: Harry S. Webb
S: Forrest Sheldon
SP: Carl Krusada

THE FIGHTING 69TH (Warner Brothers), January 5, 1940) 90 Mins.
James Cagney, Pat O'Brien, George Brent, Jeffrey Lynn, Alan Hale, Frank McHugh, Dennis Morgan, Dick Foran, William Lundigan, Guinn "Big Boy" Williams, Henry O'Neill, John Litel, Sammy Cohen, John Ridgely, Charles Throwbridge, Frank Wilcox, Herbert Anderson, J. Anthony Hughes, Frank Mayo, John Harron, George Kilgen, Richard Clayton, Eddie Dew, Wilfred Lucas, Emmett Vogan, Frank Sully, Joseph Crehan, Frank Coghlan, Jr., James Flavin, George O'Hanlon, *Jack Perrin*, Trevor Bardette, John Arledge, Frank Melton, Edmund Glover, Frank Faylen, Edgar Edwards,

Ralph Dunn, Arno Frey, Roland Verno, Robert Layne Ireland, Elmo Murray, Jacques Lory, Jack Boyle, Jr., Creighton Hale, Benny Rubin, Eddie Acuff, Jack Mower, Nat Carr, Jack Wise
D: William Keighley
SP: Norman Reilly Raine, Fred Niblo, Jr., Dean Franklin
P: Jack L. Warner
Exec. P: Hal B. Wallis

LAND OF THE SIX-GUNS (Monogram, May 9, 1940) 54 Mins.
Jack Randall, Louise Stanley, Glenn Strange, Bud Osborne, Kenne Duncan, George Chesebro, Steve Clark, Frank LaRue, Carl Mathews, Jimmy Aubrey, *Jack Perrin*
D: Raymond K. Johnson
S/SP: Tom Gibson
P: Harry S. Webb

NEW MOON (Metro-Goldwyn-Mayer, June 1940) 105 Mins.
Jeanette MacDonald, Nelson Eddy, Mary Boland, George Zucco, H. B. Warner, Grant Mitchell, Stanley Fields, Richard Purcell, John Miljan, Ivan Simpson, William Tannen, Bunty Cutler, Claude King, Cecil Cunningham, Joe Yule, George Irving, Edwin Maxwell, Paul E. Burns, Rafael Storm, Winifred Harris, Robert Warwick, *Jack Perrin*
D/P: Robert Z. Leonard
SP: Jacques Deval and Robert Arthur
S: Based on operetta by Oscar Hammerstein II

WEST OF PINTO BASIN (Monogram, November 25, 1940) 60 Mins.
("Range Busters" Series)
Ray Corrigan, John King, Max Terhune, Gwen Gaze, Tris Coffin, Dirk Thane, George Chesebro, Carl Mathews, Bud Osborne, *Jack Perrin*, Dick Cramer, Phil Dunham, Jerry Smith, Budd Buster
D: S. Roy Luby
S: Elmer Clifton
SP: Earl Snell
P: George W. Weeks

TEXAS RANGERS RIDE AGAIN (Paramount, December 13, 1940) 68 Mins.
John Howard, Ellen Drew, Akim Tamiroff, Broderick Crawford, May Robson, Charley Grapewin, John Miljan, Anthony Quinn, Tom Tyler, Donald Curtis, Eddie Acuff, Ruth Rogers, Robert Ryan, Eva Puig, Monte Blue, James Pierce, William Duncan, Harvey Stephens, Harold Goodwin, Edward Pawley, Eddie Foy, Jr., Joseph Crehan, Stanley Price, Charles Lane, *Jack Perrin*, Gordon Jones, Ruth Rogers, John Miller, Henry Rocquemore
D: James Hogan
SP: William Lipman, Horace McCoy

THE GREEN HORNET STRIKES AGAIN (Universal, 1940) 15 Chapters.
Warren Hull, Keye Luke, Wade Boteler, Anne Nagel, Eddie Acuff, Pierre Watkins, James Seay, Arthur Loft, Joe A.

Devlin, William Hall, Dorothy Lovett, Jay Michael, Charles Miller, Jeanne Kelly, Irving Mitchell, William Forrest, Eddie Dunn, Montague Shaw, *Jack Perrin*

D: Ford Beebe and John Rawlins

SP: George H. Plympton, Basil Dickey, Sherman Lowe

Chapters Titles: (1) Flaming Havoc, (2) The Plunge of Peril, (3) The Avenging Heavens, (4) A Night of Terror, (5) Shattering Doom, (6) The Fatal Flash, (7) Death in the Clouds, (8) Human Targets, (9) The Tragic Crash, (10) Blazing Fury, (11) Thieves of the Night, (12) Crashing Barriers, (13) The Flaming Inferno, (14) Racketeering Vultures, (15) Smashing the Crime Ring

THE SHADOW (Columbia, 1940) 15 Chapters.

Victor Jory, Veda Ann Borg, Robert Moore, Robert Fiske, J. Paul Jones, Jack Ingram, Charles Hamilton, Edward Peil, Sr., Frank La Rue, *Jack Perrin*

D: James W. Horne

SP: Joseph Poland, Ned Dandy, Joseph O'Donnell

P: Larry Darmour

Chapter Titles: (1) The Doomed City, (2) The Shadow Attacks, (3) The Shadow's Peril, (4) In the Tiger's Lair, (5) Danger Above, (6) The Shadow's Trap, (7) Where Horror Waits, (8) The Shadow Rides the Rails, (9) The Devil in White, (10) The Underground Trap, (11) Chinatown at Dark, (12) Murder by Remote Control, (13) Wheels of Death, (14) The Sealed Room, (15) The Shadow's Net Closes

Adapted from the Shadow Radio Program broadcast over the Mutual network.

Based on stories published in *Shadow Magazine*

RIDERS OF DEATH VALLEY (Universal, July 1, 1941) 15 Chapters.

Dick Foran, Buck Jones, Leo Carrillo, Charles Bickford, Lon Chaney, Jr., Noah Beery, Jr., "Big Boy" Williams, Jeannie Kelly (Jean Brooks), Monte Blue, James Blaine, Glenn Strange, Roy Barcroft, Ethan Laidlaw, Dick Alexander, Jack Rockwell, Frank Austin, Charles Thomas, William Hall, James Gulifoyle, Ernie Adams, Edmund Cobb, William Pagan, Jack Clifford, Richard Travis, Ivar McFadden, Jerome Harte, Ruth Rickaby, *Jack Perrin*, Don Rowan, Bud Osborne, Slim Whitaker, Frank Brownlee, Art Miles, Ed Payson, James Farley, Alonzo Price, Ted Adams, Dick Rush, Ken Nolan, Jay Michael, Gil Perkins, Duke York, "Silver" (a horse)

D: Ray Taylor, Ford Beebe

S: Oliver Drake

SP: Sherman Lowe, Basil Dickey, George Plympton, Jack Connell

P: Henry MacRae

Chapter Titles: (1) Death Marks the Trail (2) Menacing Herd, (3) Plunge of Peril, (4) Flaming Fury, (5) Avalanche of Doom, (6) Blood and Gold, (7) Death Rides the Storm, (8) Descending Doom, (9) Death Holds the Reins, (10) Devouring Flames, (11) Fatal Blast, (12) Thundering Doom, (13) The Bridge of Disaster, (14) A Fight to the Death, (15) The Harvest of Hate

DYNAMITE CANYON (Monogram, August 8, 1941) 58 Mins.

Tom Keene, Evelyn Finley, Slim Andrews, Sugar Dawn, Stanley Price, Kenne Duncan, Gene Alsace, Fred Hoose, Tom London, *Jack Perrin* "Rusty" (a horse)

D/P: Robert Emmett Tansey

SP: Robert Emmett, Frances Kavanaugh

HOLT OF THE SECRET SERVICE (Columbia, 1941) 15 Chapters.

Jack Holt, Evelyn Brent, Montague Shaw, Tristram Coffin, John Ward, Ted Adams, Joe McGuinn, Edward Hearn, Ray Parsons, Jack Cheatham, *Jack Perrin*

D: James W. Horne

SP: Basil Dickey, George Plympton, Wyndham Gittens

P: Larry Darmour

Chapter Titles: (1) Chaotic Creek, (2) Ramparts of Revenge, (3) Illicit Wealth, (4) Menaced by Fate, (5) Exits to Terror, (6) Deadly Doom, (7) Out of the Past, (8) Escape to Perio, (9) Sealed in Silence, (10) Named to Die, (11) Ominous Warnings, (12) The Stolen Signal, (13) Prison of Jeopardy, (14) Afire Afloat, (15) Yielded Hostage

THE IRON CLAW (Columbia, 1941) 15 Chapters.

Charles Quigley, Walter Sande, Joyce Bryant, Forrest Taylor, Alex Callam, Norman Willis, James Metcalfe, Allen Doone, Edythe Elliot, John Beck, Charles King, James Morton, Hal Price, *Jack Perrin*

D: James W. Horne

S: Arthur Stringer

SP: Basil Dickey, George H. Plympton, Jesse A. Duffy, Charles R. Condon, Jack Stanley

Chapter Titles: (1) The Shaft of Doom, (2) The Murderous Mirror, (3) The Drop to Destiny, (4) The Fatal Fuse, (5) The Fiery Fall, (6) The Ship Log Talks, (7) The Mystic Map, (8) The Perilous Pit, (9) The Cul-de-Sac, (10) The Curse of the Cave, (11) The Doctor's Bargain, (12) Vapors of Evil, (13) The Secret Door, (14) The Evil Eye, (15) The Claw's Collapse

SKY RAIDERS (Universal, 1941) 12 Chapters.

Donald Woods, Billy Halop, Robert Armstrong, Edward Ciannelli, Kathryn Adams, Jacqueline Dalya, Jean Fenwick, Reed Hadley, Irving Mitchell, Edgar Edwards, John Holland, Roy Gordon, Alex Callam, Bill Cody, Jr., *Jack Perrin*

D: Ford Beebe and Ray Taylor

AP: Henry MacRae

S: Eliot Gibbons

SP: Clarence Upson Young, Paul Huston

Chapter Titles: (1) Wings of Disaster, (2) Death Rides the Storm, (3) The Toll of Treachery, (4) Battle in the Clouds, (5) The Fatal Blast, (6) Stark Terror, (7) Flaming Doom, (8) The Plunge of Terror, (9) Torturing Trails, (10) The Flash of Fate, (11) Terrors of the Storm, (12) The Winning Warriors

THE SPIDER RETURNS (Columbia, 1941) 15 Chapters.
Warren Hull, Mary Ainslee, Dave O'Brien, Joe Girard,
Kenneth Duncan, Corbet Harris, Bryant Washburn, Charles
Miller, Harry Harvey, *Jack Perrin*
D: James W. Horne
SP: Jesse A. Duffy and George Plympton
Chapter Titles: (1) The Stolen Plans, (2) The Fatal Time-
Bomb, (3) The Secret Meeting, (4) The Smoke Dream,
(5) The Gargoyle's Trail, (6) The X-Ray Eye, (7) The Radio
Boomerang, (8) The Mysterious Message, (9) The Cup of
Doom, (10) The X-Ray Belt, (11) Lips Sealed by Murder,
(12) A Money Bomb, (13) Almost a Confession, (14) Suspi-
cious Telegrams, (15) The Payoff

BROADWAY BIG SHOT (PRC, February 6, 1942) 59 Mins.
Ralph Byrd, Virginia Vale, *Jack Perrin*
D: William Beaudine
P: Jed Buell

NIGHT MONSTER (Universal, October 23, 1942) 73 Mins.
Bela Lugosi, Lionel Atwill, Irene Hervey, Ralph Morgan, Don
Porter, Nils Asther, Leif Erickson, Frank Reicher, Doris Lloyd,
Robert Homans, Janet Shaw, Eddy Waller, *Jack Perrin*, Fay
Helm, Francis Pierlot, Cyril Delavanti
S/P: Ford Beebe
SP: Clarence Upson Young

DIXIE (Paramount, June 26, 1943) 89 Mins.
(Technicolor)
Bing Crosby, Dorothy Lamour, Marjorie Reynolds, Billy
De Wolfe, Lynne Overman, Raymond Walburn, Eddie
Foy, Jr., Grant Mitchell, Louis DaPron, Clara Blandick,
Tom Herbert, Olin Howland, Robert Warwick, Stanley
Andrews, Norman Varden, Hope Landin, James Burke,
George H. Reed, Harry Barris, Jimmy Conlon, George Ander-
son, Harry C. Bradley, William Halligan, Wilbur Mack, Sam
Flint, Dell Henderson, Fortunio Bonanova, Willie Best, Tom
Kennedy, Harry Tyler, Ethel Clayton, Carl "Alfalfa"
Switzer, John "Skins" Miller, Donald Kerr, Fred Santley,
Warren Jackson, Jimmy Ray, Hal Rand, Charles Mayon,
Allen Ray, Jerry James, Jimmy Clemons, *Jack Perrin*
D: A. Edward Sutherland
AP: Paul Jones
S: William Rankin
SP: Karl Tunberg, Darrell Ware
Adapt: Claude Binyon

THE NORTH STAR (RKO, October 13, 1943).
Anne Baxter, Dana Andrews, Walter Huston, Walter Bren-
nan, Ann Harding, Jane Withers, Farley Granger, Erich von
Stroheim, Dean Jagger, Eric Roberts, Carl Benton Reid, Ann
Carter, Esther Dale, Ruth Nelson, Paul Guilfoyle, Martin
Kosleck, Tonio Selwart, Peter Pohlenz, Robert Lowery, Gene
O'Donnell, Frank Wilcox, Loudie Claar, Lynn Winthrop,
Charles Bates, *Jack Perrin*
D: Lewis Milestone
S/SP: Lillian Hellman
P: Samuel Goldwyn

NORTHERN PURSUIT (Warner Brothers, November
13, 1943) 94 Mins.
Errol Flynn, Julie Bishop, Helmut Dantine, John Ridgely,
Gene Lockhart, Tom Tully, Bernard Nedell, Warren Douglas,
Monte Blue, Alec Craig, Russell Hicks, Kurt Krueger,
Tom Fadden, Bill Kennedy, Fred Kelsey, George Lynn,
John Forsythe, John Alvin, Robert Kent, Robert Hutton,
Milt Kibbee, Hugh Prosser, James Mullican, Ken Christy,
Donald Kerr, *Jack Perrin*, Richard Alden, John Royce, Rose
Higgins, Carl Harbaugh, Joe Herrera
D: Raoul Walsh
SP: Frank Gruber, Alvah Bessie
S: Leslie T. White
P: Jack Chertok

ADVENTURES OF THE FLYING CADETS (Universal,
1943) 13 Chapters.
Johnny Downs, Bobby Jordan, Ward Wood, Billy Benedict,
Regis Toomey, Eduardo Cianelli, Robert Armstrong, Jen-
nifer Holt, Selmer Jackson, *Jack Perrin*
D: Ray Taylor and Lewis D. Collins
S: Morgan B. Cox
SP: Morgan B. Cox, George H. Plympton, Paul Huston
AP: Henry MacRae
Chapter Titles: (1) The Black Hangman Strikes, (2) Menaced
by Murderers, (3) Into the Flames, (4) Door to Death, (5)
Crushed in a Crater, (6) Rendezvous with Doom, (7) Gestapo
Execution, (8) Masters of Treachery, (9) Wings of Destruc-
tion, (10) Caught in the Cavern of An-Kar-Ban (11) Hostages
for Treason, (12) The Black Hangman Strikes Again, (13)
Toll of Treason

SONG OF NEVADA (Republic, August 5, 1944) 75 Mins.
Roy Rogers, Dale Evans, Mary Lee, Bob Nolan and the Sons
of the Pioneers, Lloyd Corrigan, Thurston Hall, John Eldridge,
Forrest Taylor, George Meeker, Emmett Hoban, LeRoy
Mason, William Davidson, Kenne Duncan, Si Jenks, Frank
McCarroll, Henry Wills, Jack O'Shea, Helen Talbot, *Jack
Perrin*, "Trigger"
D: Joseph Kane
SP: Gordon Kahn, Oliver Cooper
AP: Harry Grey

THE LAST RIDE (Warner Brothers, October 7, 1944)
56 Mins.
Richard Travis, Charles Lang, Eleanor Parker, Jack LaRue,
Cy Kindall, Wade Boteler, Mary Gordon, Harry Lewis,
Michael Ames, Virginia Patton, Ross Ford, Jack Mower,
Frank Mayo, Stuart Holmes, Leah Baird, Howard Hickman,
John Maxwell, Al Hill, John Harmon, Hank Mann, Bill
Kennedy, Clancy Cooper, Norman Willis, William Hopper,
Harry Strang, Harry Tenbrook, *Jack Perrin*, Eddie Chandler
D: D. Ross Lederman
S/P: Raymond L. Schrock
AP: William Jacobs

BELLE OF THE YUKON (International/RKO, December 6, 1944) 84 Mins.
Randolph Scott, Gypsy Rose Lee, Dinah Shore, Bob Burns, Charles Winniger, William Marshall, Guinn "Big Boy" Williams, Robert Armstrong, Florence Bates, Edward Fielding, Wanda McKay, Charles Soldani, *Jack Perrin*
S/P: William A. Seiter
S: Houston Branch
SP: James Edward Grant

THE PHANTOM SPEAKS (Republic, May 10, 1945) 68 Mins.
Richard Arlen, Stanley Ridges, Lynne Roberts, Tom Powers, Charlotte Wynters, Jonathan Hale, Pierre Watkin, Marion Martin, Garry Owen, Ralf Harolde, Philip Tonge, Jack Ingram, Nolan Leary, Edmund Cobb, Tom Chatterton, Edward Cassidy, Robert Homans, *Jack Perrin*, Doreen McCann
D: John English
S/SP: John K. Butler
Exec. P: Armand Schaeffer

RADIO STARS ON PARADE (RKO, July 1945) 69 Mins.
Wally Brown, Alan Carney, Frances Langford, Ralph Edwards, Don Wilson, Skinnay Ennis, Tony Romano, Town Criers, Rufe Davis, Robert Clarke, Sheldon Leonard, May Wagner, Ralph Peters, Harry Woods, Myrna Dell, Ray Walker, Emory Parnell, Jason Robards, Sr., Jack Rice, Tom Quinn, *Jack Perrin*, Cappy Barra Boys
D: Leslie Goodwins
P: Ben Stoloff
Exec. P: Sid Rogell

DUFFY'S TAVERN (Paramount, September 28, 1945) 98 Mins.
Ed Gardner, Victor Moore, Barry Fitzgerald, Marjorie Reynolds, Barry Sullivan, Charles Cantor, Eddie Green, Ann Thomas, Howard da Silva, Billy De Wolfe, Walter Abel, Johnny Coy, Charles Quigley, Olga San Juan, Miriam Franklin, Maurice Rocco, Cass Daily, Diana Lynn, Robert Benchley, William DeMarest, James Brown, Helen Walker, Gary, Phillip, Dennis and Lindsay Crosby, Jean Heather, Barney Dean, Bobby Watson, Frank Faylen, George M. Carleton, Addison Richards, George McKay, James Millican, Emmett Vogan, Catherine Craig, Noel Neil, *Jack Perrin*, plus guest stars Bing Crosby, Betty Hutton, Paulette Goddard, Alan Ladd, Dorothy Lamour, Eddie Bracken, Brian Donlevy, Sonny Tufts, William Bendix, Veronica Lake, Arturo De Cordova, Joan Caulfield, and Gail Russell
D: Hal Walker
AP: Danny Dare
SP: Melvin Frank and Norman Panama
Based on characters created by Ed Gardner

THE POSTMAN ALWAYS RINGS TWICE (Metro-Goldwyn-Mayer, January 1946) 113 Mins. .
Lana Turner, John Garfield, Cecil Kellaway, Hume Cronyn,

Leon Ames, Audrey Totter, Alan Reed, Jeff York, Morris Ankrum, Edward Earle, Joel Friedkin, Charlie Williams, Lloyd Ingraham, *Jack Perrin*, Cameron Grant, William Halligan, Garry Owen, Byron Foulger, Sondra Morgan, Dick Crockett, Frank Mayo, Betty Blythe, Jack Chefe, George Noisom, Virginia Randolph, Tom Dillon, James Farley
D: Tay Garnett
SP: Harry Ruskin, Niven Busch
S: James M. Cain
P: Carey Wilson

THE MAN WHO DARED (Columbia, May 30, 1946).
Leslie Brooks, George Macready, Forrest Tucker, Charles D. Brown, Warren Mills, Richard Hale, Charles Evans, Trevor Bardette, William Newell, Arthur Space, Ralph Dunn, George Lloyd, Harry Tyler, Phil Arnold, *Jack Perrin*
D: John Sturges
SP: Edward Bock
S: Maxwell Shane, Alex Gottlieb
P: Leonard S. Picker

SHADOWS ON THE RANGE (Monogram, October 16, 1946) 58 Mins.
Johnny Mack Brown, Raymond Hatton, Jan Bryant, Marshall Reed, John Merton, *Jack Perrin*, Steve Clark, Terry Frost, Cactus Mack, Pierce Lyden, Ted Adams, Lane Bradford
D: Lambert Hillyer
SP: Jess Bowers (Adele Buffington)
P: Scott R. Dunlap

THE WEB (Universal, June 1947) 90 Mins.
Ella Raines, Edmond O'Brien, William Bendix, Vincent Price, John Abbott, Maria Palmer, Fritz Leiber, Howland Chamberlain, Tito Vuolo, Wilton Graff, Robin Raymond, Pierre Watkin, Ethan Laidlaw, William Haade, Russ Conway, Lee Phelps, *Jack Perrin*, Ed Begley
D: Michael Balcon
SP: William Bowers, Bertram Milhauser
S: Harry Kurnitz
P: Jerry Bresler

A DOUBLE LIFE (Universal, December 1947) 103 Mins.
Ronald Colman, Signe Hasso, Edmond O'Brien, Shelley Winters, Ray Collins, Philip Loeb, Millard Mitchell, Joe Sawyer, Charles La Torre, Whit Bissell, John Drew Colt, Peter Thompson, Elizabeth Dunne, Alan Edmiston, Art Smith, Sid Tomack, Wilton Graff, Harlan Briggs, Claire Carleton, Betsy Blair, Janet Warren, Marjory Woodworth, Fay Kanin, Frederic Worlock, Arthur Gould-Porter, Boyd Irwin, Percival Vivian, Mary Young, Guy Bates Post, Leslie Denison, David Bond, Virginia Patton, Thayer Roberts, Elliott Reid, Georgia Caine, *Jack Perrin*
D: George Cukor
SP: Ruth Gordon and Garson Kanin
P: Michael Kanin

ALWAYS TOGETHER (Warner Brothers, December 1947)
76 Mins.
Robert Hutton, Joyce Reynolds, Cecil Kellaway, Ernest Truex, Don McGuire, Ransom Sherman, Douglas Kennedy, Chester Clute, Grady Sutton, Tom Dugan, Joe Devlin, Paul Stanton, Clifton Young, Dewey Robinson, Frank Wilcox, William Ruhl, Harry Lewis, Wheaton Chambers, Jack Mower, *Jack Perrin*
D: Frederick de Cordova
SP: Phoebe and Henry Ephron and I. A. L. Diamond
P: Alex Gottlieb

I WALK ALONE (Paramount, December 1947) 97 Mins.
Burt Lancaster, Lizabeth Scott, Kirk Douglas, Wendell Corey, Kristine Miller, George Biguad, Marc Lawrence, Mike Mazurki, Mickey Knox, Roger Neury, Noll Turner, *Jack Perrin*
D: Byron Haskin
SP: Charles Schee
Adapt: Robert Smith and John Bright
S: Theodore Reeves—"Beggars are Coming to Town" (original play)

APRIL SHOWERS (Warner Brothers, March 27, 1948)
78 Mins.
Jack Carson, Ann Sothern, Robert Alda, S. Z. Sakall, Robert Ellis, Richard Rober, Joseph Crehan, Ray Walker, John Gallaudet, Philip van Zandt, Billy Curtis, Roy Gordon, Harry Shannon, Pat Flaherty, Ralph Dunn, Charlie Williams, Edward Clark, Dewey Robinson, Donald Kerr, William Haade, Jack Mower, Lester Dorr, Harold J. Stone, Fred Kelsey, *Jack Perrin*
D: James V. Kern
SP: Peter Milne
S: Joe Laurie, Jr.
P: William Jacobs

BERLIN EXPRESS (RKO, April 1948) 86 Mins.
Merle Oberon, Robert Ryan, Charles Korvin, Paul Lukas, Robert Coote, Reinhold Schunzel, Roman Toporow, Peter Von Zerneck, Otto Waldis, Fritz Kortner, Michael Harvey, Richard Powers, *Jack Perrin*
D: Jacques Tourneur
SP: Harold Medford
S: Curt Siodmak
P: Bert Granet
Exec. P: Dore Schary

THE GALLANT LEGION (Republic, May 24, 1948) 88 Mins.
William (Bill) Elliott, Adrian Booth, Joseph Schildkraut, Bruce Cabot, Andy Devine, Jack Holt, Grant Withers, Adele Mara, James Brown, Hal Landon, Max Terry, Lester Sharpe, Hal Taliaferro, Russell Hicks, Herbert Rawlinson, Marshall Reed, Steve Drake, Harry Woods, Roy Barcroft, Bud Osborne, Hank Bell, Jack Ingram, George Chesebro,

Rex Lease, Noble Johnson, Emmett Vogan, John Hamilton, Trevor Bardette, Gene Stutenroth, Ferris Taylor, Iron Eyes Cody, Kermit Maynard, Jack Kirk, Merrill McCormack, Augie Gomez, Cactus Mack, Fred Kohler, Glenn Strange, Tex Terry, Joseph Crehan, Peter Perkins, *Jack Perrin*
D/AP: Joseph Kane
S: John K. Butler, Gerald Geraghty
SP: Gerald Adams

MR. BLANDINGS BUILDS HIS DREAM HOUSE (RKO, July 1948) 94 Mins.
Cary Grant, Myrna Loy, Melvyn Douglas, Reginald Denny, Sharyn Moffett, Connie Marshall, Louise Beavers, Ian Wolfe, Harry Shannon, Tito Vuolo, Nestor Paiva, Jason Robards, Sr., Lurene Tuttle, Lex Barker, Emory Parnell, Don Brodie, Hal K. Dawson, Stanley Andrews, Robert Bray, *Jack Perrin*, Dan Tobin, Will Wright, Frank Darien, Cliff Clark, Franklin Parker, Charles Middleton, Frederich Ledebur
S: H. C. Potter
SP: Norman Panama, Melvin Frank
S: Eric Hodgins
P: Norman Panama, Melvin Frank

A WOMAN'S SECRET (RKO, February 7, 1949) 85 Mins.
Maureen O'Hara, Melvyn Douglas, Gloria Grahame, Bill Williams, Victor Jory, Mary Phillips, Jay C. Flippen, Robert Warwick, Curt Conway, Ann Shoemaker, Virginia Farmer, Ellen Corby, Emory Parnell, Rory Mallinson, John Parrish, Paul Guilfoyle, Lee Phelps, Mickey Simpson, *Jack Perrin*
D: Nicholas Ray
S: Vicki Baum
P: Herman J. Mankiewicz

BRIMSTONE (Republic, August 15, 1949) 90 Mins.
Rod Cameron, Adrian Booth, Walter Brennan, Forrest Tucker, Jack Holt, Jim Davis, James Brown, Guinn "Big Boy" Williams, Charlita, Hal Taliaferro, *Jack Perrin*
D: Joseph Kane
S: Norman S. Hall
SP: Thames Williams
AP: Joseph Kane

WHITE HEAT (Warner Brothers, November 28, 1949) 114 Mins.
James Cagney, Virginia Mayo, Edmond O'Brien, Margaret Wycherly, Steve Cochran, John Archer, Wally Cassell, Fred Clark, Mickey Knox, Ian McDonald, G. Pat Collins, Paul Guilfoyle, Fred Coby, Ford Rainey, Robert Osterloh, Ray Montgomery, Grandon Rhodes, Marshall Bradford, Milton Parsons, John Pickard, Harry Lauter, Nolan Leary, Sid Melton, Bob Carson, Jim Thorpe, Lee Phelps, Harry Strang, Robert Foulk, *Jack Perrin*
D: Raoul Walsh
S: Virginia Kellogg
SP: Ivan Goff
P: Louis F. Edelman

MONTANA (Warner Brothers, January 28, 1950) 76 Mins.
(Technicolor)
Errol Flynn, Alexis Smith, S. Z. "Cuddles" Sakall, Douglas Kennedy, Ian MacDonald, James Brown, Charles Irwin, Paul E. Burns, Tudor Owen, Lester Matthews, Nacho Galindo, Lane Chandler, Monte Blue, Billy Vincent, Warren Jackson, *Jack Perrin*
D: Ray Enright
S: Ernest Haycox
SP: James R. Webb, Borden Chase, Charles O'Neal
P: William Jacobs

DAKOTA LIL (20th Century Fox, February 1, 1950) 84 Mins.
(Cinecolor)
George Montgomery, Marie Windsor, Rod Cameron, John Emery, Wallace Ford, Jack Lambert, Larry Johns, Marian Martin, James Flavin, J. Farrell MacDonald, *Jack Perrin*
D: Leslie Selander
S: Frank Gruber
SP: Maurice Geraghty
P: Edward L. Alperson

SUNSET BOULEVARD (Paramount, April 1950) 109 Mins.
William Holden, Gloria Swanson, Eric Von Stroheim, Nancy Olson, Fred Clark, Lloyd Gough, Jack Webb, Franklyn Farnum, Larry Blake, Charles Dayton, Cecil B. De Mille, Hedda Hopper, Buster Keaton, Anna Q. Nilsson, H. B. Warner, Ray Evans, Jay Livingston, *Jack Perrin*
D: Billy Wilder
SP: Charles Brackett, Billy Wilder, D. M. Marshman
P: Charles Brackett

THE GREAT JEWEL ROBBERY (Warner Brothers, July 12, 1950) 91 Mins.
David Brian, Marjorie Reynolds, Jacqueline de Wit, Alice Talton, John Archer, Perdita Chandler, Robert B. Williams, Warren Douglas, John Morgan, Bigelow Sayre, Stanley Church, *Jack Perrin*, Kenneth Patterson, Fred Graham, Charles R. Cane, Weldon Heyburn, Jed Glass, John Pickard, Don Harvey, Harry Lauter, Lyle Latell, Creighton Hale, Tom Wilson, Edward Hearn
D: Peter Godfrey
SP: Borden Chase
P: Bryan Foy

I SHOT BILLY THE KID (Lippert, August 25, 1950) 57 Mins.
Don Barry, Robert Lowery, Wally Vernon, Tom Neal, Judith Allen, Wendy Lee, Barbara Woodell, Dick Lane, Sid Nelson, Archie Twitchell, John Merton, Claude Stroud, Henry Marud, Bill Kennedy, *Jack Perrin*
D/P William Berke
SP: Ford Beebe, Orville Hampton

THE FULLER BRUSH GIRL (Columbia, September 15, 1950) 85 Mins.
Lucille Ball, Eddie Albert, Carl Benton Reid, Gale Robbins, Jeff Donnell, Jerome Cowan, John Litel, Fred Graham, Lee Patrick, Arthur Space, Sid Tomack, Billy Vincent, Lorin Raker, Lelah Tyler, Sara Edwards, Lois Austin, Isabel Randolph, Isabel Withers, Donna Boswell, Gregory Marshall, *Jack Perrin*
D: Lloyd Bacon
SP: Frank Tashlin

KANSAS RAIDERS (Universal-International, November 20, 1950) 80 Mins.
(Technicolor)
Audie Murphy, Brian Donlevy, Marguerite Chapman, Scott Brady, Tony Curtis, Richard Arlen, Richard Long, James Best, John Kellogg, Dewey Martin, George Chandler, Charles Delaney, Richard Egan, David Wolfe, *Jack Perrin*
D: Ray Enright
SP: Robert L. Richards
P: Ted Richmond

BANDIT QUEEN (Lippert, December 22, 1950) 70 Mins.
Barbara Britton, Willard Parker, Philip Reed, Barton Mac-Lane, Martin Garralaga, John Merton, Jack Ingram, Victor Kilian, Thurston Hall, Anna Demetrio, Paul Matin, Pepe Hern, Lala Rios, *Jack Perrin*, Cecile Weston, Carl Pitti, Hugh Hooker, Mike Conrad, Elias Gamboa, Chuck Roberson, Trina Varela, Nancy Laurenz, Minna Philips, Margia Dean, Felipe Turich, Joe Dominguez, Roy Butler
D: William Berke
S: Victor West
SP: Victor West, Budd Lesser
P: William Berke, Murray Lerner

WELLS FARGO GUNMASTER (Republic, May 15, 1951) 60 Mins.
Allan Lane, Chubby Johnson, Mary Ellen Kay, Michael Chapin, Roy Barcroft, Walter Reed, Stuart Randall, William Bakewell, George Meeker, Anne O'Neal, James Craven, Forrest Taylor, Lee Roberts, "Black Jack", *Jack Perrin*
D: Philip Ford
SP: M. Doates Webster
AP: Gordon Kay

JIM THORPE—ALL AMERICAN (Warner Brothers, June 1951) 107 Mins.
Burt Lancaster, Charles Bickford, Steve Cochran, Phyllis Thaxter, Dick Wesson, Jack Bighead, Suni Wareloud, Al Mejia, Hubie Kerns, Nestor Paiva, Jimmy Moss, *Jack Perrin*
D: Michael Curtiz
SP: Douglas Morrow, Everett Freeman
P: Everett Freeman
S: Douglas Morrow, Vincent X. Flaherty

TREASURE OF LOST CANYON (Universal-International, March 1, 1952) 81 Mins.
(Technicolor)
William Powell, Julia Adams, Rosemary DeCamp, Charles Drake, Chubby Johnson, Henry Hull, Jimmy Ivo, John Doucetee, Marvin Press, Frank Wilcox, *Jack Perrin*
D: Ted Tetzlaff
S: Robert Louis Stevenson—"The Treasure of Franchard"
SP: Brainerd Duffield, Emerson Crocker
P: Leonard Goldstein

THE REDHEAD FROM WYOMING (Universal-International, January 1, 1953) 80 Mins.
(Technicolor)
Maureen O'Hara, Alex Nicol, Robert Strauss, Jeanne Cooper, William Bishop, Alexander Scourby, Palmer Lee, Jack Kelly, Claudette Thornton, Ray Bennett, Joe Bailey, Rush Williams, Dennis Weaver, David Alpert, Joe Bassett, Stacey Harris, Betty Allen, Larry Hudson, *Jack Perrin*
D: Lee Sholem
SP: Polly James, Herb Meadow
P: Leonard Goldstein

THE SUN SHINES BRIGHT (Republic, March 13, 1953) 90 Mins.
Charles Winninger, Arleen Whelan, John Russell, Stepin Fetchit, Russell Simpson, Ludwig Stossell, Francis Ford, Paul Hurst, Mitchell Lewis, Grant Withers, Milburn Stone, Dorothy Jordan, Slim Pickens, Henry O'Neill, Ernest Whitman, James Kirkwood, Jane Darwell, Trevor Bardette, Clarence Muse, Hal Baylor, Ken Williams, Mae Marsh, Jack Pennick, Mickey Simpson, Harry Tenbrook, Everett Glass, Jack Mower, Merrill McCormick, James Mason, Cactus Mack, *Jack Perrin*, Patrick Wayne
D: John Ford
P: John Ford, Merian C. Cooper
Scen: Laurence Stallings
S: Irvin S. Cobb—"The Mob from Massac, " "The Lord Provides," "The Sun Shines Bright"

TITANIC (20th Century Fox, April 1953) 97 Mins.
Clifton Webb, Barbara Stanwyck, Robert Wagner, Audrey Dalton, Thelma Ritter, Brian Aherne, Richard Basehart, Allyn Joslyn, James Todd, Frances Bergen, William Johnstone, Christopher Severn, James Lilburn, Charles Fitzsimmons, Barry Bernard, Guy Standing, Jr., Hellen Van Tuyl, Roy Gordon, Marta Mitrovich, Ivis Goulding, Dennis Fraser, Ashley Cowan, Harper Carter, Edmund Purdom, Lee Graham, Merry Anders, Gloria Gordon, Melinda Markey, Ronald F. Hagerthy, Conrad Feia, Richard West, *Jack Perrin*
D: Jean Negulesco
SP: Charles Brackett, Walter Reisch, Richard Breen
P: Charles Brackett

THE GLASS WEB (Universal-International, October 1953) 81 Mins.
Edward G. Robinson, John Forsythe, Kathleen Hughes, Marcia Henderson, Richard Denning, Hugh Sanders, Jean Willes, Eve McVeagh, Harry O. Tyler, John Hiestand, Clark Howat, Bob Nelson, John Verros, Helen Wallace, Benny Rubin, *Jack Perrin*
D: Jack Arnold
SP: Robert Blees, Leonard Lee
S: Max Simon Ehrlich
P: Albert J. Cohen

CALAMITY JANE (Warner Brothers, November 14, 1953) 101 Mins.
(Technicolor)
Doris Day, Howard Keel, Allyn McLerie, Philip Carey, Dick Wesson, Paul Harvey, Chubby Johnson, Gale Robbins, *Jack Perrin*, Rex Lease
D: David Butler
SP: James O'Hanlon
P: William Jacobs

RED RIVER SHORE (Republic, December 15, 1953) 54 Mins.
Rex Allen, Slim Pickens, Lyn Thomas, Bill Phipps, Douglas Fowley, Trevor Bardette, William Haade, Emmett Vogan, John Cason, Rayford Barnes, *Jack Perrin*, "Koko"
D: Harry Keller
SP: Arthur Orloff, Gerald Geraghty
AP: Rudy Ralston

THEM (Warner Brothers, April 1954) 93 Mins.
James Whitmore, Edmund Gwenn, Joan Weldon, James Arness, Onslow Stevens, Sean McClory, Chris Drake, Sandy Descher, Mary Ann Hokanson, Don Shelton, Fess Parker, Olin Howlin, *Jack Perrin*
D: Gordon Douglass
SP: Ted Sherdeman
Adapt: Russell Hughes
S: George Worthing Yates

UNTAMED HEIRESS (Republic, April 1954) 69 Mins.
Judy Canova, Donald Barry, George Cleveland, Taylor Holmes, Chick Chandler, Jack Kruschen, Hugh Sanders, Douglas Fowley, William Haade, Ellen Corby, *Jack Perrin*
D: Charles Lamont
SP: Barry Shipman
S: Jack Townley
AP: Sidney Picker

TEN WANTED MEN (Scott-Brown/Columbia, February 1, 1955) 80 Mins.
(Technicolor)
Randolph Scott, Jocelyn Brando, Richard Boone, Alfonso Bedoya, Donna Martell, Skip Homier, Clem Bevins, Leo Gordon, Minor Watson, Lester Matthews, Tom Powers, Dennis Weaver, Lee Van Cleef, Louis Jean Heydt, Kathleen

Crowley, Boyd "Red" Morgan, Denver Pyle, Francis McDonald, Pat Collins, Paul Maxey, *Jack Perrin*, Julian Rivero, Carlos Vera, Edna Holland, Reed Howes, Terry Frost, Franklyn Farnum, George Boyce
D: Bruce Humberstone
S: Irving Ravetch, Harriet Frank, Jr.
SP: Kenneth Gamet
P: Harry Joe Brown

SEVEN ANGRY MEN (Allied Artists, March 27, 1955) 90 Mins.
Raymond Massey, Debra Paget, Jeffrey Hunter, Larry Pennell, Leo Gordon, John Smith, James Best, Dennis Weaver, Guy Williams, Tom Irish, James Anderson, James Edwards, John Pickard, Smoki Whitfield, Jack Lomas, Robert Simon, Dabbs Greer, Ann Tyrell, Robert Osterloh, *Jack Perrin*
D: Charles Marquis Warren
SP: Daniel B. Ullman
P: Vincent M. Fennelly

LAST OF THE DESPERADOS (Associated, December 1, 1955) 70 Mins.
James Craig, Jim Davis, Barton MacLane, Margia Dean, Donna Martell, Myrna Dell, Bob Steele, Stanley Clements, *Jack Perrin*
D: Sam Newfield
SP: Orville Hampton
P: Sigmund Neufeld

A LAWLESS STREET (Scott-Brown/Columbia, December 15, 1955) 78 Mins.
(Technicolor)
Randolph Scott, Angela Lansbury, Warner Anderson, Jean Parker, Wallace Ford, John Emery, James Bell, Ruth Donnelly, Michael Pate, Don Megowan, Jeanette Nolan, Peter Ortiz, Don Carlos, Frank Hagney, Charles Williams, Frank Ferguson, Harry Tyler, Harry Antrim, Jay Lawrence, Reed Howes, Guy Teague, Hal K. Dawson, Pat Collins, Frank Scannell, Stanley Blystone, Barry Brooks, Edwin Chandler, *Jack Perrin*, Kermit Maynard
D: Joseph H. Lewis
S: Brad Ward—"Marshal of Medicine Bend"
SP: Kenneth Gamet
P: Harry Joe Brown, Randolph Scott

THE SPOILERS (Universal-International, January 2, 1956) 84 Mins.
(Technicolor)
Anne Baxter, Jeff Chandler, Rory Calhoun, Ray Danton, Barbara Britton, John McIntire, Carl Benton Reid, Wallace Ford, Raymond Walburn, Dayton Lummis, Willis Bouchey, Roy Barcroft, Ruth Donnelly, Forrest Lewis, *Jack Perrin*, Bob Steele, Arthur Spann, Lane Bradford, Terry Frost, Dave McGuire, Frank Sully, John Harmon
D: Jesse Hibbs
S: Rex Beach
SP: Oscar Brodney and Charles Hoffman
P: Ross Hunter

WHEN GANGLAND STRIKES (Republic, March 15, 1956) 70 Mins.
Raymond Greenleaf, Margie Millar, John Hudson, Anthony Caruso, Marian Carr, Slim Pickens, Mary Treen, Ralph Dumke, Morris Ankrum, Robert Emmett Keane, Addison Richards, John Gallaudet, Paul Birch, Richard Deacon, James Best, Jim Hayward, Peter Mamakos, Fred Siterman, Dick Elliott, Norman Leavitt, *Jack Perrin*
D: R. G. Springsteen
SP: Frederic Louis Fox, John K. Butler
AP: William J. O'Sullivan

THE RAWHIDE YEARS (Universal-International, July 1, 1956) 85 Mins.
(Technicolor)
Tony Curtis, Colleen Miller, Arthur Kennedy, William Demarest, William Gargan, Peter Van Eyck, Monor Watson, Donald Randolph, Chubby Johnson, James Anderson, Bob Wilke, Trevor Bardette, Robert Foulk, Leigh Snowden, Don Beddoe, *Jack Perrin*, Rex Lease, Kermit Maynard
D: Rudolph Mate
S: Norman A. Fox
SP: Earl Felton, Robert Presnell, Jr., and D. D. Beauchamp
P: Stanley Rubin

REBEL IN TOWN (Bel-Air/United Artists, July 30, 1956) 78 Mins.
John Payne, Ruth Roman, J. Carrol Naish, Ben Cooper, John Smith, James Griffith, Mary Adams, Bobby Clark, Mimi Gibson, Ben Johnson, Sterling Franck, Joel Ashley, *Jack Perrin*, Kermit Maynard
D: Alfred Werker
S/SP: Danny Arnold
P: Aubrey Schenck

RUNAWAY DAUGHTERS (American International, October 21, 1956) 91 Mins.
Marla English, Anna Sten, John Litel, Lance Fuller, Adele Jergens, Mary Ellen Kay, Gloria Castillo, Jay Alder, Steven Terrell, Nicky Blair, Frank J. Gorshin, Maureen Cassidy, Reed Howes, Anne O'Neal, Edmund Cobb, Snub Pollard, *Jack Perrin*, Kermit Maynard
S: Edward L. Cahn
P: Alex Gordon
Exec. P: Samuel Z. Arkoff

GIANT (Warner Brothers, November 24, 1956) 201 Mins. (WarnerColor)
Elizabeth Taylor, Rock Hudson, James Dean, Carroll Baker, Chill Wills, Jane Withers, Mercedes McCambridge, Sal Mineo, Dennis Hopper, Judith Evelyn, Paul Fix, Rod Taylor, Earl Holliman, Robert Nichols, Alexander Scourby, Fran Bennett, Charles Watts, Eliza Cardenas, Carolyn Craig, Monte Hale, Mary Ann Edwards, Sheb Wooley, Victor Millan, Mickey Simpson, Pilar de Rey, Maurice Java, Ray Whitley, Noreen Nash, Tina Menard, Max Terhune, *Jack Perrin*, Kermit Maynard
D: George Stevens
S: Edna Ferber
SP: Fred Gudil, Ivan Moffat
P: George Stevens

TOP SECRET AFFAIR (Warner Brothers, February 9, 1957) 100 Mins.
Susan Hayward, Kirk Douglas, Paul Stewart, Jim Backus, John Cromwell, Roland Winters, A. E. Gould-Porter, Michael Fox, Frank Gerstle, Charles Lane, Richard Cutting, Hal K. Dawson, Franklyn Farnum, Lyn Osborn, Terry Frost, James Flavin, *Jack Perrin*
D: H. C. Potter
SP: Roland Kibbee and Alan Scott
P: Martin Rackin

SPIRIT OF ST. LOUIS (Warner Brothers, April 20, 1957) 138 Mins.
James Stewart, Murray Hamilton, Patricia Smith, Bartlett Robinson, Marc Connelly, Arthur Space, Charles Watts, Robert Cornthwaite, Robert Burton, Richard Deacon, Jack Daly, Paul Birch, Dabbs Greer, Harlan Warde, Carleton Young, Olin Howlin, Virginia Christine, Robert B. Williams, John Damler, Charles Tannen, *Jack Perrin*, David McMatton
D: Billy Wilder
SP: Billy Wilder and Wendell Hayes
P: Leland Hayward

OUTLAW QUEEN (Globe Releasing Corporation, April 28, 1957) 70 Mins.
Andrea King, Harry James, Robert Clarke, Jim Harakas, Andy Ladas, Kenne Duncan, I. Stanford Jolley, William Murphy, Vince Barnett, Hal Peary, John Heldering, *Jack Perrin*
D: Herbert Greene
SP: Pete La Roche
P: Ronnie Ashcroft

BOMBERS B-52 (Warner Brothers, November 1957) 106 Mins.
Karl Malden, Natalie Wood, Marsha Hunt, Efrem Zimbalist, Jr., Don Kelly, Nelson Leigh, Robert Nichols, Ray Montgomery, Bob Hover, Stuart Whitman, Michael Emmett, Robert B. Williams, Ann Doran, Steve Pendleton, James Seay, Russ Conway, Peter Leeds, Harlan Warde, John Doucette, Mort Mills, Chris Drake, Henry Kulky, Olin Howlin, Dick Elliott, *Jack Perrin*

D: Gordon Douglas
SP: Irving Wallace
P: Richard Whorf

AUNTIE MAME (Warner Brothers, December 1958) 143 Mins.
Rosalind Russell, Forrest Tucker, Coral Browne, Fred Clark, Roger Smith, Patric Knowles, Peggy Cass, Jan Handzlik, Joanna Barnes, Pippa Scott, Lee Patrick, Willard Waterman, Robin Hughes, Connie Gilchrist, Yuki Shimoda, Brook Bryon, Carol Veazie, Henry Brandon, Dub Taylor, Gregory Gay, Jack Daly, Mark Dana, Margaret Dumont, Jack Mower, Forbes Murray, *Jack Perrin*, Fred Kelsey, Chris Alexander, Ruth Warren, Barbara Pepper, Robert Gates, Paul Davis, Booth Coleman, Gladys Roach
D: Morton DaCosta
SP: Betty Comden, Adolph Green
S: Patrick Dennis

THE BUCCANEER (Paramount, December 11, 1958) 121 Mins.
Yul Brynner, Charlton Heston, Claire Bloom, Charles Boyer, Inger Stevens, Henry Hull, E. G. Marshall, Lorne Green, Ted DeCorsia, Douglass Dumbrille, Robert F. Simon, Sir Lancelot, Fran Jeffries, John Dierkes, Ken Miller, George Mathews, Leslie Bradley, Bruce Gordon, Barry Kelley, Robert Warwick, Steven Marlo, James Todd, Jerry Hartleben, Onslow Stevens, Theodora Davitt, Wally Richard, Iris Adrian, James Seay, Reginald Sheffield, Stephen Alden Chase, Julia Faye, Woody Strode, Paul Newlan, Norma Varden, John Hubbard, Brad Johnson, Harry Shannon, Henry Brandon, Billie Lee Hart, Eric Alden, Robert Carson, Peter Coe, Ashley Cowan, Roger Creed, Pamela Danova, Rex Dante, Julio DeDiego, Stewart East, Mickey Finn, Kathleen Freeman, Mimi Gibson, Leonard Graves, Raymond Greenleaf, Ed Hinton, Judd Holdren, Robin Hughes, Fred Kohler, Jr., Mike Mazurki, Jack Pennick, Ken Terrell, Franklyn Farnum, Frank Hagney, Ethan Laidlaw, Don Megowan, *Jack Perrin*, Alex Nagy, Thayer Roberts, Manuel Rojas, Carl Saxe, Chester Jones, Walter Kray, Jack Kruschen, Syl Lamont
D: Anthony Quinn
SP: Harold Lamb
P: Henry Wilcoxon

WESTBOUND (Warner Brothers, April 25, 1959) 96 Mins. (WarnerColor)
Randolph Scott, Virginia Mayo, Karen Steele, Michael Dante, Andrew Duggan, Michael Pate, Wally Brown, John Day, Walter Barnes, Fred Sherman, Mack Williams, Ed Prentiss, Rory Mallinson, Rudi Dana, Tom Monroe, *Jack Perrin*, Buddy Roosevelt, Kermit Maynard, May Boss, William A. Green, Jack E. Henderson, Felice Richmond, Creighton Hale, Gertrude Keeler, Walter Reed, Jack C. Williams, Gerald Roberts, John Hudkins, Don Happy, Bobby Herron, Fred Stromscoe
D: Budd Boetticher
S: Berne Giler and Albert Shelby LeVino
SP: Berne Giler
P: Henry Blanke

THE YOUNG PHILADELPHIANS (Warner Brothers, May 1959) 136 Mins.
Paul Newman, Barbara Rush, Alexis Smith, Brian Keith, Diane Brewster, Billie Burke, John Williams, Robert Vaughn, Otto Kruger, Paul Picerni, Robert Douglas, Frank Conroy, Adam West, Fred Eisley, Richard Deacon, Isobel Elsom, James Burke, Louise Lorimer, Lennie Bremen, David McMatton, Murray Alper, Jack Mower, *Jack Perrin*, Forbes Murray, Franklyn Farnum, Stuart Holmes
D: Vincent Sherman
SP: James Gunn
S: Richard Powell

SERGEANT RUTLEDGE (Warner Brothers, May 18, 1960) 111 Mins.
(Technicolor)
Jeffrey Hunter, Constance Towers, Woody Strode, Billie Burke, Juano Hernandez, Willis Bouchey, Carleton Young, Judson Pratt, Bill Henry, Walter Reed, Chuck Hayward, Mae Marsh, Fred Libby, Toby Richards, Jan Styne, Cliff Lyons, Charles Seal, Jack Pennick, Hank Worden, Chuck Roberson, Eva Novak, Estelle Winwood, Shug Fisher, *Jack Perrin*
SP: Willis Goldbeck, James Warner Bellah
D: John Ford
P: Patrick Ford, Willis Goldbeck

ICE PALACE (Warner Brothers, July 1960)
Richard Burton, Robert Ryan, Carolyn Jones, Martha Hyer, Jim Backus, Ray Danton, Diane McBain, Karl Swenson, Shirley Knight, Barry Kelley, Sheridan Comerate, George Takei, Steve Harris, Robert E. Griffin, I. Stanford Jolley, Lennie Breman, Sam McDaniel, David McMahon, Charles Fredericks, Judd Holdren, Franklyn Farnum, Charles Morton, *Jack Perrin*, Max Wagner, Dorcas Brower, Chester Seveck, Mrs. Chester Seveck
D: Vincent Sherman
SP: Harry Kleiner
S: Edna Ferber
P: Henry Blanke

OCEAN'S ELEVEN (Warner Brothers, August 13, 1960) 127 Mins.
Frank Sinatra, Dean Martin, Sammy Davis, Jr., Peter Lawford, Angie Dickinson, Richard Conte, Cesar Romero, Patrice Wymore, Joey Bishop, Akim Tamiroff, Henry Silva, Ilka Chase, Buddy Lester, Richard Benedict, Jean Willes, Norman Fell, Clem Harvey, Hank Henry, Robert Foulk, Lew Gallo, Charles Meredith, Gregory Gay, Don Barry, Steve Pendleton, Nelson Leigh, Murray Alper, George E. Stone, John Holland, John Craven, Carmen Phillips, Ronnie Dapo, Louis Quinn, Anne Neyland, Joan Staley, Hoot Gibson, Paul Bryar, Johnny Bennett, Red Norvo, Laura Cornell, Shiva, Barbara Sterling, Tom Middleton, Spanky Kaye, Forrest Lederer, Rummy Bishop, William Justine, *Jack Perrin*
D/P: Lewis Milestone
SP: Harry Brown, Charles Lederer
S: George Clayton Johnson and Jack Golden Russell

SUNRISE AT CAMPOBELLO (Warner Brothers, September, 1960) 143 Mins.
Ralph Bellamy, Greer Garson, Hume Cronyn, Jean Hagen, Ann Schoemaker, Alan Bunce, Tim Considine, Zina Bethune, Frank Ferguson, Pat Close, Robin Warga, Tom Carty, Lyle Talbot, David White, Walter Sande, Janine Grandel, Otis Greene, Ivan Browning, Al McGranary, Herbert Anderson, Jerry Crews, Francis DeSales, Ed Prentiss, Don Dilloway, Robert B. Williams, Jack Mower, *Jack Perrin*, William Haddock, Floyd Curtis, Jack Henderson, Ruth March, Craig Curtis, Fern Barry, Mary Benoit
D: Vincent J. Donahue
P/SP: Dore Schary

A FEVER IN THE BLOOD (Warner Brothers, January 11, 1961) 117 Mins.
Efrem Zimbalist, Jr., Angie Dickinson, Jack Kelly, Don Ameche, Ray Danton, Herbert Marshall, Andra Martin, Jesse White, Rhodes Reason, Robert Colbert, Carroll O'Connor, Parley Baer, Saundra Edwards, June Blair, Nelson Leigh, Charles Irwin, Louise Lorimer, Lennie Bremen, Ed Prentiss, Jess Kirkpatrick, David McMahon, Frank Scannell, Robert B. Williams, Fred Graham, George DeNormand, Clark Howat, *Jack Perrin*, Frank Marlowe, Thomas E. Jackson, Charles Morton, Saul Gorss
D: Vincent Sherman
SP: Roy Huggins, Harry Kleiner
S: William Pearson—"A Fever in the Blood"
P: Roy Huggins

FLOWER DRUM SONG (Ross Hunter Productions/Fields Productions/Universal, November 9, 1961) 133 Mins.
(Technicolor) (Panavision)
Nancy Kwan, James Shegeta, Juanita Hall, Jack Soo, Miyoshi Umeki, Benson Fong, Reiko Sato, Patrick Adiarte, Kam Tong, Victor Sen Yung, Soo Young, Ching Wah Lee, James Hong, Spencer Shan, Arthur Song, Weaver Levy, Herman Rudin, Cherylene Lee, Virginia Lee, Virginia Grey, Paul Sorenson, Ward Ramsey, Laurette Luez, Robert Kino, Beal Wong, Jon Fong, Willard Lee, Frank Kumagai, *Jack Perrin*
D: Henry Foster
SP: Joseph Fields
S: Richard Rodgers, Oscar Hammerstein, II, Joseph Fields—"Flower Drum Song"
P: Ross Hunter

Rex Bell

5 · REX BELL

The Fun-Loving Cowboy

Westernophiles are likely to sigh nostalgically as a fading memory is given a rejuvenating charge at the mention of Rex Bell, the fun-loving cowboy who helped make the bleak depression years a little more bearable for the whole family. Of all the hundreds of exciting simple pleasures available to boys in the 1930s, Saturday afternoon or evening at the movies was tops—taking precedent over crawdad hunts, swimmin' holes, watermelon snitchin', softball, railroad walking, snowball fights, cowboy playing, listening 'round the old family radio, girl talk, and general goofin' off. And so, too, it was a top priority for mom and dad, who put away the frustrations of a meager existence to relax for an hour or two in a dream world housed in brick and mortar. Thus movies had never been more popular than in the Thirties, and Westerns were no exception.

It was in this setting that Rex Bell made his splash as a cowboy ace; and for some, at least, his appearance was akin to the fragrance of honeysuckle drifting across the prairie, for his personality and approach to Westerns were indeed refreshing additions in the stable of sagebrush cavaliers. Seemingly Rex had about everything it took to capture and hold a sizable portion of the cactus-and-dust audience, but circumstances worked against him and he never climbed into the top ranks of movie cowboys. It was a shame, too, for he was quite talented—far more so than a number of the cowboys who achieved more fame on screen.

Rex had a winning personality and was considered one of the more handsome Hollywood actors—reason enough for the ladies to like him. Men and boys could identify with him because he was a good athlete, a good horseman, handled action well, and injected humor into his features. There were plenty of thrills and just enough romance interwoven into the formula shoot-'em-ups to appease the romantically inclined.

Rex Bell's real name was George Beldam, and he was born in Chicago on October 16, 1903. Soon after his birth the family moved to Iowa, and later on to Los Angeles where Rex attended Hollywood High School. After graduation he was working for his dad's construction firm, building sets at Fox Studios, when his good looks and excellent physique were called to the attention of William Fox. On learning of Bell's horsemanship ability, Fox heaved him into the saddle, hoping that Rex could fill the stall left vacant when Buck Jones bolted the corral.

Wild West Romance (1928) was Bell's first starring effort, and he proved to be of pleasing countenance and manner. Most of the attributes of the screen's Western heroes were his—horsemanship, athletic prowess and pep, and fans liked the six-foot, light-haired cowpoke with the twinkling blue eyes. His second starrer, *The Cowboy Kid* (1928), was a comedy Western about a young cowboy who becomes entangled in the affairs of a girl. Bell's acting was breezy and the film gaited to win the approval of the neighborhood trade or those out in the sticks were Westerns were always surefire. Next in line were *The Girl-Shy Cowboy* and *Taking a Chance*, both up to expectations as regards gun fights, romance, adventure, and all the other accessories of a wild-west drama. But by the end of 1928, studios were struggling to cope with sound; consequently outdoor productions were temporarily discontinued by most of the big studios while they attempted to solve the technical problems involved in taking sound outdoors.

Tom Mix was dropped, and moved over to FBO for his last series of silent Westerns. Rex was retained by Fox but was cast as a handsome romantic type in such films as *Joy Street* (1929), *Pleasure Crazed* (1929), *Salute* (1929), *They Had to See Paris* (1929), *Happy Days* (1929), and *Harmony at Home* (1929). On loan to Warners, he did *Courage* (1930) and then was sent to Paramount for *True to the Navy* (1931), the Clara Bow-Fredric March starrer. At the time, Clara was the "sex symbol" of the screen. Referred to as the "IT" girl, she was every bit the equal of later-day high-living, free-swinging sex goddesses. No question about it. She was really a hot number. Since she had her pick of about any man in town, it was a shock to Hollywood society when she married the relatively unknown cowboy. Predictions were that the marriage would last only a few weeks, or at the most a few months. Many said that it only represented a fling for the fun-loving, handsome young Bell.

At this time Clara had just gone through a lurid, highly publicized, court suit in which Clara charged her secretary with embezzling $16,000. The secretary was convicted on one of thirty-seven charges and spent a year in jail. A scandal sheet, *The Coast Reporter*, printed lurid stories about Bow, supposedly authored by the secretary, and was charged with sending obscene material through the mails. Another trial resulted, and shortly afterward Bow suffered a nervous breakdown and spent time in a rest sanitarium—something she would do on several other occasions. Later she recuperated at Bell's ranch, and their romance blossomed. Rex had stood by her throughout her troubles, and Clara clung to the only man she had known who seemed to have a sincere and deep feeling for her. All the others—and there had been many—turned out to be one-night-stand pleasure seekers who

disappeared into the shadows when Clara needed a friend. So on December 4, 1931, the world-renowned "IT" girl eloped with Bell to Yuma, Arizona, where they were married.

A year before the marriage, Rex had purchased a ranch in what was then a godforsaken, under-populated nether nook of nothing—Nevada. The ranch was south of Las Vegas, on the upslope of the McCulloughs, about halfway between Searchlight and Nipton. Eventually Rex ran over 5,000 cattle on roughly 600,000 acres in Nevada and California, much of the land leased from the federal government. His ranch stretched from the mountains down to the Colorado River southeast of Searchlight, with all the varieties of physical desert—dry lakes, canyons, washes, sagebrush, cactus, and the fantastic crags of the McCullough Mountains. A mammoth Joshua-tree forest blanketed the east slope of the mountains, and in the midst of this Rex and Clara built their home—Spanish, big, impressive. Two sons were born to them, Rex Anthony Bell, on December 16, 1934, and George Bell, on June 14, 1936. After making a few talking pictures, Clara permanently retired to the ranch, while Rex alternated between it and Hollywood.

Rex made a final picture for Fox in 1930, supporting Will Rogers in *Lightnin'*. It was a full year before he again was seen in a new release; and, when he did appear, he was back in Western garb as second lead in the Tom Tyler serial, *Battling with Buffalo Bill* (1931), for Universal.

In late 1931 Rex accepted an offer from Monogram to do a series. *Forgotten Women* was hardly an auspicious beginning, but it was acceptable to fans of Bell and Marion Shilling. *Law of the Sea* was much better and had Rex supporting veteran William Farnum. Then came the nine Westerns which firmly established him as a Western star in the minds of "B" afficionados who jealously withheld recognition of an actor as a "cowboy" until it was shown that he would confine himself mostly to low-budget dust stirrers.

Rex's cactus quickies succeeded in being interesting in the face of fundamental weaknesses. Obviously produced for use on a double-harness bill, they appeased the appetites of those who appreciated this type of Western fare. The stories were cut to pattern and stuck pretty close to the formula, although there were a few frills. Trem

Carr produced the series, and Harry Fraser directed several of the films. The supporting players included George F. Hayes, Charles King, Bob Kortman, Tom London, and other noted Western character actors, as well as leading ladies of the calibre of Luana Walters, Cecilia Parker, and Helen Foster. But it was Bell himself who stood out handsomely. The films might be implausible and all that, but they stepped along so briskly that the lack of probability didn't bother anyone. The Bell charm, coupled with fast-moving, action-packed tales of frontier derring-do, were enough for entertainment-craving victims of the Great Depression.

In 1935 Rex made four gun-belchers for Resolute, each featuring Ruth Mix (Tom's daughter) and Buzz Barton in support. Colony followed up in 1936 with seven Rex Bell Westerns. Independents like Resolute and Colony represented the lower end of the sagebrush spectrum, and the quality of their products varied from good to bad, with most reviewers tending to believe that the majority were bad. But the bronc fans in the hinterlands of America paid "no-never-mind" to Hollywood and Broadway film reviewers as they trudged each week to the small-town theatres to watch Rex in these "indies" which subsequently have won an established place among Western drama addicts. There was something alluringly unique about Bell's Westerns, and the passing of over four decades have not erased the pleasant memories of such quaint little sagebrushers as *The Idaho Kid, Too Much Beef, Saddle Aces,* and *Stormy Trails.* They were downright entertaining and pleasant to watch.

By 1937 Gene Autry's success with musical Westerns had made its impact, and producers were rushing to put crooners and croakers into the saddle. "Regular" cowboys found work hard to get. Those associated with indie companies were the first to become unemployed.

Rex gave up film work to concentrate on ranching and gradually became "Mr. Nevada," unofficial ambassador of goodwill for the state. His smile, warmth, and great human qualities made him one of the most popular and genuinely loved men in the state. He had unmistakable charisma long before the word became fashionable. In 1942 Rex made a brief movie comeback by playing Virgil Earp in Paramount's *Tombstone—The Town Too Tough to Die* and by supporting Buck Jones in that

Clara Bow and husband Rex Bell at the opening of "The 'It' Cafe" in Hollywood in 1937.

star's last film, *Dawn on the Great Divide.* But after that it was back to his beloved Nevada ranch.

In 1945 Rex moved to Las Vegas and opened a Western-wear store. Later he also put in one at Reno. On the civic front, Bell was active in many organizations. He had a particular fondness for scouting and held both the Silver Beaver and Silver Antelope awards for his long meritorious service to scouting. He was also a charter member of the National Cowboy Hall of Fame.

Clara Bow has a number of breakdowns over the years and eventually moved to Los Angeles and lived in an apartment near her doctor and the medical facilities she required. Insomnia plagued her for years. Although they remained married, Rex and Clara did not live together, and Clara became practically a recluse in Los Angeles.

Rex was elected Lieutenant Governor of Nevada in 1954, and reelected in 1958 in an election year when he was the only Republican elected to a major office in Nevada. In 1962 he was chosen as his party's nominee for governor. On July 4th, after an appearance at a Republican rally to boost his candidacy, he suffered a fatal heart attack. He was buried at Forest Lawn in Glendale, attired in his familiar Western business suit, a cowboy hat near his head. Clara came out of her self-imposed exile to attend the services, after which she walked over to the casket, leaned forward and kissed Rex, said a few soft words over her deceased husband, and then kissed him again. Clara herself died of a heart attack in 1965 and was buried beside her husband.

Rex Bell's saddle is empty—but not his place in the hearts of Western film addicts.

REX BELL *Filmography*

WILD WEST ROMANCE (Fox, June 10, 1928) 5 Reels.
Rex Bell, Caryl Lincoln, Neil Neely, Billy Butts, Jack Walters, Fred Parke, Albert Baffert, Geoge Pearce, Ellen Woodston
D: R. Lee Hough
Scen: Jack Cuningham
S: John Stone

THE COWBOY KID (Fox, July 15, 1928) 5 Reels.
(Lavender Sequences)
Rex Bell, Mary Jane Temple, Brooks Benedict, Alice Belcher, Joseph De Grasse, Syd Crossley, Billy Bletcher
D: Clyde Carruth
Scen: James J. Tynan
S: Harry Sinclair Drago, Seton I. Miller

THE GIRL-SHY COWBOY (Fox, August 12, 1928) 5 Reels.
(Blue Sequences)
Rex Bell, George Meeker, Patsy O'Leary, Donald Stuart, Margaret Coburn, Betty Caldwell, Joan Lyons, Ottola Nesmith
D: R. Lee Hough
Scen: James J. Tynan
S: Seton I. Miller

TAKING A CHANCE (Fox, November 18, 1928) 5 Reels.
Rex Bell, Lola Todd, Richard Carlyle, Billy Butts, Jack Byron, Martin Cichy, Jack Henderson
D: Norman Z. McLeod
Scen: A. H. Halprin
S: Bret Harte—"The Saint of Calamity Gulch"

JOY STREET (Fox, May 12, 1929) 7 Reels.
(Sound effects and music score)
Lois Moran, Nick Stuart, *Rex Bell*, Jose Crespo, Dorothy Ward, Ada Williams, Maria Alba, Sally Phipps, Florence Allen, Mabel Vail, Carol Wines, John Breeden, Marshall Ruth, James Barnes, Allen Dale, Capt. Marco Elter, Destournelles De Constant
D/S: Raymond Cannon
Adapt/Scen: Charles Condon, Frank Gay

PLEASURE CRAZED (Fox, July 7, 1929) 7 Reels.
(Sound)
Marguerite Churchill, Kenneth MacKenna, Dorothy Burgess, Campbell Gullan, Douglas Gilmore, Henry Kolker, Frederick Graham, *Rex Bell*, Charlotte Merrian
S: Donald Gallaher
Scen: Douglas Z. Doty
Supv: Philip Klein

SALUTE (Fox, September 1, 1929) 9 Reels.
George O'Brien, Helen Chandler, William Janney, Joyce Compton, Stepin Fetchit, Frank Albertson, David Butler, *Rex Bell*, John Breeden, Ward Bond, John Wayne, Lumdsen Hare, Clifford Dempsey
D: John Ford
SP: James K. McGuinness
S: Tristram Tupper, John Stone

THEY HAD TO SEE PARIS (Fox, September 8, 1929) 95 Mins.
(Sound)
Will Rogers, Irene Rich, Edgar Kennedy, Marguerite Churchill, Fifi Dorsay, Ivan Lebedeff, *Rex Bell*, Bob Kerr, Christiane Yves, Marcelle Corday, Theodore Lodi, Marcia Manon, Andre Cheron, Gregory Gaye
D: Frank Borzage
Scen: Sonya Levien

Rex Bell and friend in *Wild West Romance* (Fox, 1928).

HAPPY DAYS (Fox, September 17, 1929) 9 Reels.
(Sound)
Charles E. Evans, Marjorie White, Richard Keene, Stuart Erwin, Martha Lee Sparks, Clifford Dempsey, Janet Gaynor, Charles Farrell, Marjorie White, Victor McLaglen, El Brendel, William Collier, Sr., Tom Patricola, George Jessel, Dixie Lee, Nick Stuart, *Rex Bell*, Frank Albertson, Sharon Lynn, Jack Smith, Lew Brice, Farrell MacDonald, Will Rogers, Edmund Lowe, Walter Catlett, Frank Richardson, Ann Pennington, David Rollins, Warner Baxter, J. Harold Murray, Paul Page, The Slate Brothers, Flo Bert, James J. Corbett, George MacFarlane, George Olsen and his Orchestra, Betty Grable
D: Benjamin Stoloff
S: Sidney Lanfield

HARMONY AT HOME (Fox, December 12, 1929) 69 Mins.
(Sound)
William Collier, Sr., Dixie Lee, *Rex Bell*, Marguerite Churchill, Charlotte Henry, Charles Eaton, Elizabeth Patterson, Dot Farley
D: Hamilton McFadden
Adapt: Clare Kummer, Seton I. Miller, William Collier, Sr., Charles J. McGuirk

VOICES OF HOLLYWOOD NO. 2 (Tiffany, January 8, 1930) 1 Reel.
(Sound)
Andy Clyde, Buddy Rogers, Ernest Torrence, Sessue Hayakawa, Tom Mix, Slim Summerville, Richard Arlen, Jackie Coogan, Edwin Booth, Dickie Moore, *Rex Bell*, George Marshall, Douglas Fairbanks, "Tony"

COURAGE (Warner Brothers, May 22, 1930) 65 Mins.
Belle Bennett, Marion Nixon, *Rex Bell*, Richard Tucker, Leon Janney, Carter De Haven, Jr., Blanche Frederici, Charlotte Henry, Dorothy Ward, Byron Sage, Don Marion
D: Archie Mayo
SP: Walter Anthony

TRUE TO THE NAVY (Paramount, May 31, 1930) 70 Mins.
(Sound)
Clara Bow, Fredric March, Harry Green, *Rex Bell*, Eddie Fetherston, Eddie Dunn, Ray Cooke, Harry Sweet, Adele Windsor, Sam Hardy, Jed Prouty
D: Frank Tuttle
SP: Keene Thompson, Doris Anderson

LIGHTNIN' (Fox, November 28, 1930) 10 Reels.
Will Rogers, Louise Dresser, Joel McCrea, Helen Cohan, Jason Robards, Luke Cosgrove, J. M. Kerrigan, Ruth Warren, Sharon Lynn, Joyce Compton, *Rex Bell*, Frank Campeau, Goodee Montgomery, Philip Tead, Walter Percival, Charlotte Walker, Blanche LeClair, Bruce Warren, Antica Nast, Moon Carroll, Bess Flowers, Gwendolyn Faye, Eva Dennison, Betty Alden, Lucille Young, Betty Sinclair, Roxanne Curtis, Thomas Jefferson, The Gypsy Dancers
D: Henry King
SP: S. N. Behrman, Sonya Levien

William Farnum and Rex Bell in a melodramatic scene from *Law of the Sea* (Monogram, 1932).

BATTLING WITH BUFFALO BILL (Universal, November 23, 1931) 12 Chapters.
Tom Tyler, *Rex Bell*, Lucile Browne, William Desmond, Chief Thunderbird, Francis Ford, Yakima Canutt, Bud Osborne, John Beck, George Regas, Joe Bonomo, Jim Thorpe, Bobby Nelson, Edmund Cobb, Fred Humes, Art Mix, Franklyn Farnum
D: Ray Taylor
S: William Cody
SP: George Plympton, Ella O'Neill
P: Henry MacRae
Chapter Titles: (1) Captured by Redskins, (2) Circling Death, (3) Between Hostile Tribes, (4) The Savage Horde, (5) The Fatal Plunge, (6) Trapped, (7) The Unseen Killer, (8) Sentenced to Death, (9) The Death Trap, (10) A Shot from Ambush, (11) The Flaming Death, (12) Cheyenne Vengeance

FORGOTTEN WOMEN (Monogram, November 24, 1931) 69 Mins.
Marion Shilling, *Rex Bell*, Beryl Mercer, Carmelita Geraghty, Edna Murphy, Virginia Lee Corbin, Edward Earle
D: Richard Thorpe
S/Scen: Adele Buffington and Wellyn Totman

LAW OF THE SEA (Chadwick Productions/Monogram, January 20, 1932) 64 Mins.
William Farnum, Sally Blane, *Rex Bell*, Priscilla Dean, Eve Southern, Ralph Ince, Syd Saylor, Jack Clifford, Frank LaRue, Wally Albright
D: Otto Brower

HOLLYWOOD ON PARADE #8 (Paramount, March 9, 1932) 1 Reel.
Eddie Borden, *Rex Bell*, Mae Questal, Bela Lugosi, Charlie Murray, George Sidney, Dorothy Burgess
P: Louis Lewyn

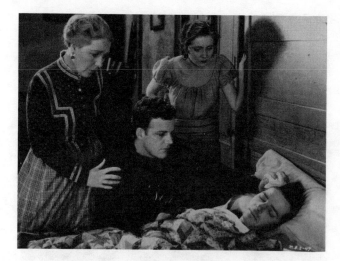

Rex Bell, Naomi Judge, and unidentified players in *The Man From Arizona* (Monogram, 1932).

ARM OF THE LAW (Monogram, April 20, 1932) 60 Mins.
Rex Bell, Lina Basquette, Dorothy Revier, Robert Frazer, Marceline Day, Gordon DeMain
D: Louis King
S: Arthur Hoerl
SP: Leon Lee
P: Trem Carr

FROM BROADWAY TO CHEYENNE (Monogram, September 10, 1932) 60 Mins.
Rex Bell, Marceline Day, Robert Ellis, Roy D'Arcy, Gwen Lee, George Hayes, Huntley Gordon, Mathew Betz, John Elliott
D: Harry Fraser
S/SP: Wellyn Totman
P: Trem Carr

THE MAN FROM ARIZONA (Monogram, October 21, 1932) 58 Mins.
Rex Bell, Charles King, Theodore Lorch, George Nash, John Elliott, Naomi Judge, Nat Carr, Les Lindsay, James Marcus, Henry Sedley, John Beck, Hank Bell, George Cooper, Bob McKenzie
D: Harry Fraser
S/SP: Wellyn Totman
P: Trem Carr

LUCKY LARRIGAN (Monogram, December 1, 1932) 58 Mins.
Rex Bell, Helen Foster, George Chesebro, John Elliott, Stanley Blystone, Julian Rivero, G. D. Wood (Gordon DeMain), Wildred Lucas
D: J. P. McCarthy
S/SP: Wellyn Totman
P: Trem Carr

THE DIAMOND TRAIL (Monogram, December 30, 1932) 60 Mins.
Rex Bell, Frances Rich, Bud Osborne, Lloyd Whitlock, Norman Feusier, Jerry Storm, John Webb Dillon, Billy West, Harry LaMont
D: Harry Fraser
SP: Harry Fraser, Sherman Lowe
P: Trem Carr

CRASHING BROADWAY (Monogram, June 1, 1933) 55 Mins.
Rex Bell, Doris Hill, Harry Bowen, George Haye., Charles King, Louis Sargent, G. D. Wood (Gordon DeMain), Ann Howard, Blackie Whiteford, Perry Murdock, Henry Rocquemore, Max Asher, Allan Lee, George Morrell, Archie Ricks, Tex Palmer
D: John P. McCarthy
SP: Wellyn Totman
P: Paul Malvern
Supv: Trem Carr

RAINBOW RANCH (Monogram, July 25, 1933) 55 Mins.
Rex Bell, Cecilia Parker, Bob Kortman, Henry Hall, George Nash, Gordon DeMain, Phil Dunham, Jerry Storm, Tiny Sanford, Van Galbert, Jackie Hoefley
D: Harry Fraser
S: Harry O. Jones (Harry Fraser)
SP: Phil Dunham
P: Trem Carr

THE FIGHTING TEXANS (Monogram, July 26, 1933) 55 Mins.
Rex Bell, Luana Walters, Betty Mack, George Hayes, Wally Wales, Yakima Canutt, Lafe McKee, Anne Howard, Al Bridge, Frank LaRue, George Nash
D: Armand Schaefer
SP: Wellyn Totman, Charles Roberts
P: Trem Carr

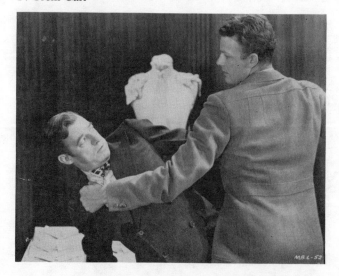

Al Bridge and Rex Bell man-to-man it in *Fighting Texans* (Monogram, 1933).

Blackie Whiteford, George Chesebro, and Charles King have the best of Rex Bell at the moment in *Crashing Broadway* (Monogram, 1933).

THE FUGITIVE (Monogram, August 1933) 56 Mins.
Rex Bell, Cecilia Parker, George Hayes, Robert Kortman, Tom London, Gordon DeMaine, Phil Dunham, Theodore Lorch, Dick Dickinson, Earl Dwire, George Nash
D: Harry Fraser
S/Adapt: Harry O. Jones

FIGHTING PIONEERS (Resolute, May 21, 1935) 60 Mins.
Rex Bell, Ruth Mix, Buss Barton, Stanley Blystone, Earl Dwire, John Elliott, Roger Williams, Guate Mozin, Chief Standing Bear, Chuck Morrison, Chief Thunder Cloud
D: Harry Fraser
S/SP: Harry Fraser, Chuck Roberts
P: Alfred T. Mannon

Rex Bell may be outlawed in *The Fugitive* (Monogram, 1933), but he has at least one faithful friend.

119

Rex Bell, James Sheridan (a.k.a. Sherry Tansey) and Earl Dwire in *Saddle Aces* (Resolute, 1935).

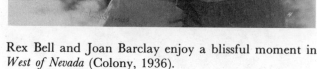

Rex Bell and Joan Barclay enjoy a blissful moment in *West of Nevada* (Colony, 1936).

GUNFIRE (Resolute, 1935).
Rex Bell, Ruth Mix, Buzz Barton, Milburn Morante, William Desmond, Theodore Lorch, Philo McCullough, Ted Adams, Lew Meehan, Jack Baston, Willie Fung, Mary Jane Irving, Fern Emmett, Howard Hickey, Chuck Morrison
D: Harry Fraser
S: Eric Howard—"Pards in Paradise"
SP: Harry C. Crist (Harry Fraser)
P: Alfred T. Mannon

SADDLE ACES (Resolute, 1935) 56 Mins.
Rex Bell, Ruth Mix, Buzz Barton, Stanley Blystone, Earl Dwire, Chuck Morrison, Mary MacLaren, John Elliott, Roger Williams, Bud Osborne, Allen Greer, Chief Thunder Cloud
D: Harry Fraser
S: J. Kaley—"Deuces Wild"
SP: Harry C. Crist (Harry Fraser)
P: Alfred T. Mannon

THE TONTO KID (Resolute, 1935).
Rex Bell, Ruth Mix, Buzz Barton, Theodore Lorch, Joseph Girard, Barbara Roberts, Jack Rockwell, Murdock McQuarrie, Bert Lindsley, Jane Keckley, Stella Adams
D: Harry Fraser
S: Christopher B. Booth—"The Daughter of Diamond D"
SP: Harry C. Crist (Harry Fraser)
P: Alfred T. Mannon

TOO MUCH BEEF (Colony, June 6, 1936) 60 Mins.
Rex Bell, Connie Bergen, Horace Murphy, Forrest Taylor, Lloyd Ingraham, Peggy O'Connell, Vincent Dennis, George Ball, Jimmy Aubrey, Jack Cowell, Fred Burns, Steve Clark, Jack Kirk, Dennis Meadows (Dennis Moore), Frank Ellis
D: Robert Hill
S: William Colt MacDonald
SP: Rock Hawley (Robert Hill)
P: Max and Arthur Alexander

WEST OF NEVADA (Colony, July 21, 1936) 57 Mins.
Rex Bell, Joan Barclay, Al St. John, Forrest Taylor, Steve Clark, Dick Bottiler, Georgia O'Dell, Frank McCarroll, Bob Woodward
D: Robert Hill
S: Charles Kyson—"Raw Gold"
SP: Rock Hawley (Robert Hill)
P: Arthur Alexander

THE IDAHO KID (Colony, August 6, 1936) 59 Mins.
Rex Bell, Marion Shilling, David Sharpe, Lane Chandler, Charles King, Lafe McKee, Earl Dwire, Phil Dunham, Dorothy Woods, Herman Hack, Edward Cassidy, George Morrell, Jimmy Aubrey, Sherry Tansey, Dick Botiller
D: Robert Hill
S: Paul Evan Lehman—"Idaho"
SP: George Plympton
P: Arthur Alexander

Rex Bell and Phil Dunham in *The Idaho Kid* (Colony, 1936).

Rex Bell and Chuck Morrison are not exactly seeing things eye to eye in *Stormy Trails* (Colony, 1936).

MEN OF THE PLAINS (Colony, September 29, 1936) 62 Mins.
Rex Bell, Joan Barclay, George Ball, Charles King, Forrest Taylor, Roger Williams, Ed Cassidy, Lafe McKee, Jack Cowell
D: Bob Hill
S/SP: Robert Emmett (Tansey)
P: Arthur and Max Alexander

LAW AND LEAD (Colony, November 15, 1936) 60 Mins.
Rex Bell, Harley Wood, Wally Wales, Lane Chandler, Earl Dwire, Soledad Jiminez, Lloyd Ingraham, Roger Williams, Karl Hackett, Edward Cassidy, Donald Reed, Lew Meehan
D: Bob Hill
S: Rock Hawley (Bob Hill)
SP: Basil Dickey
P: Arthur and Max Alexander

STORMY TRAILS (Colony, December 23, 1936) 58 Mins.
Rex Bell, Bob Hodges, Lois Wilde, Lane Chandler, Earl Dwire, Karl Hackett, Earl Ross, Lloyd Ingraham, Murdock McQuarrie, Jimmy Aubrey, Roger Williams, Chuck Morrison, George Morrell
D: Sam Newfield
S: E. B. Mann—"Stampede"
P: Arthur and Max Alexander

TOMBSTONE—THE TOWN TOO TOUGH TO DIE (Paramount, June 13, 1942) 79 Mins.
Richard Dix, Kent Taylor, Edgar Buchanan, Frances Gifford, Don Castle, Clem Bevins, Victor Jory, *Rex Bell*, Chris-Pin Martin, Jack Rockwell, Charles Stephens, Hal Taliaferro, Wallis Clark, James Ferrara, Paul Sutton, Dick Curtis, Harvey Stevens, Charles Middleton, Don Curtis, Beryl Wallace
D: William McGann
S: Dean Franklin, Charles Beisner
SP: Albert Shelby LeVino, Edward E. Paramore
P: Harry Sherman

DAWN ON THE GREAT DIVIDE (Monogram, December 18, 1942) 63 Mins.

Buck Jones, Mona Barrie, Raymond Hatton, *Rex Bell*, Robert Lowery, Harry Woods, Christine McIntyre, Betty Blythe, Robert Frazer, Tris Coffin, Jan Wiley, Roy Barcroft, Dennis Moore, Steve Clark, Reed Howes, Bud Osborne, I. Stanford Jolley, Artie Ortego, George Morrell, Milburn Morante, Ray Jones, Maude Eburne, Lee Shumway, Warren Jackson, Ben Corbett, Horace B. Carpenter, Al Haskell, Herman Hack, Denver Dixon, Merrill McCormack, "Silver"

D: Howard Bretherton

SP: Jess Bowers (Adele Buffington)

P: Scott R. Dunlap

LONE STAR (Metro-Goldwyn-Mayer, February 8, 1952) 94 Mins.

Clark Gable, Ava Gardner, Broderick Crawford, Lionel Barrymore, Beulah Bondi, Ed Begley, James Burke, William Farnum, Lowell Gilmore, Lucius Cook, Ralph Reed, Rick Roman, Victor Sutherland, Jonathan Cott, Charles Kane, Nacho Galindo, Trevor Bardette, Harry Woods, Dudley Sadler, Emmett Lynn, *Rex Bell*

D: Vincent Sherman

S/SP: Gorden Chase

P: Z. Wayne Griffin

THE MISFITS (United Artists, February 4, 1961) 124 Mins.

Clark Gable, Marilyn Monroe, Montgomery Clift, Thelma Ritter, Eli Wallich, James Barton, Estelle Winwood, Kevin McCarthy, Dennis Shaw, Philip Mitchell, Walter Ramage, Peggy Barton, J. Lewis Smith, Marietta Tree, Bobby LaSalle, Ryall Bowker, Ralph Roberts, *Rex Bell*

D: John Huston

SP: Arthur Miller

P: Frank E. Taylor

6 • HARRY CAREY

The Beloved Scout Who Pioneered the Way

Scores of milk-drinking, horse-loving, girl-shy cowboys have ridden Hollywood's cinematic trails since Broncho Billy Anderson appeared in *The Great Train Robbery* in 1903. But in the fifty years' existence of series or "B" Westerns no screen cowboy was more loved, respected, or admired than Harry Carey, one of the greatest of the great movie cowboys. He was a perennial favorite who made moviegoing such a great adventure four, five, and six decades ago. He never seemed to let his fans down, and always gave a sterling performance in spite of the sometimes incongruous dialogue and script situations handed him.

Carey was born in the Bronx, New York, on January 16, 1878, the son of a New York City judge. Little is known of his early years except that he was a good student, well adjusted, and apparently lived a normal life in a middle-class home. It was only natural that he would become interested in law. In due course he enrolled in the Hamilton Institute to study law and later transferred to New York University.

At the age of twenty-one he suffered a severe case of pneumonia and was forced to abandon, at least temporarily, thoughts of becoming a lawyer. Perhaps he would have pursued his objective had he not whiled away his time during recuperation by writing a play called *Montana*, although he had never been west until his father sent him to a

friend's ranch in Montana to convalesce. He was so taken with his writing efforts that he decided to put his play on stage and ultimately wound up both directing and starring in the play.

The play was so successful that Harry toured the eastern part of the United States for nearly three years with it in 1908, 1909, and 1910, playing what was called in those days the "ten-twenty-thirty-time." All thoughts of a law career were abandoned, and although he graduated from New York Law School (in the same class as Mayor Jimmy Walker) Carey never took the New York bar exam.

Montana was followed by a second melodrama from the Carey pen, *The Heart of Alaska*. This time he was not so fortunate with his writing, directing, and acting efforts. The play soon folded. Needing work, and now definitely intent on an acting career, Carey applied for work in the infant movie industry. So far as is known, his first work was at Biograph. *Bill Sharkey's Last Game*, a two-reeler filmed on Staten Island, is reputed to be his first film. Soon he was part of famed D. W. Griffith's stock company which consisted of Lillian and Dorothy Gish, Mae Marsh, Mary Pickford, Owen Moore, Lionel Barrymore, Blanche Sweet, Henry B. Walthall, Walter Miller, and Robert Harron. Carey remained active for Griffith for the next several years and went with him when he transferred his production to the West Coast.

Harry Carey

For several years Carey alternated between Westerns and melodramas. In 1915 he signed with Universal at $150 a week and was soon cast as a Western lead in two-reelers directed by John Ford who was just getting his start as a director. Soon Carey was appearing in three- and five-reelers, generally playing a character called "Cheyenne Harry." Often he wrote the scripts, sometimes in conjunction with Ford. By 1919 his salary had zoomed to $1,250 a week.

Carey and Ford proved a winning combination. Carey was not a young man, and, perhaps for that reason, never went in for the "showy" Westerns popularized by Mix, Thomson, and Maynard. He played up strong and often sentimental stories. Although William S. Hart is credited with creating the "realistic" Western, Carey's taciturn characterization actually predated Hart's, considering that Carey made Westerns at Biograph before Hart entered the movies. The moral rectitude of Carey's films was less than that of Hart's films. Carey never achieved the popularity of Hart, yet he continued

as a popular star and made films in the so-called "Hart mold" long after the public had tired of Hart's screen characterizations. The difference seemed to lie in the personalities of the two stars. Often likened to Will Rogers, Carey could empathize with his audience better than Hart. His personal charm somehow struck a responsive chord in his audience, and people warmed to him. That wrinkled, leathery face, those kindly eyes, and the boyishly innocent smile got to people. Also his characters were always a little more human and more flexible than those of Hart. And by no means least, Carey was a better actor than Hart. He just sort of grew on you and became a part of you without your consciously realizing it.

Desperate Trails (Universal, 1921) is an interesting example of the early work of Carey and Ford. It is typical Western fare, yet one sees shades of the later great Ford in the dramatic sequences, and it reveals that Carey is obviously capable of heavy drama. In the story, in order to protect the "brother" of a woman he thinks he loves, Carey takes the rap for a crime he didn't commit. Afterward, in prison, he learns that the brother is really a lover and that he had been duped. Carey escapes and returns with vengeance in his heart, only to give himself up to the villain's estranged wife and small son on Christmas Eve in order that they might have the reward. All ends well, however, when the temptress confesses and informs the sheriff of the real culprit.

When Carey left Universal in 1922, the Western was in a state of flux. Hart's popularity was waning, and Tom Mix was rapidly nailing down "King of the Cowboys" honors with his flashy, action-packed flickers. Hoot Gibson had been helped to stardom by Carey, and the hooter was a hot property. Carl Laemmle was so impressed by the reception Hoot received from movie patrons that he decided not to rehire Carey but instead put his money and energies into the production of Gibson Westerns. Buck Jones, too, was becoming highly popular. His Westerns were somewhat of a compromise between those of Hart and Carey on the one hand and the showmanship vehicles of Mix, Hoxie, and Acord on the other. The public seemed to prefer straightforward, nonrealistic, action-crammed range dramas, and Fred Thomson and Ken Maynard were soon to capture the Saturday matinee crowds' fancy with their acrobatics.

In spite of the trend away from realism and strong plots, however, Carey's Westerns remained unusually popular, though more so with adults than with kids. In 1922 he was forty-four years old, hardly a young man. Neither was he handsome. But he was a solid performer, his pictures were good, and people—even kids who wanted nothing but fights, riding, and stunts—came to love his craggy weatherbeaten features, the wry grin, the smiling eyes, and his taciturn characterizations. His austere visage was ideally suited to Westerns; and somehow, even back in the 1920s, it was kind of nice to see ladies treated as if they were only a little less divine than the angels. Like Hart, Carey always treated his heroines with the greatest respect—usually loving them in silence—and often riding away, heartbroken from a feeling of unworthiness to make his love known to the fair maiden. Even when his initial intentions were not honorable, his heart would be purified before the film was over—as, for example, in Pathe's *Silent Sanderson* (1925), a picture much in the Hart vein. It was convincing proof, if one needed it at this late stage in Carey's career, that he could carry off the "good badman" role just as well, if not better, than Hart, and would continue to be popular in the Hart-type characterizations until the end of the silent era.

Pathe's *Satan Town* (1926) is a great Western, reminiscent of Hart's *Hell's Hinges* made a decade earlier. Carey is at his dramatic best, and there is a balance of action and pathos in this well-constructed and beautifully photographed "B+" Western. Such films were making a profit for Pathe and providing employment for Carey long after the public had tired of Hart's austere Westerns. Heroes would come and go, but Carey was always there—there to return to when the glamorous heroes had shot their wad and ridden into the sunset for the last time.

After leaving Universal, Carey made several films for R-C Pictures in 1922–1923, then did a series for Hunt Stromberg from 1924 to 1926, and finally went to Pathe toward the end of the silent era. By this time Carey's salary had mushroomed, doubling several times since his initial employment as a cowboy star at Universal. He had no financial worries, even when his Pathe series ended in 1928. But disaster struck on March 13,

Harry Carey and his future wife, Olive Fuller Golden, in an early unidentified Universal Western.

1928, when the St. Francis Dam broke and sent an ocean of water across his ranch in the San Fernando Valley and completely wiped him out. He lost everything—buildings, cattle, sheep, and horses. In an attempt to recoup his losses, Carey and his wife, Olive, worked up a vaudeville act and hit the road. This venture was a smaller-scale disaster.

MGM came to the rescue by offering him the lead role in *Trader Horn*, the classic all-talking outdoor drama partly filmed in Africa. Carey, Olive, and their young children spent a year in Africa shooting the film. W. S. Van Dyke directed, with Harry playing Aloysius Horn, Duncan Renaldo as Peru, Edwina Booth as the white goddess, and Mutia Omoolu as Renchero the faithful native. Although the film and its crew were plagued by bad luck and MGM had to discard thousands of feet of unusable film, the finished film was a smash hit with audiences around the world. Carey was able to rebuild his ranch, but hardly had he done so when fire wiped him out again. All his buildings burned to the ground.

There was little time for tears. Carey devoted himself to his acting career, gradually recovered financially, and proved that the old cowboy was not yet ready for the pasture. Three serials for Mascot, a Western series for Artclass, and important character roles in "A" Westerns had him back in the limelight. In 1935 he starred in a series for William Berke, released on the independent market. Although cheaply produced, they were competently made horse operas with plenty of complications, fast movement, sustained suspense, and dashes of comedy. Carey, of course, easily held the center of interest. RKO starred him in the all-star Western *Powdersmoke Range* in 1935, billed as the "Barnum and Bailey of Westerns." It was followed by *The Last Outlaw* (RKO, 1935), with Carey and Hoot Gibson co-starred. And in 1938 he had the lead in RKO's exceptional programmer, *Law West of Tombstone.*

From 1936 on, Carey played important parts in a variety of features and became one of Hollywood's better character actors. In 1941 he co-starred with John Wayne in *The Shepherd of the Hills,* Paramount's popular film based on the Harold Bell Wright story. The following year the two were together in *The Spoilers* (Universal, 1942); in 1947 in *Angel and the Badman* (Republic); and in 1948 *Red River* (UA). Other big pictures for Carey were *Parachute Battalion* (RKO, 1941), *Sundown* (UA, 1941), *Airforce* (WB, 1943), *Happy Land* (Fox, 1943), *China's Little Devils* (Monogram, 1945), and *Duel in the Sun* (Selznick, 1948).

Between picture assignments Carey was in three Broadway plays—*Heavenly Express* (1940), *Ah, Wilderness* (1941), and *But not Goodbye* (1944). He also toured one season with a circus.

In 1947 Carey became ill with a heart and lung condition. A black widow spider bite complicated his condition, and on September 21 he died of coronary thrombosis. Over a thousand people attended his funeral. He was buried wearing his cowboy boots, black suit, and shoestring tie.

When John Ford remade *Three Godfathers* in 1949, he introduced it with a film clip of Carey on horseback against the setting sun and, with a footnote, dedicated it to the memory of Harry Carey, the brightest star in the Western heavens.

HARRY CAREY *Filmography*

BILL SHARKEY'S LAST GAME (O.A.C. Lund, circa 1910).
Harry Carey

GENTLEMAN JOE (American Biograph, 1910)
Harry Carey

BRUTE ISLAND (American Biograph, 1911)
Harry Carey
D: D. W. Griffith

AN UNSEEN ENEMY (American Biograph, September 7, 1912) 1 Reel.
Walter C. Miller, Lillian Gish, Dorothy Gish, Elmer Booth, Grace Henderson, Robert Harron, *Harry Carey,* Henry B. Walthall, Wallace Reid
D: D. W. Griffith
Scen: Frank Wood
S: Edward Acker
C: Billy Bitzer

FRIENDS (American Biograph, September 21, 1912).
Mary Pickford, Henry B. Walthall, Lionel Barrymore, *Harry Carey,* Charles Hill Mailes, Robert Harron
D/Scen: D. W. Griffith
C: Billy Bitzer

IN THE AISLES OF THE WILD (American Biograph, October 12, 1912) 1 Reel.
Henry B. Walthall, Claire McDowell, Lillian Gish, *Harry Carey,* Elmer Booth
D: D. W. Griffith
Scen: Stanner E. V. Taylor
S: Bret Harte
C: Billy Bitzer

MUSKETEERS OF PIG ALLEY (American Biograph, October 26, 1912).
Elmer Booth, Alfred Paget, Lillian Gish, Walter C. Miller, Miss Butler, Spike Robinson, Lionel Barrymore, *Harry Carey,* Robert Harron, Antonio Moreno, Dorothy Gish, Marie Newton, Jack Pickford, Jack Dillon, W. C. Robinson
D/Scen: D. W. Griffith
C: Billy Bitzer

HEREDITY (American Biograph, November 2, 1912) 1,015 ft.
Marion Sunshine, *Harry Carey,* Alfred Paget, Jack Pickford, Spike Robinson, George Nicholls
D: D. W. Griffith
S: George Hennessy
C: Billy Bitzer

Harry Carey (seated) and unidentified player in *Gentleman Joe* (American Biograph, 1910).

THE INFORMER (American Biograph, November 23, 1912) 1,080 ft.

Mary Pickford, Walter C. Miller, Kate Bruce, Henry B. Walthall, Gertrude Norman, Dorothy Gish, W. Christy Cabanne, *Harry Carey,* Joseph Graybill, Lionel Barrymore, Robert Harron

D: D. W. Griffith

Scen: George Hennessy

C: Billy Bitzer

THE BURGLAR'S DILEMMA (American Biograph, December 14, 1912) 998 ft.

Robert Harron, Lionel Barrymore, Henry B. Walthall, *Harry Carey,* Lillian Gish, Charles West

D: D. W. Griffith

Scen: Lionel Barrymore

C: Billy Bitzer

A CRY FOR HELP (American Biograph, December 21, 1912) 1,000 ft.

Walter C. Miller, Claire McDowell, Lionel Barrymore, *Harry Carey,* Lillian Gish, Dorothy Gish, Robert Harron

D: D. W. Griffith

Scen: Edward Acker

C: Billy Bitzer

THE GOD WITHIN (American Biograph, December 21, 1912).

Harry Carey, Blanche Sweet

D: D. W. Griffith

S: T. P. Bayer

THREE FRIENDS (American Biograph, December 28, 1912) 1 Reel.
Henry B. Walthall, Blanche Sweet, Lionel Barrymore, Jack Dillon, *Harry Carey*
D: D. W. Griffith
Scen: M. S. Reardon
C: Billy Bitzer

MY HERO (American Biograph, 1912).
Dorothy Gish, Robert Harron, Henry B. Walthall, *Harry Carey*, Charles H. Mailes, Lionel Barrymore, Kate Bruce, Walter Lewis
D: D. W. Griffith

THE TELEPHONE GIRL AND THE LADY (American Biograph, January 3, 1913).
Mae Marsh, Claire McDowell, *Harry Carey*, Alfred Paget, Lee Dougherty
D: D. W. Griffith
S: Edward Acker

PIRATE GOLD (American Biograph, January 11, 1913) 1 Reel.
J. Jiquel Lanoe, Blanche Sweet, *Harry Carey*, Donald Crisp, Wallace Reid
Scen: George Hennessy
Camera: Billy Bitzer

AN ADVENTURE IN THE AUTUMN WOODS (American Biograph, January 11, 1913).
W. Chrystie Miller, Mae Marsh, Lionel Barrymore, *Harry Carey*
Scen: W. Christy Cabanne
C: Billy Bitzer

BROTHERS (American Biograph, January 29, 1913).
Harry Carey, Mabel Normond, Mae Marsh, Wallace Reid
S: H. M. L. Nolte
D: D. W. Griffith

OIL AND WATER (American Biograph, February 1, 1913) 1,513 ft.
Henry B. Walthall, Blanche Sweet, Walter C. Miller, Lionel Barrymore, Robert Harron, Lillian Gish, Dorothy Gish, Charles Hill Mailes, Alfred Paget, *Harry Carey*, Jack Dillon
D: D. W. Griffith
Scen: E. J. Montagne
C: Billy Bitzer

A CHANCE DECEPTION (American Biograph, February 18, 1913).
Blanche Sweet, *Harry Carey*, Mildred Manning, Wilfred Lucas, Dorothy Bernard
D: Christy Cabanne
S: W. C. Cabanne
C: Billy Bitzer

LOVE IN AN APARTMENT HOTEL (American Biograph, February 22, 1913) 1 Reel.
Blanche Sweet, Henry B. Walthall, Mae Marsh, Edward Dillon, Walter C. Miller, Jack Dillon, Robert Harron, *Harry Carey*, Kate Toncray, Lionel Barrymore
D: D. W. Griffith
Scen: William M. Marston

BROKEN WAYS (American Biograph, March 1, 1913) 1 Reel.
Henry B. Walthall, Blanche Sweet, Alfred Paget, Edward Dillon, *Harry Carey*, Robert Harron, Mae Marsh
D: D. W. Griffith
Scen: T. P. Bayer

THE WRONG BOTTLE (American Biograph, March 1, 1913) 1 Reel.
Claire McDowell, Hector Dion, *Harry Carey*, Lionel Barrymore, Peal Sindelar
S: Leon J. Suckert

A GIRL'S STRATAGEM (American Biograph, March 8, 1913).
Mae Marsh, Kate Bruce, W. C. Miller, *Harry Carey*, Charles West, Del Henderson, Alfred Paget, Lionel Barrymore
D: Frank Powell
Scen: George Hennessy
Supv: S. W. Griffith

THE UNWELCOME GUEST (American Biograph, March 8, 1913) 1,004 ft.
Mary Pickford, Claire McDowell, Elmer Booth, Jack Pickford, *Harry Carey*, Lillian Gish, Walter Miller, Charles Mailes
D: D. W. Griffith
Scen: George Hennessy

NEAR TO EARTH (American Biograph, March 15, 1913).
Harry Carey, Mae Marsh, Gertrude Bambrick, Mabel Normand, Walter C. Miller, Lionel Barrymore
D: D. W. Griffith
Scen: James Orr

THE SHERIFF'S BABY (American Biograph, March 22, 1913) 1,004 ft.
Lionel Barrymore, Alfred Paget, *Harry Carey*, Dorothy Bernard, Donald Crisp, Charles Hill Mailes, Henry B. Walthall, Robert Harron, Kate Bruce, Jack Dillon, Joseph MacDermott
D: D. W. Griffith
Scen: Edward Bell

THE HERO OF LITTLE ITALY (American Biograph, March 29, 1913) 1 Reel.
Blanche Sweet, Kate Toncray, Charles West, *Harry Carey*, Charles Hill Mailes, W. J. Butler
D: D. W. Griffith
Adapt: Grace C. DeSellen

THE STOLEN BRIDE (American Biograph, April 5, 1913).
Blanche Sweet, Henry B. Walthall, Lillian Gish, *Harry Carey,*
Robert Harron
D: Tony O'Sullivan
Adapt: Kate McCabe
S: Kate McCabe

THE LEFT-HANDED MAN (American Biograph, April 19, 1913).
Lillian Gish, Charles West, *Harry Carey,* James Kirkwood
D: D. W. Griffith
Scen: Frank Woods

IF ONLY WE KNEW (American Biograph, April 26, 1913).
Blanche Sweet, Henry B. Walthall, *Harry Carey,* Mae Marsh
D: D. W. Griffith
Scen: George Hennessy

THE WANDERER (American Biograph, April 26, 1913).
Harry Carey, Lionel Barrymore
S/D: D. W. Griffith

OLAF—AN ATOM (American Biograph, May 17, 1913)
1,003 ft.
Harry Carey, Claire McDowell, Charles Hill Mailes
D: D. W. Griffith
Scen: William E. Wine

THE RANCHERO'S REVENGE (American Biograph, May 31, 1913).
Lionel Barrymore, Claire McDowell, *Harry Carey*
D: D. W. Griffith
Adapt: Charles E. Inslee

THE WELL (American Biograph, June 7, 1913).
Lionel Barrymore, *Harry Carey,* Claire McDowell
D: W. Christy Cabanne
Adapt: Minnie Meyer

THE SWITCH-TOWER (American Biograph, June 10, 1913) 1 Reel.
Lionel Barrymore, *Harry Carey*
D: D. W. Griffith
S: George Hennessy

THE SORROWFUL SHORE (American Biograph, June 28, 1913).
Harry Carey, Olive Fuller Golden
D: D. W. Griffith
Scen: W. Christy Cabanne

A GAMBLER'S HONOR (American Biograph, July 8, 1913) 1 Reel.
Harry Carey
S: *Harry Carey*

THE MISTAKE (American Biograph, July 12, 1913).
Henry B. Walthall, Charles Hill Mailes, Blanche Sweet, *Harry Carey*
D: D. W. Griffith
Scen: Anita Loos

A GAMBLER'S HONOR (American Biograph, July 8, 1913) 1 Reel.
Harry Carey
D: Tony O'Sullivan
S/Adapt: *Harry Carey*

THE MIRROR (American Biograph, July 19, 1913) 1 Reel.
Claire McDowell, Henry B. Walthall, Lionel Barrymore, *Harry Carey*
D: Dell Henderson
Scen: Frank E. Woods

UNDER THE SHADOW OF THE LAW (American Biograph, August 2, 1913).
Harry Carey
S/Adapt: *Harry Carey*

TWO MEN OF THE DESERT (American Biograph, August 16, 1913).
Harry Carey, Donald Crisp, Blanche Sweet, Henry B. Walthall, Mae Marsh, Walter Miller, Marshall Neican, Charles Hill Mailes
D: D. W. Griffith
Scen: Stanner E. V. Taylor
S: Jack London

BLACK AND WHITE (American Biograph, August 23, 1913).
Harry Carey, Donald Crisp, Grace Henderson
D: W. Christy Cabanne
Scen: William Beaudine

THE CROOK AND THE GIRL (American Biograph, August 30, 1913).
Claire McDowell, *Harry Carey,* Lionel Barrymore, Hector Dion
S/Adapt: Emil Kruschke

A MODEST HERO (American Biograph, September 6, 1913).
Lillian Gish, Walter Miller, Charles Hill Mailes, *Harry Carey*
D: D. W. Griffith
Scen: George Hennessy

THE STOLEN TREATY (American Biograph, September 13, 1913).
Claire McDowell, Dorothy Bernard, Lionel Barrymore, *Harry Carey*
S: Julia M. Purdy

A TENDER-HEARTED CROOK (American Biograph, October 4, 1913).
Claire McDowell, Charles West, *Harry Carey,* Hector Dion, Wilfred Lucas, Marion Leonard
D: Frank Powell
S: I. P. Dodge

MADONNA OF THE STORM (American Biograph, October 18, 1913) 1,000 ft.
Lillian Gish, Charles Hill Mailes, *Harry Carey*
D: D. W. Griffith
Adapt: M. B. Harvey

THE ABANDONED WELL (American Biograph, December 27, 1913) 1 Reel.
Harry Carey
D: Travers Vale
S: Paul L. Feitus

A NEST UNFEATHERED (American Biograph, February 7, 1914).
Harry Carey, Claire McDowell, Kate Bruce
Adapt: M. Krakauer

HER FATHER'S SILENT PARTNER (American Biograph, February 21, 1914).
Dorothy Gish, Claire McDowell, *Harry Carey*
D: Donald Crisp
Scen: Belle Taylor

JUDITH OF BETHULIA (American Biograph, March 8, 1914) 4 Reels.
Blanche Sweet, Henry B. Walthall, Kate Bruce, Charles Hill Mailes, Mae Marsh, Robert Harron, Lillian Gish, G. Jiguel Lanoe, *Harry Carey,* Dorothy Gish, H. Hyde, Gertrude de Babrick, Eddie Dillon, W. Chrystie Miller, Gertrude Robinson
D: D. W. Griffith
Scen: D. W. Griffith—from the Apocryphal "Book of Judith," the narrative poem "Judith and Holofernes," and the play *Judith of Bethulia* by Thomas Bailey Aldrich

THE BATTLE OF ELDERBUSH GULCH (American Biograph, March 28, 1914) 2 Reels.
Mae Marsh, Robert Harron, Henry B. Walthall, Kate Bruce, Alfred Paget, *Harry Carey* (some sources credit Carey to this film; others do not. The author has been unable to verify for certain Carey's appearance in the film)
D: D. W. Griffith
S/SP: D. W. Griffith

McVEAGH OF THE SOUTH SEAS (Progressive, November 7, 1914) 1 Reel.
Harry Carey
S: Harry Carey

THE BATTLE OF FRENCHMAN'S RUN (Vitagraph, February 8, 1915) 1 Reel.
Dorothy Kelly, George Cooper, Albert Roccardi, *Harry Carey,* Charles H. West
D: Theodore Marston
Scen: Theodore Marston
S: James Oliver Curwood

THE HEART OF A BANDIT (American Biograph, February 27, 1915) 1 Reel.
Harry Carey, Charles H. West, Violet Reid

PERILS OF THE JUNGLE (Selig, March 13, 1915) 1 Reel.
Harry Carey
D: E. A. Martin
S: Chris Lane

THE SHERIFF'S DILEMMA (American Biograph, March 26, 1915) 1 Reel.
Harry Carey

THE MISER'S LEGACY (American Biograph, April 10, 1915) 1 Reel.
Harry Carey, Charles H. West, Claire McDowell

THE GAMBLER'S I.O.U. (American Biograph, April 17, 1915) 1 Reel.
Barney Furey, Charles H. West, *Harry Carey,* Claire McDowell

A DAY'S ADVENTURE (American Biograph, May 8, 1915) 1 Reel.
Charles H. West, *Harry Carey,* Claire McDowell

TRUTH STRONGER THAN FICTION (American Biograph, May 22, 1915).
Charles H. West, *Harry Carey,* Claire McDowell, Helen Bray

HER DORMANT LOVE (American Biograph, May 29, 1915) 1 Reel.
Charles H. West, *Harry Carey,* Claire McDowell

THE WAY OUT (American Biograph, June 12, 1915) 1 Reel.
Claire McDowell, *Harry Carey,* Lewis Wells

HER CONVERT (American Biograph, June 19, 1915) 1 Reel.
Claire McDowell, *Harry Carey,* Charles H. West

AS IT HAPPENED (American Biograph, July 10, 1915) 1 Reel.
Harry Carey, Claire McDowell

JUST JIM (Universal, August 14, 1915), 4 Reels.
Harry Carey, Jean Taylor, Mr. Edmundsen, Olive Golden, William Crinley, Duke Worne, J. F. Abbott, Mr. Loraine
D/Scen: Oscar A. C. Lund

JUDGE NOT, OR THE WOMAN OF MONA DIGGINS (Universal, October 2, 1915) 6 Reels.
Harry Carey, Harry Carter, Marc Robbins, Julia Dean, Kingsley Benedict, Joe Singleton, Paul Machette, Lydia Yeamans Titus, Walter Belasco
D: Robert Leonard and Harvey Gates
S: Peter B. Kyne—"Renunciation"
AD: Joseph D. Webster

GRAFT (Universal, December 11, 1915) 20 Chapters.
Hobart Henley, *Harry Carey,* Nanine Wright, Richard Stanton, Hayward Mack, Jane Novak, Glen White, L. M. Wells, W. Horne, Mary Ruby, Edward Brown
P: Richard Stanton
S: Hugh C. Weir, Joe Brandt
Scen: Walter Woods
Chapter Titles: (1) Liquor and the Law, (2) The Tenement House Evil, (3) The Traction Grab, (4) The Power of the People, (5) Grinding Life Down, (6) The Railroad Monopoly, (7) America Saved from War, (8) Old King Coal, (9) The Insurance Swindlers, (10) The Harbor Transportation Trust, (11) The Illegal Bucket Shops, (12) The Milk Battle, (13) The Powder Trust and the War, (14) The Iron Ring, (15) The Patent Medicine Danger, (16) The Pirates of Finance, (17) Queen of the Prophets, (18) The Hidden City of Crime, (19) The Photo Badger Game, (20) The Final Conquest
(Hobart Henley starred in the first three chapters and then dropped out of the serial. Carey starred in the remaining seventeen chapters)

A KNIGHT OF THE RANGE (Universal-Red Feather, January 18, 1916) 5 Reels.
Harry Carey, Olive Fuller Golden, Hoot Gibson, Fred Church, Bill Gettinger
P: Jacques Jaccard
Scen: *Harry Carey*

A MOVIE STAR (Triangle, February 1916) 2 Reels.
Harry Carey, Mack Swain
S: Mack Sennett

STAMPEDE IN THE NIGHT (Universal-Bison, February 18, 1916) 2 Reels.
Harry Carey
P/Scen: Jacques Jaccard
S: *Harry Carey*

THE NIGHT RIDERS (Universal-Bison, February 24, 1916) 2 Reels.
Harry Carey, Hoot Gibson, Neal Hart
D/S: Jacques Jaccard

THE PASSING OF HELL'S CROWN (Universal-Bison, April 14, 1916) 2 Reels
Neal Hart, Olive Fuller Golden, *Harry Carey,* Hoot Gibson, Peggy Coudroy
Director: Jacques Jaccard
SP: Lucia Chamberlain
S: W. B. Pearson

THE THREE GODFATHERS (Universal-Bluebird, May 31, 1916) 6 Reels.
Harry Carey, Stella Razetto, George Berrell, Frank Lanning, Hart (Jack) Hoxie, Joe Rickson
D: Edward LeSaint
S: Peter B. Kyne
SP: Edward LeSaint and Harvey Gates

THE COMMITTEE ON CREDENTIALS (Universal-Bison, June 29, 1916) 3 Reels.
Harry Carey, Olive Fuller Golden
S: Peter B. Kyne
P: *Harry Carey*
Scen: Harvey Gates

LOVE'S LARIAT (Universal-Bluebird, July 12, 1916) 5 Reels.
Harry Carey, Neal Hart
SP: George E. Marshall, W. B. Pearson
P: George E. Marshall, *Harry Carey*

A WOMAN'S EYES (Universal, August 2, 1916) 1 Reel.
Harry Carey
D: George Marshall
P: George Marshall, *Harry Carey*

BLOOD MONEY (Universal-Bison, December 22, 1916) 2 Reels.
Harry Carey, Louise Lovely, Jack Richardson, William Gettinger, Vester Pegg
D: Fred Kelsey
S: *Harry Carey*

THE BAD MAN OF CHEYENNE (Universal-Bison, December 28, 1916) 2 Reels.
Harry Carey
D/Scen: Fred Kelsey
S: *Harry Carey*

THE OUTLAW AND THE LADY (Universal-Bison, January 23, 1917) 2 Reels.
Harry Carey, Louise Lovely, Jack Richardson
D: Fred A. Kelsey
S: *Harry Carey*

THE FIGHTING GRINGO (Universal-Red Feather, March, 1917) 5 Reels.
Harry Carey, Claire Du Bray, George Webb, T. D. Crittendon, Rex De Roselli, Bill Gettinger, T. Du Crow, Vester Pegg
D: Fred Kelsey
S: Henry Wallace Phillips
Scen: Maud Grange

GOIN' STRAIGHT (Universal-Bison, March 9, 1917) 2 Reels.
Harry Carey, Priscilla Dean, Vester Pegg, Teddy Brooks
D/SP: Fred A. Kelsey
S: *Harry Carey*

HAIR-TRIGGER BURK (Universal-Gold Seal, March 29, 1917) 3 Reels.
Harry Carey
D: Fred Kelsey

THE HONOR OF AN OUTLAW (Universal-Bison May, 1917) 3 Reels.
Harry Carey, Claire du Brey, T. D. Crittenden, Fred Kelsey, Jack Leonard
D: Fred A. Kelsey
S: Fred A. Kelsey

A 44-CALIBER MYSTERY (Universal-Gold Seal, May 18, 1917) 3 Reels.
Harry Carey, Hoot Gibson
(Reissued in 1922)
D: Fred Kelsey
S: T. Shelley Sutton
SP: F. A. Meredyth

THE GOLDEN BULLET (Universal-Gold Seal, June 12, 1917) 3 Reels.
Harry Carey, Fritzie Ridgeway, George Berrell, Hoot Gibson, Vester Pegg, William Gettinger
D: Fred A. Kelsey
S: T. Shelley Sutton
Scen: George Hively

THE MYSTERIOUS OUTLAW (Universal-Big U, June 11, 1917) 1 Reel
William Goettinger, Jane Bernoudy, Elizabeth James, *Harry Carey*
D: Fred A. Kelsey
S: E. B. Lewis
Scen: Karl R. Coolidge

THE WRONG MAN (Universal-Bison, June 23, 1917) 3 Reels.
Harry Carey, Hoot Gibson, Fritzie Ridgeway, George Berrell, Vester Pegg, Bill Gettinger
D: Fred A. Kelsey
S: N. P. Oakes
SP: Jack Cunningham

SIX-SHOOTER JUSTICE (Universal-Gold Seal, July 7, 1917) 3 Reels.
Harry Carey, Claire DuBrey, Bill Gettinger, Arthur Witting
D: Fred A. Kelsey
S: T. Shelley Sutton
Scen: George Hively

THE SOUL HERDER (Universal-Bison, August 7, 1917) 3 Reels.
Harry Carey, Jean Hersholt, Hoot Gibson, Fritzi Ridgeway, William Gettinger, Duke Lee, Molly Malone, Elizabeth James, Vester Pegg
D: Jack (John) Ford
S/SP: George Hively

CHEYENNE'S PAL (Universal-Star, August 13, 1917) 2 Reels.
Harry Carey, Bill Gettinger, Hoot Gibson, Vester Pegg, Gertrude Astor, Jim Corey, Steve Clemento, Ed Jones, "Cactus Pete" (a horse)
D/SP: Jack (John) Ford

STRAIGHT SHOOTING (Universal-Butterfly, August 27, 1917) 5 Reels.
Harry Carey, Mollie Malone, Duke R. Lee, Vester Pegg, Hoot Gibson, George Berrell, Ted Brooks, Milt Brown, William Gettinger
D: Jack (John) Ford
SP: George Hively

THE TEXAS SPHINX (Universal-Bison, August 31, 1917) 2 Reels.
Harry Carey, Alice Lake, Hoot Gibson, Vester Pegg
D: Fred A. Kelsey
S: T. Shelley Sutton
SP: George Hively

THE SECRET MAN (Universal-Butterfly, October 1, 1917) 5 Reels.
Harry Carey, Elizabeth Sterling, Hoot Gibson, Elizabeth James, Vester Pegg, Bill Gettinger, Steve Clemento, J. Morris Foster
D: Jack (John) Ford
W: George Hively

A MARKED MAN (Universal-Butterfly, October 19, 1917) 5 Reels.
Harry Carey, Mrs. Townsend, Mollie Malone, Vester Pegg, Bill Gettinger, Hoot Gibson, Joseph Harris, Harry L. Rattenberry
D: Jack (John) Ford
W: George Hively

BUCKING BROADWAY (Universal-Special, December 24, 1917) 5 Reels.
Harry Carey, Mollie Malone, Vester Pegg, L. M. Wells
D: Jack (John) Ford
W: George Hively
P: *Harry Carey*

THE PHANTOM RIDERS (Universal-Special, January 28, 1918) 5 Reels.
Harry Carey, Mollie Malone, Buck Connors, Vester Pegg, Bill Gettinger, Jim Corey
D: Jack (John) Ford
S: Henry MacRae
Scen: George Hively
P: *Harry Carey*

WILD WOMEN (Universal-Special, February 25, 1918) 5 Reels.
Harry Carey, Mollie Malone, Vester Pegg, Ed Jones, Martha Maddox, E. Van Beaver, W. Taylor
D: Jack (John) Ford
W: George Hively
P: *Harry Carey*

THIEVES' GOLD (Universal-Special, March 18, 1918) 5 Reels.
Harry Carey, Mollie Malone, Vester Pegg, Harry Tenbrook, M. K. Wilson, John Cook, Helen Ware, Martha Maddox
D: Jack (John) Ford
W: George Hively
S: Frederick Bechdolt—"Back to the Right Trail"

THE SCARLET DROP (Universal, April 24, 1918) 5 Reels.
Harry Carey, Molly Malone, Vester Pegg, M. K. Wilson, Betty Schade, Martha Maddox, Steve Clemento
D/S: Jack (John) Ford
Scen: George Hively

HELL BENT (Universal, June 29, 1918).
Harry Carey, Neva Gerber, Duke R. Lee, Vester Pegg, Joe Harris, M. K. Wilson, Steve Clemento
D: Jack (John) Ford
Scen/S: Jack Ford, *Harry Carey*

A WOMAN'S FOOL (Universal, August 12, 1918) 5 Reels.
Harry Carey, Mollie Malone, Betty Schade, Roy Clarke, Vester Pegg, M. K. Wilson, William Arthur Carroll
D: Jack (John) Ford
Scen: George Hively
S: Owen Wister—"Lin McLean"

THREE MOUNTED MEN (Universal, October 7, 1918) 6 Reels.
Harry Carey, Neva Gerber, Joe Harris, Harry Carter, Ella Hall
D: Jack (John) Ford
W: Eugene B. Lewis

ROPED (Universal, January 13, 1919) 6 Reels.
Harry Carey, Neva Gerber, J. Farrell McDonald, Mollie McConnell, Arthur Shirley
D: Jack (John) Ford
S: Eugene B. Lewis

HELL BENT

Duke Lee, Harry Carey, and Neva Gerber in a climactic moment from *Hell Bent* (Universal, 1918).

A FIGHT FOR LOVE (Universal-Special, March 24, 1919) 6 Reels.
Harry Carey, Neva Gerber, J. Farrell McDonald, Joe Harris, Princess Neola Mae, Mark Fenton, Betty Schade, Edith Johnson, Chief Big Tree
D: Jack (John) Ford
W: Eugene B. Lewis

BARE FISTS (Universal-Special, May 5, 1919) 6 Reels.
Harry Carey, Betty Schade, Anna Mae Walthall, Howard Ensteadt, Joseph Harris, Vester Pegg, Mollie McConnell, Joseph Girard
D: Jack (John) Ford
W: Eugene B. Lewis
P: P. A. Powers
S: Bernard McConville

RIDERS OF VENGEANCE (Universal, May 18, 1919) 6 Reels.
Harry Carey, Seena Owen, Alfred Allen, Joe Harris, J. Farrell McDonald, Jennie Lee, Vester Pegg, M. K. Wilson, Glita Lee
D: Jack (John) Ford
S: Jack Ford, *Harry Carey*
SP: Eugene B. Lewis
P: P. A. Powers

THE OUTCASTS OF POKER FLAT (Universal, July 6, 1919) 6 Reels.
Harry Carey, Cullen Landis, Gloria Hope, J. Farrell McDonald, Charles H. Mailes, Vic Potel, Joseph Harris, Louise Lester, Virginia Chester, Duke Lee, Vester Pegg
D: Jack (John) Ford
Scen: H. Tipton Steck
S: Bret Harte—"The Luck of Roaring Camp" and "Outcasts of Poker Flat"
P: P. A. Powers

ACE OF THE SADDLE (Universal, August 18, 1919) 6 Reels.
Harry Carey, Joe Harris, Duke R. Lee, Peggy Pearce, Jack Walters, Vester Pegg, Zoe Rae, Howard Ensteadt, Ed Jones, William Cartwright
D: Jack (John) Ford
S: B. J. Jackson
SP: George Hively
P: P. A. Powers

RIDER OF THE LAW (Universal, November 3, 1919) 6 Reels.
Harry Carey, Gloria Hope, Vester Pegg, Theodore Brooks, Joe Harris, Jack Woods, Duke Lee, Claire Anderson, Jennie Lee
D: Jack (John) Ford
SP: H. Tipton Steck
S: G. B. Lancaster
P: P. A. Powers

A GUN FIGHTIN' GENTLEMAN (Universal, November 30, 1919) 5 Reels.
Harry Carey, Kathleen O'Connor, J. Barney Sherry, Harry von Meter, Lydia Yeaman Titus, Duke R. Lee, Joe Harris, Theodore Brooks, Johnny Cooke
D: Jack (John) Ford
S: Jack Ford, *Harry Carey*
Scen: Hal Hoadley
P: P. A. Powers

MARKED MEN (Universal, December 21, 1919) 5 Reels.
Harry Carey, J. Farrell McDonald, Joe Harris, Winifred Westover, Ted Brooks, Charles LeMoyne, David Kirby
D: Jack (John) Ford
Scen: H. Tipton Steck
S: Peter B. Kyne—"Three Godfathers"
P: P. A. Powers

OVERLAND RED (Universal, February 19, 1920) 5 Reels.
Harry Carey, Vola Jale, Harold Goodwin, Charles LeMoyne, J. Morris Foster, Joe Harris, Capt. C. E. Anderson, David Gally
D/SP: Lynn F. Reynolds
S: N. H. Knibbs

BULLET PROOF (Universal, April 21, 1920) 5 Reels.
Harry Carey, Kathleen O'Connor, William Ryno, Fred Gamble, J. Farrell MacDonald, Beatrice Burnham, Bob McKenzie, Joe Harris, Capt. C. E. Anderson, Charles LeMoyne, Robert McKim
D/SP: Lynn F. Reynolds
S: John Frederick

HUMAN STUFF (Universal, June 16, 1920) 5 Reels.
Harry Carey, Olive Fuller Golden, Rudolph Christians, Charles LeMoyne, Joe Harris, Fontaine LaRue, Mary Charleston, Bobby Mack
D: Reeves Eason
S: Tarkington Baker
SP: Reeves Eason, *Harry Carey*

BLUE STREAK McCOY (Universal, August 16, 1920) 5 Reels.
Harry Carey, Lila Leslie, Charles Arling, "Breezy" Eason, Olive Fuller Golden, Ray Ripley, Charles LeMoyne, Ruth Royce, Ben Alexander
D: B. Reeves Eason
S: H. H. Van Loan
SP: Harvey Gates

SUNDOWN SLIM (Universal, October 7, 1920) 5 Reels.
Harry Carey, Mignonne Golden, Otto Meyers, Ed Jones, J. Morris Foster, Ted Brooks, Charles LeMoyne, Francis Conrad, Duke R. Lee, Joseph Harris, Ed Price, Genevieve Blinn
D: Val Paul
S: Henry Herbert Knibbs—"Sundown Slim"

WEST IS WEST (Universal, November 12, 1920) 5 Reels.
Harry Carey, Sue Mason, Charles LeMoyne, Joe Harris, Mignonne Golden, Ted Brooks, Ed Lattell, Otto Nelson, Jack Dill, Frank Braidwood, Arthur Millett, Adelaide Halbeck, Jim O'Neill, Scott McKee
D: Val Paul
S: Eugene Manlove Rhodes
SP: George C. Hull

HEARTS UP! (Universal, December 16, 1920) 5 Reels.
Harry Carey, Mignonne Golden, Arthur Millett, Charles LeMoyne, Frank Braidwood
D/SP: Val Paul
S: *Harry Carey*

"IF ONLY" JIM (Universal, February 28, 1921) 5 Reels.
Harry Carey, Carol Holloway, Ruth Royce, Duke Lee, Roy Coulson, Charles Brinley, George Bunny, Joseph Hazelton, Minnie Prevost, Thomas Smith, "Pal" (a dog)
D: Jacques Jaccard
Scen: George C. Hull
S: Philip Verrill Mighels—"Brewer Jim's Baby"

THE FREEZE-OUT (Universal, April 9, 1921) 5 Reels.
Harry Carey, Helen Ferguson, Joe Harris, Charles LeMoyne,
J. Farrell MacDonald, Lydia Yeamans Titus
D: Jack (John) Ford
S: George C. Hull
P: Jack Ford

THE WALLOP (Universal, May 9, 1921) 5 Reels.
Harry Carey, Mignonne Golden, William Gettinger, Charles
Le Moyne, Joe Harris, C. E. Anderson, J. Farrell MacDonald,
Mark Fenton, Noble Johnson
D: Jack (John) Ford
Scen: George C. Hull
S: Eugene Manlowe Rhodes—"The Girl He Left Behind Him"

DESPERATE TRAILS (Universal, September 7, 1921)
5 Reels.
Harry Carey, Irene Rich, Georgie Stone, Helen Field, Edward
Coxen, Barbara La Marr, George Seigman, Charles E. Insley
D: Jack (John) Ford
Scen: Elliott J. Clawson
S: Courtney Ryley Cooper—"Christmas Eve at Pilot Butte"
P: Jack Ford

THE FOX (Universal, October 11, 1921) 7 Reels.
Harry Carey, George Nichols, Gertrude Olmstead, Betty Ross
Clark, Johnny Harron, Gertrude Claire, Alan Hale, George
Cooper, Breezy Eason, Jr., Charles Le Moyne, C. E. Anderson,
Harley Chambers
D: Robert Thornby
Scen: Lucien Hubbard
S: Arthur Henry Gooden

MAN TO MAN (Universal, March 20, 1922) 6 Reels.
Harry Carey, Lillian Rich, Charles Le Moyne, Harold Goodwin,
Willis Robards
D: Stuart Paton
Scen: George C. Hull
S: Jackson Gregory—"Man to Man"

THE KICK BACK (R-C Pictures, September 3, 1922)
6 Reels.
Harry Carey, Ethel Grey Terry, Henry B. Walthall, Charles
Le Moyne, Vester Pegg, James O'Neill
D: Val Paul
Scen: George Edwardes-Hall
S: *Harry Carey*

GOOD MEN AND TRUE (R-C Pictures, November 5,
1922) 6 Reels.
Harry Carey, Vola Vale, Thomas Jefferson, Noah Beery,
Charles Le Moyne, Tully Marshall, Helen Gilmore, Jim
Wang, William Steele (Gettinger)
D: Val Paul
Adapt/Scen: George Edwardes-Hall
S: Eugene Manlowe Rhodes

Harry Carey and Marguerite Clayton in *Desert Driven*
(R-C Pictures, 1923).

CANYON OF THE FOOLS (R-C Pictures, January 21,
1923) 6 Reels.
Harry Carey, Marguerite Clayton, Fred Stanton, Joseph
Harris, Jack Curtis, Carmen Arselle, Charles Le Moyne,
Vester Pegg, Murdock MacQuarrie, Mignonne Golden
D: Val Paul
Scen: J. W. Grey
S: Richard Matthews Hallet—"The Canyon of the Fools"

CRASHIN' THRU (R-C Pictures, April 1, 1923) 6 Reels.
Harry Carey, Cullen Landis, Myrtle Stedman, Vola Vale,
Charles Le Moyne, Winifred Bryson, Joseph Harris, Donald
MacDonald, Charles Hill Mailes, Vester Pegg, Nell Craig
D: Val Paul
Adapt: Beatrice Van
S: Elizabeth Dejeans—"If a Women Will"

DESERT DRIVEN (R-C Pictures, July 8, 1923) 6 Reels.
Harry Carey, Marguerite Clayton, George Waggoner, Charles
Le Moyne, Alfred Allen, Camile Johnson, Dan Crimmins,
Catherine Key, Tom Lingham, Jack Carlyle, Jim Wang,
Ashley Cooper
D: Val Paul
Adapt: Wyndham Gittens
S: Wyndham Martin—"The Man From the Desert"

THE MIRACLE BABY (R-C Pictures, August 9, 1923)
6 Reels.
Harry Carey, Margaret Landis, Charles Le Moyne, Edward
Hearn, Hedda Nova, Edmund Cobb, Alfred Allen, Bert
Sprotte
D: Val Paul
Adapt: Isodore Bernstein, Jacques Jaccard
S: Frank Richardson Pierce—"The Miracle Baby"

THE NIGHT HAWK (Stellar Productions/Producers Distributing Corp., February 17, 1924) 6 Reels.
Harry Carey, Claire Adams, Joseph Girard, Fred Malatesta, Nicholas De Ruiz, Lee Shumway, Oreda Parrish, Billy Elmer, Myles McCarthy, Fred Kelsey, Douglas Carter
D: Stuart Paton
Adapt: Joseph Poland
S: Carlysle Graham Raht
Supv: Hunt Stromberg

THE LIGHTNING RIDER (Stellar Productions/Producers Distributing Corp., May 18, 1924) 6 Reels.
Harry Carey, Virginia Brown Faire, Thomas G. Lingham, Frances Ross, Leon Barry, Bert Hadley, Madame Sul-Te-Wan
D: Lloyd Ingraham
Adapt: Doris Dorn
S: Shannon Fife
Supv: Hunt Stromberg

TIGER THOMPSON (Stellar Productions/Producers Distributing Corp., July 13, 1924) 6 Reels.
Harry Carey, Marguerite Clayton, John Dillon, Jack Richardson, George Ring
D: B. Reeves Eason
S/Scen: Buckleigh Fritz Oxford
Supv. Hunt Stromberg

ROARING RAILS (Stellar Productions/Producers Distributing Corp., September 21, 1924) 6 Reels.
Harry Carey, Frankie Darro, Edith Roberts, Wallace MacDonald, Frank Hagney
D: Tom Forman
S: Doris Dorn, Hunt Stromberg
Supv: Hunt Stromberg

THE MAN FROM TEXAS (Stellar Productions/Producers Distributing Corp., 1924).
Harry Carey.
D: Tom Forman

THE FLAMING FORTIES (Stellar Productions/Producers Distributing Corp., December 21, 1924) 6 Reels.
Harry Carey, William Norton Bailey, Jacqueline Gadsdon, James Mason, Frank Norcross, Wilbur Higby
D: Tom Forman
Cont: Harvey Gates
SP: Elliott J. Clawson
S: Bret Harte—"Tennessee's Pardner"
Supv: Hunt Stromberg

SOFT SHOES (Stellar Productions/Producers Distributing Corp., January 1, 1925) 6 Reels.
Harry Carey, Lillian Rich, Paul Weigel, Francis Ford, Stanton Heck, Harriet Hammond, Jimmie Quinn, Sojin, Majel Coleman, John Stelling
D: Lloyd Ingraham
SP: Hunt Stromberg, Harvey Gates
S: *Harry Carey*
Supv: Hunt Stromberg

BEYOND THE BORDER (Rogstrom Productions/Producers Distributing Corp., March 2, 1925) 5 Reels.
Harry Carey, Mildred Harris, Tom Santschi, Jack Richardson, William Scott
D: Scott R. Dunlap
Adapt: Harvey Gates
S: Meredith Davis—"When Smith Meets Smith"
Supv: Hunt Stromberg

SILENT SANDERSON (Hunt Stromberg Corp./Producers Distributing Corp., April 13, 1925) 5 Reels.
Harry Carey, Trilby Clark, John Miljan, Gardner James, Edith Yorke, Stanton Heck, Sheldon Lewis
D: Scott R. Dunlap
Adapt: Harvey Gates
S: Kate Corbaley
Supv.: Hunt Stromberg

THE BAD LANDS (Hunt Stromberg Corp./Producers Distributing Corp., June 1, 1925) 5 Reels.
Harry Carey, Wilfred Lucas, Lee Shumway, Gaston Glass, Joe Rickson, Trilby Clark, Buck Black
D: Dell Henderson
S: Kate Corbaley
Adapt: Harvey Gates

THE TEXAS TRAIL (Hunt Stromberg Corp./Producers Distributing Corp., June 1, 1925).
Harry Carey, Ethel Shannon, Charles K. French, Claude Payton, Sidney Franklin
D: Scott R. Dunlap
S: Guy Morton—"Rangy Pete"
SP: Harvey Gates

THE PRAIRIE PIRATE (Hunt Stromberg Corp./Producers Distributing Corp., October 11, 1925) 5 Reels.
Harry Carey, Jean Dumas, Lloyd Whitelock, Trilby Clark, Robert Edeson, Tote Du Crow, Evelyn Selbie, Fred Kohler
D: Edmund Mortimer
Adapt: Anthony Dillon
S: W. C. Tuttle—"The Yellow Seal"

THE MAN FROM RED GULCH (Hunt Stromberg Productions/Producers Distributing Corp., December 13, 1925) 6 Reels.
Harry Carey, Harriet Hammond, Frank Campeau, Mark Hamilton, Lee Shumway, Doris Lloyd, Frank Norcross, Virginia Davis, Mickey Moore
D: Edmund Mortimer
Adapt: Elliott J. Clawson
S: Bret Harte—"The Idyll of Red Gulch"

DRIFTIN' THRU (Charles R. Rogers Productions/Pathe, February 21, 1926) 5 Reels.
Harry Carey, Stanton Heck, Ruth King, G. Raymond Nye, Joseph Girard, Harriet Hammond, Bert Woodruff
D: Scott R. Dunlap
Scen: Harvey Gates
S: Basil Dickey

THE SEVENTH BANDIT (Charles R. Rogers Productions/Pathe, April 18, 1926) 6 Reels.
Harry Carey, James Morrison, Harriet Hammond, John Webb Dillon, Trilby Clark, Walter James, Charles McHugh
D: Scott R. Dunlap
Scen: E. Richard Schayer
S: Arthur Preston Hawkins

THE FRONTIER TRAIL (Charles R. Rogers Productions/Pathe, June 20, 1926) 6 Reels.
Harry Carey, Mabel Julienne Scott, Ernest Hilliard, Frank Campeau, Nelson McDowell, Charles Mailes, Harvey Clark, Aggie Herring, Chief Big Tree
D: Scott R. Dunlap
S/Scen: E. Richard Schayer, Basil Dickey

SATAN TOWN (Charles R. Rogers Productions/Pathe, August 15, 1926).
Harry Carey, Kathleen Collins, Charles Clary, Trilby Clark, Richard Neill, Ben Hall, Charles Delaney, Ben Hendricks
D: Edmund Mortimer
Scen: Marion Jackson
S: Jack Boyle

A LITTLE JOURNEY (Metro-Goldwyn-Mayer, January 1, 1927) 7 Reels.
Claire Windsor, William Haines, *Harry Carey*, Claire McDowell, Lawford Davison
D: Robert Z. Leonard
SP: Albert Lewin
S: Rachel Crothers—"A Little Journey, A Comedy in Three Acts"

SLIDE, KELLY, SLIDE (Metro-Goldwyn-Mayer, March 12, 1927) 8 Reels.
William Haines, Sally O'Neill, *Harry Carey*, Junior Coghlan, Warner Richmond, Paul Kelly, Karl Done, Guinn "Big Boy" Williams, Mike Donlin, Irish Meusel, Bob Meusel, Tony Lazzeri
D: Edward Sedgwick
SP: A. P. Younger

BURNING BRIDGES (Charles R. Rogers Productions/Pathe, September 30, 1928) 6 Reels.
Harry Carey, Kathleen Collins, William N. Bailey, Dave Kirby, Raymond Wells, Edward Phillips, Florence Midgely, Henry A. Barrow, Sam Allen
D: James P. Hogan
Scen: Edward J. Meagher
S: Jack Boyle

THE BORDER PATROL (Charles R. Rogers Productions/Pathe, December 23, 1928) 5 Reels.
Harry Carey, Kathleen Collins, Phillips Smalley, Richard Tucker, James Neill, James Marcus
D: James P. Hogan
S/Adapt: Finis Fox

THE TRAIL OF '98 (Metro-Goldwyn-Mayer, January 5, 1929) 8,799 ft.
(Music and Sound Effects)
Dolores Del Rio, *Harry Carey*, Tully Marshall, Ralph Forbes, Tenen Holtz, Karl Dane, Russell Simpson, John Down, George Cooper, Red Thompson, Joe Bonomo, Paul Malvern, Harvey Perry, Gordon Carveth
D: Clarence Brown
S: Robert William Service—"The Trail of '98: A Northland Romance"
SP: Benjamin Glazer

TRADER HORN (Metro-Goldwyn-Mayer, January 1931).
Harry Carey, Edwina Booth, Duncan Renaldo, Mutia Omoolu, Olive Fuller Golden
D: W. S. Van Dyke
S: Aloysius Horn

THE VANISHING LEGION (Mascot, June 1, 1931) 12 Chapters.
Harry Carey, Edwina Booth, "Rex" King of Wild Horses, Frankie Darro, Philo McCullough, William Desmond, Joe Bonomo, Yakima Canutt, Edward Hearn, Al Taylor, Lafe McKee, Dick Hatton, Pete Morrison, Dick Dickinson, Bob Kortman, Paul Weigel, Frank Brownlee, Tom Dugan, Robert Walker, Olive Fuller Golden, Charlie Schaefer
D: B. Reeves Eason, Ford Beebe
S/SP: Wyndham Gittens, Ford Beebe, Helmer Bergman
P: Nat Levine
Chapter Titles: (1) The Voice from the Void, (2) The Queen of the Night, (3) The Invisible Enemy, (4) The Fatal Message, (5) The Trackless Trail, (6) The Radio Riddle, (7) The Crimson Clue, (8) The Doorway of Disaster, (9) When Time Stood Still, (10) Riding the Whirlwind, (11) The Capsule of Oblivion, (12) The Hoofs of Horror

CAVALIER OF THE WEST (Artclass, November 15, 1931) 75 Mins.
Harry Carey, Carmen LaRoux, Kane Richmond, Paul Panzer, Theodore (Ted) Adams, George Hayes, Maston Williams, Ben Corbett, Christine (Carlotta) Monti
D/S/SP: J. P. McCarthy
P: Louis Weiss

WITHOUT HONORS (Artclass, January 2, 1932) 66 Mins.
Harry Carey, Mary Jane Irving, Mae Busch, Gibson Gowland, George Hayes, Lafe McKee, Tom London, Ed Brady, Jack Richardson, Partner Jones, Lee Sage, Blackjack Ward, Jim Corey, Buck Bucko, Roy Bucko
D: William Nigh
S: Lee Sage
SP: Harry P. Crist (Harry Fraser)
P: Louis Weiss

Harry Carey and Mutia Omoolu in *Trader Horn* (Metro-Goldwyn-Mayer, 1931), the film that catapulted Carey back into the movie limelight.

LAW AND ORDER (Universal, March 7, 1932) 7 Reels. (Reissued as "Guns A'Blazing")
Walter Huston, *Harry Carey*, Raymond Hatton, Russell Hopton, Ralph Ince, Russell Simpton, Harry Woods, Dick Alexander, Andy Devine, Alphonze Ethier, Dewey Robinson, Walter Brennan, Nelson McDowell, D'Arcy Corrigan, George Dixon, Arthur Wanzer, Neal Hart, Steve Clemente
D: Edward Cahn
S: W. R. Burnett—"Saint Johnson"
SP: John Huston, Tom Reed

BORDER DEVILS (Artclass, April 4, 1932) 65 Mins.
Harry Carey, Kathleen Collins, George Hayes, Murdock Mac-Quarrie, Niles Welch, Ray Gallager, Olive Gordon, Al Smith, Maston Williams, Art Mix, Merrill McCormick, Tetsu Komai
D: William Nigh
S: Murray Lenister
SP: Harry C. Crist (Harry Fraser)
P: Louis Weiss

THE LAST OF THE MOHICANS (Mascot, May 17, 1932)
12 Chapters.
Harry Carey, Hobart Bosworth, Junior Coughlan (Frank Couglan), Edwina Booth, Lucile Browne, Walter Miller, Bob Kortman, Walter McGrail, Nelson McDowell, Edward Hearn, Mischa Auer, Yakima Canutt, Chief Big Tree, Joan Gale, Tully Marshall, Al Craver, Jewel Richford
D: B. Reeves Eason, Ford Beebe
S: James Fenimore Cooper
SP: Colbert Clark, Jack Natteford, Ford Beebe, Wyndham Gittens
C: Ernest Miller, Jack Young
P: Nat Levine
Chapter Titles: (1) Unknown, (2) Flaming Arrows, (3) Rifles or Tomahawks, (4) Riding with Death, (5) Red Shadows, (6) The Lure of Gold, (7) The Crimson Trail, (8) The Tide of Battle, (9) A Redskin's Honor, (10) The Enemy's Stronghold, (11) Paleface Magic, (12) The End of the Trail

THE NIGHT RIDER (Artclass, May 22, 1932) 72 Mins.
Harry Carey, Eleanor Fair, George Hayes, Julian Rivero, Jack Weatherby, Walter Shumway, Bob Kortman, Cliff Lyons, Tom London
D: William Nigh
SP: Harry P. Crist (Harry Fraser)
P: Louis Weiss

THE DEVIL HORSE (Mascott, November 1, 1932)
12 Chapters.
Harry Carey, Noah Beery, Frankie Darro, Greta Granstedt, Barrie O'Daniels, Edward Peil, Jack Mower, Al Bridge, Jack Byron, J. Paul Jones, Carli Russell, Lew Kelly, Dick Dickinson, Lane Chandler, Fred Burns, Yakima Canutt, Bert Goodridge, Rube Schaefer, Ken Cooper, Wes Warner, Al Taylor, Apache-King of the Wild Horses
D: Otto Brower, Richard Talmadge
SP: George Morgan, Barney Sarecky, Wyndham Gittens
P: Nat Levine
Chapter Titles: (1) Untamed, (2) The Chasm of Death, (3) The Doom Riders, (4) Vigilante Law, (5) The Silent Call, (6) The Heart of the Mystery, (7) The Battle of the Strong, (9) The Showdown, (10) The Death Trap, (11) Wild Loyalty, (12) The Double Decoy

THE THUNDERING HERD (Paramount, March 1, 1933)
59 Mins.
(Reissued as "Buffalo Stampede")
Randolph Scott, Judith Allen, Barton MacLane, *Harry Carey*, Larry "Buster" Crabbe, Dick Rush, Frank Rice, Buck Connors, Charles Murphy, Noah Beery, Sr., Raymond Hatton, Blanche Friederici, Monte Blue, Al Bridge
D: Henry Hathaway
S: Zane Grey
SP: Jack Cunningham, Mary Flannery

Harry Carey, Tom London, Robert Kortman, George F. (Gabby) Hayes, and Julian Rivero in *The Night Rider* (Artclass, 1932).

SUNSET PASS (Paramount, May 26, 1933) 16 Mins.
Randolph Scott, Tom Keene, Kathleen Burke, *Harry Carey*, Fuzzy Knight, Noah Beery, Vince Barnett, Kent Taylor, Tom London, Pat Farley, Charles Middleton, Bob Kortman, James Mason, Frank Beal, Al Bridge, Leila Bennett, Nelson McDowell, George Barbler, Patricia Farley, Christian J. Frank
D: Henry Hathaway
S: Zane Grey
SP: Jack Cunningham, Gerald Geraghty

MAN OF THE FOREST (Paramount, August 25, 1933)
62 Mins.
Randolph Scott, *Harry Carey*, Verna Hillie, Noah Beery, Larry "Buster" Crabbe, Barton MacLane, Guinn Williams, Vince Barnett, Blanche Frederici, Tempe Piggot, Tom Kennedy, Frank McGlynn, Jr., Duke Lee, Lew Kelly, Merrill McCormack
D: Henry Hathaway
S: Zane Grey
SP: Jack Cunningham, Harold Shumate

WAGON TRAIL (Ajax, April 9, 1935) 55 Mins.
Harry Carey, Gertrude Messinger, Edward Norris, Earl Dwire, Chuck Morrison, Chief Thunder Cloud, John Elliott, Roger Williams, Dick Botiller, Lew Meehan, Francis Walker, Silver Tip Baker, Allen Greer, Jack Evans, Budd Buster
D: Harry Fraser
S/SP: Monroe Talbot
P: William Berke

Harry Carey, Silver Tip Baker (with mustache), and Bob Steele in *Powdersmoke Range* (RKO-Radio, 1935).

RUSTLERS' PARADISE (Ajax, May 1, 1935) 61 Mins.
Harry Carey, Gertrude Messinger, Edmund Cobb, Carmen Bailey, Theodore Lorch, Roger Williams, Chuck Morrison, Allen Greer, Slim Whitaker, Chief Thunder Cloud
D: Harry Fraser
S: Monroe Talbot
SP: Weston Edwards
P: William Berke

POWDERSMOKE RANGE (RKO, September 27, 1935) 6 Reels.
(First of the "3 Mesquiteers" films)
Harry Carey, Hoot Gibson, Bob Steele, Tom Tyler, Guinn "Big Boy" Williams, Boots Mallory, Wally Wales, Sam Hardy, Adrian Morris, Buzz Barton, Art Mix, Frank Rice, Buddy Roosevelt, Buffalo Bill, Jr., Franklyn Farnum, William Desmond, William Farnum, Ethan Laidlaw, Eddie Dunn, Ray Meyer, Barney Furey, Bob McKenzie, James Mason, Irving Bacon, Henry Roquemore, Phil Dunham, Silver Tip Baker, Nelson McDowell, Frank Ellis
D: Wallace Fox
S: William Colt MacDonald
SP: Adele Buffington
AP: Cliff Reid

BARBARY COAST (United Artists, October 1935) 91 Mins.
Miriam Hopkins, Edward G. Robinson, Joel McCrea, Walter
Brennan, Frank Craven, Brian Donlevy, Otto Hoffman,
Rollo Lloyd, Donald Meek, Roger Gray, Clyde Cook, *Harry
Carey*, J. M. Kerrigan, Matt McHugh, Wong Chung, Russ
Powell, Frederik Vogeding, Dave Wengren, Anders Van
Haden, Jules Cowles, Cyril Thornton, Clarence Wertz, Harry
Semels, Theodore Lorch, Olin Francis, Larry Fisher, George
Simpson, Bert Sprotte, Claude Payton, Frank Benson, Bob
Stevenson, David Niven, Edward Gargan, Tom London, Art
Miles, Charles West, Heinie Conklin
D: Howard Hawks
SP: Ben Hecht, Charles MacArthur
P: Samuel Goldwyn

THE LAST OF THE CLINTONS (Ajax, November 12,
1935) 59 Mins.
Harry Carey, Betty Mack, Del Gordon, Victor Potel, Earl Dwire,
Ruth Findlay, Tom London, Slim Whitaker, Ernie Adams,
William McCall, Lafe McKee
D: Harry Fraser
S: Monroe Talbot
SP: Weston Edwards
P: William Berke

WILD MUSTANG (Ajax, 1935) 58 Mins.
Harry Carey, Barbara Fritchie, Del Gordon, Cathryn Jons,
Robert Kortman, George Chesebro, Dick Botiller, George
Morrell, Milburn Morante, Francis Walker, Budd Buster,
"Sonny" (The Marvel Horse)
D: Harry Fraser
S: Monroe Talbot
SP: Weston Edwards
P: William Berke

ACES WILD (Commodore, January 2, 1936) 57 Mins.
Harry Carey, Gertrude Messinger, Fred Toones, Phil Dunham,
Edward Cassidy, Chuck Morrison, Ted Lorch, William
McCall, Roger Williams, "Sonny" (The Marvel Horse)
D: Harry Fraser
S/SP: Monroe Talbot
P: William Berke

PRISONER OF SHARK ISLAND (20th Century Fox, Feb-
ruary 28, 1936) 95 Mins.
Warner Baxter, Gloria Stuart, Claude Gillingwater, Arthur
Byron, O. P. Heggie, *Harry Carey*, John McGuire, Francis
Ford, Francis McDonald, Paul Fix, John Carradine, J. M.
Kerrigan, Fred Kohler, Jr., Douglas Wood, Joyce Kay, Fred
Kohler, Jr., Ernest Whitman, Frank McGlynn, Sr., Frank
Shannon, Etta McDaniel, Leslie McIntyre, Arthur Loft,
Paul McVey, Maurice Murphy, Jack Pennick, Whitney
Bourne, Robert Parrish
D: John Ford
AP/SP: Nunnally Johnson

GHOST TOWN (Commodore, February 15, 1936) 60 Mins.
Harry Carey, Ruth Findlay, Jane Novak, David Sharpe, Lee
Shumway, Edward Cassidy, Roger Williams, Phil Dunham,
Earl Dwire, Chuck Morrison, "Sonny"
D: Harry Fraser
S/SP: Monroe Talbot
P: William Berke

SUTTER'S GOLD (Universal, April 9, 1936) 94 Mins.
Edward Arnold, Lee Tracy, Binnie Barnes, Katherine Alex-
ander, Montague Love, Addison Richards, John Miljan,
Robert Warwick, *Harry Carey*, Mitchell Lewis, William Janney,
Ronald Cosby, Jeannie Smith, Harry Cording, Aura DeSilva,
Byrant Washburn, William Ruhl, Pedro Regas, John Bliefer,
William Gould, Jim Thorpe, Priscilla Lawson, Oscar Apfel,
Neeley Edwards, Don Briggs, Charles Farr, Harry Stubbs,
Nan Gray, Billy Gilbert, Allen Vincent, Sidney Bracey,
Gaston Glass, Frank Reicher, Morgan Wallace, Russ Powell,
George Irving, Al Smith
D: James Cruze
S: Blaise Cendrars, Bruno Frank
SP: Jack Kirkland, Walter Woods, George O'Neil
P: Edmund Grainger

THE LAST OUTLAW (RKO, June 19, 1936) 62 Mins.
Harry Carey, Hoot Gibson, Tom Tyler, Henry B. Wathall,
Margaret Callahan, Ray Meyer, Hary Jans, Frank M. Thomas,
Russell Hopton, Frank Jenks, Maxine Jennings, Joe Sawyer,
Fred Scott
D: Christy Cabanne
S: John Ford, E. Murray Campbell
SP: John Twist, Jack Townley
P: Robert Sisk

LITTLE MISS NOBODY (20th Century Fox, June 1936)
65 Mins.
Jane Withers, Jane Darwell, Ralph Morgan, Sara Haden, *Harry
Carey*, Thomas Jackson, Jed Prouty, Clarence Wilson, Claudia
Coleman, Donald Haines, Lillian Harmer, Betty Jean Hainey,
Thomas Jackson, Jackie Murrow
D: John Blystone
P: Sol M. Wurtzel
S: Frederick Hazlitt Brennon—"The Matron's Report"
Adapt: Lou Breslow, Paul Burger, Edward Eliseu

VALIANT IS THE WORD FOR CARRIE (Paramount,
October 2, 1936) 110 Mins.
Gladys George, Arline Judge, John Howard, Dudley Digges,
Harry Carey, Isabel Jewell, Hattie McDaniel, William Collier,
Sr., John Wray, Jackie Moran, Charlene Wyatt, Maude
Eburne, Lew Payton, Grady Sutton, Janet Young, Adrienne
D'Ambricourt, Helen Lowell, Bernard Suss, George F. Hayes,
Irving Bacon, Olive Hatch, Nick Lukats
P/D: Wesley Ruggles
SP: Claude Binyon
S: Barry Benefield

THE ACCUSING FINGER (Paramount, October, 1936)
7 Reels.
Marsha Hunt, Robert Cummings, Paul Kelly, Kent Taylor, *Harry Carey*, Bernadine Hayes, Sam Flint, DeWitt Jennings, Fred Kohler, Sr., Ralf Harolde
D: James Hogan
SP: Madeleine Ruthven, Brian Marlow, John Bright, Robert Tasker

RACING LADY (RKO, January, 1937) 59 Mins.
Ann Dvorak, Smith Ballew, *Harry Carey*, Berton Churchill, Frank M. Thomas, Ray Mayer, Willie Best, Harlan Tucker, Hattie McDaniel, Harry Jans, Lew Payton
D: Wallace Fox
S: Damon Runyon—"All Scarlet" and Norman Houston and I. Robert Bren—"Odds Are Even"
Scen: Dorothy Yost, Thomas Lennon, Cortland Fitzsimmons

KID GALAHAD (Warner Brothers, March 1937) 10 Reels.
Edward G. Robinson, Bette Davis, Humphrey Bogart, Wayne Morris, Jane Bryan, *Harry Carey*, William Haade, Ben Welden, Joe Crehan, Veda Ann Borg, Frank Faylan, Hank Hankinson, Soledad Jiminez, Joe Cunningham, Harland Tucker, Bob Evans, Bob Nestell, Jack Krantz, George Blake, Charlie Sullivan, Joyce Compton, Eddie Foster, George Humbert, Emmett Vogan, I. Stanford Jolley, Harry Harvey, Lane Chandler, Don Brodie, Milton Kibbee, Ralph Dunn, Eddie Chandler, Don DeFoe (De Fore), John Shelton
D: Michael Curtiz
S: Francis Wallace
SP: Seton I. Miller

BORDER CAFE (RKO, June 4, 1937) 69 Mins.
Harry Carey, John Beal, Armida, Walter Miller, Marjorie Lord, George Irving, Leona Roberts, J. Carrol Naish, Lee Patrick, Paul Fix, Max Wagner, Alec Craig, Dudley Clements
D: Lew Landers
S: Thomas Gill—"In the Mexican Quarter"
SP: Lionel Houser
P: Robert Sisk

SOULS AT SEA (Paramount, July 1937) 90 Mins.
Gary Cooper, George Raft, Frances Dee, Henry Wilcoxen, *Harry Carey*, Olmpe Bradna, Robert Cummings, George Zucco, Virginia Weidler, Joseph Schildkraut, Lucien Littlefield, Paul Fix, Tully Marshall, Monte Blue, Stanley Fields, Lee Shumway, Charles Middleton, Lina Basquette, Robert Barrat, Porter Hall, Gilbert Emery
D: Henry Hathaway
SP: Grover Jones, Dale Van Every
S: Ted Lesser

BORN RECKLESS (20th Century Fox, July 1937) 60 Mins.
Brian Donlevy, Rochelle Hudson, Robert Kent, Barton MacLane, *Harry Carey*, Pauline Moore, Chick Chandler, William Pawley, Francis McDonald, George Wolcott, Joe Crehan
D: Malcolm St. Clair
S: Jack Andrews
SP: John Patrick, Helen Logan, Robert Ellis

ANNAPOLIS SALUTE (RKO, September 1937) 7 Reels.
James Ellison, Marsha Hunt, *Harry Carey*, Van Heflin, Ann Hovey, Authur Lake, Dick Hogan
D/S: Christy Cabanne
SP: John Twist
P: Robert Sisk

LEST WE FORGET (Metro-Goldwyn-Mayer, 1937) 1 Reel.
Harry Carey, Gary Cooper, Robert Taylor, Allan Jones
D/Scen: Frank Whitbeck
Musical Score: David Snell

DANGER PATROL (RKO, November 1937) 59 Mins.
Sally Eilers, John Beal, *Harry Carey*, Frank M. Thomas, Crawford Weaver, Lee Patrick, Edward Gargan, Paul Guilfoyle, Solly Ward
D: Lew Landers
S: Helen Vreeland, Hilda Vincent
SP: Sy Bartlett

PORT OF MISSING GIRLS (Monogram, March 1938)
63 Mins.
Judith Allen, Milburn Stone, *Harry Carey*, Betty Compson, George Cleveland, William Costello, Matty Fain, Jane Jones, Sandra Karina, Lyle Moraine
SP/D: Karl Brown
P: Lon Young

YOU AND ME (Paramount, May 1938) 90 Mins.
Sylvia Sidney, George Raft, Robert Cummings, Barton MacLane, Roscoe Karns, *Harry Carey*, George E. Stone, Warren Hymer, Guinn Williams, Carol Paige, Bernadene Hayes, Vera Gordon, Egon Breecher, Paul Newlan, Joyce Compton, Hal K. Dawson, Matt McHugh, Margaret Randall, Jack Mulhall, Sam Ash, William B. Davidson
S/P: Fritz Lang
SP: Virginia Van Upp
S: Norman Krasna

SKY GIANT (RKO, July 1938) 80 Mins.
Richard Dix, Chester Morris, *Harry Carey*, Joan Fontaine, Vicki Lester, Robert Strange, James Bush, Harold Goodwin, Gaylord Pendleton, Paul Guilfoyle, Max Hoffman, Jr., William Corson, Edwin Marr, Barry Campbell
D: Lew Landers
S/SP: Lionel Houser
P: Robert Sisk

GATEWAY (20th Century Fox, July 1938) 73 Min.
Don Ameche, Arleen Whelan, Gregory Ratoff, Binnie Barnes, Gilbert Roland, Raymond Walburn, John Carradine, Maurice Moscovich, *Harry Carey*, Marjorie Gateson, Lyle Talbot, Fritz Leiber, Warren Hymer, Eddy Conrad, E. E. Clive, Russell Hicks, Charles Coleman, Gerald Oliver Smith, Albert Conti
D: Alfred G. Werker
SP: Lamar Trotti
S: Walter Reisch
P: Samuel G. Engel

KING OF ALCATRAZ (Paramount, October 12, 1938) 56 Mins.
Gail Patrick, Lloyd Nolan, *Harry Carey*, J. Carrol Naish, Robert Preston, Anthony Quinn, Richard Stanley (Dennis Morgan), Virginia Dabney, Emory Parnell, Dorothy Howe, John Hart, Philip Warren, Porter Hall, Richard Denning, Tom Tyler, Gustav von Seyfferitz, Monte Blue, Hooper Atchley, Buddy Roosevelt, Stanley Blystone
D: Robert Florey
S/SP: Irving Reis

THE LAW WEST OF TOMBSTONE (RKO, November 18, 1938) 73 Mins.
Harry Carey, Tim Holt, Evelyn Brent, Jean Rouverol, Clarence Kolb, Esther Muir, Bradley Page, Paul Guilfoyle, Robert Moya, Allan Lane, Ward Bond, George Irving, Monte Montague, Bob Kortman, Kermit Maynard
D: Glenn Tyron
S: Clarence Upson Young
SP: John Twist, Clarence Upson Young
P: Cliff Reid

BURN 'EM UP O'CONNOR (Metro-Goldwyn-Mayer, January 1939) 70 Mins.
Dennis O'Keefe, Cecelia Parker, Nat Pendleton, *Harry Carey*, Addison Richards, Charley Grapewin, Alan Curtis, Tom Neal, Frank Orth, Tom Collins, Frank M. Thomas, Si Jenks
D: Edward Sedgwick
S: Sir Malcom Campbell
Adapt: Milton Berlin, Byron Morgan

CODE OF THE STREETS (Universal, February 1939) 72 Mins.
Harry Carey, Frankie Thomas, James McCallion, Leon Ames, Juanita Quigley, Paul Fix, Ed Brendel, Marc Lawrence, Dorothy Arnold, Stanley Hughes, Harris Berger, Hally Chester, Charles Duncan, William Benedict, David Gorcey
D: Harold Young
SP: Arthur T. Herman

STREET OF MISSING MEN (Republic, May 1939) 7 Reels.
Charles Bickford, *Harry Carey*, Tommy Ryan, Mabel Todd, Guinn Williams, Nana Bryant, Ralph Graves, John Gallaudet, Regis Toomey
D: Sidney Salkow
S: Eleanor Griffen, William Rankin
SP: Frank Dolan, Leonard Lee

INSIDE INFORMATION (Universal, June 1939) 61 Mins.
Dick Foran, June Lang, *Harry Carey*, Mary Carlisle, Addison Richards, Joe Sawyer, Grant Richards, Paul McVey, John Harmon, Selmer Jackson, Frederick Burton
D: Charles Lamont
S: Martin Mooney, Burnet Hershey—"7th Precinct"
SP: Alex Gottlieb
P: Irving Starr

MR. SMITH GOES TO WASHINGTON (Columbia, October 1939) 13 Reels.
James Stewart, Jean Arthur, Claude Rains, Edward Arnold, Guy Kibbee, Thomas Mitchell, Eugene Pallette, Beulah Bondi, *Harry Carey*, H. B. Warner, Ruth Donnally, Grant Mitchell, Porter Hall, Charles Lane, Dick Elliott, John Russell
D: Frank Capra
S: Lewis R. Foster
SP: Sidney Buchman

MY SON IS GUILTY (Columbia, December 28, 1939) 63 Mins.
Bruce Cabot, *Harry Carey*, Jacqueline Wells, Glenn Ford, Wynne Gibson, Don Beddoe, John Tyrell, Bruce Bennett, Dick Curtis, Edgar Buchanan
D: Charles Barton
S: Karl Brown
SP: Harry Shumate, Joseph Carole

OUTSIDE THE THREE MILE LIMIT (Columbia, March 7, 1940) 64 Mins.
Jack Holt, Irene Ware, *Harry Carey*, Eduardo Ciannelli, Paul Fix, Dick Purcell, Sig Ruman, Donald Briggs, Ben Welden, George J. Lewis
D: Lewis D. Collins
S: Albert DeMond
SP: Albert DeMond, Eric Taylor

BEYOND TOMORROW (Academy Productions/RKO, March 1940) 84 Mins.
Harry Carey, C. Aubrey Smith, Charles Winninger, Alex Melesh, Maria Ouspenskaya, Helen Vinson, Rod LaRocque, Richard Carlson, Jean Parker, Anthony Hughes, Robert Homans, Virginia McMullen, James Bush, William Bakewell
D: A. Edward Sutherland
S: Adele Comandini
SP: Adele Comandini, Mildred Cram
P: Lee Garmes

Alarm tinged with fright are reflected on the faces of Harry Carey and Betty Field in this tense scene from *The Shepherd of the Hills* (Paramount, 1941).

THEY KNEW WHAT THEY WANTED (RKO, 1940) 96 Mins.
Carole Lombard, Charles Laughton, William Gargan, *Harry Carey*, Frank Fay, Joe Bernard, Janet Fox, Lee Tung-Foo, Karl Malden, Victor Kilian
D: Garson Kanin
P: Erich Pommer
SP: Robert Ardrey
S: From the play by Sidney Howard

THE SHEPHERD OF THE HILLS (Paramount, July 18, 1941) 98 Mins.
John Wayne, Betty Field, *Harry Carey*, Beulah Bondi, James Barton, Samuel S. Hinds. Marjorie Main, Ward Bond, Marc Lawrence, John Qualen, Fuzzy Knight, Tom Fadden, Hank Bell, Dorothy Adams, Fern Emmet
D: Henry Hathaway
S: Harold Bell Wright
SP: Grover Jones, Stuart Anthony
P: Jack Moss

PARACHUTE BATTALION (RKO, July 1941) 75 Mins.
Robert Preston, Nancy Kelly, Edmund O'Brien, *Harry Carey*, Buddy Ebsen, Paul Kelly, Richard Cromwell, Robert Barrat, Erville Anderson, Grant Withers, Lee Bonnell, Eddie Dunn, Edward Fielding, Jack Briggs, Walter Sande, Kathryn Sheldon, Robert Smith, Wayne Whitman, Douglas Evans
D: Leslie Goodwins
SP: John Twist, Major Hugh Fite

AMONG THE LIVING (Paramount, September 1941) 67 Mins.
Albert Dekker, Susan Hayward, *Harry Carey*, Frances Farmer, Gordon Jones, Jean Phillips, Ernest Whitman, Maude Eburne, Frank M. Thomas, Harlan Briggs, Archie Twitchell, Dorothy Sebastian, William Stack, Ella Neal, Catherine Craig, Eddy Chandler, Abe Dinovitch, Jack Watson, Richard Webb, Mimi Doyle, John Kellogg, Blanche Payson, George Turner, Harry Tenbrook, Ethan Laidlaw, Charles Hamilton, Frank S. Hagney, Lee Shumway, Lane Chandler
D: Stuart Heisler
SP: Lester Cole, Garrett Fort
S: Lester Cole, Brain Marlow
AP: Colbert Clark
P: Sol C. Siegel

SUNDOWN (Wanger/United Artists, October 31, 1941) 90 Mins.
Gene Tierney, Bruce Cabot, George Sanders, *Harry Carey*, Joseph Calliea, Dorothy Dandridge, Reginald Gardner
D: Henry Hathaway
S: Barry Lyndon
SP: Charles G. Booth
P: Henry Hathaway

THE SPOILERS (Universal, April 10, 1942) 87 Mins.
Marlene Dietrich, Randolph Scott, John Wayne, Margaret Lindsay, *Harry Carey*, Richard Barthelmess, William Farnum, George Cleveland, Samuel S. Hinds, Russell Simpson, Marietta Canty, Jack Norton, Ray Bennett, Forrest Taylor, Art Miles, Charles McMurphy, Charles Halton, Bud Osborne, Robert W. Service
D: Ray Enright
S: Rex Beach
SP: Tom Reed
P: Frank Lloyd

AIRFORCE (Warner Brothers, March 20, 1943) 124 Mins.
John Garfield, Gig Young, Arthur Kennedy, Charles Drake, *Harry Carey*, George Tobias, James Brown, Stanley Ridges, Willard Robertson, Moroni Olsen, James Flavin, Faye Emerson, Addison Richards, Tom Neal, Ross Ford, Rand Brooks, James Millican, William Forrest, Henry Blair, Warren Douglas, Sol Gross, James Bush, George Offerman, Jr., Walter Sande, Theodore von Eltz, Lynne Baggett, Ann Doran
D: Howard Hawks
SP: Dudley Nichols
P: Hal B. Wallis

HAPPY LAND (20th Century Fox, November 1943) 75 Mins.
Don Ameche, Frances Dee, *Harry Carey*, Ann Rutherford, Cara Williams, Richard Crane, Henry Morgan, Dickie Moore, Minor Watson, William Weber, Oscar O'Shea, Adeline Dewalt Reynolds, Roseanne Murray, James West, Larry Olsen, Bernard Thomas, James J. Smith, Mary Wickes, Walter Baldwin, Richard Abbott, Lillian Bronson, Ferris Taylor, Larry Thompson, Paul Welgel, Ned Dobson, Jr., Jackie Averill, Joe Bernard, Housley Stevens, Milton Kibbee, John Dilson, Leigh Whipper, Marjorie Cooley, Robert Dudley, Pass LeNoir
D: Irving Pichel
P: Kenneth Macgowan
SP: Kathryn Seola, Julien Josephson
S: MacKinlay Kantor

THE GREAT MOMENT (Paramount, June 1944) 90 Mins.
Joel McCrea, Betty Field, *Harry Carey*, William Demarest, Louis Jean Heydt, Julius Tannen, Edwin Maxwell, Porter Hall, Franklin Pangborn, Grady Sutton, Donivee Lee, Harry Hayden, Torben Meyer, Vic Potel, Thurston Hall, J. Farrell MacDonald, Robert Dudley, Robert Frandsen, Sylvia Field, Reginald Sheffield, Robert Creig, Sheila Sheldon, Harry Rosenthal, Frank Moran
D/SP: Preston Sturges

CHINA'S LITTLE DEVILS (Monogram, September 1945) 74 Mins.
Harry Carey, Paul Kelly, "Ducky" Louie, Hayward Soo Hoo, Gloria Ann Chew, Fred Mah, Jr., Ralph Lewis
D: Monta Bell
P: Trem Carr and Grant Withers
SP: Sam Ornitz

ANGEL AND THE BADMAN (Republic, January 15, 1947) 100 Mins.
John Wayne, Gail Russell, *Harry Carey*, Bruce Cabot, Irene Rich, Lee Dixon, Stephen Grant, Tom Powers, Paul Hurst, Olin Howlin, John Halloran, Joan Barton, Craig Woods, Marshall Reed
D: James Edward Grant
S/SP: James Edward Grant
P: John Wayne

DUEL IN THE SUN (Selznick, April 1947) 134 Mins.
(Technicolor)
Jennifer Jones, Joseph Cotton, Gregory Peck, Lionel Barrymore, Herbert Marshall, Lillian Gish, Walter Huston, Charles Bickford, *Harry Carey*, Tilly Losch, Joan Tetzel, Sidney Blackmer, Francis McDonald, Victor Kilian, Griff Barnett, Butterfly McQueen, Frank Cordell, Scott McKay, Dan White, Otto Kruger, Steve Dunhill, Lane Chandler, Lloyd Shaw, Thomas Dillon, Robert McKenzie, Charles Kingle, Si Jenks, Kermit Maynard, Hank Worden, Hal Taliaferro, Guy Wilkerson, Rose Plummer, Johnny Bond, Hank Bell
D: King Vidor
S: Niven Busch
SP: Oliver H. P. Garrett
P: David O. Selznick

THE SEA OF GRASS (Metro-Goldwyn-Mayer, 1947)
Spencer Tracy, Katherine Hepburn, Melvyn Douglas, Phyllis Thaxter, Robert Walker, Edgar Buchanan, *Harry Carey*, James Bell, Robert Barrat, Russell Hicks, Charles Throwbridge, Robert Armstrong, Trevor Bardette, Morris Ankrum, Ruth Nelson
D: Elia Kazan
SP: Marguerite Roberts, Vincent Lawrence
S: Conrad Richter

RED RIVER (Monterey/United Artists, September 17, 1948) 125 Mins.
John Wayne, Montgomery Clift, Joanne Dru, Walter Brennan, Coleen Gray, John Ireland, Noah Beery, Jr., Chief Yowlachie, *Harry Carey, Sr.,* Harry Carey, Jr., Mickey Kuhn, Paul Fix, Hank Worden, Ivan Parry, Hal Taliaferro, Paul Fiero, Billy Self, Ray Hyke, Glenn Strange, Tom Tyler, Dan White, Lane Chandler, Lee Phelps, George Lloyd, Shelley Winters.
D: Howard Hawks
S: Borden Chase—"The Chisholm Trail" (also titled "Red River"
P: Howard Hawks

SO DEAR TO MY HEART (RKO, December 1948) 84 Mins.
Burl Ives, Beulah Bondi, Bobby Driscoll, *Harry Carey*
D: Harold Schuster
SP: John Tucker Battle
S: Sterling North

7 • BUCK JONES

An Idol Nonpareil

Author Don Miller in his book *Hollywood Corral* sums up the feeling of most Western film historians when he says:

There was about Buck Jones a mystique, an intriguing quality far apart from the rest of the cowboy performers. Astride his impressive mount Silver, silhouetted against some picturesque California cloud formations, he presented one of the more satisfying outdoor portraits. But there was more than the mere physical to Jones. Of all the Western players before and after, the feeling persists that the respect for and devotion to his milieu and his craft ran deepest in Jones.

Buck Jones was Buck Jones, and "King" and "Silver" could do no wrong—two reasons why the Jones giddyappers seldom failed at the box office in neighborhoods where juveniles were numerous. His hell-for-leather thrillers were a natural for the moppets for Buck was always the scourge of sagebrush villainy, and his films packed an unusual amount of hair-raisin' shootin'-iron stuff, slugfests, and general skullduggery. Sometimes production was just fair-to-middling; but no one seemed to mind except a few film critics, most of whom didn't like Western programmers under any circumstances. Even among critics, the consensus was that Buck Jones at his worst was pretty sure to be better than most of the Western boys' best.

Buck strove for originality, quaint touches, and new twists in his films. Sometimes these elements clicked; sometimes they didn't. At times stories were wheezened and the development slow. And like most action pictures, the Jones films contained the usual number of implausible situations and incredible stunts. But more often the Jones vehicles were snappy shoot-'em-uppers from the regular Western story batter to the red-warm plains' griddle, serving up the best elements of the good grade of old-time Westerns.

As a professional, Buck always gave his best. But he was more than just a pro. He sincerely loved the West and his job and believed that the making of "B" hoss operas was just as important, satisfying, and rewarding as working in any other type of picture. He loved the genre that made him a star and was ever loyal to it.

Buck was a small boy's idol, the larrupin' everready hero, not turning too soft at the sight of the proverbial prairie flower, and dishing out punishment with either fists or gunfire. He could be counted on to provide plenty of fodder for the kids to devour. Fights, wild rides, escapes, rescues, shootouts, comedy, and "Silver's" horsey bits were all there to make Buck's pictures the type of exciting affairs that the kids demanded. Yet there were sufficient romance, characterization, sentiment, and human touches to lift his oaters out of the ordinary cow-chip class and satisfy the more demanding adult audiences. There was little doubt that the Buck Jones Westerns possessed more box-office plausibility than the ordinary run of broncho sagas.

146

Buck Jones

Always a cinch for dualers and the grinds, the Jones films were generally able to make the grade on a solo basis in better houses. This was particularly true in those areas where family trade was paramount, and Jones films were likely to be booked into theatres not normally inclined to book "B" Westerns, for his large following was an indisputable fact. In the early 1930s he was the world's favorite cowboy, and with "Silver" he rode into the hearts of millions of people and staked out a hunk of cinema history. Youngsters, oldsters, hardened cowhands, and bank presidents cheered alike when Buck and "Silver" routed the range vipers, protected the abused lady, and either rode cavalier-like into the setting sun, or swooped the girl into his arms for the fade-out kiss. Strangely enough, the kids did not seem to mind too much when it was Buck clinching with the lovely ladies. There would be whoops and shrills when "Silver" finally nudged Buck into the receptive arms of the sagebrush sweetheart. Perhaps through Buck they were living a vicarious experience; yet, if another cowboy tried the mushy stuff, the result would likely be boos and jeers.

Five million boys are reputed to have joined the Buck Jones Rangers, a youth organizaton of the 1920s and 1930s, and in a single year he received 50,000 requests for autographed pictures from youngsters whose hero he was. At one time his fan mail exceeded that of Clark Gable and all other giants of the film world.

Buck probably did more through his exemplary life, clean films, and dedication to the welfare of impressionable youth to shape the moral fiber of adolescent boys in the 1930s than any other single individual. It was an age of heroes, and Buck Jones easily was the foremost hero of them all.

Charles Frederick Gebhard was his real name, and he was born on December 12, 1891, in Vincennes, Indiana. The family moved to Indian Territory (Oklahoma) when Buck was a baby, and it was on his dad's 3,000-acre-ranch near Red Rock that he spent his youth and learned the life of a cowboy. Wanderlust early took possession of Buck, and he joined the army at fifteen, serving on the Mexican-United States border until September 7, 1907, when his troop set sail for the Philippines to try to quell the fierce Moros who infested the jungles. Toward the end of 1909 Buck was shot in the leg during an ambush of his patrol. Discharged for disability, and barely able to walk, he returned home to recuperate. But on October 14, 1910, he signed for his second army hitch, his leg having sufficiently healed. He rose to the rank of sergeant, gained a transfer to the First Aero Squadron in hopes of becoming a pilot, but found himself a greasemonkey instead. Discouraged by not getting to fly he left the army in October of 1913, at Texas City, Texas.

The Miller Brothers 101 Ranch Wild West Show was playing Texas City, and Buck talked himself into a job of currying horses. Soon he was the show's top bronc buster. In 1914, while playing Madison Square Garden with the 101, Buck met Odelle Osborne, a beautiful young equestrienne from Philadelphia. They fell in love. And when Odelle signed with the Julia Allen Show, Buck joined too, rather than be separated from his sweetheart. Buck and Odelle were married in center ring during a performance of the show in Lima, Ohio, on August 11, 1915. They continued with the show for a while, but during World War I they settled down in Chicago where Buck worked as a horsebreaker for the British and French armies

Buck Jones and daughter Maxine (Buck Jones Wild West Show, 1929).

at a remount depot at the Chicago stockyards. Because his services were needed in this capacity, he was not drafted for military duty. After his job ended, Buck and Odelle returned to the circus world—first touring with Gollmar Brothers, and then with Ringling Brothers.

In 1918, at the end of the circus season, Buck and Odelle hit Hollywood with a twenty-dollar car and a few dollars cash. Odelle was pregnant, and they wanted to settle down. Buck easily found work at the studios. Odelle, too, was able to work as a double and rodeo performer before and after the birth of their daughter, Maxine.

Eventually Buck became part of the Tom Mix unit at Fox, after he had been prominently featured in several of Franklyn Farnum's two-reelers at Canyon Pictures. And because Tom was making demands, William Fox decided to build a second Western star, in the event that Mix decided to fly the coop. Buck was placed under contract at $150 a week. His first starring film was *The Last Straw*, released in February 1920. He quickly became a top-flight performer, and by the time he left Fox in 1928 he was making around $3,500 a week.

Buck's 62 features for Fox were mostly first-rate and mostly Western, though occasionally he put aside his cowboy duds and horse to assume non-cactus roles. And he was good in them too. Originally billed as Charles Jones, the billing soon became Charles (Buck) Jones, and, finally, just Buck Jones. He acquired "Silver" about 1922. Before that he had used black horses. He also had two other horses,

"Eagle" and "Sandy," and they, too, appeared on screen as "Silver" when doubling for the real "Silver."

As things turned out, Fox had a second goldmine in Buck Jones. His personality was quite different from that of the flamboyant Mix, yet was more palatable to a lot of people. Buck represented a sort of compromise between the austere and overrealistic films of William S. Hart and the gaudy nonrealistic pictures of Mix. He refused to dress in the type of Sunday-go-to-meeting clothes worn by Mix, preferring simple cowboy duds; and the action content of his films, though plentiful, was usually justified by the story development as opposed to the "show-off" footage injected into the Mix films. But where Buck outshined most of the other cowboys was in the acting department. He was a competent actor who could rise to the occasion when the story writers came up with something more challenging than the usual "they went that-a-way" story line.

Buck's Fox features were generally fast-moving, with good structure and acting, intelligent direction, nice backgrounding, and better-than-average photography and sound—in short, a pleasant hour for those whose photoplay interests lay in low-budget range thrillers.

In 1928 Buck voluntarily left Fox after the studio failed to honor an oral promise he was given regarding vacation salary. He formed his own production company and made *The Big Hop*, released on the states' rights market on August 31, 1928. Sound effects and synchronized music were hastily added to the completed film (more an aeroplane yarn than a Western); but it bombed at the box office, and Buck lost about $50,000. He next put together The Buck Jones Wild West Show and Roundup Days, but this too failed after struggling along for two months. Besides being a poor time in general for circuses, dishonest managers had stolen everything they could from him. He lost close to $250,000 on the venture and finished out the season with the Robbins Brothers Circus as its stellar attraction.

Scott R. Dunlap, his personal manager and oftentimes director, came to the rescue with a contract to make pictures for Sol Lesser's Beverly Productions, releasing through Columbia. His salary was only $300 a week, a mere pittance of that he had received at Fox. But in 1930, with the slump in Westerns and the tremendous problems associated with handling the cumbersome sound equipment outdoors, Buck was lucky to land any series. Even Mix's contract with Fox had not been renewed, and he had signed with FBO—quite a comedown for the cowboy who, with Buck, had literally kept the Fox studio solvent for many years.

Buck was quickly reestablished at the box office.

Within three years he shot past Ken Maynard in popularity and became the undisputed King of the Cowboys (though actually that title was not coined until Republic felt the need to hang a tag of some kind on Roy Rogers). Columbia bought up Buck's contract from Lesser, and thereafter his films were straight Columbia Westerns. Significantly Buck Jones is the only one of the silent-screen cowboys who made it big in sound Westerns and consistently worked for major studios. Maynard, McCoy, and Gibson were in-and-outers, often working for the small independents; and Mix fizzled out altogether after one series of talking pictures. But sound was what Buck needed, as he evidenced, through sound, a screen magnetism and dynamic personality comparable to that of Mix in the silent days.

Buck was able to empathize with a worldwide audience and was almost as popular abroad as he was at home. No question about it, he dominated so inclined. From 1930 to 1938, Buck made 35 Columbia features, 22 Universal features, and 4 Universal serials—every one a money-maker. At times Buck played the shy, bewildered, trusting, naive, bashful cowboy, who in the unwinding of the story invariably became aroused and provided plenty of zing in the rough-and-tumble fights—hard ridin' and heavy shootin' making up the last reel or two of the film's footage.

Though often criticized by reviewers for his attempts at comedy, Buck Jones had a comic talent that was readily accepted by his fans. Thus while reviewers sat at their typewriters grasping for words to condemn Buck's comedy, the fans poured their coins into the coffers and laughed heartily at Buck's and "Silver's" antics. No question about it—Buck satisfied the world's need for a bigger-than-life hero to ease the Depression's heart-ache, and for several years he was the undisputed number one saddle ace of the cinema.

Buck Jones looks serious as he stands by his personal railroad car (Buck Jones Wild West Show, 1929).

But times insuperably change, and success, at best, is but an ephemeral wisp of recognition before the fall into the abyss of changing tastes. Gene Autry and his imitators swept across the prairie during the years 1934–1938, plucking their guitars and exercising their vocal chords at the slightest provocation. Suddenly the singers were in, and the old-time cowboys were out. In 1938 Buck ranked third in the *Motion Picxture Herald's* poll of top Western stars, yet his contract was not renewed in spite of his standing. Studios were looking for even more guitar pickers and those with a novel gimmick of some kind.

Buck made one picture in 1939, Paramount's non-western *Unmarried*. It was the story of a broken-down prizefighter. In 1940 he played a crooked sheriff in Republic's *Wagons Westward*. It was a career at low point. At the end of the film both Buck and "Silver" perish. But then came the climb back out of the abyss. Columbia starred him in the serial *White Eagle*, released in January 1941. Although lacking in the production finesse of his Universal serials, it proved popular. As a result, Universal signed him for the million-dollar super-serial *Riders of Death Valley* as a secondary lead to Dick Foran. Having been catapulted back into the limelight, Buck was approached by Scott Dunlap with the idea of a "trio" series. The result was the formation of a production company by Dunlap and Jones to produce "The Rough Riders" series, with financing and release through Monogram. Tim McCoy and Raymond Hatton were hired as co-stars, and the series went into production in 1941. It was well received and was one of the finest produced by any studio in the Forties. Critics lauded the concept, the production quality, and the fine acting by the trio of old-timers. Buck was always given the emphasis, and "Silver," too, came in for billing.

On completion of the eight films contracted for, McCoy left the series to reenter the Army. Monogram proceeded to make a special with Buck as the star and Rex Bell and Raymond Hattan as chief support, with the intention of starring him in a series with Hatton as comedy relief. A bond-selling and publicity tour for Buck Jones followed. While in Boston, he was a guest of theatre people at the Coconut Grove Club. There, along with nearly five hundred others, Buck was trapped in the holocaust of November 28, 1942. Although taken alive from the fiery inferno, he died on Monday, November 30. It was ironic that this splendid star of sagebrush epics should die in surroundings so far removed from his beloved West.

Buck Jones was probably the most loved and most respected of all screen cowboys, and the recognition of his contributions to Western films is still ever-growing. Time only magnifies his memory and popularity with those who remember yesterday's Saturdays and a childhood never outgrown.

BUCK JONES *Filmography*

(Incomplete Listing of Unbilled Roles)

WESTERN BLOOD (Fox, April 14, 1918) 5 Reels.
Tom Mix, Victoria Forde, Pat Chrisman, Barney Fury, Frank Clark, *Buck Jones* (unbilled)
D/SP: Lynn F. Reynolds
S: Tom Mix

TRUE BLUE (Fox, May 5, 1918) 6 Reels.
William Farnum, Francis Carpenter, Charles Clary, William Scott, Genevieve Blimm, Harry Devere, G. Raymond Nye, Barney Furey, Marc Robbins, Katherine Adams, Ada Gleason, Jack Connelly, *Buck Jones* (unbilled)

THE RIDERS OF THE PURPLE SAGE (Fox, September 1, 1918) 7 Reels.
William Farnum, William Scott, M. B. Robbins, Murdock MacQuarrie, Mary Mersch, Katherine Adams, Nancy Coswell, J. Holmes, Charles Clary, *Buck Jones* (unbilled)
D/Adapt: Frank Lloyd
S: Zane Grey

THE RAINBOW TRAIL (Fox, October 13, 1918) 6 Reels.
William Farnum, Ann Forrest, Mary Mersch, William Burress, William Nye, Genevieve Blimm, George Ross, *Buck Jones* (unbilled)
D: Frank Lloyd
S: Zane Grey
SP: Charles Kenyon, Frank Lloyd

THE SHERIFF'S SON (Paramount, February 17, 1919) 5 Reels.
Charles Ray, Seena Owen, Charles K. French, Clyde Benson, Otto Hoffman, Lamar Johnstone, *Buck Jones* (unbilled)
D: Victor Schertzinger
S: William MacLeod Raine
SP: J. G. Hawks

THE PITFALLS OF A BIG CITY (Fox, April 13, 1919) 5 Reels.
William Farnum
(*Buck Jones* is reputed to have been an extra or bit player in this film but it has not been verified)
D: Frank Lloyd
S: Bennett R. Cohn

BROTHER BILL (Canyon, 1919) 2 Reels.
Franklyn Farnum, *Buck Jones*

UPHILL CLIMB (Canyon, 1919) 2 Reels.
Franklyn Farnum, *Buck Jones*

DESERT RAT (Canyon, 1919) 2 Reels.
Franklyn Farnum, *Buck Jones*

THE TWO DOYLES (Canyon, 1919) 2 Reels.
Franklyn Farnum, *Buck Jones*, Lola Maxam, Mary Bruce, Vester Pegg

WHEN PALS FALL OUT (Canyon, 1919) 2 Reels.
Franklyn Farnum, *Buck Jones*

BREEZY BOB (Canyon, 1919) 2 Reels.
Franklyn Farnum
(*Buck Jones* reported to be in this film but author unable to verify)

THE COWBOY AND THE RAJAH (Canyon, 1919) 2 Reels.
Franklyn Farnum
(*Buck Jones* reported to be in this film but author unable to verify)

THE PUNCHER AND THE PUP (Canyon, 1919) 2 Reels.
Franklyn Farnum
(*Buck Jones* reported to be in this film but author unable to verify)

VENGEANCE AND THE GIRL (Canyon, 1919) 2 Reels.
Franklyn Farnum
(*Buck Jones* reported to be in this film but author unable to verify)

CUPID'S ROUND-UP (Canyon, 1919) 2 Reels.
Franklyn Farnum
(*Buck Jones* reported to be in this film but author unable to verify)

SHACKLES OF FATE (Canyon, 1919) 2 Reels.
Franklyn Farnum
(*Buck Jones* reported to be in this film but author unable to verify)

THE WILDERNESS TRAIL (Fox, July 6, 1919) 5 Reels.
Tom Mix, Colleen Moore, Jack Nelson, Sid Jordan, George Nichols, Frank Clark, Pat Chrisman, *Buck Jones*
D: Edward J. LeSaint
S: Frank Williams
SP: Charles Kenyon

SPEED MANIAC (Fox, October 19, 1919) 5 Reels.
Tom Mix, Eva Novak, Charles K. French, Hayward Mack, L. C. Shumway, Helen Wright, Jack Curtis, Georgie Stone, George Hackathron, Ernest Shields, Charles Hill Mailes, *Buck Jones*
D: Edward J. LeSaint
S: H. H. Van Loan
SP: Denison Clift

THE CYCLONE (Fox, January 25, 1920) 5 Reels.
Tom Mix, Colleen Moore, William Ellingford, *Buck Jones*
D: Cliff Smith
SP: J. Anthony Roach

THE LAST STRAW (Fox, February 8, 1920) 5 Reels.
Buck Jones, Vivian Rich, Jane Tallent, Colin Kenny, Charles LeMoyne, Robert Chandler, Bill Gillis, H. W. Padgett, Hank Bell, Lon Poff, Zeib Morris
SP/D: Charles Swickard
S: Harold Titus

FORBIDDEN TRAILS (Fox, May 16, 1920) 5 Reels.
Buck Jones, Winifred Westover, Stanton Heck, William Elmer, George Kunkel, Fred Herzog
SP/D: Scott R. Dunlap
S: Charles Alden Seltzer

THE SQUARE SHOOTER (Fox, August 8, 1920) 5 Reels.
Buck Jones, Patsy DeForrest, Charles K. French, Al Fremont, Frederick Starr, Edwin Booth Tilton, Ernest Shields, Charles Force, Lon Poff, Orpha Alba
D: Paul Cazeneuve
S/SP: Denison Clift

FIREBRAND TREVISON (Fox, September 5, 1920) 5 Reels.
(Tinted Sequences)
Buck Jones, Winifred Westover, Martha Mattox, Stanton Heck, Katherine Van Buren, Frank Clark, Joe Ray, Pat Harnman, Fong Hong
D: Thomas Heffron
S: Charles Alden Seltzer
SP: Denison Clift

SUNSET SPRAGUE (Fox, October 3, 1920) 5 Reels.
Buck Jones, Patsy De Forrest, H. J. Hebert, Gloria Payton, Edwin Booth Tilton, Josie Sedgwick, Jack Rollens, Gus Soville, Hoble Johnson
D: Thomas Heffron, Paul Gazeneuve
S/SP: Clyde C. Westover

JUST PALS (Fox, November 14, 1920) 5 Reels.
Buck Jones, Helen Ferguson, George Stone, Duke R. Lee, William Buckley, Edwin Booth Tilton, Eunice Murdock Moore, Bert Apling, Slim Padgett, Pedro Leon, Ida Tenbrook, John J. Cooke, Helen Field
D: John Ford
S: John McDermott
SP: Paul Schofield

TWO MOONS (Fox, December 19, 1920) 5 Reels.
Buck Jones, Carol Holloway, Gus Saville, Edward Peil, Bert Sprotte, Slim Padgett, William Ellingford, Dick LaRens, May Foster, Billy Fay, Jim O'Neil, Eunice Murdock Moore, Edwin Booth Tilton, Louis Fitzroy, Eleanor Gilmore
D/Adapt.: Edward J. LeSaint
S: Robert Welles Ritchie

HOLLYWOOD TODAY #4 (Circa late 1920s) 1 Reel.
Tom Mix and "Tony," Bessie Love, *Buck Jones*, and other Hollywood personalities in brief glimpses at work and play

Buck Jones and Winifred Westover in *Firebrand Trevison* (Fox, 1920).

THE BIG PUNCH (Fox, January 30, 1921) 5 Reels.
Buck Jones, Barbara Bedford, George Siegman, Jack Curtis, Jack McDonald, Al Fremont, Jennie Lee, Edgar Jones, Irene Hunt, Eleanor Gilmore
D: John Ford
S/SP: Jules G. Furthman

THE ONE MAN TRAIL (Fox, March 27, 1921) 5 Reels.
Buck Jones, Beatrice Burnham, Helene Rosson, James Farley
D: Bernard J. Durning
S: Jack Strumwasser, Clyde C. Westover
SP: William K. Howard

GET YOUR MAN (Fox, May 22, 1921) 5 Reels.
Buck Jones, William Lawrence, Beatrice Burnham, Helen Bosson, Paul Kamp
D: George W. Hill, William K. Howard
S: Alan Sullivan
SP: John Montague

STRAIGHT FROM THE SHOULDER (Fox, June 19, 1921) 6 Reels.
Buck Jones, Helen Ferguson, Norman Selby, Frances Hatton, Herschel Mayall, Yvette Mitchell, G. Raymond Nye, Glen Cavender, Dan Crimmins, Albert Knott, Lewis King
D: B. J. Kurning
S: Roy Norton
SP: John Montague

TO A FINISH (Fox, August 21, 1921) 5 Reels.
Buck Jones, Helen Ferguson, G. Raymond Nye, Norman Selby, Herschel Mayall
D: B. J. Durning
S/SP: Jack Strumwasser

BAR NOTHING (Fox, October 2, 1921) 5 Reels.
Buck Jones, Ruth Renick, Arthur Carew, James Farley, William Buckley
D: Edward Sedgwick
S: Jack Strumwasser, Clyde C. Westover
SP: Jack Strumwasser

RIDING WITH DEATH (Fox, November 13, 1921) 5 Reels.
Buck Jones, Betty Francisco, Jack Mower, J. Farrell MacDonald, Harry Von Sickle, Bill Steele, Bill Gettinger, Bill Gillis, Art Ortego, Tina Medorri
D/S: Jacques Jaccard
SP: Agnes Parsons

PARDON MY NERVE (Fox, March 5, 1922) 5 Reels.
Buck Jones, Eileen Percy, Mae Busch, G. Raymond Nye, Joe Harris, Otto Hoffman, William Steele, Robert Daly
D: Reaves Eason
SP: Jack Strumwasser
S: William Patterson White—"The Heart of the Range"

WESTERN SPEED (Fox, April 23, 1922) 5 Reels.
Buck Jones, Eileen Percy, Jack McDonald, J. P. Lockney, Jack Curtis, Milton Ross, Walt Robbins, Charles Newton
D: Scott Dunlap, William Wallace
S: William Patterson White—"Lynch Lawyers"
SP: Scott Dunlap

ROUGH SHOD (Fox, June 4, 1922) 5 Reels.
Buck Jones, Helen Ferguson, Ruth Renick, Maurice B. Flynn, Jack Rollins, Charles LeMoyne
D: Reaves Eason
S: Charles Alden Seltzer—"West"
SP: Jack Strumwasser

TROOPER O'NEILL (Fox, July 16, 1922) 5 Reels.
Buck Jones, Beatrice Burnham, Francis McDonald, Claude Peyton, Sid Jordan, Jack Rolli, Karl Fromes
D: Scott Dunlap
S: George Goodchild
SP: William K. Howard

WEST OF CHICAGO (Fox, August 17, 1922) 5 Reels.
Buck Jones, Renee Adoree, Philo McCullough, Sidney D'Allbrook, Charles French, Marcella Daly, Kathleen Key, William H. McIlvain, Otto Matiesen
D: Scott R. Dunlap
S: George Scarborough
SP: Paul Schofield

THE FAST MAIL (Fox, August 20, 1922) 6 Reels.
Buck Jones, Eileen Percy, James Mason, William Steele, Adolphe Menjou, Harry Dunkinson, Nick Cogley
D: Bernard J. Durning
S: Lincoln J. Carter
SP: Agnes Parsons, Jacques Jaccard

BELLS OF SAN JUAN (Fox, October 15, 1922) 5 Reels.
Buck Jones, Fritzie Brunette, G. Raymond Nye, Francis Ford, Sid Jordan, Milton Ross, Kathleen Kay, Otto Matiesen, Hardee Kirkland, Claude Payton, William A. Steele, Harry Todd
D: Scott Dunlap
S: Jackson Gregory
SP: Rex Taylor

THE BOSS OF CAMP 4 (Fox, November 26, 1922) 5 Reels.
Buck Jones, Fritzie Brunette, G. Raymond Ney, Francis Ford, Sid Jordan, Milton Ross
D: W. S. Van Dyke
S: Arthur Preston Hankins—"The Boss of Camp Four, A Western Story"
SP: Paul Schofield

FOOTLIGHT RANGER (Fox, January 14, 1923) 5 Reels.
Buck Jones, Fritzie Brunette, James Mason, Lillian Langdon, Lydia Yeamans Titus, Henry Barrows, Otto Hoffman
D: Scott R. Dunlap
S: William Branch
SP: Dorothy Yost

SNOW DRIFT (Fox, April 22, 1923) 5 Reels.
Buck Jones, Irene Rich, G. Raymond Nye, Dorothy Manners, Lalo Encinas, Lee Shumway, Charles Anderson, Evelyn Selbie, Gertrude Ryan, Colin Chase, Annette Jean
D: Scott R. Dunlap
S: James B. Hendryx
SP: Jack Strumwasser

SKID PROOF (Fox, July 22, 1923) 6 Reels.
Buck Jones, Laura Anson, Fred Eric, Jacqueline Gadsden, Peggy Shaw, Earl Metcalf, Claude Peyton, Harry Tracey, Fred Kelsey
D: Scott R. Dunlap
S: Byron Morgan
SP: Harvey Gates

THE ELEVENTH HOUR (Fox, July 20, 1923) 7 Reels.
Buck Jones, Shirley Mason, Richard Tucker, Alan Hale, Walter McGrail, June Elvidge, Fred Kelsey, Nigel DeBrolier, Fred Kohler, Bernard Siegel
D: Bernard J. Durning
S: Lincoln J. Carter
SP: Louis Sherwin

SECOND HAND LOVE (Fox, August 26, 1923) 5 Reels.
Buck Jones, Ruth Dwyer, Charles Coleman, Harvey Clark, Frank Weed, James Quinn, Gus Leonard
D: William Wellman
S: Shannon Fife
SP: Charles Kenyon

HELL'S HOLE (Fox, September 23, 1923) 6 Reels.
Buck Jones, Maurice B. Flynn, Eugene Pallette, George Siegman, Ruth Clifford, Kathleen Key, Hardee Kirkland, Charles K. French, Henry Miller, Fred Kohler, Dick Sutherland
D: Emmett J. Flynn
S: George Scarborough
SP: Bernard McConville

BIG DAN (Fox, October 14, 1923) 6 Reels.
Buck Jones, Marion Nixon, Ben Hendricks, Charles Coleman, Lydia Yeamans Titus, Monty Collins, Eileen O'Malley, Trilby Clark, Jacqueline Gadsden, Charles Smiley, Harry Lonsdale, Mattie Peters, J. P. Lockney, Jackie Herrick
D: William A. Wellman
S/SP: Frederick Hatton, Fanny Hatton

CUPID'S FIREMAN (Fox, December 16, 1923) 57 Mins. (5 Reels).
Buck Jones, Marion Nixon, Brooks Benedict, Eileen O'Malley, Lucy Beaumont, Al Freemont, Charles McHugh, Mary Warren, L. H. King
D: William A. Wellman
S: Richard Harding Davis—"Andy M'Gee's Chorus Girl" in "Van Bibber and Others"
SP: Eugene B. Lewis

NOT A DRUM WAS HEARD (Fox, January 27, 1924) 5 Reels.
Buck Jones, Betty Bouton, Frank Campeau, Rhody Hathaway, Al Fremont, William Scott, Mickey McBan
D: William A. Wellman
S: Ben Ames Williams
SP: Doty Hobart

THE VAGABOND TRAIL (Fox, March 9, 1924) 5 Reels.
Buck Jones, Marion Nixon, Charles Coleman, L. C. Shumway, Virginia Warwick, Harry Lonsdale, Frank Nelson, George Reed, George Romain
D: William A. Wellman
S: George O. Baxter—"Donnegan"

THE CIRCUS COWBOY (Fox, May 11, 1924) 65 Mins.
Buck Jones, Marion Nixon, Jack McDonald, Ray Hallor, Marguerite Clayton, George Romain
D: William A. Wellman
S: Louis Sherwin
SP: Doty Hobart

WESTERN LUCK (Fox, June 22, 1924) 53 Mins.
Buck Jones, Beatrice Burnham, Pat Hartigan, Tom Lingham, J. Farrell MacDonald, Edith Kennick, Bruce Gordon, George Lewis
D: G. Beranger
S/SP: Robert N. Lee

AGAINST ALL ODDS (Fox, June 27, 1924) 5 Reels.
Buck Jones, Dolores Rousse, William Scott, William N. Bailey, Thais Valdmer, Ben Hendricks, Bernard Seigel, Jack McDonald
D: Edmund Mortimer
S: Max Brand—"Cuttle's Hired Man"

THE DESERT OUTLAW (Fox, August 24, 1924) 65 Mins.
Buck Jones, Evelyn Brent, DeWitt Henning, William Haynes, Claude Peyton, William Gould, Bob Klein
D: Edmund Mortimer
S/SP: Charles Kenyon

WINNER TAKE ALL (Fox, October 12, 1924) 6 Reels.
Buck Jones, Peggy Shaw, Edward Hearn, Lilyan Tashman, William Norton Bailey, Ben Deeley, Tom O'Brien
D: William S. Van Dyke
S: Larry Evans—"Winner Take All"
Scen: Ewart Adamson

THE MAN WHO PLAYED SQUARE (Fox, November 23, 1924) 65 Mins.
Buck Jones, Ben Hendricks, Jr., David Kirby, Wanda Hawley, Hank Mann, Howard Foster, William Scott
D: Al Santell
S: William Wallace Cook
SP: John Stone

ARIZONA ROMEO (Fox, January 4, 1925) 5 Reels.
Buck Jones, Lucy Fox, Thomas R. Mills, Maine Geary, Hardie Kirkland, Marcella Daly, Lydia Yeamans Titus, Harvey Clark, Hank Mann, "Silver"
D: Edmund Mortimer
S: Charles Kenyon, Edmund Mortimer
SP: Charles Kenyon

THE TRAIL RIDER (Fox, February 22, 1925) 57 Mins.
Buck Jones, Nancy Deaver, Lucy Fox, Carl Stockdale, Jack McDonald, George Berrell, Jacques Rollens, William Walling, "Silver"
D: W. S. Van Dyke
S: George W. Ogden—"The Trail Rider; A Romance of the Kansas Range"
SP: Thomas Dixon, Jr.

GOLD AND THE GIRL (Fox, April 5, 1925) 5 Reels.
Buck Jones, Elinor Fair, Bruce Gordon, Claude Peyton, Lucien Littlefield, Alphonse Ethier, "Silver," "Pal" (a dog)
D: Edmund Mortimer
S/SP: John Stone

HEARTS AND SPURS (Fox, June 7, 1925) 5 Reels.
Buck Jones, Carole Lombard, William Davidson, Freeman Wood, Jean La Motte, J. Gordon Russell, Walt Robbins, Charles Eldridge, Lucien Littlefield, "Silver"
D: W. S. Van Dyke
S: Jackson Gregory—"The Outlaw"
SP: John Stone

DURAND OF THE BADLANDS (Fox, November 1, 1925) 6 Reels.
(Tinted Sequences)
Buck Jones, Marion Nixon, Malcolm Waite, Fred Desilva, Luke Cosgrove, George Lessey, Buck Black, Seesel Ann Johnson, Jim Corrigan, Carole Lombard, Jack Durtis, "Silver"
D/SP: Lynn Reynolds

LAZYBONES (Fox, November 6, 1925) 8 Reels.
(Tinted Sequences)
Buck Jones, Madge Bellamy, Virginia Marshall, Edythe Chapman, Leslie Fenton, Jane Novak, Emily Fitzroy, ZaSu Pitts, William Norton Bailey
D: Frank Borzage
S: Owen Davis—"Lazybones"
SP: Frances Marion

TIMBER WOLF (Fox, November 20, 1925) 59 Mins.
(Tinted Sequences)
Buck Jones, Elinor Fair, David Dyas, Sam Allen, William Walling, Jack Craig, Robert Mack, "Silver"
D: W. S. Van Dyke
S: Jackson Gregory—"Timber Wolf"
SP: John Stone

THE DESERT'S PRICE (Fox, December 13, 1925) 6 Reels.
(Tinted Sequences)
Buck Jones, Florence Gilbert, Edna Marion, Ernest Butterworth, Arthur Houseman, Montague Love, Carl Stockdale, Harry Dunkinson, Pauline Garon, "Silver"
D: W. S. Van Dyke
S: William McLeod Raine—"The Desert's Price"
SP: Charles Darnton

THE COWBOY AND THE COUNTESS (Fox, January 31, 1926) 6 Reels.
(Tinted Sequences)
Buck Jones, Helen D'Argy, Diana Miller, Chappell Dossett, Fletcher Norton, Monte Collins, Jr., Harvey Clark, Jere Austin, "White Eagle"
D: R. William Neill
S: Maxine Alton, Adele Buffington
SP: Charles Darnton

THE FIGHTING BUCKAROO (Fox, April 4, 1926) 5 Reels.
(Tinted Sequences)
Buck Jones, Sally Long, Lloyd Whitlock, Frank Butler, E. J. Ratcliffe, Ben Hendricks, Jr., Ray Thompson, Frank Rice, "Silver"
D: R. William Neil
S: Frank Howard Clark
SP: Charles Darnton, John Stone

A MAN FOUR-SQUARE (Fox, May 9, 1926) 5 Reels.
(Tinted Sequences)
Buck Jones, Marion Harlan, Harry Woods, William Lawrence, Jay Hunt, Sidney Bracey, Florence Gilbert, Frank Beal
D: R. William Neill
Scen: Charles Darnton, John Stone
S: William MacLeod Raine—"A Man Four-Square"

THE GENTLE CYCLONE (Fox, June 27, 1926) 5 Reels (65 Mins).
(Tinted Sequences)
Buck Jones, Rose Blossom, Will Walling, Reed Howes, Stanton Heck, Grant Withers, Kathleen Myers, Jay Hunt, Oliver Hardy, Marion Harlan, "Silver"
D: W. S. Van Dyke
S: Frank R. Buckley—"Peg Leg and the Kidnapper" in *Western Story Magazine*
SP: Thomas Dixon, Jr.

THE FLYING HORSEMAN (Fox, September 5, 1926) 5 Reels.
(Tinted Sequences)
Buck Jones, Gladys McConnell, Bruce Covington, Walter Percival, Hank Mann, Harvey Clark, Vester Pegg, Joe Rickson, "Silver"
D: Orville Dull
S: Max Brand—"Dark Rosaleen" in *Country Gentleman Magazine*
SP: Gertrude Orr

30 BELOW ZERO (Fox, October 31, 1926) 5 Reels.
(Tinted Sequences)
Buck Jones, Eva Novak, E. J. Ratcliffe, Frank Butler, Paul Panzer, Harry Woods, Fred Walton, Henry Murdock, Howard Vincent
D: Robert P. Kerr, Lambert Hillyer
S/SP: John Stone

DESERT VALLEY (Fox, December 26, 1926) 5 Reels.
(Tinted Sequences)
Buck Jones, Virginia Brown Faire, Malcolm Waite, J. W. Johnson, Charles Brinley, Eugene Pallette, "Silver"
D: Scott R. Dunlap
S: Jackson Gregory
SP: Randall H. Faye

THE WAR HORSE (Fox, February 6, 1926) 5 Reels.
Buck Jones, Lola Todd, Lloyd Whitlock, Stanley Taylor, Yola D'Avril, James Gordon, Robert Kortman, "Silver"
D/SP: Lambert Hillyer
S: Buck Jones, Lambert Hillyer

WHISPERING SAGE (Fox, March 20, 1927) 5 Reels.
Buck Jones, Natilie Joyce, Emile Chautard, Carl Miller, Albert J. Smith, Joseph Girard, William A. Steele, Ellen Winston, Hazel Keener, Joseph Rickson, Enrique Acosta, "Silver"
D: Scott R. Dunlap
S: Harry Sinclair, Drago & Joseph Noel
SP: Harold Shumate

Murdock MacQuarrie, Buck Jones, and Barbara Bennett in *Black Jack* (Fox, 1927).

HILLS OF PERIL (Fox, May 1, 1927) 5 Reels.
Buck Jones, Georgia Hale, Albert J. Smith, Buck Black, William Welch, Marjorie Beebe, Duke Green, Bob Kortman, Charles Athloff, "Silver"
D: Lambert Hillyer
S: Winchelle Smith and George Abbott—"The Holy Terror: A None-Too-Serious Drama"
SP: Jack Jungmeyer

GOOD AS GOLD (Fox, June 12, 1927) 5 Reels (52 Mins).
(Tinted Sequences)
Buck Jones, Frances Lee, Carl Miller, Charles K. French, Adele Watson, Arthur Ledwig, Mickey Moore, Duke Green, "Silver"
D: Scott R. Dunlap
S: Murray Leinster—"The Owner of the Aztec" in *Western Magazine*
SP: Jack Jungmeyer

CHAIN LIGHTNING (Fox, August 14, 1927) 6 Reels.
(Tinted Sequences)
Buck Jones, Diane Ellis, Tex McNamara, William Welsh, Jack Batson, Gene Cameron, William Carress, "Eagle"
D: Lambert Hillyer
S: Charles Alden Seltzer—"The Brass Commandments"
SP: Lambert Hillyer

BLACK JACK (Fox, September 25, 1927) 5 Reels.
Buck Jones, Barbara Bennett, George Berrell, Sam Allen, William Carress, Buck Moulton, Theodore Lorch, Harry Cording, Murdock McQuarrie, "Silver"
D: Orville Dull
S: Johnston McCulley—"The Broken Dollar" in *Far West Illustrated Magazine*
SP: Harold Shumate

BLOOD WILL TELL (Fox, November 13, 1927) 5 Reels.
Buck Jones, Kathryn Perry, Lawford Davidson, Bob Kortman, Harry Grippe, Austin Jewell, Arthur Housman, "Silver"
D: Ray Flynn
S: Adele Buffington
SP: Paul Gangelin

LIFE IN HOLLYWOOD #4 (1927) 10 Mins.
John Barrymore, Ernst Lubitsch, Harry Myers, Mae Marsh, William Seiter, Monte Blue, Baby Priscilla Moran, Marie Prevost, Alice Calhoun, Tom Mix and Tony, *Buck Jones*, Shirley Mason, Francis MacDonald, Bessie Love, Hal Goodwin, L. C. Wellman, Alan Hale, Corrinne Griffith

BRANDED SOMBRERO (Fox, January 8, 1928) 5 Reels.
Buck Jones, Leila Hyams, Jack Batson, Stanton Heck, Frances Ford, Josephine Borio, Lee Kelly, "Eagle"
D/SP: Lambert Hillyer
S: Cherry Wilson

THE BIG HOP (Buck Jones Productions, August 31, 1928) 7 Reels.
(Sound effects added; no dialogue)
Buck Jones, Jobyna Ralston, Ernest Hilliard, Charles K. French, Charles Clary, Duke Lee, Edward Hearne, Jack Dill
D: James W. Horne
S/SP: J. B. Mack

Sound Features

THE LONE RIDER (Beverly/Columbia, July 13, 1930) 5118 ft.
(Remade as "The Man Trailer" in 1934)
Buck Jones, Vera Reynolds, Harry Woods, George Pearce, "Silver"
D: Louis Kins
S: Frank Clark
SP: Forrest Sheldon
P: Sol Lesser

Robert Kortman is shot by Buck Jones while Kathryn Perry and Kortman's cutthroats look on in *Blood Will Tell* (Fox, 1929).

SHADOW RANCH (Beverly/Columbia, September 28, 1930) 5,766 ft.

Buck Jones, Marguerite De La Motte, Kate Price, Frank Rive, Ben Wilson, Al Smith, Ernie Adams, Slim Whitaker, Robert McKenzie, Lafe McKee

D: Louis King
S: George M. Johnson, Clark Silvernail
SP: Frank Clark
P: Sol Lesser

MEN WITHOUT LAW (Beverly/Columbia, October 15, 1930) 6,090 ft.

Buck Jones, Carmelita Geraghty, Tom Carr, Lydia Knott, Harry Woods, Fred Burns, Syd Saylor, Fred Kelsey, Victor Sarno, Ben Corbett, Lafe McKee, Art Mix, "Silver"

D: Louis King
S: Lou Seiler
SP: Dorothy Howell
P: Sol Lesser

Buck Jones in *The Big Hop* (Buck Jones Productions, 1928), a film failure that cost Jones a bundle of money—as did a wild west show venture shortly afterwards.

THE DAWN TRAIL (Beverly/Columbia, November 23, 1930) 66 Mins.
Buck Jones, Miriam Seegar, Charles Morton, Erville Alderson, Edward J. LeSaint, Charles King, Hank Mann, Vester Pegg, Charles Brinley, Charles Whittaker, Inez Gomez, Robert Burns, Robert Fleming, Violet Axzelle, Buck Connors, Jack Curtis
D: Christy Cabanne
S: Forrest Sheldon
SP: John Thomas Neville
P: Sol Lesser

DESERT VENGEANCE (Beverly/Columbia, January 25, 1931) 59 Mins.
Buck Jones, Barbara Bedford, Buck Connors, Pee Wee Holmes, Slim Whitaker, Douglas Gilmore, Al Smith, Ed Brady, Robert Ellis, Bob Fleming, Joe Girard, Barney Bearsley, "Silver"
D: Louis King
S/SP: Stuart Anthony

THE AVENGER (Beverly/Columbia, March 6, 1931) 65 Mins.
Buck Jones, Dorothy Revier, Edward Piel, Sr., Otto Hoffman, Sidney Bracey, Edward Hearn, Walter Percival, "Silver"
D: Roy William Neill
S: Jack Townley
SP: George Morgan

THE TEXAS RANGER (Beverly/Columbia, May 10, 1931) 61 Mins.
Buck Jones, Carmelita Geraghty, Harry Woods, Ed Brady, Nelson McDowell, Billy Bletcher, Harry Todd, Budd Fine, Bert Woodruff, Edward Piel, Sr., Blackie Whiteford, Lew Meehan, "Silver"
D: D. Ross Lederman
S/SP: Roffest Sheldon
P: Sol Lesser

THE FIGHTING SHERIFF (Beverly/Columbia, May 15, 1931) 67 Mins.
Buck Jones, Loretta Sayers, Robert Ellis, Harlan Knight, Paul Fix, Lillian Worth, Nena Quartero, Clarence Muse, Lilliane Leighton, Tom Bay, Charles Whitaker, "Silver"
D: Louis King
S/SP: Stuart Anthony

BRANDED (Columbia, September 1, 1931) 61 Mins.
Buck Jones, Ethel Kenton, Wallace MacDonald, Fred Burns, Al Smith, Philo McCullough, John Oscar, Bob Kortman, Clark Burroughs, Sam MacDonald, "Silver"
D: D. Ross Lederman
S/SP: Randall Faye

BORDER LAW (Columbia, September 15, 1931) 63 Mins.
Buck Jones, Lupita Tovar, James Mason, Frank Rice, Don Chapman, Louis Hickus, F. R. Smith, John Wallace, Robert Burns, Glenn Strange, Fred Burns, Art Mix, "Silver"
D: Louis King
S/SP: Stuart Anthony

DEADLINE (Columbia, October 14, 1931) 59 Mins.
Buck Jones, Loretta Sayers, Robert Ellis, Ed Brady, Raymond Nye, Knute Erickson, George Ernest, Harry Todd, Jack Curtis, James Farle, Edward LeSaint, "Silver"
D: Lambert Hillyer
S/SP: Lambert Hillyer

THE RANGE FEUD (Columbia, November 22, 1931) 54 Mins.
Buck Jones, John Wayne, Susan Fleming, Edward J. LeSaint, William Walling, Wallace MacDonald, Harry Woods, Frank Austin, Glenn Strange, Lew Meehan, Jim Corey, Frank Ellis, Bob Reeves, Hank Bell, Rube Palroy, Archie Ricks, Merrill McCormack, Blackjack Ward, "Silver"
D: D. Ross Lederman
S: Milton Krims
SP: George Plympton

Who says cowboys only kiss their horses? Buck Jones is seen here in a romantic interlude with Loretta Sayers in *High Speed* (Columbia, 1932), one of the author's favorite movie stills.

RIDIN' FOR JUSTICE (Columbia, January 4, 1932) 64 Mins.
Buck Jones, Mary Doran, Russell Simpson, Walter Miller, Bob McKenzie, William Walling, Billy Engle, Hank Mann, Lafe McKee, "Silver"
D: D. Ross Lederman
S/SP: Harold Shumate

ONE MAN LAW (Columbia, January 11, 1932) 63 Mins.
Buck Jones, Shirley Grey, Robert Ellis, Murdock McQuarrie, Harry Todd, Henry Sedley, Ernie Adams, Dick Alexander, Wesley Giraud, Edward J. LeSaint, "Silver"
D: Lambert Hillyer
S/SP: Lambert Hillyer

SOUTH OF SANTA FE (Columbia, March 5, 1932) 60 Mins.
Buck Jones, Mona Maris, Philo McCullough, Doris Hill, George J. Lewis, Paul Fix, Charles Reque, James Durkin, Harry Semels, Charles Stevens, "Silver"
D: Lambert Hillyer
S: Harold Shumate
SP: Milton Krims

HIGH SPEED (Columbia, March 1932) 60 Mins.
Buck Jones, Loretta Sayers, Mickey McGuire (Rooney), Ed LeSaint, William Walling, Ward Bond, Dick Dickinson, Martin Faust, Joe Bardeaux, Pat O'Malley, Edward Chandler, Wallace MacDonald
D: Ross Lederman
S: Harold Shumate
Adapt: Adele Buffington

Buck Jones and Mickey McGuire (Rooney) in *High Speed* (Columbia, 1932).

HELLO TROUBLE (Columbia, July 15, 1932) 67 Mins.
Buck Jones, Lina Basquette, Russell Simpson, Otto Hoffman, Wallace MacDonald, Allan Roscoe, Morgan Galloway, Ruth Warren, Frank Rice, Lafe McKee, Ward Bond, Al Smith, Spec O'Donnell, King Baggott, "Silver"
D: Lambert Hillyer
S/SP: Lambert Hillyer

MCKENNA OF THE MOUNTED (Columbia, August 26, 1932) 66 Mins.
Buck Jones, Greta Granstedt, James Glavin, Walter McGrail, Niles Welch, Mitchell Lewis, Claude King, Glen Strange, Buz Osborne, Edmund Cobb, "Silver"
D: D. Ross Lederman
SP: Stuart Anthony
S: Randall Faye

WHITE EAGLE (Columbia, October 7, 1932) 67 Mins.
Buck Jones, Barbara Weeks, Ward Bond, Robert Ellis, Jason Robards, Jim Thorpe, Frank Campeau, Bob Kortman, Robert Elliott, Clarence Geldert, Jimmy House, Frank Hagney, Russell Simpson, "Silver"
D: Lambert Hillyer
S/SP: Fred Myton

FORBIDDEN TRAIL (Columbia, November 18, 1932) 71 Mins.
Buck Jones, Barbara Weeks, Mary Carr, George Cooper, Ed Brady, Frank Rice, Al Smith, Frank LaRue, Won Chung, Wallis Clark, Tom Forman, Gertrude Howard, Dick Rush, Charles Berner, "Silver"
D: Lambert Hillyer
S/SP: Milton Krims

CHILD OF MANHATTAN (Columbia, December, 1932) 70 Mins.
Nancy Carroll, John Boles, *Charles "Buck" Jones*, Jessie Ralph, Luis Alberni, Betty Grable, Warburton Gamble, Clara Blandick, Tyler Brooke, Gary Owen, Jane Darwell, Betty Kendall, Nat Pendleton, John Sheehan
D: Eddie Buzzell
S: Preston Sturges
Adapt: Gertrude Purcell, Maurine Watkins

TREASON (Columbia, February 10, 1933) 63 Mins.
Buck Jones, Shirley Grey, Robert Ellis, Edward J. LeSaint, Frank Lackteen, Frank Ellis, Ivar McFadden, Nick Cogley, "Silver"
D: George B. Seitz
S: Gordon Battle

THE CALIFORNIA TRAIL (Columbia, March 24, 1933) 67 Mins.
Buck Jones, Helen Mack, George Humbart, Luis Alberni, Charles Stevens, Emile Chautard, Evelyn Sherman, Chris-Pin Martin, Carmen LaRoux, Carlo Villar, Qugie Gomez, John Paul Jones, Allan Garcia, Juan DuVal, William Steele, "Silver"
D: Lambert Hillyer
S/SP: Jack Nattford

THE THRILL HUNTER (Columbia, April 30, 1933) 60 Mins.
Buck Jones, Dorothy Revier, Arthur Rankin, Robert Ellis, Edward J. LeSaint, Frank LaRue, Al Smith, Harry Semels, Eddie Kane, John Ince, Alf James, Harry Todd, Willie Fung, Jay Wilsey (Buffalo Bill, Jr.), Buddy Roosevelt, Alice Dahl, Glenn Strange, Hank Bell, Frank Ellis
D: George Seitz
S/SP: Harry O. Hoyt

UNKNOWN VALLEY (Columbia, May 5, 1933) 69 Mins.
Buck Jones, Cecilia Parker, Bret Black, Carlota Warwick, Arthur Wanzer, Wade Boteler, Frank McGlynn, Charles Thurston, Ward Bond, Gaylord Pendleton, Alf James, "Silver"
D: Lambert Hillyer
S: Donald W. Lee
SP: Lambert Hillyer

GORDON OF GHOST CITY (Universal, August 14, 1933) 12 Chapters.
Buck Jones, Madge Bellamy, Walter Miller, William Desmond, Tom Ricketts, Francis Ford, Edmund Cobb, Hugh Enfield (Craig Reynolds), Bud Osborne, Ethan Laidlaw, Dick Rush, Jim Corey, William Steele, Bob Kerrick, Cecil Kellogg, Artie Ortego, "Silver"
D: Ray Taylor
S: Peter B. Kyne—"Oh Promise Me!"
SP: Ella O'Neill, Basil Dickey, George Plympton, Harry O. Hoyt, and Het Mannheim
P: Henry MacRae
Chapter Titles: (1) A Lone Hand, (2) The Stampede, (3) Trapped, (4) The Man of Mystery, (5) Riding for Life, (6) Blazing Prairies, (7) Entombed in the Tunnel, (8) Stampede, (9) Flames of Fury, (10) Swimming in the Torrent, (11) A Wild Ride, (12) Mystery of Ghost City

Buck Jones and Madge Bellamy are apprehensive in this scene from *Gordon of Ghost City* (Universal, 1933).

THE FIGHTING CODE (Columbia, December 30, 1933) 65 Mins.
Buck Jones, Diane Sinclair, Ward Bond, Niles Welch, Dick Alexander, Louis Natheaux, Alf James, Erville Alderson, Gertrude Howard, Bob Kortman, Charles Brinley, Buck Moulton, "Silver"
D: Lambert Hillyer
S/SP: Lambert Hillyer

THE SUNDOWN RIDER (Columbia, December 30, 1933) 69 Mins.
Buck Jones, Barbara Weeks, Pat O'Malley, Wheeler Oakman, Niles Welch, Bradley Page, Frank LaRue, Ward Bond, Ed Brady, Harry Todd, Glenn Strange, "Silver"
D: Lambert Hillyer
S: John T. Neville
SP: Lambert Hillyer

THE FIGHTING RANGER (Columbia, March 17, 1934) 60 Mins.
(Remake of "Border Law")
Buck Jones, Dorothy Revier, Frank Rice, Bradley Page, Ward Bond, Paddy O'Flynn, Art Smith, Denver Dixon, Frank LaRue, Jack Wallace, Mozelle Britton, Bud Osborne, Lew Meehan, Jim Corey, Steve Clemente, Frank Ellis, "Silver"
D: George B. Seitz
S: Stuart Anthony
SP: Harry O. Hoyt

THE MAN TRAILER (Columbia, March 24, 1934) 59 Mins.
Buck Jones, Cecilia Parker, Arthur Vinton, Clarence Geldert, Lew Meehan, Steve Clark, Charles West, Dick Botiller, Artie Ortego
D/SP: Lambert Hillyer

THE RED RIDER (Universal, July 1934) 15 Chapters.
Buck Jones, Marion Schilling, Grant Withers, Walter Miller, J. P. McGowan, Dick Cramer, Margaret LaMarr, Charles K. French, Edmund Cobb, William Desmond, Mert Lavarre (John Merton), Frank Rice, Jim Thorpe, Monte Montague, Dennis Moore, Jim Corey, Bud Osborne, Al Ferguson, Artie Ortego, Tom Ricketts, J. Frank Glendon, Charles Brinley, William Steele, Fred Burns, Hank Bell, Chester Gan, Jim Toney, Art Mix, Jack Rockwell, Jack O'Shea, Frank Ellis, "Silver"
D: Louis Friedlander (Lew Landers)
S: W. C. Tuttle—"The Redhead From Sun Dog"
SP: George Plympton, Vin Moore, Ella O'Neill, George Morgan
P: Henry MacRae
Chapter Titles: (1) Sentenced to Die, (2) A Leap for Life, (3) The Night Attack, (4) Treacherous Attack, (5) Trapped, (6) The Brink of Death, (7) The Fatal Plunge, (8) The Stampede, (9) The Posse Rider, (10) The Avenging Trail, (11) The Lost Diamond, (12) Double Trouble, (13) The Night Raiders, (14) In the Enemy's Hideout, (15) Brought to Justice

A CYCLONE of WESTERN ACTION and THRILLS!

UNIVERSAL presents

Buck Jones in "The RED RIDER"

with
GRANT WITHERS · MARIAN SHILLING
WALTER MILLER · WILLIAM DESMOND
EDMUND COBB · · · JIM THORPE..
BUD OSBORNE and FRANK RICE...

CHAPTER No 12 "DOUBLE TROUBLE!"

A UNIVERSAL PICTURE

Buck Jones was one of the few serial stars to have his name above the title. Shown here with Marion Shilling in *The Red Rider* (Universal, 1934).

ROCKY RHODES (Universal, September 1934) 7 Reels.
Buck Jones, Sheila Terry, Stanley Fields, Walter Miller, Alf James, Paul Fix, Lydia Knott, Lee Shumway, Jack Rockwell, Carl Stockdale, Monte Montague, Bud Osborne, Harry Semels, "Silver"
D: Al Raboch
S: W. C. Tuttle
SP: Edward Churchill
P: *Buck Jones*

WHEN A MAN SEES RED (Universal, November 24, 1934) 60 Mins.
Buck Jones, Dorothy Revier, Syd Saylor, Peggy Campbell, LeRoy Mason, Frank LaRue, Libby Taylor, Jack Rockwell, Charles K. French, Bob Kortman, William Steele
D: Alan James
S: Basil Dickey
SP: Alan James
P: *Buck Jones*

THE CRIMSON TRAIL (Universal, March 8, 1935) 60 Mins.
Buck Jones, Polly Ann Young, Carl Stockdale, Charles K. French, Ward Bond, John Bliefer, Bob Kortman, Bud Osborne, Charles Brinley, Hank Pott, George Sowards, Paul Fix, Robert Walker, "Silver"
D: Al Raboch
S: Wilton West
SP: Jack Natteford
P: *Buck Jones*

STONE OF SILVER CREEK (Universal, April 2, 1935) 61 Mins.
Buck Jones, Noel Francis, Niles Welch, Murdock McQuarrie, Marion Shilling, Peggy Campbell, Rodney Hilderbrand, Harry Semels, Grady Sutton, Kernan Cripps, Frank Rice, Bob McKenzie, Lew Meehan, "Silver"

Dorothy Revier, Buck Jones, Peggy Campbell, and Jack Rockwell in *When a Man Sees Red* (Universal, 1934).

BORDER BRIGANDS (Universal, June 4, 1935) 56 Mins.
Buck Jones, Lona Andre, Fred Kohler, Frank Rice, Edward Keane, J. P. McGowan, Hank Bell, Al Bridge, Lew Meehan, "Silver"
D: Nick Grinde
S/SP: Stuart Anthony
P: *Buck Jones*, Irving Starr

OUTLAWED GUNS (Universal, July 29, 1935) 7 Reels.
Buck Jones, Pat O'Brien, Ruth Channing, Frank McGlynn, Sr., Charles King, Joan Gale, Roy D'Arcy, Joseph Girard, Monte Montague, Lee Shumway, Jack Rockwell, Bob Walker, Carl Stockdale, Cliff Lyons, Babe DeTreest, Jack Montgomery
D: Ray Taylor
S: Cliff Farrell
SP: Jack Neville
P: *Buck Jones*

THE ROARING WEST (Universal, July 1935) 15 Chapters.
Buck Jones, Muriel Evans, Walter Miller, Frank McGlynn, Sr., Harlan Knight, William Desmond, William Thorne, Eole Galli, Pat O'Brien, Charles King, Slim Whitaker, Tom London, Edmund Cobb, Dick Rush, Cecil Kellogg, Paul Palmer, Harry Tenbrook, Jay Wilsey (Buffalo Bill, Jr.), Tiny Skelton, George Ovey, Fred Humes, Cliff Lyons, John Bose, Lafe McKee, "Silver"
D: Ray Taylor
S: Ed Earl Repp
SP: George Plympton, Nate Gatzert, Basil Dickey, Robert C. Rothafel, Ella O'Neill
P: Henry MacRae
Chapter Titles: (1) The Land Rush, (2) Torrent of Terror, (3) Flaming Peril, (4) Stampede of Death, (5) Danger in the Dark, (6) Death Rides the Plain, (7) Hurled to the Depths, (8) Ravaging Flames, (9) Death Holds the Reins, (10) The Fatal Blast, (11) The Baited Trap, (12) The Mystery Shot, (13) Flaming Torrents, (14) Thundering Fury, (15) The Conquering Cowpunchers

THE THROWBACK (Universal, September 1, 1935) 6 Reels. Reels.

Buck Jones, Muriel Evans, Eddie Phillips, George Hayes, Paul Fix, Frank LaRue, Earl Pinegree, Bob Walker, Charles K. French, Bryant Washburn, Allan Ramsay, Margaret Davis, Bobby Nelson, Mickey Martin, "Silver"
D: Ray Taylor
S: Cherry Wilson
SP: Frances Guihan
P: *Buck Jones*

THE IVORY-HANDLED GUN (Universal, November 1935) 60 Mins.

Buck Jones, Charlotte Wynters, Walter Miller, Carl Stockdale, Frank Rice, Joseph Girard, Robert Kortman, Stanley Blystone, Lafe McKee, Lee Shumway, Charles King, Ben Corbett, Eddie Phillips, Niles Welch, "Silver"
D: Ray Taylor
S: Charles E. Barnes
SP: John Neville
P: *Buck Jones*

SUNSET OF POWER (Universal, January 22, 1936) 7 Reels.

Buck Jones, Dorothy Dix, Charles Middleton, Donald Kirke, Ben Corbett, Charles King, William Lawrence, Joe De LaCruz, Nina Campana, Humenco Blanco, Murdock Mc-Quarrie, Alan Sears, Monty Vandergrift, Glenn Strange, "Silver"
D: Ray Taylor
S: J. E. Grinstead
SP: Earle Snell
P: *Buck Jones*

SILVER SPURS (Universal, January 29, 1936) 6 Reels.

Buck Jones, Muriel Evans, J. P. McGowan, George Hayes, Dennis Moore, Robert Frazer, Bruce Lane, William Lawrence, Earl Askam, Charles K. French, Beth Marion, Kernan Cripps, "Silver"
D: Ray Taylor
S: Charles Alden Seltzer
SP: Joseph Poland
P: *Buck Jones*

FOR THE SERVICE (Universal, May 6, 1936) 64 Mins.

Buck Jones, Fred Kohler, Beth Marion, Frank McGlynn, Sr., Clifford Jones, Ben Corbett, Chief Thunderbird, Edward Keane, "Silver"
D: *Buck Jones*
S/SP: Isadore Bernstein
P: *Buck Jones*

THE COWBOY AND THE KID (Universal, May 25, 1936) 58 Mins.

Buck Jones, Billy Burrud, Dorothy Revier, Harry Worth, Charles LeMoy, Dick Rush, Lafe McKee, Bob McKenzie, Burr Caruth, Eddie Lee, Kernan Cripps, Oliver Eckhart, Mary Mersch, Mildred Gober, "Silver"
D: Ray Taylor
S: *Buck Jones*
SP: Frances Guihan
P: *Buck Jones*

THE PHANTOM RIDER (Universal, July 6, 1936) 15 Chapters.

Buck Jones, Marla Shelton, Diana Gibson, Joey Ray, Harry Woods, Frank LaRue, George Cooper, Eddie Gribbon, Helen Shipman, James Mason, Jim Corey, Lee Sumway, Charles LeMoyne, Clem Bevins, Cecil Weston, Matt McHugh, Jim Thorpe, Charles King, Curtis McPeters (Cactus Mack), Charles K. French, Tom London, Wally Wales, Slim Whitaker, Frank Ellis, Bob Fite, "Hi Pockets" Busse, Bill Scott, Jimmy Carroll, Hank Bell, Lafe McKee, Priscilla Lawson, Drew Stanfield, Art Mix, George Plues, Tom Carter, Scoop Martin, Fred Warren, Olin Francis, Iron Eyes Cody, Paul Regas, Eva McKenzie, Orrin Burke, George Ovey, Cliff Lyons, "Silver"
D: Ray Taylor
Original SP: George Plympton, Basil Dickey, Ella O'Neill
P: Henry MacRae
Chapter Titles: (1) Dynamite, (2) The Maddened Herd, (3) The Brink of Disaster, (4) The Phantom Rides, (5) Trapped by Outlaws, (6) Shot Down, (7) Stark Terror, (8) The Night Attack, (9) The Indian Raid, (10) Human Targets, (11) The Shaft of Doom, (12) Flaming Gold, (13) Crashing Timbers, (14) The Last Chance, (15) The Outlaw's Vengeance

RIDE 'EM COWBOY (Universal, September 20, 1936) 59 Mins.

Buck Jones, George Cooper, Luana Walters, J. P. McGowan, William Lawrence, Joe Girard, Donald Kirke, Charles LeMoyne, Edmund Cobb, Lester Dorr, "Silver"
D: Lesley Selander
S: *Buck Jones*
SP: Frances Guihan
P: *Buck Jones*

BOSS RIDER OF GUN CREEK (Universal, November 1, 1936) 65 Mins.

Buck Jones, Muriel Evans, Harvey Clark, Lee Phelps, Tom Chatterton, Joseph Swickard, Ernest Hillard, Mahlon Hamilton, Alphonse Ethier, Alan Sears, William Lawrence, Edward Hearn, "Silver"
D: Lesley Selander
S: E. B. Mann
SP: Frances Guihan
P: *Buck Jones*

EMPTY SADDLES (Universal, December 20, 1936) 67 Mins.
Buck Jones, Louise Brooks, Harvey Clark, Gertrude Astor, Frank Campeau, Niles Welch, Lloyd Ingraham, Charles Middleton, Claire Rochelle, Mary Mersh, Ruth Cherrington, Oliver Eckhart, Robert Adair, Charles LeMoyne, Ben Corbett, Buck Moulton, Earl Askam, William Lawrence, "Silver"
D: Lesley Selander
S: Cherry Wilson
SP: Frances Guihan
P: *Buck Jones*

SANDFLOW (Universal, February 14, 1937) 58 Mins.
Buck Jones, Lita Chevret, Bob Kortman, Arthur Aylesworth, Robert Terry, Enrique DeRosas, Josef Swickard, Lee Phelps, Harold Hodge, Tom Chatterton, Arthur Van Slyke, Malcolm Graham, Ben Corbett, "Silver"
D: Lesley Selander
S: Carey Wilson
SP: Frances Guihan
P: *Buck Jones*

LEFT HANDED LAW (Universal, April 18, 1937) 63 Mins.
Buck Jones, Noel Francis, Frank LaRue, Lee Phelps, Matty Fain, George Regas, Robert Frazer, Lee Shumway, Nena Quartero, "Silver"
D: Lesley Selander
S: Charles M. Martin
SP: Frances Guihan
P: *Buck Jones*

SMOKE TREE RANGE (Universal, June 6, 1937) 59 Mins.
Buck Jones, Muriel Evans, John Elliott, Edmund Cobb, Ben Hall, Ted Adams, Donald Kirke, Dickie Jones, Lee Phelps, Charles King, Earle Hodgins, Mable Concord, Bob Kortman, Eddie Phillips, Bob McKenzie, Slim Whitaker, "Silver"
D: Lesley Selander
S: Arthur Henry Gordon
P: *Buck Jones*

BLACK ACES (Universal, September 5, 1937) 59 Mins.
Buck Jones, Kay Linaker, Charles King, Bob Kortman, Fred MacKaye, William Lawrence, Robert Frazer, Raymond Brown, Bernard Phillips, Frank Campeau, Charles LeMoyne, Arthur Van Slyke, Bob McKenzie, "Silver"
D/P: *Buck Jones*
S: Stephen Payne
SP: Frances Guihan

Buck Jones and "Silver" having a man-to-horse talk in *Sandflow* (Universal, 1932).

LAW FOR TOMBSTONE (Universal, October 10, 1937) 59 Mins.
Buck Jones, Muriel Evans, Harvey Clark, Carl Stockdale, Earle Hodgins, Alexander Cross, Chuck Morrison, Mary Carney, Charles LeMoyne, Ben Corbett, Harold Hodge, Arthur Van Slyke, Ezra Paulette, Francis Walker, Bob Kortman, Slim Whitaker, Tom Forman, Bill Patton, Frank McCarroll, D. V. Tannlinger, Carlos Bernardo, "Silver"
D: *Buck Jones*, B. Reeves Eason
S: Charles M. Martin
SP: Frances Guihan

HOLLYWOOD ROUNDUP (Columbia, November 6, 1937) 64 Mins.
Buck Jones, Helen Twelvetrees, Grant Withers, Shemp Howard, Dickie Jones, Eddie Kane, Monty Collins, Warren Jackson, Lester Dorr, Lee Shumway, Edward Keane, George Berlinger, Bob Woodward
D: Ewing Scott
SP: Joseph Hoffman, Monroe Schaff

165

A typical lobby card from Buck Jones' peak years as America's favorite cowboy.

SUDDEN BILL DORN (Universal, November 10, 1937) 60 Mins.
Buck Jones, Noel Francis, Evelyn Brent, Frank McGlynn, Harold Hodge, Ted Adams, William Lawrence, Lee Phelps
D: Ray Taylor
S: Jackson Gregory
SP: Frances Guihan
P: *Buck Jones*

BOSS OF LONELY VALLEY (Universal, November 14, 1937) 59 Mins.
Buck Jones, Muriel Evans, Harvey Clark, Walter Miller, Lee Phelps, Dickie Howard, Ezra Paulette, Matty Fain, Grace Goodall, Virginia Dabney, "Silver"
D: Ray Taylor
S: Forrest Brown
SP: Frances Guihan
P: *Buck Jones*

HEADIN' EAST (Columbia, December 13, 1937) 67 Mins.
Buck Jones, Ruth Coleman, Shemp Howard, Donald Douglas, Elaine Arden, Earle Hodgins, John Elliott, Stanley Blystone, Harry Lash, Frank Faylen, Dick Rich, Al Herman
D: Ewing Scott
S: Joseph Hoffman, Monroe Schaff
SP: Ethel La Blanche, Paul Franklin
P: L. G. Leonard

THE OVERLAND EXPRESS (Columbia, April 11, 1938) 55 Mins.
Buck Jones, Marjorie Reynolds, Carlyle Moore, Maston Williams, William Arnold, Lew Kelly, Bud Osborne, Ben Taggart, Ben Corbett, Gene Alsace (Rocky Camron), Blackie Whiteford, Bob Woodward, "Silver"
D: Drew Eberson
SP: Monroe Schaff
P: L. G. Leonard

UNMARRIED (Paramount, May 26, 1938) 64 Mins.
Buck Jones, Helen Twelvetrees, Donald O'Connor, John Hartley, Robert Armstrong, Sidney Blackmer, Larry Buster Crabbe, Edward Pawley, William Haade, Philip Warren, Dorothy Howe, Lucien Littlefield, Jack Roper
D: Kurt Neumann
SP: Lillie Hayward, Brian Marlow
S: Grover Jones, William Slavens McNutt

THE STRANGER FROM ARIZONA (Columbia, September 22, 1938) 54 Mins.
Buck Jones, Dorothy Fay, Hank Mann, Roy Barcroft, Hank Worden, Bob Terry, Horace Murphy, Budd Buster, Dot Farley, Walter Anthony, Stanley Blystone, Ralph Peters, Loren Ziebe, Horace B. Carpenter, "Silver"
D: Elmer Clifton
S/SP: Monroe Schaff

LAW OF THE TEXAN (Columbia, October 24, 1938) 54 Mins.
Buck Jones, Dorothy Fay, Kenneth Harlan, Don Douglas, Matty Kemp, Joe Whitehead, Forrest Taylor, Jose Tortosa, Tommy Mack, Melissa Sierra, Bob Kortman, Dave O'Brien, Buck Morgan, Jack Ingram, Carl Mathews, Ray Henderson, "Silver"
D: Elmer Clifton
S/SP: Monroe Schaff, Arthur Hoerl

CALIFORNIA FRONTIER (Columbia, December 15, 1938) 54 Mins.
Buck Jones, Carmen Bailey, Milburn Stone, Jose Perez, Soledad Jiminez, Stanley Blystone, Carlos Villanos, Glenn Strange, Paul Ellis, Ernie Adams, Forrest Taylor, "Silver"
D: Elmer Clifton
SP: Monroe Schaff, Arthur Hoerl

WAGONS WESTWARD (Republic, June 19, 1940) 70 Mins.
Chester Morris, Anita Louise, *Buck Jones,* Ona Munson, George Hayes, Guinn Williams, Douglas Fowley, Edmund Cobb, Charles Stevens, Selmer Jackson, Virginia Brissac, Wayne Hull, Joe McGuinn, Trevor Bardette, John Gallaudent, Tex Landers, "Silver"
D: Lew Landers
SP: Harrison Jacobs, Joseph M. Marsh
AP: Armand Schaefer

WHITE EAGLE (Columbia, January 31, 1941) 15 Chapters.
Buck Jones, Raymond Hatton, Dorothy Fay, James Craven, Chief Yowlachie, Jack Ingram, Charles King, John Merton, Roy Barcroft, Edward Hearn, Al Ferguson, J. Paul Jones, Edward Cecil, Chick Hannon, Bob Woodward, Horace B. Carpenter, Steve Clark, Merrill McCormack, Constantine Romanoff, Yakima Canutt, Kit Guard, Harry Tenbrook, Hank Richardson, Charles Hamilton, Edward Peil, Hank Bell, Lloyd Whitlock, Eddie Featherston, George Chesebro, Kenne Duncan, Bud Osborne, Edmund Cobb, Dick Cramer, Jack O'Shea, Richard Ellis, Robert Elliott, "Silver"
D: James W. Horne
S: Fred Myton—Adapted from the 1932 "White Eagle" feature

SP: Arch Heath, Morgan B. Cox, John Cutting, Lawrence Taylor
P: Larry Darmour
Chapter Titles: (1) Flaming Tepees, (2) The Jail Delivery, (3) The Dive Into Quicksand, (4) The Warning Death Knife, (5) Treachery at the Stockdale, (6) The Gun-Cane Murder, (7) The Revealing Blotter, (8) Bird-Calls of Deliverance, (9) The Fake Telegram, (10) Mystic Dots and Dashes, (11) The Ear at the Window, (12) The Massacre Invitation, (13) The Framed-up Showdown, (14) The Fake Army General, (15) Treachery Downed

RIDERS OF DEATH VALLEY (Universal, July 1, 1941) 15 Chapters
Dick Foran, Buck Jones, Leo Carrillo, Charles Bickford, Lon Chaney, Jr., Noah Beery, Jr., "Big Boy" Williams, Jeannie Kelly (Jean Brooks), Monte Blue, James Blaine, Glenn Strange, Roy Barcroft, Ethan Laidlaw, Dick Alexander, Jack Rockwell, Frank Austin, Charles Thomas, William Hall, James Gulifoyle, Ernie Adams, Edmund Cobb, William Pagan, Jack Clifford, Richard Travis, Ivar McFadden, Jerome Harte, Ruth Rickaby, Jack Perrin, Don Rowan, Bud Osborne, Slim Whitaker, Frank Brownlee, Art Miles, Ed Payson, James Farley, Alonzo Price, Ted Adams, Dick Rush, Ken Nolan, Jay Michael, Gil Perkins, Duke York, Bob Burns, Art Dillard, Jack Casey, Tex Palmer, "Silver"
D: Ray Taylor, Ford Beebe
S: Oliver Drake
SP: Sherman Lowe, Basil Dickey, George Plympton, Jack Connell
P: Henry MacRae
Chapter Titles: (1) Death Marks the Trail, (2) Menacing Herd, (3) Plunge of Peril, (4) Flaming Fury, (5) Avalanche of Doom, (6) Blood and Gold, (7) Death Rides the Storm, (8) Descending Doom, (9) Death Holds the Reins, (10) Devouring Flames, (11) Fatal Blast, (12) Thundering Doom, (13) The Bridge of Disaster, (4) A Fight to the Death, (15) The Harvest of Hate

ARIZONA BOUND (Monogram, July 19, 1941) 57 Mins.
("Rough Riders" Series)
Buck Jones, Tim McCoy, Raymond Hatton, Tris Coffin, Dennis Moore, Luana Walters, Kathryn Sheldon, Gene Alsace, Slim Whitaker, Artie Ortego, I. Stanford Jolley, Horace Murphy, Hal Price, Jack Daley, Augie Gomez, Slim Whitaker, Hal Price, "Silver"
D: Spencer G. Bennet
S: Oliver Drake
SP: Jess Bowers (Adele Buffington)
P: Scott R. Dunlap

THE GUNMAN FROM BODIE (Monogram, September 26, 1941) 62 Mins.
("Rough Rider" Series)
Buck Jones, Tim McCoy, Raymond Hatton, Christine McIntyre, David O'Brien, Robert Frazer, Frank LaRue, Charles King, Lynton Brent, Max Walzman, Gene Alsace, John Merton, Jerry Sheldon, Jack King, Earl Douglas, Warren Jackson, Billy Carro, Frederick Gee, "Silver"
D: Spencer G. Bennet
SP: Jess Bowers (Adele Buffington)
P: Scott R. Dunlap

Buck Jones, Charles King, and Lynton Brent talk it over in *Gunman From Bodie* (Monogram, 1941).

FORBIDDEN TRAILS (Monogram, December 26, 1941) 54 Mins.
("Rough Riders" Series)
Buck Jones, Tim McCoy, Raymond Hatton, Tris Coffin, Charles King, Glenn Strange, Lynton Brent, Jerry Sheldon, Hal Price, Dave O'Brien, Christine McIntyre, Dick Alexander, Tom London, Frank Yaconelli, Eddie Phillips, Milburn Morante, Tex Palmer, Lee Shumway, Edward Peil, Sr., Herman Hack, Silvertip Baker, Dan White, Jess Cavan, Jack Kirk, Sarah Padden, "Silver"
D: Robert North Bradbury
SP: Jess Bowers (Adele Buffington)
S: Oliver Drake
P: Scott R. Dunlap

BELOW THE BORDER (Monogram, January 30, 1942) 57 Mins.
("Rough Riders" Series)
Buck Jones, Tim McCoy, Raymond Hatton, Linda Brent, Eva Puig, Charles King, Dennis Moore, Roy Barcroft, Ted Mapes, Bud Osborne, Merrill McCormack, Jack Rockwell, "Silver"
D: Howard Bretherton
SP: Jess Bowers (Adele Buffington)
P: Scott R. Dunlap

GHOST TOWN LAW (Monogram, March 27, 1942) 62 Mins.
("Rough Rider" Series)
Buck Jones, Tim McCoy, Raymond Hatton, Virginia Carpenter, Murdock McQuarrie, Charles King, Howard Masters, Ben Corbett, Tom London, "Silver"
D: Howard Bretherton
SP: Jess Bowers (Adele Buffington)
P: Scott R. Dunlap

DOWN TEXAS WAY (Monogram, May 22, 1942) 57 Mins.
("Rough Riders" Series)
Buck Jones, Tim McCoy, Raymond Hatton, Luana Walters, Dave O'Brien, Glenn Strange, Lois Austin, Harry Woods, Tom London, Kansas Moehring, Jack Daley, "Silver"
D: Howard Bretherton
SP: Jess Bowers (Adele Buffington)
P: Scott R. Dunlap

RIDERS OF THE WEST (Monogram, August 21, 1942) 58 Mins.
("Rough Riders" Series)
Buck Jones, Tim McCoy, Raymond Hatton, Sarah Padden, Dennis Moore, Harry Woods, Christine McIntyre, Walter McGrail, Harry Frazer, Bud Osborne, Charles King, Lee Phelps, Kermit Maynard, Milburn Morante, Edward Piel, Sr., Lynton Brent, J. Merrill Holmes, George Morrell, Tom London, "Silver"
D: Howard Bretherton
SP: Jess Bowers (Adele Buffington)
P: Scott R. Dunlap

WEST OF THE LAW (Monogram, October 2, 1942) 60 Mins.
("Rough Riders" Series)
Buck Jones, Tim McCoy, Raymond Hatton, Evelyn Cook, Milburn Morante, Harry Woods, Roy Barcroft, Bud McTaggart, George DeNormand, Jack Daley, Bud Osborne, Lynton Brent, "Silver"
D: Howard Bretherton
SP: Jess Bowers (Adele Buffington)
P: Scott R. Dunlap

DAWN ON THE GREAT DIVIDE (Monogram, December 18, 1942) 63 Mins.
Buck Jones, Mona Barrie, Raymond Hatton, Rex Bell, Robert Lowery, Harry Woods, Christine McIntyre, Betty Blythe, Robert Frazer, Tris Coffin, Jan Wiley, Roy Barcroft, Dennis Moore, Steve Clark, Reed Howes, Bud Osborne, I. Stanford Jolley, Artie Ortego, George Morrell, Milburn Morante, Ray Jones, Maude Eburne, Lee Shumway, Warren Jackson, Ben Corbett, Denver Dixon, Herman Hack, Merrill McCormack, "Silver"

SCREEN SNAPSHOTS (Columbia, September 4, 1947) 9½ Mins.
(Segment called "Hollywood Cowboys")
Buck Jones, Gene Autry, Roy Rogers, Will Rogers, Tom Mix, John Mack Brown, Hoot Gibson, William S. Hart, William Boyd, Robert Young, Jackie Coogan
D: Ralph Staub

HOLLYWOOD BRONC BUSTERS (Columbia, 1956) 9 Mins.
("Screen Snapshots" Series)
Jack Lemmon, Ralph Staub; Film clips featuring Gene Autry, Roy Rogers, Tom Mix, William Boyd, William S. Hart, *Buck Jones,* Hoot Gibson, Charles Starrett
D/P: Ralph Staub

8 • REB RUSSELL

A Refreshing Breeze Through Gower Gulch

Almost forty-five years ago a handsome young athlete could be seen come charging on the screen as a rip-snortin', hell-bent-for-leather cowboy in the tradition laid down by Tom Mix. The picture was *The Man From Hell* (Kent, 1934) and the star was Reb Russell.

Reb was born in Osawatomie, Kansas, on May 31, 1905, and still ranks as probably the greatest football player ever produced by the state of Kansas. Knute Rockne called him "the greatest plunging fullback I ever saw." As a quarterback at the University of Nebraska he made the then All-Big-Six team, but after one year he transferred to Northwestern where he was destined to become a football immortal. The year was 1929, and because of the transfer he was ineligible to play football his first season. But he stayed to graduate from Northwestern in 1932 as an All-American fullback who led the Big Ten in scoring, and made Ripley's "Believe It or Not" by averaging six yards every time he carried the pigskin. And he was no slouch in wrestling, either.

Not a dull or introverted person, Reb was elected both president of the senior class and top man on campus. He also received other forms of recognition. Sustaining a back injury in his senior year, he was able to play in only one regular-season game. But he did play in the East-West Shrine game on January 1, 1932, in San Francisco, gained more yards than the entire West team,

and led the East to a 7-0 win. Reb came out of his back cast three weeks ahead of schedule in order to play in this game.

One of the more interesting sidelights of his football glory is that there never was any promotion of Reb as a football star. When he went to Nebraska, he received no athletic scholarships; likewise, when he went to Northwestern, there was no stipend of any kind. Reb was proud of not ever having taken a penny of the taxpayers' educational dollar as a college athlete.

Hollywood beckoned in the summer of 1932. Universal was making *The All-American,* a football picture, and for authenticity and box-office appeal the studio decided to cast fourteen All-Americans in it. Thus Reb Russell, along with thirteen other football greats, found himself at work on the Universal lot.

No one was in a hurry in 1932, it seemed, as shooting of the picture dragged on for six weeks. So nightly entertainment for the ex-collegians was the order of the day. And they had a ball. Somehow, in this mad whirl of social activity, Reb made the acquaintance of Tom Mix, one of filmdom's greatest money-makers who was completing his last series at Universal. Tom took a liking to the husky, good-natured Russell and became, in effect, his mentor. He liked football games and went to them religiously but could never fully understand what was going on. So he insisted that Reb accompany him and interpret

Reb Russell

is commendable, but there was a little more to his stardom than merely being able to mount and ride a steed. For one thing, he was a perfect physical specimen; and for another, he was good-looking and already had a name as a football great.

Lesser hired Reb with the intention of starring him in a film of Harold Bell Wright's novel *When a Man's a Man* as an opener for the series. Before filming could start, however, Lesser and Wright became embroiled in a legal squabble as to whether Lesser had the right to make a talkie instead of a silent film. Several producers who had bought screen rights before the advent of talkies found themselves tied up in litigation over the matter. While Lesser fumed and hassled with Wright and planned a Tarzan movie, Reb played a season of professional football with the Philadelphia Eagles—with Lesser's permission—drawing a salary from both Lesser and the Eagles.

Since it looked as though the Lesser picture would never be made, Reb asked for and obtained his release. He had a chance to star in a series of Westerns for another independent producer, Willis Kent, who planned to market his pictures through states' rights distribution. This could have been a costly mistake for Reb, since Lesser finally did make his proposed film with George O'Brien in the lead role. Lesser had both more money to plow into his films and a better distribution hookup than did Kent.

Before going further, it should be mentioned that, before signing with Lesser, Reb had come close to becoming a Columbia Western star as replacement for Ken Maynard whom the studio was ready to drop because of his erratic behavior and salary and other demands. Tom Mix was excited about the prospect of Reb's joining the Columbia stable of stars and was also a little peeved at Maynard at the time. Mix promised Reb all sorts of support, but to no avail; Maynard and Columbia resolved their differences, and Russell signed with Kent. Reb's initial film for Kent was *Fighting To Live,* a dog story featuring Gaylord Pendleton and Marion Shilling. His role as third principal gave Reb a modicum of acting experience and camera savvy.

Reb's first starrer, *The Man From Hell,* was a fast-paced shoot-'em-up that was well received on the independent market. Eight other oaters followed.

for him and was perpetually amazed at Reb's insight into the game and savvy of what was happening or was about to happen. Tom was quite a flamboyant cowboy and got around and into places that no mere All-American or lesser cowboy actor could expect to gain admittance. So it was that Reb, through the auspices of Mix, was able to meet and know some of the big stars of the day. For some reason Tom thought that Reb would be just the right fellow as a husband for his daughter Ruth and tried to promote a romance—but to no avail. Ruth and Reb were only friends.

Reb made a film test for Universal with Walter Brennan and a dog. Universal never followed up on the test. But Sol Lesser, the independent producer of Tarzan and Western movies, did. On the basis of it, he offered Reb a contract to star in eighteen Westerns. As Reb much later put it, "They found out I could get on and off a horse, so I made some Westerns." Reb's modesty

And rough and tough they were, utilizing Reb's athletic prowess to the maximum degree. What he lacked in acting ability he amply made up for in mile-a-minute thrills which satisfied the neighborhood matinee audiences of 1934–1935. He rode a beautiful white gelding, named "Rebel" by a script girl who thought the name went well with "Reb." Reb had bought "Rebel" in Parsons, Kansas, and brought him to California for the Western series.

According to Reb, "I loved that old horse. We'd be out on location, and all the cast would either be asleep or playing gin rummy. But when it came time for old Rebel to work, they all came to watch. There was one scene where Rebel had to act as if he was looking at a picture I was holding. So we put a carrot on my knee—oh, he loved carrots—and when I called him over he would look down, see the carrot and grab it. We went through this three or four times when we didn't have any carrot there. But Rebel looked, and it looked just like he was looking at a picture. That's how they do some of those things."

"Rebel" was trained for his picture assignments by Tracey Lane, the same man who had trained "Tarzan" for Ken Maynard. And, at Reb's request, he helped Gene Autry find a suitable horse to ride, one that became famous as "Champion."

Western film historians will immediately realize that Reb Russell preceded Gene Autry and Smiley Burnette on the Hollywood scene by a couple of years. These two would-be actors, on being hired by Nat Levine for Mascot, looked up Russell when they got to Hollywood. Autry knew of Reb through his football fame and that he was from down Oklahoma for several weeks, he turned his house over to them; later, the three of them lived together for over a month. Reb helped Gene pick out his first saddle and in innumerable ways helped him become acclimated to life as a not-yet-successful cowboy in the Hollywood hills.

The Russell Westerns were shot in about ten days each. Like most independent Westerns of that era, they did not have a musical score. But they made money. For example, Paramount might take most of the proceeds of, say, a Mae West film as rental; a theatre manager could book a Reb Russell Western for a weekend, pay a flat rental of twenty-five dollars, pack his theatre, and pocket

nearly all the proceeds. The films were made on location on the Hearst ranches in southern California and at Lone Pine, California. Interiors were done on a lease arrangement with one of the Poverty Row studios.

When the Kent series ended, Reb declined to sign for another, although he could have. Those film historians who have implied that he simply washed out as a Western star are misinformed. He left Hollywood because he could see what it was doing to those who stayed there too long. Like the rest, he was making good money but was unable to save any. And he was an educated man. He knew that in all likelihood, if he remained, ten or fifteen years later he would be grinding out Westerns of the same caliber. Worse, he could wind up as many of the old-timers had—working for peanuts and living in the glories of the past. Reb wanted more out of life than to say, "Come on, Rebel, we can head them off at the pass." Or, in later years, perhaps merely, "They went that-a-way" as an extra. So he saddled up and voluntarily left Hollywood. Although Reb's Westerns for Kent had been good, solid, albeit low-budget affairs, they did not afford him the credentials for breaking into the highly-paid stable of film cowboys of the time.

Reb developed a "wild west" act and toured with the popular Russell Brothers Circus (the name is coincidental; he was not related to the owners), performing a whip act and engaging in unbelievable feats of stunt-riding. He also took a second circus outing with the Downey Brothers Circus, but after two years of traveling he began to long for the tranquility of the range. And so, putting show business behind him, Reb returned to his beloved south-central homeland to become a successful farmer and rancher, with ranches in both Kansas and Oklahoma.

Reb Russell died on March 16, 1978, in Coffeyville, Kansas. In the three years before his death he had appeared at Western film festivals around the country, proving he was still a popular favorite with the fans and enjoying a return to the limelight after so many years of obscurity. He was a gentleman in every sense of the word, and the Western genre was blessed by his interlude as a cowboy star. Lucky was the boy who, having adopted Reb as a hero, attempted to emulate him. For, in so doing, he was not likely to stray far from

Reb Russell gets in a little practice while the Downie Brothers Circus sets up (1937).

the proper range—the one that provided the best nourishment for the development of soul, mind, and body. As old cowboys might say, "He done himself proud" and was truly a man "fittin' to ride the range with." What more could a kid expect for the dimes he spent "way back when. . . ."? He got his dime's worth many times over.

REB RUSSELL *Filmography*

THE ALL-AMERICAN (Universal, October 1932) 9 Reels. Richard Arlen, Andy Devine, Gloria Stuart, James Gleason, John Darrow, Preston Foster, Merna Kennedy, Harold Waldridge, June Clyde, and the All-Star and All-American football teams (with *Reb Russell* of Northwestern and other football players)
D: Russell Mack
S: Dale Van Every, Richard Schayer
SP: Frank W. Wead, Ferdinand Reyher
P: Carl Laemmle, Jr.

THE LOST SPECIAL (Universal, 1932) 12 Chapters. Frank Albertson, Cecilia Parker, Ernie Nevers, Caryl Lincoln, Francis Ford, Frank Glendon, Tom London, Al Ferguson, Edmund Cobb, George Magrill, Joe Bonomo, Harold Nelson, Jack Clifford, *Reb Russell*
D: Henry McRae
S: Arthur Conan Doyle
SP: Ella O'Neill, George Plympton, Basil Dickey, George Morgan
Chapter Titles: (1) The Lost Special, (2) Racing Death, (3) The Red Lantern, (4) Devouring Flames, (5) The Lightning Strikes, (6) The House of Mystery, (7) The Tank-Room Terror, (8) The Fatal Race, (9) Into the Depths, (10) The Jaws of Death, (11) The Flaming Forest, (12) Retribution

FIGHTING TO LIVE (Principal, May 6, 1934) 60 Mins. Marion Shilling, Gaylord Pendleton, *Reb Russell*, Eddie Phillips, Ted Stroback, Bruce Mitchell, Lloyd Ingraham, Henry Hall, "Captain" (a dog)
D: Edward F. Cline
S: Robert Ives
P: Sol Lesser

THE MAN FROM HELL (Kent/Cristo, August 29, 1934) 58 Mins.
Reb Russell, Fred Kohler, Ann D'Arcy, George Hayes, Jack Rockwell, Yakima Canutt, Slim Whitaker, Roy D'Arcy, "Rebel"
D: Lew Collins
S: Ed Earl Repp
SP: Melville Shyer
P: Willis Kent

Downie Brothers Circus poster (1937).

Reb Russell and Yakima Canutt in *Fighting Thru* (Kent, 1934).

Ben Corbett, Mary Jane Carey, and Reb Russell in *Border Vengeance* (Kent, 1935).

FIGHTING THROUGH (Kent, August 29, 1934) 55 Mins.
Reb Russell, Lucille Lund, Yakima Canutt, Edward Hearn, Chester Gans, Steve Clemente, Bill Patton, Frank McCarroll, Ben Corbett, Hank Bell, Slim Whitaker, Nelson McDowell, Lew Meehan, Jack Jones, Jack Kirk, Chuck Baldra, Wally Wales, "Rebel"
D/S/SP: Harry Fraser
P: Willis Kent

OUTLAW RULE (Kent, February 1935).
Reb Russell, Betty Mack, Yakima Canutt, Jack Rockwell, John McGuire, Al Bridge, Joseph Girard, Jack Kirk, Henry Hall, "Rebel"
D: S. Roy Luby
P: Willis Kent

RANGE WARFARE (Kent, March 1935).
Reb Russell, Lucille Lund, Wally Wales, Lafe McKee, Roger Williams, Slim Whitaker, Ed Boland, Dick Botiller, Chief Blackhawk, Ed Porter, Gene Alsace (Rocky Camron), Bart Carre, "Rebel"
D: S. Roy Luby
P: Willis Kent
S: E. B. Mann—"The Death Whistler"

ARIZONA BAD MAN (Kent, 1935) 58 Mins.
Reb Russell, Lois January, Edmund Cobb, Tommy Bupp, Slim Whitaker, Dick Botiller, Ben Corbett, Anne Howard, Tracy Layne, Walter James, Silver Harr, "Rebel"
D: S. Roy Luby
P: Willis Kent

BLAZING GUNS (Kent/Marcy, 1935).
Reb Russell, Marion Shilling, Lafe McKee, Joseph Girard, Frank McCarroll, Charles "Slim" Whitaker, Charles Murray, Jr., "Rebel"
D: Ray Heinz
SP: Forbes Parkhill
P: Willis Kent

BORDER VENGEANCE (Kent/Marcy, 1935).
Reb Russell, Mary Jane Carey, Kenneth MacDonald, Ben Corbett, Hank Bell, Glenn Strange, June Bupp, Norman Feusuer, Clarence Geldert, Charles "Slim" Whitaker, Ed Phillips, Marty Joyce, Fred Burns, Pat Harmon, Bart Carre, "Rebel"
D: Ray Heinz
P: Willis Kent

Reb Russell and Charles Whitaker in *Arizona Badman* (Kent, 1935).

Reb Russell, Roger Williams, Tracey Lane, Art Dillard, and Edmund Cobb in *Cheyenne Tornado* (Kent, 1935).

CHEYENNE TORNADO (Kent, 1935).
Reb Russell, Victoria Vinton, Edmund Cobb, Roger Williams, Tina Menard, Dick Botiller, Ed Porter, Winton Perry, Hank Bell, Bart Carre, Lafe McKee, Jack Evans, Oscar Gahan, Clyde McClary, "Rebel"
D: William O'Connor
P: Willis Kent

LIGHTNING TRIGGERS (Kent/Marcy, 1935).
Reb Russell, Yvonne Pelletier, Fred Kohler, Jack Rockwell, Edmund Cobb, Lillian Castle, Lew Meehan, William McCall, Dick Botiller, Olin Francis, Artie Artego, Steve Clark, Ed Porter, "Rebel," and with song over opening credits sung by Smiley Burnette
D: S. Roy Luby
P: Willis Kent

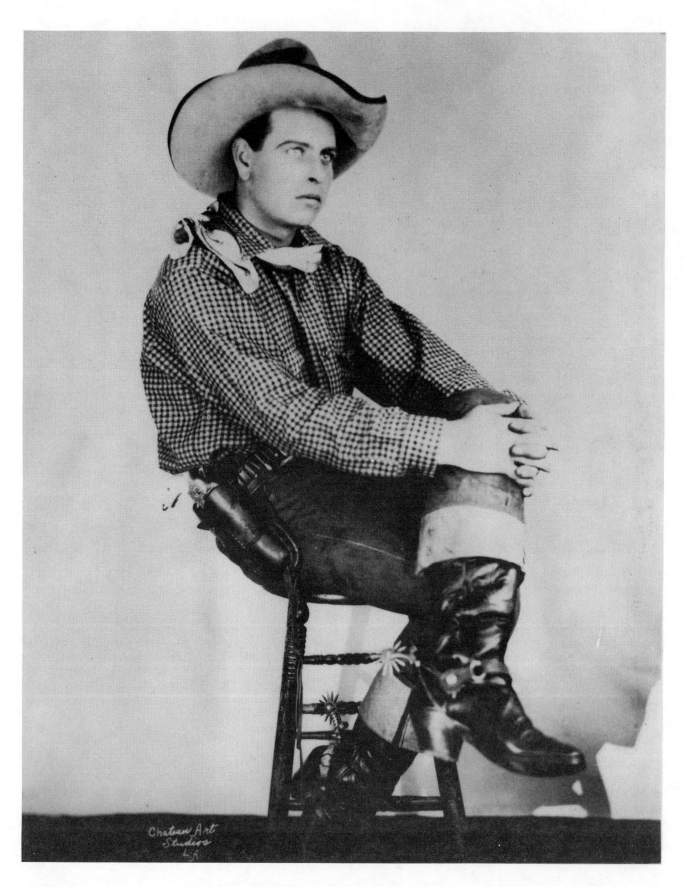

Al Hoxie

9 • AL HOXIE

A Hard-Riding Galoot

"Al Hoxie? Al Hoxie? Can't say I've ever heard of him, but let me think. . . . Say, wasn't he one of those cowboy stars who used to be in silent pictures? Sure, now I remember. But his name was Jack, wasn't it? Yeah, you mean *Jack* Hoxie."

A typical reaction to the mention of Al Hoxie? Well, not really. Very likely there are few today who can even recall Al's much-better-known brother, Jack Hoxie, one of the greatest of the silent Western stars. Call it one more instance of the ephemerality of fame.

The Western aficionado will, of course, recognize the name of Jack Hoxie, Harry Carey, Buck Jones, Ken Maynard, Tom Mix, and those of other great Western stars of the 1920s. And the more astute devotee of the genre will probably not stumble in recognizing names like Wally Wales, Buddy Roosevelt, Jack Perrin, and Bob Steele. But Al Hoxie? Ah, here we come to one of a group of cowboy stars whose careers are no longer remembered—except by a handful of film historians and those with aging memories who, as youngsters clutching their nickels and dimes, always attended the Saturday matinees at the second- and third-rate movie houses of fifty years ago.

The 1920s comprised a rich decade in terms of the quality of B Westerns of the major producers of such films. And some independent companies that produced for the states' rights market also turned out surprisingly good Western fare. Every-

thing considered, these sagebrushers rated rather high in production value. Their direction and acting were acceptable, they were well scripted, had plenty of action, and usually were well photographed and edited.

But a raft of independent producing companies, looking for a fast buck in exchange for a cheap product, jumped into Western film production to turn out what I call cow-dung Westerns. Understand, now, I'm not really knocking these dregs of the Western field. They met a need, filled a void, and entertained thousands of noncritical moviegoers of that golden era. And so far as the enthusiastic intensity they engendered in their audiences is concerned, why, nothing since has come close to matching it. Anyway, action was what Western matinee audiences wanted, and action is what they got—all the way, from one- or two-reel featurettes to five- and six-reel features and those magnificent 10- to 20-chapter serials.

Yep, Al Hoxie was just one of the dozens of minor Western stars who held the public's fancy for a time, helped Poverty Row producers reap some neat profits from cheap and virtually plotless cowboy flickers, and then, when their popularity waned, either reverted to minor roles or just disappeared from the screen altogether. But as one of the more interesting personalities to ride the trails (well marked by cow-dung, perhaps) of Western filmdom, Al Hoxie fought and rode his way across the screens of many a neighborhood picture palace.

Al (for Alton) Hoxie was born in Nez Perce, Idaho, on October 7, 1901, his parents having migrated from Oklahoma Territory where his brother Jack was born six years earlier. Here on the Salmon River in northern Idaho Al spent his youth. At the age of eighteen, wanderlust got the best of him—as it had his brother—and he wound up in California in November, 1919, to visit Jack and see at firsthand the fascinating world of make-believe in which Jack had been working with ho-hum success for six or seven years. You see, Brother Jack was working in pictures.

Jack had just signed a contract to co-star with Ann Little in the Western serial *Lightning Bryce* for National Film Corporation. And, knowing his way around Hollywood, he was able to introduce Al to producers and directors who could give him work as a stuntman, double, or rider. Al's first work was as a bit player in *Kentucky Colonel,* which starred Joseph Dowling.

After scoring in *Lightning Bryce,* Jack was starred in *Thunderbolt Jack,* a National Film serial release of 1920. Playing opposite him was Marin Sais—whom he married within the year—and playing Marin's brother was Al. It was a good beginning for the husky nineteen-year-old who was listed fifth in the cast.

Al worked with his brother for the next several years, playing in practically every picture Jack made until 1925. Al doubled for Jack in several films and did stunts in many of them. He also worked in other cowboy films.

During 1920-1925 Al stayed busy in films, depending more on his athletic prowess than on his acting ability. But he did appear as a soldier in Lon Chaney's unforgettable classic of 1923, *The Hunchback of Notre Dame,* filmed by Universal. In 1924 Al played in a second serial, *Days of '49,* starring Neva Gerber and Edmund Cobb. This 15-chapter Arrow serial was directed by Jacques Jaccard and Ben Wilson, the latter a famous serial star himself. Al played the part of an Indian chief, and his friend and fellow stuntman, Yakima Canutt, had an important role.

During this period Al also played the part of a down-and-out tramp in *Back Trail,* a film starring his brother Jack. He played the heavy in several two-reelers starring Edmund Cobb, and also in some which starred Fred Gilman. He was the heavy in a couple of Ted Wells pictures, a heavy in a second Reginald Denny picture, and a cowboy in William S. Hart's last film, *Tumbleweeds.* Al estimates that he was in thirty-five to forty pictures in the early 1920s.

In 1925 filmdom was cluttered with cowboy actors—good, mediocre, and downright bad. But the small movie houses that were growing in number demanded Westerns, which made money even when they were bad. Quite often an independent Western, rented for ten dollars a day by a theatre manager, would outgross a non-Western from a major studio renting for $100 to $150 a day. And an independent Western might do almost as well as a Buck Jones, a Hoot Gibson, or a Tom Mix Western renting for $50 a day. Kids made up the bulk of the matinee audiences in the lesser movie houses, and they settled for anyone on a horse that could fight, ride, shoot well, and did not fool around with women very much. Thus, many independent series destined for the states' rights market were produced during the 1920s.

Against this background, it was only natural that Al Hoxie should be elevated to stardom. He had a famous name (because of Jack); he could ride and stunt with the best of them; and he had a pleasant personality which came across on screen reasonably well. Not as big as Jack—Al weighed about one hundred ninety pounds and stood five feet ten inches—Al nevertheless looked a good deal like him, and this was a distinct advantage. In addition, Al was quite a handsome young man in his own right.

Seeing potential in Al, Anchor Film Distributors signed him to star in a series of eight Westerns released in 1926. All were directed by J. P. McGowan, so far as is known, and, you're right, I guess you could call them cow-dung Westerns. In Al's defense, however, it should be pointed out that although his Anchor pictures were his worst films, his other pictures were much better.

There was something about Al that caught the fancy of Western fans, something that has endeared him to them to this day. He still gets fan mail. I think it can be fairly said that Al was limited more by the cheapness of his films and their often shoddy production than by any ineptitude of his own as an actor.

Al next signed with Bud Barsky for a series of eight Westerns that were released in 1926-1927. All were filmed at one time up near Three rivers in Sequoia National Forest and directed by Paul Hurst. They literally shot the eight films simultaneously, Al jumping from one film to another in the same day. Paul would say, "Now, Al, this scene is for Picture No. 2." Later, "Now this shot is for No. 6, and we'll follow with the chase scene for No. 5, and the romantic interlude for No. 1." Al recalls that it was a madhouse. His biggest headache was to remember the correct wardrobe for each film. He was constantly changing clothes.

Following the Barsky series, Al was signed by Bill Pizor Productions, at the same salary of $100 a week, to do a series of eight films down around San Diego at what was known as La Mesa Studios. The films were released through Krelbar Pictures. Al moved down to La Mesa, and the company paid his house rent while they shot there. Evelyn Miller was the leading lady in three or four of the films. Then they returned to Hollywood to make the rest, where Pizor had a deal with the Bailey School for Aspiring Actors to provide the heroines for Al. For a sizable sum Pizor would cast a star-struck girl opposite Al and thereby not only eliminate an expense but also generate revenue.

One of the best entries in this last series, and one of the best of all Al's features, was *The Rustler's End*, in which he was supported by Bill Mostell and Betty Gates. The film begins with Al's making like Clark Gable or Rudolph Valentino as he sweeps the lovely Miss Gates into his arms for a long kissing embrace. But the real shooting action soon begins, and there is even a scene or two where effective tinting was employed. Quite unusual for independent Westerns of that era.

By 1928 the film industry was in turmoil over the advent of sound. Al, his contract with William M. Pizor not renewed, ambled out of movies altogether. He made a personal appearance tour in Texas in 1929, and then went north to Oregon. There he worked in the woods for a year, and afterward just roamed around until 1934. Then he returned to Los Angeles, took a job as a streetcar conductor, and stayed on until 1939.

In 1940 Al joined the California State Forestry Service as an assistant ranger and worked in that

Al Hoxie and Ronald Reagan at ceremonies wherein Hoxie received California Medal of Honor for bravery in the line of duty as a security officer (1968).

capacity until 1944, when he joined the Anaheim Police Department. He put in fifteen and a half years as a policeman and quit in 1958. But he couldn't stay inactive and went back to the forestry service to work eight months as a lookout. Realizing he still liked law-enforcement work, he then went to work for the State of California as chief security officer at Patton State Hospital in San Bernardino County. Just fourteen days before retiring, Al had an exceptional encounter at the hospital. Called to the admitting room, he found an ex-patient with a loaded revolver and a hostage. This man had already shot two people, his wife and his employer. Al talked him into letting the hostage go and handing over the gun. As a result, Al received the California Medal of Honor, the state's highest award. Presentation was made by Governor Ronald Reagan, who reminisced with Al about moviemaking days.

While working at the hospital, Al met a secretary who is now his wife Marie. Married in 1964, they both continued working until 1968, when they retired. Since then, they have been living in Redlands, California, where Al has pursued his hobbies of woodcraft, gardening, landscaping, and sports.

Luckily Al has lived to see, after forty-five years of obscurity, a rebirth of interest in his films. Long forgotten, Al has been swept up and carried along by the nostalgia craze. In 1975 he was a hit at the Western Film Festival in Nashville. The following year he returned there and was also a featured guest at the Los Angeles Western Film Festival. One of his greatest honors was to be invited to the stuntmen's hall of fame in California and have his footprints permanently placed in cement there.

"A rarin', roarin' two-gun man of the West." "The screen's most daring rider!" "The greatest stunt rider in the history of the screen." These catchlines for *His Last Bullet* may or may not have validly described Al Hoxie, Western film star. One would need to see a fair sampling of his movies to decide.

AL HOXIE *Filmography*

RUTH OF THE ROCKIES (Pathe, August 29, 1920) 15 Chapters.
Ruth Roland, Herbert Heyess, Thomas Lingham, Fred Burns, Norma Bichole, William Gilliss, Jack Rollens, Alton *(Al) Hoxie* (as a double)
D: George Marshall
S: Johnston McCulley—"Broadway Bab"
P: Ruth Roland
Chapter Titles: (1) The Mysterious Trunk, (2) The Inner Circle, (3) The Tower of Danger, (4) Between Two Fires, (5) Double Crossed, (6) The Eagle's Nest, (7) Troubled Waters, (8) Danger Trails, (9) The Perilous Path, (10) Outlawed, (11) The Fatal Diamond, (12) The Secret Order, (13) The Surprise Attack, (14) The Secret of Regina Island, (15) The Hidden Treasure

THUNDERBOLT JACK (Arrow, November 1, 1920) 10 Chapters.
Jack Hoxie, Marin Sais, Chris Frank, Steve Clemento, Alton *(Al) Hoxie*, Edith Stayart
D: Murdock MacQuarrie, Francis Ford
(No copyright records indicating the copyrighting of Chapters 3-10 by title)

THE HUNCHBACK OF NOTRE DAME (Universal-Super Jewel, September 2, 1923) 12 Reels.
Lon Chaney, Ernest Torrence, Patsy Ruth Miller, Norman Kerry, Kate Lester, Brandon Hurst, Raymond Hatton, Tully Marshall, Nigel De Brulier, Harry Van Meter, Gladys Brockwell, Eulalie Jensen, Winifred Bryson, Nick De Ruiz, Edwin Wallock, W. Ray Meyers, William Parke, Sr., John Cossar, Roy Laidlaw, George MacQuarrie, Jay Hunt, Harry De Vere, Pearl Tupper, Eva Lewis, Jane Sherman, Helen Bruneau, Gladys Johnston, Cesare Gravina, *Al Hoxie*
D: Wallace Worsley
Scen: Edward T. Lowe, Tony Kornman
S: Victor Hugo—*Notre-Dame de Paris*

THE RED WARNING (Universal, December 17, 1923) 5 Reels.
Jack Hoxie, Elinor Field, Fred Kohler, Frank Rice, Jim Welsh, William Welsh, Ben Corbett, Ralph Fee McCullough, *Al Hoxie*, "Scout"
D: R. N. Bradbury
S/Scen: Isadore Bernstein

THE DAYS OF '49 (Arrow, March 15, 1924) 15 Chapters.
(Alternate Title: CALIFORNIA IN '49—also released in a feature version)
Neva Gerber, Edmund Cobb, Ruth Royce, Wilbur McGaugh, Yakima Canutt, Charles Brinley, Clark Coffey, *Al Hoxie*
D: Jacques Jaccard, Jay Marchant
S/Scen: Karl Coolidge
Chapter Titles: (1) Soldiers of Fortune, (2) Red Man and White, (3) A Night of Terror, (4) The Empire Builders, (5) A Web of Lies, (6) Demetroff's Vow, (7) Facing Death, (8) Under the Bear Flag, (9) A Ride of Peril, (10) Yellow Metal and Blue Blood, (11) Gold Madness, (12) Crimson Nights, (13) Vigilantes Justice, (14) For Life and Love, (15) Trail's End

THE BACK TRAIL (Universal, June 16, 1924) 6 Reels.
Jack Hoxie, Eugenia Gilbert, Alton Stone *(Al Hoxie)*, Claude Payton, William Lester, Bill McCall, Buck Connors, Pat Harmon
D: Cliff Smith
Scen: Isadore Bernstein
S: Walter J. Coburn

RIDIN' THUNDER (Universal, June 14, 1925) 5 Reels.
Jack Hoxie, Katherine Grant, Jack Pratt, Francis Ford, George (Buck) Connors, Bert De Mare, William McCall, Broderick O'Farrell, *Al Hoxie*, "Scout"
D: Cliff Smith
Cont: Carl Krusada
Adapt: Isadore Bernstein
S: B. M. Bower—"Jean of Lazy A"

TUMBLEWEEDS (United Artists, December 20, 1925) 7 Reels.
William S. Hart, Barbara Bedford, Lucien Littlefield, J. Gordon Russell, Richard R. Neill, Jack Murphy, Lillian Leighton, Gertrude Claire, George F. Marion, Capt. T. E. Duncan, Fred Gamble, Turner Savage, Monte Collins, *Al Hoxie*
D: King Baggot and William S. Hart
S: Hal G. Evarts
P: William S. Hart

BURIED GOLD (Anchor/Rayart, April 1926) 5 Reels.
Al Hoxie, Ione Reed, Lew Meehan, Andrew Waldron
D: J. P. McGowan
P: Morris R. Schlank

Al Hoxie and player in *Buried Gold* (Anchor, 1926).

UNSEEN ENEMIES (Anchor, April 2, 1926) 5 Reels.
Al Hoxie
D: J. P. McGowan
P: Morris R. Schlank

THE LOST TRAIL (Anchor/Rayart, May 1926) 5 Reels.
Al Hoxie, Alma Rayford, Leon Kent, Frank Ellis, Charles Whitaker, Andrew Waldron, Lew O'Connor
D: J. P. McGowan
S: Charles Saxton
P: Morris R. Schlank

THE ROAD AGENT (Anchor/Rayart, May 1926) 5 Reels
Al Hoxie, Ione Reed, Lew Meehan, Leon De La Motte, Florence Lee, Cliff Lyons
D: J. P. McGowan
S/Scen: Charles Saxton
AD: Mack V. Wright
P: Morris R. Schlank

THE ACE OF CLUBS (Anchor/Rayart, August 14, 1926) 5 Reels.
Al Hoxie, Peggy Montgomery, Andrew Waldron, Jules Cowles, Minna Ferry Redman, Charles Whitaker, Frank Ellis, "Mutt" (a dog)
D: J. P. McGowan
S/Scen: G. A. Durlam
AD: Mack V. Wright
P: Morris R. Schlank

RIDING ROMANCE (Anchor/Rayart, August 15, 1926) 5 Reels.
Al Hoxie, Marjorie Bonner, Arthur Morrison, Steve Clemento
D: J. P. McGowan
AD: Mack V. Wright
S: William Lester
Scen: G. A. Durlam
P: Morris R. Schlank

RED BLOOD (Anchor/Rayart, August 25, 1926) 5 Reels.
Al Hoxie, Marjorie Warfield, Lew Meehan, Eddie Barry, J. P. McGowan, Frances Kellogg, Walter Patterson, Len Sewards
D: J. P. McGowan
AD: Mack V. Wright
S/Scen: G. A. Durlam
P: Morris R. Schlank

THE FIGHTING RANGER (Bud Barsky Productions, September 15, 1926) 5 Reels.
Al Hoxie, Ione Reed, Alfred Hewston, Cliff Lyons, Paul Hurst
D: Paul Hurst
C: Frank Cotner

BATTLING KID (Bud Barsky Productions, October 15, 1926) 5 Reels.
Al Hoxie, Ione Reed, Alfred Hewston, Cliff Lyons, Paul Hurst
D: Paul Hurst
C: Frank Cotner

THE TEXAS TERROR (Anchor/Rayart, October 28, 1926) 5 Reels.
Al Hoxie, Ione Reed, Ed Burns, George Williams, Louise Gallagher, Bob Fleming, Gordon Sackville, Harry Tenbrook, Mike Donovan
D: J. P. McGowan
AD: Mack V. Wright
P: Morris R. Schlank

SON OF A GUN (Bud Barsky Productions, November 15, 1926) 5 Reels.
Al Hoxie, Ione Reed, Alfred Hewston, Cliff Lyons, Paul Hurst
D: Paul Hurst
C: Frank Cotner

BLUE STREAK O'NEIL (Bud Barsky Productions, December 15, 1926) 5 Reels.
Al Hoxie, Ione Reed, Alfred Hewston, Cliff Lyons, Paul Hurst
D: Paul Hurst
C: Frank Cotner

Al Hoxie in *Blue Streak O'Neill* (Wild West, 1926). That's Cliff Lyons with his foot on running board.

RIDER OF THE LAW (Bud Barsky Productions, January 15, 1927) 5 Reels.
Al Hoxie, Ion Reed, Alfred Hewston, Cliff Lyons, Paul Hurst
D: Paul Hurst
C: Frank Cotner

THE RANGE RAIDERS (Bud Barsky Productions/Wild West Pictures, February 1927) 5 Reels.
Al Hoxie, Ione Reed, Alfred Hewston, Cliff Lyons, Paul Hurst
D: Paul Hurst
C: Frank Cotner

OUTLAW'S PARADISE (Bud Barsky Productions/Wild West Pictures, March 1927) 5 Reels.
Al Hoxie, Ione Reed, Alfred Hewston, Cliff Lyons, Paul Hurst
D: Paul Hurst
C: Frank Cotner

SMOKING GUNS (Bud Barsky Productions/Wild West Pictures, April 1927) 5 Reels.
Al Hoxie, Ione Reed, Alfred Hewston, Cliff Lyons, Paul Hurst
D: Paul Hurst
C: Frank Cotner

THROWING LEAD (William M. Pizor Productions, 1928) 5 Reels.
Al Hoxie
D: Robert J. Horner
Scen: L. V. Jefferson
C: Lauren A. Draper

RIP ROARING LOGAN (William M. Pizor Productions, 1928) 5 Reels.
Al Hoxie
D: Robert J. Horner
Scen: L. V. Jefferson
C: Lauren A. Draper

An austere Al Hoxie and players in unidentified Western, circa 1927.

THE RANGER'S OATH (William M. Pizor Productions, 1928) 5 Reels.
Al Hoxie
D: Robert J. Horner
Scen: L. V. Jefferson
C: Lauren A. Draper

BATTLING THRU (William M. Pizor Productions, 1928) 5 Reels.
Al Hoxie
D: Robert J. Horner

HIS LAST BULLET (Krelbar Pictures/Collwyn Pictures, March 19, 1928) 5 Reels.
Al Hoxie, Peggy O'Day, Ben Wilson, Jr., Houston Ellis, Slim Parelda, Ed LaNeice, Jed Thompson, Phil Randall, "Sunflash" (a horse)
S/Cont: Robert Dillon
D: Ben Wilson
C: Frank Cotner and Jack Jackson
P: William M. Pizor

BATTLING BURKE (Krelbar Pictures/Collwyn Pictures, March 19, 1928) 5 Reels.
Al Hoxie, "Sunflash"
D: Robert Horner
P: William Pizor

OUTLAWED (Krelbar Pictures/Collwyn Pictures, April 17, 1928) 5 Reels.
Al Hoxie, "Sunflash"
D: Robert Horner
P: William M. Pizor

DEADSHOT CASEY (Krelbar Pictures/Collwyn Pictures, July 21, 1928) 5 Reels.
Al Hoxie, Berth Rae, Chris Allen
D: Robert J. Horner
P: William M. Pizor

TWO GUN MURPHY (Krelbar Pictures/Collwyn Pictures, September 20, 1928) 5 Reels.
Al Hoxie
D: Robert J. Horner
P: William M. Pizor

Al Hoxie and Ione Reed in *Smoking Guns* (Wild West, 1927).

THE RUSTLER'S END (Krelbar Pictures/Collwyn Pictures, November 14, 1928) 5 Reels.
(Tinted Sequences)
Al Hoxie, Betty Gates, Bill Nestell, Carl Berlin, Herbert Walter
D: Robert J. Horner
P: William Pizor

THE WHITE OUTLAW (J. Charles Davis Productions/ Exhibitors Film Corp., Janaury 7, 1929) 5 Reels.
Art Acord, Lew Meehan, Walter Maly, Howard Davies, Vivian May, Bill Patton, *Al Hoxie*, Slim Mathews, Dick Nores, Betty Carter, Sherry Tansey
D: Robert J. Horner
S: Bob McKenzie
(Note: The footage showing Al as a sheriff in this film was spliced in from one of his old films. He never worked with Art Acord or for the J. Charles Davis organization)

ROARING GUNS (Krelbar Pictures/Collwyn Pictures, March 7, 1930) 5 Reels.
Al Hoxie
D: Robert J. Horner (?)
P: William M. Pizor (?)
(This film may be a re-release or one made up of footage previously used in other films. Probably it is a re-release either of a Pizor film or of one of the earlier Anchor films.)

FIGHTING COWBOY (Krelbar Pictures/Collwyn Pictures, March 14, 1930) 5 Reels.
Al Hoxie
D: Robert J. Horner (?)
P: William M. Pizor (?)
(This film may be a re-release or one made up of footage previously used in other films. Probably it is a re-release either of a Pizor film or of one of the earlier Anchor films.)

CARRYING THE MAIL (Imperial, 1934) 27 Mins.
Wally Wales, Peggy Djarling, Yakima Canutt, *Al Hoxie*, Sherry Tansey, Franklyn Farnum, "Silver King"
D: Robert Emmett
SP: Al Lane
P: William M. Pizor

Al Hoxie reminising in 1973. Album photo on left is Al; one on right is of brother Jack.

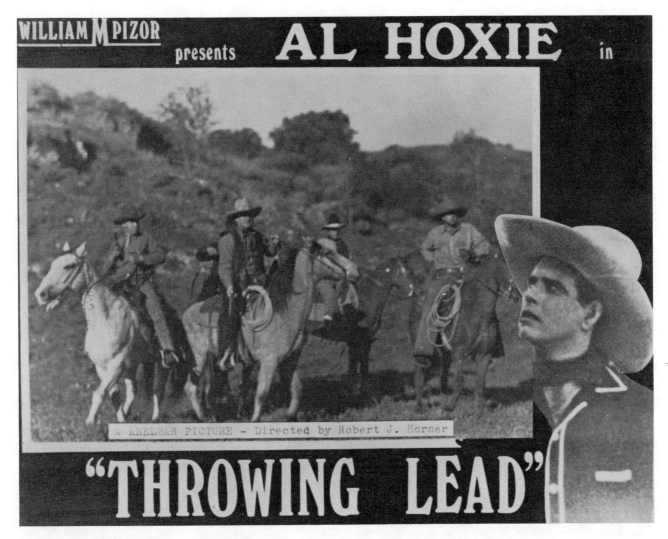

Al Hoxie in *Throwing Lead* (Pizor, 1928).

DESERT MAN (Imperial, 1934) 3 Reels.
Wally Wales, Peggy Djarling, Yakima Canutt, Franklyn
Farnum, Sherry Tansey, *Al Hoxie*, "Silver King" (a horse)
D/SP: Robert Emmett
P: William M. Pizor

PALS OF THE WEST (Imperial, 1934) 29 Mins.
Walley Wales, Dorothy Gritten, Yakima Canutt, Franklyn
Farnum, Sherry Tansey, *Al Hoxie*, Fred Parker, "Silver King"
D/SP: Robert Emmett
P: William M. Pizor

Al Hoxie sits alongside Tris Coffin at Western film
festival in Nashville, TN in 1976.

Ken Maynard

10 • KEN MAYNARD

The Cowboy Enigma

"Ken Maynard was one of the greatest movie cowboys ever to sit a saddle." Few Western devotees would take issue with this statement, for it would be like arguing against motherhood, the Fourth of July, and apple pie—a losing battle all the way. Ken was a man uniquely fitted for his time, and he succeeded where greater talents failed. Although he was the first singing cowboy, a dozen others had better voices. His brother Kermit and Yak Canutt could outride him. Reb Russell and Jack Hoxie were better circus performers. Just about anyone— but *anyone*—could handle dialogue better; yet Maynard had the necessary charisma to make him the most popular cowboy in the world in the early 1930s. One can only extend sympathy to those who might have been deprived of seeing his rooftop chases, jumps from balconies into a saddle, leaps with Tarzan from cliffs into churning waters, shootouts, slugfests, trick riding, wild prairie dashes aboard "Tarzan," and the musical and comedy interludes at which he was adept.

Ken's screen personality was at variance with his real one. On screen he projected as the All-American hero—nondrinking, woman respecting, disciplined, delightful, bashful, unemotional, happy-go-lucky, friendly. And he had a disarming smile. Yet in actuality Ken was often cantankerous, self-indulgent, undisciplined, and flirtatious. Throughout his life he had a drinking problem, and after a few drinks he sometimes became mean. On various occasions he shot hotel lights out or tires off studio trucks and was inclined to throw tantrums on the set when things displeased him. He could be the most personable guy imaginable or the rudest, depending on his mood. He was a man of extremes, but an honest one. He seldom took a tactful middle position on anything. One knew exactly where Ken stood on an issue.

Ken was born on July 21, 1895, in Vevey, Indiana, the eldest of five children. His father was a working man and had a small construction firm. Ken early demonstrated his rebellious nature by running away from home at the age of 12 to join a wagon show. He was brought back. But at the age of sixteen, with his parents' consent, he joined a touring carnival. One job led to another, and Ken moved from show to show—Buffalo Bill's Wild West (1913), Kit Carson's Wild West (1914), Hagginback and Wallace (1915 and 1918), Pawnee Bill's Wild West (1919), and finally Ringling Brothers Circus (1920).

During World War I Ken volunteered for the army and served as one of its youngest civil engineers. Most of his time he was stationed at Camp Knox, Kentucky. In 1920 John Ringling and Tex Richard talked Ken into entering rodeo competition. His first year out he won the World's All-Around Champion Cowboy award and picked up $42,000 for his arena accomplishments. For the next couple of years he traveled with Ringling

Brothers as its top cowboy attraction and also competed in rodeos. His income remained near the $40,000-a-year mark.

In late 1922 Ken was signed by Fox, after being coaxed by Buck Jones and Tom Mix to visit Hollywood. He liked the glamour associated with movies, and accepted Fox's $100-a-week offer. It was far less than he had made as a rodeo-circus rider, but money as such mattered little to him. He was seeking new thrills and was challenged by the success that Jones and Mix were having, figuring that he was just as good a cowboy as they were.

Ken's initial film appearances were in *Bra Commandments* (1923), *The Gunfighter* (1923), and *The Man Who Won* (1923). His small parts went unnoticed. Finally Fox put him into cowboy duds in a two-reeler titled *Somebody Lied* (1923), the story of a braggart cowboy whose talk was more potent than his deeds. Jean Arthur played the female lead. This picture, too, failed to attract much attention, as did his role as a riverboat gambler in *Cameo Kirby* (1923). His salary climbed to $750 a week, strangely enough, but Ken spent most of his time sitting around doing nothing. In 1924 he obtained his release from Fox, which had no interest in picking up his option, and accepted an offer from director Lynn Reynolds to appear as Paul Revere in the movie *Janice Meredith*, produced by William Randolph Hearst's Cosmopolitan Pictures. Ken's salary was $1,000 a week. The big-budget ($1.5 million) film was a success, and Ken attracted favorable notice as one of the featured players. His career as an outdoor hero was launched.

The Davis Corporation, a small independent outfit, hired Ken at $1,000 a picture to star in a series of program Westerns in late 1924. The first of these was *$50,000 Reward*. Four others followed. And then the studio edited the five features into a 10-chapter serial for release in 1926. In 1929 it would be re-released with music, synchronized sound, and a spoken prologue.

Ken was a convincing cowboy and came off well in the Davis films, which were released on the states' rights market. Appearing with him was "Tarzan," often referred to as "The Wonder Horse." The complimentary tag was well earned. Ken had just acquired the white palomino before starting the series. It was one of the wisest purchases he ever made. "Tarzan" was probably the smartest

horse in the movies and certainly performed more tricks than any of the others. He was a consummate actor and took direction well. As the years went by, he learned a whole repertoire of tricks which he could perform on cue; a grinding camera had almost the same effect on him as it did on egotistical actors—"Tarzan" was a ham at heart and capable of almost human emotion.

During the 1930s "Tarzan" was almost a co-star rather than just a beautiful horse ridden by the hero. Special scenes were written into the scripts to allow him to do his horsey bits—play dead, dance, jump chasms, laugh, act as cupid between hero and heroine, perform rescues from burning buildings and surging waters, chase and capture villains, break down doors and pull out jail windows, buck and rear on command, *ad infinitum*. "Tony," "Starlight," "Champion," "Rebel," "Trigger," "Fritz," and even "Silver," had to take a backseat to "Tarzan" in intelligence and showmanship. He was the "Rin-Tin-Tin" of the equestrian world, with his own fan club and several doubles.

Following the Davis features, Ken co-starred with "Strongheart," the canine competitor of "Rin-Tin-Tin," in *North Star* (1926) for Associated Exhibitors. Clark Gable was one of the supporting players.

First National signed Ken in 1926, and it was in the eighteen features for that organization that Ken became a major star. First National spared no cost in producing the finest series of silent Westerns of that era, and for years studios would incorporate action footage from the Maynards into their cheaper-made programmers to give them a more expensive look. Ken was a whale of a rider and his trick riding feats were just short of miraculous. He quickly became an equal in popularity with Tom Mix, Buck Jones, Hoot Gibson, and Fred Thomson—the big guns at the time.

In 1929 Ken signed a lucrative contract with Universal for a series directed by Harry Joe Brown. Most of the films were released in both the silent and sound version. And to Ken goes credit as the first singing cowboy and the first to introduce musical interludes into Westerns. Ken had a pleasant enough voice and was a dandy fiddle player. The music was never allowed to take over the pictures, as in the case of Autry and Rogers, and

Ken's singing and playing were usually in a humorous vein rather than a romantic one.

The Wagon Master (1929), Ken's first Universal feature, was a pioneer in the field of dialogue and sound effects for small-time Westerns. A fight scene in an old-time beer saloon seemed an excerpt from a burlesque blackout and had audiences rocking. A wagon train racing across the desert and open plains provided plenty of red-blooded meller personified by the shouts of the wagon drivers and the swift thuds of the hoofs of the racing nags. Universal did a lot to lift the Maynards out of the old oaken bucket, and the saddle-and-spurs audiences perked up noticeably at the sight of Ken in chaps, riding "Tarzan." Only Buck Jones on "Silver" could match the ecstasy of that moment in the hearts and minds of Saturday matinee audiences.

Afraid of what effect sound might ultimately have on Westerns, Universal czar, Carl Laemmle, dropped Ken after the initial series, even though Ken was rapidly becoming the most popular cowboy on the screen. Tiffany picked him up, and it was in the "all-talkies" of that studio that Ken made the transition from silent to sound techniques of film-making. Eleven slam-bang Westerns, filled with flying hoofs, winded mustangs, skull-cracking, and belching guns were completed by Ken, most of which were directed by Phil Rosen. A series of eight films followed for World Wide, without letup in the spectacular horsemanship displayed by Ken. Frail and pretty heroines continued to endanger their lives so that handsome Ken could come to their rescue, sometimes pulling his favorite stunt of riding six horses at once. And "Tarzan" had more to do than just run his fetlocks sore. He got a chance to act as well as push Ken into the arms of the receptive heroine at the finis. *Come On Tarzan* (1932) and *Dynamite Ranch* (1932) were probably the best of this series. But all the entries from both Tiffany and World Wide had good photography, intelligent direction, plenty of thrills, and better-than-average sound.

Ken was almost able to write his own ticket, once Carl Laemmle realized that sound was going to help rather than kill off the program Western. Ken got his own production company at Universal in 1933 and complete control of all facets of production. Budgets approached $100,000 a film.

Strawberry Roan stands out as probably the best of the eight films in the 1933–34 series, although *The Fiddlin' Buckaroo* and *Trail Drive* are nearly as good. All three had entertaining musical interludes which the audiences seemed to like. But Ken left Universal when he couldn't get his way in an argument with Laemmle. It was a bad career move, for never again would he have the freedom and the budgets given him by Universal.

Nat Levine of Mascot signed Ken for two pictures in 1934—the serial *Mystery Mountain* and the feature *In Old Santa Fe*, which served to introduce Gene Autry and Smiley Burnette to the cinema world. Ken was paid $10,000 a week. During filming, his tantrums grew worse. Both films, however, were profitable, and *In Old Santa Fe* is considered one of the finest Westerns Ken made.

In 1935–36 Ken was at Columbia under an agreement similar to the one he had at Universal, only with reduced budgets approximating $70,000 a picture. *Western Frontier* (1935) was a charming film, enhanced by the original story by Ken and the presence of two lovely ladies, Lucille Browne and Nora Lane. It stands as his finest Columbia film, though Spencer G. Bennet set a fast pace in his direction of the last seven films in the series, injecting plenty of chases, fights, and the proper amount of comedy in guiding Ken and "Tarzan" to new victories.

By 1936 Ken had lost much of his enthusiasm for picture-making. His wife Mary had divorced him after ten years of marriage, primarily because of his drinking and general carousing. She had provided much of his inspiration. Also, he was unhappy about studio domination, limited budgets, salary, and shooting schedules. The circus became his driving passion, and he put all his energies into organizing the Ken Maynard Diamond K Ranch and Wild West Circus and Indian Congress. It folded after two weeks, costing him thousands of dollars. But in 1937, 1938, and 1940 Ken headed up the wild west concert of Cole Brothers Circus, proving to be a popular attraction with "Tarzan" (who died in 1940). The circus tours were worked into his schedule along with films.

Ken made four films for Grand National in 1937–1938, and four for Colony in 1939–1940, but the Maynard magic was no longer working. Younger cowboys dominated the range now. He made a brief return to film-making in 1943–44 as co-star with Hoot Gibson and Bob Steele in Monogram's "Trail Blazers" series. The films were cheaply made and the stories hackneyed, but the mere fact that the old-timers were back in the saddle made them interesting. As usual, however, Ken was unhappy over salary and other things and quit after six entries in the series. His last starring Western was *Harmony Trail* (1944), made for a cheapie outfit called Mattox Productions. He then retired from movies to make personal appearances with rodeos for a number of years. His last circus appearances were with the Biller Brothers and Arthur Brothers circuses in 1945, though his edacious passion for the sawdust trail, never quite abated, found release in rodeo appearances through the 1950s.

Ken Maynard's last years were tragic ones. His third wife, Bertha, a former Ringling Brothers aerialist to whom he was married for twenty years, died suddenly in 1968. Thereafter Ken lived alone in a trailer in the San Fernando Valley. His drinking and his disposition grew worse. In 1970, director Robert Slatzer gave him a supporting role in *Big Foot* (1970), his first film in twenty-five years. The role led nowhere and his health failed. A woman who variously claimed to be his wife, his agent, and his daughter took him for whatever he might have had and sold all his personal effects. Finally, unable to care for himself, he was admitted to the Motion Picture Country Hospital on January 18, 1973, for treatment of nutritional deficiency, arthritis, and general physical deterioration. He passed away on March 23, 1973, at age seventy-seven.

Ken Maynard, despite his human failings, was truly one of the sons of the great West and will always be remembered as a great pioneer in the field of Western movie-making. At his best Ken Maynard was unmatchable for fast-action thrills, and it is in that capacity that history will remember him.

KEN MAYNARD *Filmography*

BRASS COMMANDMENTS (Fox, January 28, 1923) 5 Reels.
William Farnum, Wanda Hawley, Tom Santschi, Claire Adams, Charles LeMoyne, Joe Rickson, Lon Poff, Al Fremont, Joseph Gordon, Charles Anderson, *Ken Maynard*
D: Lynn Reynolds
S: Charles A. Seltzer
Scen: Charles Kenyon

THE MAN WHO WON (Fox, September 1, 1923) 5 Reels.
(Tinted Sequences)
Dustin Farnum, Jacqueline Gadsden, Lloyd Whitlock, Ralph Cloninger, Mary Warren, Pee Wee Holmes, Harvey Clark, Lon Poff, Andy Waldron, *Ken Maynard*, Merrill McCormack, Mickey McBan, Bob Marks
D: William A. Wellman
S: Ridgwell Cullum—"Twins of Suffering Creek"
Scen: Ewart Adamson

THE GUNFIGHTER (Fox, September 2, 1923) 5 Reels.
William Farnum, Doris May, Lee C. Shumway, J. Morris Foster, Irene Hunt, Virginia True Boardman, Cecil Van Auker, *Ken Maynard*, Arthur Morrison, Jerry Campbell
D/SP: Lynn F. Reynolds
S: Max Brand—"Hired Guns"

SOMEBODY LIED (Fox, October 14, 1923) 2 Reels.
Ken Maynard, Jean Arthur
D: Stephen Roberts and Bryan Foy

CAMEO KIRBY (Fox, October 21, 1923) 7 Reels.
(Tinted Sequences)
John Gilbert, Gertrude Olmstead, Alan Hale, Eric Mayne, William E. Lawrence, Richard Tucker, Phillips Smalley, Jack McDonald, Jean Arthur, Eugene Ford, *Ken Maynard*
D: John Ford
S: Based on play by Booth Tarkington and Harry Leon Wilson.
Scen: Robert N. Lee

JANICE MEREDITH (Cosmopolitan/Metro-Goldwyn Distributing Corp., January 5, 1925) 153 Mins.
Marion Davies, Holbrook Blinn, Harrison Ford, Maclyn Arbuckle, Hattie Delaro, Joseph Kilgour, George Nash, Tyrone Power, Robert Thorne, Walter Law, Lionel Adams, Nicolai Koesberg, George Siegmann, W. C. Fields, Edwin Argus, Princess DeBourbon, Wilfred Noy, *Ken Maynard*, Helen Lee Worthing, Spencer Charters, Olin Howland, May Vokes, Douglas Stevenson, Harlan Knight, Mildred Arden, Lee Beggs, Joe Raleigh, Wilson Reynolds, Jerry Peterson, Isadore Marcel, Keane Waters, Edgar Nelson, Byron Russell, Colonel Patterson, George Clive, Burton McEvilly, Wilfred Noy, Mrs. Maclyn Arbuckle, Florence Turner
D: E. Mason Hopper
S: Paul Leicester Ford—"Janice Meredith: A Story of the American Revolution"
Scen/Adapt: Lillie Hayward

FIGHTING COURAGE (Clifford S. Elfelt Productions/
Davis Distributing Corp., July 7, 1925) 5 Reels.
Ken Maynard, Peggy Montgomery, Melbourne MacDowell,
Muriel Montrose, Frank Whitson, Henry Ward, Gus Saville,
James Barry, Jr., Nancy Zann, Harry Woods
P/D: Clifford S. Elfelt
S/SP: Frank Howard Clark

THE DEMON RIDER (Davis Distributing Corp., December
3, 1925) 5 Reels.
Ken Maynard, Alma Rayford, Fred Burns, Tom London,
James Low, Hollywood Beauty Sextette, "Tarzan"
D: Paul Hurst
S: Jay Inman Kane
P: Clifford S. Elfelt

$50,000 REWARD (Clifford S. Elfelt Productions/Davis
Distributing Corp., December 24, 1925) 5 Reels.
Ken Maynard, Esther Ralston, Bert Lindley, Edward Peil,
Lillian Leighton, Charles Newton, Frank Whitson, William
Moran, Ananias Beery, Jr., Augusta Ain, Nancy Zann, Fern
Lorraine, Olive Trevor, Grace Fay, Kathryn De Forrest,
Edith Flynn, "Tarzan" (a horse)
P/D: Clifford S. Elfelt
S/SP: Frank Howard Clark

NORTH STAR (Howard Estabrook Productions/Associated
Exhibitors, December 27, 1925) 53 Mins.
Ken Maynard, Virginia Lee Corbin, Stuart Holmes, Harold
Austin, Clark Gable, William Riley, Martin Faust, Syd
Crossley, Jerry Mandy, Jack Fowler, "Strongheart"
D: Paul Powell
SP: Charles Horan
P: Howard Estabrook

THE GREY VULTURE (Davis Distributing Corp., January
11, 1926) 50 Mins.
Ken Maynard, Hazel Deane, Sailor Sharkey, Boris Bullock, Fred
Burns, Nancy Zann, Whitehorse, Olive Trevor, Marie Woods,
Flora Maitland, Dorothy Dodd, Fern Lorraine, "Tarzan"
D: Forrest Sheldon
S/SP: George Hively
P: Clifford S. Elfelt

THE HAUNTED RANGE (Davis Distributing Corp.,
January 11, 1926) 5 Reels.
Ken Maynard, Alma Rayford, Harry Moody, Al Hallett, Fred
Burns, Bob Williamson, Tom London, "Tarzan"
D: Paul Hurst
S/SP: Frank Howard Clark
P: Clifford S. Elfelt

THE RANGE FIGHTER (Davis Distributing Corp., 1926)
10 Chapters.
Ken Maynard, Alma Rayford, Hazel Deane, Peggy Mont-
gomery, Esther Ralston, Tom London, Bert Lindley, Melford
McDowell, Harry Moody, Sailor Sharkey, "Tarzan"
(This serial was put together from segments of "$50,000
Reward," "Fighting Courage," "The Demon Rider," "The
Haunted Range," and "The Grey Vulture")

Ken Maynard and player in *Overland Stage* (First National, 1927).

SENOR DAREDEVIL (Charles R. Rogers Productions/First
National, August 1, 1926) 70 Mins.
Ken Maynard, Dorothy Devore, George Nicholls, J. P. Mc-
Gowan, Sheldon Lewis, Joseph Swickard, Buck Black, Billy
Franey, Billy Gillis, Charles Whitaker, Frank Ellis, Dick
Sutherland, Hank Bell, "Tarzan"
D: Albert Rogell
S/SP: Marion Jackson
P: Charles R. Rogers
Supv: Harry Joe Brown

THE UNKNOWN CAVALIER (Charles R. Rogers Pro-
ductions/First National, November 14, 1926) 73 Mins.
Ken Maynard, Kathleen Collins, David Torrence, T. Roy
Barnes, James Mason, Otis Harlan, Joseph Swickard, Pat
Harmon, Frank Lackteen, Raymond Wells, Bruce Gordon,
Fred Burns, Jimmy Boudwin, "Tarzan"
D: Albert S. Rogell
S: Kenneth Perkins—"Ride Him Cowboy"
SP: Marion Jackson
P: Charles R. Rogers
Supv: Harry Joe Brown

THE OVERLAND STAGE (Charles R. Rogers Productions/
First National, January 30, 1927) 71 Mins.
Ken Maynard, Kathleen Collins, Tom Santschi, Sheldon
Lewis, Jay Hunt, Dot Farley, Florence Turner, Paul Hurst,
William Malan, Fred Burns, "Tarzan"
D: Albert S. Rogell
S/SP: Marion Jackson
P: Charles R. Rogers

SOMEWHERE IN SONORA (Charles R. Rogers Productions/First National, April 3, 1927) 63 Mins.
Ken Maynard, Kathleen Collins, Frank Leigh, Joseph Bennett, Charles Hill Mailes, Carl Stockdale, Yvonne Howell, Ben Corbett, Richard Neill, Monte Montague, Charles Whitaker, Hank Bell, Frank Ellis, "Tarzan"
D: Albert Rogell
Adapt: Marion Jackson
S: Will Levington Comfort—"Somewhere South in Sonora"
Supv: Harry Joe Brown
P: Charles R. Rogers

LAND BEYOND THE LAW (Charles R. Rogers Productions/First National, June 5, 1927) 68 Mins.
Ken Maynard, Dorothy Dwan, Tom Santschi, Noah Young, Billy Butts, Gibson Gowland, Charles Whitaker, Frank Ellis, Buck Bucko, Fred Burns, Hank Bell, Joseph Girard, Lafe McKee, "Tarzan"
D: Harry Joe Brown
S/SP: Marion Jackson
P: Charles R. Rogers
Supv: Harry Joe Brown

THE DEVIL'S SADDLE (Charles R. Rogers Productions/First National, July 11, 1927) 6 Mins.
Ken Maynard, Kathleen Collins, Earle Metcalfe, William R. Walling, Paul Hurst, Francis Ford, Art Mix, Buck Bucko, Ernie Adams, Hank Bell, "Tarzan"
D: Albert Rogell
S: Kenneth Perkins
SP: Marion Jackson
P: Charles R. Rogers
Supv: Harry Joe Brown

THE RED RAIDERS (Charles R. Rogers Productions/First National, September 4, 1927) 7 Reels.
Ken Maynard, Ann Drew, J. P. McGowan, Paul Hurst, Chief Yowlache, Harry Shutan, Tom Bay, Ben Corbett, Harold Salter, "Tarzan"
D: Albert Rogell
S/SP: Marion Jackson
P: Charles R. Rogers
Supv: Harry Joe Brown

GUN GOSPEL (Charles R. Rogers Productions/First National, November 6, 1927) 70 Mins.
Ken Maynard, Virginia Brown Faire, Romaine Fielding, J. P. McGowan, Bob Fleming, Bill Dyer, Noah Young, Jerry Madden, Charles Whitaker, "Tarzan"
D: Harry Joe Brown
Adapt: Marion Jackson
S: W. D. Hoffman
P: Charles R. Rogers

THE WAGON SHOW (Charles R. Rogers (Productions/First National, February 19, 1928) 69 Mins.
Ken Maynard, Marion Douglas (Ena Gregory), Maurice Costello, Fred Malatesta, George Davis, May Boley, Sidney Jarvis, Paul Weigel, Henry Roquemore, "Tarzan"
D: Harry Joe Brown
S/SP: Ford I. Beebe
P: Charles R. Rogers

THE CANYON OF ADVENTURE (Charles R. Rogers Productions/First National, April 22, 1928) 64 Mins.
Ken Maynard, Virginia Brown Faire, Eric Mayne, Theodore Lorch, Tyrone Brereton, Harold Salter, Billy Franey, Charles Whitaker, "Tarzan"
D: Albert S. Rogell
S/SP: Marion Jackson
P: Charles R. Rogers

THE UPLAND RIDER (Charles R. Rogers Productions/First National, June 3, 1928) 75 Mins.
Ken Maynard, Marion Douglas (Ena Gregory), Lafe McKee, Sidney Jarvis, Bobby Dunn, Robert Walker, David Kirby, Robert Milash, Art Mix, Ben Corbett, "Tarzan"
D: Albert Rogell
S/SP: Marion Jackson
Supv: Harry Joe Brown
P: Charles R. Rogers

CODE OF THE SCARLET (Charles R. Rogers Productions/First National, July 1, 1928) 62 Mins.
Ken Maynard, Gladys McConnell, Edwin J. Brady, J. P. McGowan, Robert Walker, Dot Farley, Joseph W. Girard, Nelson McDowell, Joe Rickson, Harold Salter, Sheldon Lewis, Lafe McKee, Charles Whitaker, "Tarzan"
D: Harry Joe Brown
S: Bennett R. Cohen
SP: Ford I. Beebe
P: Charles R. Rogers

THE GLORIOUS TRAIL (Charles R. Rogers Productions/First National, October 28, 1928) 65 Mins.
Ken Maynard, Gladys McConnell, Les Bates, Frank Hagney, James Bradbury, Jr., Billy Franey, Chief Yowlache, Lafe McKee, Buck Bucko, Fred Burns, Bud McClure, Jack Ward, "Tarzan"
D: Albert S. Rogell
S/SP: Marion Jackson
Supv: Harry Joe Brown
P: Charles R. Rogers

THE PHANTOM CITY (Charles R. Rogers Productions/First National, December 23, 1928) 65 Mins.
Ken Maynard, Eugenia Gilbert, James Mason, Charles Hill Mailes, Jack McDonald, Jackie Combes, Blue Washington, Charles Whitaker, Ben Corbett, Fred Burns, "Tarzan"
D: Albert S. Rogell
S/SP: Adele Buffington
Supv: Harry Joe Brown
P: Charles R. Rogers

CHEYENNE (Charles R. Rogers Productions/First National, January 12, 1929) 65 Mins.
Ken Maynard, Gladys McConnell, James Bradbury, Jr., Charles Whitaker, Billy Franey, Tom London, Ben Corbett, Chuck Baldra, "Tarzan"
D: Albert S. Rogell
S/SP: Bennett R. Cohen
Supv: Harry Joe Brown
P: Charles R. Rogers

THE LAWLESS LEGION (Charles R. Rogers Productions/First National, February 17, 1929) 68 Mins.
Ken Maynard, Nora Lane, Paul Hurst, J. P. McGowan, Howard Truesdell, Frank Rice, Ernie Adams, Tom London, Al Ferguson, Charles Whitaker, Richard Talmadge, Buck Bucko, Bud McClure, "Tarzan"
D/Supv: Harry Joe Brown
S/SP: Bennett R. Cohen
P: Charles R. Rogers

CALIFORNIA MAIL (Charles R. Rogers Productions/First National, February 17, 1929) 60 Mins.
Ken Maynard, Dorothy Dwan, Lafe McKee, C. E. Anderson, Paul Hurst, Fred Burns, "Tarzan"
D: Albert S. Rogell
S/SP: Marion Jackson
Supv: Harry Joe Brown
P: Charles R. Rogers

THE ROYAL RIDER (Charles R. Rogers Productions/First National, February 17, 1929) 67 Mins.
(One version released with synchronized effects, no dialogue)
Ken Maynard, Olive Hasbrouck, Philip de Lacey, Theodore Lorch, Joseph Burke, Harry Semels, Frank Rice, Bobby Dunn, Ben Corbett, Billy Franey, Johnny Sinclaire, "Tarzan"
D/Supv: Harry Joe Brown
S: Nate Gatzert
SP: Jacques Jaccard and Sylvia Seid
P: Charles R. Rogers

THE WAGON MASTER (Universal, September 8, 1929) 70 Mins.
(Talking sequences and music score)
Ken Maynard, Edith Roberts, Tom Santschi, Jackie Hanlon, Al Ferguson, Bobby Dunn, Frank Rice, Fred Dana
D: Harry Joe Brown
S: Marion Jackson
P: *Ken Maynard*

SENOR AMERICANO (Universal, November 10, 1929) 71 Mins.
(Part Talking)
Ken Maynard, Kathryn Crawford, Frank Yaconelli, J. P. McGowan, Frank Beal, Gino Corrado, "Tarzan"
D: Harry Joe Brown
SP: Lesley Mason
P: *Ken Maynard*

THE RANGE FIGHTER (Exhibitor's Pictures Corp., 1929) 10 Chapters.
(A re-issue of the 1926 serial with music, synchronized effects, and a spoken prologue)
Ken Maynard

PARADE OF THE WEST (Universal, January 19, 1930) 75 Mins.
(Part Talking)
Ken Maynard, Gladys McConnell, Frank Yaconelli, Otis Harlan, Jackie Hanlon, Frank Rice, Fred Burns, Bobbie Dunn, Blue Washington, Stanley Blystone, "Tarzan," "Rex"
D: Harry Joe Brown
S: Bennett Cohen

LUCKY LARKIN (Universal, March 2, 1930) 66 Mins.
(Synchronized and Musical Effects)
Ken Maynard, Nora Lane, Paul Hurst, Blue Washington, James Farley, Charles Clary, Harry Todd, Jack Rockwell, "Tarzan"
D: Harry Joe Brown
S/SP: Marion Jackson
P: *Ken Maynard*, Harry Joe Brown

VOICE OF HOLLYWOOD No. 9 (Tiffany, April 1, 1930)
Bert Wheeler, Sally Starr, Dorothy Jordan, *Ken Maynard*, Aimee Semple McPherson, Marceline Day, Wesley Barry, Marjorie Kane, "Tarzan"
D: Mack D'Agostino

THE FIGHTING LEGION (Universal, April 6, 1930) 75 Mins.
(Part Talking)
Ken Maynard, Dorothy Dawn, Frank Rice, Charles Whitaker, Ernie Adams, Harry Todd, Robert Walker, Stanley Blystone, Les Bates, Bill Nestell, Jack Fowler, "Tarzan"
D: Harry Joe Brown
S: Bennett Cohen
SP: Bennett Cohen, Lesley Mason
P: *Ken Maynard*

MOUNTAIN JUSTICE (Universal, May 4, 1930) 6,797 ft.
(Title changed from KETTLE CREEK)
Ken Maynard, Kathryn Crawford, Fred Burns, Otis Harlan, Pee Wee Holmes, Paul Hurst, Ricard Carlyle, Les Bates, Blue Washington, "Tarzan"
D: Harry Joe Brown
S/SP: Bennett Cohen
P: *Ken Maynard*, Harry Joe Brown

SONG OF THE CABALLERO (Universal, June 29, 1930) 72 Mins.
Ken Maynard, Doris Hill, Francis Ford, Frank Rice, William Irving, Joyzelle, Evelyn Sherman, Josef Swickward, Gino Corrado
D: Harry Joe Brown
S: Kenneth Bonton
SP: Bennett Cohen
P: *Ken Maynard*

193

SONS OF THE SADDLE (Universal, August 3, 1930) 76 Mins.
Ken Maynard, Doris Hill, Francis Ford, Joe Girard, Harry Todd, Caroll Nye, Frank Rice
D: Harry Joe Brown
S/SP: Bennett Cohen
P: *Ken Maynard*

FIGHTIN' THRU (Tiffany, December 25, 1930) 61 Mins. (Also known as "California 1878")
Ken Maynard, Carmelita Geraghty, Charles King, Wallace MacDonald, W. L. Thorne, Jeanette Loff, Fred Burns, Bill Nestell, Tommy Bay, John (Jack) Fowler, Charles Baldra, Art Mix, Jack Kirk, Bud McClure, Jim Corey, "Tarzan"
D: William Nigh
S/SP: Jack Natteford
P: Phil Goldstone

THE TWO GUN MAN (Tiffany, May 15, 1931) 60 Mins.
Ken Maynard, Lucille Powers, Lafe McKee, Nita Martin, Charles King, Tom London, Murdock McQuarrie, Walter Perry, Will Stanton, William Jackie, Ethan Allen, Buck Bucko, Roy Bucko, Jim Corey, Jack Ward, "Tarzan"
D: Phil Rosen
S/SP: Jack Natteford
P: Phil Goldstone

ALIAS THE BAD MAN (Tiffany, July 15, 1931) 66 Mins.
Ken Maynard, Virginia Brown Faire, Charles King, Lafe McKee, Frank Mayo, Robert Homans, Irving Bacon, Ethan Allen, Earl Dwire, Jack Rockwell, Jim Corey, "Tarzan"
D: Phil Rosen
AP: Ford Beebe
SP: Earle Snell
P: Phil Goldstone

THE ARIZONA TERROR (Tiffany, September 1, 1931) 64 Mins.
Ken Maynard, Lina Basquette, Edmund Cobb, Hooper Atchley, Tom London, Charles King, Nena Quartero, Michael Visaroff, Murdock McQuarrie, Fred Burns, Jack Rockwell, Jim Corey, Roy Bucko, Buck Bucko, "Tarzan"
D: Phil Rosen
S/SP: Jack Natteford
P: Phil Goldstone

RANGE LAW (Tiffany, October 11, 1931) 63 Mins.
Ken Maynard, Frances Dade, Charles King, Frank Mayo, Lafe McKee, Jack Rockwell, Tom London, Aileen Manning, William Duncan, Blackjack Ward, "Tarzan"
D: Phil Rosen
S/SP: Earle Snell
P: Phil Goldstone

BRANDED MEN (Tiffany, November 8, 1931) 70 Mins.
Ken Maynard, June Clyde, Charles King, Irving Bacon, Billy Bletcher, Donald Keith, Jack Rockwell, Hooper Atchley, Edmund Cobb, Slim Whitaker, Roy Bucko, Buck Bucko, Al Taylor, Bud McClure, "Tarzan"
D: Phil Rosen
SP: Earle Snell
P: Phil Goldstone

THE POCATELLO KID (Tiffany, December 6, 1931) 61 Mins.
Ken Maynard, Marceline Day, Dick Cramer, Charles King, Lafe McKee, Lew Meehan, Jack Rockwell, Bert Lindley, Bob Reeves, Jack Ward, "Tarzan"
D: Phil Rosen
S/SP: W. Scott Darline
P: Phil Goldstone

THE SUNSET TRAIL (Tiffany, January 17, 1932) 62 Mins.
Ken Maynard, Ruth Hiatt, Philo McCullough, Frank Rice, Buddy Hunter, Dick Alexander, Frank Ellis, Slim Whitaker, Jack Rockwell, Lew Meehan, Bud Osborne, Bud McClure, "Tarzan"
D: B. Reeves Eason
S/SP: Bennett Cohen
P: Phil Goldstone

TEXAS GUN-FIGHTER (Tiffany, February 14, 1932) 63 Mins.
Ken Maynard, Sheila Mannors, Harry Woods, James Mason, Bob Fleming, Edgar Lewis, Lloyd Ingraham, Jack Rockwell, Frank Ellis, Jack Ward, Roy Bucko, Buck Bucko, Bud McClure, Bob Burns, "Tarzan"
D: Phil Rosen
S/SP: Bennett Cohen

HELL FIRE AUSTIN (Tiffany, March 3, 1932) 70 Mins.
Ken Maynard, Ivy Merton, Jack Perrin, Charles LeMayne, Lafe McKee, Nat Pendleton, Allan Roscoe, William Robyns, Fargo Bussey, Jack Rockwell, Jack Ward, Bud McClure, Lew Meehan, Ben Corbett, "Tarzan"
D: Forrest Sheldon
S: Forrest Sheldon
SP: Betty Burbridge

WHISTLIN' DAN (Tiffany, March 20, 1932) 65 Mins.
Ken Maynard, Joyzelle Joyner, Georges Renevant, Don Terry, Harlan E. Knight, Jack Rockwell, Jessie Arnold, Bud McClure, Lew Meehan, Merrill McCormack, Roy Bucko, Buck Bucko, Frank Ellis, Hank Bell, Iron Eyes Cody, Wesley Giraud, "Tarzan"
D: Phil Rosen
SP: Stuart Anthony
S: Stuart Anthony
P: Phil Goldstone

DYNAMITE RANCH (KBS/World Wide, July 31, 1932)
59 Mins.
Ken Maynard, Ruth Hall, Jack Perrin, Arthur Hoyt, Allan
Roscoe, Al Smith, John Beck, George Pierce, Lafe McKee,
Mortha Mattox, Edmund Cobb, Charles Le Moyne, Cliff
Lyons, Kermit Maynard (stuntman and double), "Tarzan"
D: Forrest Sheldon
S/SP: Barry Barrington, Forrest Sheldon
P: Burt Kelly, Sam Bischoff, William Saal

COME ON, TARZAN (KBS/World Wide, September 11,
1932) 61 Mins.
Ken Maynard, Kate Campbell, Roy Stewart, Niles Welch, Ben
Corbett, Bob Kortman, Jack Rockwell, Nelson McDowell,
Jack Mower, Merna Kennedy, Edmund Cobb, Robert
Walker, Hank Bell, Jim Corey, Slim Whitaker, Al Taylor,
Jack Ward, Bud McClure, "Tarzan"
D: Alan James
SP: Alan James
P: Burt Kelly, Sam Bischoff, William Saal

BETWEEN FIGHTING MEN (KBS/World Wide, October
16, 1932) 62 Mins.
Ken Maynard, Ruth Hall, Josephine Dunn, Wallace Mac-
Donald, Albert J. Smith, Walter Law, James Bradbury, Jr.,
John Pratt, Charles King, Edmund Cobb, Jack Rockwell,
Jack Kirk, Bud McClure, Roy Bucko, Jack Ward, Jack
Perrin, "Tarzan"
D: Forrest Sheldon
S/SP: Betty Burbridge, Forrest Sheldon
P: Burt Kelly, Sam Bischoff, William Saal

TOMBSTONE CANYON (KBS/World Wide, December
25, 1932) 62 Mins.
Ken Maynard, Cecilia Parker, Lafe McKee, Sheldon Lewis,
Frank Brownlee, Jack Clifford, George Gerwing, Edward
Peils, Sr., George Chesebro, Jack Kirk, Merrill McCormack,
Bud McClure, "Tarzan"
D: Alan James
S/SP: Claude Rister

DRUM TAPS (KBS/World Wide, January 24, 1933) 61 Mins.
Ken Maynard, Dorothy Dix, Hooper Atchley, Junior Coghlan,
Charles Stevens, Kermit Maynard, Al Bridge, Harry Semels,
Slim Whitaker, James Mason, Leo Willis, Hooper Atchley,
Los Angeles Boy Scout Troop 107, "Tarzan"
D: J. P. McGowan
SP: Alan James

THE PHANTOM THUNDERBOLT (KBS/World Wide/
Distributed by Fox, March 1933) 63 Mins.
Ken Maynard, Frances Dade, Frank Rice, William Gould,
Bob Kortman, Harry Holman, Frank Beal, Wilfred Lucas,
William Robyns, Nelson McDowell, Bud McClure, Roy
Bucko, William Patton, Jack Rockwell, "Tarzan"
D: Alan James
S: Forrest Sheldon, Betty Burbridge
SP: Alan James
P: KBS

Ken Maynard receives a little assistance from "Tarzan"
in *Phantom Thunderbolt* (World Wide, 1933).

THE LONE AVENGER (KBS/World Wide/Distributed by
Fox, May 14, 1933) 61 Mins.
Ken Maynard, Muriel Gordon, Jack Rockwell, Charles King,
Al Bridge, James Mason, Niles Welch, William N. Bailey,
Ed Brady, Clarence Gelder, Lew Meehan, Horace B. Car-
penter, Jack Ward, Roy Bucko, Buck Bucko, Bud McClure,
"Tarzan"
D: Alan James
S: Forrest Sheldon, Betty Burbridge
SP: Alan James
P: KBS

KING OF THE ARENA (Universal, June 1, 1933) 59 Mins.
Ken Maynard, Lucile Browne, John St. Polis, Michael Visaroff,
Bob Kortman, James Marcus, Frank Rice, Fred McKay, Blue
Washington, William Steele, Jack Rockwell, Ed Coxen, Robert
Walker, Jack Mower, Bobby Nelson, Steve Clemente, Robert
Burns, Merrill McCormack, Artie Ortego, Chief Big Tree,
Buck Bucko, Jack Kirk, Horace B. Carpenter, Pascale Perry,
Bud McClure, Helen Gibson, Lafe McKee, Iron Eyes Cody,
"Tarzan"
D: Alan James
S: Hal Berger, Ray Bouk
SP: Alan James
P: *Ken Maynard*

THE FIDDLIN' BUCKAROO (Universal, July 20, 1933)
65 Mins.
Ken Maynard, Gloria Shea, Fred Kohler, Frank Rice, Jack
Rockwell, Joe Girard, Jack Mower, Slim Whitaker, Al Bridge,
Bob Kortman, Bob McKenzie, Hank Bell, Frank Ellis, Roy
Bucko, Buck Bucko, Bud McClure, Pascale Perry, Clem
Horton, Robert Walker, Jack Kirk, "Tarzan"
D: *Ken Maynard*
S/SP: Nate Galzert
P: *Ken Maynard*

THE TRAIL DRIVE (Universal, September 4, 1933) 60 Mins.

Ken Maynard, Cecilia Parker, William Gould, Wally Wales, Ben Corbett, Lafe McKee, Alan Bridge, Bob Kortman, Frank Rice, Fern Emmett, Jack Rockwell, Slim Whitaker, Frank Ellis, Hank Bell, Edward Coxen, Bob Reeves, Art Mix, Jack Kirk, Buck Bucko, Bud McClure, "Tarzan"

D: Alan James

S: *Ken Maynard*, Nate Gatzert

SP: Nate Gatzert

P: *Ken Maynard*

STRAWBERRY ROAN (Universal, October 26, 1933) 59 Mins.

Ken Maynard, Ruth Hall, Harold Goodwin, Frank Yaconelli, Charles King, William Desmond, James Marcus, Jack Rockwell, Robert Walker, Ben Corbett, Bill Patton, Art Mix, Roy Bucko, Buck Bucko, Bud McClure, "Tarzan"

D: Alan James

SP: Nate Gatzert

P: *Ken Maynard*

S: Nate Gatzert

FARGO EXPRESS (KBS/World Wide/Distributed by Fox, November 20, 1933) 61 Mins.

Ken Maynard, Helen Mack, Roy Stewart, William Desmond, Paul Fix, Jack Rockwell, Claude Payton, Joe Rickson, Bud McClure, Hank Bell, "Tarzan"

D: Alan James

SP: Alan James, Earle Snell

GUN JUSTICE (Universal, December 11, 1933) 59 Mins.

Ken Maynard, Cecilia Parker, Hooper Atchley, Walter Miller, Jack Rockwell, Francis Ford, Fred McKaye, William Dyer, Jack Richardson, Ed Coxen, William Gould, Sheldon Lewis, Lafe McKee, Ben Corbett, Slim Whitaker, Hank Bell, Blackie Whiteford, Horace B. Carpenter, Bob McKenzie, Frank Ellis, Bud McClure, Roy Bucko, Buck Bucko, Pascale Perry, Jack Ward, Cliff Lyons, "Tarzan"

D: Alan James

S/SP: Robert Quigley

P: *Ken Maynard*

WHEELS OF DESTINY (Universal, February 19, 1934) 64 Mins.

Ken Maynard, Dorothy Dix, Philo McCullough, Fred McKay, Jay Wilsey (Buffalo Bill, Jr.), Fred Sale, Jr., Jack Rockwell, Frank Rice, Nelson McDowell, William Gould, Ed Coxen, Merrill McCormack, Slim Whitaker, Hank Bell, Robert Burns, Artie Ortego, Wally Wales, Jack Evans, Helen Gibson, Bud McClure, Fred Burns, Chief Big Tree, Roy Bucko, Marin Sais, Chuck Baldra, Arkansas Johnny, Bobby Dunn, Blackjack Ward, Al Taylor, "Tarzan"

D: Alan James

S/SP: Nate Gatzert

P: *Ken Maynard*

HONOR OF THE RANGE (Universal, April 16, 1934) 61 Mins.

Ken Maynard, Cecilia Parker, Fred Kohler, Jack Rockwell, Frank Hagney, James Marcus, Franklyn Farnum, Al Bridge, Jack Kirk, Art Mix, Eddie Barnes, Jack Kirk, Albert J. Smith, Charles Whitaker, Fred McKaye, Wally Wales, Hank Bell, Lafe McKee, William Patton, Bud McClure, Nelson McDowell, Ben Corbett, Pascale Perry, Jack Ward, Roy Bucko, Buck Bucko, Fred Burns, Cliff Lyons, Jim Corey, "Tarzan"

S/SP: Nate Gatzert

P: *Ken Maynard*

SMOKING GUNS (Universal, June 11, 1934) 65 Mins.

Ken Maynard, Gloria Shea, Walter Miller, Harold Goodwin, William Gould, Bob Kortman, Jack Rockwell, Etta McDaniels, Martin Turner, Ed Coxen, Slim Whitaker, Hank Bell, Horace B. Carpenter, Blue Washington, Wally Wales, Edmund Cobb, Bob Reeves, Fred McKaye, Jim Corey, Roy Bucko, Buck Bucko, Ben Corbett, Jack Ward, Bud McClure, Cliff Lyons, "Tarzan"

D: Alan James

S/SP: Nate Gatzert

P: *Ken Maynard*

IN OLD SANTA FE (Mascot, November 15, 1934) 64 Mins.

Ken Maynard, Evalyn Knapp, George Hayes, H. B. Warner, Kenneth Thompson, Gene Autry, Lester "Smiley" Burnette, Wheeler Oakman, George Chesebro, George Burton, Jack Rockwell, Jim Corey, Jack Kirk, Edward Hearn, Frank Ellis, Horace B. Carpenter, "Tarzan"

D: David Howard

S: Wallace MacDonald, John Rathmell

P: Nat Levine

Supv: Victor Zobel

MYSTERY MOUNTAIN (Mascot, December 1, 1934) 12 Chapters.

Ken Maynard, Verna Hillie, Edward Earle, Edmund Cobb, Lynton Brent, Syd Saylor, Carmencita Johnson, Lafe McKee, Al Bridge, Edward Hearn, Bob Kortman, Gene Autry, Lester "Smiley" Burnette, Wally Wales, Tom London, George Chesebro, Philo McCullough, Frank Ellis, Steve Clark, James Mason, Lew Meehan, Jack Rockwell, Art Mix, William Gould, Hooper Atchley, Dick Dickinson, Al Haskel, Pascale Perry, "Tarzan"

D: B. Reeves Eason, Otto Brower

S: Sherman Lowe, Barney Sarecky, B. Reeves Eason

SP: Bennett Cohen, Armand Schaefer

P: Nat Levine

Supv: Victor Zobel

Chapter Titles: (1) The Rattler, (2) The Man Nobody Knows, (3) The Eye That Never Sleeps, (4) The Human Target, (5) Phantom Outlaws, (6) The Perfect Crime, (7) Tarzan the Cunning, (8) The Enemy's Stronghold, (9) The Fatal Warning, (10) The Secret of the Mountain, (11) Behind the Mask, (12) The Judgment of Tarzan.

Cecilia Parker and Fred Kholer are pictured with Ken Maynard in this lobby card for *Honor of the Range* Universal, 1934).

WESTERN FRONTIER (Columbia, August 7, 1935) 59 Mins.

Ken Maynard, Lucile Browne, Nora Lane, Robert Henry, Frank Yaconelli, Otis Harlan, Harold Goodwin, Frank Hagney, Gordon S. Griffith, Jim Marcus, Tom Harris, Nelson McDowell, Frank Ellis, Art Mix, Slim Whitaker, William Gould, Dick Curtis, Budd Buster, Herman Hack, Horace B. Carpenter, Oscar Gahan, Joe Weaver, "Tarzan"

D: Al Herman
S: Ken Maynard
SP: Nate Gatzert
P: Larry Darmour

WESTERN COURAGE (Columbia, October 29, 1935) 61 Mins.

Ken Maynard, Geneva Mitchell, Charles K. French, Betty Blythe, Cornelius Keefe, Ward Bond, E. H. Calbert, Renee Whitney,

Dick Curtis, Bob Reeves, Wally West, Roy Bucko, Buck Bucko, Bud McClure, Bart Carre, Arkansas Johnny, "Tarzan"

D: Spencer G. Bennet
S: Charles Francis Royal
SP: Nate Gatzert
P: Larry Darmour

LAWLESS RIDERS (Columbia, December 6, 1935) 57 Mins.

Ken Maynard, Geneva Mitchell, Harry Woods, Frank Yaconelli, Hal Taliaferro (Wally Wales), Slim Whitaker, Frank Ellis, Jack Rockwell, Bob McKenzie, Hank Bell, Bud Jamison, Horace B. Carpenter, Jack King, Bud McClure, Pascale Perry, Oscar Gahon, "Tarzan"

D: Spencer G. Bennet
S/SP: Nate Gatzert
P: Larry Darmour

197

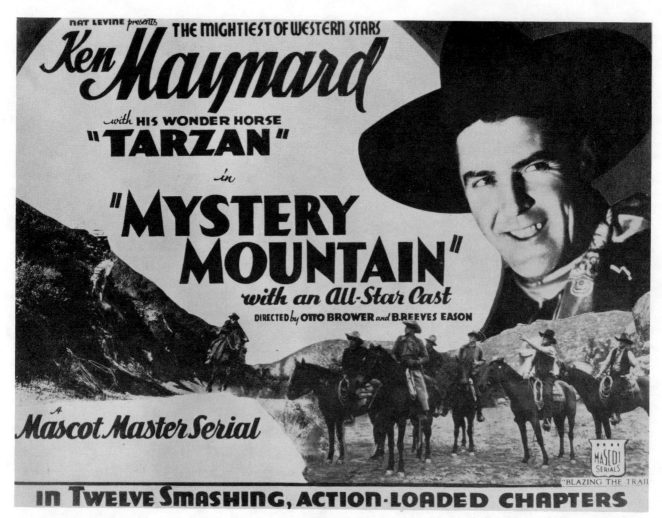

This Ken Maynard serial (Mascot, 1934) was a popular one in the mid-1930s.

HEIR TO TROUBLE (Columbia, December 17, 1935) 59 Mins.
Ken Maynard, Joan Perry, Harry Woods, Wally Wales, Martin Faust, Harry Brown, Dorothy Wolbert, Fern Emmett, Pat O'Malley, Art Mix, Frank Yaconelli, Frank LaRue, Hal Price, Jim Corey, Lafe McKee, Jack Rockwell, Slim Whitaker, Roy Bucko, Buck Bucko, Jack Ward, Bud McClure, Artie Ortego, "Tarzan"
D: Spencer G. Bennet
S: Ken Maynard
SP: Nate Gatzert
P: Larry Darmour

THE CATTLE THIEF (Columbia, May 26, 1936) 50 Mins.
Ken Maynard, Geneva Mitchell, Ward Bond, Roger Williams, Jim Marcus, Sheldon Lewis, Edward Cecil, Jack Kirk, Edward Hearn, Glenn Strange, Jack King, Al Taylor, Dick Rush, Bud McClure, "Tarzan"
D: Spencer G. Bennet
S/SP: Nate Gatzert
P: Larry Darmour

AVENGING WATERS (Columbia, July 8, 1936) 57 Mins.
Ken Maynard, Beth Marion, Ward Bond, John Elliott, Zella Russell, Wally Wales, Tom London, Edmund Cobb, Edward Hearn, Buck Moulton, Glenn Strange, Cactus Mack, Buffalo Bill, Jr., Sterling Holloway, Jack King, Buck Bucko, Bud McClure, "Tarzan"
D: Spencer G. Bennet
S/SP: Nate Gatzert
P: Larry Darmour

HEROES OF THE RANGE (Columbia, August 18, 1936) 58 Mins.
Ken Maynard, June Gale, Harry Woods, Harry Ernest, Bob Kortman, Bud McClure, Tom London, Bud Osborne, Frank Hagney, Jack Rockwell, Lafe McKee, Wally Wales, Jay Wilsey (Buffalo Bill, Jr.), Jerome Ward, Bud McClure, Bud Jamison, Bob Reeves, Jack King, "Tarzan"
D: Spencer G. Bennet
S/SP: Nate Gatzert
P: Larry Darmour

Harry Woods and henchmen seem to have the upper hand of Ken Maynard in this scene from *Heir to Trouble* (Columbia, 1935).

THE FUGITIVE SHERIFF (Columbia, October 20, 1936) 58 Mins.

Ken Maynard, Beth Marion, Walter Miller, Hal Price, John Elliott, Arthur Millet, Virginia True Boardman, Frank Ball, Edmund Cobb, Lafe McKee, Art Mix, William Gould, Bob Burns, Horace Murphy, Vernon Dent, Tex Palmer, Bud Osborne, Slim Whitaker, Al Taylor, Frank Ellis, Horace B. Carpenter, Oscar Gahan, Glenn Strange, Fred Burns, Lew Meehan, Blackjack Ward, Tex Cooper, Roy Bucko, Buck Bucko, Art Dillard, Jack King, Bud Jamison, Bud McClure, "Tarzan"

D: Spencer G. Bennet

S/SP: Nate Gatzert

P: Larry Darmour

BOOTS OF DESTINY (Grand National, July 16, 1937) 56 Mins.

Ken Maynard, Claudia Dell, Vince Barnett, Walter Patterson, Martin Garralaga, George Morrell, Fred Cordova, Sid D'Albrook, Ed Cassidy, Carl Mathews, Wally West, "Tarzan"

D: Arthur Rosson

SP: Philip White

P: M. K. Hoffman

TRAILING TROUBLE (Grand National/Condor, August 27, 1937) 57 Mins.

Ken Maynard, Lona Andre, Vince Barnett, Roger Williams, Grace Woods, Fred Burns, Phil Dunham, Edward Cassidy, Horace B. Carpenter, Marin Sais, Tex Palmer, "Tarzan"

D: Arthur Rosson

SP: Philip Graham White

P: M. K. Hoffman

John Elliott, Ward Bond, Ken Maynard, and Tom London in *Avenging Waters* (Columbia, 1936).

WHIRLWIND HORSEMAN (Grand National, April 29, 1938) 58 Mins.
Ken Maynard, Joan Barclay, Bill Griffith, Joe Girard, Kenny Dix, Roger Williams, Dave O'Brien, Walter Shumway, Budd Buster, Lew Meehan, Glenn Strange, "Tarzan"
D: Bob Hill
SP: George Plympton
P: Max and Arthur Alexander

SIX-SHOOTIN' SHERIFF (Grand National, May 20, 1938) 59 Mins.
Ken Maynard, Marjorie Reynolds, Lafe McKee, Harry Harvey, Jane Keckely, Walter Long, Bob Terry, Tom London, Warner Richmond, Dick Alexander, Ben Corbett, Earl Dwire, Glenn Strange, Roger Williams, Bud Osborne, Ed Piel, Milburn Morante, Carl Mathews, "Tarzan"
D: Harry Fraser
S: Weston Edwards (Harry Fraser)
P: Max and Arthur Alexander

FLAMING LEAD (Colony, November 1939) 57 Mins.
Ken Maynard, Eleanor Stewart, Dave O'Brien, Ralph Peters, Walter Long, Tom London, Carleton Young, Reed Howes, Bob Terry, Kenne Duncan, Ethan Allen, Joyce Rogers, John Merton, Carl Mathews
D: Sam Newfield
SP: Joseph O'Donnell
P: Max and Arthur Alexander

DEATH RIDES THE RANGE (Colony, January 1940) 58 Mins.
Ken Maynard, Fay McKenzie, Ralph Peters, Julian Rivero, Charles King, John Elliott, William Costello, Saen Hugh Borg, Michael Vallon, Julian Madison, Kenneth Rhodes, Murdock McQuarrie, Wally West, Dick Alexander, Bud Osborne, "Tarzan"
D: Sam Newfield
SP: William Lively
P: Max and Arthur Alexander

200

PHANTOM RANCHER (Colony, March 1940) 61 Mins.
Ken Maynard, Dorothy Short, Harry Harvey, Dave O'Brien, Ted Adams, Tom London, John Elliott, Reed Howes, Steve Clark, Carl Mathews, Sherry Tansey, Wally West, George Morrell, Herman Hack, "Tarzan"
D: Harry Fraser
SP: William Lively
P: Max and Arthur Alexander

LIGHTNING STRIKES WEST (Colony, June 1940) 56 Mins.
Ken Maynard, Claire Rochelle, Charles King, Bob Terry, Michael Vallon, Reed Howes, Dick Dickinson, George Chesebro, John Elliott, William Gould, Chick Hannon, Tex Palmer, Carl Mathews, "Tarzan"
D: Harry Fraser
S: Monroe Talbot
SP: Martha Chapin
P: Max and Arthur.Alexander

WILD HORSE STAMPEDE (Monogram, April 16, 1943) 59 Mins.
("Trail Blazers" Series)
Ken Maynard, Hoot Gibson, Betty Miles, Bob Baker, Ian Keith, Si Jenks, Donald Stewart, John Bridges, Glenn Strange, Reed Howes, Kenneth Harlan, Tom London, Tex Palmer, Forrest Taylor, I. Stanford Jolley, Kenne Duncan, Bob McKenzie, Chick Hannon
D: Alan James
S: Frances Kavanaugh
SP: Elizabeth Beecher
P: Robert Tansey

THE LAW RIDES AGAIN (Monogram, August 6, 1943) 58 Mins.
("Trail Blazers" Series)
Ken Maynard, Hoot Gibson, Betty Miles, Jack LaRue, Chief Thunder Cloud, Hank Bell, Bryant Washburn, Emmett Lynn, Kenneth Harlan, John Bridges, Fred Hoose, Charles Murray, Jr., Chief Many Treaties, John Merton
D: Alan James
SP: Frances Kavanaugh
P: Robert Tansey

BLAZING GUNS (Monogram, October 8, 1943) 55 Mins.
("Trail Blazers" Series)
Ken Maynard, Hoot Gibson, Kay Forrester, LeRoy Mason, Roy Brent, Lloyd Ingraham, Charles King, Weldon Heyburn, Dan White, Frank Ellis, Kenne Duncan, Emmett Lynn
D: Robert Tansey
SP: Frances Kavanaugh
P: Robert Tansey

DEATH VALLEY RANGERS (Monogram, December 3, 1943) 59 Mins.
("Trail Blazers" Series)
Ken Maynard, Hoot Gibson, Bob Steele, Linda Brent, Kenneth Harlan, Bob Allen, Charles King, George Chesebro, John Bridges, Al Ferguson, Steve Clark, Wally West, Glenn Strange, Forrest Taylor, Lee Roberts, Weldon Heyburn, Karl Hackett
D: Robert Tansey
SP: Robert Emmett, Frances Kavanaugh, Elizabeth Beecher
P: Robert Tansey

WESTWARD BOUND (Monogram, January 17, 1944) 54 Mins.
("Trail Blazers" Series)
Ken Maynard, Hoot Gibson, Bob Steele, Betty Miles, John Bridges, Harry Woods, Karl Hackett, Weldon Heyburn, Hal Price, Roy Brent, Frank Ellis, Curley Dresden, Dan White, Al Ferguson
D/P: Robert Tansey
SP: Frances Kavanaugh

ARIZONA WHIRLWIND (Monogram, February 21, 1944) 59 Mins.
("Trail Blazers" Series)
Ken Maynard, Hoot Gibson, Bob Steele, Ian Keith, Myrna Dell, Donald Stewart, Charles King, Karl Hackett, George Chesebro, Dan White, Charles Murray, Jr., Frank Ellis, Chief Soldani, Willow Bird
D: Robert Tansey
SP: Frances Kavanaugh
P: Robert Tansey

HARMONY TRAIL (Mattox Productions, December 1, 1944) 57 Mins.
(Released in 1947 by Astor Pictures as "White Stallion")
Ken Maynard, Eddie Dean, Max Terhune, Rocky Camron, Ruth Roman, Glenn Strange, Bob McKenzie, Charles King, Bud Osborne, Al Ferguson, Dan White, Fred Gildart, Jerry Shields, Hal Price, John Bridges
D: Robert Emmett (Tansey)
S: Frank Simpson
SP: Frances Kavanaugh
P: Walt Mattox

BIG FOOT (Gemini/American/Ellman Enterprises, October 21, 1970) 95 Mins.
(Eastman Color)
Joi Lansing, Christopher Mitchum, John Carradine, Lindsay Crosby, Judy Jordon, James Craig, John Mitchum, Jay Wilkerson, James Stellar, *Ken Maynard*, Doodles Weaver, Dorothy Keller, Noble "Kid" Chissell, Nick Raymond, Sonny West, Walt Zachrich, Ray Cantrell, Suzy Marlin, Lois Red Elk, Jenifer Bishop, Holly Kamen, Walt Swanner, Billy Record, Carolyn Gilbert, Sonny Incontro, Kathy Andrews, Andrews, Denise Gilbert, Tony Cardoza, Kenny Marlowe
D/S: Robert Slatzer
SP: Robert Slatzer, James Gordon White
P: Anthony Cardoza

William Duncan

11 • WILLIAM DUNCAN

The Revered Serial King

William Duncan was Selig's foremost Western star in 1910–1911 (when Tom Mix worked with him making one-reelers in Canyon City, Colorado) and one of the most fearless men on the screen in the era 1910–1925. He displayed athletic prowess in practically every scene of his ten serials and in many shorter films—scenes that always moved with kaleidoscopic swiftness.

A five-foot-ten-inch Irish-Scotsman born in 1880, he came to the United States at the age of ten. Later he attended the University of Pennsylvania, and, while working his way through college, he still found time to make records on the cinder-path and in field events. He played football, baseball, and other major sports and was a crack swimmer and water-polo player. His great natural strength helped him immensely, and after graduation he became a teacher of physical training.

Duncan's prowess reached the ears of Sandow, the famous strongman, and he invited Duncan to tour the country with him. Having gone to the best instructors in wrestling, boxing, fencing, and juggling, Duncan had become adept in each of these sports.

After he appeared with Sandow for several seasons, Duncan decided that his talents would be utilized to better advantage in dramatic work. His versatility led him to repertory work, and he again toured the country, this time with the Forepaugh Stock Company, finally managing, writing, and starring

in his own productions. Motion pictures presented even wider possibilities, and Duncan became that phenomenon: a leading man, director, and scenario writer at the same time. He signed with Selig Polyscope Company about 1910, and, because of his athletic prowess, he was put to work making one-reel Westerns. It was in the Duncan films that Tom Mix got his early Selig experience prior to his own series of one- and two-reelers.

During the years 1910–1915 Duncan starred for Selig in scores of short films which long since have deteriorated and are lost forever to the screen world. He was prolific and innovative as an actor/director/writer, and the Western genre owes much to Duncan for creating many of its classic situations and technical procedures. As a pathfinder he blazed a trail, followed first by Mix and later by every cowboy in the business.

In 1915 Duncan switched to Vitagraph, a progressive firm that became part of the Warner Brothers group in 1925. There he appeared in countless short films, mostly outdoor adventures, and both directed and acted in serials. Typical of Duncan's Vitagraph Westerns were *The Man From the Desert* (1915) and *The Wanderers* (1915), both three-reelers. In the former, Duncan is left to die in the desert by his mining partner who steals his $20,000 share of their earnings from three years' hard labor. Instead of dying, Duncan is rescued, becomes immensely rich, and then returns to the city and breaks his treacherous companion through the market. And then, just as he contemplates killing his old partner to complete his revenge, he discovers that he is in love with the man's daughter. And so we are given a reconciliation and a happy ending. In the latter film Duncan is a blacksmith, known as "The Wanderer," who buys out a blacksmith shop in a little town. He falls in love with the village schoolmarm, but overhears her address a stranger in apparently endearing fashion, and, brokenhearted, he follows the wanderlust. During a series of exciting events Bill becomes partners with the stranger seen talking to his sweetheart (although he does not know he is the same man). In the end both men become rich through some oil stock an old man gives them in gratitude for saving his life, and Bill discovers that his partner is the brother of his former sweetheart. The conversation incident is satisfactorily explained, and Bill gives his girl a bear hug, indicating that the wanderer has found the end of the trail.

In 1916 Duncan was sent by Vitagraph president, Albert E. Smith, out into the mountain wilds to film a serial based on Jack London's *Hearts of Three*. Six or seven chapters of the intended serial were filmed before it was discovered that London had sold what no longer belonged to him. It seems that he had already entered into several contracts for the story, and, as it turned out, William Randolph Hearst had the first claim. Vitagraph could do nothing except call its crew home and scrap the footage already shot.

In 1917, however, Duncan hit the big time by starring in and directing his first serial, *The Fighting Trail*, a story revolving about a secret mine which contains munitions materials of great interest to German agents. The serial was 15 chapters in length (as were all the Vitagraph serials), with the first chapter being three reels long rather than the customary two. At this point a word of explanation is in order for the benefit of those whose memories of serials extend back only to the late 1930s or the 1940s.

The serials of 1910–1930 were taken seriously by both fans and the studios. Their production quality was considerably greater than the serials produced after 1935, as a general rule, and there was not the stigma attached to them then that developed later. Serial performers were not looked down on as "has-beens" or "never-weres"; rather, serial stars were universally idolized, and serials played the best theatres, as well as those in the boondocks. Carol Holloway had the femme lead, and, unlike most serials of the sound era, romance played a vital part in the action-crammed adventure film. A second serial, *Vengence and the Woman* (1917), followed, and it too featured Holloway as the love interest. That same year she also co-starred with Duncan in two Western features, *Deadshot Baker* and *The Tenderfoot*. Beginning with *A Fight for Millions* (1918), third in the series of the Duncan serials, Edith Johnson became his screen heroine and co-starred with him in eight chapter plays. She worked with him until the two retired from serial production in 1924, and she also became Mrs. Duncan in real life.

Duncan became so popular as a serial star that in 1919 Vitagraph tore up his contract and rewrote it to call for six serials budgeted at $1,500,000, with Duncan to receive an average salary of $10,000 a week for directing and starring in two serials a year. Few Hollywood personalities have ever matched this kind of salary—certainly no serial stars. And today, because of the inflated dollar and high income taxes, it would take something like $60,000 a week to equal the purchasing power of Duncan's salary.

The Duncan-Johnson team proved a winning combination for Vitagraph. Their serials and features were the principal assets of the firm, not only keeping the wolf from the door but allowing the studio the luxury of other film production financed by the huge profits on the couple's films. Four more serials were made by the team for Vitagraph, titled *Man of Might* (1918), *Smashing Barriers* (1919), *The Silent Avenger* (1920), and *Fighting Fate* (1921). Space does not permit an account of all the Duncan serials, but they were sure-fire box-office, and their bloodthirsty, adventurous, and artificial thrills never ceased to satisfy serial patrons of the 1920s. Both Duncan and Johnson consistently risked their lives for the sake of screen realism, performing stunts that no stars would be allowed to perform today. One such stunt was a double leap from a lofty cliff into a turbulent river. The stars actually risked their lives to get the utmost out of this thrill, without doubles or the use of safety nets.

Duncan's work at Vitagraph was not confined to serials. He and Edith also starred in seven feature films, all directed by Duncan. *No Defense* (1921) is set primarily in the North where Duncan and two partners, one a crook, seek gold. Bill Duncan is accused of murder and flees for his life. His wife, although still married to Bill, marries another and kills the crook who tries to blackmail her by threatening to expose her secret. Bill returns and takes the blame for the killing. Edith forces her husband, the governor, to pardon Bill by threatening to expose his shady dealings. Ultimately Bill and Edith are reunited. *Steelheart* (1921) is a Western in which Bill saves Edith from an unsavory cabaret owner when she arrives in a mining town looking for her husband. *Where Men are Men* (1921) is a good Western with a good story based on Ralph Cummins' "The Princess of the Desert Dream." Duncan, weary and broke, straggles out of Death Valley only to have the deed to his mine stolen from him and then be accused of murdering his partner. In *The Silent Vow* (1922) Bill is a mountie assigned to track down the supposed killers of his father; whereas in *The Fighting Guide* (1922) he uncovers a plot to swindle a girl out of her valuable land after her father had been framed for murder. *When Danger Smiles* (1922) finds Duncan back in the saddle as a cowboy who blunders into trouble through infatuation with a girl and an attempt to help a robbery victim; and in *Playing it Wild* (1923) he is a devilish cowpoke masquerading as a bandit to rid the town of a crooked sheriff.

When Vitagraph decided to discontinue serial production, Duncan and his wife moved to Universal under an arrangement similar to that which Bill had enjoyed at Vitagraph. He continued to direct and to have his own production unit, and his serials remained a potent sorce of income for the producer. Bill, however, was not happy with the setup at Universal. He was constantly ensnarled in red tape, so much so that he finally decided he could get along nicely without Carl Laemmle as boss. So the Duncans retired in 1925, making personal appearances for a while and then settling down to enjoy life with each other and their children. They had no financial problems.

In the 1930s, just to have something to do and to indulge in the nostalgia of being back in front of a camera, Bill appeared in a few features. The most notable of these were the Hopalong Cassidy westerns in which he played "Buck Peters," Hoppy's boss.

William Duncan died on February 8, 1961. His passing drew hardly a mention by the press. But in his day Bill commanded many pages of news-copy as King of the Silent Serials. Hopefully, more of his work will be salvaged and made available in 16mm or 8mm versions for the appreciation and edification of modern-day thrill hunters who are seeking vicarious cinematic adventures through vintage films from Hollywood's glory days.

WILLIAM DUNCAN *Filmography*

THE NEW EDITOR (Selig, July 1, 1911) 1,000 ft.
William Duncan, Otis Thayer

THE TELLTALE KNIFE (Selig, November 25, 1911) 1 Reel.
William Duncan, Tom Mix
D: *William Duncan*

THE BROTHERHOOD OF MAN (Selig, March 2, 1912) 1,000 ft.
William Duncan, Myrtle Stedman, Kathlyn Williams

HYPNOTIZED (Selig, March 2, 1912) 1,000 ft.
Mr. Cox, *William Duncan*, William Stowell, Rex DeRosselli, Winnifred Greenwood

HIS CHANCE TO MAKE GOOD (Selig, March 30, 1912).
William Duncan, Rex DeRosselli, Winnifred Greenwood, Myrtle Stedman
D: *William Duncan*

DRIFTWOOD (Selig, April 6, 1912) 1,000 ft.
Kathlyn Williams, Myrtle Stedman, *William Duncan*, Frank Weed

THE LAW OF THE NORTH (Selig, April 20, 1912) 1,000 ft.
Charles Clary, *William Duncan*, Adrienne Kroell
D: George L. Cox

A CITIZEN IN THE MAKING (Selig, May 18, 1912) 1,000 ft.
William Duncan, Winnifred Greenwood

THE POLO SUBSTITUTE (Selig, July 13, 1912) 1,000 ft.
Hobart Bosworth, *William Duncan*

THE DOUBLE-CROSS (Selig, July 20, 1912) 1,000 ft.
Myrtle Stedman, *William Duncan*, Lester Cuneo

A WARTIME ROMANCE (Selig, July 20, 1912).
Myrtle Stedman, *William Duncan*, Richard Garrick, Vera Hamilton, Mattie Fitzgerald, Rex DeRosselli, William Stowell

AN UNEXPECTED FORTUNE (Selig, August 3, 1912) 1,000 ft.
Charles Clary, *William Duncan*, Frank Weed, Lester Cuneo, Walter Roberts, Clara Reynolds Smith, Adrienne Kroell, Harry Lonsdale, Kathlyn Williams

CIRCUMSTANTIAL EVIDENCE (Selig, September 7, 1912) 1,000 ft.
William Duncan, Lester Cuneo, Myrtle Stedman, Marshall Stedman, Josephine West, Otis B. Thayer, Rex DeRosselli, Warden Tynon
D: Otis B. Thayer
Adapt: Hapsbure Liebe

THE FIGHTING INSTINCT (Selig, September 7, 1912) 1,000 ft.
William Duncan, Marshall Stedman, Myrtle Stedman
D/Scen: *William Duncan*

THE CATTLE RUSTLERS (Selig, September 21, 1912) 1,000 ft.
William Duncan, Myrtle Stedman

THE BRAND BLOTTER (Selig, September 21, 1912) 1,000 ft.
William Duncan, Myrtle Stedman, Rex DeRosselli, Lester Cuneo, Shorty DeLong, C. E. Reeves, C. S. Tipton, B. Jacobs
D: Marshall Stedman
Adapt: Elizabeth Fraser

WHY JIM REFORMED (Selig, September 28, 1912) 1,000 ft.
William Duncan, Myrtle Stedman, C. E. Reeves, Rex De-Rosselli, Lester Cuneo
D/Scen: William Duncan

THE COUNT OF MONTE CRISTO (Selig, October 12, 1912) 3,000 ft.
Hobart Bosworth, Tom Santschi, Herbert Rawlinson, Eugenie Besserer, *William Duncan*, Robert Chandler, George Hernandez, Nick Cogley, William Hutchinson, Roy Watson, Frank Clark, Fred Huntly, Bessie Eyton, Lillian Hayward, Al Garcia
D: Colin Campbell
Scen: Colin Campbell
S: Alexander Dumas—*The Count of Monte Cristo*

THE OPIUM SMUGGLERS (Selig, October 12, 1912) 1,000 ft.
William Duncan, Myrtle Stedman, Lester Cuneo, Rex De-Rosselli

JIM'S VINDICATION (Selig, October 26, 1912) 1,000 ft.
William Duncan, Lester Cuneo, Rex DeRosselli, Frank Mc-Clintock, Marshall Stedman, Charles Reeves
D/Scen: *William Duncan*

BETWEEN LOVE AND THE LAW (Selig, November 9, 1912) 1,000 ft.
William Duncan, Myrtle Stedman

THE DYNAMITERS (Selig, November 9, 1912) 1,000 ft.
William Duncan, Myrtle Stedman, Lester Cuneo
D/Scen:*William Duncan*

THE RANGER AND HIS HORSE (Selig, December 7, 1912) 1,000 ft.
William Duncan, Lester Cuneo, Myrtle Stedman, Rex DeRosselli
D/Scen: *William Duncan*

BUCK'S ROMANCE (Selig, December 14, 1912) 1,000 ft.
Myrtle Stedman, Lester Cuneo, *William Duncan*, Rex DeRosselli, Florence Dye
D/Scen: *William Duncan*

A ROUGH RIDE WITH NITROGLYCERINE (Selig, December 28, 1912) 1,000 ft.
William Duncan, Myrtle Stedman, Lester Cuneo, Charles F. Reaves, Rex DeRosselli
D: *William Duncan*

THE GUNFIGHTER'S SON (Selig, January 4, 1913) 1,000 ft.
William Duncan, Rex DeRosselli, Myrtle Stedman, Florence Dye, Lester Cuneo
D/Scen: *William Duncan*

RUD'S HEIRESS (Selig, January 11, 1913) 1,000 ft.
William Duncan
D/Scen: *William Duncan*

A CANINE MATCHMAKER (Selig, January 25, 1913) 1,000 ft.
William Duncan
D/Scen: *William Duncan*

A MATRIMONIAL DELUGE (Selig, January 25, 1913) 1,000 ft.
William Duncan, Myrtle Stedman, Florence Dye
D/Scen: *William Duncan*

THE SUFFRAGETTE (Selig, January 25, 1913).
William Duncan, Myrtle Stedman
Adapt: Marshall Stedman

HOW IT HAPPENED (Selig, February 1, 1913) 1,000 ft.
William Duncan, Myrtle Stedman, Lester Cuneo, Tom Mix
D/Scen: *William Duncan*

SELIG presents

William Duncan

in

BILL'S BIRTHDAY PRESENT

A Western Comedy -- Drama

William Duncan and players in *Bill's Birthday Present* (Selig, 1913).

BILL'S BIRTHDAY PRESENT (Selig, February 8, 1913) 1,000 ft.
William Duncan, Myrtle Stedman, Lester Cuneo
D/Sc: *William Duncan*

RANGE LAW (Selig, February 15, 1913) 1,000 ft.
William Duncan, Myrtle Stedman, Lester Cuneo
Adapt: William Duncan
D: *William Duncan*

THE BANK'S MESSENGER (Selig, February 22, 1913).
William Duncan, Myrtle Stedman, Lester Cuneo
D/Scen: *William Duncan*

THE DEPUTY'S SWEETHEART (Selig, March 1, 1913) 1,000 ft.
William Duncan, Myrtle Stedman, Lester Cuneo, Rex De-Rosselli
Adapt: *William Duncan*

JUGGLING WITH FATE (Selig, March 10, 1913).
William Duncan
D: *William Duncan*
Scen: Edward McWade

THE SHERIFF OF YAWAPAI COUNTY (Selig, March 15, 1913) 1,000 ft.
William Duncan, Myrtle Stedman, Lester Cuneo, Tom Mix, Rex DeRosselli
D/Scen: *William Duncan*

THE LIFETIMER (Selig, March 22, 1913).
William Duncan, Myrtle Stedman, Florence Dye, Tom Mix, Lester Cuneo
D/Scen: *William Duncan*

THE SHOTGUN MAN AND THE STAGE DRIVER (Selig, April 5, 1913).
William Duncan, Tom Mix
D/Scen: *William Duncan*

HIS FATHER'S DEPUTY (Selig, May 17, 1913) 1 Reel.
William Duncan, Tom Mix, Lester Cuneo, Rex De Rosselli
D/Scen: *William Duncan*

RELIGION AND GUN PRACTICE (Selig, May 24, 1913) 1 Reel.
William Duncan, Myrtle Stedman, Tom Mix
D: *William Duncan*
Adapt: A. W. Corey

AN EMBARRASSED BRIDEGROOM (Selig, May 31, 1913) 1 Reel.
William Duncan
D: *William Duncan*
Adapt: C. G. Philips

THE JEALOUSY OF MIGUEL AND ISABELLA (Selig, June 7, 1913) 1 Reel.
Myrtle Stedman, *William Duncan*, Lester Cuneo, Florence Dye, Rex DeRosselli
D: *William Duncan*
Adapt: Cornelius Shea

THE LAW AND THE OUTLAW (Selig, June 7, 1913) 1 Reel.
William Duncan, Tom Mix, Myrtle Stedman, Lester Cuneo
D: *William Duncan*
S: Tom Mix and U. E. Hungerford

TAMING A TENDERFOOT (Selig, June 14, 1913) 1 Reel.
William Duncan
D: *William Duncan*
Adapt: Cornelius Shea

THE MARSHAL'S CAPTURE (Selig, June 28, 1913) 1 Reel.
William Duncan, Tom Mix
D: *William Duncan*
Adapt: Elizabeth Frazer

SALLIE'S SURE SHOT (Selig, June 28, 1913) 1 Reel.
William Duncan, Tom Mix
D: *William Duncan*
Adapt: Cornelius Shea

MADE A COWARD (Selig, July 11, 1913) 1 Reel.
William Duncan, Tom Mix
D: *William Duncan*
Adapt: A. W. Collins

THE ONLY CHANCE (Selig, July 12, 1913) 1,000 ft.
William Duncan, Lester Cuneo
D: *William Duncan*
Scen: C. Chester Wesley

THE SENORITA'S REPENTANCE (Selig, July 22, 1913) 1,000 ft.
William Duncan
D: *William Duncan*
Adapt: William A. Corey

THE TAMING OF TEXAS PETE (Selig, July 24, 1913) 1,000 ft.
William Duncan, Tom Mix
D: *William Duncan*
Adapt: Joseph F. Poland

AN APACHE'S GRATITUDE (Selig, August 1, 1913) 1,000 ft.
William Duncan, Tom Mix, Myrtle Stedman, Jim Robson, Rex DeRosselli
D/Sc: *William Duncan*

THE GALLOPING ROMEO (Selig, August 9, 1913) 500 ft.
William Duncan
D: *William Duncan*
Adapt: Aaron E. Bishop

THE STOLEN MOCCASINS (Selig, August 9, 1913) 1,000 ft.
William Duncan, Myrtle Stedman, Lester Cuneo, Tom Mix
D: *William Duncan*
Adapt: Cornelius Shea

THE GOOD INDIAN (Selig, August 13, 1913) 1,000 ft.
William Duncan, Tom Mix
D: *William Duncan*
Adapt: Ethel C. Unland

HOW BETTY MADE GOOD (Selig, August 23, 1913) 1,000 ft.
Myrtle Stedman, Lester Cuneo, *William Duncan*
D: *William Duncan*
Adapt: Ethel C. Unland

HAWLIN' JONES (Selig, September 6, 1913).
William Duncan, Myrtle Stedman
D: *William Duncan*
Adapt: O. H. Nelson

THE CAPTURE OF BAD BROWN (Selig, September 20, 1913) 1,000 ft.
William Duncan, Myrtle Stedman
D: *William Duncan*
Adapt: Cornelius Shea

THE REJECTED LOVER'S LUCK (Selig, September 20, 1913) 1,000 ft.
William Duncan
D: *William Duncan*
Adapt: Cornelius Shea

THE CATTLE THIEF'S ESCAPE (Selig, October 4, 1913).
Myrtle Stedman
D: *William Duncan*
Adapt: R. E. Hicks

SAVED FROM THE VIGILANTES (Selig, October 4, 1913) 1,000 ft.
William Duncan
D: *William Duncan*
Adapt: Malcolm Douglas

DISHWASH DICK'S COUNTERFEIT (Selig, October 18, 1913).
Myrtle Stedman, *William Duncan*
D: *William Duncan*
Adapt: B. L. Williams

THE SILVER GRINDSTONE (Selig, October 18, 1913) 1,000 ft.
William Duncan
D: *William Duncan*
Adapt: Eugene P. Lyle

TWO SACKS OF POTATOES (Selig, October 25, 1913).
William Duncan, Hugh Mosher, Clyde Morris
D: *William Duncan*
Scen: Ethel C. Unland

CUPID IN THE COW CAMP (Selig, November 29, 1913) 1,000 ft.
William Duncan
D: *William Duncan*
Adapt: J. A. Dunn

THE RUSTLER'S REFORMATION (Selig, November 29, 1913) 1,000 ft.
D: *William Duncan*
Adapt: Cornelius Shea

BUSTER'S LITTLE GAME (Selig, December 13, 1913) 1,000 ft.
William Duncan, Myrtle Stedman
Adapt: C. W. Van Sant

PHYSICAL CULTURE ON THE QUARTER CIRCLE V BAR (Selig, December 13, 1913) 1,000 ft.
William Duncan, Lester Cuneo
D: *William Duncan*
Scen: Edwin Ray Coffin

MOTHER LOVE VS. GOLD (Selig, December 20, 1913) 1,000 ft.
William Duncan, Myrtle Stedman
D: *William Duncan*
Adapt: John M. Kiskadden

GOOD RESOLUTIONS (Selig, December 27, 1913) 1,000 ft.
William Duncan, Myrtle Stedman, Florence Dye
D/Scen: *William Duncan*

A FRIEND IN NEED (Selig, January 24, 1914) 1,000 ft.
William Duncan
D/Adapt: *William Duncan*

ROMANCE OF THE FOREST RESERVE (Selig, April 13, 1914)
William Duncan
D: *William Duncan*
S: William Alfred Cory

MARRYING GRETCHEN (Selig, May 2, 1914).
William Duncan
D: *William Duncan*
Adapt: Edwin Ray Coffin

HUNGER KNOWS NO LAW (Vitagraph, May 7, 1914) 1 Reel.
William Duncan, Margaret Gibson, Jane Novak
S: Alice A. Methley

MARIAN, THE HOLY TERROR (Selig, May 9, 1914).
William Duncan
D: *William Duncan*
Adapt: W. E. Wing

THE SERVANT QUESTION OUT WEST (Selig, June 24, 1914).
William Duncan
D: *William Duncan*
Adapt: William Alfred Corey

AN INNOCENT DELILAH (Vitagraph, August 4, 1914).
William Duncan, George Stanley, Jane Novak
D: Ulysses Davis
S: Elizabeth Kendricks

WARD'S CLAIM (Vitagraph, August 22, 1914).
Myrtle Gonzales, *William Duncan*
D: Ulysses Davis
Adapt: W. A. Tremayne

ANNE OF THE MINES (Vitagraph, October 17, 1914) 2 Reels.
William Duncan, Myrtle Gonzales
Scen: Grace Adele Pierce

THE CHOICE (Vitagraph, October 31, 1914).
Myrtle Gonzales, Alfred Vosburen, *William Duncan*, Jack Mower
D: Ulysses S. Davis
Adapt: Guernsey Fraser

ANN THE BLACKSMITH (Vitagraph, November 7, 1914) 2 Reels.
Anne Schaeffer, Alfred Vosburgh, Jack Mower, George Kunkel, *William Duncan*, C. E. Thompson
D: Ulysses Davis
Adapt: Grace Hoele Pierce

THE LEVEL (Vitagraph, November 21, 1914).
Myrtle Gonzales, *William Duncan*, Alfred D. Vosburgh, Al Mower, Duke (a dog)
D: Ulysses Davis
Adapt: Ethel Hill

PURE GOLD (Vitagraph, December 5, 1914).
Anne Schaeffer, *William Duncan*
D: Ulysses Davis
Adapt: Joseph F. Whelan

THE NAVAJO RING (Vitagraph, January 16, 1915).
Anne Schaeffer, Margaret Gibson, *William Duncan*
D: Ulysses Davis
Adapt: Fred R. Ashfield

THE GAME OF LIFE (Vitagraph, January 26, 1915) 2 Reels.
Myrtle Gonzales, William Burke, Alfred D. Vosburen, William S. Smith, George Kunkel, Jack Mower, *William Duncan*
D: Ulysses Davis
Adapt: Dave Smith

A CHILD OF THE NORTH (Vitagraph, May 1, 1915) 2 Reels.
William Duncan, George Holt, Myrtle Gonzales
D: Rollin S. Sturgeon
Adapt: Frederick Chapin

THE MAN FROM THE DESERT (Broadway Star/Vitagraph, June 7, 1915) 3 Reels.
Myrtle Gonzales, *William Duncan*, George Holt, Otto Lederer, George Kunkel
D: Ulysses Davis
Adapt: Jack Wolf

THE RED STEPHANO (Vitagraph, July 24, 1915) 2 Reels.
William Duncan, Alfred Vosburgh, Anne Schaeffer
D: Ulysses Davis
Scen: Charles Lofquist

THE REPENTANCE OF DR. BLINN (Vitagraph, July 31, 1915).
George Holt, *William Duncan*, Myrtle Gonzales, Jack Mower
D: Dave Smith
Adapt: V. E. Rowe

THE CHALICE OF COURAGE (Vitagraph, August 14, 1915) 6 Reels.
Myrtle Gonzales, *William Duncan*, George Holt, W. V. Ranous, Otto Lederer, Natalie De Lontan
D: Rollin S. Sturgeon
Adapt: from a story by Cyrus Townsend Brady

HIS GOLDEN GRAIN (Vitagraph, September 11, 191 2 Reels.
William Duncan, Jack Mower, Myrtle Gonzales, George Kunkel, Alice Neice, George Stanley, Otto Lederer
D: Ulysses Davis
Adapt: Joseph F. Poland

THE OFFENDING KISS (Vitagraph, September 11, 1915) 2 Reels.
William Duncan, Myrtle Gonzales, Alfred Vosburgh, Otto Lederer, George Stanley, Anne Schaeffer, Marguerite Reid, George Kunkel
D: Ulysses Davis
Adapt: Anna L. Heath

THE QUARREL (Vitagraph, September 11, 1915).
William Duncan, Myrtle Gonzales, Jack Mower, Anne Schaeffer, George Kunkel, Otto Lederer
Adapt: Henry M. Neff

THE EBONY CASKET (Vitagraph, October 30, 1915).
William Duncan, Anne Schaeffer, Myrtle Gonzales, Alfree Vosburen, George Kunkel, Otto Lederer, Carlton Weatherby, George Stanley
D: Ulysses Davis
Adapt: Elsie Robertson

LOVE AND LAW (Vitagraph, November 13, 1915).
William Duncan, George Stanley, Ann Drew
D: Rollin S. Sturgeon
Adapt: William Duncan

CAL MARVIN'S WIFE (Broadway Star/Vitagraph, December 4, 1915) 3 Reels.
Mary Anderson, Anne Schaeffer, *William Duncan*, Otto Lederer, Carlton Weatherby, George Kunkel
D: Ulysses Davis
Scen: Lulu Case Russell

A SCANDAL IN HICKVILLE (Vitagraph, December 4, 1915).
George Stanley, Anne Schaeffer, Otto Lederer, Alfred Vosburgh, *William Duncan*, Marguerite Reid, Carlton Weatherby
D: Ulysses Davis
Adapt: David Morrison

THE WANDERERS (Broadway Star/Vitagraph, December 25, 1915) 3 Reels.
William Duncan, George Holt, Mary Ruby, Jack Mower, Otto Benninger, Hazel Buckham, Otto Lederer, J. C. Weatherby, Chris Enriquez
D: William Wolbert
Adapt: Ronald E. Bradberry

GOD'S COUNTRY AND THE WOMAN (Vitagraph, April 1916) 8 Reels.
William Duncan, Nell Shipman, George Holt
D: Rollin S. Sturgeon
S: James Oliver Curwood

William Duncan in *God's Country and the Woman* (Vitagraph, 1916).

THROUGH THE WALL (Vitagraph, September 21, 1916) 6 Reels.
William Duncan, Nell Shipman, George Holt, Webster Campbell, Corrinne Griffith, Anne Schaeffer, Otto Lederer, George Kunkel
D: Roland S. Sturgeon
S: Cleveland Moffett

THE LAST MAN (Vitagraph, October 10, 1916) 7 Reels.
William Duncan, Mary Anderson, Corinne Griffith, Jack Mower, Otto Lederer
P: William Wolbert
S: James Oliver Curwood

THE COST OF HIGH LIVING (Vitagraph, 1916)
William Duncan, Corinne Griffith

William Duncan and Carol Holloway in *The Fighting Trail* (Vitagraph, 1917).

MONEY MAGIC (Vitagraph, January 27, 1917) 5 Reels.
William Duncan, Antonio Moreno, Edith Storey, Florence Dye
D: William Holbert
Adapt: A. Van Buren Powell

ALADDIN FROM BROADWAY (Vitagraph, March 10, 1917) 5 Reels.
William Duncan, Antonio Moreno, Edith Storey, Laura Winston, Otto Lederer, George Holt
D: William Wolbert
Scen: Helmer Walton Bergman
S: F. S. Isham

THE FIGHTING TRAIL (Vitagraph, September 10, 1917) 15 Chapters.
William Duncan, Carol Holloway, George Holt, Joe Ryan, Walter Rodgers, Fred Burns
D: *William Duncan*
Chapter Titles: (1) The Priceless Ingredient, (2) The Story of Ybarra, (3) Will Yaqui Joe Tell, (4) The Other Half, (5) The Torrent Rush, (6) The Ledge of Despair, (7) The Lion's Prey, (8) Strands of Doom, (9) The Bridge of Death, (10) The Sheriff, (11) Parched Trails, (12) The Desert of Torture, (13) The Water Trap, (14) The Trestle of Horrors, (15) Out of the Flame

DEAD SHOT BAKER (Vitagraph, October 6, 1917) 5 Reels.
William Duncan, Carol Holloway, Joe Ryan, S. E. Jennings, R. L. Rodgers, Otto Lederer, Charles Wheelock
D: *William Duncan*
Scen: George H. Plympton
S: Alfred Henry Lewis—"Wolfville Stories"

THE TENDERFOOT (Vitagraph, November 30, 1917) 5 Reels.
William Duncan, Carol Holloway, Florence Dye, Joe Ryan, Walter L. Rodgers, Charles Wheelock, Hattie Buskirk, Fred Forrester
D: *William Duncan*
S: Alfred Henry Lewis

VENGEANCE AND THE WOMAN (Vitagraph, December 24, 1917) 15 Chapters.
William Duncan, Carol Holloway, George Holt, Tex Allen, Vincente Howard, Fred Burns, S. E. Jennings, Walter Rodgers
D: *William Duncan*
S: Albert E. Smith, Cyrus Townsend Brady
Picturized: Garfield Thompson, Edward J. Montague
Chapter Titles: (1) The Oath, (2) Loaded Dice, (3) The Unscaled Peak, (4) The Signalling Cipher, (5) The Plunge of Destruction, (6) Lure of Hate, (7) Wolf Trap, (8) Mountain of Devastation, (9) Buried Alive, (10) The Leap for Life, (11) The Cavern of Terror, (12) The Desperate Chance, (13) Sands of Doom, (14) The Hand of Fate, (15) The Reckoning

THE DECISION (Vitagraph, 1918) 1 Reel.
(An entry in the Liberty Bond series of World War I)
William Duncan

A FIGHT FOR MILLIONS (Vitagraph, July 15, 1918) 15 Chapters.
William Duncan, Edith Johnson, Joe Ryan, Walter Rodgers
D: *William Duncan*
S: Albert E. Smith, Cyrus Townsend Brady
Adapt: Graham Baker
Chapter Titles: (1) The Snare, (2) Flames of Peril, (3) The Secret Stockade, (4) Precipice of Horror, (5) Path of Thrills, (6) Spell of Evil, (7) Gorge of Destruction, (8) In the Clutches, (9) The Estate, (10) The Secret Tunnel, (11) The Noose of Death, (12) The Tide of Disaster, (13) The Engine of Terror, (14) The Decoy, (15) The Sealed Envelope

MAN OF MIGHT (Vitagraph, January 1919) 15 Chapters.
William Duncan, Edith Johnson, Joe Ryan, Walter Rodgers, Del Harris, Frank Tokanaga, Otto Lederer, Willie Calles
D: *William Duncan*
S: Albert E. Smith, C. T. Brady
Scen: Graham Baker
Chapter Titles: (1) The Riven Flag, (2) The Leap Through Space, (3) The Creeping Death, (4) The Gripping Hand, (5) The Human Shield, (6) The Height of Torment, (7) Into the Trap, (8) The One Chance, (9) The Crashing Horror, (10) Double Crossed, (11) The Ship of Dread, (12) The Volcano's Prey, (13) The Flood of Despair, (14) The Living Catapult, (15) The Rescue

SMASHING BARRIERS (Vitagraph, September 1919) 15 chapters.
William Duncan, Edith Johnson, Walter Rodgers, George Stanley, Fred Darnton, Slim Cole, William McCall
D: *William Duncan*
S: Albert E. Smith, Cyrus T. Brady
Scen: Graham Baker, R. Cecil Smith
Chapter Titles: (1) Test of Courage, (2) Plunge of Death, (3) Tree-Hut of Torture, (4) Deed of a Devil, (5) Living Rave, (6) Downward to Doom, (7) The Fatal Flight, (8) The Murder Car, (9) The Dynamite Tree, (10) Overpowered, (11) The Den of Deviltry, (12) Explosive Bullets, (13) Dead Fall, (14) Trapped Like Rats, (15) The Final Barrier

THE SILENT AVENGER (Vitagraph, April 1920) 15 Chapters.
William Duncan, Edith Johnson, Jack Richardson, Virginia Nightingale, Ernest Shields, Willis L. Robards, William S. Smith
D: *William Duncan*
S: Albert E. Smith, Cleveland Moffett
Scen: Graham Baker, William B. Courtney
Chapter Titles: (1) The Escape, (2) Fighting Back, (3) Within the Noose, (4) Tearing Through, (5) Blotted Out, (6) The Hidden Blow, (7) Dynamite Doom, (8) The Crusher, (9) Into the Jaws, (10) Blades of Horror, (11) Shot into Space, (12) Facing Eternity, (13) A Human Pendulum, (14) The Lakes of Fire, (15) The Final Trump

FIGHTING FATE (Vitagraph, January, 1921) 15 Chapters.
William Duncan, Edith Johnson, Ford West, Frank Weed, William McCall, George Stanley, C. L. Davidson, Burwell Hamrick, Laddie Earle, Jean Carpenter
D: *William Duncan*
S: Albert E. Smith, Arthur P. Hankins
Scen: C. Graham Baker, William B. Courtney
Chapter Titles: (1) A Borrowed Life, (2) Playing the Game, (3) A Modern Daniel, (4) A Desperate Dilemma, (5) Double-Crossed, (6) The Crown Jewel Clue, (7) A Demon's Bluff, (8) The Treasure Hunt, (9) The Air Avenger, (10) The Stolen Bride, (11) A Choice of Death, (12) Indian Vengeance, (13) Mystery Mountain, (14) When Thieves Fall Out, (15) Cleaning the Bolt

WHERE MEN ARE MEN (Vitagraph, September 1, 1921) 5 Reels.
William Duncan, Edith Johnson, George Stanley, Tom Wilson, Gertrude Wilson, Harry Lonsdale, George Kunkel, William McCall, Charles Dudley
D: *William Duncan*
Scen: Thomas Dixon, Jr.

STEELHEART (Vitagraph, November 6, 1921) 6 Reels.
William Duncan, Edith Johnson, Jack Curtis, Walter Rodgers, Euna Luckey, Ardeta Malino, Earl Crain, Charles Dudley
D: *William Duncan*
Scen: Bradley J. Smollen

William Duncan and Edith Johnson in *Fighting Fate*
(Vitagraph, 1921).

NO DEFENSE (Vitagraph, December 25, 1921) 6 Reels.
William Duncan, Edith Johnson, Jack Richardson, Henry
Hebert, Mathilde Brundage, Charles Dudley
D: *William Duncan*
Scen: C. Graham Baker

THE SILENT VOW (Vitagraph, April 16, 1922) 5 Reels.
William Duncan, Edith Johnson, Dorothy Dwan, Maud Emery,
J. Morris Foster, Henry Hebert, Fred Burley, Jack Curtis,
Charles Dudley
D: *William Duncan*
Scen: Bradley J. Smollen

WHEN DANGER SMILES (Vitagraph, October 3, 1922)
5 Reels.
William Duncan, Edith Johnson, James Farley, Henry Hebert,
Charles Dudley, William McCall
D: *William Duncan*
Scen: Bradley J. Smollen
S: John B. Clymer

THE FIGHTING GUIDE (Vitagraph. October 15, 1922)
5 Reels.
William Duncan, Edith Johnson, Harry Lonsdale, William
McCall, Sidney D'Albrook, Charles Dudley, Fred De Silva,
Mrs. Harry Burns
D: *William Duncan*, Don Clark
S/Scen: Bradley J. Smollen

PLAYING IT WILD (Vitagraph, April 19, 1923) 6 Reels.
William Duncan, Edith Johnson, Francis Powers, Dick La
Reno, Edmund Cobb, Frank Beal, Frank Weed
D: *William Duncan*
S/Scen: C. Graham Baker

William Duncan and Edith Johnson in *The Fighting Guide* (Vitagraph, 1922)

SMASHING BARRIERS (Vitagraph, June 17, 1923) 6 Reels.
(feature version of the 1919 serial of the same title)
William Duncan, Edith Johnson, Joe Ryan, Walter Rogers, George Stanley, Frederick Darnton, Slim Cole, William McCall
D: *William Duncan*
Scen: Graham Baker, R. Cecil Smith, Harvey Gates
S: Albert E. Smith, Cyrus Townsend Brady

THE STEEL TRAIL (Universal, August 27, 1923) 15 Chapters.
William Duncan, Edith Johnson, Harry Carter, John Cossar, Harry Woods, Mabel Randall
D: *William Duncan*
S/Scen: George Plympton, Karl Coolidge, Paul M. Bryan
Chapter Titles: (1) Intrigue, (2) Dynamite, (3) Wildfire, (4) Blown from the Cliff, (5) Head On, (6) Crushed, (7) The Gold Rush, (8) Judith's Peril, (9) The Dam Bursts, (10) The Trap, (11) The Fight on the Cliff, (12) The Tottering Bridge, (13) Between Two Fires, (14) Burning Fumes, (15) Ten Seconds to Go

William Duncan in *The Fast Express* (Universal, 1924).

THE FAST EXPRESS (Universal, March 19, 1924) 15 Chapters.
William Duncan, Edith Johnson, Albert J. Smith, Harry Woods, John Cossar, Harry Carter
D: *William Duncan*
S: Courtney Ryley Cooper—"Crossed Wires"
Adapt: Frank H. Clark
Chapter Titles: (1) Facing the Crisis, (2) Vanishing Diamonds, (3) Woman of Mystery, (4) Haunted House, (5) Perils of the City, (6) Cipher Message, (7) Bandit Raiders, (8) Imposter's Scheme, (9) Falsely Accused, (10) Path of Danger, (11) The Abduction, (12) The Trial Run, (13) The False Summons, (14) Black Treasure, (15) Retribution

WOLVES OF THE NORTH (Universal, September 21, 1924) 10 Chapters.
William Duncan, Edith Johnson, Esther Ralston, Joseph W. Girard, Frank Rice, Joe Bonomo, Clarke Comstock, Edward Cecil, Harry Woods, Melvina Polo, Robert Homans
D: *William Duncan*
S: Katherene and Robert Pinkerton—"The Free Trader"
Scen: Frank H. Clark
Chapter Titles: (1) The Fur Pirates, (2) The Wolf Pack, (3) The Avalanche, (4) Passions of War, (5) The Blizzard, (6) Flames of Peril, (7) The Manhunt, (8) The Trail of Gold, (9) A Trick of Fate, (10) The Stolen Map

NEVADA (Paramount, November 29, 1935) 7 Reels.
Larry "Buster" Crabbe, Kathleen Burke, Monte Blue, Raymond Hatton, Glenn Erikson, Syd Saylor, *William Duncan*, Richard Carle, Stanley Andrews, Frank Sheridan, Jack Kennedy, Henry Roquemore, William L. Thorne, Harry Dunkinson, Barney Furey. William Desmond, Frank Rice, Dutch Hendrian
D: Charles Barton
S: Zane Grey—"Nevada"
SP: Barnett Weston, Stuart Anthony

FORLORN RIVER (Paramount, July 2, 1937) 56 Mins.
Larry "Buster" Crabbe, June Martel, John Patterson, Harvey Stephen, Chester Conklin, Lew Kelly, Syd Saylor, *William Duncan*, Rafael Bennett, Ruth Warren, Lee Powell, Oscar Hendrian, Robert Homans, Purnell Pratt, Larry Lawrence, Tom Long, Merrill McCormick, Vester Pegg, Barlowe Barland
D: Charles Barton
S: Zane Grey
SP: Stuart Anthony, Robert Yost

HOPALONG RIDES AGAIN (Paramount, September 30, 1937) 65 Mins.
("Hopalong Cassidy" Series)
William Boyd, George Hayes, Russell Hayden, Harry Worth, Nora Lane, *William Duncan*, Lois Wilde, Billy King, John Rutherford, Ernie Adams, Frank Ellis, Artie Ortego, Ben Corbett, John Beach, Blackjack Ward, Bud McClure
D: Les Selander
S: Clarence E. Mulford—"Black Buttes"
SP: Norman Houston
P: Harry Sherman

BAR 20 JUSTICE (Paramount, June 24, 1938) 70 Mins.
("Hopalong Cassidy" Series)
William Boyd, George Hayes, Russell Hayden, Paul Sutton, Gwen Gaze, Pat O'Brien, Joseph DeStefani, *William Duncan*, Walter Long, John Beach, Bruce Mitchell, Frosty Royce, Jim Toney, Hank Bell
D: Lesley Selander
S: Clarence E. Mulford
SP: Arnold Belgard, Harrison Jacobs
P: Harry Sherman

THE FRONTIERSMAN (Paramount, December 16, 1938)
74 Mins.
("Hopalong Cassidy" Series)
William Boyd, George Hayes, Russell Hayden, Evelyn
Venable, *William Duncan*, Clara Kimball Young, Charles
(Tony) Hughes, Dickie Jones, Roy Barcroft, Emily Fitzroy,
John Beach, Blackjack Ward, George Morrell, Jim Corey,
Saint Brendan Boys Choir, Robert Mitchell
D: Lesley Selander
S: Clarence E. Mulford
SP: Norman Houston, Harrison Jacobs
P: Harry Sherman

THE FARMER'S DAUGHTER (Paramount, February 2,
1940) 60 Mins.
Martha Raye, Charles Ruggles, Richard Denning, Gertrude
Michael, William Frawley, Jack Norton, William Demarest,
William Duncan, Ann Shoemaker, Benny Baker, Tom Dugan,
Lorraine Krueger, Betty McLaughlin, Ann Harrison
D: James Hogan
AP: William C. Thomas
S: Delmar Daves
SP: Lewis R. Foster

TEXAS RANGERS RIDE AGAN (Paramount, December 13, 1940) 68 Mins.
John Howard, Ellen Drew, Akim Tamiroff, Broderick
Crawford, May Robson, Charley Grapewin, John Miljan,
Anthony Quinn, Tom Tyler, Donald Curtis, Eddie Acuff,
Ruth Rogers, Robert Ryan, Eva Puig, Monte Blue, James
Pierce, *William Duncan*, Harvey Stephens, Harold Goodwin,
Edward Pawley, Eddie Foy, Jr., Joseph Crehan, Stanley
Price, Charles Lane, Jack Perrin, Gordon Jones, Ruth Rogers,
John Miller, Henry Roquemore
D: James Hogan
SP: William Lipman, Horace McCoy

12 • HOOT GIBSON

The Human Cowboy

During the years 1937–1939 an aging cowpoke, already a stranger to a new generation of kids, endeavored to keep creditors from his door through milking his past glories as Western star for all they were worth. This he did by headlining Wallace Brothers Circus, Hagenbeck-Wallace Circus, Robbins Brothers Circus, and Russell Brothers Circus. He didn't especially want to hit the sawdust trail again; it was a matter of necessity. After making and spending a fortune during his years as a superstar at Universal, he needed work to keep the wolf from the door. Bad investments and bad marriages had hurt him financially. His popularity had waned with the coming of sound, and it was possible for him to work only for the independents—and even that possibility had dried up in 1937.

The cowboy, of course, was Edmund Richard Gibson, better known as "Hoot." And in case there is any doubt, Hoot was a genuine cowboy. He first came into the limelight when a howling mob of Westerners declared him the World's Champion Cowboy at the Pendleton, Oregon, Roundup and presented him with a diamond-studded belt. That was in 1912.

But back to the beginning. Hoot was born at Tekamah, Nebraska, on August 6, 1892. His early youth was spent in and around that small hamlet lying just north of Omaha and not far from the Missouri River. But as soon as he was old enough he took to the range as a wandering cowboy, tossing his cheap worn saddle over any cayuse a ranch boss might want broken. He was only fifteen when he began his meanderings. For three years he gravitated from range to range, developing a reputation as one of the saltiest cowboys around. Outlaw horses were his specialty, and the steer had not been born that he couldn't throw in short order.

As early as 1907, Hoot had been a performer with the Miller Brothers 101 Ranch Show. Prior to winning the world's championship at Pendleton in 1912, Hoot spent a year or two touring with the Dick Stanley-Bud Atkinson Wild West Show as broncrider and bulldogger along with his friend, Art Acord, who likewise would become a mainstay at Universal in the golden years of the silent era. But at the time, absolutely no one could see in the cards or tea leaves *any* future for the two devil-may-care cowboys who nonchalantly risked their lives as if there were no tomorrow.

Hoot was a fine athlete. He loved horses and show business, and his skill and riding ability made him a popular cowpoke with the wild-west-show fans. The rowdy ways of wild-west shows and rodeo competitions were Hoot's idea of living. Education for him came mostly through a closeness to the earth, cowpunchers, and animals, and no school could have ever taught him the skills he attained as a trick roper, broncbuster, and bull-dogger.

It was in 1910 that he and pal Art Acord managed

Hoot Gibson

and threats of eviction from his living quarters lest there not be a rent payment. Universal was only too glad to put him on as a wrangler, stuntman, and double, and he was soon working in the Harry Carey Westerns. Harry liked the youth and helped him go from double to actor in the Carey two-reelers. John Ford, too, was just getting a start at the studio as a director and, in 1916, was put in charge of the Carey Westerns. Hoot and Ford shared a room and became fast friends. And so, when the first Ford-Carey, five-reel Western, *Straight Shooting* (1917) was filmed, Hoot was promoted to featured player.

Hoot was just getting his career in gear when patriotism engulfed him. He joined the army, serving throughout World War I in the Tank Corps in France. It was nearly two years before he returned to Hollywood. Carey and Ford helped him land a series after he first supported Pete Morrison in a group of two-reelers. Old reliable Pete was the star of these early, action oaters, but Hoot gained much needed experience and worked well with Pete, whose own competency at mild humor and adherence to cowboy traditions probably influenced to some degree the Gibson format when Hoot was catapulted into stardom.

In mid-1919 Hoot began starring in his own series of two-reel Western thrillers. He assumed the role of the typical, hearty, lighthearted young Westerner who was the antithesis of the grim-visaged William S. Hart or the taciturn Carey, yet was less flamboyant than Tom Mix. Flamboyant he was, but in a way different from that of Mix. His characterizations of the cowboy were a little more believable than those of the other fellows. Hoot dared to be human and found a profitable niche in the hearts of Western fandom. Sagebrush eaters liked his rollicking horse frolics, backgrounded by plenty of Western scenery. The action in his prairie epics was usually at a frenzied pace, and the comedy refreshing. He was the first to emphasize comedy, with himself as the clowning, fumbling, all-thumbs hero who seldom wore a gun and often got knocked on his butt by the heavies. His popularity transcended a following by kids alone. In fact, Hoot's films appealed as much to mommy and daddy as to junior. Probably more

to appear as stuntmen in a D. W. Griffith film, *Two Brothers*. But his real entrance into motion pictures as a professional actor was yet two years away.

At the Pendleton Roundup Hoot won a "bride" as well as the world championship. Her name was Helen Wenger, and she was one of the Congress riders. Because lodging was hard to come by and preference was given to married couples, Hoot and Helen, unknown to each other before the Roundup, registered as "Mr. and Mrs." It is not certain whether they actually were married. But Miss Wenger adopted the name of Gibson and went on to fame as Helen Gibson, heroine of the railroad films so popular in the World War I era. She even threw some work Hoot's way, and he appeared in a number of the episodes of Kalem's *The Hazards of Helen*, first with Helen Holmes and then with Helen Gibson.

In 1914 or 1915 Hoot was enticed to Universal City—enticed by the hunger pains in his stomach

In 1921 Carl Laemmle, surprised at the Hooter's fantastic popularity, rushed to capitalize on it by casting him in features running five, six, and sometimes seven reels. The first was called simply *Action*. It was aptly titled. Hoot's deadpan comedy was played up even more in the features than it had been in the two-reelers. Every indignity imaginable, it seems, happened to this one-hundred-sixty-pound, five-foot-ten-inch, plain-looking cowboy with the mischievous disarming smile. He kept his audiences on the edge of their seats wondering from one second to the next what calamity was going to befall him. Just as likely as not, he would get his fool head knocked off. Audiences loved having a hero who was human, one they could worry about and empathize with. He didn't give them an inferiority complex—as was likel to happen with bigger-than-life hero, Tom Mix.

Sixty-eight Hoot Gibson features were made through 1930, ending with *The Concentratin' Kid*, released on November 26, 1930. So profitable had been Hoot's pictures that he was paid aroun $14,000 a week during his peak years, 1924–1930. The money disappeared as fast as it was earned.

Gibson's bantering comedy style was well received during the 1920s, although many a child grew exasperated at the lack of action in some of his films, expectantly awaiting the final reel when Hoot invariably came to life in a whirlwind finale. As Universal's most popular Western ace, Hoot was cast in specials apart from his regular series. Costs of such films as *The Flaming Frontier*, *Calgary Stampede*, and *Painted Ponies* went over $100,000 and were four to six weeks in production. *The Flaming Frontier*, the story of Custer at the Little Big Horn, is generally conceded to be Hoot's best film, enhanced by a strong supporting cast.

In 1922 Hoot married Helen Johnson. The marriage resulted in a daughter, Hoot's only child, and lasted until the early part of 1930 when Helen was granted a divorce and half of Hoot's property. In her suit she charged Hoot with infidelity. Sally Eilers was the lady Hoot had fallen madly in love with, and he married her as soon as he legally could.

Because Carl Laemmle was running scared about the feasibility and profitablity of sound Westerns, he did not renew Hoot's contract for 1931; consequently, Gibson signed for a series with Allied Pictures, an independent serving the states' rights market. Max H. Hoffman owned the company. The eleven oaters Hoot made for him were sadly lacking in production values as compared with the Universal product, but they were enjoyable Saturday matinee fare and returned a reasonable profit to the producer. Hoot's characterization remained the same—that of the nonpistol-packing, rope-twirling, devilishly humorous and bumbling cowpoke who just "happens into trouble." "Skeeter Bill" Robbins, a tall lanky cowboy who looked surprisingly like Slim Summerville, supplied what additional humor was needed in several of the films.

Three films for First Division followed, then a couple of excellent Westerns for RKO in which he was reunited with pal Harry Carey. In 1936 and 1937 he made five oaters for Diversion Pictures and had a featured role in the Republic serial *The Painted Stallion*. After that it was the sawdust arena and odds-and-ends for Hoot, until Monogram brought him out of forced retirement for "The Trail Blazers" series, which co-starred him with Ken Maynard and/or Bob Steele. Both Hoot and Ken had put on weight and each looked every bit his age. But producer Robert Tansey felt that they would have sufficient nostalgic appeal, when combined with the intake from "the every Saturday, regardless" audience, to make a series starring the two a profitable venture. The films were to be made on budgets of around $15,000 and shot in four to five days each. The stars were to receive around $800 per picture in salary, an amount they would have considered as coffee money a decade earlier. Bob Steele was brought in after the third film to bolster the series, Tansey hoping that Steele's personal drawing power would further enhance the series. It did. Maynard dropped out after the sixth entry over a salary dispute. Gibson and Steele continued for five more features before Monogram stopped production, having reached a decision to invest its money in younger stars like Jimmy Wakely and Whip Wilson.

After the Tansey series, things began to get rough for Hoot. For a time he tried operating a restaurant. Then he organized his own rodeo. Ventures were plentiful, but for the most part unprofitable. The years rolled by. A brief respite from obscurity came in 1953 when Ken Murray chose Hoot to co-star with him in *The Marshal's Daughter* for United Artists release. Over the years there were brief appearances here and there, but the Hooter was now a part of past history and not a participator in the on-going creation of history.

Gibson ultimately settled in Las Vegas with his wife, Dorothy Dunstan, a rodeo performer he had married in 1942. They remained together for the rest of Hoot's life. In Las Vegas, Hoot worked for a while as a greeter for one of the casinos, and even did some carnival work. As best they could, Hoot and Dorothy survived and struggled to meet the enormous debts incurred for a series of cancer operations for Hoot. His health deteriorated, and the pain in his stomach intensified.

Hoot Gibson died on August 23, 1962—broke, humble, not bitter, and at peace with his creator and mankind. An important part of Hollywood history was laid to rest, assured of a special kind of immortality among Western film aficionados.

HOOT GIBSON *Filmography*

THE TWO BROTHERS (American/Biograph, May 14, 1910) 1 Reel.
Arthur Johnson, George Nicholls, Kate Bruce, Mary Pickford, W. Chrystie Miller, Mack Sennett, Marion Leonard, Billy Quirk, Henry B. Walthall, *Hoot Gibson*, Art Acord
D: D. W. Griffith
SP: Elinore Hicks

PRIDE OF THE RANGE (Selig, circa 1910) 1 Reel.
Tom Santschi, Tom Mix, Betty Harte, *Hoot Gibson*, Milt Brown, Al Green
D: Francis Boggs

THE NEW SUPERINTENDENT (Selig, November 16, 1911) 1 Reel.
Herbert Rawlinson, Nick Coglen, *Hoot Gibson*

HIS ONLY SON (Nestor, October 12, 1912) 1 Reel.
Wallace Reid, Dorothy Davenport, Jack Conway, Victoria Forde, *Hoot Gibson*
D: Milton Fahrney and Jack Conway

COWBOY SPORTS AND PASTIMES (101/Bison, 1913) 2 Reels.
Hoot Gibson, Bertha Blanchard

SHOTGUN JONES (Selig, April 2, 1914) 2 Reels.
Wheeler Oakman, Joseph Girard, Bessie Eyton, *Hoot Gibson*
D: Colin Campbell
S: Bertrand W. Sinclair

THE HAZARDS OF HELEN (Kalem, November 13, 1914) 119 Episodes.
Helen Holmes, Helen Gibson, Robyn Adair, Ethel Clisbee, Tom Trent, G. A. Williams, Pearl Anibus, P. S. Pembroke, Roy Watson, *Hoot Gibson*
D: J. P. McGowan and James Davis
(Gibson was featured prominently in Episode No. 26, THE WILD ENGINE; in Episode No. 33, IN DANGER'S PATH; and in Episode No. 83, TREASURE TRAIN, and appeared in several other episodes of this lengthy and loosely connected serial. Each episode was 1 reel in length.)

THE MAN FROM THE EAST (Selig, November 28, 1914) 1 Reel.
Tom Mix, Goldie Colwell, Leo Maloney, Pat Chrisman, Inez Walker, *Hoot Gibson*
D/SP: Tom Mix

THE MAN FROM TEXAS (Selig, February 1915) 2 Reels.
Tom Mix, Sid Jordan, Leo Maloney, *Hoot Gibson*
D/SP: Tom Mix

JUDGE NOT: OR, THE WOMAN OF MONA DIGGINGS (Universal-Broadway, September 16, 1915) 6 Reels.
Harry Carey, Julia Dean, Harry Carter, *Hoot Gibson*, Marc Robbins, Kingsley Benedict, Joe Singleton, Paul Nachette, Lydia Yeamans Titus, Walter Belasco
D: Robert Leonard
S: Peter B. Kyne—"Renunciation"

THE RING OF DESTINY (Universal-Rex, November 20, 1915) 2 Reels.
Cleo Madison, Joe King, *Hoot Gibson*, William Gettinger
D: Cleo Madison
S: Marshall Stedman
Scen: Olga Printzlaw

A KNIGHT OF THE RANGE (Universal-Red Feather, January 1916) 5 Reels.
Harry Carey, *Hoot Gibson*, Fred Church, Olive Fuller Golden, William Gettinger
D/P: Jacques Jaccard
S: Harry Carey

THE NIGHT RIDERS (Universal-Bison, February 24, 1916) 2 Reels.
Harry Carey, *Hoot Gibson*, Neal Hart
D/ Jacques Jaccard

THE PASSING OF HELL'S CROWN (Universal-Bison, April 14, 1916) 2 Reels.
Harry Carey, Oliver Fuller Golden, *Hoot Gibson*, Peggy Coudroy
D: Jacques Jaccard
Scen: Lucia Chamberlain
S: W. B. Pearson

THE VOICE ON THE WIRE (Universal, March 18, 1917)
15 Chapters.
Neva Gerber, Ben Wilson, Francis McDonald, Ernest Shields, Joseph W. Girard, Frank Tokonaga, Howard Crampton, *Hoot Gibson*
D: Stuart Paton
Scen: J. Grubb Alexander
S: Eustace Hale Ball
Chapter Titles: (1) The Oriental Death Punch, (2) The Mysterious Man in Black, (3) The Spider's Web, (4) The Next Victim, (5) The Spectral Hand, (6) The Death Warrant, (7) The Marked Room, (8) High Finance, (9) A Stern Chase, (10) The Guarded Heart, (11) The Thought Machine, (12) The Sign of the Thumb, (13) Twixt Death and Dawn, (14) The Light of Dawn, (15) The Living Death

A 44-CALIBER MYSTERY (Universal-Gold Seal, May 18, 1917) 3 Reels.
Harry Carey, *Hoot Gibson*
D: Fred Kelsey
S: T. Shelley Sutton
SP: F. A. Meredyth

THE GOLDEN BULLET (Universal-Gold Seal, June 12, 1917) 3 Reels.
Harry Carey, *Hoot Gibson*, Fritzie Ridgeway, George Berrell, Vester Pegg, William Gettinger
D: Fred Kelsey
S: T. Shelley Sutton
Scen: George Hively

THE WRONG MAN (Universal-Bison, June 23, 1917) 3 Reels.
Harry Carey, *Hoot Gibson*
D: Fred A. Kelsey
S: N. P. Oakes
SP: Jack Cunningham

THE SOUL HERDER (Universal-Bison, August 6, 1917) 3 Reels.
Harry Carey, Fritzi Ridgeway, Jean Hersholt, *Hoot Gibson*, Bill Gettinger
D: Jack (John) Ford
W: George Hively

CHEYENNE'S PAL (Universal-Star, August 14, 1917) 2 Reels.
Harry Carey, Gertrude Astor, Bill Gettinger, *Hoot Gibson*, Vester Pegg, Jim Corey, "Cactus Pete" (a horse)
D: Jack (John) Ford
SP: Jack (John) Ford

STRAIGHT SHOOTING (Universal-Butterfly, August 27, 1917) 5 Reels.
Harry Carey, Molly Malone, *Hoot Gibson*, Duke Lee, George Berrell, Ted Brooks, Milton Brown, Vester Pegg, William Gettinger
D: Jack (John) Ford
SP: George Hively

THE TEXAS SPHINX (Universal-Bison, August 31, 1917) 2 Reels.
Harry Carey, Alice Lake, *Hoot Gibson*, Vester Pegg
D: Fred C. Kelsey
S: T. Shelley Sutton
SP: George Hively

THE SECRET MAN (Universal-Bison, October 1, 1917) 5 Reels.
Harry Carey, Elizabeth Sterling, *Hoot Gibson*, Elizabeth James, Vester Pegg, Bill Gettinger, Steve Clemento, J. Morris Foster
D: Jack (John) Ford
SP: George Hively

A MARKED MAN (Universal-Butterfly, October 19, 1917) 5 Reels.
Harry Carey, Molly Malone, Mrs. Townsend, Vester Pegg, *Hoot Gibson*, Bill Gettinger, Joseph Harris, Harry L. Rattenberry
D: Jack (John) Ford
SP: George Hively

HEADIN' SOUTH (Artcraft Famous Players, February 22, 1918) 5 Reels.
Douglas Fairbanks, Katherine MacDonald, Frank Campeau, James Mason, Jack Holt, Marjorie Daw, Bob Emmons, Alice Smith, *Hoot Gibson*, Art Acord
D: Arthur Rosson
S: Allan Dwan
P: Douglas Fairbanks

A WOMAN IN THE WEB (Vitagraph, April 8, 1918) 15 Chapters.
Hedda Nova, J. Frank Glendon, Robert Bradbury, Otto Lederer, Chet Bryan, *Hoot Gibson*, Patricia Palmer, George Kuwa
D: David Smith, Paul C. Hurst
SP: Albert E. Smith, Cyrus Townsend Brady
Chapter Titles: (1) Caught in the Web, (2) The Open Switch, (3) The Speeding Doom, (4) The Clutch of Terror, (5) The Hand of Mystery, (6) Full Speed Ahead, (7) The Crater of Death, (8) The Plunge of Horror, (9) The Fire Trap, (10) Out of the Dungeon, (11) In the Desert's Grip, (12) Hurled to Destruction, (13) The Hidden Menace, (14) The Crash of Fate, (15) Out of the Web

PLAY STRAIGHT OR FIGHT (Universal, May 29, 1918) 2 Reels.
Hoot Gibson, Helen Gibson, Noble Johnson
P: Paul Hurst
S: Leon de la Motte

THE MIDNIGHT FLYER (Universal, June 13, 1918) 2 Reels.
Hoot Gibson, Helen Gibson

THE BRANDED MAN (Universal, June 26, 1918) 2 Reels.
Hoot Gibson, Helen Gibson

DANGER, GO SLOW (Universal, December 2, 1918) 6 Reels.
Mae Murray, Jack Mulhall, *Hoot Gibson*
D: Robert Leonard

THE BLACK HORSE BANDIT (Universal, February 3, 1919) 2 Reels.
Hoot Gibson, Helen Gibson, M. K. Wilson, Vester Pegg, Noble Johnson, Bill Nye, George Berrell, George Sowards, Neal Hart, Jack Walters
D: Harry Harvey
SP: George Hively

THE FIGHTING BROTHERS (Universal, March 1919) 2 Reels.
Pete Morrison, *Hoot Gibson,* Yvette Mitchell, Duke Lee, Jack Woods
D: Jack (John) Ford
S: George C. Hall

BY INDIAN POST (Universal, April 3, 1919) 2 Reels.
Pete Morrison, Magda Lane, Duke Lee, *Hoot Gibson,* Ed "King Fisher" Jones, Jack Woods, Harley Chambers, Jack Walters, Otto Myers, Jim Moore
D: Jack (John) Ford
S: William Wallace Cook
SP: H. Tipton Steck

THE RUSTLERS (Universal, April 16, 1919) 2 Reels.
Pete Morrison, *Hoot Gibson,* Helen Gibson
D: Reginald Barker
S/SP: George Hively

GUN LAW (Universal, April 28, 1919) 2 Reels.
Pete Morrison, *Hoot Gibson,* Helen Gibson

THE GUN PACKER (Universal, May 12, 1919) 2 Reels.
Pete Morrison, Ed "King Fisher" Jones, Magda Lane, Jack Woods, *Hoot Gibson,* Jack Walters, Duke Lee, Howard Enstedt
D: Jack (John) Ford
SP: Karl Coolidge

ACE HIGH (Universal, May 23, 1919) 2 Reels.
Hoot Gibson
D: George Holt
S: W. Pigott
SP: Karl Coolidge

KINGDOM COME (Universal, June 11, 1919) 2 Reels.
Pete Morrison, Josie Sedgwick, *Hoot Gibson,* Hall Wilson
D: George Holt
S: Dorothy Rochfort
SP: Karl Coolidge

THE FIGHTING HEART (Universal, August 5, 1919) 2 Reels.
Jack Perrin, *Hoot Gibson,* Josephine Hill, William Pattle
D: Reaves Eason
S: William Piggott
SP: Anthony Coldeway

THE FOUR-BIT MAN (Universal, August 21, 1919) 2 Reels.
Jack Perrin, *Hoot Gibson,* Josephine Hill, Andres Waldron, William Dyer
D: Reaves Eason
S: Judith and Erick Howard
SP: Anthony Coldeway

THE JACK OF HEARTS (Universal, September 2, 1919) 2 Reels.
Jack Perrin, *Hoot Gibson,* Josephine Hill
D: Reeves Eason
S: Dorothy Rochfort
SP: Anthony Coldeway

THE CROW (Universal, September 15, 1919) 2 Reels.
Hoot Gibson
D: B. Reeves Eason
S: Alvin J. Neitz, Neal Hart
SP: Karl Coolidge

THE TELLTALE WIRE (Universal, October 18, 1919) 2 Reels.
Hoot Gibson, Josephine Hill
D: B. Reeves Eason
S: Lillian Valentine
SP: Philip Hubbard

THE FACE IN THE WATCH (Universal, October 28, 1919) 2 Reels.
Hoot Gibson, Josephine Hill
D: Edward Kull
S: Harvey Gates
SP: Arthur Henry Gooden

THE TRAIL OF THE HOLD-UP MAN (Universal, November 18, 1919) 2 Reels.
Hoot Gibson
D: George Holt
S: Dorothy Rochfort
SP: Jack Jevne

THE LONE HAND (Universal, November 25, 1919) 2 Reels.
Hoot Gibson, Josephine Hill
D: George Holt
S: Arthur Henry Gooden

THE DOUBLE HOLDUP (Universal, December 6, 1919) 2 Reels.
Hoot Gibson, Josephine Hill
D: Philip E. Rosen
S: Elizabeth Logan
SP: Arthur Henry Gooden

THE JAY BIRD (Universal, December 30, 1919) 2 Reels.
Hoot Gibson, Josephine Hill
D: Philip Rosen
S: J. A. Roche
SP: Jack Jevne

WEST IS BEST (Universal, January 7, 1920) 2 Reels.
Hoot Gibson, Josephine Hill
D: Philip Rosen
S: Gwendolyn Logan
SP: Philip Hubbard

ROARIN' DAN (Universal, January 15, 1920) 2 Reels.
Hoot Gibson, Ethel Shannon
D: Philip E. Rosen
S/SP: Arthur Henry Gooden

THE SHERIFF'S OATH (Universal, February 13, 1920) 2 Reels.
Hoot Gibson, Josephine Hill, Arthur Mackley, Bert Frank, Jim O'Neill, Martha Mattox, William Harrison
D: Philip Rosen
S: Paul Annitzer

HAIR-TRIGGER STUFF (Universal, February 19, 1920) 2 Reels.
Hoot Gibson, Mildred Moore, George Field, Beatrice Dominquez
D: Reeves Eason
S: Dorothy Rochefort
SP: Philip Hubbard

RUNNIN' STRAIGHT (Universal, February 26, 1920) 2 Reels.
Hoot Gibson, Virginia Brown Faire, L. M. Wells
D: Art Flavers
S/SP: Philip Hubbard

HELD UP FOR THE MAKIN'S (Universal, March 11, 1920) 2 Reels.
Hoot Gibson
D: Reeves Eason
S: George Hull
SP: Philip Hubbard

THE RATTLER'S HISS (Universal, March 15, 1920) 2 Reels.
Hoot Gibson, Mildred Moore
D: Reeves Eason
S/SP: George Hively

THE TEXAS KID (Universal, April 2, 1920) 2 Reels.
Hoot Gibson, Reeves Eason, Jr., Ben Corbett
D/SP: Reeves Eason
S: Henry Murray

WOLF TRACKS (Universal, April 23, 1920) 2 Reels.
Hoot Gibson, Thelma Percy, Leonard Clapham (Tom London), Jim Corey
D: Mack V. Wright
S: Arthur Henry Gooden
SP: Hope Loring, Mack V. Wright

MASKED (Universal, May 4, 1920) 2 Reels.
Hoot Gibson, Virginia Brown Faire
D: Mack V. Wright
S: Harvey Gates
SP: Hope Loring

THIEVES' CLOTHES (Universal, May 6, 1920) 2 Reels.
Hoot Gibson
D: Mack V. Wright
S: Arthur Henry Gooden
SP: Hope Loring

THE BRONCHO KID (Universal, May 28, 1920) 2 Reels.
Hoot Gibson, Yvette Mitchell, Jim Corey, D. C. Hendricks
D: Mack V. Wright
S/SP: Arthur Henry Gooden

THE FIGHTIN' TERROR (Universal, June 9, 1920) 2 Reels.
Hoot Gibson, Yvette Mitchell, Mark Fenton
D: *Hoot Gibson*
S/SP: Harvey Gates

THE SHOOTIN' KID (Universal, July 1, 1920) 2 Reels.
Hoot Gibson
D: *Hoot Gibson*
S/SP: George W. Pyper

THE SMILIN' KID (Universal, August 14, 1920) 2 Reels.
Hoot Gibson, Dorothy Wood
D: *Hoot Gibson*
S: Arthur Henry Gooden
SP: Bob Horner

THE CHAMPION LIAR (Universal, September 3, 1920)
2 Reels.
Hoot Gibson
D: Hoot Gibson
S: Louis D. Lighton
SP: Bob Horner

THE BIG CATCH (Universal, September 11, 1920) 2 Reels.
Hoot Gibson
D: Leo Maloney
S: Louis D. Lighton
SP: Ford Beebe

A GAMBLIN' FOOL (Universal, September 17, 1920) 2 Reels.
Hoot Gibson, Dorothy Wood, Jim Corey
D: Leo Maloney
S/SP: Ford Beebe

THE GRINNING GRANGER (Universal, September 25, 1920) 2 Reels.
Hoot Gibson
D: Leo Maloney
S/SP: Ford Beebe

ONE LAW FOR ALL (Universal, October 2, 1920) 2 Reels.
Hoot Gibson, Dorothy Wood, Leo Maloney
D: Leo Maloney
S/SP: Ford Beebe

SOME SHOOTER (Universal, October 11, 1920) 2 Reels.
Hoot Gibson
D: Hoot Gibson
S/SP: Hadden Ware, Jeanne Spencer

IN WRONG WRIGHT (Universal, October 20, 1920) 2 Reels.
Hoot Gibson, Dorothy Wood
D: Albert Russell
S/SP: Ford Beebe

CINDERS (Universal, October 25, 1920) 2 Reels.
Hoot Gibson, Dorothy Wood
D: Edward Laemmle
S: W. C. Tuttle
SP: George Hively

DOUBLE DANGER (Universal, November 5, 1920) 2 Reels.
Hoot Gibson
D: Albert Russell
S/SP: Ford Beebe

THE TWO-FISTED LOVER (Universal, November 5, 1920)
2 Reels.
Hoot Gibson, Dorothy Wood, Jim Corey, Charles Newton,
Walter Crowley, Katherine Bates, Nancy Caswell
D: Edward Laemmle
S/SP: Ford Beebe

TIPPED OFF (Universal, November 12, 1920) 2 Reels.
Hoot Gibson
S/SP: Ford Beebe
D: Albert Russell

SUPERSTITION (Universal, November 20, 1920) 2 Reels.
Hoot Gibson, Dorothy Wood
D: Edward Laemmle
SP: Ford Beebe
P: Alfred Russell
S: Arthur H. Gooden

FIGHT IT OUT (Universal, December 1, 1920) 2 Reels.
Hoot Gibson, Dorothy Wood, Jim Corey, Charles Newton,
Ben Corbett
D: Albert Russell
S: W. C. Tuttle
SP: Ford Beebe

THE MAN WITH THE PUNCH (Universal, December 7, 1920) 2 Reels.
Hoot Gibson, Dorothy Wood, Jim Corey, Ben Corbett,
Charles Newton
D: Edward Laemmle
S: W. C. Tuttle
SP: Burl Armstrong

THE TRAIL OF THE HOUND (Universal, December 11, 1920) 2 Reels.
Hoot Gibson
D: Albert Russell
S: Ford Beebe

THE SADDLE KING (Universal, December 18, 1920)
2 Reels.
Hoot Gibson, Jim Corey, Dorothy Wood
D: Edward Laemmle
SP: Ford Beebe
S: George Morgan

MARRYIN' MARION (Universal, 1920) 2 Reels.
Hoot Gibson, Gertrude Olmstead, Jim Corey, Jack Walters,
Charles Newton
D: Albert Russell
S: Ford Beebe

A PAIR OF TWINS (Universal, 1920) 2 Reels.
Hoot Gibson, Dorothy Wood, Jim Corey, Charles Newton,
Georgia Davey
D: Albert Russell
S: Ford Beebe

HARMONY RANCH (Universal, 1920) 2 Reels.
Hoot Gibson

WINNING A HOME (Universal, 1920) 2 Reels.
Hoot Gibson

THE STRANGER (Universal, 1920) 2 Reels.
Hoot Gibson
S: W. C. Tuttle

RANSOM (Universal, 1920) 2 Reels.
Hoot Gibson, Virginia Brown Faire, Leonard Clapham (Tom London)
D: Mack V. Wright
S: Harvey Gates

THE TEACHER'S PET (Universal, 1920) 2 Reels.
Hoot Gibson, Dorothy Wood
S: Ford Beebe

THE SHOOTIN' FOOL (Universal, 1920) 2 Reels.
Hoot Gibson, Dorothy Wood
SP: F. H. Ware, Jeanne Spencer

A NOSE IN THE BOOK (Universal, 1920) 2 Reels.
Hoot Gibson, Mildred Moore, George Field, Billy Eason
D: B. Reeves Eason
S: Henry Murray

THE DRIFTIN' KID (Universal, January 6, 1921) 2 Reels.
Hoot Gibson, Gertrude Olmstead, Otto Nelson, Artie Ortego
D: Albert Russell
S: James Edward Hungerford
SP: Ford Beebe

SWEET REVENGE (Universal, January 13, 1921) 2 Reels.
Hoot Gibson, Gertrude Olmstead, Jim Corey
D: Edward Laemmle
S/SP: Ford Beebe

KICKAROO (Universal, January 22, 1921) 2 Reels.
Hoot Gibson
D: Albert Russell
S: George Morgan
SP: Ford Beebe

OUT O'LUCK (Universal, February 25, 1921) 2 Reels.
Hoot Gibson
D: Hoot Gibson
S/SP: George Morgan

THE FIGHTING FURY (Universal, February 28, 1921) 2 Reels.
Hoot Gibson, Gertrude Olmstead, Ben Corbett
D: Hoot Gibson
S: Arthur Henry Gooden
SP: George Morgan

THE CACTUS KID (Universal, March 12, 1921) 2 Reels.
Hoot Gibson, Consuela Henley
D/P: *Hoot Gibson*
S/SP: George Morgan

WHO WAS THE MAN? (Universal, April 1, 1921) 2 Reels.
Hoot Gibson
D: Lee Kohlmar
S: W. Craft, G. H. Plympton
SP: George Morgan

CROSSED CLUES (Universal, April 13, 1921) 2 Reels.
Hoot Gibson
P: William Craft
S: James Edwards Hungerford
SP: George Morgan

DOUBLE-CROSSERS (Universal, May 6, 1921) 2 Reels.
Hoot Gibson
D: William J. Craft
SP: George Plympton, *Hoot Gibson*

THE WILD, WILD WEST (Universal, May 21, 1921) 2 Reels.
Hoot Gibson
D: Lee Kohlmar
S: Fred V. Williams
SP: George H. Plympton

BANDITS BEWARE (Universal, June 10, 1921) 2 Reels.
Hoot Gibson
D: Lee Kohlmar
SP: George Morgan

THE MOVIE TRAIL (Universal, June 24, 1921) 2 Reels.
Hoot Gibson
P: Charles Thompson
S/SP: George Morgan

THE MAN WHO WOKE UP (Universal, July 12, 1921) 2 Reels.
Hoot Gibson
D: Lee Kohlmar
S: L. Underwood
SP: Robert Dillon

BEATING THE GAME (Universal, July 21, 1921) 2 Reels.
Hoot Gibson
D: Lee Kohlmar
S: Evelyn McKinney
SP: Robert Dillon

TOO-TIRED JONES (Universal, 1921) 2 Reels.
Hoot Gibson
D: Lee Kohlmar

THE WINNING TRACK (Universal, 1921) 2 Reels.
Hoot Gibson

Francis Ford, Hoot Gibson, and J. Farrell MacDonald
in *Action* (Universal, 1921).

ACTION (Universal, September 12, 1921) 5 Reels.
Hoot Gibson, Francis Ford, J. Farrell MacDonald, Buck
Connors, Clara Horton, William Robert Daly, Dorothea
Wolbert, Byron Munson, Charles Newton, Jim Corey, Ed
"King Fisher" Jones
D: Jack (John) Ford
S: J. Allen Dunn—"The Mascot of the Three Star"
SP: Harvey Gates

RED COURAGE (Universal, October 10, 1921) 5 Reels.
Hoot Gibson, Joel Day, Molly Malone, Joe Girard, William
Merrill McCormick, Charles Newton, Arthur Hoyt, Joe
Harris, Dick Cummings, Mary Philbin, Jim Corey, Mac V.
Wright
D: Reeves Eason
S: Peter B. Kyne—"The Sheriff of Cinnabar"
Scen: Harvey Gates

SURE FIRE (Universal, November 7, 1921) 5 Reels.
Hoot Gibson, Molly Malone, Breezy Eason, Jr., Harry Carter,
Fritzi Brunette, Murdock MacQuarrie, George Fisher, Charles
Newton, Jack Woods, Jack Walters, Joe Harris, Steve Clemente
D: Jack (John) Ford
S: Eugene Manlove Rhodes
Scen: George C. Hull

THE FIRE-EATER (Universal, December 24, 1921) 5 Reels.
Hoot Gibson, Louise Lorraine, Walter Perry, Tom Lingham,
Fred Lancaster, Carmen Philips, George Berrell, W. Bradley
Ward, George A. Williams
D: Reaves Eason
Scen: Harvey Gates
S: Ralph Cummings—"The Badge of Fighting Hearts"

Lillian Rich and Hoot Gibson in *Bearcat* (Universal, 1922,

HEADIN' WEST (Universal, February 13, 1922) 5 Reels.
Hoot Gibson, Gertrude Short, Charles Le Moyne, Jim Corey, Leo White, Louise Lorraine, George A. Williams, Frank Whitson, Mark Fenton
D: William J. Craft
S/Scen: Harvey Gates

THE BEARCAT (Universal, April 3, 1922) 5 Reels.
Hoot Gibson, Lillian Rich, Charles French, Joe Harris, Alfred Hollingsworth, Harold Goodwin, William Buckley, Fontaine La Rue, James Alamo, J. J. Allen, Stanley Fitz, Joe De La Cruz, Sam Pobo
D: Edward Sedgwick
Scen: George Hively
S: F. R. Buckley

STEP ON IT! (Universal, May 29, 1922) 5 Reels.
Hoot Gibson, Edith Yorke, Frank Lanning, Barbara Bedford, Vic Potel, Gloria Davenport, Joe Girard, L. C. Shumway
D: Jack Conway
S: Courtney Riley Cooper
Scen: Arthur F. Statter

TRIMMED (Universal, July 3, 1922) 5 Reels.
Hoot Gibson, Patsy Ruth Miller, Alfred Hollingsworth, Fred Kohler, Otto Hoffman, Dick La Reno, R. Hugh Sutherland
D: Harry Pollard
Scen: Arthur F. Statter
S: Hapsburg Liebe—"Trimmed and Burning"

THE LOADED DOOR (Universal, August 4, 1922) 5 Reels.
Hoot Gibson, Gertrude Olmstead, Bill Ryno, Eddie Sutherland, Noble Johnson, Joseph Harris, Charles Newton, Charles A. Smiley, Victor Potel, C. L. Sherwood
D: Harry A. Pollard
Scen: George Hively
S: Ralph Cummins—"Cherub of Seven Bar"

THE GALLOPING KID (Universal, September 11, 1922) 5 Reels.
Hoot Gibson, Edna Murphy, Lionel Belmore, Leon Bary, Jack Walters, Percy Challenger
D: Nat Ross
Scen: A. P. Younger, Arthur Statter
S: William Hamby

THE LONE HAND (Universal, October 16, 1922) 5 Reels.
Hoot Gibson, Marjorie Daw, Helen Holmes, Hayden Stevenson, Jack Pratt, William Welsh, Robert Kortman
D: Reaves Eason
Scen: A. P. Younger
S: Ralph Cummins—"Laramie Ladd"

RIDIN' WILD (Universal, November 19, 1922) 5 Reels.
Hoot Gibson, Edna Murphy, Wade Boteler, Jack Walters, Otto Hoffman, William Taylor, Bert Wilson, Gertrude Claire, William Walsh, Wallace Beery, Charles Whitaker, Steve Reeves
D: Nat Ross
Cont: Roy Myers, Edward T. Lowe, Jr.
S: Roy Myers

KINDLED COURAGE (Universal, December 1922) 5 Reels.
Hoot Gibson, Beatrice Burnham, Harold Goodwin, Harry Tenbrook, James Gordon, Russell Powell, Albert Hart
D: William Worthington
Scen: Raymond L. Schrock
S: Llete R. Brown

THE GENTLEMAN FROM AMERICA (Universal, February 19, 1923) 5 Reels.
Hoot Gibson, Tom O'Brien, Louise Lorraine, Carmen Phillips, Frank Leigh, Jack Crane, Bob McKenzie, Albert Prisco, Rosa Rosanova
D: Edward Sedgwick
Scen: George C. Hull
S: Raymond L. Schrock

SINGLE-HANDED (Universal, March 25, 1923) 5 Reels.
Hoot Gibson, Elinor Field, Percy Challenger, William Steele, Philip Sleeman, Dick La Reno, Mack V. Wright, Tom McGuire, Gordon McGregor, W. T. McCulley, C. B. Murphy, Bob McKenzie, Sidney De Grey
D/S: Edward Sedgwick
Scen: George C. Hull

DEAD GAME (Universal, April 23, 1923) 5 Reels.
Hoot Gibson, Laura La Plante, Alfred Allen, William Welsh, William Steele, Arthur Mackley, W. T. McCulley, Kansas Moehring, Robert McKim, Harry Carter
D/S/SP: Edward Sedgwick

DOUBLE DEALING (Universal, May 21, 1923) 5 Reels.
Hoot Gibson, Helen Ferguson, Eddie Gribbon, Betty Francisco, Frank Hayes, Gertrude Claire, Otto Hoffman, Jack Dillon
D/S: Henry Lehrman
Scen: George C. Hull

SHOOTIN' FOR LOVE (Universal, June 28, 1923) 5 Reels.
Hoot Gibson, Laura La Plante, Alfred Allen, William Welsh, William Steele, Arthur Mackley, W. T. McCulley, Kansas Moehring
D: Edward Sedgwick
Scen: Albert Kenyon, Raymond L. Schrock
S: Raymond L. Schrock, Edward Sedgwick

OUT OF LUCK (Universal, July 23, 1923) 6 Reels.
Hoot Gibson, Laura La Plante, Howard Druesdell, Elinor Hancock, De Witt Jennings, Freeman Wood, Jay Morley, Kansas Moehring, John Judd
D/S: Edward Sedgwick
Scen: George C. Hull, Raymond L. Schrock

BLINKY (Universal, August 17, 1923) 6 Reels.
Hoot Gibson, Esther Ralston, Mathile Brundage, De Witt Jennings, Elinor Field, Donald Hatswell, Charles K. French, John Judd, William E. Lawrence, W. T. McCulley
D/Scen: Edward Sedgwick
S: Gene Markey—"Blinky"

THE RAMBLIN' KID (Universal, September 3, 1923) 6 Reels.
Hoot Gibson, Laura La Plante, Harold Goodwin, William Welsh, W. T. McCulley, Charles K. French, G. Raymond Nye, Carol Holloway, Goober Glenn, George King, Gyp Streeter, John Judd
D: Edward Sedgwick
Scen: E. Richard Schayer
S: Earl Wayland Bowman—"The Ramblin' Kid"

THE THRILL CHASER (Universal, November 26, 1923) 6 Reels.
Hoot Gibson, James Neill, Billie Dove, William E. Lawrence, Bob Reeves, Gino Gerrado, Lloyd Whitlock, Maty Philbin, Norman Kerry, Reginald Denny, Laura La Plante, Hobart Helley, King Baggot, Edward Sedgwick
D/S: Edward Sedgwick
Scen: Richard Schayer
S: Edward Sedgwick, Raymond L. Schrock

HOOK AND LADDER (Universal, January 7, 1924) 6 Reels.
Hoot Gibson, Mildred June, Frank Beal, Edward Davis, Philo McCullough
D: Edward Sedgwick
Scen: E. Richard Schayer
S: Edward Sedgwick, Raymond L. Schrock

RIDE FOR YOUR LIFE (Universal, February 25, 1924) 6 Reels.
Hoot Gibson, Laura La Plante, Harry Todd, Robert McKim, Howard Truesdell, Fred Humes, Clark Comstock, Mrs. George Hernandez, William Robert Daley
D: Edward Sedgwick
Adapt: Raymond L. Schrock, E. Richard Schayer
S: Johnston McCulley

FORTY-HORSE HAWKINS (Universal, April 21, 1924) 6 Reels.
Hoot Gibson, Anne Cornwall, Richard Tucker, Helen Holmes, Jack Gordon Edwards, Ed Burns, Edward Sedgwick, John Judd
D: Edward Sedgwick
S/Scen: Edward Sedgwick, Raymond L. Schrock

BROADWAY OR BUST (Universal, June 9, 1924) 6 Reels.
Hoot Gibson, Ruth Dwyer, King Zany, Gertrude Astor, Stanhope Wheatcroft, Fred Malatesta
D: Edward Sedgwick
Scen: Dorothy Yost
S: Edward Sedgwick, Raymond L. Schrock

HIT-AND-RUN (Universal, August 10, 1924) 6 Reels.
Hoot Gibson, Marion Harlan, Cyril Ring, Harold Goodwin, De Witt Jennings, Mike Donlin, William A. Steele
D: Edward Sedgwick
S/Scen: Edward Sedgwick, Raymond L. Schrock

THE SAWDUST TRAIL (Universal, August 10, 1924) 6 Reels.
Hoot Gibson, Josie Sedgwick, David Torrence, Charles K. French, Harry Todd, G. Raymond Nye, Pat Harmon, Taylor Carroll, W. T. McCulley
D: Edward Sedgwick
Scen: E. Richard Schayer
Adapt: Raymond L. Schrock
S: William Dudley Pelley

THE RIDIN' KID FROM POWDER RIVER (Universal, November 30, 1924) 6 Reels.
(Also known as "The Lone Outlaw"; working title was "The Saddle Hawk")
Hoot Gibson, Gladys Hulette, Gertrude Astor, Tully Marshall, Walter Long, Sidney Jordan, William A. Steele, Howard Truesdell, Frank Rice, Nelson McDowell, Fred Humes, Bowditch Turner, Newton House
D: Edward Sedgwick
S: Henry Herbert Knibbs—"The Ridin' Kid from Powder River" or "The Saddle Hawk"
Scen: Raymond L. Schrock and Rex Taylor
Adapt: Raymond L. Schrock, LeRoy Armstrong
P: *Hoot Gibson*

THE CITY OF STARS (Universal, 1924) 28 Mins.
William Desmond, Norman Kerry, Jean Hersholt, Reginald Denny, Jack Hoxie, Laura LaPlante, Pat O'Malley, Alice Joyce, Clive Brook, *Hoot Gibson*, May McAvoy, Marian Nixon
D: H. Bruce Humberstone
(This was some kind of promotional release filmed in and around Universal City, with many of the studio's stars being seen at work and play)

THE HURRICANE KID (Universal, January 25, 1925)
6 Reels.
Hoot Gibson, Marion Nixon, William A. Steele, Arthur
Mackley, Violet La Plante, Harry Todd, Fred Humes, "Pal"
D: Edward Sedgwick
Scen: E. Richard Schayer
Adapt: Raymond L. Schrock
S: Lambert Hillyer

THE TAMING OF THE WEST (Universal, March 1, 1925)
6 Reels.
Hoot Gibson, Marceline Day, Morgan Brown, Edwin Tilton,
Herbert Prior, Louise Hippe, Albert J. Smith, Francis Ford,
Frona Hale
D: Arthur Rosson
Cont: Raymond L. Schrock
S: Bertha Muzzy Sinclair (B. M. Bower)—"The Range
Dwellers"

LET 'ER BUCK (Universal, March 8, 1925) 6 Reels.
Hoot Gibson, Marion Nixon, Charles K. French, G. Raymond
Nye, William A. Steele, Josie Sedgwick, Fred Humes
D: Edward Sedgwick
S/Scen: Edward Sedgwick, Raymond L. Schrock

THE SADDLE HAWK (Universal, March 8, 1925) 6 Reels.
Hoot Gibson, Marion Nixon, G. Raymond Nye, Josie Sedg-
wick, Charles French, Tote Du Crow, Fred Humes, William
Steele, Frank Campeau
D: Edward Sedgwick
S/Scen: Edward Sedgwick, Raymond L. Schrock

SPOOK RANCH (Universal-Jewel, September 20, 1925)
6 Reels.
Hoot Gibson, Helen Ferguson, Ed Cowles, Tote Du Crow,
Robert McKim, Frank Rice, Dick Sutherland
D: Edward Laemmle
Scen: Raymond L. Schrock
S: Edward Sedgwick, Raymond L. Schrock

HOLLYWOOD TODAY #8 (Circa mid-1920s) 10 Mins.
Hoot Gibson, Laura La Plante and other Universal stars

THE CALGARY STAMPEDE (Universal-Jewel, Novem-
ber 1, 1925) 6 Reels.
Hoot Gibson, Virginia Brown Faire, Clark Comstock, Ynez
Sabury, Jim Corey, Philo McCullough, W. T. McCulley,
Ena Gregory, Charles Sellon, Tex Young, Bob Gillis
D: Herbert Blache
S: Raymond L. Schrock, Donald W. Lee, E. Richard
Schayer

ROADS TO HOLLYWOOD (Hollywood Enterprises, 1925).
Art Acord, *Hoot Gibson*, Pete Morrison, William Dyer
(No other information available on this film)

THE ARIZONA SWEEPSTAKES (Universal-Jewel, Jan-
uary 10, 1926) 6 Reels.
Hoot Gibson, Helen Lynch, Philo McCullough, George Ovey,
Emmett King, Ted Brown, Kate Price, Jackie Morgan,
Billy Kent Schaeffer, Turner Savage
D: Clifford S. Smith
Scen: Isadore Bernstein
S: Charles Logue

CHIP OF THE FLYING U (Universal-Jewel, March 14,
1926) 7 Reels.
Hoot Gibson, Virginia Brown Faire, Philo McCullough,
Nora Cecil, De Witt Jennings, Harry Todd, Pee Wee
Holmes, Mark Hamilton, Willie Sung, Steve Clemente
D: Lynn Reynolds
Scen: Lynn Reynolds, Harry Dittmar
S: B. M. Bower

THE PHANTOM BULLET (Universal-Jewel, May 9, 1926)
6 Reels.
Hoot Gibson, Eileen Percy, Allan Forrest, Pat Harmon,
Nelson McDowell, William H. Turner, John T. Prince,
Pee Wee Holmes, Rosemary Cooper
D: Clifford S. Smith
Adapt/Cont: Curtis Benton
S: Oscar J. Friend—"Click of the Triangle T"

THE MAN IN THE SADDLE (Universal-Jewel, July 11,
1926) 6 Reels.
Hoot Gibson, Fay Wray, Charles Mailes, Clark Comstock,
Sally Long, Boris Karloff, Emmett King, Lloyd Whitlock,
Duke R. Lee, Yorke Sherwood, William Dyer
D: Clifford S. Smith
SP: Charles A. Logue

THE SHOOT 'EM UP KID (Universal-Mustang, August 25,
1926) 2 Reels.
Hoot Gibson
D: Hoot Gibson
S: Carol Holloway
SP: William Lester

THE TEXAS STREAK (Universal-Jewel, September 26,
1926) 7 Reels.
Hoot Gibson, Blanche Mehaffey, Alan Roscoe, James Marcus,
Jack Curtis, George "Slim" Summerville, Les Bates, Jack
Murphy, William H. Turner
D/S/SP: Lynn Reynolds

THE BUCKAROO KID (Universal-Jewel, October 19,
1926) 6 Reels.
Hoot Gibson, Newton House, Ethel Shannon, Burr McIntosh,
Harry Todd, James Gordon, Charles Colby, Joe Rickson,
Clark Comstock
D/Adapt: Lynn Reynolds
S: Peter Bernard Kyne—"Oh, Promise Me"

THE FLAMING FRONTIER (Universal-Jewel, November 12, 1926) 9 Reels.
Hoot Gibson, Anne Cornwall, Dustin Farnum, Ward Crane, Kathleen Key, Eddie Gribbon, Harry Todd, Harold Goodwin, George Fawcett, Noble Johnson, Charles K. French, William Steele, Walter Rodgers, Ed Wilson, Joe Bonomo, William Orlamonde
D/S: Edward Sedgwick
Scen: Edward J. Montague, Charles Kenyon
Adapt: Raymond L. Schrock

THE SILENT RIDER (Universal-Jewel, January 2, 1927) 6 Reels.
Hoot Gibson, Blanche Mehaffey, Ethan Laidlaw, Otis Harlan, Wendell Phillips Franklin, Arthur Morrison, Nora Cecil, Dick La Reno, Lon Poff, Dick L'Estrange
D: Lynn Reynolds
Cont: Joseph Franklin Poland
S: Katherine Newlin Burt—"The Redheaded Husband"

THE DENVER DUDE (Universal-Jewel, February 13, 1927) 6 Reels.
Hoot Gibson, Blanche Mehaffey, Robert McKim, George Summerville, Glenn Tryon, Howard Truesdell, Mathilde Brundage, Rolfe Sedan, Grace Cunard, Buck Carey, Pee Wee Holmes
D: B. Reeves Eason
S: Earle Snell
Adapt: Carl Krusada, William B. Lester

HEY! HEY! COWBOY (Universal-Jewel, April 3, 1927) 6 Reels.
Hoot Gibson, Nick Cogley, Kathleen Key, Wheeler Oakman, Clark Comstock, Monte Montague, Milla Davenport, Jim Corey, Slim Summerville
D/S/Scen: Lynn Reynolds

THE PRAIRIE KING (Universal-Jewel, May 15, 1927) 6 Reels.
Hoot Gibson, Barbara Worth, Albert Prisco, Charles Sellon, Rosa Gore, Sidney Jarvis, George Periolat
D: Reaves Eason
Adapt/Cont: Frank Howard Clark
S: William Wallace Cook

A HERO ON HORSEBACK (Universal-Jewel, July 10, 1927) 6 Reels.
Hoot Gibson, Ethlyne Clair, Edwards Davis, Edward Hearn, Dan Mason
D: Del Andrews
Adapt: Mary Alice Scully, Arthur Statter
S: Peter B. Kyne—"Bread Upon the Waters"

PAINTED PONIES (Universal-Special, September 25, 1927) 6 Reels.
Hoot Gibson, Ethlyne Clair, William Dunn, Charles Sellon, Otto Hoffman, Slim Summerville, Chief White Spear, Black Hawk, Chief Big Tree, Mary Lopez
D: Reeves Eason
Scen: Arthur Statter
Adapt: Frank Beresford
S: John Harold Hamlin—"Painted Ponies"

GALLOPING FURY (Universal-Jewel, November 20, 1927) 6 Reels.
Hoot Gibson, Otis Harlan, Sally Rand, Frank Beal, Gilbert "Pee Wee" Holmes, Max Asher, Edward Coxen, Duke R. Lee, "Silver" (a horse, but not the more famed "Silver" ridden by Buck Jones)
D: Reeves Eason
Scen: Arthur Statter
S: Peter B. Kyne—"Tidy Toreador"

THE RAWHIDE KID (Universal-Jewel, January 29, 1928) 6 Reels.
Hoot Gibson, Georgia Hale, Frank Hagney, William H. Strauss, Harry Todd, Tom Lingham
D: Del Andrews
Cont: Arthur Statter
Adapt: Isadore Bernstein
S: Peter B. Kyne

A TRICK OF HEARTS (Universal-Jewel, March 18, 1928) 6 Reels.
Hoot Gibson, Georgia Hale, Heinie Conklin, Joe Rickson, Rosa Gore, Howard Truesdell, George Ovey, Nora Cecil, Grace Cunard, Dan Crimmins
D: Reeves Eason
Scen: Arthur Statter
S: Henry Irving Dodge

THE FLYIN' COWBOY (Universal-Jewel, May 12, 1928) 6 Reels.
Hoot Gibson, Olive Hasbrouck, Harry Todd, William Bailey, Buddy Phillips, Ann Carter
D/Cont: Reeves Eason
S/Adapt: Arthur Statter

THE WILD WEST SHOW (Universal-Jewel, May 20, 1928) 6 Reels.
Hoot Gibson, Dorothy Gulliver, Allan Forrest, Gale Henry, Monte Montague, Roy Laidlaw, John Hall
D: Del Andrews
Cont: John B. Clymer
Adapt: Isadore Bernstein
S: Del Andrews, St. Elmo Boyce

RIDING FOR FAME (Universal-Jewel, August 19, 1928) 6 Reels.
Hoot Gibson, Ethlyne Clair, Charles K. French, George "Slim" Summerville, Allan Forrest, Ruth Cherrington, Chet Ryan, Robert Burns
D/SP: Reeves Eason
Cont: Reeves Eason, Slim Summerville
S: Arthur Statter

CLEARING THE TRAIL (Universal-Jewel, October 7, 1928) 6 Reels.
Hoot Gibson, Dorothy Gulliver, Fred Gilman, Cap Anderson, Philo McCullough, Andy Waldron, Duke Lee, Monte Montague, Universal Ranch Riders
D: Reeves Eason
Adapt/Scen: John F. Natteford
S: Charles Maigne

THE DANGER RIDER (Universal-Jewel, November 18, 1928) 6 Reels.
Hoot Gibson, Eugenia Gilbert, Reeves Eason, Monte Montague, King Zany, Frank Beal, Milla Davenport, Bud Osborne
D: Henry MacRae
Adapt/Scen: Arthur Statter
S: Wynn James

KING OF THE RODEO (Universal-Jewel, January 6, 1929) 6 Reels.
Hoot Gibson, Kathryn Crawford, Slim Summerville, Charles K. French, Monte Montague, Joseph W. Girard, Jack Knapp, Harry Todd, Bodil Rosing
D: Henry MacRae
Cont: George Morgan
S: B. M. Bower
P: *Hoot Gibson*

BURNING THE WIND (Universal-Jewel, February 10, 1929) 6 Reels.
Hoot Gibson, Virginia Brown Faire, Cesare Gravina, Boris Karloff, Pee Wee Holmes, Robert Homans, George Grandee
D: Henry MacRae, Herbert Blacke
S: William MacLeod Raine—"A Daughter of the Dons: A Story of New Mexico"
SP: George Plympton, Raymond L. Schrock

SMILIN' GUNS (Universal-Jewel, March 31, 1929) 6 Reels.
Hoot Gibson, Blanche Mehaffey, Virginia Pearson, Robert Graves, Leo White, Walter Brennan, Jack Wise, James Bradbury, Jr., Dad Gibson
D: Henry MacRae
Scen: George Morgan
S: Shannon Fife

THE LARIAT KID (Universal-Jewel, May 12, 1929) 6 Reels.
Hoot Gibson, Ann Christy, Cap Anderson, Mary Foy, Walter Brennan, Andy Waldron, Bud Osborne, Joe Bennett, Jim Corey, Francis Ford, Joe Rickson
D: Reaves Eason
S: Buckleigh Fritz Oxford
Cont: Jacques Jaccard, Sylvia Berstein

THE WINGED HORSEMAN (Universal-Jewel, May 24, 1929) 6 Reels.
Hoot Gibson, Ruth Elder, Charles Schaeffer, Allan Forrest, Herbert Prior
D: Arthur Rosson
S/Cont: Raymond L. Schrock

POINTS WEST (Universal-Jewel, June 16, 1929) 6 Reels.
Hoot Gibson, Alberta Vaughn, Frank Campeau, Jack Raymond, Martha Franklin, Milt Brown, Jim Corey, Ann Christy, Andy Waldron, Mary Foy, Joe Rickson
D: Arthur Rosson
Cont: Rowland Brown
S: B. M. Bower—"Points West"
Adapt: George Morgan

THE LONG LONG TRAIL (Universal, October 27, 1929) 6 Reels.
(Part-talking)
Hoot Gibson, Sally Eilers, Kathryn McGuire, James Mason, Archie Ricks, Walter Brennan, Howard Truesdale
D: Arthur Rosson
SP: Howard Green and Earl Bowman
S: Earl Bowman—"Ramblin Kid"
P: *Hoot Gibson*

COURTIN' WILDCATS (Universal, December 22, 1929) 6 Reels.
(Part-talking)
Hoot Gibson, Eugenie Gilbert, Harry Todd, Joseph Girard, Monte Montague, John Oscar, Jim Corey, James Farley, Pete Morrison, Joe Bonomo
D: Jerome Storm
SP: Dudley McKenna
S: William Dudley Peller—"Courtin' Calamity"

THE MOUNTED STRANGER (Universal, February 8, 1930) 55 Mins.
Hoot Gibson, Louise Lorraine, Buddy Hunter, Milton Brown, Fred Burns, James Corey, Francis Ford, Walter Patterson, Francelia Billington
D: Arthur Rosson
S: H. H. Knibbs—"Ridin' Kid from Powder River"
SP: Arthur Rosson

TRAILIN' TROUBLE (Universal, March 23, 1930) 6 Reels
57 Mins.
Hoot Gibson, Margaret Quimby, Pete Morrison, Olive Young,
William McCall, Bob Perry
D: Arthur Rosson
SP/S: Arthur Rosson—"Hand 'Em Over"
P: *Hoot Gibson*

ROARING RANCH (Universal, April 27, 1930) 65 Mins.
Hoot Gibson, Sally Eilers, Wheeler Oakman, Bobby Nelson,
Frank Clark, Leo White
D: Reeves Eason
S/SP: Reeves Eason—"Howdy, Cowboy"
P: *Hoot Gibson*

TRIGGER TRICKS (Universal, June 1, 1930) 60 Mins.
Hoot Gibson, Sally Eilers, Robert Homans, Jack Richardson,
Monte Montague, Neal Hart, Walter Perry, Max Asher
D/S/SP: B. Reeves Eason
P: *Hoot Gibson*

SPURS (Universal, August 24, 1930) 60 Mins.
Hoot Gibson, Helen Wright, Robert Homans, Frank Clark,
Buddy Hunter, Gilbert Holmes, William Bertram, Philo
McCullough, Cap Anderson, Pete Morrison, Artie Ortega
D/S/SP: B. Reeves Eason
P: *Hoot Gibson*

THE CONCENTRATIN' KID (Universal, November 26,
1930) 57 Mins.
Hoot Gibson, Kathryn Crawford, Duke R. Lee, James Mason,
Robert E. Homans
D: Arthur Rosson
SP: Harold Tarshie
S: Harold Tarshie, Charles Sexton
P: Hoot Gibson

CLEARING THE RANGE (Allied, April 1, 1931) 61 Mins.
Hoot Gibson, Sally Eilers, Hooper Atchley, George Mendoza,
Robert Homans, Maston Williams, Edward Peil, Jack Byron,
Jim Fremont, Mme. Eva Grippon, Edward Hearn
D: Otto Brower
S: Jack Cunningham
SP: Jack Natteford
P: M. H. Hoffman, Jr.

WILD HORSE (Allied, August 2, 1931) 77 Mins.
Hoot Gibson, Alberta Vaughn, Stepin Fetchit, Neal Hart,
Edmund Cobb, "Skeeter Bill" Robbins, George Bunny,
Edward Peil, Joe Rickson, Glenn Strange, Fred Gilman
D: Richard Thorpe, Sidney Algier
S: Peter B. Kyne
SP: Jack Natteford
P: M. H. Hoffman, Jr.
(Reissued by Astor Films as "Silver Devil")

Hoot Gibson and player in *The Gay Buckaroo* (Allied,
1932).

HARD HOMBRE (Allied, September 20, 1931) 65 Mins.
Hoot Gibson, Lina Basquette, Mathilda Comont, Jesse Arnold,
G. Raymond Nye, Christian Frank, Jack Byron, Frank
Winkelmann, Fernando Galvez, Rosa Gore, "Skeeter Bill"
Robbins, Glenn Strange, Tiny Sanford, Fred Burns, Milton
Brown
D: Otto Brower
S/SP: Jack Natteford
P: M. H. Hoffman, Jr.

THE LOCAL BAD MAN (Allied, January 15, 1932) 59 Mins.
Hoot Gibson, Sally Blane, Hooper Atchley, Edward Peil, Edward
Hearn, "Skeeter Bill" Robbins, Jack Clifford, Milton Brown
D: Otto Brower
S: Peter B. Kyne—"All For Love"
SP: Philip G. White
P: M. H. Hoffman

THE GAY BUCKAROO (Allied, January 17, 1932) 56 Mins.
Hoot Gibson, Merna Kennedy, Roy D'Arcy, Edward Peil,
Charles King, Lafe McKee, Jimmy Engles, Sidney de Grey,
The Hoot Gibson Cowboys
D: Phil Rosen
S: Lee R. Brown
SP: Philip G. White
P: M. H. Hoffman, Jr.

SPIRIT OF THE WEST (Allied, March 1, 1932) 62 Mins.
Hoot Gibson, Doris Hill, Hooper Atchley, Alan Bridge, Lafe
McKee, George Mendoza, Charles Brinley, Walter Perry,
Tiny Sanford
D: Otto Brower
S: Jack Natteford
SP: Philip G. White
P: M. H. Hoffman, Jr.

Walter McGrail, Mary Doran, Hoot Gibson, and an unidentified player in *Sunset Range* (First Division, 1935).

A MAN'S LAND (Allied, June 11, 1932) 65 Mins.
Hoot Gibson, Marion Shilling, Ethel Wales, Robert Ellis, Charles King, Bill Nye, "Skeeter Bill" Robbins, Alan Bridge, Hal Burney, Merrill McCormack, Slim Whitaker
D: Phil Rosen
S/SP: Adele Buffington
P: M. H. Hoffman, Jr.

THE COWBOY COUNSELLOR (Allied, October 15, 1932) 62 Mins.
Hoot Gibson, Sheila Manners (later Sheila Bromley), "Skeeter Bill" Robbins, Bobby Nelson, Fred Gilman, Jack Rutherford, Alan Bridge, William Humphreys, Gordon De Main, William Merrill McCormick, Sam Allen, Frank Ellis
D: George Melford
S/SP: Jack Natteford
P: M. H. Hoffman, Jr.

THE BOILING POINT (Allied, November 12, 1932) 64 Mins.
Hoot Gibson, Helen Foster, Wheeler Oakman, "Skeeter Bill" Robbins, Lafe McKee, Billy Bletcher, Tom London, George F. (later Gabby) Hayes, Charles Bailey, William Nye, Lew Meehan, Hattie McDaniel, Robert Burns, Art Mix, Merrill McCormick, Artie Ortego, Frank Ellis
D: George Melford
S: Donald W. Lee
P: M. H. Hoffman, Jr.

THE DUDE BANDIT (Allied, May 1, 1933) 62 Mins.
Hoot Gibson, Gloria Shea, "Skeeter Bill" Robbins, Hooper Atchley, Neal Hart, Lafe McKee, Gordon DeMain, Fred Burns, Fred Gilman, Art Mix, George Morrell, Merrill McCormick, Hank Bell, Horace B. Carpenter, Pete Morrison, Charles Whitaker, Blackie Whiteford, Frank Ellis, Charles Brinley, Charles King, Bill Gillis
D: George Melford
S/Scen: Jack Natteford
P: M. H. Hoffman, Jr.

THE FIGHTING PARSON (Allied, August 2, 1933) 61 Mins.
Hoot Gibson, Marceline Day, Robert Frazer, Stanley Blystone, "Skeeter Bill" Robbins, Ethel Wales, Phil Dunham, Jules Cowles, Charles King, Frank Nelson
D: Harry Fraser
P: M. H. Hoffman, Jr.
S: Edward Weston
Scen: Harry Fraser, Edward Weston

SUNSET RANGE (First Division, April 3, 1935) 60 Mins.
Hoot Gibson, Mary Doran, James Eagles, Walter McGrail, John Elliott, Eddie Lee, Ralph Lewis, Kitty McHugh, Fred Gilman, Martha Sleeper
D: Ray McCarey
S/SP: Paul Schofield

RAINBOW'S END (First Division, 1935) 54 Mins.
Hoot Gibson, June Gale, Warner Richmond, Oscar Aphel, Charles Hill, Buddy Roosevelt, Ada Ince, Stanley Blystone, John Elliott, Henry Roquemore, Fred Gilman
D: Norman Spencer
S: Rollo Ward

POWDERSMOKE RANGE (RKO-Radio, September 27, 1935) 71 Mins.
Harry Carey, *Hoot Gibson*, Bob Steele, Tom Tyler, Guinn "Big Boy" Williams, Boots Mallory, Wally Wales, Sam Hardy, Adrian Morris, Buzz Barton, Art Mix, Frank Rice, Buddy Roosevelt, Buffalo Bill, Jr. (Jay Wilsey), Franklyn Farnum, William Desmond, William Farnum, Ethan Laidlaw, Eddie Dunn, Ray Mayer, Barney Furey, Bob McKenzie, James Mason, Irving Bacon, Henry Roquemore, Phil Dunham, Silver Tip Baker, Nelson McDowell, Frank Ellis
D: Wallace Fox
S: William Colt MacDonald
SP: Adele Buffington
P: Cliff Reid

Harry Carey, Hoot Gibson, Boots Mallory, Guinn (Big Boy) Williams, and William Farnum in *Powdersmoke Range* (RKO-Radio, 1935).

SWIFTY (Diversion, December 12, 1935) 59 Mins.
Hoot Gibson, June Gale, Lafe McKee, Art Mix, Ralph Lewis, George F. (Gabby) Hayes, Robert Kortman, Wally Wales, Duke Lee, William Gould, "Starlight" (a horse, but available information does not indicate whether it is the famous mount of Jack Perrin)
D: Alan James
S: Stephen Payne
SP: Bennett Cohen
P: Walter Futter

LUCKY TERROR (Diversion/Grand National, February 20, 1936) 61 Mins.
Hoot Gibson, Lona Andre, Charles Hill, George Chesebro, Robert McKenzie, Jack Rockwell, Frank Yaconelli, Charles King, Horace Carpenter, Hank Bell, Wally Wales, Art Mix, Horace Murphy, Fargo Bussey, Nelson McDowell
D: Alan James
S/SP: Roger Allman, Alan James
P: Walter Futter

FEUD OF THE WEST (Diversion, April 15, 1936) 62 Mins.
Hoot Gibson, Joan Barclay, Buzz Barton, Reed Howes, Robert Kortman, Edward Cassidy, Nelson McDowell, Lew Meehan, Bob McKenzie, Allen Greer, Roger Williams
D: Harry Fraser
SP: Phil Dunham, Walton Farrar, Roger Allmon
S: Russell A. Bankson
P: Walter Futter

THE RIDING AVENGER (Diversion, June 15, 1936) 58 Mins.
Hoot Gibson, June Gale, Ruth Mix, Buzz Barton, Stanley Blystone, Roger Williams, Francis Walker, Slim Whitaker, Budd Buster, Blackie Whiteford
D: Harry Fraser
SP: Norman Houston
S: Walton West—"Big Bud Buckaroo"
P: Walter Futter

THE LAST OUTLAW (RKO-Radio, June 19, 1936) 62 Mins.
Harry Carey, *Hoot Gibson,* Margaret Callahan, Henry B. Walthall, Tom Tyler, Ray Mayer, Harry Jans, Frank M. Thomas, Russell Hopton, Frank Jenks, Maxine Jennings, Fred Scott, Joe Sawyer
D: Christy Cabanne
SP: John Twist, Jack Townley
S: John Ford, E. Murray Campbell
P: Robert Sisk

CAVALCADE OF THE WEST (Diversion, October 1936) 59 Mins.
Hoot Gibson, Marion Shilling, Rex Lease, Adam Goodman, Nina Guilbert, Steve Clark, Earl Dwire, Phil Dunham, Robert McKenzie, Jerry Tucker, Barry Downing, Budd Buster, Blackie Whiteford
D: Harry Fraser
S/SP: Norman Houston
P: Walter Futter

FRONTIER JUSTICE (Diversion, 1936) 58 Mins.
Hoot Gibson, Jane Barnes, Richard Cramer, Franklyn Farnum, Lloyd Ingraham, John Elliott, Lafe McKee, Joe Girard, Fred Toones, Roger Williams, George Yoeman, John Elliott, Lafe McKee, Silver Harr
D: Robert McGowan
SP: W. Scott Darling
S: George B. Rodney
P: Walter Futter

THE PAINTED STALLION (Republic, June 5, 1937) 12 Chapters.
Ray Corrigan, *Hoot Gibson,* LeRoy Mason, Duncan Renaldo, Jack Perrin, Sammy McKim, Hal Taliaferro, Ed Platt, Lou Fulton, Julia Thayer, Yakima Canutt, Maston Williams, Duke Taylor, Loren Riebe, George DeNormand, Gordon DeMain, Charles King, Vinegar Roan, Lafe McKee, Frank Leyva, Frankie Marvin, John Big Tree, Pascale Perry, Don Orlando, Henry Hale, Edward Peil, Sr., Horace Carpenter, Lee White, Joe Yrigoyen, Paul Lopez, Monte Montague, Gregg Star Whitespear, Buck Bucko, Roy Bucko, Leo Dupee, Babe DeFreest, Jose Dominguez, Jack Padjan, Al Haskell, Augie Gomez, Curley Dresden, James Marcus, Oscar & Elmer
D: William Witney, Alan James, Ray Taylor
SP: Barry Shipman, Winston Miller
AP: J. Laurence Wickland
S: Morgan Cox and Ronald Davidson

WILD HORSE STAMPEDE (Monogram, April 16, 1943) 57 Mins.
Ken Maynard, *Hoot Gibson,* Betty Miles, Bob Baker, Ian Keith, Si Jenks, Donald Stewart, John Bridges, Glenn Strange, Reed Howes, Kenneth Harlan, Tom London, Tex Palmer, Forrest Taylor, I. Stanford Jolley, Kenne Duncan, Bob McKenzie, Chick Hannon, Cliff Lyons (stunting)
D: Alan James
S: Frances Kavanaugh
SP: Elizabeth Beecher
P: Robert Tansey

THE LAW RIDES AGAIN (Monogram, August 6, 1943) 58 Mins.
Ken Maynard, *Hoot Gibson,* Betty Miles, Jack LaRue, Chief Thunder Cloud, Hank Bell, Bryant Washburn, Emmett Lynn, Kenneth Harlan, John Bridges, Fred Hoose, Charles Murray, Jr., Chief Many Treaties, John Merton, Keene Duncan, Roy Brent, Steve Clark, Budd Buster, Wally West, Carleton Young, Kenneth MacDonald, Cliff Lyons (stunting)
D: Alan James
S/SP: Frances Kavanaugh
P: Robert Tansey

BLAZING GUNS (Monogram, October 8, 1943) 55 Mins.
Ken Maynard, *Hoot Gibson,* Kay Forrester, LeRoy Mason, Roy Brent, Lloyd Ingraham, Charles King, Weldon Heyburn, Dan White, Frank Ellis, Kenne Duncan, Emmett Lynn, Eddie Gribbon, George Kamel, Bobbie Cavanaugh, Virginia Baxter, Charles Murray, Jr., John Bridges, Robert Allen, Cliff Lyons (stunting)
D/P: Robert Tansey
S/SP: Frances Kavanaugh

Jack Perrin, Hoot Gibson, Ray Corrigan, and Hal Taliaferro (Wally Wales, in *The Painted Stallion* (Republic, 1937.

DEATH VALLEY RANGERS (Monogram, December 3, 1943) 59 Mins.

Ken Maynard, *Hoot Gibson*, Bob Steele, Linda Brent, Kenneth Harlan, Bob Allen, Charles King, George Chesebro, John Bridges, Al Ferguson, Steve Clark, Wally West, Glenn Strange, Forrest Taylor, Lee Roberts, Weldon Heyburn, Karl Hackett, Bryant Washburn, Frank Ellis, Cliff Lyons (stunting)

D/P: Robert Tansey
S: Robert Emmett, Frances Kavanaugh
SP: Elizabeth Beecher

ARIZONA WHIRLWIND (Monogram, February 21, 1944) 59 Mins.

Ken Maynard, *Hoot Gibson*, Bob Steele, Ian Keith, Myrna Dell, Donald Stewart, Charles King, Karl Hackett, George Chesebro, Dan White, Charles Murray, Jr., Frank Ellis, Chief Soldani, Willow Bird, Cliff Lyons (stunting)

D/P: Robert Tansey
S/SP: Frances Kavanaugh

Betty Miles, Hoot Gibson, and Ken Maynard in *The Law Rides Again* (Monogram, 1943).

OUTLAW TRAIL (Monogram, April 18, 1944) 53 Mins.
Hoot Gibson, Bob Steele, Chief Thunder Cloud, Jennifer Holt, Cy Kendall, Rocky Camron, George Eldredge, Charles King, Hal Price, John Bridges, Bud Osborne, Jim Thorpe, Frank Ellis, Al Ferguson, Warner Richmond, Tex Palmer
D/P: Robert Tansey
S: Alvin J. Neitz (Alan James)
SP: Frances Kavanaugh

SONORA STAGECOACH (Monogram, June 10, 1944) 61 Mins.
Hoot Gibson, Bob Steele, Chief Thunder Cloud, Rock Camron, Betty Miles, Glenn Strange, George Eldredge, Karl Hackett, Henry Hall, Charles King, Bud Osborne, Charles Murray, Jr., John Bridges, Al Ferguson, Forrest Taylor, Frank Ellis, Hal Price, Rodd Redwing, John Cason, Horace B. Carpenter
D/S/P: Robert Tansey
SP: Frances Kavanaugh

THE UTAH KID (Monogram, July 26, 1944) 55 Mins.
Hoot Gibson, Bob Steele, Beatrice Gray, Evelyn Eaton, Ralph Lewis, Mike Letz, Mauritz Hugo, Jammison Shade, Dan White, George Morrell, Bud Osborne, Earle Hodgins
D: Vernon Keyes
S/SP: Victor Hammond
P: William Strobach

MARKED TRAILS (Monogram, July 29, 1944) 58 Mins.
Hoot Gibson, Bob Steele, Veda Ann Borg, Ralph Lewis, Mauritz Hugo, Steve Clark, Charles Stevens, Lynton Brent, Bud Osborne, George Morrell, Allen B. Sewell, Ben Corbett, John Cason
D: J. P. McCarthy
SP: J. P. McCarthy, Victor Hammond
P: William Strobach
S: J. P. McCarthy

TRIGGER LAW (Monogram, September 30, 1944) 56 Mins.
Hoot Gibson, Bob Steele, Beatrice Gray, Ralph Lewis, Edward Cassidy, Jack Ingram, George Eldridge, Pierce Lyden, Lane Chandler, Bud Osborne, George Morrell
D: Vernon Keyes
S/SP: Victor Hammond
P: Charles J. Bigelow

FLIGHT TO NOWHERE (Screen Guild, July 1947) 65 Mins.
Alan Curtis, Evelyn Ankers, Michaline Cheirel, Jack Holt, Jerome Cowan, John Craven, Inez Cooper, Roland Varno, Michael Visaroff, Gordon Richards, *Hoot Gibson*
D: William Rowland
SP: Arthur V. Jones
P: William B. David

SCREEN SNAPSHOTS (Columbia, September 4, 1947) 10 Mins.
(Segment called "Hollywood Cowboys")
Buck Jones, Gene Autry, Roy Rogers, Will Rogers, Tom Mix, John Mack Brown, *Hoot Gibson*, William S. Hart, William Boyd, Robert Young, Jackie Coogan
D/P: Ralph Staub

THE MARSHAL'S DAUGHTER (United Artists, June 26, 1953) 71 Mins.
Hoot Gibson, Lauri Enders, Harry Lauter, Ken Murray, Robert Bray, Bob Duncan, Forrest Taylor, Tom London, Bruce Norman, Cecil Elliott, Bettie Lou Walters, Francis Ford, Julian Upton, Ted Jordan, and guest stars Preston Foster, Johnny Mack Brown, Jimmy Wakely, Buddy Baer
D: William Berke
SP: Bob Duncan
P: Ken Murray

HOLLYWOOD BRONC BUSTERS (Columbia, 1956) 9 Mins.
("Screen Snapshot" Series)
Jack Lemmon, Ralph Staub; Film clips featuring Gene Autry, Roy Rogers, Tom Mix, William Boyd, William S. Hart, Buck Jones, *Hoot Gibson*, and Charles Starrett
D/P: Ralph Staub

THE HORSE SOLDIERS (Mahin-Rackin/Mirisch/United Artists, June 12, 1960)
119 Mins. (Color by DeLuxe)
John Wayne, William Holden, Constance Towers, Althea Gibson, *Hoot Gibson*, Anna Lee, Russell Simpson, Stan Jones, Carleton Young, Basil Ruysdael, Willis Bouchey, Ken Curtis, O. Z. Whitehead, Judson Pratt, Denver Pyle, Strother Martin, Hank Worden, Walter Reed, Jack Pennick, Fred Graham, Chuck Hayward, Charles Seel, Stuart Holmes, Major Sam Harris, Richard Cutting, Bing Russell, William Leslie, Ron Haggerty, William Forrest, Fred Kennedy, Bill Henry, Dan Borzage
D: John Ford
SP: John Lee Mahin, Martin Rackin
S: Harold Sinclair
P: John Lee Mahin, Martin Rackin

OCEANS 11 (Warner Brothers, August 13, 1960) 127 Mins. Frank Sinatra, Dean Martin, Sammy Davis, Jr., Peter Lawford, Angie Dickinson, Richard Conte, Cesar Romero, Patrice Wymore, Joey Bishop, Akim Tamiroff, Henry Silva, Ilka Chase, Buddy Lester, Richard Benedict, Jean Willes, Norman Fell, Clem Harvey, Hank Henry, Robert Foulk, Lew Gallo, Charles Meredith, Gregory Gay, Don Barry, Steve Pendleton, Nelson Leigh, Murray Alper, George E. Stone, John Holland, John Craven, Carmen Phillips, Ronnie Dapo, Louis Quinn, Anne Neyland, Joan Staley, *Hoot Gibson*, Jack Perrin, Paul Bryar, Johnny Indrisano, Red Skelton, George Raft, Shirley MacLaine, Marjorie Bennett, Red Norvo, Laura Cornell, Barbara Sterling, Tom Middleton, Sparky Kaye, Forrest Lederer, Rummy Bishop, William Justine
D/P: Lewis Milestone
SP: Harry Brown and Charles Lederer
S. George Clayton Johnson and Jack Golden Russell

Hoot Gibson and Harold Lloyd when Hollywood was at its zenith.

Gene Autry

13 • GENE AUTRY

A Cowboy Phenomenon

The story of Gene Autry's phenomenal rise as the world's most popular cowboy star has been told many times and probably needs little embellishment here. Few movie fans, even at this late date—twenty-five years after the release of his last theatrical film—are not sufficiently familiar with the name of Autry to identify him as the screen's first* and foremost singing cowboy, and they are at least vaguely aware that he somehow revolutionized cinema Westerns. Revolutionized indeed!

Gene was born in Tioga, Texas, on September 29, 1907, the son of a cattle buyer and the grandson of a Baptist minister. When in his teens, Gene moved to Oklahoma to work for the railroad and for a while lived around Tishomingo, the old capital of the Chickasaw Nation. Old-timers there still talk about Gene's sitting on the street corner on Saturdays, strummin' his cheap guitar and acting every bit the country-boy-come-to-town. Gene's job for the railroad was as a telegrapher. One night in Chelsea, as he was whiling away the lonely hours by plucking and singing for his own amusement, Will Rogers dropped in to send a telegram, heard him singing, listened awhile, and suggested to Gene that he give radio a try. Bashfully Gene thanked him, not realizing until later that it was Rogers. Shortly thereafter, heeding Will's advice, he

set out for New York to try his luck in the entertainment field. He was turned down consistently for lack of experience.

Disappointed, but still determined, he returned to Oklahoma where he was able to get a radio show on KVOO in Tulsa, billed as "Oklahoma's Singing Cowboy." It was a popular show; and, his courage bolstered by his local success, after a year he returned to New York, armed not only with experience but with a song he had written in conjunction with a friend—a song called "That Silver-Haired Daddy of Mine." It was a hit, and NBC's affiliate station WLS in Chicago hired Gene. Soon he was appearing regularly on the "National Barn Dance," an exceedingly popular country-western radio show. The sandy-haired, blue-eyed, gum-chewing ballad-eer became a familiar voice to millions who "listened round the old box" each Saturday evening, and his melodious yipee-yi-ays won him a host of record and radio fans. He stayed at WLS for four years, also cutting records for the American Record Company.

Gene wanted to get in the movies and for months wrote letters to Mascot president, Nat Levine, asking for a chance. Finally convinced that his radio and record popularity should not be ignored, Levine signed both Gene (at $100 a week) and Smiley Burnette (at $75 a week) to a contract. Smiley had been working for Gene for a couple of years on the "National Barn Dance" and was also a recognized radio personality.

---

*Purists will readily recognize that the dubious honor of being the first singing cowboy belongs more appropriately to Ken Maynard, but songs and music in his films were always secondary to the action and not emphasized.

Levine's intention was to use Gene and Smiley as support for Ken Maynard in a proposed series of musical Westerns in both serial and feature format. Ken had introduced musical interludes into his Universal features, and the result had been quite palatable to audiences. True, he wasn't much of a singer, but that's where Gene figured in. Ken was the most innovative and popular cowboy at the time, and, while Nat dickered with him about money and such, Gene underwent several months of training in acting and riding. Tracey Layne and Yak Canutt, Mascot employees, were assigned the task of teaching Gene how to ride. And Reb Russell, with whom Gene lived for a while, also assisted him in the transformation from country hick to movie hero.

Levine finally signed Maynard, and *In Old Santa Fe* (1934) went into production, with Gene and Smiley given several songs to do. Evelyn Knapp and George F. Hayes provided chief support for Ken. As things turned out, it was one of Maynard's best pictures, and Gene surprisingly came across on screen more pleasantly than even Levine had hoped for. In Maynard's next, the serial *Mystery Mountain* (1934), Gene and Burnette had small non-singing and nonriding roles. Gene was still a novice horseman. Maynard walked out, or was fired, after completion of the serial. He was a difficult man to work with, and Levine had had more of Ken's temper tantrums than he could stomach. He took the big gamble, and cast Autry in *The Phantom Empire* (1935) in the lead role originally intended for Maynard.

Movie history was in the making. The science-fiction motif in a western setting struck a responsive cord, and for twelve weeks on end depression-weary people flocked to their small hometown theatres to see the singing cowboy from Melody Ranch cavort in the underground kingdom of Murania. The story was a wild one, its incongruity of ingredients unbelievable; yet this bizarre bit of weekly make-believe clicked. Not only did audiences like the fantasy story, they also liked the guitar-plucking young hero with the friendly, natural, honest manner and pleasant, nasal-twang voice. Physically he wasn't much to write home about, and the histrionic abilities he demonstrated could easily have been the outcome of a three-day stint in a high-school senior play, yet his enthralling personality attracted a considerable coterie of

fans. He was lucky in that a combination of high technical skills gave the film a physical wallop, and that suspense was forcefully pounded home in the pile-driver direction job by Otto Brower and B. Reeves Eason, coupled with an intriguing musical score.

Unquestionably there was a charisma about Gene Autry. Any doubts on the subject were dispelled with the fantastic success of his first starring feature, *Tumbling Tumbleweeds* (1935), a $75,000 investment that quickly grossed over $500,000. Levine had merged his Mascot pictures with Monogram, Consolidated Film Laboratories, and several smaller outfits to form Republic, and Autry's first feature was released as a Republic product.

The Autry phenomenon was in motion, as uncontrollable, it would seem, as a "Conestoga and eight up" on a downhill run. Nat Levine continued to produce Autry films through 1936, with Joseph Kane most often at the directorial helm. The Autry fantasy was gradually constructed. Gene, with one exception, was always "Gene Autry" on screen, and his image was built around the ten commandments he had devised for himself. His hero was always as pure as the driven snow, moved, not by selfish motives, but by respect for women, parents, old folks, children and animals; by fair play, truthfulness, cleanliness of thought and speech; by racial and religious tolerance; by abstinence from liquor, smoking, and sex, and so forth. His cowboy code was really not as original as it is given credit for being, as most "B" cowboys in the 1920s and 1930s had adhered to the basic tenets of it long before Gene put it in writing. But he never once deviated from his code and went to greater lengths than anyone had previously gone to create a "pure" cowboy whom youngsters could admire and emulate. His westerns were almost completely divorced from reality—quite understandable when it became apparent that there was a strong correlation between the degree of fantasy in his prairie musicals and his popularity.

By 1936 Gene ranked third in popularity among cowboy stars. From 1937 through 1942 he was America's favorite cowboy, and in 1940 he was the fourth most popular movie star in the world, slipping to sixth rank in 1941 and seventh rank in 1942. He was the first "B" cowboy to ever crash the "Big Ten"—the top money-making, box-office stars other than the Western category. From 1947 through 1954, the last year the poll was taken, Gene ranked second behind Roy Rogers in the Top Ten Cowboy Popularity Poll.

Astride his horse Champion, Gene sang, smiled, and philosophized his way into the hearts of millions. Through movies, records, rodeos, personal appearance tours, radio, comic books, and merchandise bearing his name, he built a financial empire that quickly made him a millionaire several times over. Shrewd investments in oil wells, hotels, radio and television stations, a baseball team, music publishing, ranches, and a multitude of other things eventually put his wealth at an estimated $100 million.

At the height of his career Gene Autry received more fan mail than anyone in Hollywood, an average of 80,000 letters a month! His records sold in the millions. The Autry Westerns were Republic's bread-and-butter and, as such, received the gloss that others did not. Gradually the action content was lessened and the musical content intensified until it was a question of whether his films were musical westerns or western musicals. It seemed not to matter to the fans. Prewar films, such as *The Big Show* (1936), *Gold Mine in the Sky* (1938), *Mexicali Rose* (1939), *South of the Border* (1939), *Melody Ranch* (1940), *Down Mexico Way* (1940), and *Sierra Sue* (1941), set a high in standards for programmer Westerns. So popular were the Autry films that they were shown in first-rate theatres which had never before booked the "B" product.

Gene's last film before entering the U.S. Air Force in 1942 was *Bells of Capistrano* (1942), his fifty-second starring film. With the exception of *Shooting High* (Fox, 1940), all had been done for Republic with Smiley Burnette as his rotund sidekick. After three years in the service Gene returned to find that Republic had been giving Roy Rogers the big push as King of the Cowboys. Gene was still under contract. His first postwar film was *Sioux City Sue* (1946), a disappointment in comparison with most of his prewar oaters. Neither the music nor the action seemed up to snuff, and Sterling Holloway was not nearly so funny as Smiley Burnette, who by this time was working elsewhere. Four more entries followed for Gene at Republic before his contract expired. Although certainly above par as "B" Westerns, some of the magic that had characterized the prewar films was lacking.

Gene could not come to terms with Republic's Herbert Yates on a new contract and formed his own company to make his films for Columbia release, taking with him John English as director and Armand Schaefer as producer. His first Columbia release, *The Last Round-Up* (1947), proved that he still had the charisma when given a decent screenplay and adequate production. Succeeding entries were just as good. Gene made a total of thirty-one Columbia Westerns from late 1947 through 1953. Appropriately titled, his last theatrical film was *Last of the Pony Riders* (1953). Most of the Columbia releases were photographed in Cinecolor or Sepiatone, and running time ranged from 82 minutes for *The Big Sombrero* (1949) to 56 minutes for *Saginaw Trail* (1953). Pat Buttram was comedy foil in six films, and Smiley Burnette rejoined Gene for the final six films.

Gene lasted to the very end of the "B" era, voluntarily withdrawing from the production of theatrical films when it seemed that they would no longer be profitable; instead he devoted himself to television, starring in over ninety segments of his own Gene Autry Show, as well as producing several other Western series through his Flying A Productions.

It has been nearly twenty-five years since Gene gave up active performing to devote full time to the management of his financial empire. And just as that empire has continued to grow, so has the recognition for Gene's show-business achievements. His election to both the Country Music Hall of Fame and the National Cowboy Hall of Fame were well-deserved honors for the Oklahoma singing cowboy who instilled new life into the Western and provided vicarious thrills and romance for millions who could never hope to have it directly.

Gene Autry's Westerns were fun to watch. What more could an overall-clad, towheaded, freckled-faced kid desire in those golden years of long ago? To walk on a pleasant summer evening to the local "picture show" to watch Gene and "Champion" and to wistfully and bashfully offer popcorn to the pretty little girl one "just happened to sit next to" was ecstasy personified. Beautiful little girls there will always be, no doubt, and let's hope that they will continue to quicken the pulse rate of little boys; but how sad it is that today's youngsters, on their sojourns to the cinema palaces, must watch semifilth or raw pornography instead of Gene and "Champion" in good, clean, fantasy entertainment.

No, not everything changes for the better—not by a long shot! The memory of Gene Autry and his Gower Gulch contemporaries is well worth retaining, for the simple product they made not only entertained but also taught the moral lessons that sustained a generation.

GENE AUTRY *Filmography*

IN OLD SANTA FE (Mascot, November 15, 1934) 64 Mins.
Ken Maynard, Evalyn Knapp, George Hayes, H. B. Warner, Kenneth Thompson, *Gene Autry*, Lester "Smiley" Burnette, Wheeler Oakman, George Chesebro, George Burton, Jack Rockwell, Jim Corey, Jack Kirk, Edward Hearn, Frank Ellis, Horace B. Carpenter, "Tarzan"
D: David Howard
S: Wallace MacDonald, John Rathmell
SP: Colbert Clark
P: Nat Levine

MYSTERY MOUNTAIN (Mascot, December 1, 1934) 12 Chapters.
Ken Maynard, Verna Hillie, Edward Earle, Edmund Cobb, Lynton Brent, Syd Saylor, Carmencita Johnson, Lafe McKee, Al Bridge, Edward Hearn, Bob Kortman, *Gene Autry*, Lester "Smiley" Burnette, Wally Wales, Tom London, George Chesebro, Philo McCullough, Frank Ellis, Steve Clark, James Mason, Lew Meehan, Jack Rockwell, Art Mix, William Gould, "Tarzan"
D: B. Reeves Eason, Otto Brower
S: Sherman Lowe, Barney Sarecky, B. Reeves Eason
SP: Bennett Cohen, Armand Schaefer
P: Nat Levine
Chapter Titles: (1) The Rattler, (2) The Man Nobody Knows, (3) The Eye That Never Sleeps, (4) The Human Target, (5) Phantom Outlaws, (6) The Perfect Crime, (7) Tarzan the Cunning, (8) The Enemy's Stronghold, (9) The Fatal Warning, (10) The Secret of the Mountain, (11) Behind the Mask, (12) The Judgment of Tarzan

THE PHANTOM EMPIRE: (Mascot, February 23, 1935) 12 Chapters.
Gene Autry, Frankie Darro, Betsy King Ross, Dorothy Christie, Wheeler Oakman, Charles K. French, Warner Richmond, J. Frank Glendon, Smiley Burnette, William Moore, Edward Peil, Jack Carlyle, Wally Wales, Jay Wilsey (Buffalo Bill, Jr.), Stanley Blystone, Richard Talmadge, Frank Ellis, Peter Potter, Bob Burns, Bob Card, Bruce Mitchell, "Champion"
D: Otto Brower, B. Reeves Eason
S: Wallace MacDonald, Gerald Geraghty, Hy Freedman, Maurice Geraghty
SP: John Rathmell, Armand Schaefer
P: Nat Levine

Chapter Titles: (1) The Singing Cowboy, (2) The Thunder Riders, (3) The Lightning Chamber, (4) Phantom Broadcast, (5) Beneath the Earth, (6) Disaster from the Skies, (7) From Death to Life, (8) Jaws of Jeopardy, (9) Prisoners of the Ray, (10) The Rebellion, (11) A Queen in Chains, (12) The End of Murania.
(Two feature versions edited from this serial: MEN WITH STEEL FACES, and RADIO RANCH)

TUMBLING TUMBLEWEEDS (Republic, September 5, 1935) 57 Mins.
Gene Autry, Smiley Burnette, Lucile Browne, Norma Taylor, George Hayes, Edward Hearn, Jack Rockwell, Frankie Marvin, George Chesebro, Eugene Jackson, Charles King, Charles Whitaker, George Burton, Tom London, Cornelius Keefe, Tommy Coats, Cliff Lyons, Bud Pope, Tracy Layne, "Champion"
D: Joseph Kane
S: Alan Ludwig
SP: Ford Beebe
P: Nat Levine

MELODY TRAIL (Republic, September 24, 1935) 60 Mins.
Gene Autry, Smiley Burnette, Ann Rutherford, Wade Boteler, Willy Costello, Al Bridge, Marie Quillan, Gertrude Messinger, Tracy Layne, Abe Lefton, George DeNormand, Jane Barnes, Ione Reed, Marion Downing, "Champion"
D: Joseph Kane
S: Sherman Lowe, Betty Burbridge
SP: Sherman Lower
P: Nat Levine

THE SAGEBRUSH TROUBADOUR (Republic, November 19, 1935) 54 Mins.
Gene Autry, Smiley Burnette, Barbara Pepper, J. Frank Glendon, Dennis Moore, Hooper Atchley, Fred Kelsey, Julian Rivero, Tom London, Wes Warner, Frankie Marvin, Bud Pope, Tommy Gene Fairey, "Champion"
D: Joseph Kane
S: Oliver Drake
SP: Oliver Drake, Joseph Poland
P: Nat Levine

THE SINGING VAGABOND (Republic, December 11, 1935) 52 Mins.
Gene Autry, Smiley Burnette, Ann Rutherford, Barbara Pepper, Warner Richmond, Frank LaRue, Grace Goodall, Niles Welch, Tom Brower, Robinson Neeman, Henry Rocquemore, Ray Benard (Ray Corrigan), Allan Sears, Robert Burns,

Thompson, Marion O'Connell, Marie Quillan, Elaine Shepherd, George Letz (Montgomery), "Champion"
D: Carl Pierson
S: Bill Witney
SP: Oliver Drake, Betty Burbridge

Gene Autry (left), with scrubby face, menaces Ken Maynard, along with Art Mix (right) and Edward Hearn (on horse) in *Mystery Mountain* (Mascot, 1934).

RED RIVER VALLEY (Republic, March 2, 1936) 56 Mins.
Gene Autry, Smiley Burnette, Frances Grant, Booth Howard, Jack Kinney, Sam Flint, George Chesebro, Charles King, Eugene Jackson, Edward Hearn, Frank LaRue, Ken Cooper, Frankie Marvin, Cap Anderson (C. E. Anderson), Monty Cass, John Wilson Lloyd Ingraham, Hank Bell, "Champion"
D: B. Reeves Eason
S/SP: Dorrell and Stuart McGowan
P: Nat Levine

COMIN' ROUND THE MOUNTAIN (Republic, March 31, 1936) 55 Mins.
Gene Autry, Ann Rutherford, Smiley Burnette, LeRoy Mason, Raymond Brown, Ken Cooper, Tracy Layne, Bob McKenzie, Laurita Puente, John Ince, Frank Lackteen, Jim Corey, Al Taylor, Steve Clark, Frank Ellis, Hank Bell, Dick Botiller, "Champion"
D: Mack V. Wright
S: Oliver Drake
SP: Oliver Drake, Dorrell and Stuart McGowan
P: Nat Levine

The science fiction Western serial that started the Autry
phenomena (Mascot, 1935).

THE SINGING COWBOY (Republic, May 13, 1936)
56 Mins.
Gene Autry, Smiley Burnette, Lois Wilde Creighton (Lon)
Chaney, John Van Pelt, Earle Hodgins, Ken Cooper, Harrison
Green, Wes Warner, Jack Rockwell, Tracy Lane, Fred Toones,
Oscar Gahan, Frankie Marvin, Jack Kirk, Audry Davis, George
Pierce, Charles McAvoy, Ann Gillis, Earl Erby, Harvey Clark,
Alf James, Pat Caron, "Champion"
D: Mack V. Wright
S: Tom Gibson
SP: Dorrell and Stuart McGowan
P: Nat Levine

OH, SUSANNA! (Republic, August 19, 1936) 59 Mins.
Gene Autry, Smiley Burnette, Frances Grant, Earle Hodgins,
Donald Kirke, Booth Howard, Clara Kimball Young, Edward
Peil, Sr., Frankie Marvin, Carl Stockdale, Gerall Roscoe,
Roger Gray, Fred Burns, Walter James, Fred Toones, Earl
Dwire, Bruce Mitchell, Jack Kirk, George Morrell, The Light
Crust Doughboys, "Champion"
D: Joseph Kane
S/SP: Oliver Drake
P: Nat Levine

RIDE, RANGER, RIDE (Republic, September 30, 1936) 59 Mins.

Gene Autry, Smiley Burnette, The Tennessee Ramblers, Kay Hughes, Monte Blue, Max Terhune, George J. Lewis, Robert Homans, Chief Thunder Cloud, Frankie Marvin, Iron Eyes Cody, Sunny Chorre, Bud Pope, Nelson McDowell, Shooting Star, Arthur Singley, Greg Whitespear, Robert Thomas, "Champion"

D: Joseph Kane
S: Bernard McConville, Karen DeWolf
SP: Dorrell and Stuart McGowan
P: Nat Levine

THE BIG SHOW (Republic, November 16, 1936) 59 Mins.

Gene Autry, Smiley Burnette, Kay Hughes, Max Terhune, Sally Payne, William Newill, Charles Judels, Rex King, Harry Worth, Mary Russell, Christine Maple, Jerry Larkin, Jack O'Shea, Wedgewood Norrell, Antrim Short, June Johnson, Grace Durkin, Slim Whitaker, George Chesebro, Edward Hearn, Cliff Lyons, Tracy Layne, Jack Rockwell, Frankie Marvin, Cornelius Keefe, Martin Stevenson, Horace B. Carpenter, Helen Servis, Frances Morris, Richard Beach, Jeanne Lafayette, Art Mix, I. Stanford Jolley, Vic Lacardo, Sally Rand, The SMU 50, Sons of the Pioneers (Roy Rogers, Bob Nolan, Tim Spencer, Hugh and Karl Farr), The Light Crust Doughboys, The Beverly Hill Billies, The Jones Boys, "Champion"

D: Mack V. Wright
S/SP: Dorrell and Stuart McGowan
P: Nat Levine

THE OLD CORRAL (Republic, December 21, 1936) 56 Mins.

Gene Autry, Smiley Burnette, Hope Manning, Cornelius Keefe, Sons of the Pioneers (Roy Rogers, Bob Nolan, Hugh Farr, Karl Farr, Tim Spencer), Lon Chaney, Jr., John Bradford, Milburn Morante, Abe Lefton, Merril McCormack, Charles Sullivan, Buddy Roosevelt, Lynton Brent, Oscar and Elmer (Ed Platt and Lou Fulton), Jack Ingram, "Champion"

D: Joseph Kane
S: Bernard McConville
SP: Sherman Lowe, Joseph Poland
P: Nat Levine

GUNS AND GUITARS (Republic, December 22, 1936) 56 Mins.

Gene Autry, Smiley Burnette, Dorothy Dix, Tom London, Charles King, J. P. McGowan, Earle Hodgins, Frankie Marvin, Eugene Jackson, Ken Cooper, Jack Rockwell, Harrison Greene, Pascale Perry, Bob Burns, Jack Don, Tracy Layne, Frank Stravenger, Jack Kirk, Audry Davis, Al Taylor, George Morrell, Sherry Tansey, Jack Evans, George Plues, Denver Dixon, Wes Warner, Jim Corey, "Champion"

D: Joseph Kane
S/SP: Dorrell and Stuart McGowan
P: Nat Levine

Gene Autry apparently has the attention of George Chesebro, Charles King, and cronies in this scene from *Red River Valley* (Republic, 1936).

ROUND-UP TIME IN TEXAS (Republic, April 22, 1937) 58 Mins.

Gene Autry, Smiley Burnette, Maxine Doyle, The Cabin Kids, LeRoy Mason, Earle Hodgins, Buddy Williams, Dick Wessell, Cornie Anderson, Frankie Marvin, Ken Cooper, Elmer Fain, Al Ferguson, Slim Whitaker, Al Knight

D: Joseph Kane
SP: Oliver Drake
P: Armand Schaefer

ROOTIN' TOOTIN' RHYTHM (Republic, May 12, 1937) 60 Mins.

Gene Autry, Smiley Burnette, Armida, Monte Blue, Ann Pendleton, Hal Taliaferro, Charles King, Max Hoffman, Jr., Frankie Marvin, Nina Campana, Charles Mayer, Karl Hackett, Al Clauser and his Oklahoma Outlaws, Jack Rutherford, "Champion"

D: Mack Wright
S: Johnston McCulley
SP: Jack Natteford
P: Armand Schaefer

YODELIN' KID FROM PINE RIDGE (Republic, June 14, 1937) 60 Mins.

Gene Autry, Smiley Burnette, Betty Bronson, The Tennessee Ramblers (Dick Hartman, W. J. Blair, Elmer Warren, Happy Morris & Pappy Wolf), LeRoy Mason, Charles Middleton, Russell Simpson, Jack Dougherty, Guy Wilkerson, Frankie Marvin, Henry Hall, Fred Toones, Jack Kirk, Bob Burns, Al Taylor, George Morrell, Lew Meehan, Jim Corey, Jack Ingram, Art Dillard, Art Mix, Bud Osborne, Oscar Gahan, "Champion"

D: Joseph Kane
S: Jack Natteford
SP: Dorrell & Stuart McGowan, Jack Natteford
P: Armand Schaefer

PUBLIC COWBOY NO. 1 (Republic, August 23, 1937) 59 Mins.

Gene Autry, Smiley Burnette, Ann Rutherford, William Farnum, James C. Morton, Maston Williams, Arthur Loft, Frankie Marvin, House Peters, Jr., Frank LaRue, Milburn Morante, King Mojave, Hal Price, Jack Ingram, Rafael Bennett, George Plumes, Frank Ellis, James Mason, Doug Evans, Bob Burns, "Champion"

D: Joseph Kane
S: Bernard McConville
SP: Oliver Drake
P: Sol C. Siegel

BOOTS AND SADDLES (Republic, October 11, 1937) 59 Mins.

Gene Autry, Smiley Burnette, Judith Allen, Ra Hould, Guy Usher, Gordon (Bill) Elliott, John Ward, Frankie Marvin, Chris-Pin Martin, Stanley Blystone, Bud Osborne, Merrill McCormack, "Champion"

D: Joseph Kane
S: Jack Natteford
SP: Oliver Drake
P: Sol C. Siegel

MANHATTAN MERRY-GO-ROUND (Republic, November 13, 1937)

Phil Regan, Leo Carrillo, Ann Dvorak, Tamara Geva, James Gleason, Henry Armetta, Luis Alberni, Selmer Jackson, Moroni Olsen, Eddie Kane, Nellie V. Nichols, Gennaro Curoi, Sam Finn, Al Herman, Jack Jenny, Max Terhune, Smiley Burnette, *Gene Autry*, Ted Lewis and his Band, Cab Calloway and his Orchestra, Kay Thompson, Joe DiMaggio, Louis Prima, Rosalean and Seville

D: Charles F. Riesner
P: Harry Sauber
SP: Harry Sauber

SPRINGTIME IN THE ROCKIES (Republic, November 15, 1937) 60 Mins.

Gene Autry, Smiley Burnette, Polly Rowles, Ula Love, Ruth Bacon, Jane Hunt, George Chesebro, Alan Bridge, Tom London, Edward Hearn, Frankie Marvin, William Hale, Edmund Cobb, Fred Burns, Art Davis, Lew Meehan, Jack Kirk, Frank Ellis, George Letz (Montgomery), Robert Dudley, Jack Rockwell, Jimmy LeFuer's Saddle Pals, Oscar Gahan, "Champion"

D: Joseph Kane
SP: Betty Burbridge, Gilbert Wright
P: Sol C. Siegel

THE OLD BARN DANCE (Republic, January 29, 1938) 60 Mins.

Gene Autry, Smiley Burnette Helen Valkis, Sammy McKim, Ivan Miller, Earl Dwire, Hooper Atchley, Ray Bennett, Carleton Young, Frankie Marvin, Earle Hodgins, Gloria Rich, Dick Weston (Roy Rogers), Denver Dixon, The Stafford Sisters, The Maple City Four, Walt Shrum and his Colorado Hillbillies, "Champion"

D: Joseph Kane
SP: Bernard McConville, Charles Francis Royal
AP: Sol C. Siegel

GOLD MINE IN THE SKY (Republic, July 5, 1938) 60 Mins.

Gene Autry, Smiley Burnette, Carol Hughes, Craig Reynolds, Cupid Ainsworth, LeRoy Mason, Frankie Marvin, Robert Homans, Eddie Cherkose, Ben Corbett, Milburn Morante, Jim Corey, George Guhl, Jack Kirk, Fred Toones (Snowflake), George Letz (Montgomery), Charles King, Lew Kelly, Joe Whitehead, Matty Roubert, Anita Bolster, Earl Dwire, Maude Prickett, Al Taylor, Art Dillard, Stafford Sisters, J. L. Franks, Golden West Cowboys, "Champion"

D: Joseph Kane
S: Betty Burbridge
SP: Betty Burbridge, Jack Natteford
AP: Charles E. Ford

MAN FROM MUSIC MOUNTAIN (Republic, August 14, 1938) 58 Mins.

Gene Autry, Smiley Burnette, Carol Hughes, Polly Jenkins and her Plowboys, Sally Payne, Ivan Miller, Al Terry, Dick Elliott, Hal Price, Cactus Mack, Edward Cassidy, Howard Chase, Lew Kelly, Frankie Marvin, Earl Dwire, Lloyd Ingraham, Lillian Drew, Al Taylor, Joe Yrigoyen, Gordon Hart, Rudy Sooter, Harry Harvey, Meredith McCormack, Chris Allan, "Champion"

D: Joseph Kane
S: Bernard McConville
SP: Betty Burbridge, Luci Ward
AP: Charles E. Ford

PRARIE MOON (Republic, October 7, 1938) 58 Mins.
Gene Autry, Smiley Burnette, Shirley Deane, Tommy Ryan, Tom London, Warner Richmond, William Pawley, Walter Tetley, David Gorcey, Stanley Andrews, Peter Potter, Bud Osborne, Ray Bennett, Jack Rockwell, Merrill McCormack, Hal Price, Lew Meehan, Jack Kirk, "Champion"

D: Ralph Staub
SP: Betty Burbridge, Stanley Roberts
AP: Harry Grey

RHYTHM OF THE SADDLE (Republic, November 5, 1938) 58 Mins.
Gene Autry, Smiley Burnette, Peggy Moran, Pert Kelton, LeRoy Mason, Arthur Loft, Ethan Laidlaw, Walter De Palma, Archie Hall, Eddie Hart, Eddie Acuff, Tom London, William Norton Bailey, Roger Williams, Curley Dresdon, Rudy Sooter, Douglas Wright, Kelsey Sheldon, Lola Monte, Alan Gregg, James Mason, Jack Kirk, Emmett Vogan, "Champion"
D: George Sherman
SP: Paul Franklin
AP: Harry Grey

WESTERN JAMBOREE (Republic, December 2, 1938) 56 Mins.
Gene Autry, Smiley Burnette, Jean Rouveral, Esther Muir, Frank Darien, Joe Frisco, Kermit Maynard, Jack Perrin, Jack Ingram, Margaret Armstrong, Harry Holman, Edward Raquello, Bentley Hewitt, George Walcott, Ray Teal, Frank Ellis, Eddie Dean, Davidson Clark, "Champion"
D: Ralph Staub
S: Patricia Harper
SP: Gerald Geraghty
AP: Harry Grey

HOME ON THE PRAIRIE (Republic, February 3, 1939) 58 Mins.
Gene Autry, Smiley Burnette, June Storey, Jack Mulhall, George Cleveland, Walter Miller, Gordon Hart, Hal Price, Earle Hodgins, Ethan Laidlaw, John Beach, Jack Ingram, Bob Woodward, Sherven Brothers Rodeoliers, "Champion"
D: Jack Townley
SP: Arthur Powell, Paul Franklin
AP: Harry Grey

MEXICALI ROSE (Republic, March 29, 1939) 60 Mins.
Gene Autry, Smiley Burnette, Noah Beery, Luana Walters, William Farnum, LeRoy Mason, William Royle, Wally Albright, Kathryn Frey, Roy Barcroft, Dick Botiller, Vic Demourelle, John Beach, Henry Otho, Joe Dominguez, Al Hackell, Merrill McCormack, Fred Toones, Sherry Hall, Al Taylor, Josef Swickward, Tom London, Jack Ingram, Eddie Parker, "Champion"
D: George Sherman
S: Luci Ward, Connie Lee
SP: Gerald Geraghty
AP: Harry Grey

BLUE MONTANA SKIES (Republic, May 4, 1939) 56 Mins.
Gene Autry, Smiley Burnette, June Storey, Walt Shrum and his Colorado Hillbillies, Harry Woods, Tully Marshall, Al Bridge, Glenn Strange, Dorothy Granger, Edmund Cobb, Robert Winkler, Jack Ingram, John Brach, Elmo Lincoln, Allan Cavan, Jay Wilsey (Buffalo Bill, Jr.), Augie Gomez, "Champion"
D: B. Reeves Eason
S: Norman S. Hall, Paul Franklin
SP: Gerald Geraghty
AP: Harry Grey

Gene Autry and Jack Ingram in *Colorado Sunset* (Republic, 1939).

MOUNTAIN RHYTHM (Republic, June 29, 1939) 61 Mins.
Gene Autry, Smiley Burnette, June Storey, Maude Eburne, Ferris Taylor, Walter Fenner, Jack Pennick, Hooper Atchley, Edward Cassidy, Jack Ingram, Tom London, Frankie Marvin, Roger Williams, Charles Whitaker, "Champion"
D: B. Reeves Eason
S: Connie Lee
SP: Gerald Geraghty
AP: Harry Grey

COLORADO SUNSET (Republic, July 31, 1939) 61 Mins.
Gene Autry, Smiley Burnette, June Storey, Larry "Buster" Crabbe, Barbara Pepper, Robert Barrat, Patsy Montana, Parnell Pratt, William Farnum, Kermit Maynard, Jack Ingram, Elmo Lincoln, Frank Marvin, Ethan Laidlaw, Fred Burns, Jack Kirk, Bud Buster, Ed Cassidy, Slim Whitaker, Murdock McQuarrie, Ralph Peters, The CBS-KMBC Texas Rangers, "Champion"
D: George Sherman
S: Luci Ward, Jack Natteford
SP: Betty Burbridge, Stanley Roberts
AP: William Berke

IN OLD MONTEREY (Republic, August 14, 1939) 73 Mins.
Gene Autry, Smiley Burnette, June Storey, George "Gabby" Hayes, Stuart Hamblen, Billy Lee, Jonathan Lee, Robert Warwick, William Hall, Eddy Conrad, Curley Dresden, Victor Cox, Ken Carson, Robert Wilke, Hal Price, Tom Steele, Jack O'Shea, Rex Lease, Edward Earle, James Mason, Fred Burns, Dan White, Frank Ellis, Jim Corey, Sarie and Sallie, the Ranch Boys, "Champion"
D: Joe Kane
AP: Armand Schaefer
SP: Gerald Geraghty, Dorrell and Stuart McGowan
S: Gerald Geraghty, George Sherman

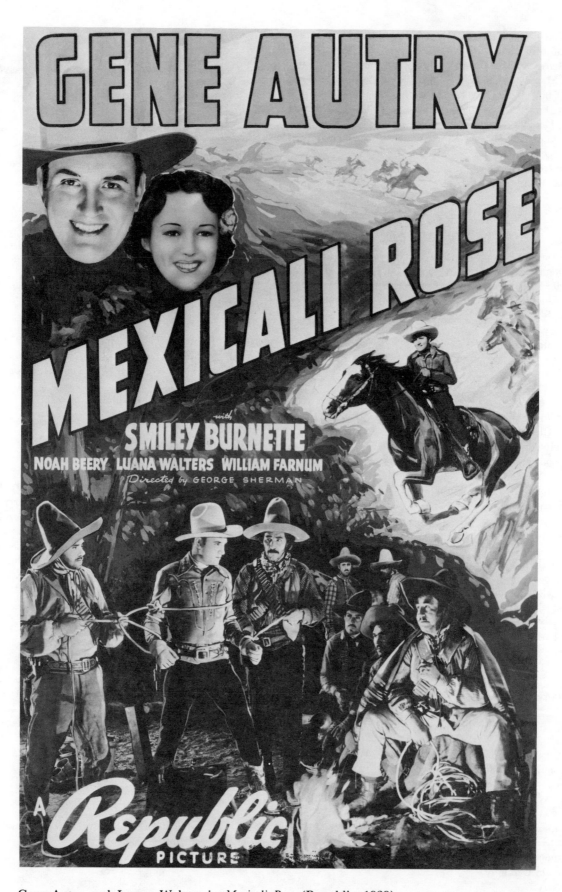

Gene Autry and Luana Walters in *Mexicali Rose* (Republic, 1939).

ROVIN' TUMBLEWEEDS (Republic, November 16, 1939)
64 Mins.
(Also known as "Washington Cowboy")
Gene Autry, Smiley Burnette, Mary Carlisle, Douglass Dumbrille, William Farnum, Lee "Lasses" White, Ralph Peters, Gordon Hart, Vic Potel, Sammy McKim, Jack Ingram, Reginald Barlow, Eddie Kane, Guy Usher, Horace Murphy, David Sharpe, Jack Kirk, Rose Plummer, Robert Burns, Art Mix, Horace B. Carpenter, Fred Toones, Frank Ellis, Fred Burns, Edward Cassidy, Forrest Taylor, Tom Chatterton, Crauford Kent, Maurice Costello, Charles K. French, Lee Shumway, Bud Osborne, Harry Semels, Chick Morrison, Nora Lou Martin and the Pals of the Golden West, "Champion"
D: George Sherman
SP: Betty Burbridge, Dorrell and Stuart McGowan
AP: William Berke

SOUTH OF THE BORDER (Republic, December 15, 1939)
71 Mins.
Gene Autry, Smiley Burnette, June Storey, Lupita Tovar, Mary Lee, Duncan Renaldo, Frank Reicher, Alan Edwards, Claire DuBrey, Dick Botiller, William Farnum, Selmer Jackson, Sheila Darcy, Rex Lease, Charles King, Reed Howes, Jack O'Shea, Slim Whitaker, Hal Price, Julian Rivero, Curley Dresden, The Checkerboard Band, "Champion"
D: George Sherman
S: Dorrell and Stuart McGowan
AP: William Berke

RANCHO GRANDE (Republic, March 22, 1940) 68 Mins.
Gene Autry, Smiley Burnette, June Storey, Mary Lee, Dick Hogan, Ellen Lowe, Ferris Taylor, Joseph DeStefami, Roscoe Ates, Rex Lease, Ann Baldwin, Roy Barcroft, Edna Lawrence, Jack Ingram, Bud Osborne, Slim Whitaker, The Brewer Kids, The Boys Choir of Saint Joseph's School, The Pals of the Golden West, "Champion"
D: Frank McDonald
S: Peter Milne, Connie Lee
SP: Bradford Ropes, Betty Burbridge, Peter Milne
AP: William Berke

SHOOTING HIGH (20th Century Fox, April 26, 1940)
65 Mins.
Jane Withers, *Gene Autry*, Marjorie Weaver, Frank M. Thomas, Robert Lowery, Katherine (Kay) Aldridge, Hobart Cavanaugh, Jack Carson, Hamilton McFadden, Charles Middleton, Ed Brady, Tom London, Eddie Acuff, Pat O'Malley, George Chandler
D: Alfred E. Green
SP: Lou Breslow, Owen Francis
AP: John Stone

Jane Withers and Gene Autry in *Shooting High* (Fox, 1940).

MEN WITH STEEL FACES (Times Pictures) 70 Mins.
(A feature edited from 1935s "The Phantom Empire" serial. Also released as RADIO RANCH. For more complete credits, see THE PHANTOM EMPIRE listing)
Gene Autry, Frankie Darro, Betsy King Ross, Dorothy Christie, Wheeler Oakman, Charles K. French, Warner Richmond, J. Frank Glendon, Smiley Burnette, Jack Carlyle, Edward Peil, William Moore
D: Otto Brower, B. Reeves Eason

GAUCHO SERENADE (Republic, May 10, 1940) 66 Mins.
Gene Autry, Smiley Burnette, June Storey, Mary Lee, Duncan Renaldo, Cliff Severn, Jr., Lester Matthews, Smith Ballew, Joseph Crehan, William Ruhl, Wade Boteler, Ted Adams, Fred Burns, Julian Rivero, George Lloyd, Edward Cassidy, Joe Dominguez, Olaf Hytten, Fred Toones, Gene Morgan, Jack Kirk, Harry Strang, Hank Worden, Kernan Cripps, Jim Corey, Tom London, Walter Miller, "Champion"
D: Frank McDonald
S/SP: Betty Burbridge, Bradford Ropes
AP: William Berke

CAROLINA MOON (Republic, July 15, 1940) 65 Mins.
Gene Autry, Smiley Burnette, June Storey, Mary Lee, Eddy Waller, Hardie Albright, Frank Dale, Terry Nibert, Robert Fiske, Etta McDaniel, Paul White, Fred Ritter, Ralph Sanford, Jack Kirk, Jimmie Lewis and his Texas Cowboys, "Champion"
D: Frank McDonald
S: Connie Lee
SP: Winston Miller
AP: William Berke

RIDE, TENDERFOOT, RIDE (Republic, September 6, 1940) 65 Mins.
Gene Autry, Smiley Burnette, June Storey, Mary Lee, Warren Hull, Forbes Murray, Joe McGuinn, Joe Frisco, Isobel Randolph, Herbert Clifton, Si Jenks, Mildred Shay, Cindy Walker, Patty Saks, Jack Kirk, Slim Whitaker, Fred Burns, The Pacemakers, Robert Burns, Fred Toones, Chuck Morrison, Frank O'Connors, Curley Dresden, "Champion"
D: Frank McDonald
S: Betty Burbridge, Connie Lee
SP: Winston Miller
AP: William Berke

MELODY RANCH (Republic, November 15, 1940) 70 Mins.
Gene Autry, Jimmy Durante, Ann Miller, Barton MacLane, Barbara Allen, George Hayes, Jerome Cowan, Mary Lee, Horace MacMahon, Clarance Wilson, Billy Benedict, Ruth Gifford, Maxine Ardell, Veda Ann Borg, George Chandler, Jack Ingram, Horace Murphy, Lloyd Ingraham, Tom London, John Merton, Edmund Cobb, Slim Whitaker, Curley Dresden, Dick Elliott, Billy Bletcher, Art Mix, George Chesebro, Tiny Jones, Herman Hack, Jack Kirk, Merrill McCormack, Wally West, Bob Wills and the Texas Playboys, "Champion"
D: Joseph Santley
SP: Jack Moffitt, F. Hugh Herbert, Sid Culler, Ray Golden
AP: Sol C. Siegel

RIDIN' ON A RAINBOW (Republic, January 24, 1941) 79 Mins.
Gene Autry, Smiley Burnette, Mary Lee, Carol Adams, Ferris Taylor, Georgia Caine, Byron Foulger, Ralf Harolde, Jimmy Conlin, Guy Usher, Anthony Warde, Forrest Taylor, Burr Caruth, Ed Cassidy, Ben Hall, Tom London, William Mong, "Champion"
D: Lew Landers
SP: Bradford Ropes, Doris Malloy
S: Bradford Ropes
AP: Harry Grey

BACK IN THE SADDLE (Republic, March 14, 1941) 73 Mins.
Gene Autry, Smiley Burnette, Mary Lee, Edward Norris, Jacqueline Wells, Addison Richards, Arthur Loft, Edmund Elton, Joe McGuinn, Edmund Cobb, Robert Barron, Reed Howes, Stanley Blystone, Curley Dresden, Fred Toones, Frank Ellis, Jack O'Shea, Victor Cox, Herman Hack, Bob Burns, "Champion"
D: Lew Landers
SP: Richard Murphy, Jesse Lasky, Jr.
AP: Harry Grey

THE SINGING HILL (Republic, April 26, 1941) 75 Mins.
Gene Autry, Smiley Burnette, Virginia Dale, Mary Lee, Spencer Charters, Gerald Oliver Smith, George Meeker, Wade Botiller, Harry Stubbs, Cactus Mack, Jack Kirk, Chuck Morrison, Monte Montague, Sam Fling, Hal Price, Fred Burns, Herman Hack, Jack O'Shea, "Champion"
D: Lew Landers
S: Jesse Lasky, Jr., Richard Murphy
SP: Olive Cooper
AP: Harry Grey

MEET ROY ROGERS (Republic, June 24, 1941) 10 Mins.
(Harriet Parsons Series)
Roy Rogers, *Gene Autry*, Judy Canova, Bill Elliott, George "Gabby" Hayes, Billy Gilbert, Bob Baker, Roscoe Ates, Mary Lee
D/P: Harriet Parsons

SUNSET IN WYOMING (Republic, July 14, 1941) 65 Mins.
Gene Autry, Smiley Burnette, Maris Wrixon, George Cleveland, Robert Kent, Sarah Padden, Monte Blue, Dick Elliott, John Dilson, Stanely Blystone, Eddie Dew, Fred Burns, Reed Howes, Ralph Peters, Syd Saylor, Tex Terry, Lloyd Whitlock, Herman Hack, "Champion"
D: William Morgan
S: Joe Blair
SP: Ivan Goff, Anne Morrison Chapin
AP: Harry Grey

UNDER FIESTA STARS (Republic, August 25, 1941) 94 Mins.
Gene Autry, Smiley Burnette, Carol Hughes, Frank Darien, Joe Straugh, Jr., Pauline Drake, Ivan Miller, Sam Flint, Elias Gamboa, John Merton, Jack Kirk, Inez Palange, Curley Dresden, Hal Taliaferro, "Champion"
D: Frank McDonald
S: Karl Brown
SP: Karl Brown, Eliot Gibbons
AP: Harry Grey

DOWN MEXICO WAY (Republic, October 15, 1941) 73 Mins.
Gene Autry, Smiley Burnette, Fay McKenzie, Harold Huber, Duncan Renaldo, Arthur Loft, Murry Alper, Joe Sawyer, Paul Fix, Julian Rivero, Eddie Dean, Thornton Edwards, Ruth Robinson, Andrew Tombes, Herrera Sisters, Sidney Blackmer, Esther Estrella, Sam Appel, Helen MacKellar, Elias Gamboa, Rico de Montez, Charles Rivero, Paquita del Rey, Jose Manero, Carmela Cansino, Reed Howes, Hank Bell, Fred Burns, Al Haskell, Jack O'Shea
D: Joseph Santley
S: Dorrell and Stuart McGowan
SP: Oliver Cooper, Albert Duff
AP: Harry Grey

Gene Autry and players in *Down Mexico Way* (Republic, 1941).

SIERRA SUE (Republic, November 12, 1941) 64 Mins.
Gene Autry, Smiley Burnette, Fay McKenzie, Frank M. Thomas, Robert Homans, Earle Hodgins, Dorothy Christy, Jack Kirk, Eddie Dean, Kermit Maynard, Budd Buster, Rex Lease, Hugh Prosser, Vince Barnett, Hal Price, Syd Saylor, Roy Butler, Sammy Stein, Eddie Cherkose, Bob McKenzie, Marin Sais, Bud Brown, Gene Eblen, Buel Bryant, Ray Davis, Art Dillard, Frankie Marvin, "Champion"
D: William Morgan
SP: Earl Felton, Julian Zimet
AP: Harry Grey

COWBOY SERENADE (Republic, January 30, 1942) 66 Mins.
Gene Autry, Smiley Burnette, Fay McKenzie, Cecil Cunningham, Randy Brooks, Addison Richards, Tris Coffin, Slim Andrews, Melinda Leighton, Johnny Berkes, Forrest Taylor, Hank Worden, Si Jenks, Ethan Laidlaw, Hal Price, Otto Ham, Loren Raker, Bud Wolfe, Forbes Murray, Bud Geary, Frankie Marvin, Tom London, Ken Terrell, Ralph Kirny, Ken Cooper, Rich Anderson, "Champion"
D: William Morgan
SP: Olive Cooper
AP: Harry Grey

HEART OF THE RIO GRANDE (Republic, March 11, 1942) 70 Mins.
Gene Autry, Smiley Burnette, Fay McKenzie, Edith Fellows, Pierre Watkin, Joe Strauch, Jr., William Haade, Sarah Padden, Jean Porter, Milton Kibbee, Edmund Cobb, Jimmy Wakely Trio (Jimmy Wakely, Johnny Bond, Dick Rinehart), Budd Buster, Frank Mills, Howard Mitchell, Allan Wood, Nora Lane, Mady Lawrence, Buck Woods, Harry Deep, George Porter, Frankie Marvin, Jeannie Heners, Kay Frye, Jane Graham, Patsy Fay Northup, Jan Lester, Floria and Gladys Gardner, "Champion"
D: William Morgan
S: Newlin B. Wilds
SP: Lillie Hayward, Winston Miller
AP: Harry Grey

HOME IN WYOMIN' (Republic, April 29, 1942) 67 Mins.
Gene Autry, Smiley Burnette, Fay McKenzie, Olin Howlin, Chick Chandler, Joe Strauch, Jr., Forrest Taylor, James Seay, George Douglas, Charles Lane, Hap Price, Bud Geary, Ken Cooper, Jean Porter, James McNamara, Kermit Maynard, Roy Butler, Billy Benedict, Cyril Ring, Spade Cooley, Ted Mapes, Jack Kirk, William Kellogg, Betty Farrington, Rex Lease, Tom Hanlon, Lee Shumway, "Champion"
D: William Morgan
S: Stuart Palmer
SP: Robert Tasker, M. Coates Webster
SP: Harry Grey

STARDUST ON THE SAGE (Republic, May 25, 1942) 65 Mins.
Gene Autry, Smiley Burnette, Bill Henry, Edith Fellows, Louise Currie, George Ernest, Emmett Vogan, Vince Barnett, Betty Farrington, Roy Barcroft, Tom London, Tex Lease, Frank Ellis, Edward Cassidy, Fred Burns, Frank LaRue, Franklyn Farnum, Edmund Cobb, Jerry Jerome, Merrill McCormack, Bert LeBaron, Monte Montague, George DeNormand, Bill Jamison, Jimmy Fox, George Sherwood, William Nestell, Frank O'Connor, Griff Barnett, Frankie Marvin, Lee Shumway, "Champion"
D: William Morgan
S: Dorrell and Stuart McGowan
SP: Betty Burbridge
AP: Harry Grey

CALL OF THE CANYON (Republic, August 17, 1942) 71 Mins.
Gene Autry, Smiley Burnette, Ruth Terry, Joe Strauch, Jr., Thurston Hall, Cliff Nazarro, Dorthea Kent, Bob Nolan, Pat Brady, Edmund McDonald, Marc Lawrence, John Holland, Eddy Waller, Budd Buster, Frank Jacquet, Loren Raker, Johnny Duncan, Broderick O'Farrell, Ray Bennett, Carey Harrison, Anthony Marsh, Fred Santley, Frank Ward, Freddie Walburn, Earle Hodgins, John Harmon, Red Knight, Al Taylor, Jimmy Lucas, Edna Johnson, Frankie Marvin, Charles Flynn, Bob Burns, Charles Williams, Sons of the Pioneers, Joy Barton, "Champion"

D: Joseph Santley
S: Olive Cooper, Maurice Raff
SP: Olive Cooper
P: Harry Grey

BELLS OF CAPISTRANO (Republic, September 15, 1942) 73 Mins.
Gene Autry, Smiley Burnette, Virginia Grey, Lucien Littlefield, Morgan Conway, Claire DuBrey, Charles Cane, Joe Strauch, Jr., Marla Shelton, Tris Coffin, Jay Novello, Al Bridge, Terrisita Osta, Eddie Acuff, Jack O'Shea, Julian Rivero, William Forrest, Bill Telaak, Ken Christy, Dick Wessell, Ed Jauregui, Guy Usher, Ralph Peters, Joe McGuinn, Howard Hickman, William Kellogg, Carla Ramos, Fernando Ramos, Peggy Satterlee, Ray Jones, "Champion"
D: William Morgan
SP: Lawrence Kimble
AP: Harry Grey

SIOUX CITY SUE (Republic, November 21, 1946) 69 Mins.
Gene Autry, Lynne Roberts, Sterling Holloway, Cass County Boys, Richard Lane, Ralph Sanford, Ken Lundy, Helen Wallace, Pierre Watkin, Edwin Wills, Minerva Urecal, Frank Marlowe, LeRoy Mason, Harry Cheshire, George Carleton, Sam Flint, Michael Hughes, Tex Terry, Tris Coffin, Frankie Marvin, Forrest Burns, Tommy Coates, "Champion"
D: Frank McDonald
SP: Olive Cooper
AP: Armand Schaefer

TRAIL TO SAN ANTONE (Republic, January 25, 1947) 67 Mins.
Gene Autry, Peggy Stewart, Sterling Holloway, William Henry, John Duncan, Tris Coffin, Dorothy Vaughn, Edward Keane, Ralph Peters, The Cass County Boys, "Champion"
D: John English
SP: Luci Ward, Jack Natteford
AP: Armand Schaefer

TWILIGHT ON THE RIO GRANDE (Republic, April 1, 1947) 71 Mins.
Gene Autry, Sterling Holloway, Adele Mara, Bob Steele, Charles Evans, Martin Garralaga, Howard J. Negley, George J. Lewis, Nacho Galindo, Tex Terry, George Magril, Bob Burns, Enrique Acosta, Frankie Marvin, Barry Norton, Gil Perkins, Nina Campana, Kenne Duncan, Tom London, Alberto Morin, Keith Richards, Anna Camargo, Donna Martell, Jack O'Shea, Steve Soldi, Bud Osborne, Frank McCarroll, Bob Wilke, Alex Montoya, Connie Menard, Joaquin Elizondo, The Cass County Boys, "Champion, Jr."
D: Frank McDonald
SP: Dorrell and Stuart McGowan
AP: Armand Schaefer

SADDLE PALS (Republic, June 1947) 72 Mins.
Gene Autry, Lynne Roberts, Sterling Holloway, Irving Bacon, Damain O'Flynn, Charles Arnt, Jean Van, Tom London, Charles Williams, Francis McDonald, Edward Gargan, Carl Sepulveda, George Chandler, Paul E. Burns, Joel Friedkin, LeRoy Mason, Larry Steers, Edward Keane, Maurice Cass, Nolan Leary, Minerva Urecal, John S. Roberts, James Carlisle, Sam Ash, Frank O'Connor, Neal Hart, Frank Henry, Edward Peil, Sr., Bob Burns, Joe Yrigoyen, Johnny Day, The Cass County Boys, "Champion, Jr."
D: Lesley Selander
S: Dorrell and Stuart McGowan
SP: Bob Williams and Jerry Sackheim
AP: Sidney Picker

ROBIN HOOD OF TEXAS (Republic, July 14, 1947) 71 Mins.
Gene Autry, Sterling Holloway, Lynn Roberts, Adele Mara, James Cardwell, John Kellogg, Ray Walker, Michael Branden, Paul Bryar, James Flavin, Dorothy Vaughn, Stanley Andrews, Alan Bridge, Hank Patterson, Edmund Cobb, Lester Dorr, William Norton Bailey, Irene Mack, Opal Taylor, Eva Novak, Norma Brown, Frankie Marvin, Billy Wilkerson, Duke Greene, Ken Terrell, Joe Yrigoyen, The Cass County Boys, "Champion, Jr."
D: Lesley Selander
SP: John Butler, Earle Snell
AP: Sidney Picker

SCREEN SNAPSHOTS (Columbia, September 4, 1947) 9½ Mins.
(Segment called "Hollywood Cowboys")
Buck Jones, *Gene Autry*, Roy Rogers, Will Rogers, Tom Mix, John Mack Brown, Hoot Gibson, William S. Hart, William Boyd, Robert Young, Jackie Coogan
D: Ralph Staub

THE LAST ROUND-UP (Columbia, November 5, 1947) 77 Mins.
Gene Autry, Jean Heather, Ralph Morgan, Carol Thurston, Mark Daniels, Bobby Blake, Russ Vincent, Shug Fisher, Trevor Bardette, Lee Bennett, John Halloran, Sandy Saunders, Roy Gordon, Silverheels Smith, Frances Rey, Bob Cason, Dale Van Sickle, Billy Wilkinson, Ed Peil Sr., George Carleton, Don Kay Reynolds, Nolan Leary, Ted Adams, Jack Baxley, Steve Clark, Chuck Hamilton, Bud Osborne, Frankie Marvin, Kernan Cripps, Jose Alvarado, J. W. Cody, Iron Eyes Cody, Blackie Whiteford, Robert Walker, Virginia Carroll, Arline Archuletta, Louis Crosby, Brian O'Hara, Rodd Redwing, Alex Montoya, The Texas Rangers, "Champion, Jr."
D: John English
S: Jack Townley
SP: Jack Townley, Earle Snell
P: Armand Schaefer

LOADED PISTOLS (Columbia, January 1949) 79 Mins.
Gene Autry, Barbara Britton, Chill Wills, Jack Holt, Russell Arms, Robert Shayne, Fred Kohler, Jr., Vince Barnett, Leon Weaver, Clem Bevins, Sandy Sanders, Budd Buster, John R. McKee, Stanley Blystone, Hank Bell, Felice Raymond, Dick Alexander, Frank O'Connor, Reed Howes, William Sundholm, Snub Pollard, Heinie Conklin, "Champion, Jr."
D: John English
SP: Dwight Cummings, Dorothy Yost
P: Armand Schaefer

THE BIG SOMBRERO (Columbia, March 1949) 82 Mins.
(Cinecolor)
Gene Autry, Elena Verdugo, Stephen Dunne, George J. Lewis, Vera Marshe, William Edmunds, Martin Garralaga, Gene Stutenroth, Neyle Morrow, Bob Cason, Pierce Lyden, Rian Valente, Antonio Filauri, Sam Bernard, Jasper Palmer, Jose Alvarado, Robert Espinosa, Cosmo Sardo, Alex Montoya, Jose Portugal, Joe Kirk, Artie Ortego, Joe Domiguez, "Champion, Jr."
D: Frank McDonald
SP: Olive Cooper
P: Armand Schaefer

RIDERS OF THE WHISTLING PINES (Columbia, May 1949) 70 Mins.
Gene Autry, Patricia White, Jimmy Lloyd, Douglass Dumbrille, Damian O'Flynn, Clayton Moore, Britt Wood, Harry Cheshire, Leon Weaver, Lois Bridge, Jerry Scroggings, Fred Martin, Bert Dodson, Roy Gordon, Jason Robards, Sr., Len Torrey, Lane Chandler, Lynn Farr, Al Thompson, Emmett Vogan, Virginia Carroll, Nolan Leary, Steve Benton, The Cass County Boys, The Pinafores, "Champion, Jr."
D: John English
SP: Jack Townley
P: Armand Schaefer

RIM OF THE CANYON (Columbia, July 1949) 70 Mins.
Gene Autry, Nan Leslie, Thurston Hall, Clem Bevins, Walter Sande, Jock Mahoney, Francis McDonald, Alan Hale, Jr., Amelita Ward, John R. McKee, Denver Pyle, Bobby Clark, Boyd Stockman, Sandy Sanders, Lynn Farr, Rory Mallison, Frankie Marvin, "Champion, Jr."
D: John English
S: Joseph Chadwick—"Phantom 45's Talk Loud" *Western Aces Magazine*
SP: John K. Butler
P: Armand Schaefer

THE COWBOY AND THE INDIANS (Columbia, September 15, 1949) 70 Mins.
Gene Autry, Sheila Ryan, Frank Richards, Hank Patterson, Jay Silverheels, Claudia Drake, George Nokes, Charles Stevens, Alex Frazer, Frank Lackteen, Chief Yowlachie, Lee Roberts, Nolan Leary, Maudie Prickett, Harry Macklin, Charles Quigley, Gilbert Alonzo, Roy Gordon, Jose Alvarado, Ray Beltram, Felipe Gomez, Iron Eyes Cody, Shooting Star, Romere Darling, "Champion, Jr."
D: John English
SP: Dwight Cummings, Dorothy Yost
P: Armand Schaefer

RIDERS IN THE SKY (Columbia, November 1, 1949) 70 Mins.
Gene Autry, Gloria Henry, Pat Buttram, Mary Beth Hughes, Robert Livingston, Steve Darrell, Alan Hale, Jr., Tom London, Hank Patterson, Ben Welden, Dennis Moore, Joe Forte, Kenne Duncan, Frank Jacquet, Roy Gordon, Loi Bridge, Boyd Stockman, Vernon Johns, Pat O'Malley, John Parrish, Kermit Maynard, Bud Osborne, Lynton Brent, Isobel Withers, Sandy Sanders, Denver Dixon, Robert Walker, "Champion, Jr."
D: John English
S: Herbert A. Woodbury
SP: Gerald Geraghty
P: Armand Schaefer

SONS OF NEW MEXICO (Columbia, January 14, 1950) 71 Mins.
Gene Autry, Gail Davis, Robert Armstrong, Dick Jones, Frankie Darro, Clayton Moore, Irving Bacon, Russell Arms, Marie Blake, Sandy Sanders, Roy Gordon, Frankie Marvin, Paul Raymond, Pierce Lyden, Kenne Duncan, Harry Mackin, Bobby Clark, Gaylord Pendleton, Billy Lechner, "Champion, Jr."
D: John English
SP: Paul Gangelin
P: Armand Schaefer

MULE TRAIN (Columbia, February 22, 1950) 70 Mins. (SepiaTone)
Gene Autry, Pat Buttram, Sheila Ryan, Robert Livingston, Frank Jacquet, Vince Barnett, Syd Saylor, Sandy Danders, Gregg Barton, Kenne Duncan, Roy Gordon, Stanley Andrews, Robert Hilton, Bob Wilke, John Miljan, Robert Carson, Pat O'Malley, Eddie Parker, George Morrell, John R. McKee, George Slocum, Frank O'Connor, Norman Leavitt, "Champion, Jr."
D: John English
P: Armand Schaefer
S: Alan James
SP: Gerald Geraghty

COW TOWN (Columbia, May 19, 1950) 70 Mins. (SepiaTone)
Gene Autry, Gail Davis, Harry Shannon, Jock O'Mahoney, Clark Burroughs, Harry Harvey, Steve Darrell, Sandy Sanders, Ralph Sanford, Bud Osborne, Robert Hilton, Ted Mapes, Chuck Roberson, House Peters, Jr., Walt LaRue, Herman Hack, Ken Cooper, Victor Cox, Holly Bane, Felice Raymond, Frank McCarroll, Pat O'Malley, Blackie Whiteford, Frankie Marvin, "Champion, Jr."
D: John English
SP: Gerald Geraghty
P: Armand Schaefer

BEYOND THE PURPLE HILLS (Columbia, July 1, 1950) 70 Mins.
(SepiaTone)
Gene Autry, Pat Buttram, Jo Dennison, Don Beddoe, James Millican, Don Kay Reynolds, Hugh O'Brian, Bob Wilke, Roy Gordon, Harry Harvey, Gregg Barton, Ralph Peters, Frank Ellis, John Cliff, Sandy Sanders, Merrill McCormack, Tex Terry, Fenton Jones, Maudie Prickett, Pat O'Malley, Herman Hack, Cliff Barnett, Frank O'Connor, Frankie Marvin, Bobby Clark, Boyd Stockman, Lynton Brent, Victor Cox, Jerry Ambler, "Champion, Jr."
D: John English
SP: Norman S. Hall
P: Armand Schaefer

INDIAN TERRITORY (Columbia, September 30, 1950) 70 Mins.
(SepiaTone)
Gene Autry, Pat Buttram, Gail Davis, Kirby Grant, James Griffith, Philip Van Zant, Pat Collins, Roy Gordon, Charles Stevens, Robert Carson, Chief Thunder Cloud, Chief Yowlachie, Frank Lackteen, Boyd Stockman, Sandy Sanders, Frank Ellis, Frankie Marvin, John R. McKee, Bert Dodson, Nick Rodman, Wesley Hudman, Robert Hilton, Roy Butler, Kenne Duncan, Chief Thundersky, "Champion, Jr."
D: John English
SP: Norman S. Hall
P: Armand Schaefer

THE BLAZING SUN (Columbia, November 20, 1950) 70 Mins.
(SepiaTone)
Gene Autry, Pat Buttram, Lynne Roberts, Anne Gwynne, Edward Norris, Kenne Duncan, Alan Hale, Jr., Gregg Barton, Steve Darrell, Tom London, Sandy Sanders, Frankie Marvin, Bob Woodward, Boyd Stockman, Lewis Martin, Virginia Carroll, Sam Fling, Chris Allen, Charles Colean, Pat O'Malley, Almira Sessions, Nolan Leary, "Champion, Jr."
D: John English
SP: Jack Townley
P: Armand Schaefer

GENE AUTRY AND THE MOUNTIES (Columbia, January 30, 1951) 70 Mins.
(SepiaTone)
Gene Autry, Pat Buttram, Elena Verdugo, Carleton Young, Richard Emory, Herbert Rawlinson, Trevor Bardette, Francis McDonald, Jim Frasher, Gregg Barton, House Peters, Jr., Jody Gilbert, Nolan Leary, Boyd Stockman, Bruce Carruthers, Robert Hilton, Teddy Infuhr, Billy Gray, John R. McKee, Roy Butler, Steven Elliott, Chris Allen, "Chapion, Jr."
D: John English
SP: Norman S. Hall
P: Armand Schaefer

TEXANS NEVER CRY (Columbia, March 15, 1951) 70 Mins.
(SepiaTone)
Gene Autry, Pat Buttram, Mary Castle, Gail Davis, Russell Hayden, Richard Powers (Tom Keene), Don Harvey, Roy Gordon, Michael Ragan (Holly Bane), Frank Fenton, Sandy Sanders, John R. McKee, Harry McKim, Minerva Urecal, Richard Flato, I. Stanford Jolley, Duke York, Roy Cutler, "Champion, Jr."
D: Frank McDonald
SP: Norman S. Hall
P: Armand Schaefer

WHIRLWIND (Columbia, April 1951) 70 Mins.
(SepiaTone)
Gene Autry, Smiley Burnette, Gail Davis, Thurston Hall, Harry Lauter, Dick Curtis, Harry Harvey, Gregg Barton, Tommy Ivo, Kenne Duncan, Al Wyatt, Gary Goodwin, Pat O'Malley, Bud Osborne, Boyd Stockman, Frankie Marvin, Stan Jones, Leon DeVoe, "Champion, Jr."
D: John English
SP: Norman S. Hall
P: Armand Schaefer

SILVER CANYON (Columbia, June 20, 1951) 70 Mins.
(SepiaTone)
Gene Autry, Pat Buttram, Gail Davis, Jim Davis, Bob Steele, Edgar Dearing, Dick Alexander, Terry Frost, Peter Mamakos, Steve Clark, Stanley Andrews, Duke York, Eugene Borden, Bobby Clark, Frankie Marvin, Boyd Stockman, Sandy Sanders, Kenne Duncan, Bill Hale, Jack O'Shea, Frank Matts, Stanley Blystone, John Merton, Jack Pepper, Pat O'Malley, Martin Wilkins, Jim Magill, John R. McKee, "Champion, Jr."
D: John English
S: Alan James
SP: Gerald Geraghty
P: Armand Schaefer

HILLS OF THE UTAH (Columbia, September 30, 1951) 70 Mins.
(SepiaTone)
Gene Autry, Pat Buttram, Elaine Riley, Onslow Stevens, Denver Pyle, Donna Martell, William Fawcett, Harry Lauter, Tom London, Kenne Duncan, Sandy Sanders, Teddy Infuhr, Lee Morgan, Boyd Stockman, Billy Griffith, Tommy Ivo, Bob Woodward, Stanley Price, "Champion, Jr."
D: John English
S: Les Savage, Jr.
SP: Gerald Geraghty
P: Armand Schaefer

VALLEY OF FIRE (Columbia, November 20, 1951) 70 Mins.
(SepiaTone)
Gene Autry, Pat Buttram, Gail Davis, Russell Hayden, Christine Larsen, Harry Lauter, Bud Osborne, Terry Frost, Barbara Stanley, Riley Hill, Duke York, Teddy Infuhr, Marjorie Liszt, Victor Sen Young, Gregg Barton, Sandy Sanders, Fred Sherman, James Magill, Frankie Marvin, Pat O'Malley, Wade Crosby, William Fawcett, Syd Saylor, John Miller, "Champion, Jr."
D: John English
S: Gerald Geraghty
SP: Earle Snell
P: Armand Schaefer

THE OLD WEST (Columbia, January 15, 1952) 61 Mins.
(SepiaTone)
Gene Autry, Gail Davis, Pat Buttram, Lyle Talbot, Louis Jean Heydt, House Peters, Sr., House Peters, Jr., Dick Jones, Kathy Johnson, Don Harvey, Dee Pllack, Raymond L. Morgan, James Craven, Tom London, Frank Marvin, Syd Saylor, Bob Woodward, Buddy Roosevelt, Tex Terry, Pat O'Malley, Bobby Clark, Robert Hilton, John Merton, Frank Ellis, "Champion, Jr."
D: George Archainbaud
SP: Gerald Geraghty
P: Armand Schaefer

NIGHT STAGE TO GALVESTON (Columbia, March 18, 1952) 60 Mins.
(SepiaTone)
Gene Autry, Pat Buttram, Virginia Huston, Thurston Hall, Judy Nugent, Robert Livingston, Harry Cording, Robert Bice, Frank Sully, Clayton Moore, Frank Rawls, Steve Clark, Harry Lautr, Robert Peyton, Lois Austin, Kathleen O'Malley, Riley Hill, Dick Alexander, Boyd Stockman, Bob Woodward, Sandy Sanders, Ben Welden, Gary Goodwin, "Champion, Jr."
D: George Archainbaud
SP: Norman S. Hall
P: Armand Achaefer

Virginia Huston, Thurston Hall and Gene Autry in
Night Stage to Galveston (Columbia, 1952).

APACHE COUNTRY (Columbia, May 30, 1952) 62 Mins.
(SepiaTone)
Gene Autry, Pat Buttram, Carolina Cotton, Harry Lauter,
Mary Scott, Sideney Mason, Francis X. Bushman, Gregg
Barton, Tom London, Byron Foulger, Frank Matts, Mickey
Simpson, Iron Eyes Cody, Tony Whitecloud's Jemez Indians,
Cass County Boys, "Champion, Jr."
D: George Archainbaud
SP: Norman S. Hall
P: Armand Schaefer

BARBED WIRE (Columbia, July 25, 1952) 61 Mins.
(SepiaTone)
Gene Autry, Pat Buttram, Anne James, William Fawcett,
Leonard Penn, Michael Vallon, Terry Frost, Clayton Moore,
Edwin Parker, Sandy Sanders, Stuart Whitman, Zon Murray,
Frankie Marvin, Alan Bridge, Victor Cox, Bobby Clark,
Pat O'Malley, Bud Osborne, Bob Woodward, Wesley Hudman,
Duke York, Harry Harvey, "Champion, Jr."
D: George Archainbaud
SP: Gerald Geraghty
P: Armand Schaefer

WAGON TEAM (Columbia, September 30, 1952) 61 Mins.
(SepiaTone)
Gene Autry, Pat Buttram, Gail Davis, Dick Jones, Harry
Harvey, Gordon Jones, Henry Rowland, George J. Lewis,
John Cason, Gregg Barton, Carlo Tricoli, Pierce Lyden,
Syd Saylor, Sandy Sanders, Cass County Boys (Jerry Scroggins,
Fred Martin, and Fred Dodson), "Champion, Jr."
D: George Archainbaud
SP: Gerald Geraghty
P: Armand Schaefer

BLUE CANADIAN ROCKIES (Columbia, November 30,
1952) 58 Mins.
(SepiaTone)
Gene Autry, Pat Buttram, Gail Davis, Caroline Cotton, Russ
Ford, Tom London, Mauritz Hugo, Don Beddoe, Gene Roth,
John Merton, David Garcia, Bob Woodward, W. C. "Billy"
Wilkerson, The Cass County Boys, "Champion, Jr."
D: George Archainbaud
SP: Gerald Geraghty
P: Armand Schaefer

WINNING OF THE WEST (Columbia, January 20, 1953)
57 Mins.
(SepiaTone)
Gene Autry, Smiley Burnette, Gail Davis, Richard Crane,
Robert Livingston, House Peters, Jr., Gregg Barton, William
Fawcett, Ewing Mitchell, Rodd Redwing, George Chesebro,
Frank Jacquet, Charles Delaney, Charles Soldani, Eddie
Parker, Terry Frost, James Kirkwood, Boyd Morgan, Bob
Woodward, "Champion, Jr."
D: George Archainbaud
SP: Norman S. Hall
P: Armand Schaefer

ON TOP OF OLD SMOKY (Columbia, March 25, 1953)
59 Mins.
(SepiaTone)
Gene Autry, Smiley Burnette, Gail Davis, Grandon Rhodes,
Sheila Ryan, Kenne Duncan, Robert Bice, Zon Murray,
Fred S. Martin, Jerry Scroggins, Bert Dodson, Pat O'Malley,
"Champion, Jr."
D: George Archainbaud
SP: Gerald Geraghty
P: Armand Schaefer

GOLDTOWN GHOST RAIDERS (Columbia, May 30,
1953) 59 Mins.
(SepiaTone)
Gene Autry, Smiley Burnette, Gail Davis, Kirk Riley, Carleton
Young, Neyle Morrow, Denver Pyle, Steve Conte, John
Doucette, "Champion, Jr."
D: George Archainbaud
SP: Gerald Geraghty
P: Armand Schaefer

PACK TRAIN (Columbia, July 30, 1953) 57 Mins.
(SepiaTone)
Gene Autry, Smiley Burnette, Gail Davis, Kenne Duncan,
Sheila Ryan, Tom London, Harry Lauter, Melinda Plowman,
B. G. Norman, Louise Lorimer, Frankie Marvin, Norman
E. Westcott, Tex Terry, Wesley Hudman, Kermit Maynard,
Frank Ellis, Frank O'Connor, Dick Alexander, Jill Zeller,
Herman Hack, "Champion, Jr."
D: George Archainbaud
SP: Norman S. Hall
P: Armand Schaefer

SAGINAW TRAIL (Columbia, September 20, 1953) 56 Mins.
(SepiaTone)
Gene Autry, Smiley Burnette, Connie Marshall, Eugene Borden, Ralph Reed, Henry Blair, Myron Healey, Mickey Simpson, John War Eagle, Rodd Redwing, Billy Wilkerson, Gregg Barton, John Parrish, John Merton, Charlie Hayes, "Champion, Jr."
D: George Archainbaud
SP: Dorothy Yost, Dwight Cummings
P: Armand Schaefer

LAST OF THE PONY RIDERS (Columbia, November 30, 1953) 59 Mins.
(SepiaTone)
Gene Autry, Smiley Burnette, Kathleen Case, Dick Jones, Howard Wright, Arthur Space, Gregg Barton, Buzz Henry, Harry Mackin, Harry Hines, "Champion, Jr."
D: George Archainbaud
SP: Ruth Woodman
P: Armand Schaefer

HOLLYWOOD BRONC BUSTERS (Columbia, 1956) 9 Mins.
(Screen Snapshot Series)
Jack Lemmon, Ralph Staub; Film clips featuring *Gene Autry*, Roy Rogers, Tom Mix, William Boyd, William S. Hart, Buck Jones, Hoot Gibson, Charles Starrett
D/P: Ralph Staub

ALIAS JESSE JAMES (United Artists, April 2, 1959) 92 Mins.
(DeLuxe Color)
Bob Hope, Rhonda Fleming, Wendell Corey, Jim Davis, Gloria Talbot, Will Wright, Mary Young, Sid Melton, George E. Stone, James Burke, Joe Vitale, Lyle Latell, Harry Tyler, Mike Mazurki, Mickey Finn, Nestor Paiva, Mike Ross, Emory Parnell, I. Stanford Jolley, Richard Alexander, Oliver Blake, Jack Lambert, Ethan Laidlaw, Glenn Strange, J. Anthony Hughes, Bob Gunderson, Fred Kohler, Jr., Iron Eyes Cody, and unbilled cameo appearances by *Gene Autry*, Hugh O'Brian, Ward Bond, James Arness, Roy Rogers, Fess Parker, Gail Davis, James Garner, Jay Silverheels, Bing Crosby, and Gary Cooper
D: Norman McLeod
S: Robert St. Aubrey, Bert Lawrence
SP: D. D. Beauchamp, William Bowers
P: Jack Hope

THE SILENT TREATMENT (Ralph Andrews Productions, 1967).
(This film has never been released. Done in silent film technique)
Marty Ingels, Jackie Coogan, Sherry Jackson, George Raft, Paul Lynde, *Gene Autry*, Wally Cox, Milton Berle, Jerry Lewis
D: Ralph Andrews

14 • FRED THOMSON

Great but Forgotten Hero

Fred Thomson's popularity transcended a following by Western fans alone. Next to Tom Mix he was the most successful cowboy star of the 1920s, earning nearly $2.5 million in a career that lasted only six years. But in that brief time he zoomed past the likes of William S. Hart, Hoot Gibson, Buck Jones, Ken Maynard, Harry Carey, and Jack Holt as a box-office draw and was about to leave Tom Mix biting the dust when a sudden illness and death put an end to his meteoric rise to the heights as a Western luminary. Thomson was one of the most-liked actors in Hollywood because of his exemplary off-screen life. Only Buck Jones commanded as much respect for both personal morals and the high standards of his films. Mix, Gibson, and Maynard, for example, were respected for their superior Westerns but not for their free-swinging personal life style.

Thomson's life story is unique. A native Californian, he was born in Pasadena on February 26, 1890, the son of a Presbyterian minister. He grew up in the atmosphere of a religious home and as a full participant in the life of the church. There were no thoughts of rebellion; Fred, although athletic and very popular, was a serious youth who planned to be a minister himself. He attended Occidental College from 1905 to 1910, during which time he took the sports spotlight as an all-around star. He was a letterman in every branch of major collegiate sports. He played on the varsity football, basketball, and baseball teams and was captain of the track team, breaking many college records in these sports.

At Chicago in 1910 and 1911 he won the all-around amateur track-and-field championship of America. His records in these mets stood for many years. After leaving Occidental, he went to Princeton to continue his studies for the ministry. Here he became the champion "all-around Athlete of the World," a title he won in competition with the most brilliant contenders from all outstanding athletic nations. He won the U.S. decathlon championship in 1910, 1911, and 1913.

After three years at Princeton, Fred was ordained and served as a minister at charges in Washington, DC, Los Angeles, and in Goldfield, Nevada. While in Nevada, he served as Boy Scout Commissioner. Like a later Nevadan, Rex Bell, Fred was quite active in boy-scout work. One of his later features, *A Regular Scout,* was a tribute to the Boy Scouts and an attept to boost membership in the organization. Fred, because of both his athletic prowess and his personality, had a way with boys that was amazing; sensing his influence with them, he always strived to set a good example in moral and ethical conduct.

Fred was a popular minister and seemed destined to follow in his father's footsteps. Tragedy struck him in 1916 when his wife of less than three years died following a short illness. Fred was crushed. Then came World War I. Fred felt the call to serve

Fred Thomson

first screen work was as a double for nonathletic stars, but the truth or falsity of this report is not known. However, it is doubtful that such was the case. So far as is known, he began the motion picture career that was to make him America's hero by playing Mary Pickford's husband in *The Love Light* in 1921. A third of the way through the film he is killed off; the only other time he would die on the screen was in *Jesse James*, his spectacular for Paramount.

Also in 1921, Fred appeared in another drama, written by his wife, entitled *Just Around the Corner*. In 1922 he was in Dustin Farnum's *Oath-Bound* and *Penrod*; in 1923, *One Chapter in Her Life*.

Fred got a chance to put his athletic ability to good use when Universal gave him the male lead in *The Eagle's Talons*, a 15-episode serial. Ann Little had the feminine lead. Principal supporting roles went to Joe Bonomo, the strong man, and Al Wilson, a stunt flyer. The story, a nonwestern, revolved around a gang's attempts to corner the wheat market. (The vintage automobiles and airplanes would fascinate nostalgia buffs of today.) Fred actually was second fiddle to Miss Little who was an established serial queen and quite adept at athletics herself. But it served to introduce him to Saturday matinee audiences and the movie world of action epics; likewise, it convinced Fred that his desires and his forte were for roles of the Western hero type.

Fred deliberately planned his rise in Westerns. Feeling that he must have a horse capable of sharing honors with him, one that could outperform Tom Mix's "Tony" or Buck Jones' "Silver," he went looking for such an animal. While at a riding academy in New York, he was attracted to a horse that appeared unmanageable. Fred tried him out and soon brought him under control. He bought the horse, named him "Silver King," and returned to California ready to start making Westerns.

His first picture as a Western star was *The Mask of Lopez*, made in 1923 for Harry Joe Brown on Poverty Row at a cost of $10,000. Fred was an instant hit. His early Westerns were made for an independent; but he soon became associated with FBO, an outgrowth of the old Robertson-Cole Company and later to become RKO-Radio, Inc.

Fred was lucky to become associated with both Harry Joe Brown and FBO. Brown was an excellent

his country and its fighting boys, and "to get away" for a while. He was made chaplain of the 143rd Field Artillery—called the "Mary Pickford Regiment" (Mary was its honorary colonel)—and went overseas with the 40th Division.

At the Inter-Allied games in Paris, immediately following the armistice, Fred won a pentathlon and shattered the world's record for the hand-grenade throw. He broke his right leg in a football game as a member of the 143rd F. A. team, after proving himself the hero of the contest. Some sources indicate it was at this game that Fred met Frances Marion, an attractive and talented young scenario writer who was a close friend of Mary Pickford. Other sources place the meeting some-time before the game, back in the states. Regardless, they met, fell in love, and were married in Paris.

On returning home they settled in southern California, where, with his wife's help, Fred attempted to break into the movies. He had not necessarily lost his zeal for the ministry but wanted to try something else for awhile. It is reputed that his

Fred Thomson on "Silver King"

producer of Westerns, as he proved with Fred and, later, with both Ken Maynard and Randolph Scott. FBO insisted on quality in its Westerns, and they were always superior products in about every respect—story, photography, acting, action, editing, and a score of technical qualities that, all together, distinguished quality from mediocrity. The FBO's were slick and fast-paced Westerns, especially written to match the personality, athletic prowess, and acting ability of their star.

In his film performances Fred himself was a sort of combination of Tom Mix, Douglas Fairbanks, Ken Maynard, Buck Jones, and Harry Carey. His films were very much in the mold of Tom Mix and Ken Maynard (although he preceded Ken in becoming a star) so far as flamboyant action was concerned. He probably was a better athlete than either Tom or Ken; and his effortless acrobatics were often introduced in the interest of comedy, as was often the case in the early Doug Fairbanks Westerns at Triangle. Like Fairbanks and

Jones, he had a penchant for comedy which went over well with his audiences. And, like Jones and Carey, he could act—a statement which, if applied to either Mix or Maynard, would stretch credibility considerably.

Following *The Mask of Lopez*, Fred completed several more Westerns in 1923-1924. As already mentioned, these FBO programmers were expertly staged and excellent in all technical aspects. "Silver King" was given good scenes in every picture in which to demonstrate his superior equine intelligence. Thus, because his first series was such a hit Fred was able to form his own production unit in 1925, with continuing release of the films through FBO. By 1927 he was rapidly overtaking the aging Tom Mix in popularity; William S. Hart was retired, and Buck Jones and Hoot Gibson were falling slightly behind Fred in the rankings. He bought an estate in Beverly Hills, reputedly paying in excess of $600,000. Paramount beckoned, and Fred left FBO to make bigger-budget pictures for the major studio. His contract called for four pictures at a salary of $100,000 each, and he was to have his own production unit.

His first film under the new contract was *Jesse James* (Paramount, 1927). Although a very whitewashed account of the bandit, it grossed close to $1.5 million. Critics and public alike, however, came down hard on the film for its making heroes of Jesse and Frank, and Paramount found it hard to market the film. It finished Fred as a major star before his Paramount career even got off the ground. He spared no effort in making *The Pioneer Scout* (Paramount, 1928) and *The Sunset Legion* (Paramount, 1928). Paramount played up Fred as filmdom's ranking Western star, although a lot of Tom Mix fans were ready to argue the point. But the lover of thrills could hardly ask for more, for there is one big punch after another; the photography is also striking—and the scenery! No Western programmer, these! Yet they fizzled at the box office. So did his last—*Kit Carson* (Paramount, 1928)— and his career was in deep trouble.

Fred Thomson's career came to an unexpected and tragic end. He was taken ill in December and died on Christmas Day. The cause of death was tetanus, the result of stepping on a rusty nail. He was only thirty-eight years old.

FRED THOMSON *Filmography*

THE LOVE LIGHT (Mary Pickford Productions/United Artists, January 9, 1921) 8 Reels.
Mary Pickford, Evelyn Dumo, *Fred Thomson*, Edward Phillips, Albert Prisco, Raymond Bloomer, George Rigas, Jean De Briac
D/Scen: Frances Marion

JUST AROUND THE CORNER (Cosomopolitan/Paramount, December 11, 1921) 7 Reels.
Margaret Seddon, Lewis Sargeant, Sigrid Holmquist, *Fred Thomson*, Edward Phillips, Peggy Parr, Madame Rosa Rosanove, William Nally
D/Scen: Frances Marion
S: Fannie Hurst

PENROD (Marshall Neilan Productions/Assoc. First National, January 29, 1922) 8 Reels.
Wesley Barry, Tully Marshall, Claire McDowell, John Harron, Gordon Griffith, Newton Hall, Harry Griffith, *Fred Thomson*, Harry Todd, Lina Basquette, Noah Beery, Jr., Virginia True Boardman
D: Marshall Neilan
Scen: Lucita Squier
S: Booth Tarkington—"Penrod" and "Penrod, A Comedy in Four Acts"

OATH-BOUND (Fox, August 13, 1922) 5 Reels.
Dustin Farnum, Ethel Grey Terry, *Fred Thomson*, Maurice (Lefty) Flynn, Norman Selby, Aileen Pringle, Bob Perry, Herschel Mayall
D: Bernard J. Durning
S/Scen: Edward J. Le Saint

THE EAGLE'S TALONS (Universal, March 30, 1923) 15 Chapters.
Ann Little, *Fred Thomson*, Al Wilson, Joe Bonomo
D: Duke Worne
S: Theodore Wharton, Bertram Milhauser
Scen: Anthony Coldeway, Jefferson Moffitt, Bertram Milhauser
Chapter Titles: (1) House of Mystery, (2) Edge of Eternity, (3) Hulk of Horror, (4) Daring Hearts, (5) A Deal in Diplomacy, (6) The Flood of Fury, (7) The Road to Doom, (8) Against Odds, (9) A Fighting Chance, (10) Into the Chasm, (11) The Betrayal, (12) The Sacrifice, (13) Dodging the Conspirators, (14) The Inferno, (15) The Eagle Foiled

A CHAPTER IN HER LIFE (Universal/Jewel, September 17, 1923) 6 Reels.
Claude Gillingwater, Jane Mercer, Jacqueline Gadsden, Frances Raymond, Robert Frazer, Eva Thatcher, Ralph Yearsley, *Fred Thomson*, Beth Rayon
D: Lois Weber
Adapt: Lois Weber
S: Clara Louise Burnham—"Jewel: A Chapter in Her Life"

THE MASK OF LOPEZ (Monogram/FBO, January 27, 1924) 5 Reels.
Fred Thomson, Hazel Keener, Wilfred Lucas, David Kirby, Frank Hagney, George Magrill, "Pee Wee" Holmes, Bob Reeves, Dick Sutherland, Dot Farley, "Silver King" (a horse)
D: Albert Rogell
P: Harry Joe Brown
S/Scen: Marion Jackson

NORTH OF NEVADA (Monogram/FBO, February 24, 1924) 5 Reels.
Fred Thomson, Hazel Keener, Joseph Swickard, Taylor Graves, Joe Butterworth, Chester Conklin, George Magrill, Wilfred Lucas, "Silver King"
D: Albert Rogell
P: Harry Joe Brown
S/Scen: Marion Jackson

GALLOPING GALLAGHER (Monogram/FBO, March 5, 1924) 5 Reels.
Fred Thomson, Hazel Keener, Frank Hagney, Nelson McDowell, Shorty Hendrix, Andy Morris, "Silver King"
(Working titles: "The Sheriff of Tombstone" and "The Sheriff of Gopher Flats")
D: Albert Rogell
P: Hary Joe Brown
S/Scen: Marion Jackson

THE SILENT STRANGER (Monogram/FBO, April 21, 1924) 5 Reels.
Fred Thomson, Hazel Keener, George Williams, Richard Headwick, Frank Hagney, Horace Carpenter, Bud Osborne, Bob Reeves, George Nicholls, "Silver King"
D: Albert Rogell
P: Harry Joe Brown
S/Scen: Marion Jackson

THE DANGEROUS COWARD (Monogram/FBO, May 26, 1924) 5 Reels.
Fred Thomson, Hazel Keener, Frank Hagney, Andrew Arbuckle, David Kirby, Al Kaufman, Lillian Adrian, Jim Corey, "Silver King"
D: Albert Rogell
P: Harry Joe Brown
S/Scen: Marion Jackson

THE FIGHTING SAP (Monogram/FBO, June 30 1924) 5 Reels.
Fred Thomson, Hazel Keener, Wilfred Lucas, Frank Hagney, George Williams, Ralph Yearsley, Bob Williamson, Robert Fleming, "Silver King"
D: Albert Rogell
P: Harry Joe Brown
S/Scen: Marion Jackson

Fred Thomson in *The Silent Stranger* (FBO, 1924).

THUNDERING HOOFS (Monogram/FBO, October 26, 1924) 5 Reels.
Fred Thomson, Ann May, Fred Huntley, Charles Mailes, Charles DeRevenna, Carrie Clark Ward, William Lowery, "Silver King"
D: Albert Rogell
S/Cont: Marion Jackson—"Pal O' Mine"

THAT DEVIL QUEMADO (R-C/FBO, April 5, 1925) 5 Reels.
Fred Thomson, Nola Luxford, Albert Priscoe, Byron Douglas, Joseph Bell, Pat Harmon, Gloria Hope, Alan Roscoe, Robert Cantiero, "Silver King"
D: Del Andrews
S: Marvin Wilhite, William W. Winter—"Quemado"

THE BANDIT'S BABY (R-C/FBO, May 17, 1925) 5 Reels.
Fred Thomson, Helen Foster, Harry Woods, Mary Louise Miller, Clarence Geldert, David Kirby, Charles W. Mack, "Silver King"
D: James P. Hogan
Scen: Marion Jackson
S: Leete Renick Brown

THE WILD BULL'S LAIR (R-C/FBO, June 28, 1925) 6 Reels.
Fred Thomson, Catherine Bennett, Herbert Prior, Tom Carr, Frank Hagney, Kenneth Gibson, Louise Barnes, Frank Abbott, "Silver King"
D: Del Andrews
S/Scen: Marion Jackson

RIDIN' THE WIND (Monogram/FBO, September 27, 1925) 6 Reels.
Fred Thomson, Jacqueline Gadsdon, Lewis Sargeant, David Dunbar, Betty Scott, David Kirby, "Silver King"
D: Del Andrews and Al Werker
S/Scen: Marion Jackson

ALL-AROUND FRYING PAN (R-C/FBO, November 8, 1925) 6 Reels.
Fred Thomson, Clara Horton, James Marcus, William Courtwright, John Ince, Monte Collins, Elmo Lincoln, Newton Barbar, John Pierce, Garrety Lichtz, "Silver King"
D/SP: David Kirkland
S: Frank R. Pierce

Fred Thomson, Elmo Lincoln, and Clara Horton in *All Around Frying Pan* (R-C/FBO, 1925).

THE TOUGH GUY (FBO, February 1, 1926) 6 Reels.
Fred Thomson, Lola Todd, Robert McKim, William Courtwright, Billy Butts, Leo Willis, "Silver King"
D: David Kirkland
Scen: Buckleigh Fritz Oxford
S: Frank M. Clifton and Marion Jackson

HANDS ACROSS THE BORDER (R-C/FBO, May 1, 1926) 6 Reels.
Fred Thomson, Bess Flowers, Tyrone Power, Sr., William Courtwright, Clarence Geldert, Tom Santschi, "Silver King"
D: David Kirkland
Scen: William E. Wing
S: Frank M. Clifton

THE TWO-GUN MAN (R-C/FBO, June 13, 1926) 6 Reels.
Fred Thomson, Olive Hasbrouck, Joseph Dowling, Sheldon Lewis, Frank Hagney, Ivor McFadden, William Courtwright, Billy Butts, Arthur Millett, Willie Fung, Spottiswood Aitken, "Silver King"

LONE-HAND SAUNDERS (R-C/FBO, September 13, 1926) 6 Reels.
Fred Thomson, Bess Flowers, Billy Butts, Frank Hagney, Albert Priscoe, Bill Dyer, William Courtwright, "Silver King"
D: B. Reeves Eason
Scen: Del Andrews
S: Frank M. Clifton

A REGULAR SCOUT (R-C/FBO, December 1926) 6 Reels.
Fred Thomson, Olive Hasbrouck, William Courtwright, T. Roy Barnes, Margaret Seddon, Buck Black, Robert McKim, Harry Woods, Mary Carr, "Silver King"
D: David Kirkland
Scen: David Kirkland
S: Buckleigh F. Oxford

DON MIKE (R-C/FBO, January 25, 1927) 6 Reels.
Fred Thomson, Ruth Clifford, Noah Young, Albert Priscoe, William Courtwright, Tom Bates, Norma Marie, Carmen Le Roux, "Silver King"
D: Lloyd Ingraham
Cont: Lloyd Ingraham
S: Frank M. Clifton

SILVER COMES THROUGH (R-C/FBO, May 29, 1927) 6 Reels.
(Also known as "Silver King Comes Thru")
Fred Thomson, Edna Murphy, William Courtwright, Harry Woods, Mathilde Brundage, "Silver King"
D: Lloyd Ingraham
Adapt/Cont: Lloyd Ingraham
S: Frank M. Clifton

Fred Thomson and Nora Lane in *Pioneer Scout* (Paramount, 1928).

Fred Thomson and Nora Lane in *Arizona Nights* (FBO, 1927).

ARIZONA NIGHTS (R-C/FBO, August 28, 1927) 7 Reels.
Fred Thomson, Nora Lane, J. P. McGowan, William Court-wright, Lottie Williams, William McCormick, Dan Peterson, "Silver King"
D: Lloyd Ingraham
Adapt/Cont: Hal Conklin
S: Stewart Edward White

JESSE JAMES (Paramount-Famous Lasky Corp., October 15, 1927) 8 Reels.
Fred Thomson, Nora Lane, Montague Love, Mary Carr, James Pierce, Herbert Pryor, Harry Woods, William Courtwright, Milton Brown, "Silver King"
D: Lloyd Ingraham
S/Scen: Frank M. Clifton

THE PIONEER SCOUT (Paramount-Famous Lasky Corp., January 21, 1928) 7 Reels.
Fred Thomson, Nora Lane, William Courtwright, Tom Wilson, George Marion, Fred Burns, Lloyd Ingraham, "Silver King"
D: Lloyd Ingraham, Alfred Werker
S/Scen: Frank M. Clifton

Fred Thomson, Harry Woods, and players in *The Sunset Legion* (Paramount, 1928).

THE SUNSET LEGION (Paramount-Famous Lasky Corp., April 21, 1928) 7 Reels.
Fred Thomson, Edna Murphy, William Courtwright, Harry Woods, Jim Corey, Lew Meehan, "Silver King"
("Silver King" plays a dual role in this film; when Thomson's part calls for a black horse, "Silver King" appears in a tailor-made suit of black cloth.)
D: Lloyd Ingraham
S/Scen: Frank M. Clifton

KIT CARSON (Paramount-Famous Lasky Corp., June 23, 1928) 8 Reels.
Fred Thomson, Nora Lane, Dorothy Janis, Raoul Paoli, William Courtwright, Albert Priscoe, Nelson McDowell, Raymond Turner, Augustine Lopez, "Silver King"
D: Alfred L. Werker, Lloyd Ingraham
S: Frank M. Clifton
Scen: Paul Powell

Jack Holt

15 • JACK HOLT

Granite-Jawed Hero

Steel-nerved, iron-jawed, Jack Holt was not a great actor and he personally had no pretentions that he was. He was, however, a popular screen star which he considered to be ridiculous. He played his career he was featured in just about every type of motion picture except slapstick comedy—which he considered to be rediculuos. He played both heroic and villainous roles with equal aplomb, in a screen career that spanned from the days of silent movies, made with hand-cranked cameras in barns and open lots, to the era of talking pictures, technicolor, sound stages, exotic locations, and million-dollar budgets.

Jack was the embodiment of the well-bred gentleman who could be rough and tough when the occasion demanded. This type of man was the *beau ideal* of the 1920s. Born in New York City on May 31, 1888, he preferred to have people believe that he was born in Virginia, where, in fact, he did grow up as the son of an aristocratic Episopal clergyman. Wanderlust possessed him at an early age, and, after expulsion from Virginia Military Institute for a series of pranks, he became, in turn, a prospector in Alaska, civil engineer, government mail carrier, and cowpuncher in Oregon. In 1914 he was working for a surveying crew that wound up jobless in San Francisco. On learning that a movie company on location near San Raphael was looking for a man to make a daring jump on horseback over a thirty-five foot

cliff into a river, Holt applied for the job, got it, and accomplished the feat. His screen career was launched, for he was also given a bit in the film, *Salomy Jane.*

On his way down to Hollywood, he spent the remainder of 1914 as an extra and stuntman, specializing in fight scenes and often working at Univer-Universal. That same year he had a small role in Universal's serial *The Master Key*, and in 1915 he was one of the villains in another serial titled *The Broken Coin*, also for Universal. In 1916 Universal cast him as the hero opposite serial queen Marie Walcamp in *Liberty*, the first Western serial ever made. He also was featured in two short Westerns, *What the River Foretold* and *The Desperado*, as well as in a number of other one- and two-reelers.

At Universal Jack made his early mark in the movies playing mainly caddish roles. But when he changed to Paramount in 1917, the studio switched him to hero parts. Early Westerns starring Jack were *A Desert Wooing* (1918), *The Squaw Man* (1918), *Kitty Kelly, M.D.* (1919), and *North of the Rio Grande* (1922). But the studio did not follow up with more Westerns until 1924 when Jack was given the lead in *North of '36* and *Wanderer of the Wasteland*. Both features were a tremendous success and Jack, finding his true metier, was launched on a Western career and brought to the screen many of the Zane Grey characters. He stayed in the saddle for Paramount in these financially and artistically successful sagebrushers until the advent of sound temporarily put the quietus to outdoor films, continuing to star in fine mellers such as *The Ancient Highway* (1925), *The Blind Goddess* (1926), *The Tigress* (1927) and *The Smart Set* (1928).

The Holt Westerns were good—no question about that. Paramount did not skimp on budgets. The films were usually shot on location, the casts were loaded with talent, scripts were well written, competent directors and technical crews were assigned to the Holt unit, excellent photography was achieved, and time was taken to create a quality product. There was little similarity between the Holt Westerns of the 1920s, with budgets exceeding $100,000, and the shoddy "B" Westerns churned out by many producers during the 1930s, 1940s, and 1950s at costs of $10,000 to $15,000 and with three- and four-day shooting schedules. The Holt Westerns played the regular Paramount circuit of first-class theatres and were comparable in quality to the Gary Cooper, Randolph Scott, Joel McCrea, and Richard Dix Westerns of a few years later. In fact, much of the Scott films of the early 1930s was cannibalized footage from the Holt features. Paramount followed the practice of cutting up the Holt films for insertion into remakes to the point where no complete copies exist of most of the Holt Westerns.

The Wanderer of the Wasteland (Paramount, 1924) is singled out for especial comment. It was one of the most talked-about films of 1924 because of its breathtaking technicolor sequences. Audiences were enraptured with the color. The story is laid on the great desert in the Southwest, including Death Valley, back in the early 1870s when the gold rush was on. The country, with its colors and the picturesque attire of the day and location, lent itself admirably to the color process. Jack played the wanderer and received many plaudits for his work.

No better Zane Grey Westerns have ever been filmed than those by Paramount and starring Holt. Jack had in plenitude the gift of realism—uncompromising, courageous fidelity to character and atmosphere. He never seemed to hurry in that hectic movie fear that he might "drag"; his make-ups were neither prettied up to give him beauty nor smeared on to add ferocity. Jack was usually a no-nonsense cowboy and his jutting jaw (Chester Gould modeled his famous comic-strip character "Dick Tracy" after Holt) and piercing eyes usually were sufficient to turn the villains pale with fear. Interesting to note is that he was the one cowboy star who could sport a moustache and still play the "good guy." He looked and acted exactly like what he played, and that is as full a compliment as may be accorded an artist.

In late 1927 Jack began to make pictures for Columbia and starred in the company's first talkie, *The Donovan Affair*. His rich, resonant voice exactly suited his appearance, and he became Columbia's top male star. His most memorable pictures at Columbia were *Submarine* (1928), *Flight* (1929), and *Dirigible* (1931), all directed by Frank Capra. The latter film was the first Columbia movie ever booked into Grauman's Chinese Theatre, Theatre, the top prestige house on the West Coast. All three films were top box office, and had long engagements on Broadway at top prices.

During the period 1930 to 1941 Jack made a long series of adventure pictures, most of them generally dismissed as routine programmers. But this is precisely where many critics have missed the point. It was the time of the Great Depression, and the pictures Holt made were purely escapist entertainment and exactly what people wanted. That was the purpose of the films. And it was the profit from the Holt films that allowed Columbia to initially engage in more "artistic" experiments. Jack was especially popular with the male audience, being the personification of a "man's man." Titles such as *Fifty Fathoms Deep, War Correspondent, Storm Over the Andes, Outlaws of the Orient, Trapped by G-Men, Flight into Nowhere, Reformatory, Trapped in the Sky, Prison Camp, Dangerous Waters,* and *Roaring Timber* are indicative of the action content of these escape-for-the-moment films. Western fans especially liked *End of the Trail* (Columbia, 1936), loosely based on Zane Grey's "Outlaws of Palouse." Jack was at his best in a film beautiful in its pathos and simplicity.

It was a credit to him that in those halcyon years of the 1930s he became one of the "B" programmers top drawing cards and achieved a reputation for excellent action melodramas that to this day has sustained his name among Hollywood's elite. The name Holt became synonomous with hard-fisted, low-budget films that truly held one engrossed for an hour, and his films had tremendous pulling power in those years when for just a few cents one could live a vicarious life with rugged, he-man Holt.

In 1940 Jack starred in *Outside the Three-Mile Limit, Passport to Alcatraz, Fugitive from a Prison Camp*, and *The Great Plane Robbery*. Although entertaining to dyed-in-the-wool Holt fans, these features were indicative of the slow decay of the long-running series. There was little to distinguish them from any other "quickies" produced along poverty row—nothing, that is, except the Holt name. *The Great Swindle* (1941) was the last feature produced in the Holt series, bringing the total of his Columbia starrers to fifty-two. In the final film under his Columbia contract the studio cast him in the serial *Holt of the Secret Service* (1941), billing him as "the greatest action star of all times" and capitalizing through the title on his name. Jack was then fifty-four years of age.

In 1942 Jack entered the U.S. Army, serving two years and attaining the rank of major before receiving a medical discharge. While in the service he made two training films for the military. Returning to Hollywood, he played supporting roles in Westerns with Roy Rogers, Rocky Lane, Bill Elliott, Don Barry, Gene Autry, Rod Cameron, and even Lash LaRue. But his best Western roles were in RKO's *The Arizona Ranger* (1948), in which he co-starred with his son Tim, and in Warner Brothers' *Return of the Frontiersman* (1950), in which he had a top-featured role. His last film was *Across the Wide Missouri* (MGM, 1951), made with his pal, Clark Gable.

After suffering a series of heart attacks, he died in the Veterans Hospital in West Hollywood on January 18, 1951. His final resting place was Sawtelle, California.

Today's moviegoers find it difficult to realize the magnetism of Jack Holt in his prime and that he was a top-ranking star with unfathomable charisma for the many thousands of people who enjoyed slipping into a theatre to relax for an hour or so with a Holt meller or shoot-'em-up. It is also strange that most Western historians have either overlooked or failed to pay due respect to Jack as a Western star. To ignore him in this respect is unforgivable for the record speaks for itself. The problem seems to lie in the fact that the Holt

Jack Holt, Tim Holt, and Conrad Nagel out for a ride in the Hollywood hills.

Westerns have long since become nonexistent, and many of those who currently write did not have the good fortune to see his films; thus they have felt obliged to ignore Jack's Western career, rationalizing that he was primarily an action melodrama star. This he obviously was—one of the best. But he also earned his spurs as one of the best cowboys of the 1920s before putting aside his saddle to take on assorted he-man roles.

Many people mourned his death, but none more than the "little people" of Hollywood whom he had befriended. Jack was never above a slap on the back, a wave of a hand in greeting, or a smile for and a little idle chitchat with the technical crews and roustabouts on the studio lot. He prided himself on being a gentleman and always behaved as one. Lesser men subconsciously realized that Jack was an idol whose station in life was above what they could ever hope for, but they never had the idea that Jack himself thought he was different from them. It was a fine quality to pass o to his son and daughter.

JACK HOLT *Filmography*

SALOMY JANE (Alco/California Motion Picture Corp., November 2, 1914).
Beatriz Micheleana, House Peters, Mabel Hilliard, Fred W. Snook, William Nigh, Ernest Joy, Bill Pike, Forrest Halsey, *Jack Holt*
D: William Nigh
S/Adapt: Paul Armstrong
Based on Bret Harte's "Salomy Jane's Kiss"

THE MASTER KEY (Universal, November 16, 1914) 15 Chapters
Robert Leonard, Ella Hall, Harry Carter, Alan Forest, Jean Hathaway, Rupert Julian, Alfred Hickman, William Higby, Charles E. Manly, Cleo Madison, *Jack Holt*
D: Robert Leonard
(Chapter Titles Unknown)

THE BROKEN COIN (Universal, June 21, 1915) 22 Chapters.
Francis Ford, Grace Cunard, Harry Mann, Eddie Polo, John Ford, Mina Cunard, Harry Schumm, Ernest Shields, *Jack Holt*
D: Francis Ford
Scen: Frace Cunard
S: Emerson Hough
Chapter Titles: (1) The Broken Coin, (2) The Satan of the Sands, (3) When the Throne Rocked, (4) The Face at the Window, (5) The Underground Foe, (6) A Startling Discovery, (7) Between Two Fires, (8) The Prison in the Palace, (9) Room 22, (10) Cornered, (11) The Clash of Arms, (12) A Cry in the Dark, (13) War, (14) On the Battlefield, (15) The Deluge, (16) Kitty in Danger, (17) The Castaways, (18) The Underground City, (19) The Sacred Fire, (20) Between Two Fires, (21) A Timely Rescue, (22) An American Queen

A CIGARETTE, THAT'S ALL (Universal-Gold Seal, August 3, 1915) 2 Reels.
Phillip Smalley, Maude George, *Jack Holt*, Rupert Julian, H. Scott Leslie
D: Phillip Smalley
S: Helena Evans
Scen: Lois Weber

THE CAMPBELLS ARE COMING (Universal-Broadway, October 6, 1915) 4 Reels.
Francis Ford, Grace Cunard, M. Denecke, Duke Worme, Harry Schumm, Lew Short, *Jack Holt*
P/D: Francis Ford
Scen: Grace Cunard
S: Emerson Hough

AS THE TWIG IS BENT (Lubin, November 13, 1915) 3 Reels.
Lee C. Chumway, Doris Baker, Louis Fitzroy, Eleanor Blevins, *Jack Holt*, Helen Eddy, Melvin Mayo, Velma Whitman
D: Wilbert Melville

WHAT THE RIVER FORETOLD (Universal-Bison, November 13, 1915) 3 Reels.
Edythe Sterling, *Jack Holt*, Mrs. Marvin, Sherman Bainbridge
D: William Franey and Joseph Franz
S: Peter B. Kyne
Scen: Ben Cohn
P: Joseph Franz

THE POWER OF FASCINATION (Universal-Rex, December 3, 1915) 1 Reel.
Cleo Madison, *Jack Holt*, Thomas Chatterton, Carrie Fowler, Jack Francis, Jack Wells
D: Charles Saksby
P: Cleo Madison

HER BETTER SELF (Universal-Victor, January 12, 1916) 2 Reels.
Grace Cunard, *Jack Holt*, Irving Lippner, Genevieve Abbot, Roy Russell
P/S/Scen: Grace Cunard

HIS MAJESTY, DICK TURPIN (Universal-Bison, February 4, 1916) 2 Reels.
Grace Cunard, Francis Ford, *Jack Holt*, Peter Gerald, Irving Lippner, Neal Harding, Peter Gerald, Irving Lippner, Neil Haron
P/D: Francis Ford
Scen: Grace Cunard

BORN OF THE PEOPLE (Universal-Gold Seal, March 7, 1916) 2 Reels.
Jack Holt, Grace Cunard, Neal Harding
P/D/S: Grace Cunard

THE MADCAP QUEEN OF CRONA (Universal-Gold Seal, March 13, 1916) 2 Reels.
Grace Cunard, Francis Ford, *Jack Holt*, Neil Harding
P/D: Francis Ford
Scen: Grace Cunard

THE DESPERADO (Universal, March 15, 1916) 1 Reel.
Rupert Julian, *Jack Holt*, Zoe Bech
P: Rupert Julian
S: Hugh Johnson
Scen: Calder Johnstone

BEHIND THE MASK (Universal-Bison, April 8, 1916) 2 Reels.
Peter Gerald, Grace Cunard, *Jack Holt*, Francis Ford, Irving Lippner, Neal Harding, Lou Short, Robert Murdock, Burtos S. Witson
P: Francis Ford
Scen: Grace Cunard

THE DUMB GIRL OF PORTICI (Universal, April 13, 1916)
10 Reels.
Anna Pavlova, Rupert Julian, Douglas Gerrard, Betty
Schade, John (*Jack*) *Holt*, Hartford (Jack) Hoxie, Wadsworth
Harris, Edna Maison, Laura Oakley, Lois Wilson
(From the Opera based on the life of Masanicello by Daniel
Francois and Esprit Auber)
P: Phillips Smalley
Adapt: Lois Weber

THE UNEXPECTED (Universal-Rex, April 1916) 1 Reel.
Grace Cunard, Francis Ford, *Jack Holt*
P/D/S: Francis Ford and Grace Cunard

NAKED HEARTS (Universal-Bluebird, May 8, 1916) 5 Reels.
Rupert Julian, Zoe Bech, Gordon Griffith, Douglas Gerrard,
Jack Holt, George Hupp, Ben Horning, Nanine Wright
D/S: Rupert Julian
Scen: Olga Printzlau
Suggested by the Poem "Maud" by Lord Tennyson

THE FALSE PART (Universal-Gold Seal, June 10, 1916)
2 Reels.
Herbert Rawlinson, Dorothy Moore, *Jack Holt*, Ethel Clarke
P/D: William Worthington
S: Pliny Horne
Scen: Jack Wells

THE WIRE PULLERS (Universal-Laemmle, June 10, 1916)
1 Reel.
Herbert Rawlinson, Agnes Vernon, *Jack Holt*, Yona Landowska
D: William Worthington
Scen: Ben Cohn

THE 'PHONE MESSAGE (Universal-Rex, July 22, 1916)
1 Reel.
Allen Holubar, Ruth Stonehouse, *Jack Holt*
D: Allen Holubar

BRENNON O' THE MOOR (Universal-Special, August 12,
1916) 2 Reels.
Francis Ford, Grace Cunard, *Jack Holt*, Jack Francis, Orin
Jackson, Robert Murdock, Daddy Manley, Harry Mann
P/D: Francis Ford
Scen: Grace Cunard

LIBERTY (Universal, August 14, 1916) 20 Chapters.
(Also known as "Liberty, A Daughter of the U.S.A."—The
first Western Serial ever made)
Marie Walcamp, *Jack Holt*, Neal Hart, G. Raymond Nye,
L. M. Wells, Eddie Polo, Hazel Buckham, Roy Stewart,
Maude Emory, Bertram Grassby
D: Jacques Jaccard, Henry McRae
P/S/Adapt: Jacques Jaccard
Chapter Titles: (1) The Fangs of the Wolf, (2) Riding with
Death, (3) American Blood, (4) Dead or Alive, (5) Love and
War, (6) The Desert of Lost Souls, (7) Liberty's Sacrifice,
(8) Clipped Wings, (9) Trapped, (10) The Human Target,

(11) A Daughter of Mars, (12) For the Flag, (13) Strife and
Sorrow, (14) A Modern Joan of Arc, (15) The Flag of Truce,
(16) Court-Martialled, (17) A Trail of Blood, (18) The Wolf's
Nemesis, (19) An Avenging Angel, (20) A Daughter of the
U.S.A.

THE PRINCELY BANDIT (Universal-Bison, August 23, 1916)
2 Reels.
Francis Ford, Grace Cunard, *Jack Holt*, Peter Gerald
D: Francis Ford
Scen: Grace Cunard

SAVING THE FAMILY NAME (Universal-Bluebird, Sep-
tember 16, 1916) 5 Reels.
Mary McLaren, Phillips Smalley, Miss Girrard Alexander,
Carl Von Schiller, *Jack Holt*, Harry Depp
D: Lois Weber and Phillips Smalley
Scen: Lois Weber
S: Evelyn Heath

THE CHALICE OF SORROW (Universal-Bluebird, Sep-
tember 28, 1916) 5 Reels.
Cleo Madison, Wedgewood Nowell, Blanche White, Charles
Cummings, *Jack Holt*
D/Adapt: Rex Ingram

THE BLACK SHEEP OF THE FAMILY (Universal-Red
Feather, October 2, 1916) 5 Reels.
Jay Hunt, *Jack Holt*, Francelia Billington, Gilmore Hammond,
Paul Byron, Helen Leslie, Mina Jeffreys, Norton Hammond,
Mrs. Jay Hunt, Hector V. Serno
D: Jay Hunt
S: Frank M. Wiltermood, Jay Hunt

THE BETTER MAN (Universal-Bison, October 13, 1916)
2 Reels.
Jack Holt, Lucille Younge, Jack Nelson, Albert MacQuarrie
P/D: Jay Hunt
S: Ben Cohn

PATRIA (International Film Service/Pathe, January 14, 1917)
15 Chapters.
Irene Castle, Warner Oland, Milton Sills, Floyd Buckley,
Marie Walcamp, George Maharoni, Allen Murnane, Dorothy
Green, Wallace Beery, Nigel Barrie, Charles Brimley, *Jack
Holt*, George Lessey, M. W. Rale, Leroy Baker, Rudolph
Valentino, Dick Stewart
D: Theodore and Leo Wharton (Ithaca scenes), Jacques
Jaccard (Hollywood scenes)
S: Louis Joseph Vance—"The Last of the Fighting Channings"
SP: J. B. Clymer, Louis Joseph Vance, Charles W. Goddard
Chapter Titles: (1) Last of the Fighting Channings, (3 reels)
(2) The Treasure, (3) Winged Millions, (4) Double-Crossed,
(5) The Island God Forgot, (6) Alias Nemesis, (7) Red Dawn,
(8) Red Night, (9) Cat's Paw and Scapegoat, (10) War in the
Dooryard, (11) Sunset Falls, (12) Peace on the Border, or Peace
Which Passeth All Understanding, (13) Wings of Death,
(14) Border Peril, (15) For the Flag

THE COST OF HATRED (Paramount/Lasky, April 9, 1917)
5 Reels.
Kathlyn Williams, Theodore Roberts, Tom Forman, J. W. Johnston, *Jack Holt*, Charles Ogle, Walter Long, Horace B. Carpenter, Mayme Kelso, Louise Mineveh
P/D: George H. Melford
Scen: Beulah Marie Dix

SACRIFICE (Paramount/Lasky, April 30, 1917) 5 Reels.
Margaret Illington, *Jack Holt*, Winter Hall, Noah Beery, Sr.
D: Frank Reicher
S: Charles Kenyon
Scen: Beatrice de Mille, Leighton Osmun

GIVING BECKY A CHANCE (Paramount/Lasky, June 7, 1917) 5 Reels.
Vivian Martin, *Jack Holt*, Jack Richardson, P. H. Sasso, Alice Knowland
D: Howard Estabrook
S: Lois Zellner
Scen: Edith Kennedy

THE LITTLE AMERICAN (Paramount/Artcraft, July 12, 1917) 6 Reels.
Mary Pickford, *Jack Holt*, Hobart Bosworth, Raymond Hatton, Walter Long, Ben Alexander, Norman Kerry, Wallace Beery, Raymond Griffith, Colleen Moore, Sam Wood, Jame Neill, Guy Oliver, Edythe Chapman, Lillian Leighton, Gordon Griffith, Ramon Novarro
P/D: Cecil B. DeMille
S: Jeanie MacPherson
Scen: Jeanie MacPherson, Cecil B. DeMille

THE INNER SHRINE (Paramount/Lasky, August 2, 1917) 5 Reels.
Margaret Illington, Hobart Bosworth, Elliott Dexter, *Jack Holt*
D: Frank Reicher
S: Basil King
Adapt: Beatrice de Mille, Leighton Osmun

THE CALL OF THE EAST (Paramount/Lasky, November 29, 1917) 5 Reels.
Sessue Hayakawa, Tsuru Aiko, *Jack Holt*, Margaret Loomis, James Cruze, Ernest Joy
D: George H. Melford
S: Beulah Marie Dix

THE SECRET GAME (Paramount/Lasky, November 24, 1917) 5 Reels.
Sessue Hayakawa, Florence Vidor, *Jack Holt*, Raymond Hatton, Charles Ogle, Mayme Kelso
D: William de Mille
S: Marion Fairfax

HIDDEN PEARLS (Paramount/Lasky, February 4, 1918)
5 Reels.
Sessue Hayakawa, Margaret Loomis, Florence Vidor, *Jack Holt*, James Cruze, Theodore Roberts, Noah Beery, Clarence Geldhart, Gustav VovSeffertitz
D: George Melford
S: Beulah Marie Dix

HEADIN' SOUTH (Artcraft-Famous Players, February 22, 1918) 5 Reels.
Douglas Fairbanks, Katherine MacDonald, Frank Campeau, James Mason, *Jack Holt*, Marjorie Daw, Bob Emmons, Alice Smith, Hoot Gibson, Art Acord
D: Arthur Rosson
S: Allan Dwan
P: Douglas Fairbanks

ONE MORE AMERICAN (Paramount/Lasky, March 7, 1918) 5 Reels.
Charles Beban, Camille Ankewich, Hector Dion, Horace B. Carpenter, Helen Jerome Eddy, Raymond Hatton, *Jack Holt*
D: William C. de Mille
Scen: Olga Printzlau
Based on play *The Land of the Free* by William C. de Mille

LOVE ME (Paramount-Thomas Ince, March 28, 1918)
5 Reels.
Dorothy Dalton, *Jack Holt*, Robert McKim, William Conklin, Dorcas Mathews, Melborne MacDowell, Elinor Hancock
D: R. William Neill
S: C. Gardner Sullivan
Supr: Thomas H. Ince

THE HONOR OF HIS HOUSE (Paramount/Lasky, April 18, 1918) 5 Reels.
Sessue Hayakawa, Florence Vidor, *Jack Holt*, Mayme Kelso, Forrest Seabury, Thomas Kuraha
D: William de Mille
S: Marion Fairfax

THE CLAW (Select, June 9, 1918) 5 Reels.
Clara Kimball Young, Milton Sills, *Jack Holt*, Mary Mersch, Edward M. Kimball, Henry Woodward, Marcia Manon
D: Robert Vignola
S: Cynthia Stockley
Scen: Charles E. Whitaker

A DESERT WOOING (Paramount-Thomas Ince, June 18, 1918) 5 Reels.
Enid Bennett, *Jack Holt*, Donald MacDonald, John P. Lockney, Charles Spere, Elinor Hancock
D: Jerome Storm
Supr: Thomas H. Ince

GREEN EYES (Paramount-Thomas Ince, August 18, 1918) 5 Reels.
Dorothy Dalton, *Jack Holt,* Robert McKim, Emery Johnson, Doris Lee, Clyde Benson
D: R. William Neill
Supr.: Thomas H. Ince

THE MARRIAGE RING (Paramount-Thomas Ince, September 18, 1918) 5 Reels.
Enid Bennett, *Jack Holt,* Robert McKim, Maude George, Lydia Knott
D: Fred Niblo
S: John Lynch
Supr.: Thomas Ince
Picturization: R. Cecil Smith

THE ROAD THROUGH 'THE DARK (Select, December 15, 1918) 5 Reels.
Clara Kimball Young, *Jack Holt,* Elinor Fair, Henry Woodward, Robby Connolly
D: Edmund Mortimer
S: Maud Radford Warren
Scen: Kathryn Stuart

THE SQUAW MAN (Paramount-Artcraft, December 15, 1918) 6 Reels.
Elliott Dexter, Katherine MacDonald, Ann Little, Theodore Roberts, *Jack Holt,* Thurston Hall, Tully Marshall, Noah Beery, Sr., James Mason, Monte Blue, Charles Ogle, Pat Moore, Herbert Standing, Edwin Stevens, Helen Dunbar, Winter Hall, Julia Faye, William Brunton, Guy Oliver, Jack Herbert, M. Hallward, Clarence Geldart
D: Cecil B. DeMille
Scen: Beulah Marie Dix
Adapt: Edwin Milton Royle

THE WHITE MAN'S LAW (Paramount-Lasky, April 10, 1918) 5 Reels.
Sessue Hayakawa, Florence Vidor, *Jack Holt,* Herbert Standing, Mayme Kelso, Ernest Joy, Noah Beery, Clarissa Selwyn, Fred Deshon, Forrest Seabury, Joseph Swickard, Charles West
D: James Young
S: Marion Fairfax, John B. Browne

CHEATING CHEATERS (C.K.Y. Film Corp., January 14, 1919) 5 Reels.
Clara Kimball Young, *Jack Holt,* Anna Q. Nilsson, Edwin Stevens, Nicholas Dunsew, Tully Marshall, Mayme Kelso, Frank Campeau, Frederick Burton, Jess Singleton, Eleanor Hancock, W. A. Corrall
D: Allan Dwan
S: Max Marcin
Scen: Kathryn Stuart
P: Lewis J. Selznick

Elliott Dexter and Jack Holt in *The Squaw Man* (Artcraft, 1918).

A MIDNIGHT ROMANCE (First National, March 16, 1919) 6 Reels.
Jack Holt, Anita Stewart, Juanita Hansen, Edward Tilton, Elinor Hancock, Helen Yoder, Montagu Dumont
D: Lois Weber
Scen: Marion Orth

FOR BETTER, FOR WORSE (Famous Players-Lasky, May 4, 1919) 7 Reels.
Gloria Swanson, Elliott Dexter, Tom Foreman, *Jack Holt,* Raymond Hatton, Sylvia Ashton, Theodore Roberts, Wanda Hawley, Winter Hall, Fred Huntly
D: Cecil B. DeMille
Scen: Jeanie Macpherson
S: Edgar Selwyn
Adapt: William C. de Mille
P: Cecil B. DeMille

THE WOMAN THOU GAVEST ME (Famous Players-Lasky, June 15, 1919) 6 Reels.
Katherine MacDonald, Milton Sills, *Jack Holt,* Theodore Roberts
D: Hugh Ford
Scen: Beulah Marie Dix
S: Hall Caine

A SPORTING CHANCE (Famous Players-Lasky/Paramount, July 20, 1919) 5 Reels.
Ethel Clayton, *Jack Holt,* Howard Davies, Anna Q. Nilsson, Herbert Standing
D: George Melford
Scen: Will M. Ritchey
S: Roger Hartman—"Impulses"

THE LIFE LINE (Paramount/Artcraft, October 12, 1919)
6 Reels.
Jack Holt, Seena Owen, Lew Cody, Wallace Beery, Pauline
Starke, Tully Marshall
D: Charles E. Whitaker
Adapt: Charles E. Whitaker
S: George R. Sims—"The Roman Eye"

KITTY KELLY, M. D. (Robertson-Cole, October 18,
1919) 5 Reels.
Bessie Barriscale, *Jack Holt*, J. J. Dowling, Wedgewood
Nowell, Mildred Manning
D: Howard Hickman
Scen: H. C. Hickman
S: M. B. Haver

VICTORY (Paramount-Artcraft, December 7, 1919) 8 Reels.
Jack Holt, Lon Chaney, Seena Owen, Wallace Beery, Ben
Deely, Laura Winston, Bull Montana, George Nichols
D: Maurice Tourneur
Scen: Stephen Fox
S: Based on Novel by Joseph Conrad
P: Maurice Tourneur

THE BEST OF LUCK (Screen Classics/Metro, July 11,
1920) 6 Reels.
Jack Holt, Kathryn Adams, Fred Malatesta, Lilie Leslie,
Frances Raymond, Emmett King, Robert Dunbar, Effie
Conley, Jack Underhill
D: Ray C. Smallwood
Scen: Albert Shelby LeVino
S: Cecil Raleigh and Harry Hamilton
Dir-Gen: Maxwell Karger

CROOKED STREETS (Paramount-Artcraft, August 1,
1920) 5 Reels.
Ethel Clayton, *Jack Holt*, Frederick Starr, Clarence Geldhart,
Clyde Fillmore, Josephine Crowell
D: Paul Powell
Scen: Edith Kennedy
S: Samuel Merwin—"Dinner at Eight"

THE SINS OF ROSANNE (Paramount-Lasky, October 17,
1920) 5 Reels.
Ethel Clayton, *Jack Holt*, Fontaine LaRue, Mabel Van Buren,
Clarence Geldhart, Dorothy Messinger, Grace Moore, James
Smith, Guy Oliver
D: Tom Forman
Scen: Mary O'Connor
S: Cynthia Stockley—"Rosanne Ozanne"

HELD BY THE ENEMY (Paramount-Lasky, October 30,
1920) 6 Reels.
Agnes Ayres, Lewis Stone, *Jack Holt*, Wanda Hawley,
Josephine Crowell
D: Donald Crisp
Adapt: Beulah Dix
S: William Gillette

MIDSUMMER MADNESS (Paramount-Artcraft, December 12, 1920) 6 Reels.
Jack Holt, Lila Lee, Conrad Nagel, Lois Wilson, Betty
Francisco, Claire McDowell, Charlotte Jackson, Ethel
Wales, Charles Ogle, Lillian Leighton, George Kuwa
D: William de Mille
Scen: Olga Printzlau
S: Cosmo Hamilton—"His Friend and His Wife"

THE GRIM COMEDIAN (Goldwyn Pictures, January 29,
1921) 6 Reels.
Phoebe Hunt, *Jack Holt*, Gloria Hope, Bert Woodruff,
Laura La Varnie, May Hopkins, John Harron, Joseph J.
Dowling
D: Frank Lloyd
S: Rita Weiman
SP: Bess Meredyth

ALL SOULS' EVE (Realart Pictures, February 20, 1921)
6 Reels.
Mary Miles Minter, *Jack Holt*, Carmen Phillips, Clarence
Geldhart, Mickey Moore, Fanny Midgley, Lottie Williams
D: Chester Franklin
SP: Elmer Harris
S: Anne Crawford Flexner

THE MASK (Selig, March 13, 1921) 7 Reels.
Jack Holt, Hedda Nova, Mickey Moore, Fred Malatesta,
Larry Lonsdale, Byron Munson, Janice Wilson, William
Clifford
D: Bertram Bracken
SP: Arthur Lavon
S: Arthur Hornblow

DUCKS AND DRAKES (Realart Pictures, April 3, 1921)
5 Reels.
Bebe Daniels, *Jack Holt*, Mayme Kelso, Edward Martindel,
William E. Lawrence, Wade Boteler, Maurie Newell, Elsie
Andrean
D: Maurice Campbell
S/SP: Elmer Harris

THE LOST ROMANCE (Famous Players-Lasky/Paramount, May 15, 1921) 7 Reels.
Jack Holt, Lois Wilson, Fontaine LaRue, Conrad Nagel,
Mickey Moore, Wayne Kelso, Robert Brower, Barbara
Gurney, Clarence Geldhart, Clarence Burton, Lillian Leighton
D: William C. de Mille
SP: Olga Printzlau
S: Edward Knoblock

AFTER THE SHOW (Famous Players-Lasky/Paramount,
October 9, 1921) 7 Reels.
Jack Holt, Lila Lee, Charles Ogle, Eve Southern, Shannon
Day, Carlton King, Stella Seager, Ethel Wales
D: William C. de Mille
SP: Hazel Christie
S: Rita Weiman

THE CALL OF THE NORTH (Famous Players-Lasky/ Paramount, December 4, 1921) 5 Reels.
Jack Holt, Madge Bellamy, Noah Beery, Francis McDonald, Edward Martindel, Helen Ferguson, Jack Herbert
D: Joseph Henabery
S: Stuart Edward White—"Conjuror's House"
P: Jesse L. Lasky

BOUGHT AND PAID FOR (Famous Players-Lasky/Paramount, March 19, 1922) 6 Reels.
Agnes Ayres, *Jack Holt*, Walter Hiers, Leigh Wyant, George Kuwa, Bernice Frank, Ethel Wales
D: William C. de Mille
SP: Clara Beranger
S: George H. Broadhurst
P: Adolph Zukor

NORTH OF THE RIO GRANDE (Famous Players-Lasky/ Paramount, May 21, 1922) 5 Reels.
Jack Holt, Bebe Daniels, Charles Ogle, Alec B. Francis, Will R. Walling, Jack Carlyle, Fred Huntley, Shannon Day, Edythe Chapman, George Field, W. B. Clarke
D: Rollin Sturgeon, Joseph Henabery
SP: Will M. Ritchie
S: Vingie E. Roe—"Val of Paradise"

WHILE SATAN SLEEPS (Famous Players-Lasky/Paramount, July 2, 1922) 7 Reels.
Jack Holt, Wade Boteler, Mabel Van Buren, Fritzi Brunette, Will R. Walling, F. P. Lockney, Fred Huntley, Bobby Mack, Sylvia Ashton, Herbert Standing
D: Joseph Henabery
SP: Albert S. LeVino
S: Peter B. Kyne—"The Parson of Panamint"

A TRIP TO PARAMOUNT TOWN (Famous Players-Lasky/Paramount, July 10, 1922) 2 Reels.
Jack Holt and other famous stars are seen in this studio-promotion film
Sup: Jerome Beatty
Scen: Jack Cunningham

THE MAN UNCONQUERABLE (Famous Players-Lasky/ Paramount, July 10, 1922) 2 Reels.
Jack Holt, Sylvia Breamer, Clarence Burton, Ann Schaeffer, Jean De Briac, Edwin Stevens
D: Joseph Henabery
SP: Julien Josephson
S: Hamilton Smith

ON THE HIGH SEAS (Famous Players-Lasky/Paramount, October 8, 1922) 6 Reels.
Jack Holt, Dorothy Dalton, Mitchell Lewis, Winter Hall, Michael Dark, Otto Brower, William Boyd, James Gordon, Alice Knowland, Vernon Tremaine
D: Irvin Willat
SP: E. Magnus Ingleton
S: Edward Brewster Sheldon

Newspaper ads such as this one brought out 1921 audiences and swelled the coffers of Paramount. That's Noah Beery and Madge Bellamy seen in the advertisement with Jack Holt.

MAKING A MAN (Famous Players-Lasky/Paramount, December 24, 1922) 6 Reels.
Jack Holt, J. P. Lockney, Eva Novak, Bert Woodruff, Frank Nelson, Robert Dudley
D: Joseph Henabery
SP: Albert Shelby
S: Peter B. Kyne

NOBODY'S MONEY (Famous Players-Lasky/Paramount, February 4, 1923) 6 Reels.
Jack Holt, Wanda Hawley, Harry Depp, Robert Schable, Walter McGrail, Josephine Crowell, Julia Faye, Charles Clary, Will R. Walling, Clarence Burton, Aileen Manning, James Neill
D: Wallace Worsley
S: William Le Baron

THE TIGER'S CLAW (Famous Players-Lasky/Paramount, March 23, 1923) 6 Reels.
Jack Holt, Eva Novak, George Periolat, Bertram Grassby, Aileen Pringle, Carl Stockdale, Frank Butler, George Field, Evelyn Selbie, Frederick Vroom, Lucien Littlefield, Robert Cain, Robert Dudley, "Robin Hood"
D: Joseph Henabery
S/SP: Jack Cunningham

Twenty years away from stardom herself, Jennifer Holt receives a kiss from her cowboy hero dad, Jack Holt (1923).

A GENTLEMAN OF LEISURE (Famous Players-Lasky/Paramount, August 5, 1923) 6 Reels.
Jack Holt, Casson Ferguson, Sigrid Holmquist, Alec Francis, Adele Farrington, Frank Nelson, Alfred Allen, Nadeen Paul, Alice Queensberry
D: Joseph Henabery
S: John Stapleton and Pelham Grenville Wodehouse

HOLLYWOOD (Famous Players-Lasky/Paramount, August 5, 1923) 8 Reels.
Hope Drown, Luke Cosgrave, George K. Arthur, Ruby Lafayette, Harris Gordon, Bess Flowers, Eleanor Lawson, King Zany, Roscoe Arbuckle, Gertrude Astor, Mary Ayres, Baby Peggy, T. Roy Barnes, Noah Beery, William Boyd, Clarence Burton, Robert Caine, Edythe Chapman, Betty Compson, Ricardo Cortez, Viola Dana, Cecil B. DeMille, William de Mille, Charles De Roche, Dinky Dean, Helen Dunbar, Snitz Edwards, George Fawcett, Julia Faye, James Finlayson, Alec Francis, Jack Gardner, Sid Grauman, Alfred E. Green, Alan Hale, Lloyd Hamilton, Hope Hampton, William S. Hart, Gale Henry, Walter Heirs, Mrs. Walter Heirs, Stuart Holmes, Sigrid Holmquist, *Jack Holt,* Leatrice Joy, Mayme Kelso, J. Warren Kerrigan, Theodore Kosloff, Kosloff Dancers, Lila Lee, Lillian Leighton, Jacqueline Logan, May McAvoy, Robert McKim, Jeanie MacPherson, Hank Mann, Joe Martin, Thomas Meighan, Bull Montana, Owen Moore, Nita Naldi, Pola Negri, Anna Q. Nilsson, Charles Ogle, Guy Oliver, Kalla Pasha, Eileen Percy, Carmen Phillips, Jack Pickford, Chuck Reisner, Fritzi Ridgeway, Will Rogers, Sennett Girls, Ford Sterling, Anita Stewart, George Stewart, Gloria Swanson, Estelle Taylor, Ben Turpin, Bryant Washburn, Maude Wayne, Claire West, Laurence Wheat, Lois Wilson
D: James Cruze
S: Frank Condon

THE CHEAT (Famous Players-Lasky/Paramount, September 2, 1923) 8 Reels.
Pola Negri, *Jack Holt,* Charles De Roche, Dorothy Cumming, Robert Schable, Charles Stevenson, Helen Dunbar, Richard Wayne, Guy Oliver, Edward Kimball
P/D: George Fitzmaurice
S: Hector Turnbull
Adapt: Ovida Bergere

THE MARRIAGE MAKER (Famous Players-Lasky/Paramount, September 9, 1923) 7 Reels.
Agnes Ayres, *Jack Holt,* Charles De Roche, Robert Agnew, Mary Astor, Ethel Wales, Bertram Johns
D: William de Mille
SP: Clara Beranger
S: Edward Knoblock

THE LONE WOLF (Associated Exhibitors, May 11, 1924) 6 Reels.
Jack Holt, Dorothy Dalton, Wilton Lackaye, Tyrone Power, Charlotte Walker, Lucy Fox, Edouard Durand, Robert T. Haines, Gustav von Seyffertitz, Alphonse Ethier, William Tooker, Paul McAllister
D: S. E. V. Taylor
S: Louis Joseph Vance
SP: S. E. V. Taylor

THE WANDERER OF THE WASTELAND (Famous Players-Lasky/Paramount, September 30, 1924) 73 Mins. (Technicolor)
Jack Holt, Noah Beery, Billie Dove, Kathlyn Williams, George Irving, James Mason, Richard R. Neill, James Gordon, William Carroll, Willard Cooley
D: Irvin Willat
SP: George C. Hull, Victor Irvin
S: Zane Grey

Jack Holt spending a little time with son Tim on location for a Paramount Western.

EMPTY HANDS (Famous Players-Lasky/Paramount, August 24, 1924) 7 Reels.
Jack Holt, Norma Shearer, Charles Clary, Hazel Keener, Gertrude Olmstead, Ramsey Wallace, Ward Crane, Charles Stevens, Hank Mann, Charles Green
D: Victor Fleming
SP: Carey Wilson
S: Arthur Stringer

NORTH OF 36 (Famous Players-Lasky/Paramount, December 7, 1924) 8 Reels.
Jack Holt, Ernest Torrence, Lois Wilson, Noah Beery, David Dunmar, Stephen Carr, Guy Oliver, William Carroll, Clarence Geldert, George Irving, Ella Miller
D: Irvin Willat
SP: James Shelley Hamilton
S: Emerson Hough

DON'T CALL IT LOVE (Famous Players-Lasky/Paramount, December 30, 1924) 7 Reels.
Agnes Ayres, *Jack Holt,* Nita Naldi, Theodore Kosloff, Rod La Rocque, Robert Edeson, Julia Faye
D: William C. de Mille
SP: Clara Beranger
S: Julian Leonard Street

THE THUNDERING HERD (Famous Players-Lasky/Paramount, March 1, 1925) 7 Reels.
Jack Holt, Lois Wilson, Noah Beery, Raymond Hatton, Charles Ogle, Colonel Tim McCoy, Lillian Leighton, Eulalie Jensen, Stephen Carr, Maxine Elliott Hicks, Edward J. Brady, Pat Hartigan, Fred Kohler, Robert Perry, Gary Cooper
D: William K. Howard
SP: Lucien Hubbard
S: Zane Grey

Jack Holt and Arlette Marchal in *Forlorn River* (Paramount, 1926).

EVE'S SECRET (Famous Players-Lasky/Paramount, June 21, 1925) 6 Reels.
Betty Compson, *Jack Holt,* William Collier, Jr., Vera Lewis, Lionel Belmore, Mario Carillo
D: Clarence Badger
SP: Adlaide Heilbron
S: Zoe Axins and Lajos Biro

THE LIGHT OF WESTERN STARS (Famous Players-Lasky/Paramount, July 26, 1925) 90 Mins.
Jack Holt, Billie Dove, Noah Beery, Alma Bennett, William Scott, George Nichols, Mark Hamilton, Robert Perry, Eugene Pallette
D: William K. Howard
SP: George C. Hull, Lucien Hubbard
S: Zane Grey

WILD HORSE MESA (Famous Players-Lasky/Paramount, August 16, 1925) 75 Mins.
Jack Holt, Noah Beery, Billie Dove, Douglas Fairbanks, Jr., George Magrill, George Irving, Edith Yorke, Bernard Siegel, Margaret Morris, Gary Cooper
D: George B. Seitz
SP: Lucien Hubbard
S: Zane Grey

THE ANCIENT HIGHWAY (Famous Players-Lasky/Paramount, November 22, 1925) 60 Mins.
Jack Holt, Billie Dove, Montagu Love, Stanley Taylor, Lloyd Whitlock, William A. Carroll, Marjorie Bonner, Christian J. Frank
D: Irvin Willat
SP: James Shelley Hamilton, Eve Unsell
S: James Oliver Curwood

THE ENCHANTED HILL (Famous Players-Lasky/Paramount, January 10, 1926) 68 Mins.
Jack Holt, Florence Vidor, Noah Beery, Mary Brian, Richard Arlen, George Bancroft, Ray Thompson, Brandon Hurst, Henry Herbert, George Kuwa, Mathilde Comont, Willard Colley, George Magrill, Gary Cooper
D: Irvin Willat
SP: James Shelley Hamilton
S: Peter B. Kyne

SEA HORSES (Famous Players-Lasky/Paramount, March 7, 1926) 7 Reels.
Jack Holt, Florence Vidor, William Powell, George Bancroft, Mack Swain, Frank Campeau, Allan Simpson, George Nichols, Mary Dow, Dick La Reno, Frank Austin
P/D: Allan Dwan
SP: James Shelley Hamilton
Adapt: Becky Gardiner
S: Francis Brett Young

THE BLIND GODDESS (Famous Players-Lasky/Paramount, April 12, 1926) 8 Reels.
Jack Holt, Esther Ralston, Ernest Torrence, Louise Dresser, Ward Crane, Richard Tucker, Louis Payne, Charles Clary, Erwin Connelly, Charles Laine
D: Victor Fleming
SP: Gertrude Orr
S: Arthur Chesney Train

MAN OF THE FOREST (Famous Players-Lasky/Paramount, July 14, 1926) 6 Reels.
Jack Holt, Georgia Hale, El Brendel, Warner Oland, Tom Kennedy, George Fawcett, Ivan Christie, Bruce Gordon, Vester Pegg, Willard Colley, Guy Oliver, Walter Ackerman, Duke R. Lee
D: John Waters
SP: Fred Myton
S: Zane Grey

BORN TO THE WEST (Famous Players-Lasky/Paramount, August 15, 1926) 6 Reels.
Jack Holt, Margaret Morris, Raymond Hatton, Arlette Marchal, George Seigmann, Bruce Gordon, William A. Carroll, Tom Kennedy, Richard Neill, Edith Yorke, E. Allyn Warren, Billy Aber, Jean Johnson, Joe Butterworth
D: John Waters
SP: Lucien Hubbard
S: Zane Grey

FORLORN RIVER (Famous Players-Lasky/Paramount, September 19, 1926) 6 Reels.
Jack Holt, Raymond Hatton, Arlette Marchal, Edmund Burns, Tom Santschi, Joseph Girard, Christian J. Frank, Albert Hart, Nola Luxford, Chief Yowlache, Jack Moore
D: John Waters
SP: George C. Hull
S: Zane Grey

Jack Holt, Tom Kennedy, and players in *The Mysterious Rider* (Paramount, 1927).

THE MYSTERIOUS RIDER (Famous Players-Lasky/ Paramount, March 27, 1927) 6 Reels.
Jack Holt, Betty Jewel, Charles Sellon, David Torrence, Tom Kennedy, Guy Oliver, Albert Hart, Ivan Christie, Arthur Hoyt
D: John Waters
SP: Fred Myton, Paul Gangelin
S: Zane Grey

THE TIGRESS (Columbia, December 11, 1927) 54 Mins.
Jack Holt, Dorothy Revier, Frank Leigh, Philipee De Lacy, Howard Truesdell, Frank Nelson
D: George B. Seitz
SP: Harold Shumate

THE WARNING (Columbia, January 8, 1928) 6 Reels.
Jack Holt, Dorothy Revier, Frank Lackteen, Pat Harmon, Eugene Strong, George Kuwa, Norman Trevor
D: George B. Seitz
S: Lillian Ducey, H. Milner Kitchin

THE SMART SET (Metro-Goldwyn-Mayer, March 24, 1928) 7 Reels.
William Haines, *Jack Holt,* Alice Day, Hobart Bosworth, Coy Watson, Jr., Constance Howard, Paul Nicholson, Julia Swayne Gordon
D: Jack Conway
SP/S: Byron Morgan

Dorothy Revier and Jack Holt each scored big in *Submarine* (Columbia, 1928) and were often cast together as a romantic team.

THE VANISHING PIONEER (Famous Players-Lasky/Paramount, August 12, 1928) 6 Reels.
Jack Holt, Sally Blane, William Powell, Fred Kohler, Guy Oliver, Roscoe Karns, Tim Holt, Marcia Manon
D: John Waters
Scen: J. Walter Ruben
Adapt: John Goodrich, Ray Harris
S: Zane Grey (An Original Screenplay)

SUBMARINE (Columbia, September 2, 1928) 108 Mins.
(Some Sound Effects)
Jack Holt, Dorothy Revier, Ralph Graves, Clarence Burton, Arthur Rankin
D: Frank R. Capra
Cont: Dorothy Howell
Adapt: W. Dunn
S: Norman Springer
P: Irvin Willat

THE WATER HOLE (Famous Players-Lasky/Paramount, September 9, 1928) 7 Reels.
Jack Holt, Nancy Carroll, John Boles, Montague Shaw, Ann Cristy, Lydia Yeamans Titus, Jack Perrin, Jack Mower, Paul Ralli, Tex Young, Bob Miles, Greg Whitespear
D: F. Richard Jones
S: Zane Grey
P: F. Richard Jones
(Some Technicolor sequences)

AVALANCHE (Famous Players-Lasky/Paramount, December 9, 1928) 6 Reels.
Jack Holt, Doris Hill, Olga Baclanova, John Darrow, Guy Oliver, Dick Winslow, Dorothy Daw
D: Otto Brower
SP: Sam Mintz, Herman Mankiewicz, J. Walter Ruben
S: Zane Grey

COURT-MARTIAL (Columbia, December 28, 1928) 7 Reels.
Jack Holt, Betty Compson, Pat Harmon, Doris Hill, Frank Lackteen, Frank Austin, George Cowl, Zack Williams
D: George B. Seitz
S: Elmer Harris
Cont: Anthony Coldeway
P: Harry Cohn

SUNSET PASS (Paramount/Famous-Lasky Corp., March 4, 1929) 6 Reels.
Jack Holt, Nora Lane, John Loder, Christian J. Frank, Pee Wee Holmes, Chester Conklin, Pat Harmon, Alfred Allen, Guy Oliver, James Mason
D: Otto Brower
SP: J. Walter Ruben, Ray Harris
S: Zane Grey

THE DONOVAN AFFAIR (Columbia, May 5, 1929) 8 Reels.
(Columbia's first all-talking picture)
Jack Holt, Dorothy Revier, William Collier, Jr., Agnes Ayres, John Roche, Fred Kelsey, Hank Mann, Wheeler Oakman, Virginia Browne Faire, Alphonse Ethier, Edward Hearn, Ethel Wales, John Wallace
D: Frank R. Capra
SP: Dorothy Howell
S: Owen Davis

FATHER AND SON (Columbia, June 9, 1929) 7 Reels.
(Talking sequences, music score, sound effects)
Jack Holt, Dorothy Revier, Helen Chadwick, Mickey McBan, Wheeler Oakman
D: Erle C. Kenton
S: Elmer Harris
Cont: Jack Townley
P: Harry Cohn

FLIGHT (Columbia, December 4, 1929) 12 Reels.
(Columbia's first outdoor sound picture)
Jack Holt, Lila Lee, Ralph Graves, Alan Roscoe, Harold Goodwin, Jimmy De La Cruze
D: Frank R. Capra
Scen: Howard J. Green
S: Ralph Graves
P: Harry Cohn
C: Elmer Dyer and Joe Novak

VENGEANCE (Columbia, March 9, 1930) 7 Reels.
Jack Holt, Dorothy Revier, Philip Strange, George Pearce, Hayden Stevenson, Irma Harrison, Onest Conly
D: Archie Mayo
Cont: F. Hugh Herbert
S: Ralph Graves
P: Harry Cohn

THE BORDER LEGION (Paramount/Publix Corp., June 28, 1930) 8 Reels.
Jack Holt, Richard Arlen, Fay Wray, Eugene Pallette, Stanley Fields, E. H. Calvert, Ethan Allen, Sid Saylor
D: Otto Brower, Edwin H. Knopf
SP: Percy Heath, Edward E. Paramore, Jr.
S: Zane Grey

HELL'S ISLAND (Columbia, July 20, 1930) 8 Reels.
Jack Holt, Ralph Graves, Dorothy Sebastian, Richard Cramer, Harry Allen, Lionel Belmore, Otto Lang, Carl Stockdale
D: Edward Sloman
S: Thomas Buckingham
Adapt/Cont: Jo Swerling
P: Harry Cohn

THE SQUEALER (Columbia, September 14, 1930) 65 Mins.
Jack Holt, Dorothy Revier, Davey Lee, Matt Moore, ZaSu Pitts, Robert Ellis, Mathew Betz, Arthur Housman, Louis Natheaux, Eddie Kane, Eddie Sturgis, Elmer Ballard
D: Harry J. Brown
SP: Dorothy Howell
Cont: Casey Robinson
S: Mark Linder
P: Harry Cohn

THE LAST PARADE (Columbia, March 1, 1931) 9 Reels.
Jack Holt, Tom Moore, Constance Cummings, Edmund Breese, Clarence Muse, Gino Corrado, Gaylord Pendleton, Robert Ellis, Ed Le Saint, Earl D. Bunn, Robert Graham
D: Erle C. Kenton
SP: Dorothy Howell
S: Casey Robinson
P: Jack Cohn

SUBWAY EXPRESS (Columbia, March 29, 1931) 7 Reels.
Jack Holt, Aileen Pringle, Jason Robards, Sr., Fred Kelsey, Alan Roscoe, Sidney Macy, Selmer Jackson, Lillianne Leighton, James Goss, Marston Williams, Harry Semeles, Robert S. Angelo, John Kelly
D: Fred Newmeyer
Adapt: Earl Snell
S: EvaKay Flint (Eva Finklestein) and Martha Madison (Martha O'Dwyer)

DIRIGIBLE (Columbia, April 12, 1931) 100 Mins.
Jack Holt, Ralph Graves, Fay Wray, Hobart Bosworth, Roscoe Karns, Clarence Muse, Harold Goodwin, Emmet Corrigan, Al Roscoe, Selmar Jackson
D: Frank R. Capra
Adapt: Jo Swerling
Cont: Dorothy Howell
S: Frank Wilber Wead
Aerial C: Elmer Dyer
P: Harry Cohn

WHITE SHOULDERS (RKO, June 6, 1931) 9 Reels.
Jack Holt, Mary Astor, Ricardo Cortez, Sidney Toler, Kitty Kelly
D: Melville Brown
Adapt: J. Walter Ruben
AD: Henry Hobart
S: Rex Beach

FIFTY FATHOMS DEEP (Columbia, August 16, 1931) 7 Reels.
Jack Holt, Mary Doran, Richard Cromwell, Loretta Sayers, Wallace MacDonald, Mary Doran, Christina Monti, Henry Mowbray
D: Roy W. Neill
S/SP: Dorothy Howell

A DANGEROUS AFFAIR (Columbia, September 30, 1931) 8 Reels.
Jack Holt, Ralph Graves, Sally Blane, Susan Fleming, Edward Brophy, William V. Mong, Charles Middleton, Blanche Fredericki, DeWitt Jennings, Tyler Brooks, Fred Santley, Sidney Bracy, Ester Muir
D: Edward Sedgwick
S: Howard J. Green

MAKER OF MEN (Columbia, December 20, 1931) 7 Reels.
Jack Holt, Richard Cromwell, Joan Marsh, Natalie Moorhead, Walter Catlett, John Wayne, Robert Alden, Richard Tucker, Ethel Wales, Buster Crabbe
D: Edward Sedgwick
SP: Howard J. Green, Edward Sedgwick
S: Howard J. Green

BEHIND THE MASK (Columbia, February 25, 1932) 7 Reels.
Jack Holt, Constance Cummings, Boris Karloff, Claude King, Bertha Mann, Edward Van Sloan, Willard Robertson
D: John F. Dillon
S/Adapt: Jo Swerling
Cont: Dorothy Howell

WAR CORRESPONDENT (Columbia, August 13, 1932) 77 Mins.
Jack Holt, Lila Lee, Ralph Graves, Victor Wong, Tetsu Komai
D: Paul Sloane
Adapt: Jo Swerling
S: Keene Thompson

THIS SPORTING AGE (Columbia, October 1, 1932) 7 Reels.
Jack Holt, Evalyn Knapp, Hardie Albright, Walter Byron, J. Farrell MacDonald, Ruth Westan, Nora Lane, Shirley Palmer, Hal Price
D: Andrew Bennison and A. F. Erickson
S: James Kevin McGuinness
Adapt: Dudley Nichols

MAN AGAINST WOMAN (Columbia, December 17, 1932) 7 Reels.
Jack Holt, Lillian Miles, Walter Connally, Gavin Gordon, Arthur Vinton, Jack LaRue, Clarence Muse, Emmett Corrigan, Harry Seymour, Katherine Claire Ward
D: Irving Cummings
SP: Jo Swerling
S: Keene Thompson

MASTER OF MEN (Columbia, May 25, 1933) 8 Reels.
Jack Holt, Fay Wray, Walter Connally, Berton Churchill, Theodore Von Eltz
D: Lambert Hillyer
SP: Edward Paramore, Seton I. Miller
S: Chester Erskin, Eugene Solow

WHEN STRANGERS MARRY (Columbia, May 25, 1933) 7 Reels.
Jack Holt, Lillian Bond, Arthur Vinton, Barbara Barondess, Ward Bond, Paul Porcasi, Gustav Von Seffertitz, Rudolph Amendt, Charles Stevens
D: Clarence Badger
SP: James Kevin McGuinness
S: Maximilian Foster

THE WOMAN I STOLE (Columbia, June 30, 1933) 7 Reels. (Originally released as TAMPICO)
Jack Holt, Fay Wray, Noah Beery, Sr., Donald Cook, Raquel Torres, Edwin Maxwell, Ferdinand Munier, Charles Browne, Lee Phelps
D: Irving Cummings
SP: Jo Swerling
S: Joseph Hergesheimer—"Tampico"

THE WRECKER (Columbia, August 5, 1933) 8 Reels.
Jack Holt, Genevieve Tobin, George F. Stone, Sidney Blackmer, Ward Bond, Irene White, Russell Waddle, Wally Albright, Edward LeSaint, Clarence Muse
D: Albert Rogell
SP: Jo Swerling
S: Albert Rogell

BLACK MOON (Columbia, June 28, 1934) 7 Reels.
Jack Holt, Fay Wray, Dorothy Burgess, Clarence Muse, Cora Sue Collins, Eleanor Wesselhoeft, Madame Sul-te-wan, Lawrence Criner, Lumsden Hare
D: Roy W. Neill
SP: Wells Root
S: Clements Ripley
AP: Everett Riskin

THE WHIRLPOOL (Columbia, July 29, 1934) 8 Reels.
Jack Holt, Jean Arthur, Lila Lee, Rita LaRoy, Donald Cook, John Miljan, Ward Bond, Allen Jenkins, Willard Robertson
D: Roy W. Neill
SP: Dorothy Howell, Ethel Hill
S: Howard Emmet Rogers

THE DEFENSE RESTS (Columbia, August 15, 1934) 7 Reels.
Jack Holt, Jean Arthur, Harold Huber, Shirley Grey, Nat Pendleton, Arthur Hohl, Raymond Hatton, John Wray, Raymond Walburn, Robert Glecker, Sara Padden, Shirley Grey, Donald Meek, Vivian Oakland, Selmer Jackson, J. Carrol Naish, Samuel S. Hinds
D: Lambert Hillyer
S/SP: Jo Swerling

I'LL FIX IT (Columbia, November 10, 1934) 7 Reels.
Jack Holt, Mona Barrie, Ed Brophy, Winnie Lightner, John Wray, Jimmy Butler, Charles Moore, Edward Van Sloan, Clarence Wilson, Selmer Jackson, Harry Holman, Robert Gunn, Dorian Johnson, Wallis Clark
D: Roy W. Neill
SP: Ethel Hill, Dorothy Howell
S: Leonard Spigelgass

THE BEST MAN WINS (Columbia, January 2, 1935) 7 Reels.
Jack Holt, Florence Rice, Edmund Lowe, Bela Lugosi, J. Farrell MacDonald, Forrester Harvey, Bradley Page, Mitchell Lewis, Frank Sheridan
D: Erle C. Kenton, E. Roy Davidson
SP: Ethel Hill, Bruce Manning
S: Ben G. Kohn

UNWELCOME STRANGER (Columbia, April 6, 1935) 64 Mins.
Jack Holt, Mona Barrie, Jackie Searl, Ralph Morgan, Frankie Darro, Bradley Page, Sam McDaniel, Frank Orth
D: Phil Rosen
SP: Crane Wilbur
S: William Jacobs

THE AWAKENING OF JIM BURKE (Columbia, May 18, 1935) 65 Mins.
Jack Holt, Florence Rice, Kathleen Burke, Jimmie Butler, Robert Middlemass, Wyrley Birch, George McKay, Ralph M. Remley, Frank Yaconelli
D: Lambert Hillyer
S/SP: Michael Simmons

HOLLYWOOD HOBBIES
(Paramount, July 5, 1935) 10 Mins.
Richard Arlen, Boris Karloff, Charles Farrell, *Jack Holt,* Buster Crabbe, Clark Gable, James Gleason, Guy Kibbee, Walter Huston, Grantland Rice
P: Grantland Rice
Narrator: Ted Husing

Florence Rice and Jack Holt in *The Awakening of Jim Burke* (Columbia, 1935), a typical Holt thriller.

STORM OVER THE ANDES (Universal, September 25, 1935) 9 Reels.
Jack Holt, Mona Barrie, Antonio Moreno, Gene Lockhart, Grant Withers, Barry Norton, George J. Lewis, Juanita Garfias, Alma Real, Lucia Villegas, Juanita Quigley, June Gittelson
D: Christy Cabanne
SP: Albert De Mond, Frank Wead, Eve Green
S: Eliot Gibbons, La Clade Christy
AP: Maurice Pivar

THE LITTLEST REBEL (Fox, November 22, 1935) 6,618 ft.
Shirley Temple, John Boles, *Jack Holt,* Karen Morely, Bill Robinson, Guinn "Big Boy" Williams, Willie Best, Frank McGlynn, Sr., Bessie Lyle, Hannah Washington, James Flavin
D: David Butler
SP: Edwin Burke
S: Edward Peple

DANGEROUS WATERS (Universal, January 23, 1936) 7 Reels.
Jack Holt, Robert Armstrong, Grace Bradley, Willard Robertson, Ed Gargan, Diana Gibson, Charlie Murray, Dewey Robinson, Guy Usher, Richard Alexander, Billy Gilbert, Edwin Maxwell
D: Lambert Hillyer
SP: Richard Schayer, Hazel Jamieson, Malcolm Stuart Boylan
S: Theodore Reeves—"Glory Hole"
P: Fred S. Meyer

SAN FRANCISCO (Metro-Goldwyn-Mayer, June 26, 1936) 12 Reels.
Clark Gable, Spencer Tracy, Jeannette MacDonald, *Jack Holt,* Ted Healy, Margaret Irving, Jesse Ralph, Harold Huber, Al Shean, Kenneth Harlan, Roger Imhof, Frank Mayo, Tom Dugan, Charles Judels, Russell Simpson, Bert Roach, Warren Hymer, Edgar Kennedy, Gertrude Alton, Jason Robards, Sr., Vernon Dent, Carl Stockdale, Ralph Lewis, Chester Gan, Jack Kennedy, Cy Kendall, Don Rowan
D: W. S. Van Dyke
S: Robert Hopkins
SP: Anita Loos
P: W. S. Van Dyke, John Emerson, Bernard H. Hyman

CRASH DONOVAN (Universal, August 11, 1936) 6 Reels.
Jack Holt, Nan Grey, Ward Bond, John King, Eddie Acuff, Hugh Buckler, Douglas Fowley, William Tannen, Huey White, Al Hill, Gardner James, Paul Porcasi, Joe Sawyer
D: William Nigh
SP: Eugene Solow, Charles Grayson, Karl Detzer
S: Harold Shumate
AP: Julius Bernheim

END OF THE TRAIL (Columbia, October 31, 1936) 70 Mins.
Jack Holt, Louise Henry, Douglass Dumbrille, Guinn "Big Boy" Williams, George McKay, Gene Morgan, John McGuire, Edward J. LeSaint, Frank Shannon, Erle C. Kenton, Hank Bell, Art Mix, Blackie Whiteford, Blackjack Ward, Edgar Dearing
D: Erle C. Kenton
SP: Harold Shumate
S: Zane Grey—"Outlaws of Palouse" (Also published as "The Horse Thieves")

NORTH OF NOME (Columbia, October 28, 1936) 63 Mins.
Jack Holt, Evelyn Venable, Guinn "Big Boy" Williams, John Miljan, Roger Imhof, Dorothy Appleby, Paul Hurst, Frank McGlynn, Robert Glecker, Ben Hendricks, Mike Morita, George Cleveland, Blackhawk
D: William Nigh
S: Houston Branch
SP: Albert DeMond
P: Larry Darmour

TROUBLE IN MOROCCO (Columbia, March 9, 1937) 7 Reels.
Jack Holt, Mae Clarke, Harold Huber, C. Henry Gordon, Victor Varconi, Paul Hurst
D: Ernest B. Schoedsack
S: J. D. Newsom
SP/Adapt: Paul Franklin
P: Larry Darmour

Guinn (Big Boy) Williams, Louise Henry, and Jack
Holt in a tear-jerker scene from *End of the Trail* (Columbia,
1936).

ROARING TIMBER (Columbia, July 4, 1937) 65 Mins.
Jack Holt, Grace Bradley, Ruth Donnelly, Raymond Hatton,
Willard Robertson, J. Farrell MacDonald, Charles Wilson,
Fred Kohler, Jr., Tom London, Ernest Wood, Philip Ahn,
Ben Hendricks
D: Phil Rosen
S: Robert James Cosgriff
SP: Paul Franklin, Robert James Cosgriff
P: Larry Darmour

OUTLAWS OF THE ORIENT (Columbia, August 20,
1937) 7 Reels.
Jack Holt, Mae Clarke, Harold Huber, Ray Walker, James
Bush, Joe Crehan, Bernice Roberts, Harry Worth
D: Ernest B. Schoedsack
S: Ralph Graves
SP: Charles Francis Royal, Paul Franklin

TRAPPED BY G-MEN (Columbia, September 9, 1937)
65 Mins.
(Also released briefly as THE RIVER OF MISSING MEN)
Jack Holt, Wynne Gibson, Jack LaRue, Ed Brophy, C. Henry
Gordon, Arthur Hohl, Robert Emmett O'Connor, William
Bakewell, William Pawley, Eleanor Stewart, Charles Lane,
Frank Darien, Lucian Prival, Richard Tucker, Wallis Clark,
George Cleveland
D: Lewis D. Collins
SP: Tom Kilpatrick
S: Bernard McConville
P: Larry Darmour

UNDER SUSPICION (Columbia, November 22, 1937)
7 Reels.
Jack Holt, Katherine De Mille, Luis Alberni, Purnell Pratt, Rosalind Keith, Esther Muir, Maurice Murphy, Morgan Wallace, Granville Bates, Craig Reynolds, Robert Emmett Keane, Margaret Irving, Clyde Dilson, George Anderson
D: Lewis D. Collins
SP: Joseph Hoffman, Jefferson Parker
S: Philip Wylie
P: Larry Darmour

MAKING THE HEADLINES (Columbia, March 10, 1938)
60 Mins.
(Also released briefly under title HOUSE OF MYSTERY)
Jack Holt, Beverly Roberts, Craig Reynolds, Marjorie Gateson, Dorothy Appleby, Gilbert Emery, Tom Kennedy, Corbet Morris, Sheila Bromley, John Wray, Maurice Cass, Tully Marshall
D: Lewis D. Collins
SP: Jefferson Parker, Howard J. Green
S: Howard J. Green
P: Larry Darmour

FLIGHT INTO NOWHERE (Columbia, April 19, 1938)
63 Mins.
Jack Holt, Jacqueline Wells, Dick Purcell, James Burke, Karen Sorrell, Fritz Leiber, Howard Hickman, Robert Fiske, Hector Sarno
D: Lewis D. Collins
SP: Jefferson Parker, Gordon Rigby
S: William Bloom, Clarence Jay Schneider
P: Larry Darmour

CRIME TAKES A HOLIDAY (Columbia, May 9, 1938)
61 Mins.
Jack Holt, Marcia Ralston, Paul Fix, Arthur Hohl, Thomas Jackson, John Wray, Douglass Dumbrille, Russell Hopton, William Pawley, Harry Woods, Joe Crehan
D: Lewis D. Collins
SP: Jefferson Parker, Henry Altimus, Charles Logue
S: Henry Altimus
P: Larry Darmour

REFORMATORY (Columbia, July 21, 1938) 59 Mins.
Jack Holt, Bobby Jordan, Ward Bond, Frankie Darro, Grant Mitchell, Charlotte Winter, Tommy Bupp, Sheila Bromley, Paul Everton, Lloyd Ingraham, Joe Caits, Robert Emmett Keane, Vernon Dent, Greta Granstedt, Guy Usher, Al Bridges, Kent Rogers, John Wray
D: Lewis D. Collins
SP/S: Gordon Rigby

THE STRANGE CASE OF DR. MEADE (Columbia, October 26, 1938) 66 Mins.
(Originally released as OUTSIDE THE LAW)
Jack Holt, Beverly Roberts, Noah Beery, Jr., John Qualen, Paul Everton, Charles Middleton, Helen Jerome Eddy, Arthur Aylesworth, Barbara Pepper, Vic Potel
D: Lewis D. Collins
SP: Gordon Rigby
S: Gordon Rigby, Carleton Sand
P: Larry Darmour

TRAPPED IN THE SKY (Columbia, February 16, 1939)
60 Mins.
Jack Holt, Katherine DeMille, Sidney Blackmer, C. Henry Gordon, Ralph Morgan, Ivan Lebedeff, Paul Everton, Regis Toomey, Holmes Herbert
D: Lewis D. Collins
SP: Eric Taylor, Gordon Rigby
P: Larry Darmour

WHISPERING ENEMIES (Columbia, March 24, 1939)
62 Mins.
Jack Holt, Dolores Costello, Addison Richards, Joseph Crehan, Donald Briggs, Bert Kelton, Paul Everton
D: Lewis D. Collins
S: John Rawlins, Harold Tarshis
SP: Gordon Rigby, Tom Kilpatrick
P: Larry Darmour

FUGITIVE AT LARGE (Columbia, August 22, 1939)
63 Mins.
Jack Holt, Patricia Ellis, Stanley Fields, Arthur Hohl, Leon Ames, Cy Kendall, Weldon Heyburn, Guinn "Big Boy" Williams, Jonathan Hale, Don Douglas, Ben Welden, Leon Beaumont
D: Lewis D. Collins
S: Eric Taylor
SP: Eric Taylor and Harvey Gates
P: Larry Darmour

HIDDEN POWER (Columbia, September 7, 1939) 59 Mins.
Jack Holt, Gertrude Michael, Dickie Moore, Henry Kolker, Regis Toomey, William B. Davidson, Helen Browne, Marilyn Knowden, Harry Hayden, Holmes Herbert, Christian Rub
D: Lewis D. Collins
S/SP: Gordon Rigby
P: Larry Darmour

OUTSIDE THE THREE-MILE LIMIT (Columbia, March 7, 1940) 64 Mins.
Jack Holt, Irene Ware, Harry Carey, Eduardo Cianelli, Paul Fix, Dick Purcell, Sig Ruman, Donald Briggs, Ben Welden, George J. Lewis
D: Lewis D. Collins
SP: Albert DeMond
S: Eric Taylor, Albert DeMond
P: Larry Darmour

Jack Holt in the chapter play *Holt of the Secret Service* (Columbia, 1941). A quarter of a century had elapsed since he starred in the first Western serial ever made, *Liberty* (Universal, 1916).

PASSPORT TO ALCATRAZ (Columbia, June 6, 1940) 60 Mins.
Jack Holt, Noah Beery, Jr., Ivan Lebedeff, Cecilia Callejo, Maxie Rosenblum, C. Henry Gordon, Guy Usher, Clay Clement, Ben Welden, Robert Fiske, Harry Cording
D: Lewis D. Collins
S: Eric Taylor, Albert DeMond
SP: Albert DeMond
P: Larry Darmour

FUGITIVE FROM A PRISON CAMP (Columbia, August 6, 1940) 58 Mins.
(Also Released as PRISON CAMP)
Jack Holt, Marian Marsh, Jack LaRue, Robert Barratt, Phillip Terry, Dennis Moore, George Offerman, Jr., Fankie Burke, Donald Haines, Alan Baldwin, Frank LaRue, Ernest Morrison
D: Lewis D. Collins
S: Stanley Roberts, Albert DeMond
SP: Albert DeMond
P: Larry Darmour

THE GREAT PLANE ROBBERY (Columbia, December 9, 1940) 59 Mins.
Jack Holt, Stanley Fields, Paul Fix, Milburn Stone, Vicki Lester, Noel Madison, Theodore Von Eltz, Hobart Cavanaugh, Lane Chandler, Doris Lloyd, Harry Cording, John Hamilton, Granville Owen (Jeff York)
D: Lewis D. Collins
S: Harold Green, Albert DeMond
SP: Albert DeMond
P: Larry Darmour

THE GREAT SWINDLE (Columbia, April 10, 1941) 58 Mins.
Jack Holt, Jonathan Hale, Marjorie Reynolds, Sidney Blackmer, Douglas Fowley, Tom Kennedy, Henry Kolker, Don Douglas, Boyd Irwin
D: Lewis D. Collins
S: Eric Taylor
SP: Albert DeMond
P: Larry Darmour

HOLT OF THE SECRET SERVICE (Columbia, 1941) 15 Chapters
Jack Holt, Evelyn Brent, Montague Shaw, Tristram Coffin, John Ward, Ted Adams, Joe McGuinn, Edward Hearn, Ray Parsons, Jack Cheatham
D: James W. Horne
SP: Basil Dickey, George Plympton, Wyndham Gittens
P: Larry Darmour
Chapter Titles: (1) Chaotic Creek, (2) Ramparts of Revenge, (3) Illicit Wealth, (4) Menaced by Fate, (5) Exits to Terror, (6) Deadly Doom, (7) Out of the Past, (8) Escape to Peril, (9) Sealed in Silence, (10) Named to Die, (11) Ominous Warnings, (12) The Stolen Signal, (13) Prison of Jeopardy, (14) Afire Afloat, (15) Yielded Hostage

THUNDER BIRDS (Fox, October 19, 1942).
Gene Tierney, Preston Foster, Dame May Whitty, John Sutton, *Jack Holt*, Iris Adrian, Reginald Denny, George Barbier, Richard Haydn, Ted North, Janis Carter, Joyce Compton, Peter Lawford, Montagu Shaw, Viola Moore, Nana Bryant, Bess Flowers, Selmer Jackson, Charles Tannen, Harry Strang, Walter Tetley
D: William Wellman
S: Melville Crossman (Darryl F. Zanuck)
SP: Lamar Trotti
P: Lamar Trotti

NORTHWEST RANGERS (Metro-Goldwyn-Mayer, December 1, 1942) 64 Mins.
James Craig, William Lundigan, Patricia Dane, John Carradine, *Jack Holt*, Keenan Wynn, Grant Withers, Darryl Hickman, Drew Roddy
D: Joe Newman
S: Arthur Caesar
SP: Gordon Kahn
P: Samuel Marx

THE CAT PEOPLE (RKO, November 16, 1942) 73 Mins.
Simone Simon, Tom Conway, Kent Smith, *Jack Holt*, Jane
Randolph, Alan Napier, Elizabeth Russell, Alec Craig,
Elizabeth Donne, Mary Halsey, Dot Farley, Teresa Harris,
Charles Jordan, Betty Roadman, Don Kerr
D: Jacques Tournier
SP: DeWitt Bodeen
P: Val Lewton

CUSTOMS OF THE SERVICE (U.S. Army Signal Corps.,
1943) 40 Mins.
Jack Holt

THE ARTICLES OF WAR (U.S. Army Signal Corps., 1944)
30 Mins.
Jack Holt

THEY WERE EXPENDABLE (Metro-Golden-Mayer,
November 23, 1945) 136 Mins.
Robert Montgomery, John Wayne, Donna Reed, *Jack Holt*,
Marshall Thompson, Paul Langton, Leon Ames, Arthur
Walsh, Donald Curtis, Cameron Mitchell, Jeff York, Harry
Tenbrook, Jack Pennick, Charles Trowbridge, Robert Barrat,
Bruce Kellogg, Russell Simpson, Tom Tyler, Sammy Stein,
William Davidson, Kermit Maynard, Tim Murdock, Louis
Jean Heydt, Lee Tung Foo, Vernon Steele, Robert Emmett
O'Connor, Alex Havier, Pedro De Cordoba, Betty Blythe,
Blake Edwards, Philip Ahn
D: John Ford
SP: Commander Frank Wead
S: William L. White
P: John Ford

MY PAL TRIGGER (Republic, July 10, 1946) 79 Mins.
Roy Rogers, George F. Hayes, Dale Evans, *Jack Holt*, Bob
Nolan and the Sons of the Pioneers, LeRoy Mason, Roy
Barcroft, Sam Flint, Kenne Duncan, Ralph Sanford, Francis
McDonald, Harlan Briggs, William Haade, Alan Bridge,
Paul E. Burns, Frank Reicher, Fred Graham, Ted Mapes,
"Trigger"
D: Frank McDonald
S: Paul Gangelin
SP: Jack Townley, John K. Butler
AP: Armand Schaefer

THE CHASE (United Artists, October 15, 1946) 86 Mins.
Robert Cummings, Michele Morgan, Peter Lorre, Steve
Cochran, Lloyd Corrigan, *Jack Holt*, Don Wilson, Alexis
Minotis, Nina Koshetz, Yolanda Lacca, James Westerfield,
Shirley O'Hara
D: Arthur Ripley
SP: Philip Yordan
S: Cornell Woolrich
P: Seymour Nebenzal

RENEGADE GIRL (Affiliated/Screen Guild, December 25,
1946) 65 Mins.
Alan Curtis, Ann Savage, Edward Brophy, Russell Wade,
Jack Holt, Ray Corrigan, John King, Chief Thunder Cloud,
Edmund Cobb, Claudia Drake, Dick Curtis, Nick Thompson,
James Martin, Harry Cording, Kermit Maynard
D/P: William Berke
SP: Edwin K. Westrate

FLIGHT TO NOWHERE (Screen Guild, July 1947) 65 Mins.
Alan Curtis, Evelyn Ankers, Michaline Cheirel, *Jack Holt*,
Jerome Cowan, John Craven, Inez Cooper, Roland Varno,
Michael Visaroff, Goordon Richards, Hoot Gibson
D: William Rowland
SP: Arthur V. Jones
P: Wiliam B. David

THE WILD FRONTIER (Republic, October 1, 1947)
59 Mins.
Allan Lane, *Jack Holt*, Eddy Waller, Pierre Watkin, John
James, Roy Barcroft, Budd Buster, Wheaton Chambers, Tom
London, Sam Flint, Ted Mapes, Bob Burns, Art Dillard, Silver
Harr, Bud McClure
D: Philip Ford
SP: Albert DeMond
AP: Gordon Kay

THE TREASURE OF SIERRA MADRE (Warner Brothers,
January 24, 1948) 127 Mins.
Humphrey Bogart, Tim Holt, Walter Huston, Barton Mac-
Lane, Bruce Bennett, Alfonso Bedoya, Jacqualine Dalya,
Bobby Blake (later Robert Blake), Julian Rivero, John
Houston, Harry Vejar, Pat Flaherty, Martin Garralaga,
Clifton Young, Ralph Dunn, A. Soto Rangel, Manuel Donde,
Jose Torvay, Margarito Luna, and with cameo roles by
Ann Sheridan and *Jack Holt*
D/SP: John Huston
S: B. Traven
P: Henry Blanke
Music Score: Max Steiner

THE ARIZONA RANGER (RKO, May 18, 1948) 63 Mins.
Tim Holt, *Jack Holt*, Nan Leslie, Richard Martin, Steve
Brodie, Paul Hurst, Jim Nolan, Robert Bray, Richard Bene-
dict, William Phipps, Harry Harvey
D: John Rawlins
SP: Norman Houston
P: Herman Schlom

THE GALLANT LEGION (Republic, May 24, 1948) 88
Mins.
William (Bill) Elliott, Adrian Booth, Joseph Schildkraut,
Bruce Cabot, Andy Devine, *Jack Holt*, Grant Withers, Adele
Mara, James Brown, Hal Landon, Max Terry, Lester Sharpe,
Hal Taliaferro, Russell Hicks, Herbert Rawlinson, Marshall

Reed, Steve Drake, Harry Woods, Roy Barcroft, Bud Osborne, Hank Bell, Jack Ingram, George Chesebro, Rex Lease, Noble Johnson, Emmett Vogan, John Hamilton, Trevor Bardette, Gene Stutenroth, Ferris Taylor, Iron Eyes Cody, Kermit Maynard, Jack Kirk, Merrill McCormack, Augie Gomez, Cactus Mack, Fred Kohler, Glenn Strange, Tex Terry, Joseph Crehan, Peter Perkins, Jack Perrin
D/AP: Joseph Kane
S: John K. Butler, Gerald Geraghty
SP: Gerald Adams

THE STRAWBERRY ROAN (Columbia, August 15, 1948) 79 Mins.
(Cinecolor)
Gene Autry, Gloria Henry, *Jack Holt*, Dick Jones, Pat Buttram, Rufe Davis, Eddy Waller, John McGuire, Rodd Harper, Jack Ingram, Eddie Parker, Ted Mapes, San Flint, "Champion, Jr."
D: John English
SP: Dwight Cummings, Dorothy Yost
P: Armand Schaefer

LOADED PISTOLS (Columbia, January 1949) 79 Mins.
Gene Autry, Barbara Britton, Chill Wills, *Jack Holt*, Russell Arms, Robert Shayne, Fred Kohler, Jr., Vince Barnett, Leon Weaver, Clem Bevins, Sandy Sanders, Budd Buster, John R. McKee, Stanley Blystone, Hank Bell, Felice Raymond, Dick Alexander, Frank O'Connor, Reed Howes, William Sundholm, Snub Pollard, Heinie Conklin, "Champion, Jr."
D: John English
SP: Dwight Cummings, Dorothy Yost
P: Armand Schaefer

THE LAST BANDIT (Republic, April 23, 1949) 80 Mins.
(Trucolor)
William (Bill) Elliott, Andy Devine, *Jack Holt*, Forrest Tucker, Adrian Booth, Grant Withers, Minna Gombell, Virginia Brissac, Louis Faust, Stanley Andrews, Martin Garralaga, Joseph Crehan, Charles Middleton, Rex Lease, Emmett Lynn, Eugene Roth, George Chesebro, Hank Bell, Jack O'Shea, Tex Terry, Steve Clark, Stanley Blystone, Budd Buster, Clem Bevins
D: Joseph Kane
S: Luci Ward, Jack Natteford
SP: Thomas Williamson
AP: Joseph Kane

BRIMSTONE (Republic, August 15, 1949) 90 Mins.
Rod Cameron, Adrian Booth, Walter Brennan, Forrest Tucker, *Jack Holt*, Jim Davis, James Brown, Guinn "Big Boy" Williams, Charlita, Hal Taliaferro, Jack Perrin
D: Joseph Kane
S: Norman S. Hall
SP: Thames Williams
AP: Joseph Kane

RED DESERT (Lippert, December 17, 1949) 60 Mins.
Donald Barry, Tom Neal, *Jack Holt*, Margia Dean, Byron Foulger, Joseph Crehan, John Cason, Tom London, Holly Bane, Hank Bell, George Slocum
D: Ford Beebe
S: Daniel B. Ullman
SP: Daniel B. Ullman, Ron Ormond
P: Ron Ormond

TASK FORCE (Warner Brothers, August 30, 1949).
Gary Cooper, Jane Wyatt, Walter Brennan, Wayne Morris, Julie London, *Jack Holt*, Bruce Bennett, Stanley Ridges, Art Baker, Moroni Olson, Richard Rober, Ray Montgomery, Harlan Warde, James Holden, Rory Mallison, John Gallaudet, Warren Douglas, Charles Waldron, Jr., Robert Rockwell, William Gould, Sally Corner, Ken Tobey, Tetsu Komai, Beal Wong, Reed Howes, Basil Ruysdael, Edwin Fowler, Laura Treadwell, Mary Lawrence, William Hudson
D/SP: Delmer Daves
P: Jerry Wald

THE DALTONS' WOMEN (Western Adventure/Howco, February 25, 1950) 80 Mins.
Lash LaRue, Al St. John, Jack Holt, Tom Neal, Pamela Blake, Jacqueline Fontaine, Raymond Hatton, Lyle Talbot, Tom Tyler, J. Farrell MacDonald, Terry Frost, Stanley Price, Bud Osborne, Cliff Taylor, Buff Brown, Clarke Stevens, Lee Bennett, Jimmie Martin, Archie Twitchell
D: Thomas Carr
SP: Ron Ormond and Maurice Tombragel
P: Ron Ormond

RETURN OF THE FRONTIERSMAN (Warner Brothers, June 24, 1950) 74 Mins.
(Technicolor)
Gordon MacRae, *Jack Holt*, Rory Calhoun, Julie London, Fred Clark, Edwin Rand, Raymond Bond, Britt Wood, Matt McHugh
D: Richard Bare
S/SP: Edna Anhalt
P: Saul Elkins

TRAIL OF ROBIN HOOD (Republic, December 15, 1950) 67 Mins.
(Trucolor)
Roy Rogers, Penny Edwards, Gordon Jones, *Jack Holt*, Emory Parnel, Clifton Young, James Magill, Carol Nugent, George Chesebro, Edward Cassidy, Foy Willing and the Riders of the Purple Sage, "Trigger," and guest stars Tom Tyler, Kermit Maynard, Ray Corrigan, Tom Keene, Monte Hale, Rex Allen, Allan Lane, and William Farnum
D: William Witney
SP: Gerald Geraghty
AP: Eddy White

KING OF THE BULLWHIP (Western Adventure, February 1, 1951) 59 Mins.

Lash LaRue, Al St. John, *Jack Holt*, Tom Neal, Anne Gwynne, Michael Whalen, Willis Houck, George J. Lewis, Dennis Moore, Cliff Taylor, Frank Jacquet, Tex Cooper, Hugh Hooker, Jimmie Martin, Roy Butler

D/P: Ron Ormond

SP: Jack Lewis, Ira Webb

ACROSS THE WIDE MISSOURI (Metro-Goldwyn-Mayer, October 23, 1951) 78 Mins.

(Technicolor)

Clark Gable, Ricardo Montalban, John Hodiak, Adolphe Menjou, Maria Elena Marques, J. Carroll Naish, *Jack Holt*, Alan Napier, George Chandler, Richard Anderson, Douglas Fowley, Russell Simpson, Frankie Darro, John Hartman

D: William Wellman

S: Talbot Jennings, Frank Cavett

S: Talbot Jennings

P: Robert Sisk

EPILOGUE

The dust has long since settled over the trails once ridden so often and proudly by the saddle aces of the cinema. Those trails over which virginal cowboys rode in defense of equally virginal Sunbonnet Sues and battled heinous villains shaken from the broom which swept hell are now but celluloid memories. No heroes in white hats astride white chargers ride them to bring gunsmoke justice to the range, engage in teeth-rattling fistic brawls, display fantastic horsemanship virtuosity, and bashfully respond to the heroine's manifestations of appreciation with an "Aw, shucks, ma'am, it weren't nothing."

For all practical purposes, the recipe coyote drama made for the nickel and dime lower main street grinds and the rural and small-town houses bit the dust in 1954. The "B" horse opera, founded on an individualism which seemed no longer to exist in the complexities of modern life, was unacceptable to cosmopolitan audiences. Television, urbanization, and rising production costs did what ace villains Charles Whitaker, Charles King, Tom London, and Bud Osborne were never able to do—gun down our beloved cowboy heroes from the age of innocence.

But the old memories of the movies and personalities that gave them life constitute a bit of nostalgic history that is pleasant to remember, to savor, to cherish, and to perpetuate. It matters not that the sagebrushers of yesteryear were devoid of much substance. They inexorably played a part in molding the values of three generations who loved them then and remember them now as the greatest movies ever made and the finest aggregation of stars ever to populate the Hollywood hills.

As William S. Hart so aptly exclaimed in his spoken prologue to the re-release of *Tumbleweeds* (United Artist, 1939), "Oh, the thrill of it all!" Yes, the thrill of it all! The memory brings goosepimples to the flesh and sends ripples of ecstasy through the bodies of those old enough to remember.

INDEX
OF FILMS

D

S

Sacrifice, 274
Saddle Aces, 115, 120
Saddle Girth, The, 71
Saddle Hawk, The, 230
Saddle King, The, 225
Saddle Mates, 36
Saddle Pals, 255
Saga of Death Valley, 49
Sagebrush Tom, 68
Sagebrush Trail, The (1922), 24
Sagebrush Trail (1933), 39
Sagebrush Troubador, The, 244
Sagebrusher, The, 23
Saginaw Trail, 243, 259
Sallie's Sure Shot, 64, 208
Salomy Jane, 269, 272
Salute, 114, 116
San Francisco, 285
Sandflow, 165
Santa Fe Trail, The, 84, 88
Satan Town, 125, 137
Savage Horde, The, 56
Saved by a Watch, 67
Saved by Her Horse, 68
Saved by the Pony Express, 65
Saved from the Vigilantes, 209
Saving the Family Name, 273
Sawdust Trail, The, 229
Scandal in Hickville, A, 210
Scapegoat, The, 66
Scarlet Drop, The, 133
Schoolmaster of Mariposa, The, 63
Screen Snapshots, 168, 238, 255
Sea Horses, 280
Sea of Grass, The, 145
Sealed Orders, 90
Second Hand Love, 154
Secret Code, The, 18, 25
Secret Game, The, 274
Secret Man, The, 132, 222
Secret of Treasure Island, The, 100
Secrets of Hollywood, 39
Señor Americano, 193
Señor Daredevil, 191
Señorita's Repentance, The, 208
Sergeant Rutledge, 111
Servant Question Out West, The, 209
Seven Angry Men, 109
Seventh Bandit, The, 137
Shackles of Fate, 151
Shadow, The, 103
Shadow Ranch, 157
Shadows on the Range, 105
Shane, 61
Shepherd of the Hills, The, 126, 144
Sheriff and the Rustler, The, 65
Sheriff of Tombstone, 51
Sheriff of Yawapai County, The, 64, 207
Sheriff's Baby, The, 128
Sheriff's Blunder, The, 71
Sheriff's Dilemma, The, 130

Sheriff's Duty, The, 70
Sheriff's Oath, The, 224
Sheriff's Reward, The, 66
Sheriff's Secret, The, 95
Sheriff's Son, The, 150
Shoot 'Em Up Kid, The, 230
Shootin' Fool, The, 226
Shootin' For Love, 229
Shootin' Kid, The, 224
Shootin' Square, 92
Shooting High, 243, 251
Shooting up the Movies, 70
Shotgun Jones, 65, 221
Shotgun Man and the Stage Driver, The, 64, 207
Showdown, The, 18, 26
Sierra Sue, 243, 253
Sign of the Wolf, The, 95
Silent Avenger, The, 204, 213
Silent Rider, The (1917), 22
Silent Rider, The (1927), 231
Silent Sanderson, 136
Silent Sheldon, 93
Silent Stranger, The, 263, 264
Silent Treatment, The, 259
Silent Valley, 45
Silent Vow, The, 205, 214
Silver Bullet, The, 43
Silver Canyon, 257
Silver Comes Through, 265
Silver Grindstone, The, 209
Silver Lining, The, 20
Silver Spurs (1936), 164
Silver Spurs (1943), 53
Silver Valley, 77
Singing Cowboy, The, 246
Singing Hill, The, 252
Singing Vagabond, The, 244
Single Handed, 228
Sins of Rosanne, The, 276
Sioux City Sue, 243, 254
Six Cylinder Love, 71
Six-Gun Justice, 42
Six-Shooter Andy, 71
Six-Shooter Justice, 132
Six-Shootin' Sheriff, 200
Skedaddle Gold, 35
Skid Proof, 153
Sky Giant, 142
Sky High, 74
Sky Raiders, 103
Slide, Kelly, Slide, 137
Slim Higgins, 67
Smart Set, The, 270, 281
Smashing Barriers, 204, 213, 215
Smilin' Guns, 232
Smilin' Kid, The, 224
Smoke Tree Range, 165
Smoking Guns (1927), 182, 184
Smoking Guns (1934), 40, 196
Snow Drift, 153
Snowshoe Trail, The, 18, 24
So Dear to my Heart, 145
So This is Arizona, 38

Soda Water Cowboy, 36
Soft Boiled, 75
Soft Shoes, 136
Soft Tenderfoot, A, 71
Solution of the Mystery, The, 20
Some Duel, 70
Some Shooter, 225
Somebody Lied, 188, 190
Somewhere in Sonora, 192
Son of a Gun, 181
Son of Oklahoma, 95
Son of the Golden West, 78
Song of Nevada, 104
Song of the Caballero, 193
Songs of Truce, 64
Sonora Stagecoach, 238
Sons of New Mexico, 256
Sons of the Pioneers, 52
Sons of the Saddle, 194
Sorrowful Shore, The, 129
Soul Herder, The, 132, 222
Soul Mate, The, 67
Souls at Sea, 142
South of Arizona, 48
South of Northern Lights, 90
South of Santa Fe, 159
South of the Border, 243, 251
Sparrows, 27
Speed Maniac, The, 72, 151
Spider Returns, The, 104
Spirit of St. Louis, 110
Spirit of the West, 233
Spoilers, The (1942), 126, 144
Spoilers, The (1956), 109
Spook Ranch, 230
Sporting Chance, A, 275
Springtime in Texas, 54
Springtime in the Rockies, 248
Spurs, 233
Square Shooter, The, 151
Squaw Man, The, 269, 275
Squealer, The, 283
Stagecoach Days, 47
Stagecoach Driver and the Girl, The, 67
Stagecoach Guard, The, 69
Stampede in the Night, 131
Stand up and Fight, 87
Stardust on the Sage, 254
Starlight, the Untamed, 84, 93
Starlight's Revenge, 84, 93
Starring in Western Stuff, 71
Steel Trail, The, 215
Steelheart, 205, 213
Step on it!, 228
Stepping Fast, 75
Stolen Bride, The, 129
Stolen Moccasins, The, 64, 208
Stolen Treaty, The, 129
Stone of Silver Creek, 161
Storm over the Andes, 270, 285
Stormy Trailers, 115, 121
Stormy Waters, 19, 27
Straight from the Shoulder, 152

302

INDEX
OF NAMES